MW01624120

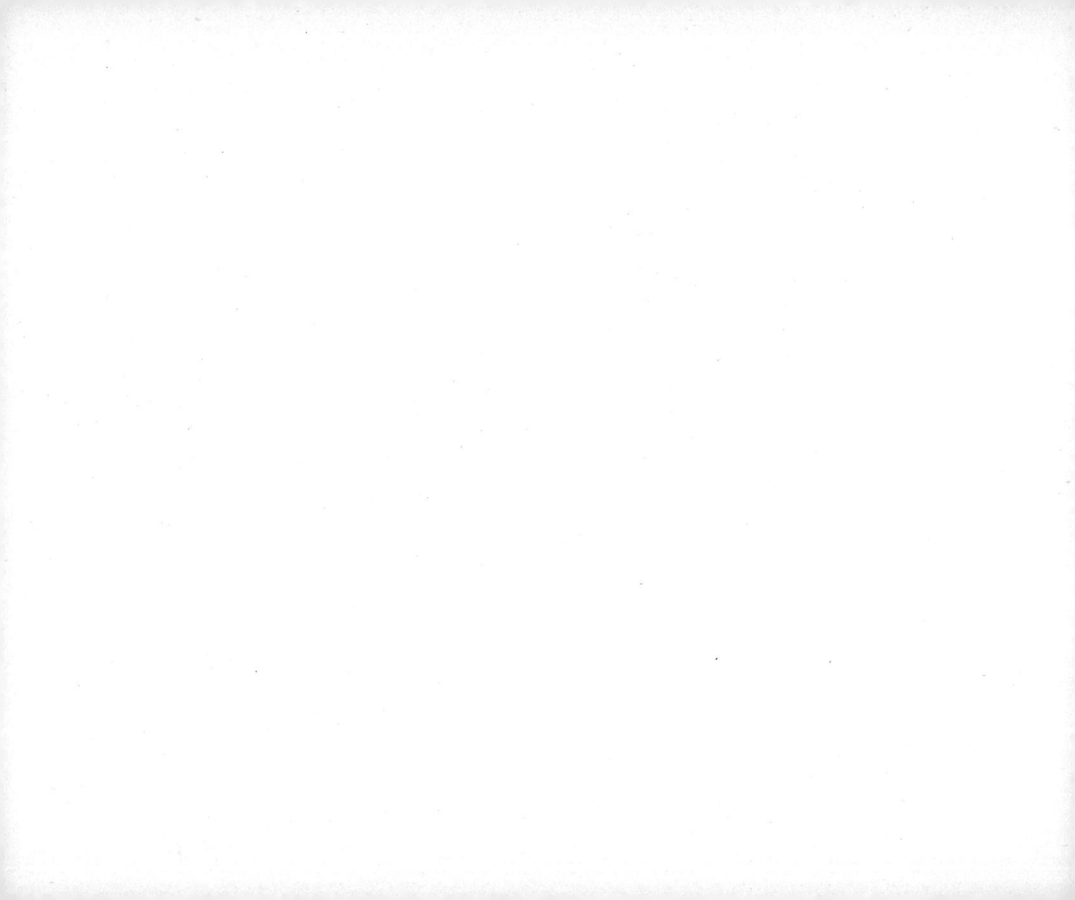

FLORIDA

THEN AND NOW®

People and Places

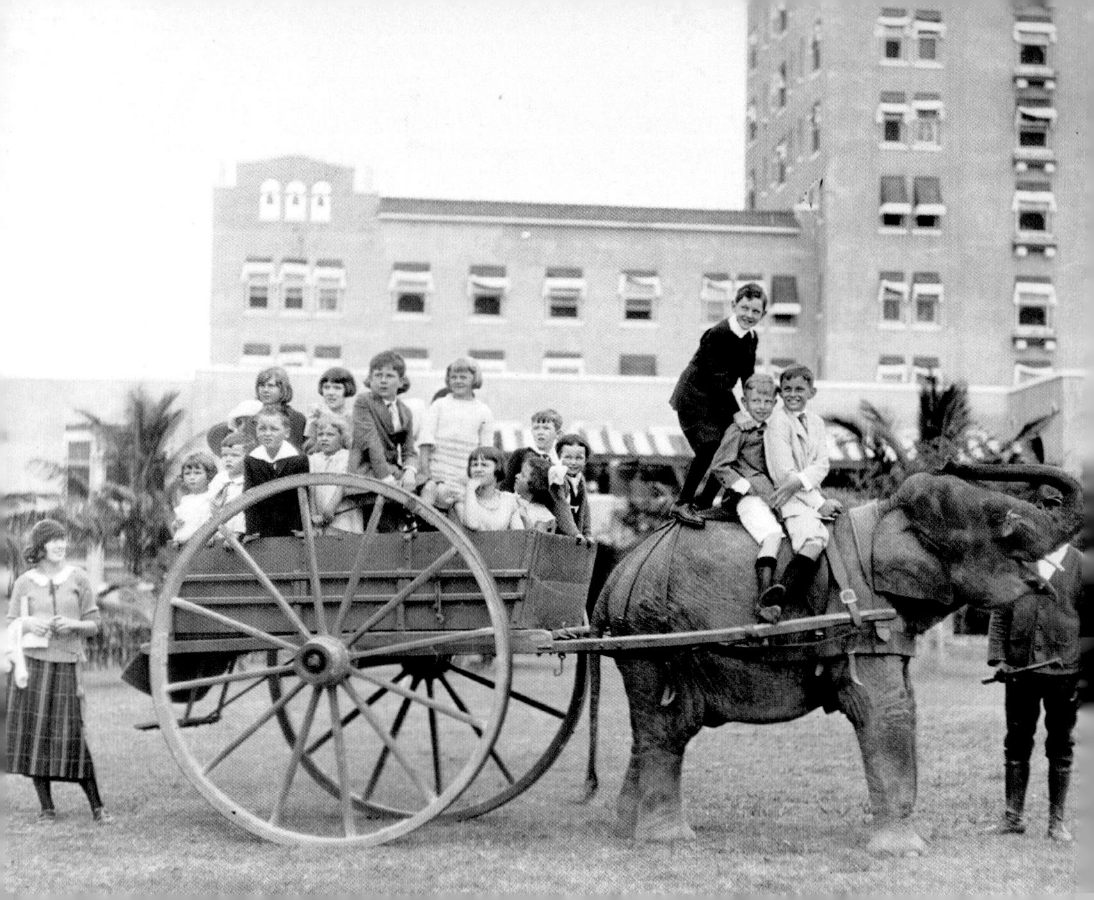

FLORIDA

THEN AND NOW®
People and Places

David Watts

First published in the United Kingdom in 2013 by
PAVILION BOOKS
10 Southcombe Street, London W14 0RA
An imprint of Anova Books Company Ltd

ISBN: 978-1-90910-865-3

A CIP catalogue record for this book is available from the British Library.

Printed by 1010 Printing International Limited, China.

10 9 8 7 6 5 4 3 2 1

FLORIDA THEN AND NOW

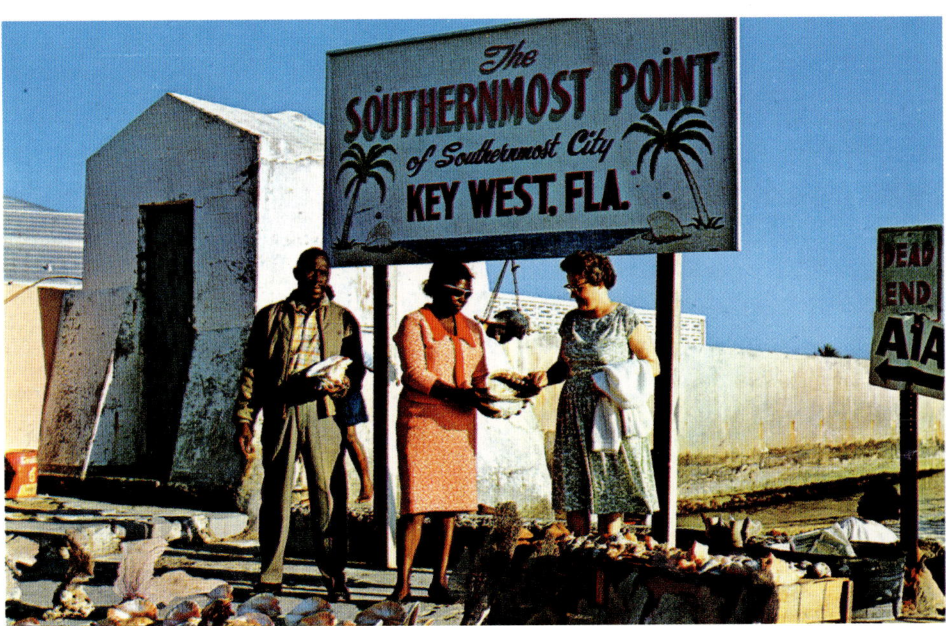

Southernmost Point, Key West, c. 1960

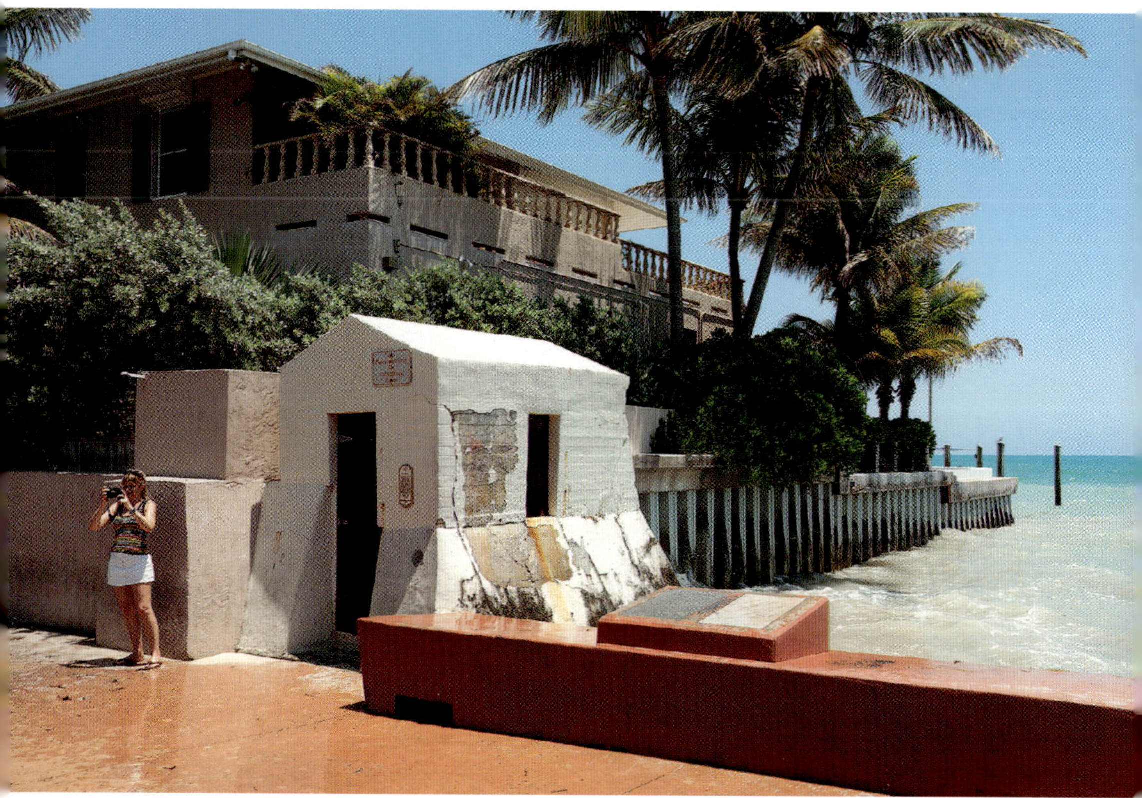

Sponge Exchange on Wharf, Key West, c. 1900

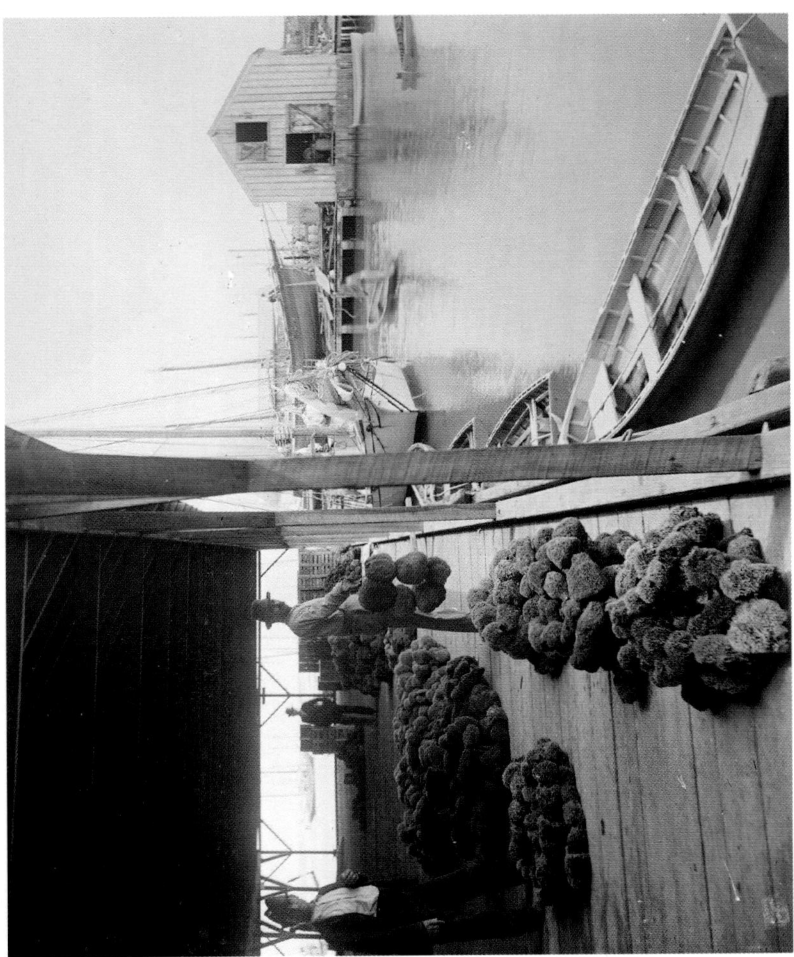

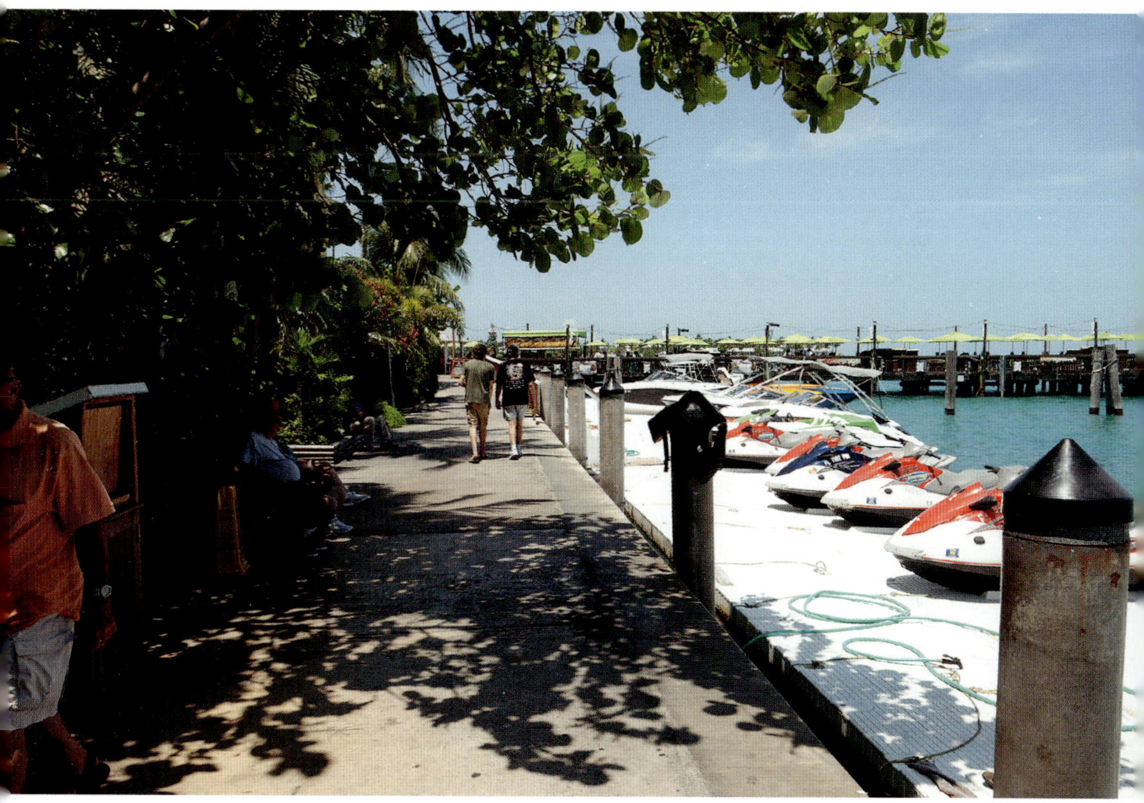

Pepe's Café, Caroline Street, Key West, 1938

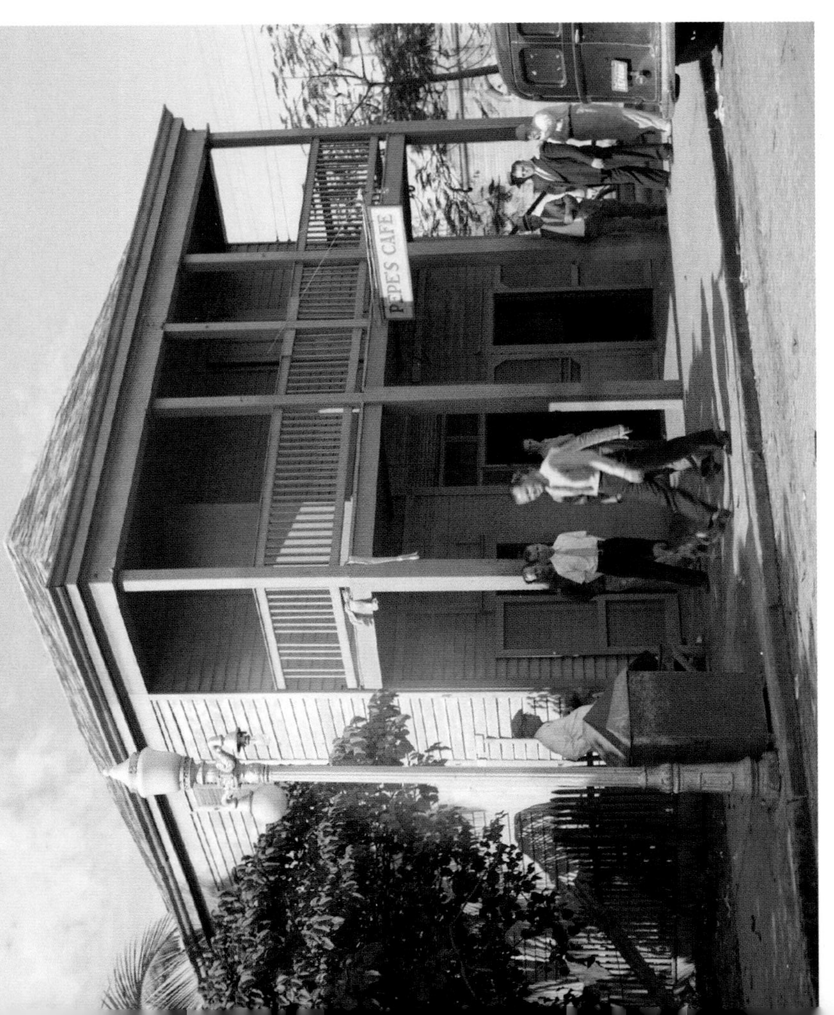

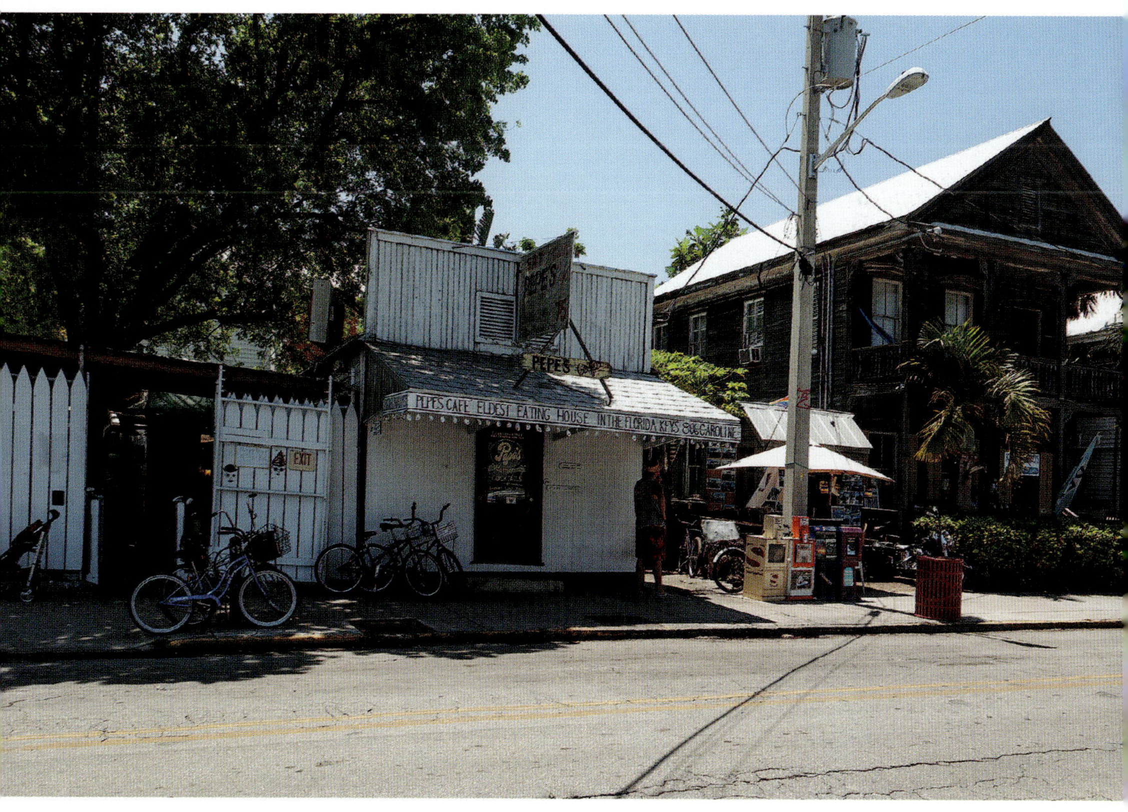
PEPES
PEPES CAFE ELDEST EATING HOUSE IN THE FLORIDA KEYS 806 CAROLINE
EXIT

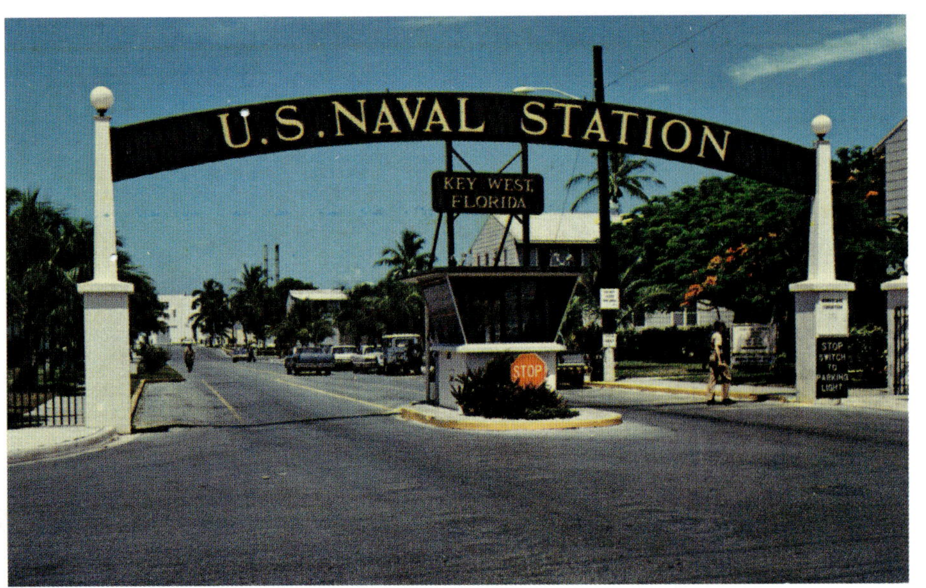

U.S. Naval Station, Key West, c. 1970

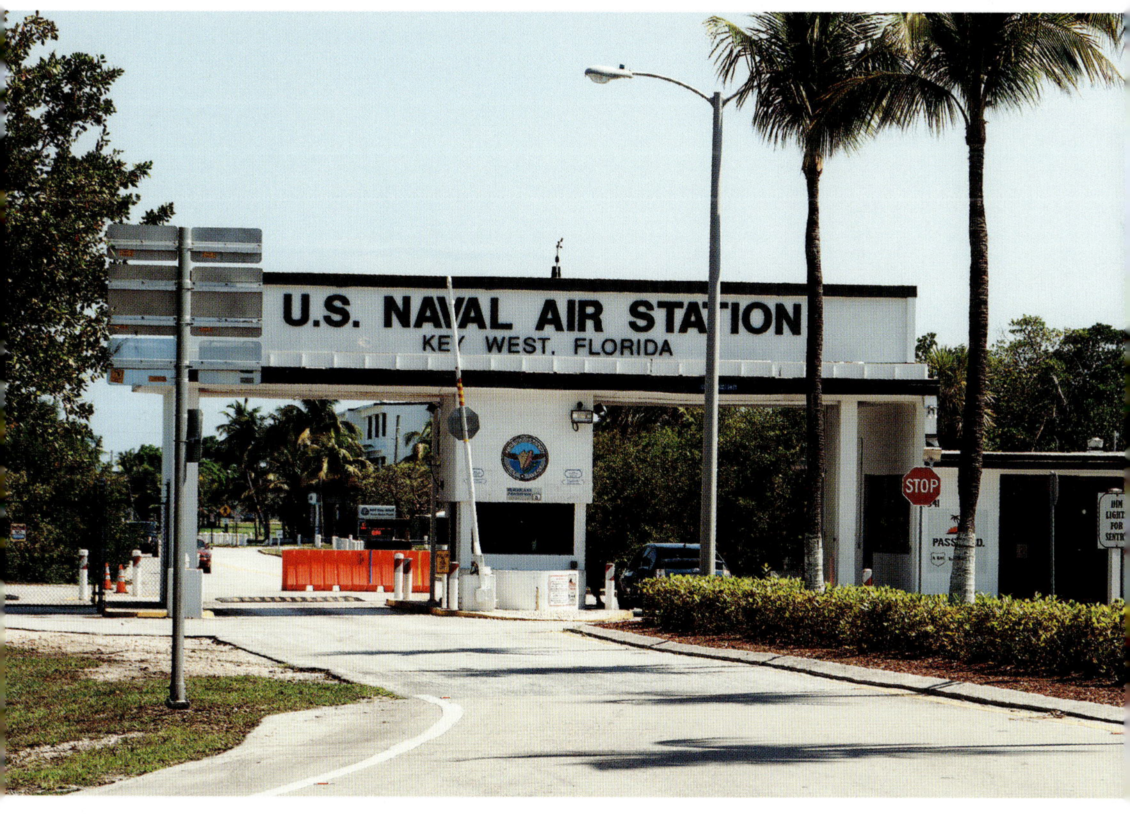
U.S. NAVAL AIR STATION
KEY WEST, FLORIDA
STOP

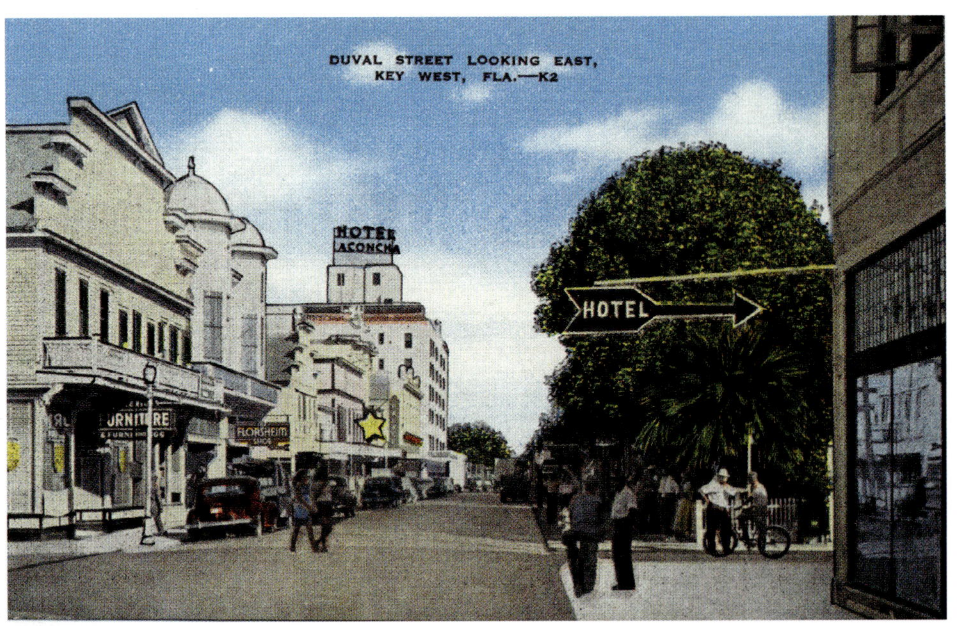

Duval Street, Key West, c. 1955

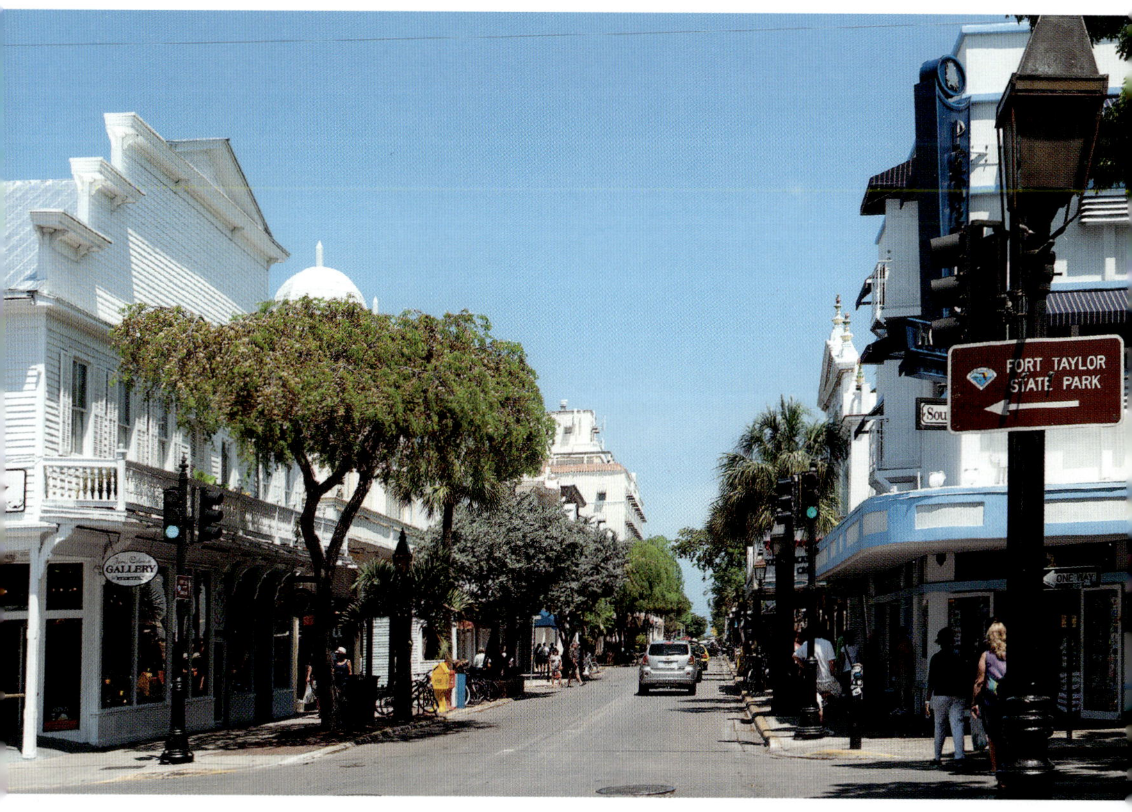
GALLERY
FORT TAYLOR
STATE PARK
ONE WAY

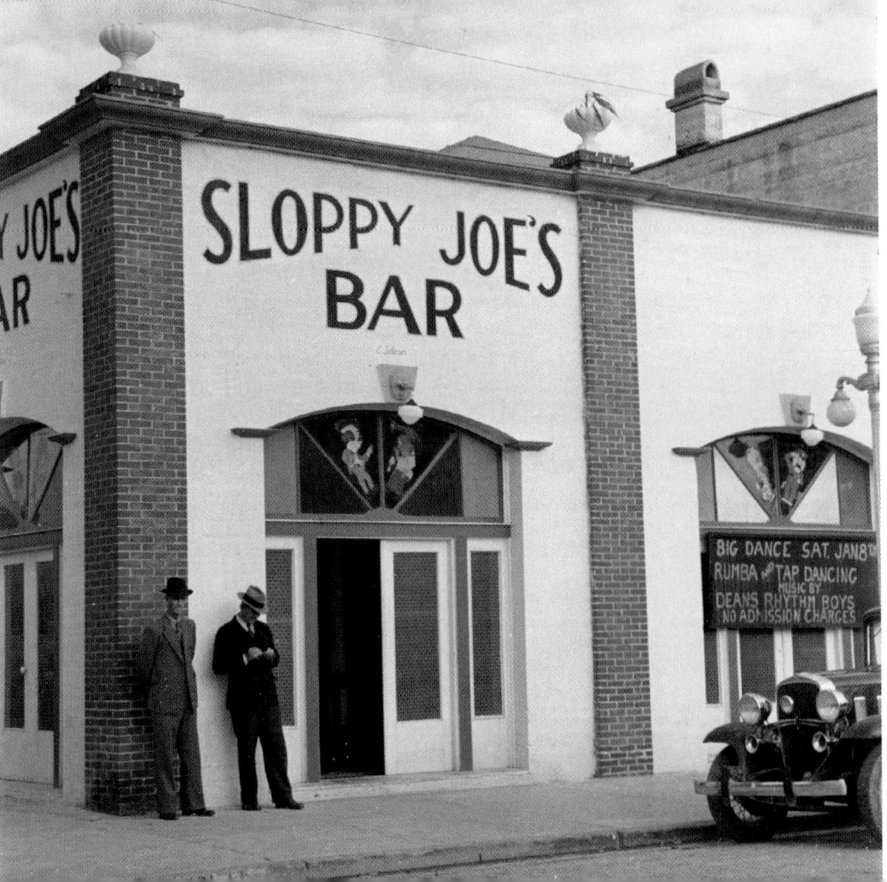

Sloppy Joe's Bar, Duval Street, Key West, 1938

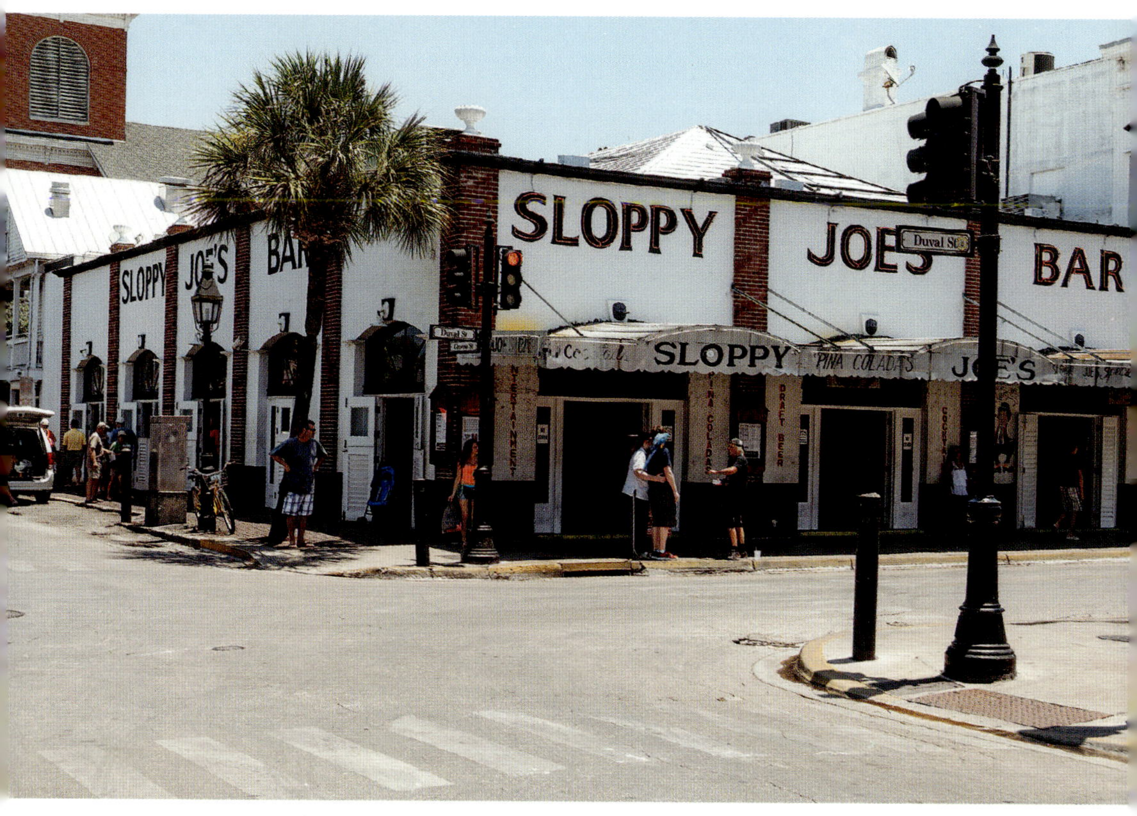
SLOPPY JOE'S BAR
SLOPPY
JOES
BAR
Duval St
SLOPPY
PINA COLADAS
JOE'S
DRAFT BEER

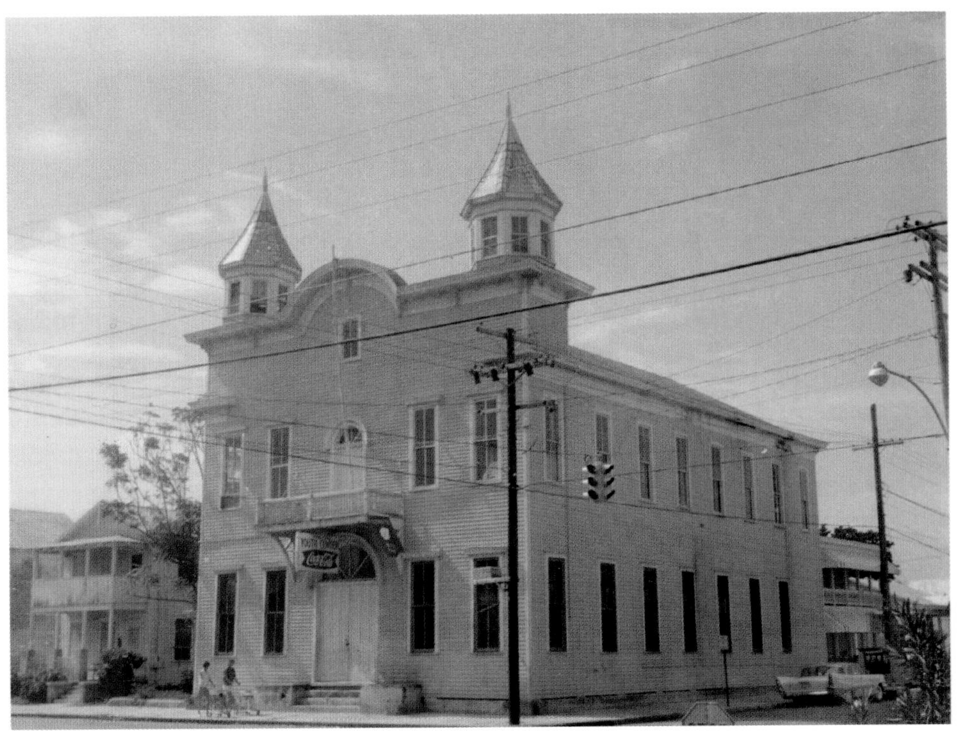

The Armory, White Street, Key West, c. 1965

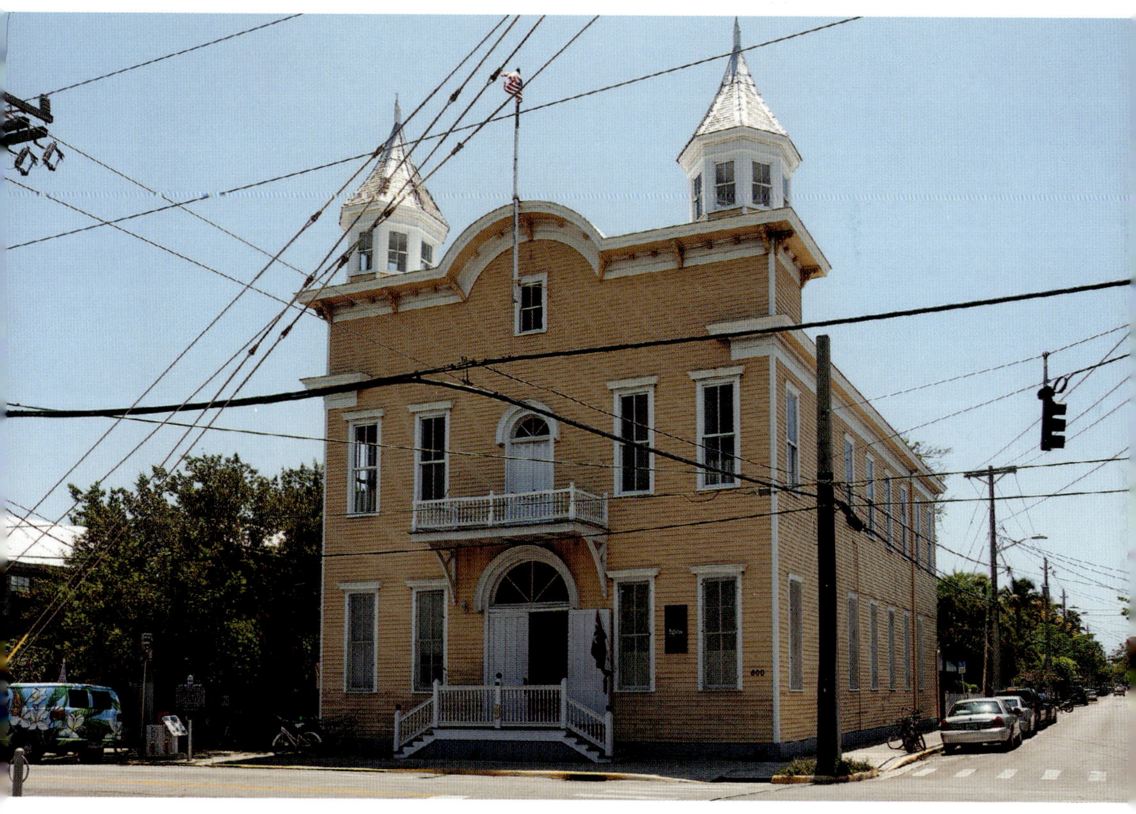

Ernest Hemingway House, Whitehead Street, Key West, 1966

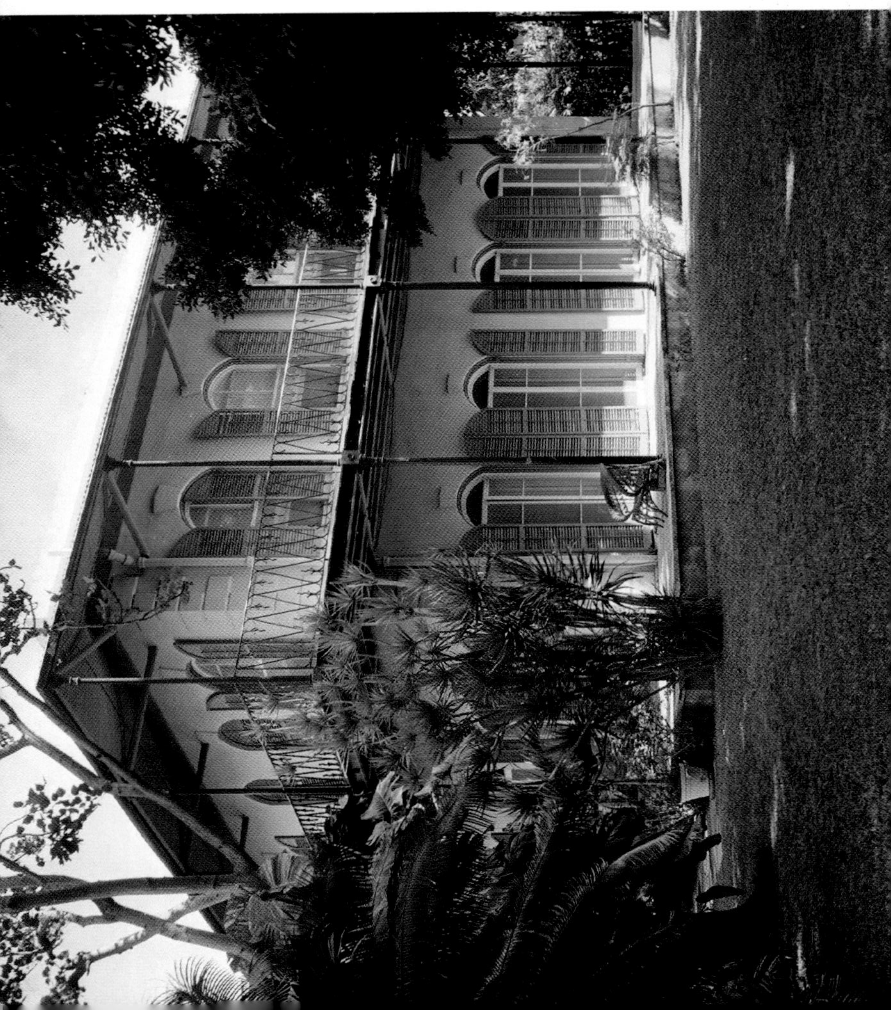

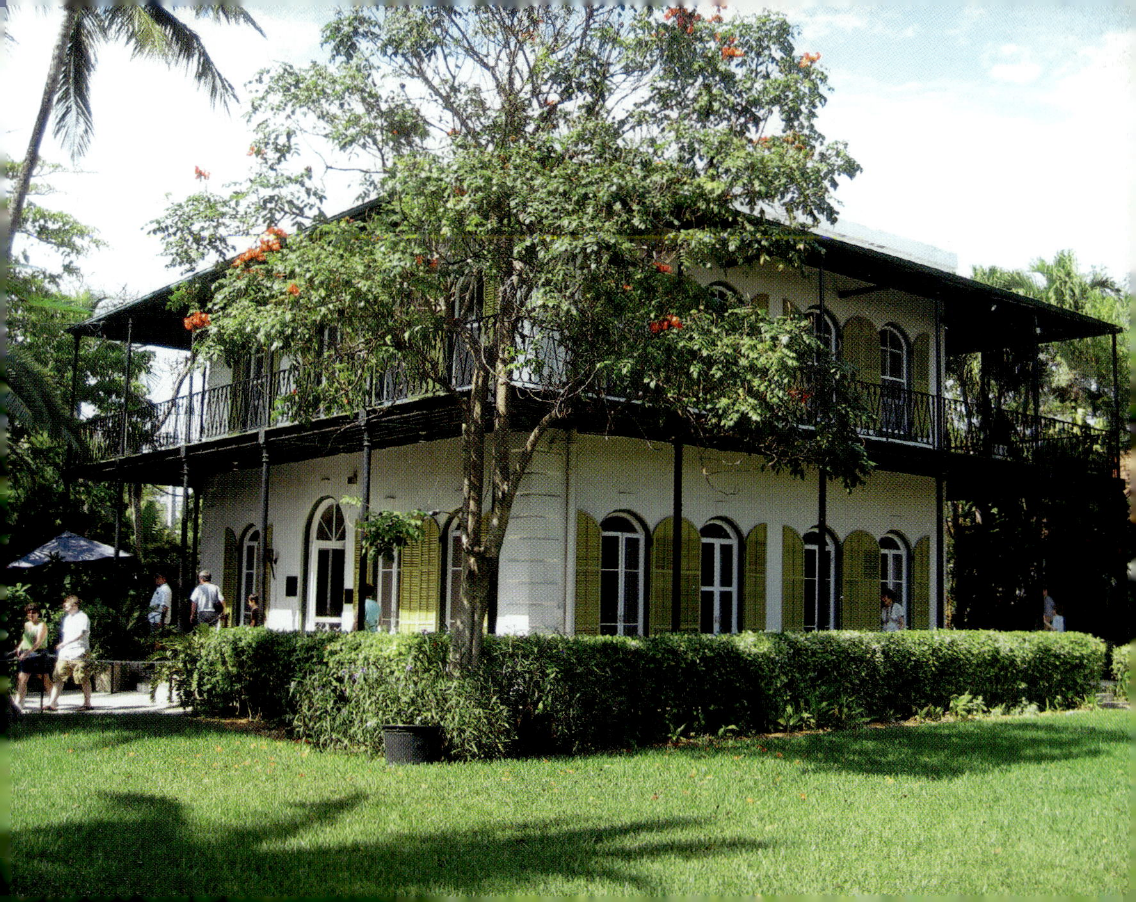

First Florida East Coast Railway train to enter Key West, 1912

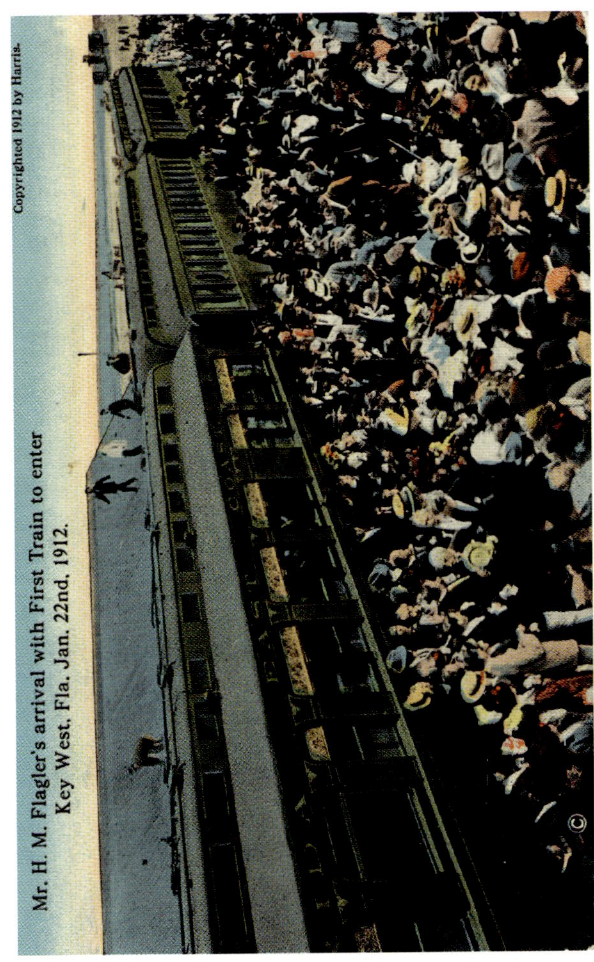

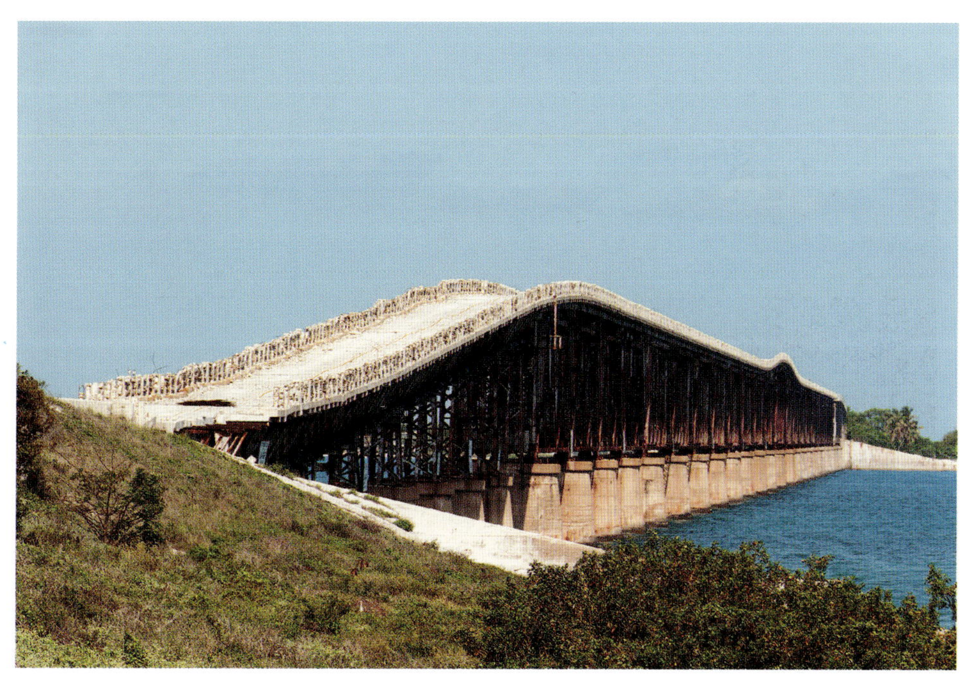

Remains of Key West railway (closed 1935), later U.S. Route 1

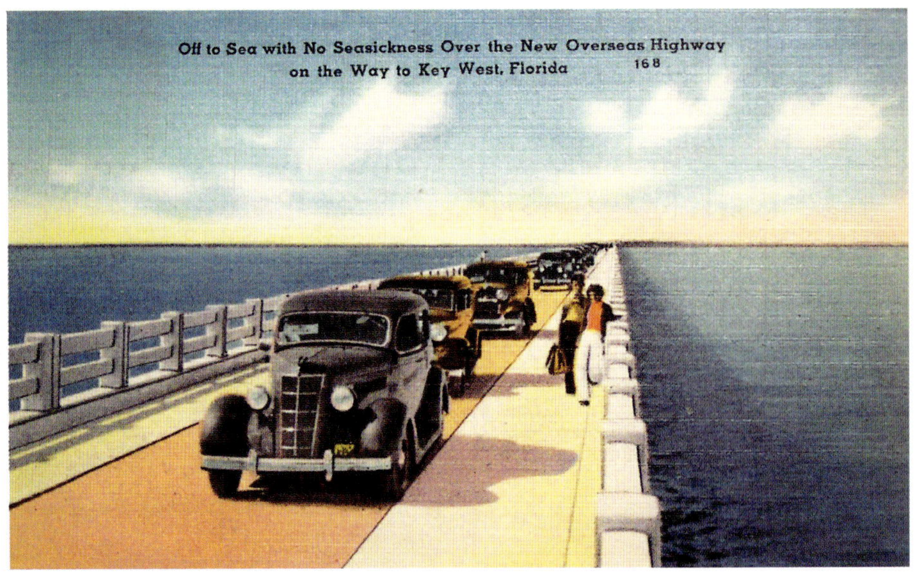

Overseas Highway to Key West, c. 1940

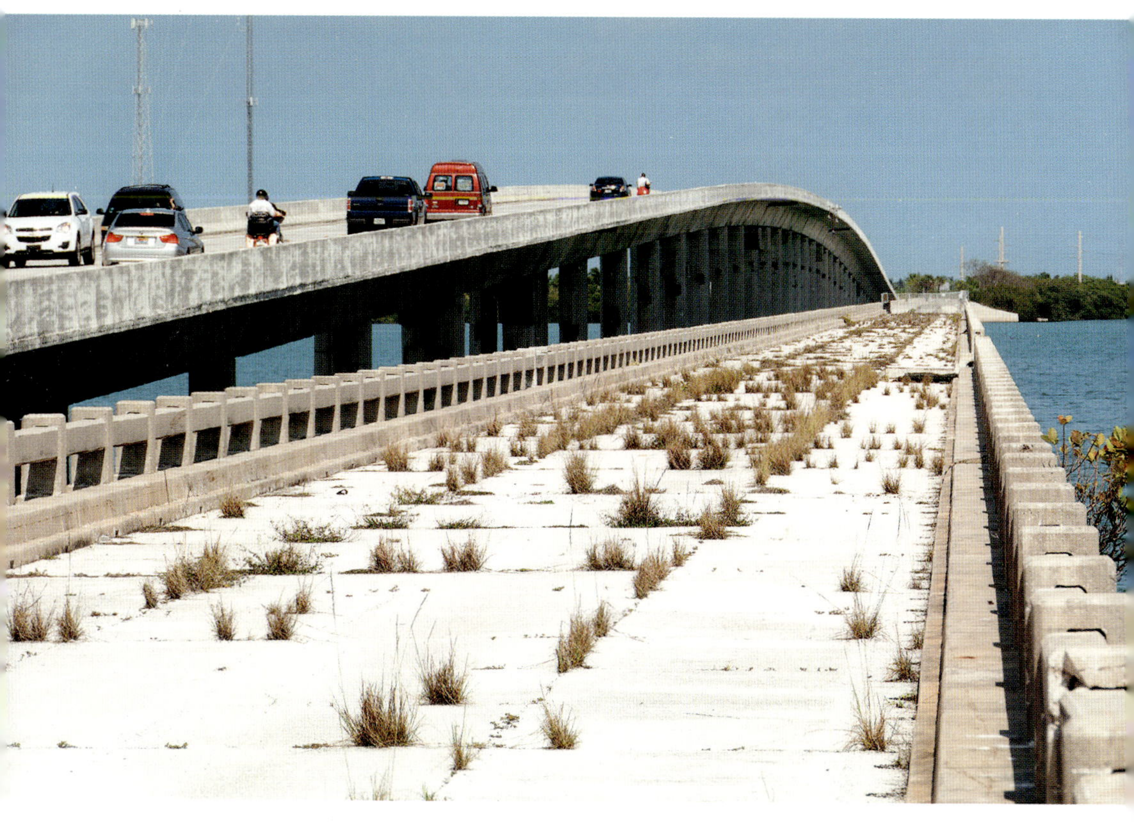

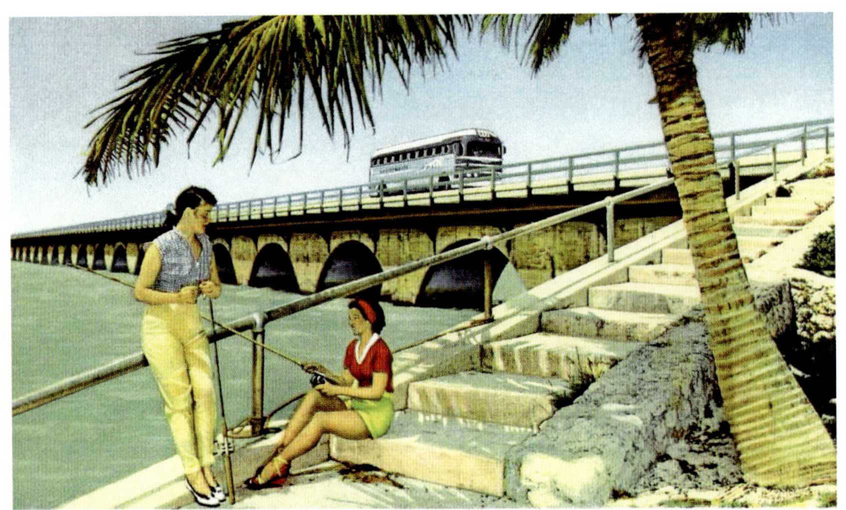

"*The bus that goes to Sea*" — **The Seven Mile Bridge Between Miami and Key West**

Overseas Highway between Key West and Miami, c. 1950

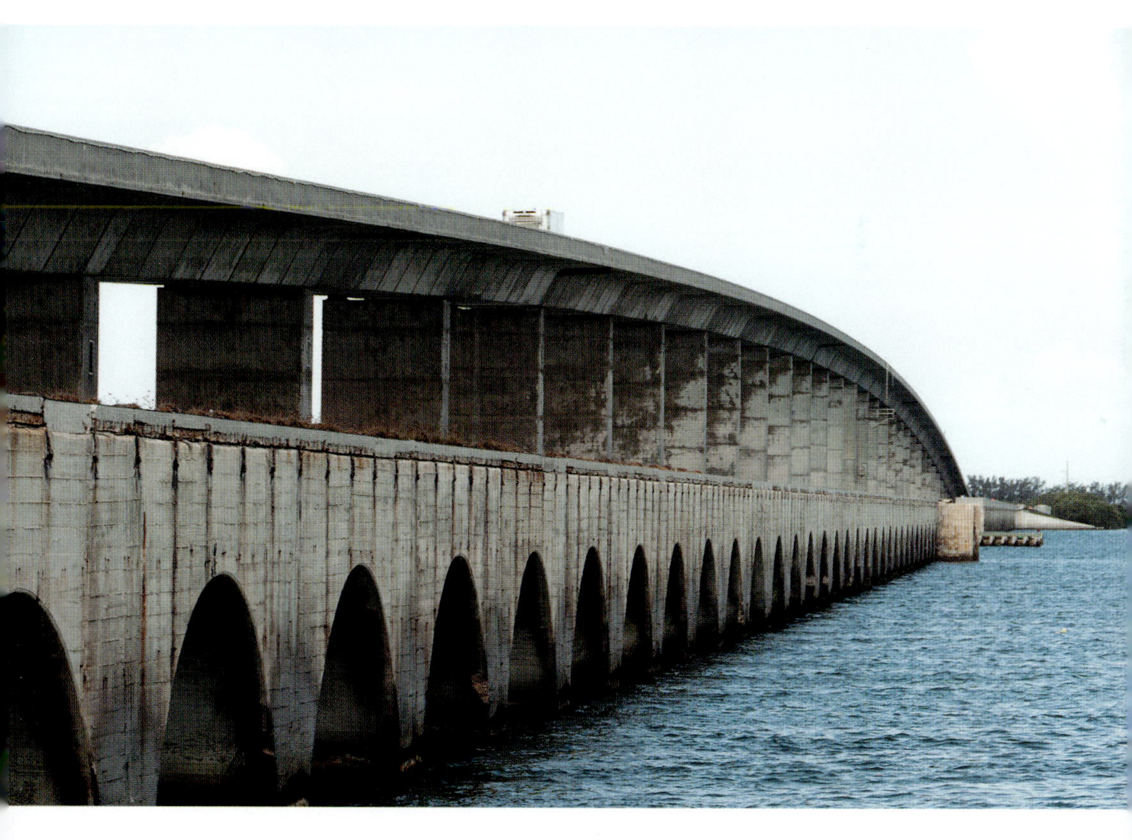

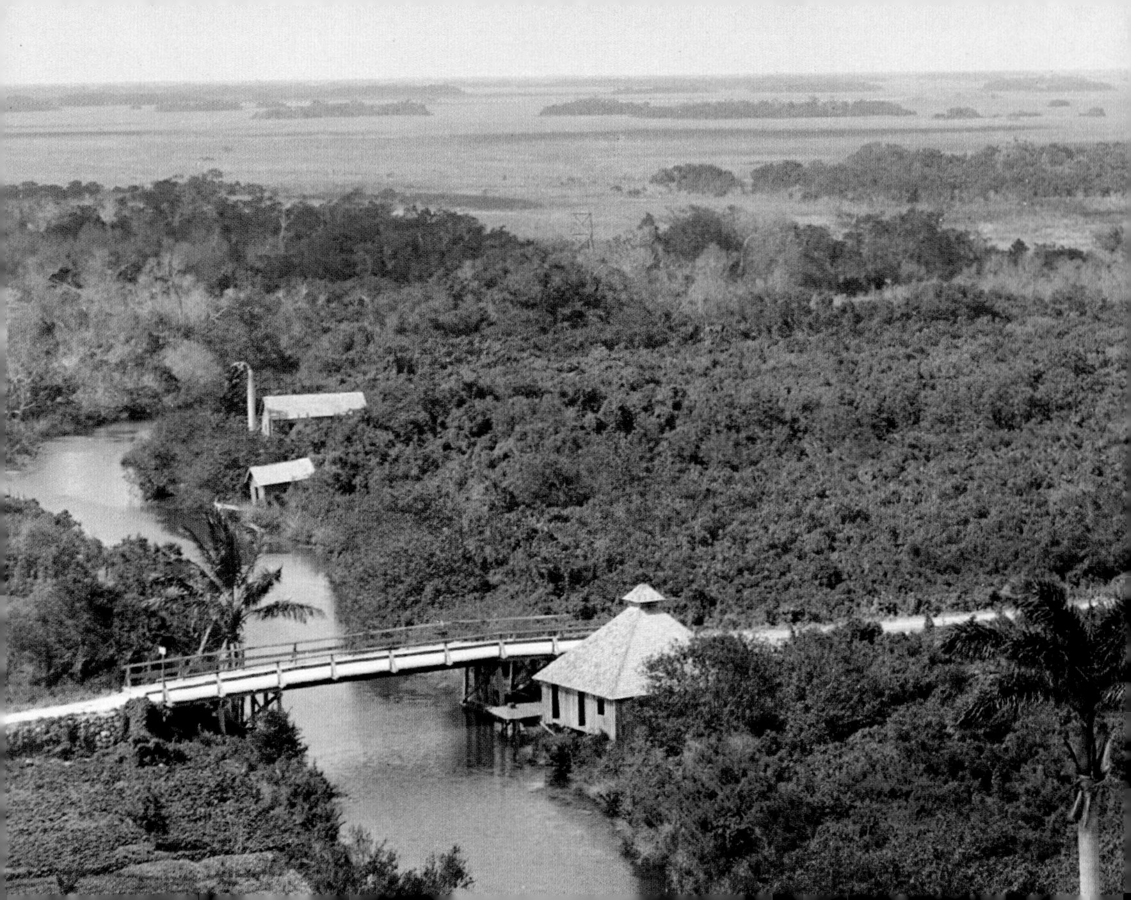

Drainage Canal, The Everglades, c. 1915

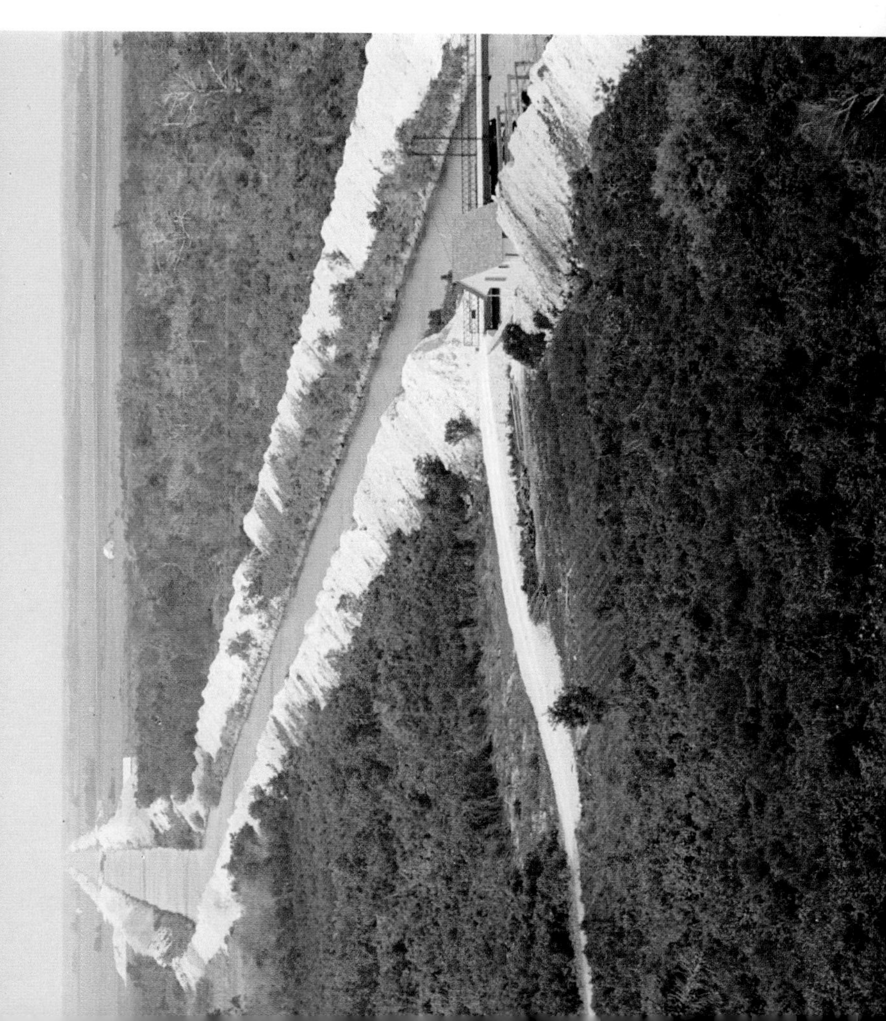

Seminole Village, The Everglades, c. 1915

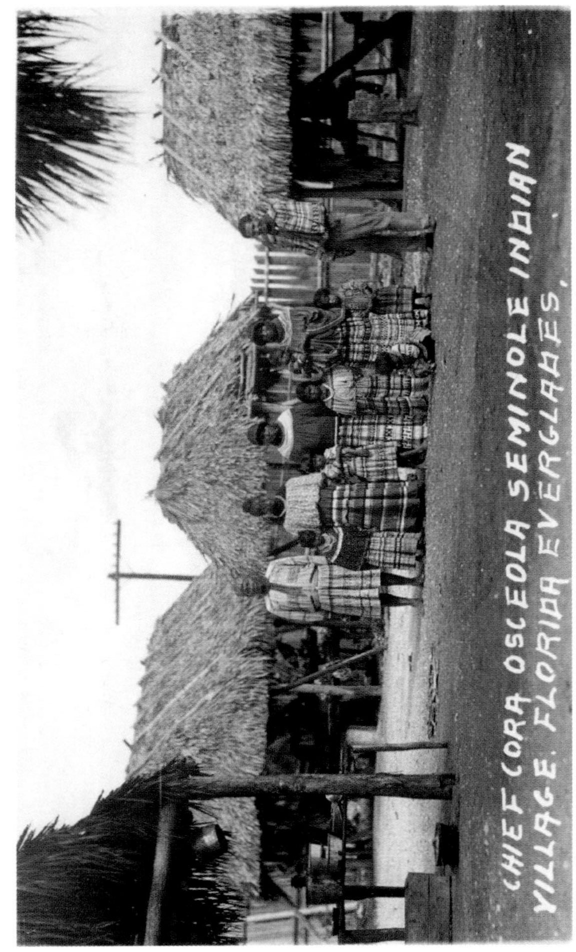

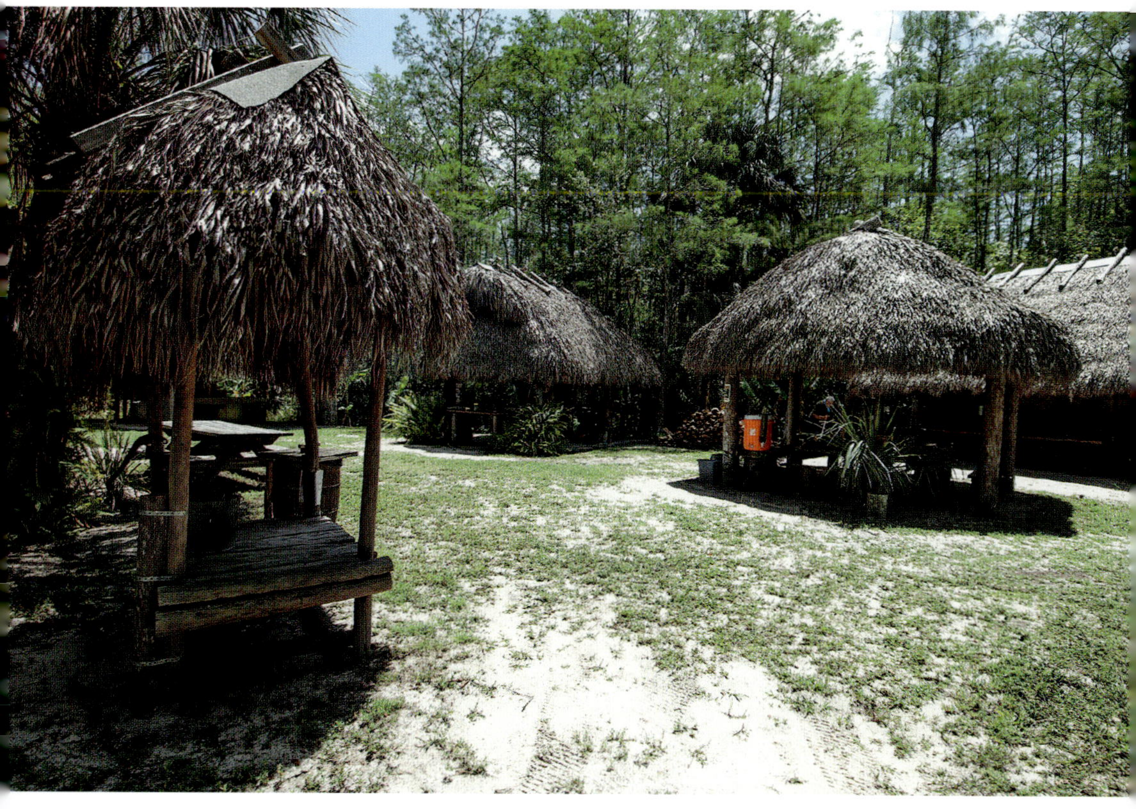

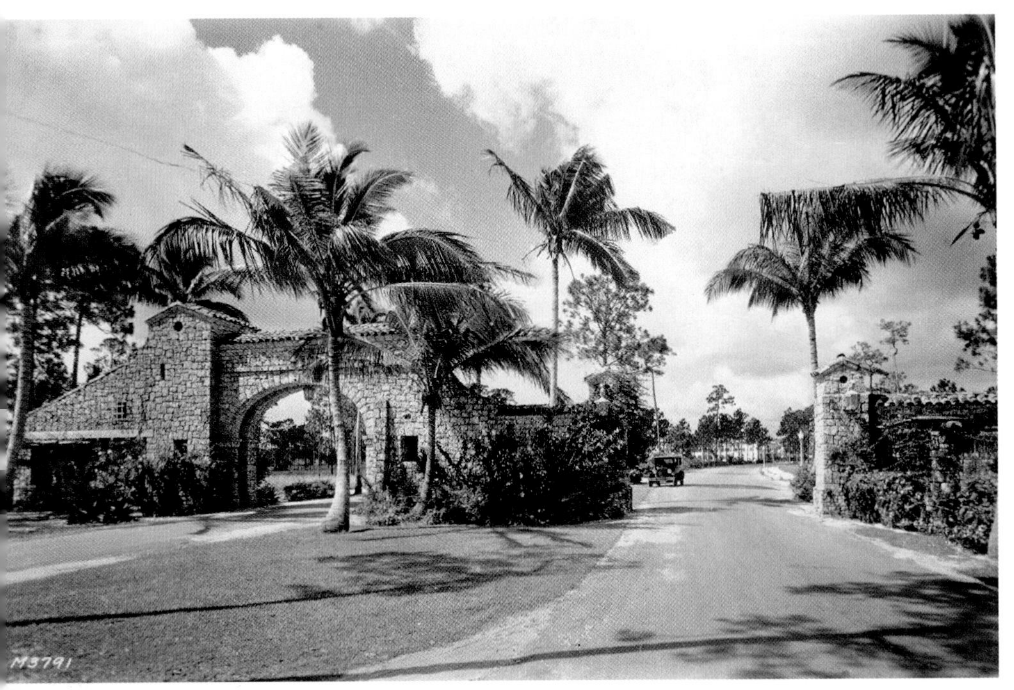

Alhambra Entrance, Coral Gables, c. 1925

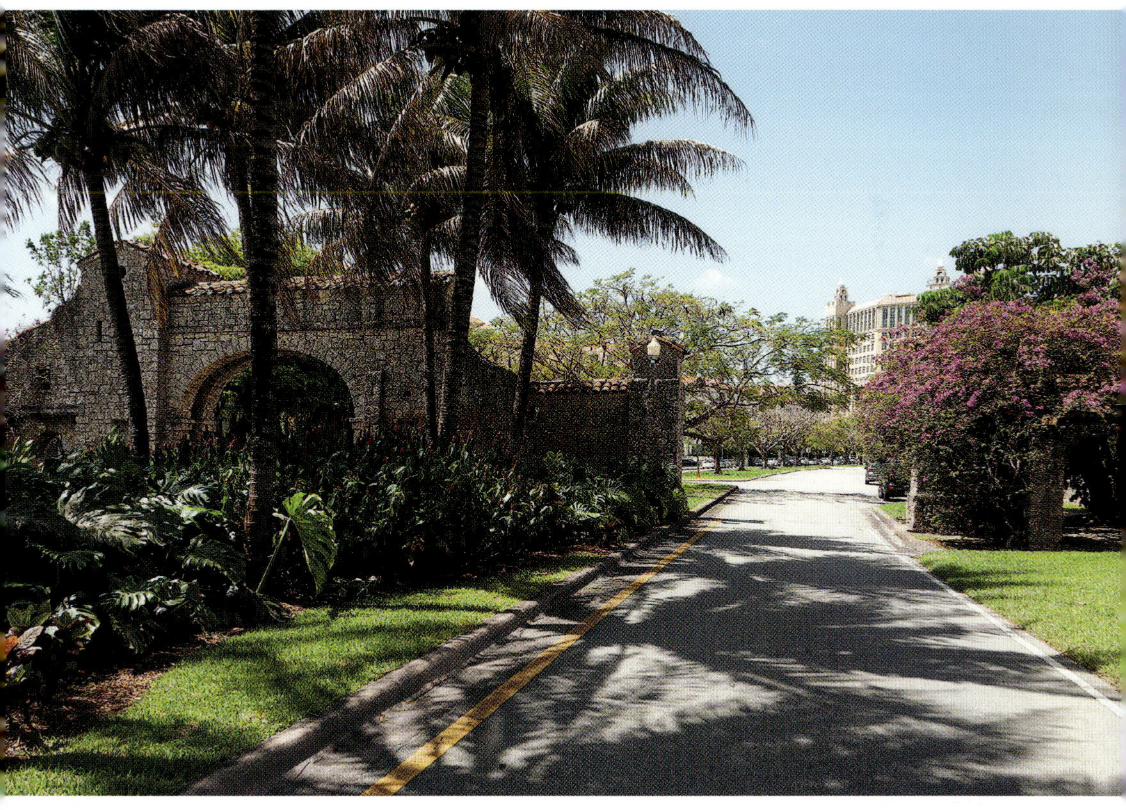

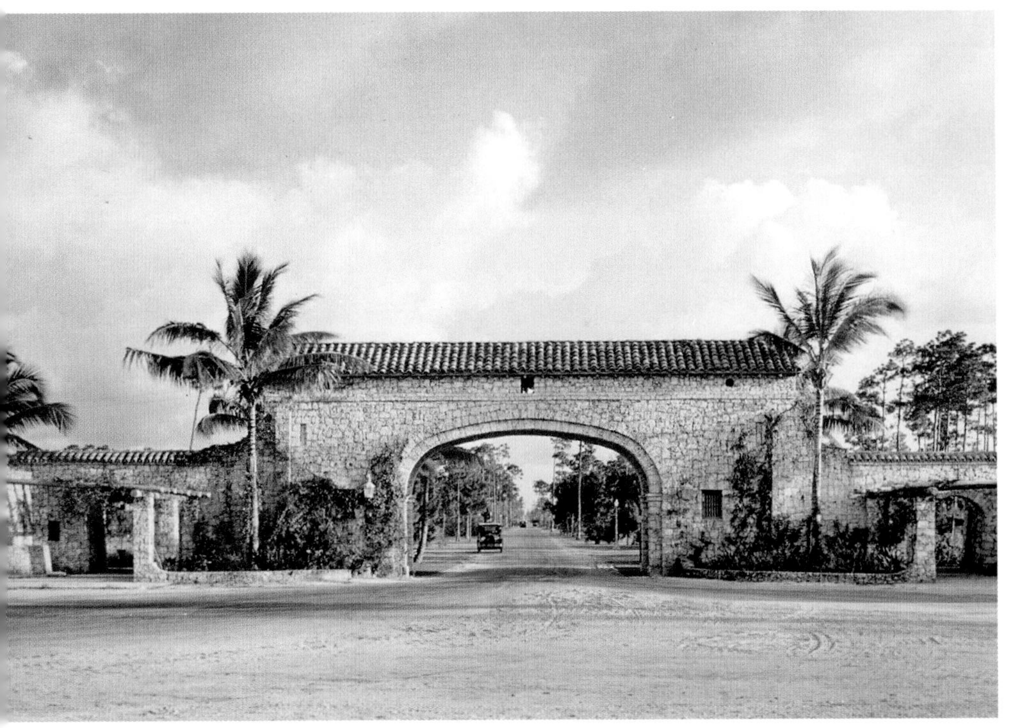

Granada Entrance, Coral Gables, c. 1925

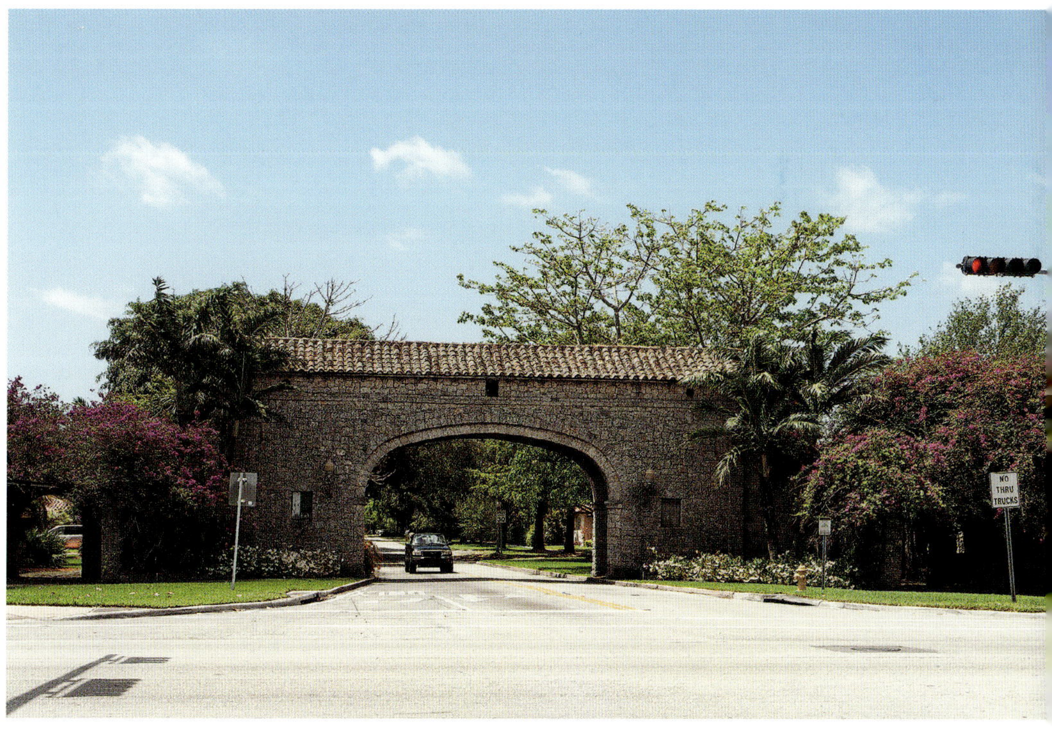
NO
THRU
TRUCKS

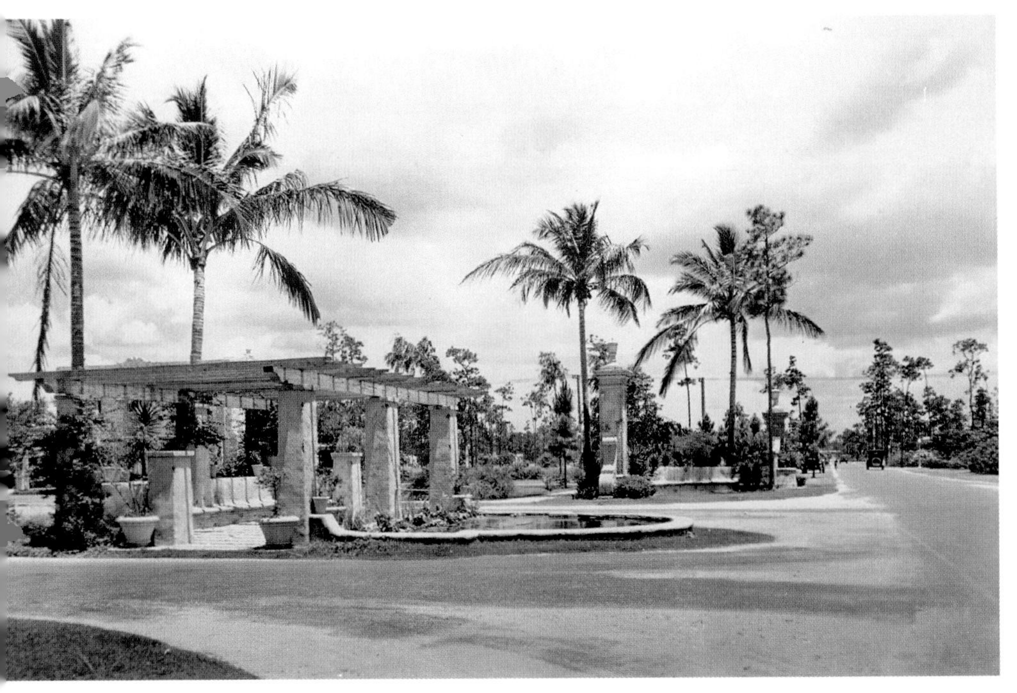

Granada Plaza, Coral Gables, c. 1925

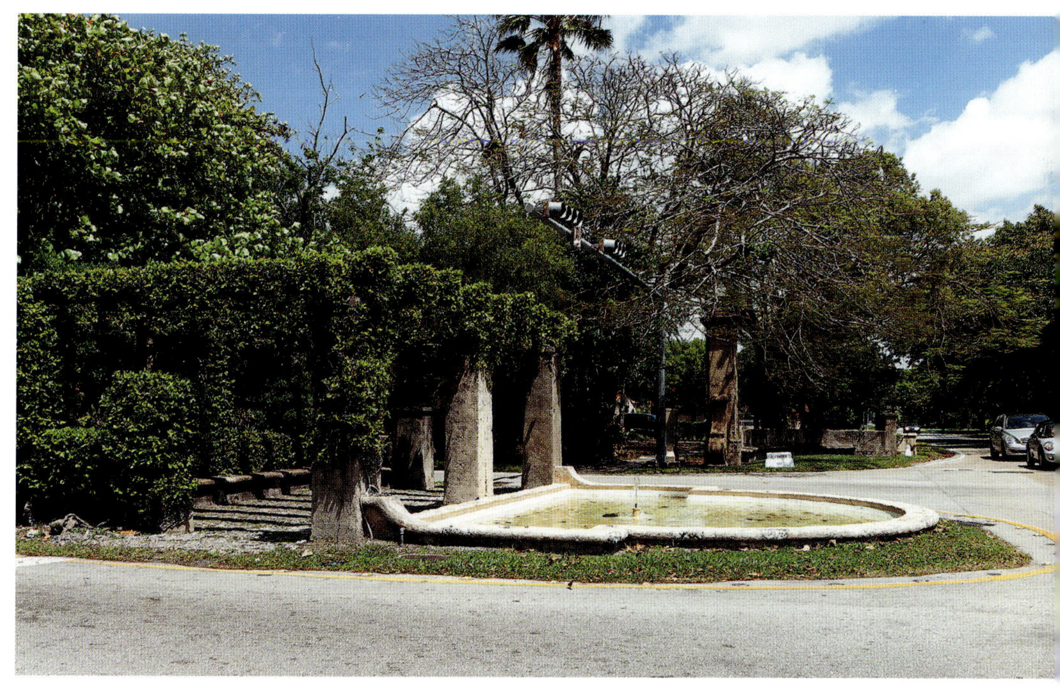

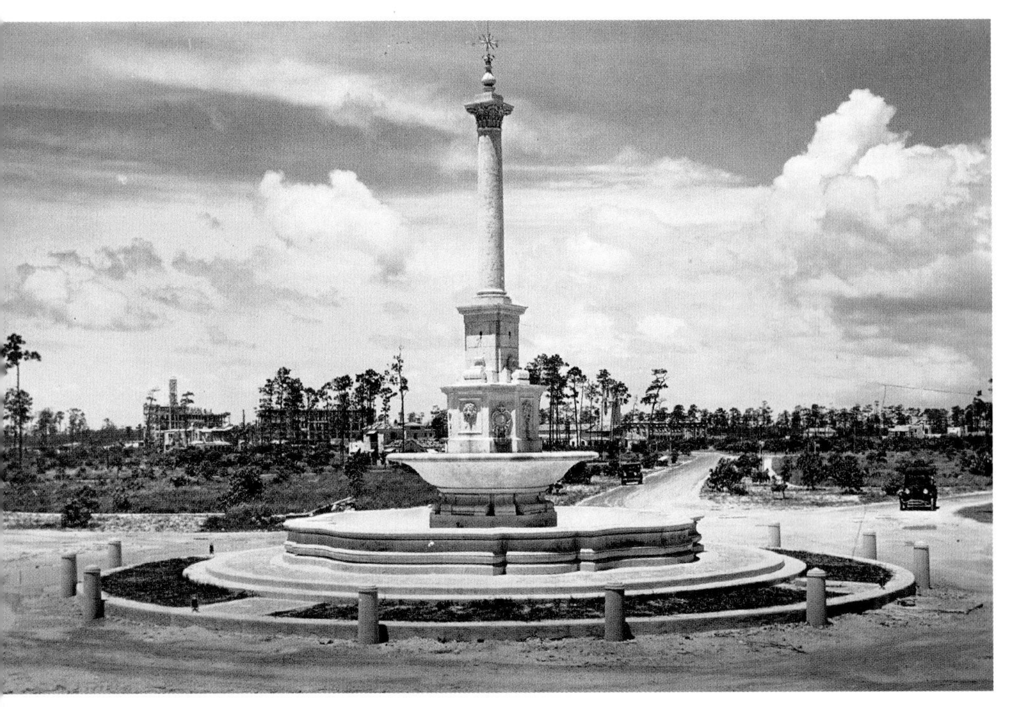

Desoto Plaza, Coral Gables, c. 1925

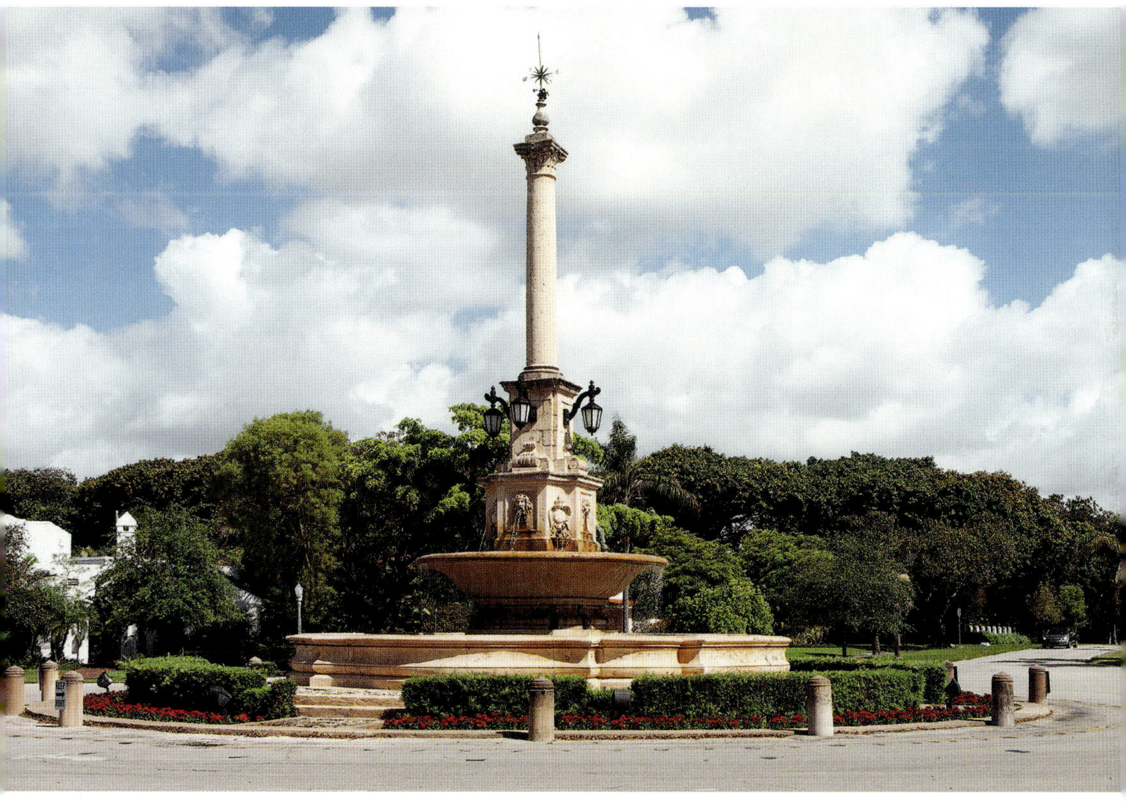

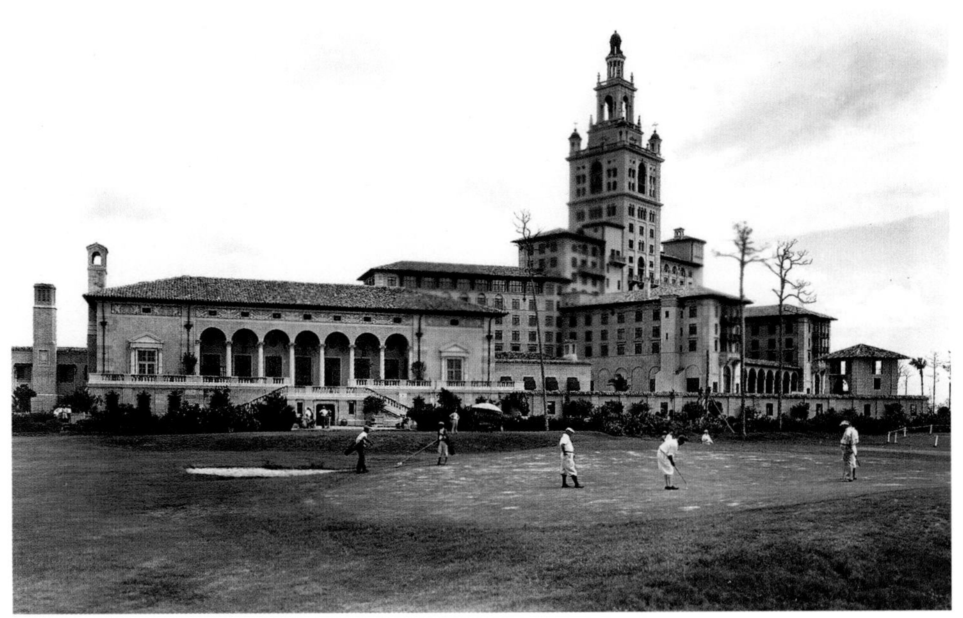

Biltmore Hotel, Coral Gables, c. 1930

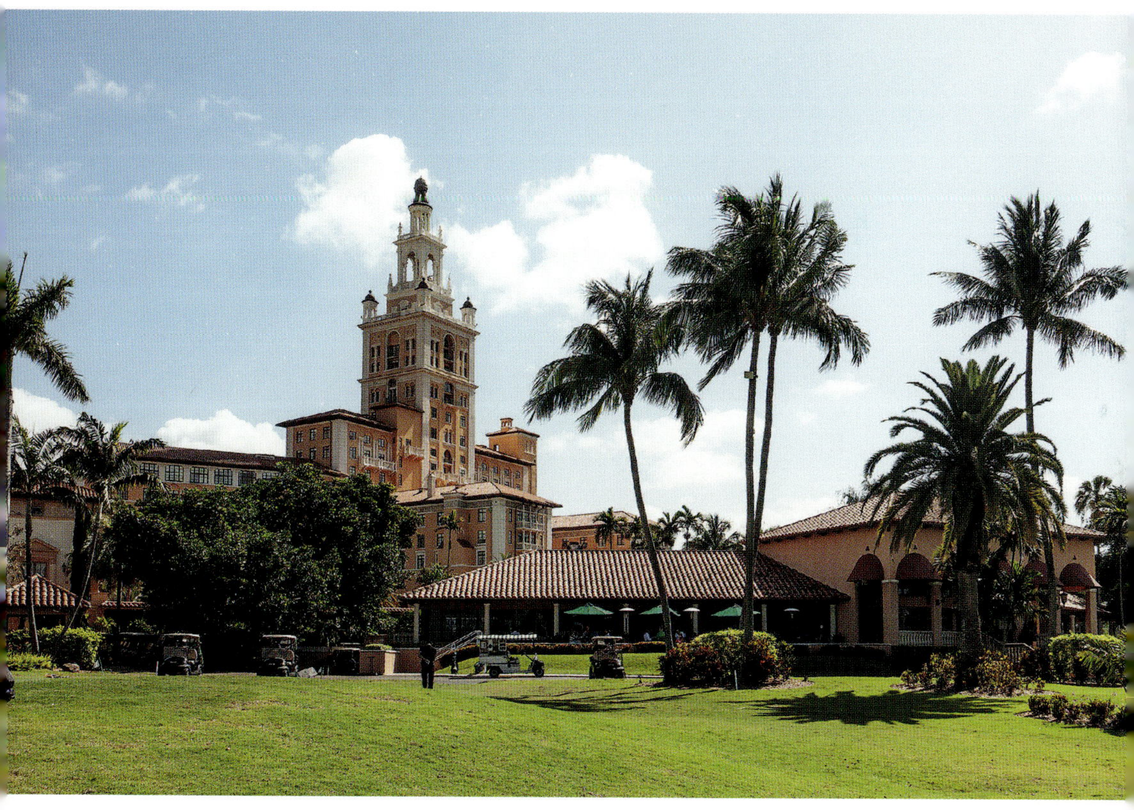

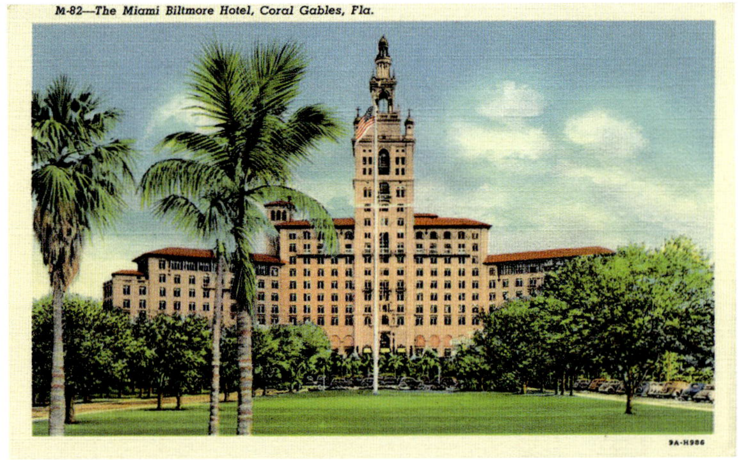

Biltmore Hotel, Coral Gables, c. 1930

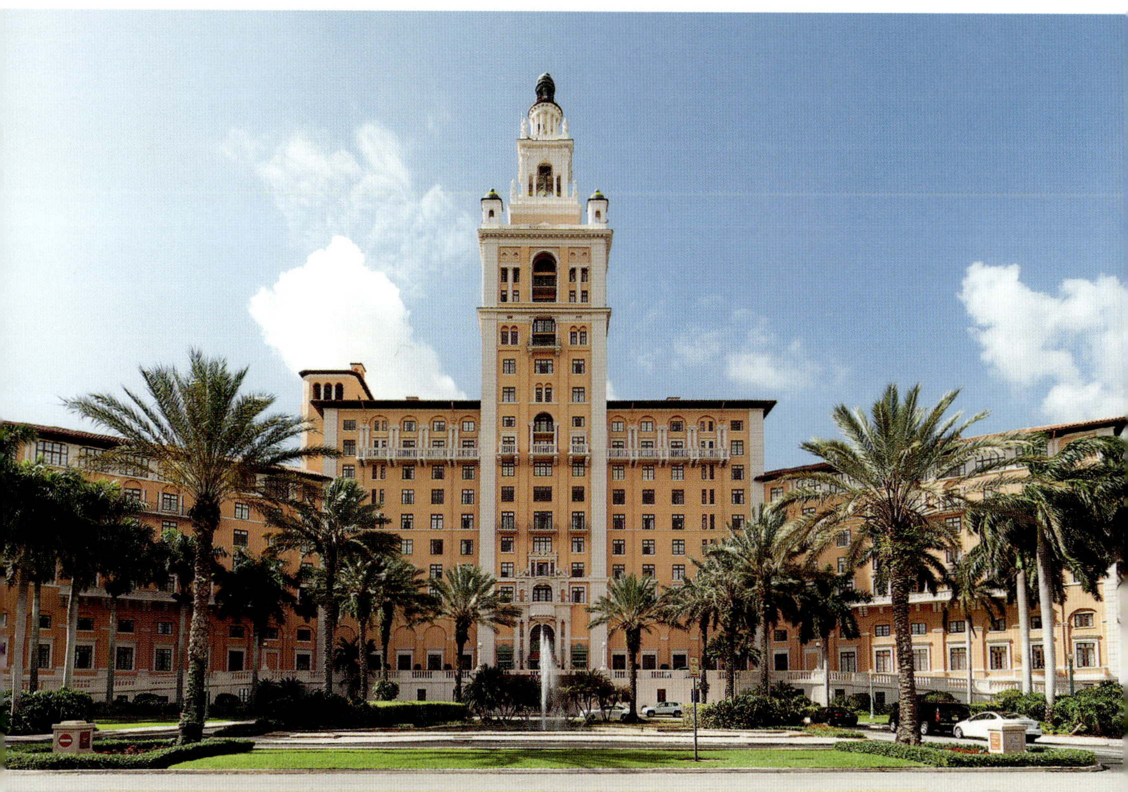

Merrick Building, University of Miami, Coral Gables, c. 1960

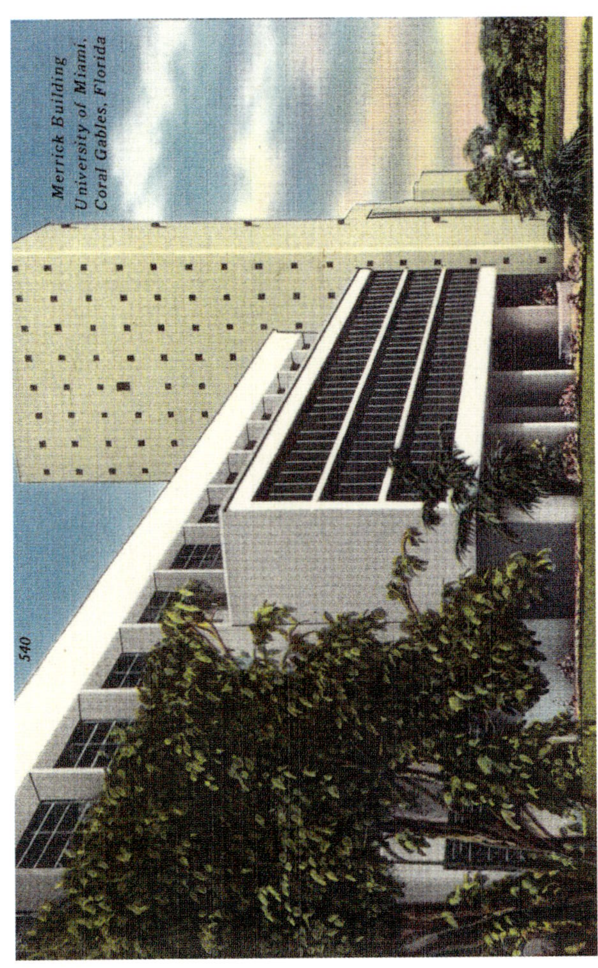

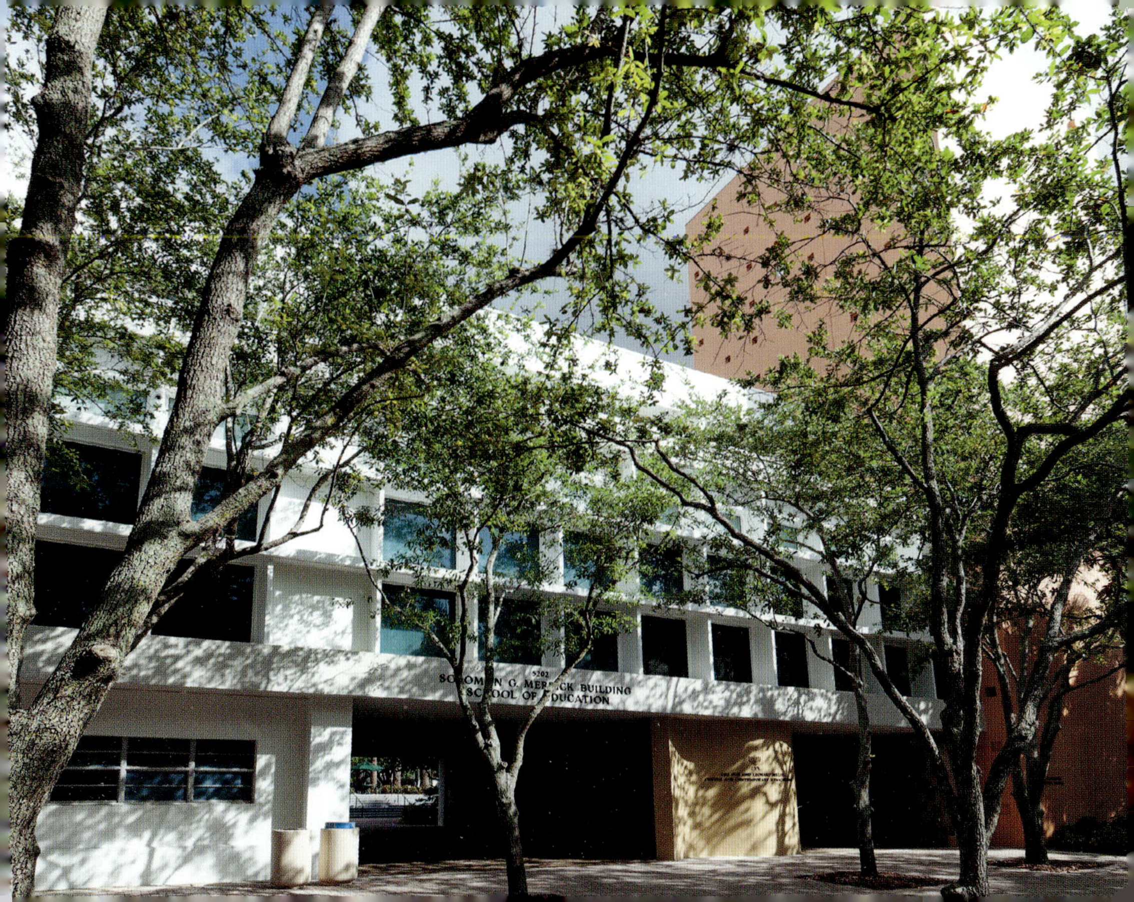
5202
G. BUILDING
SCHOOL OF

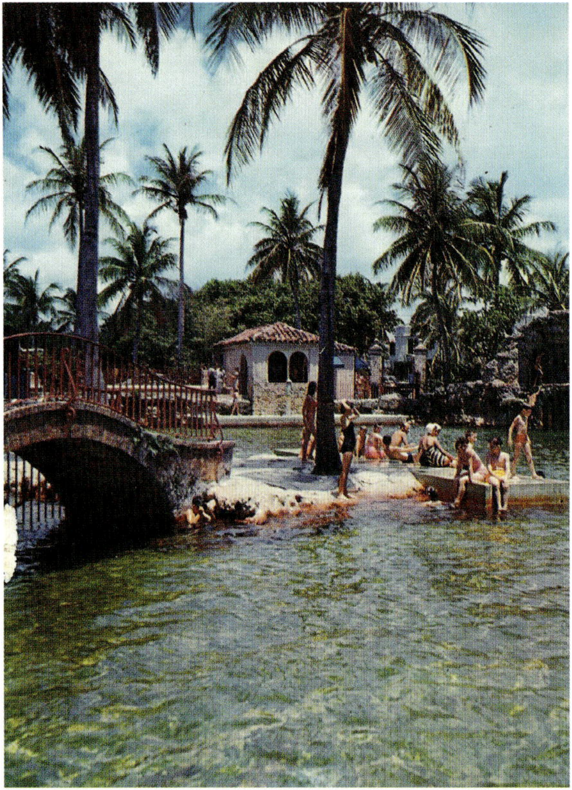

Venetian Pool, Coral Gables, c. 1960

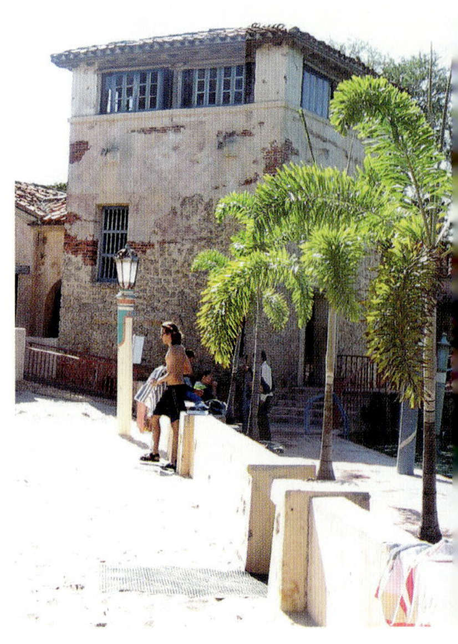

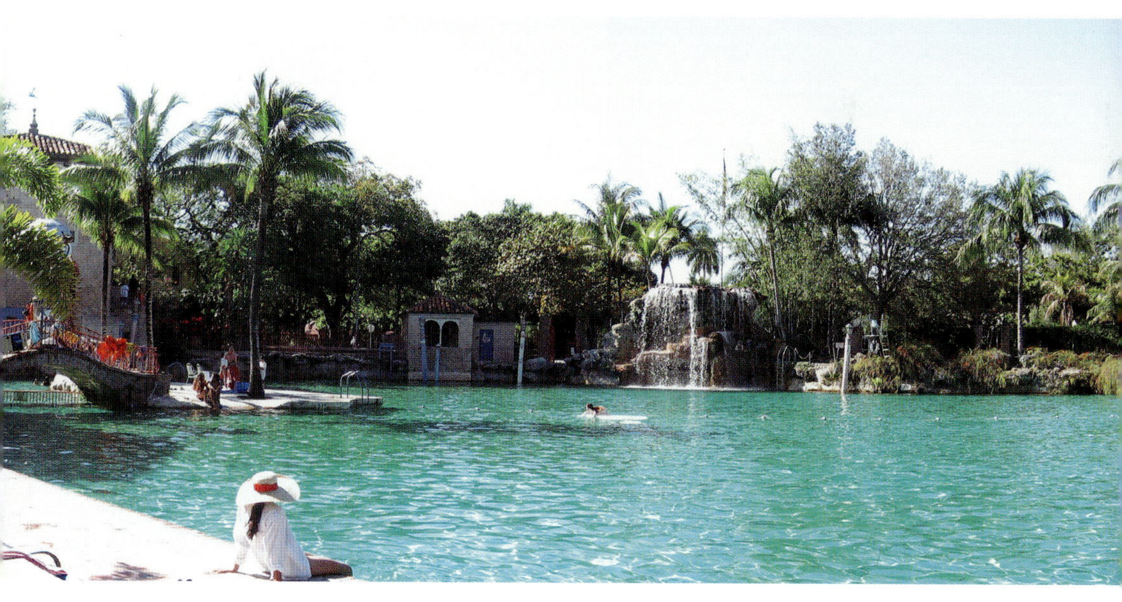

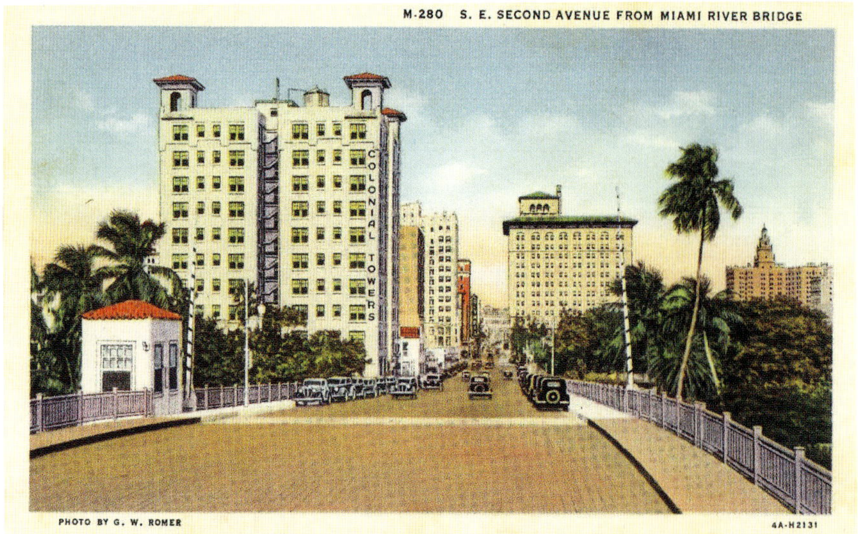

Second Avenue from Miami River Bridge, Miami, c. 1940

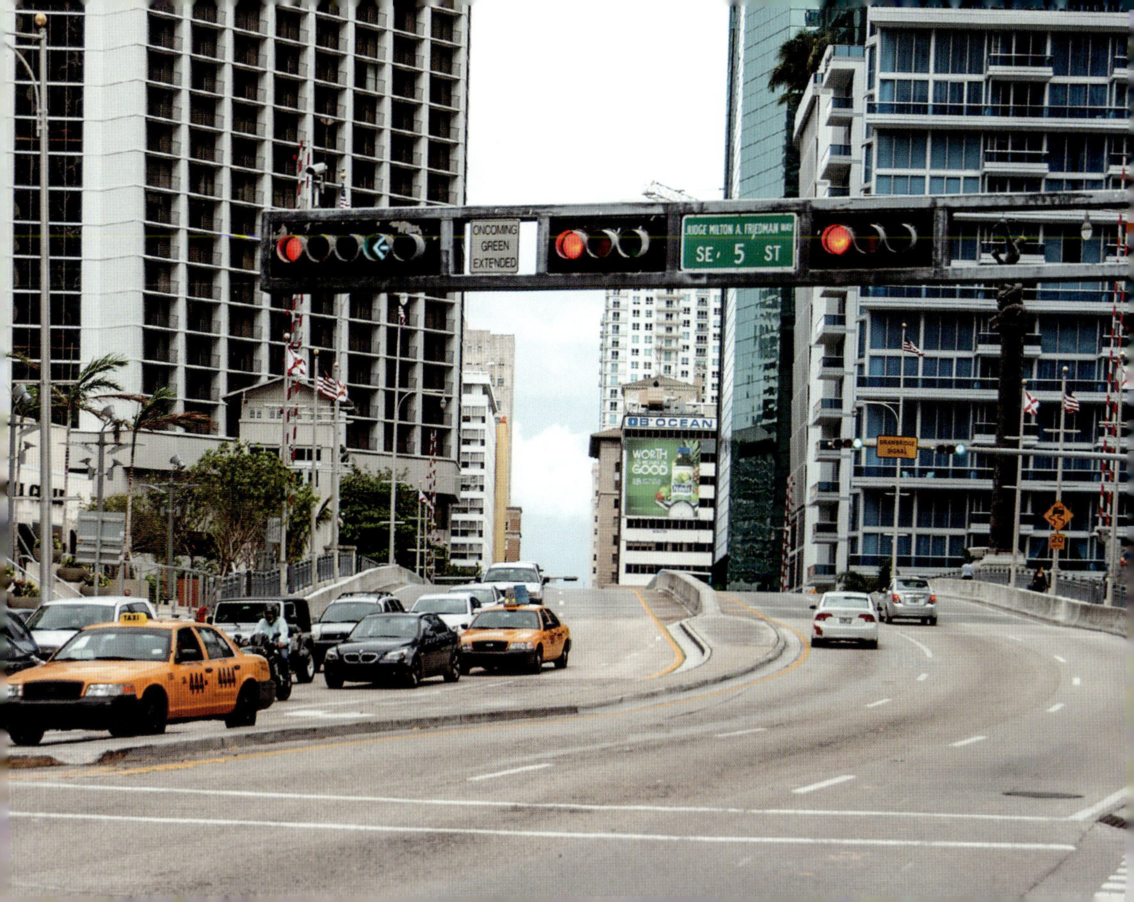
ONCOMING
GREEN
EXTENDED
JUDGE MILTON A. FRIEDMAN WAY
SE 5 ST
TAXI
4444
OCEAN
WORTH
GOOD
20

Collins Avenue at 26th Street, Miami, c. 1955

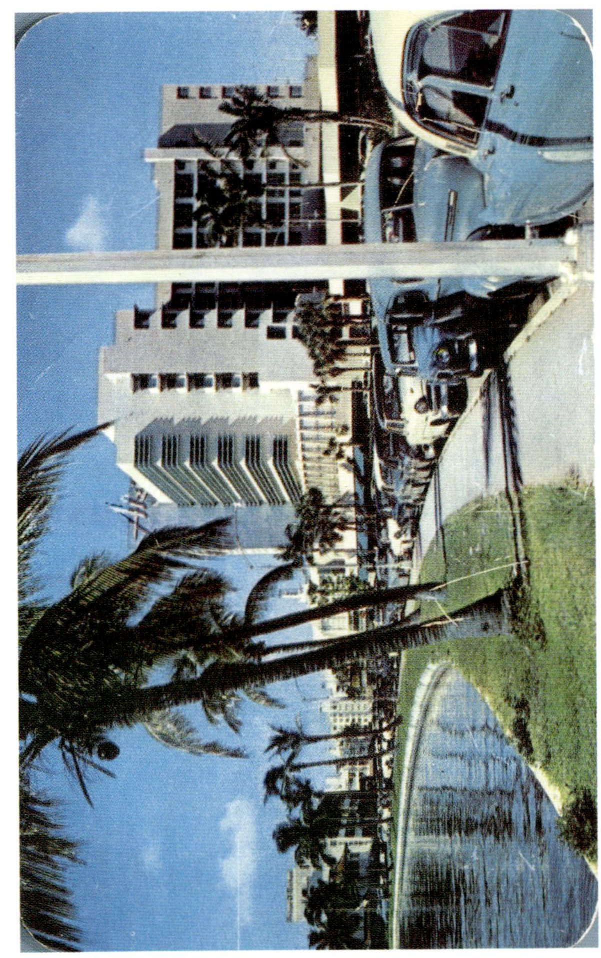

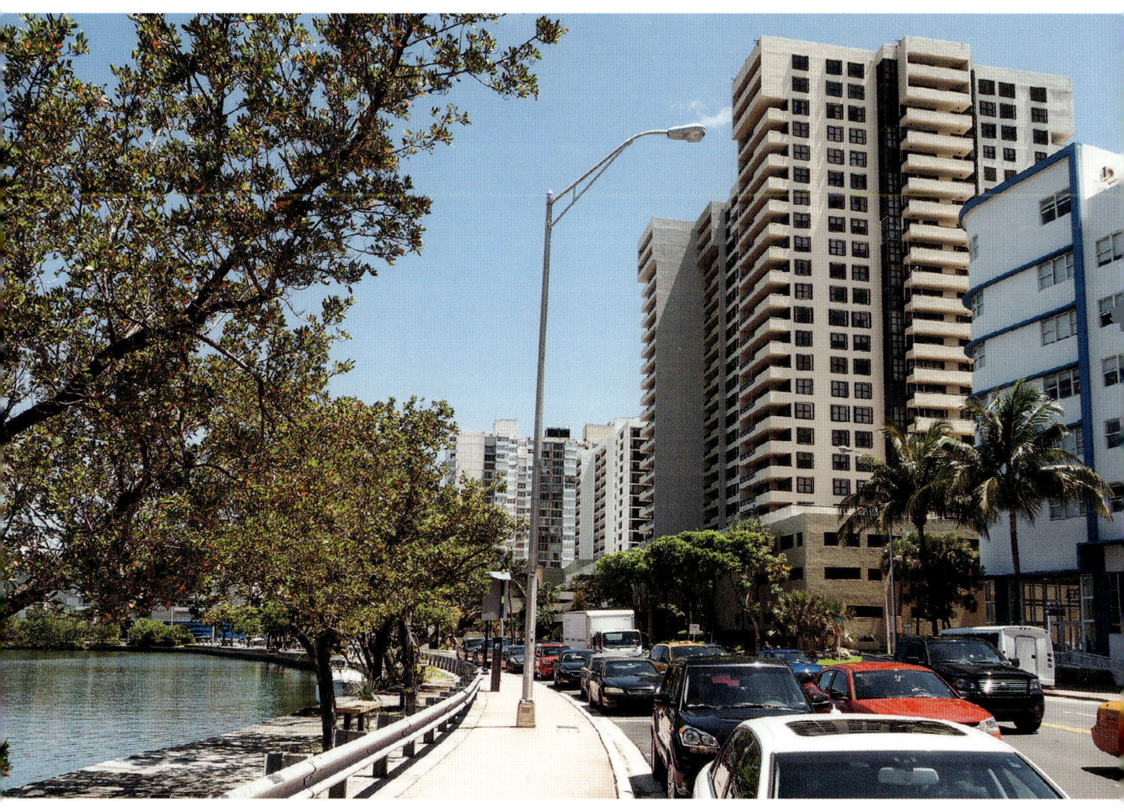

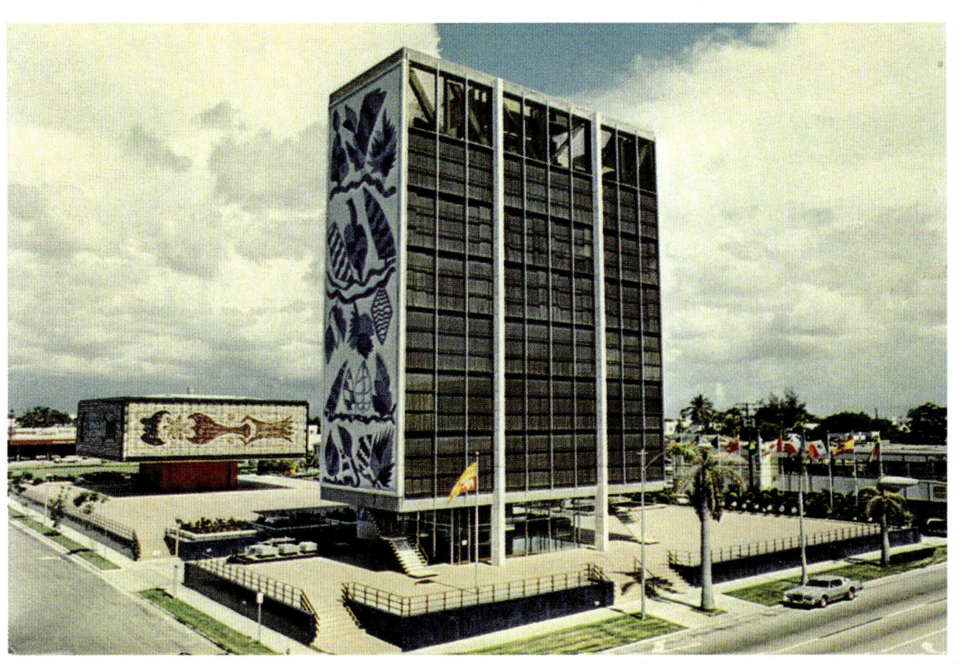

Bacardi Building, Biscayne Boulevard, Miami, c. 1975

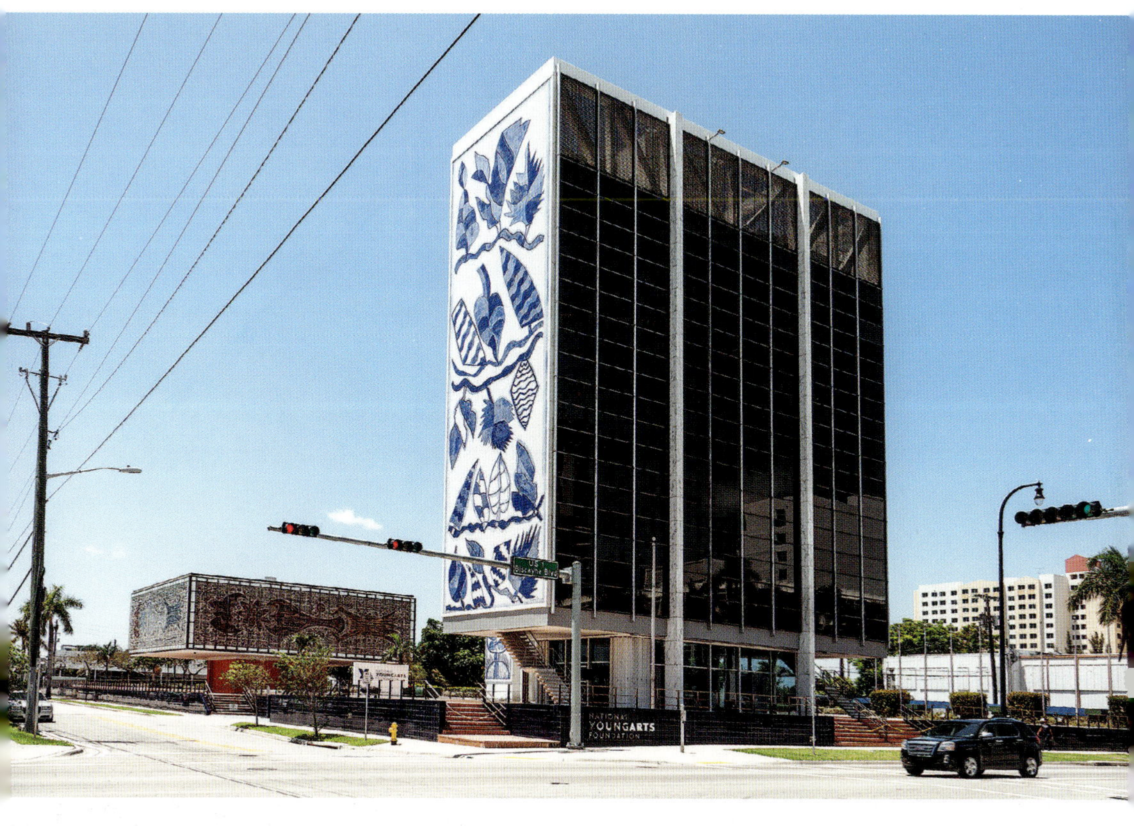
US 1
Biscayne Blvd
NATIONAL
YOUNGARTS
FOUNDATION

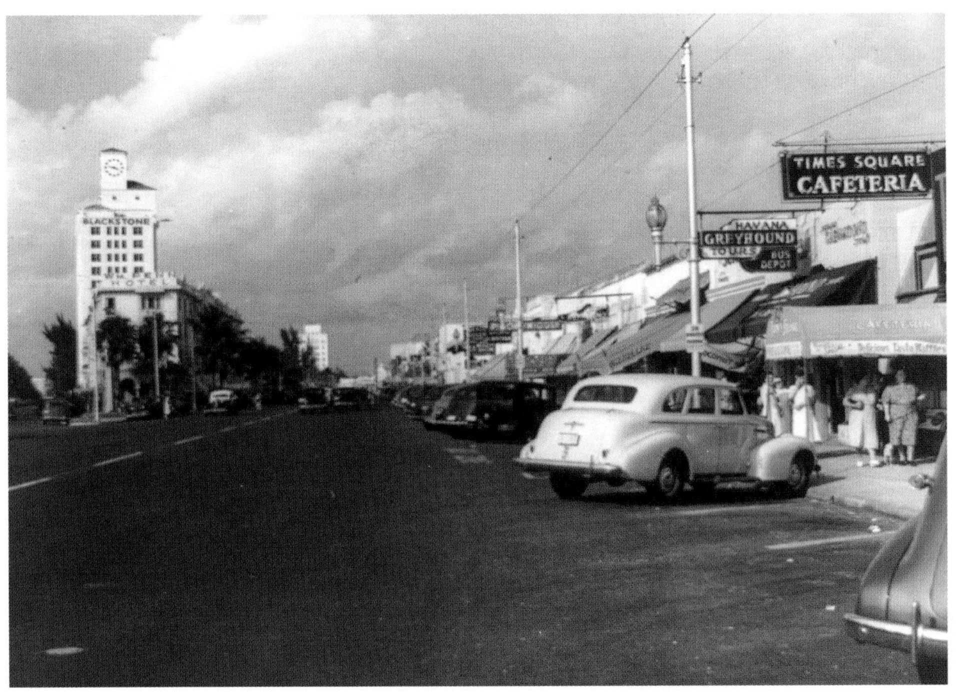

Washington Avenue, Miami, 1939

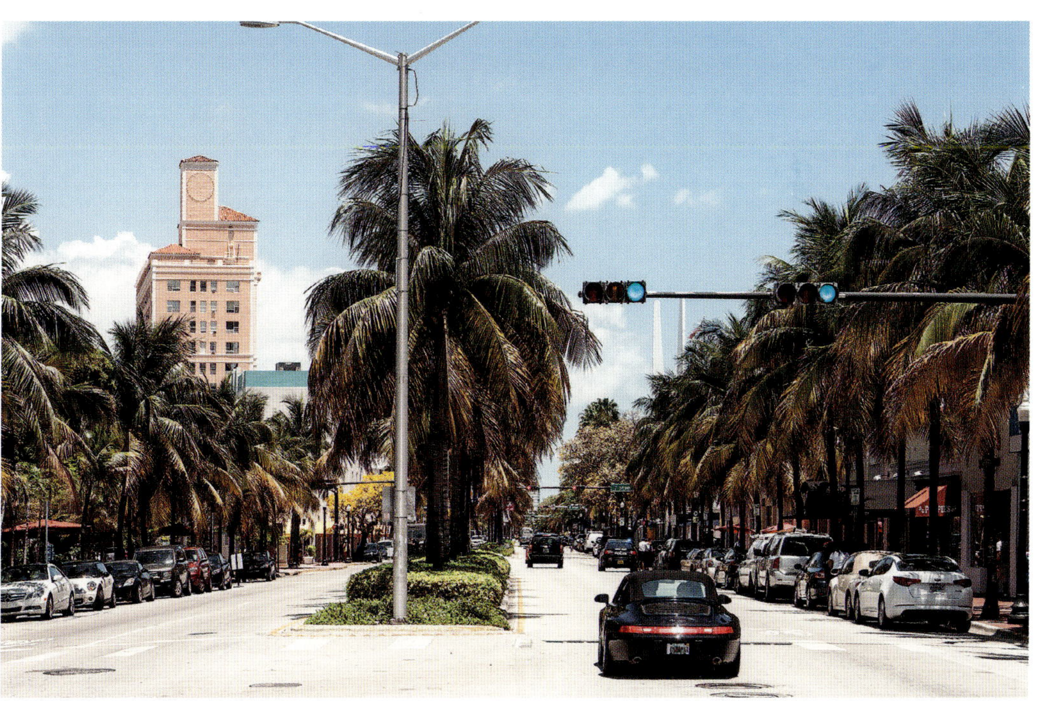

Washington Avenue at Espanola Way, Miami, 1941

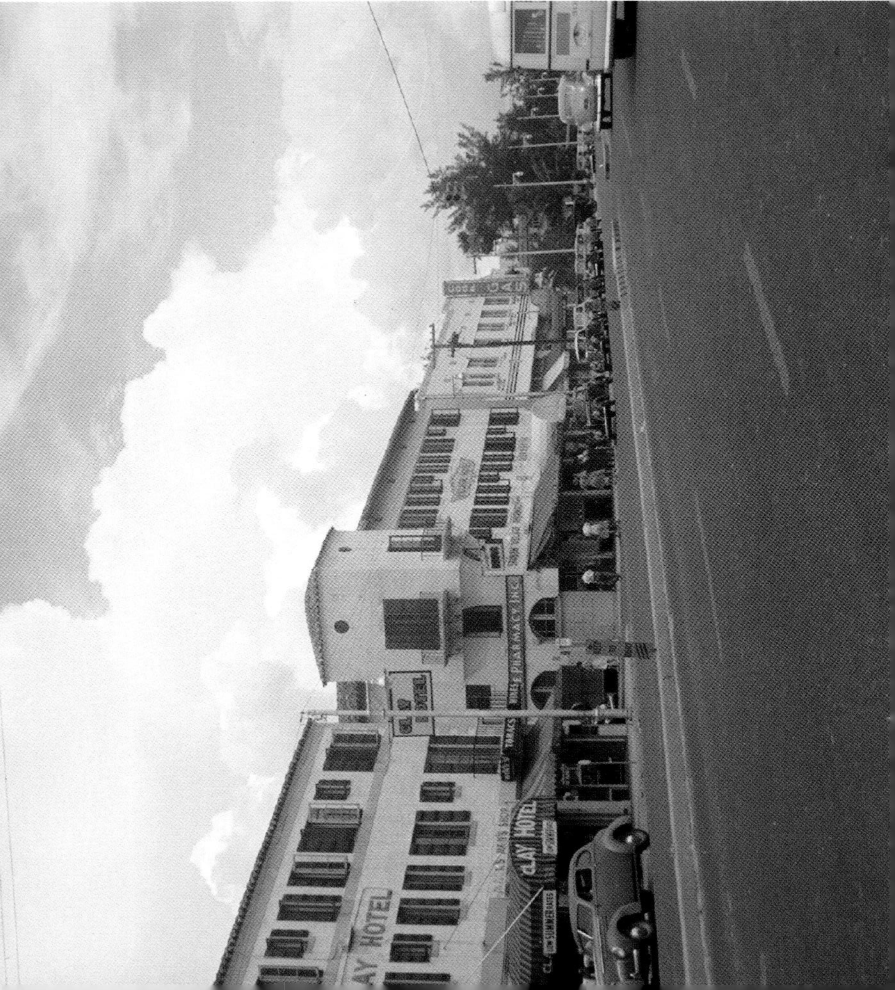

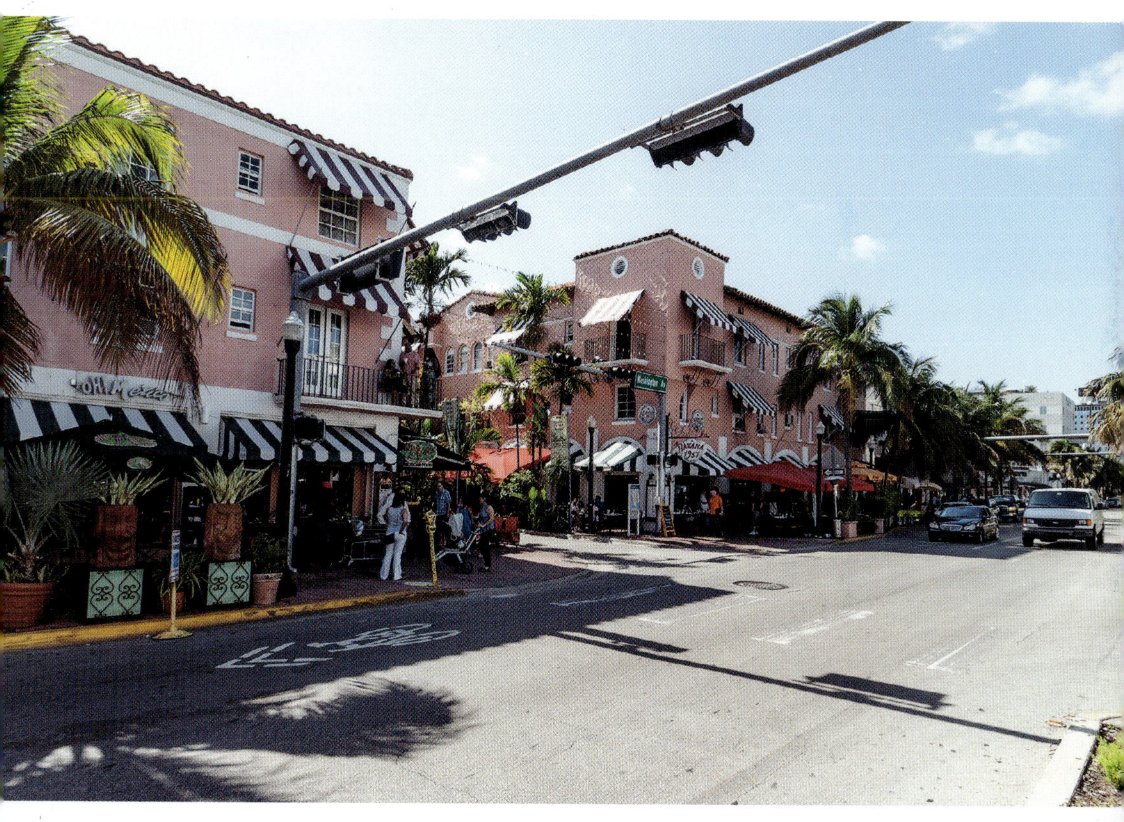

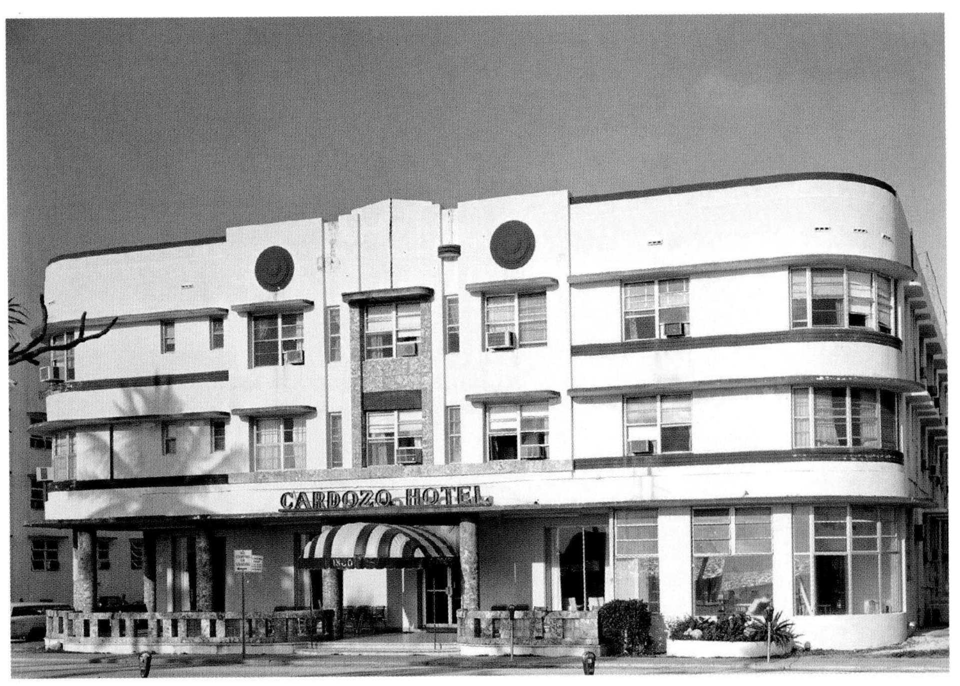

Cardozo Hotel, Ocean Drive, Miami, 1980

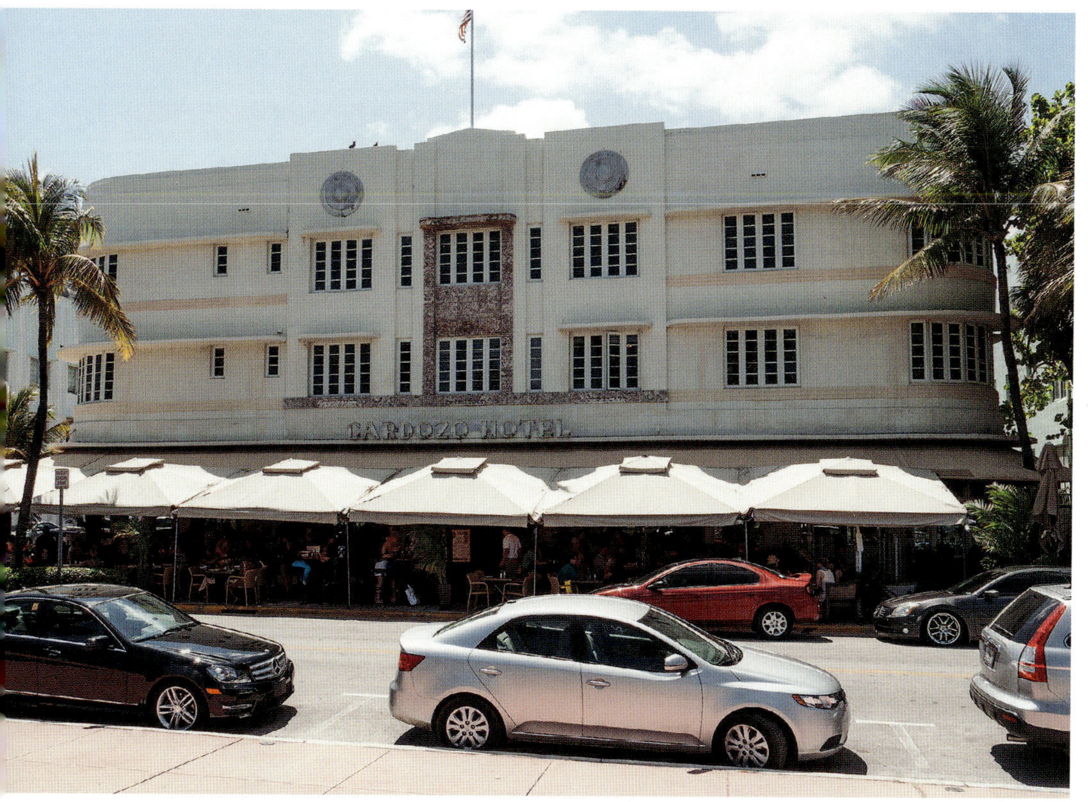
CARDOZO HOTEL

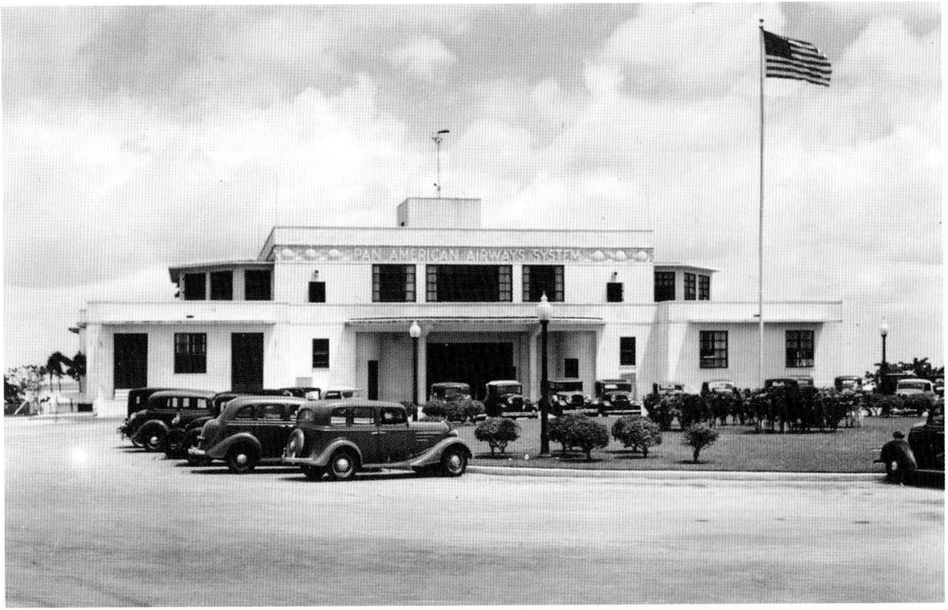

Pan American Airways Terminal (now City Hall), Miami, c. 1935

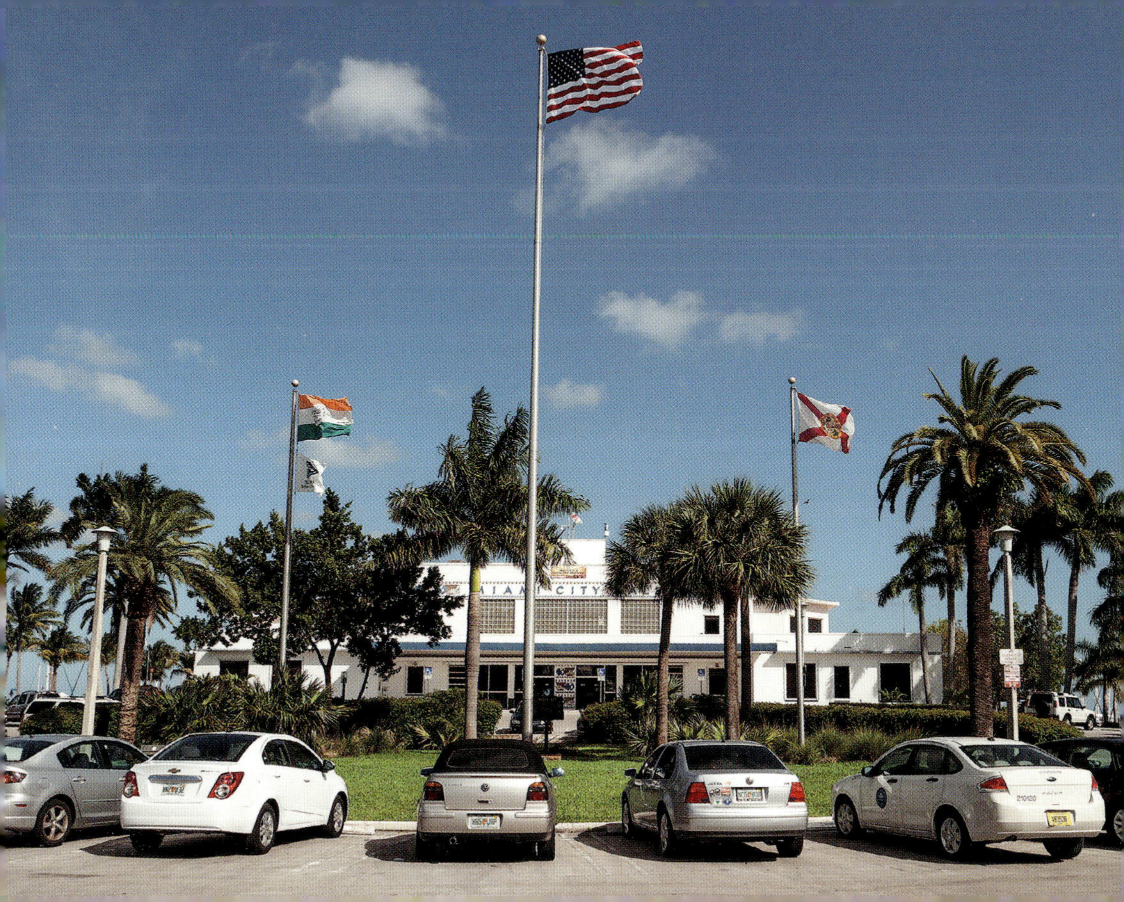

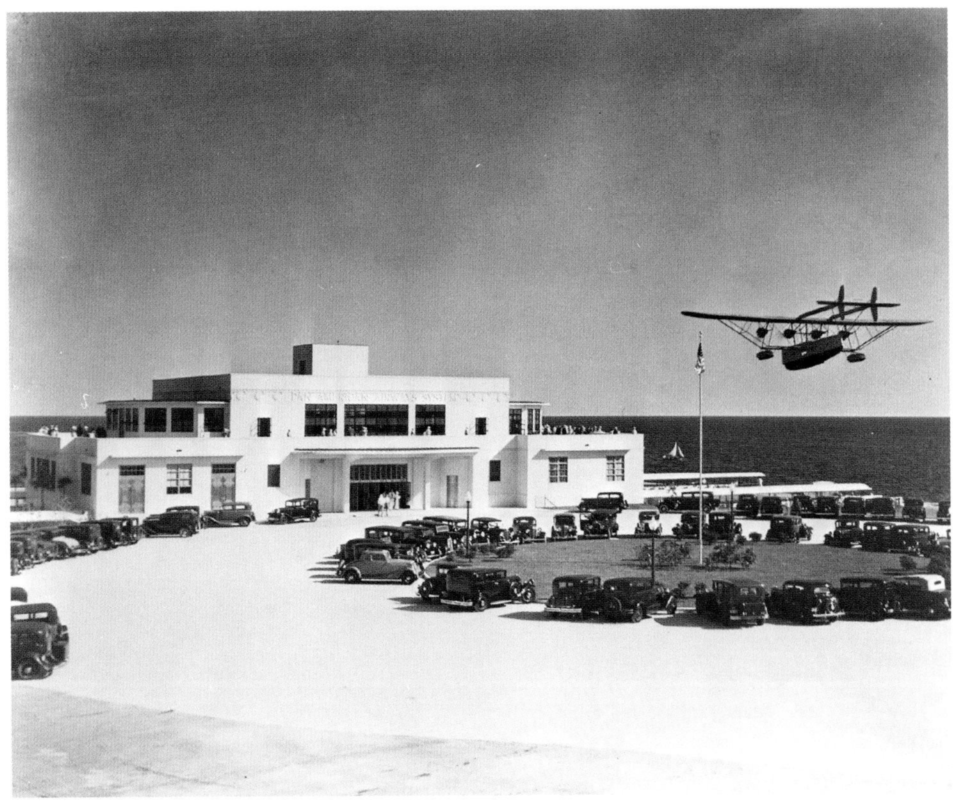

Pan American Airways Terminal (closed 1945), Miami, 1934

Miami International Airport

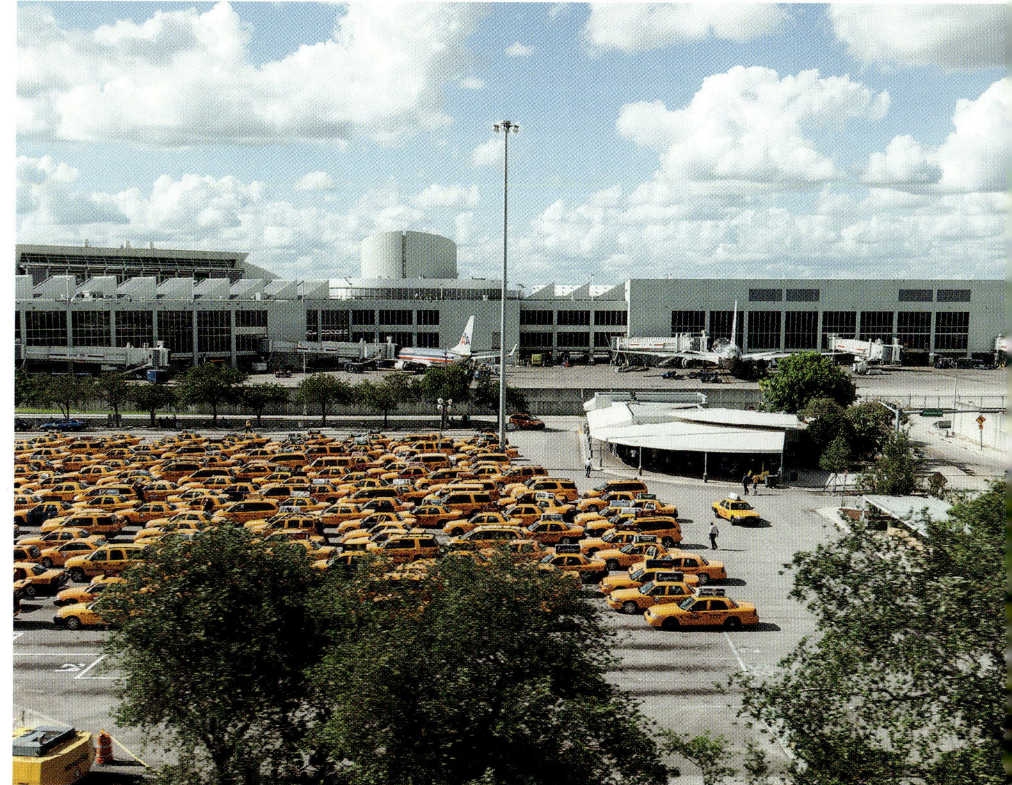

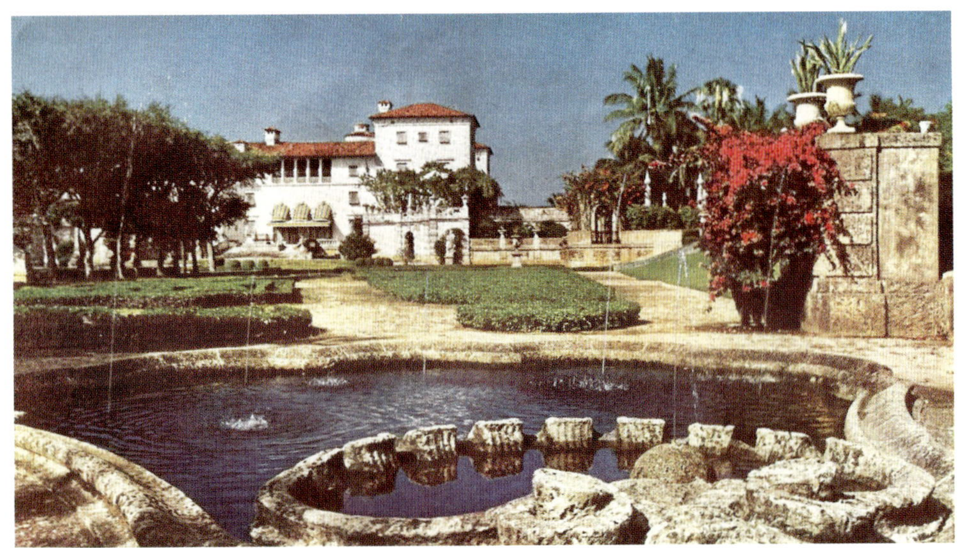

Villa Vizcaya, Miami, c. 1960

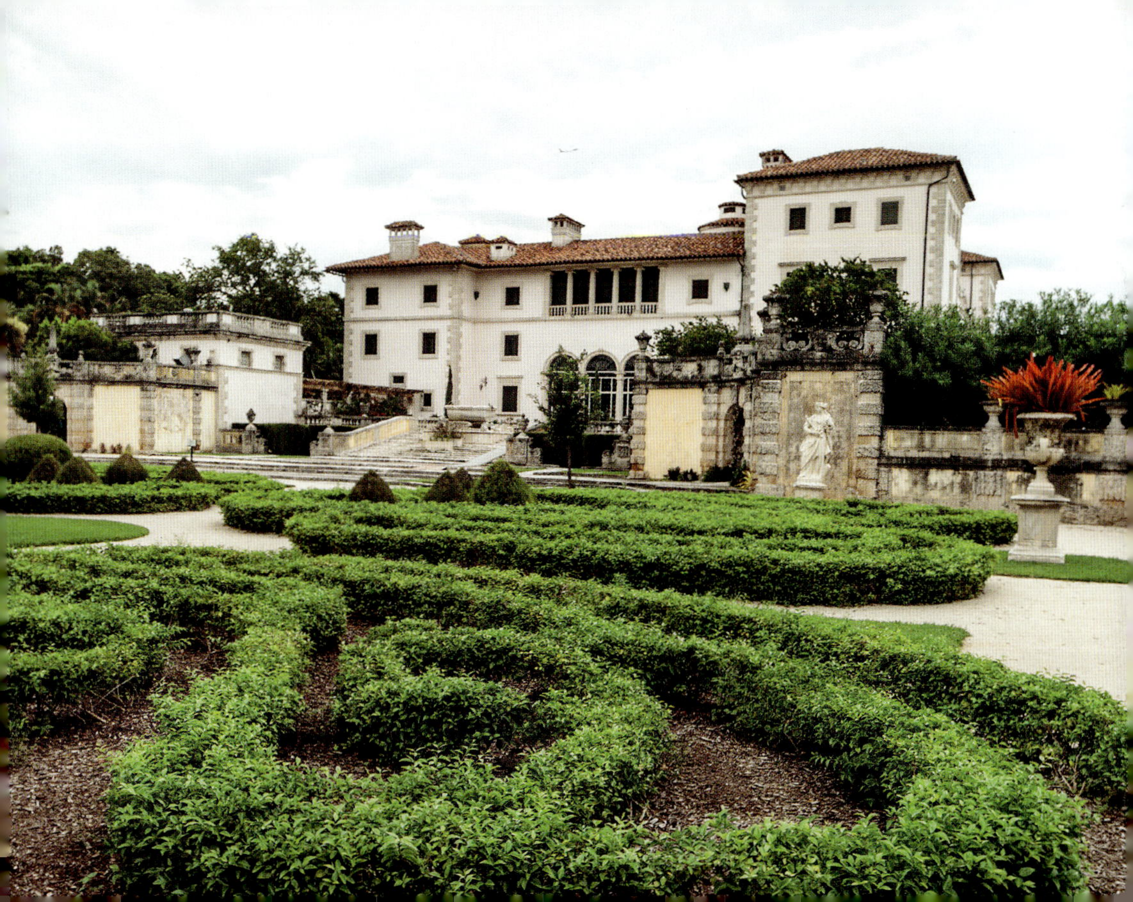

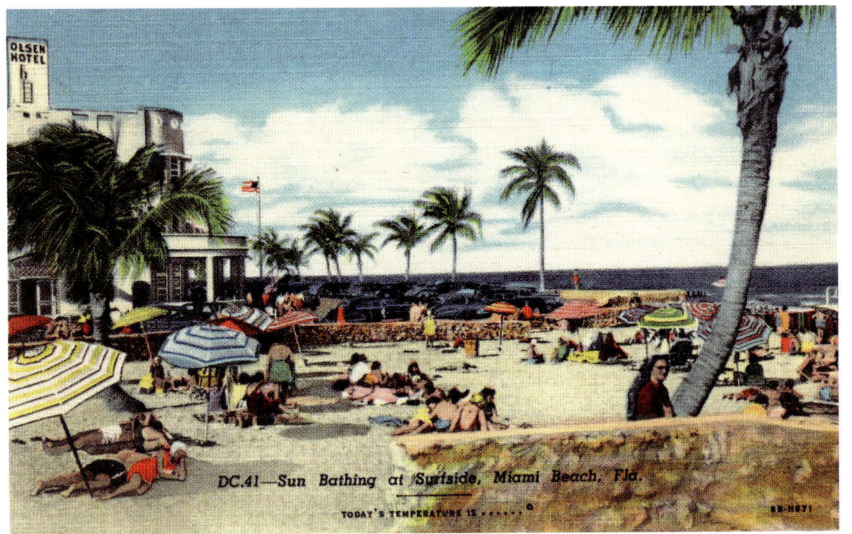

Olsen Hotel, Ocean Terrace, Miami, c. 1950

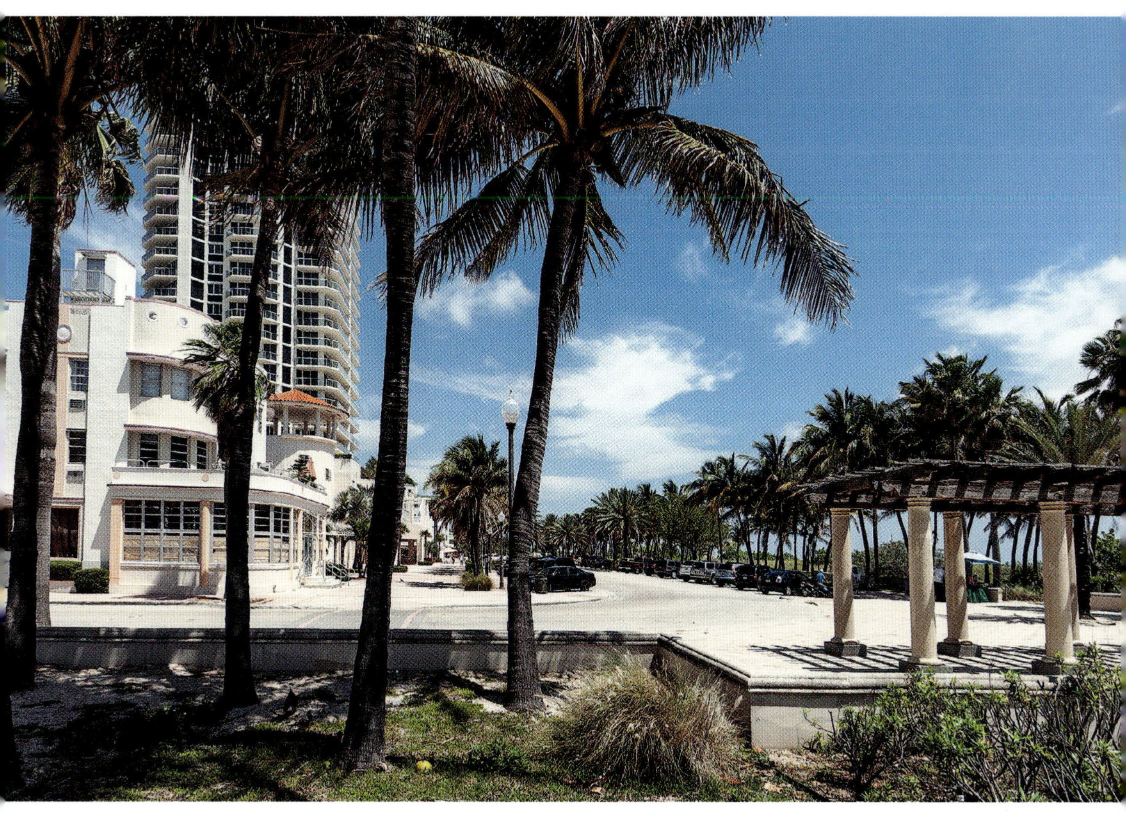

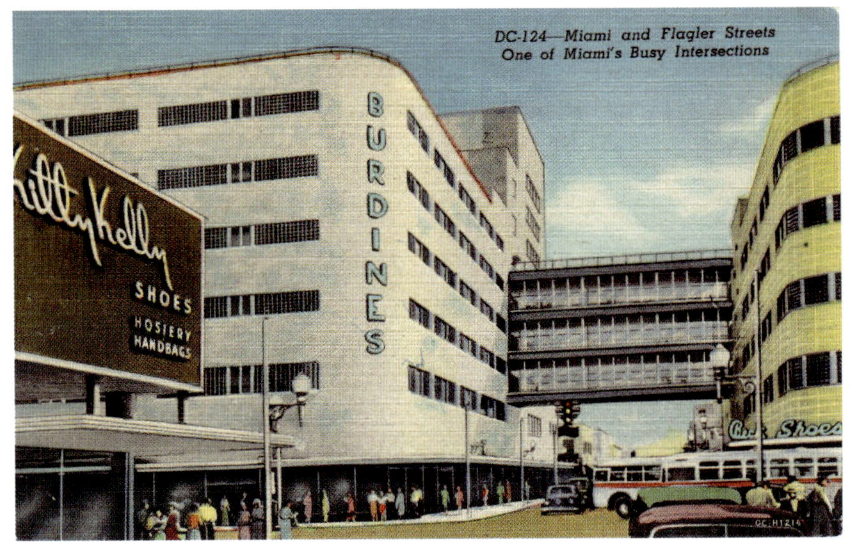

Miami and East Flagler Streets, Miami, c. 1950

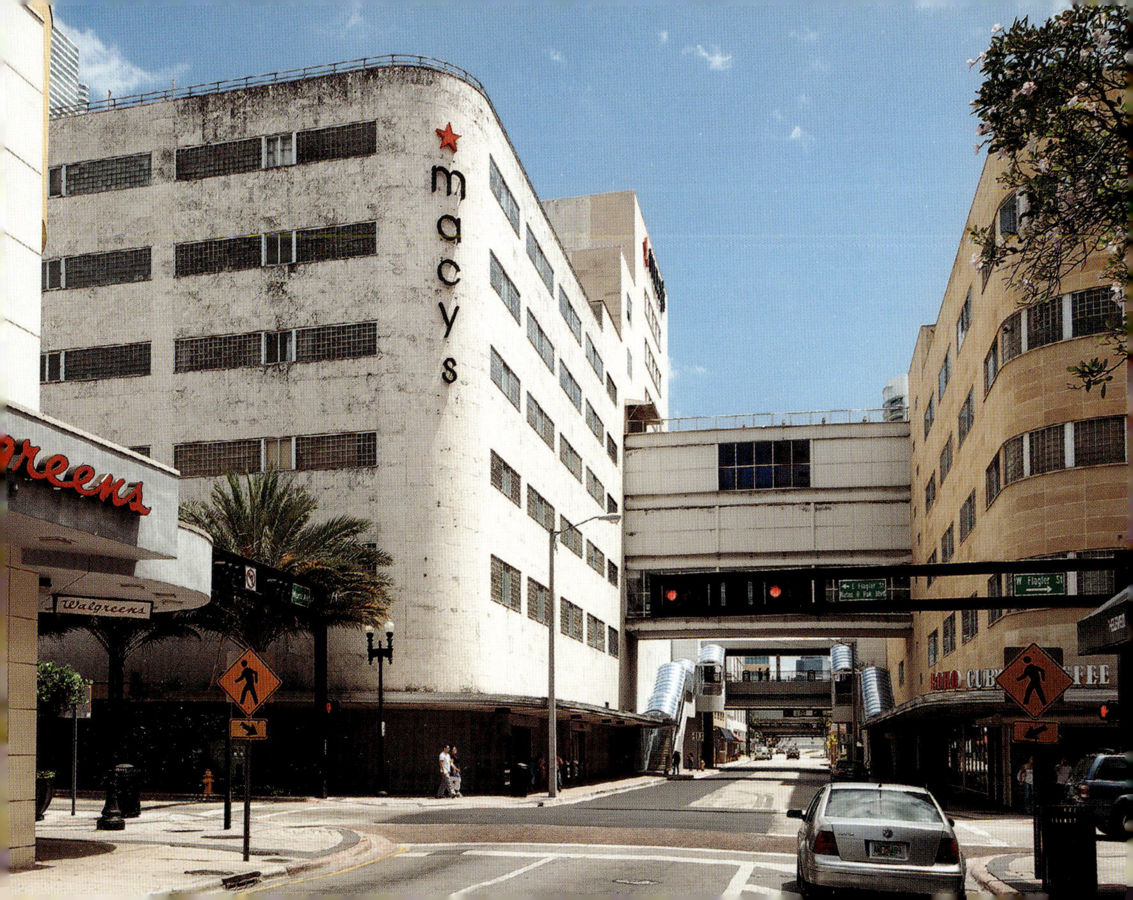
macys
Walgreens
W Flagler St

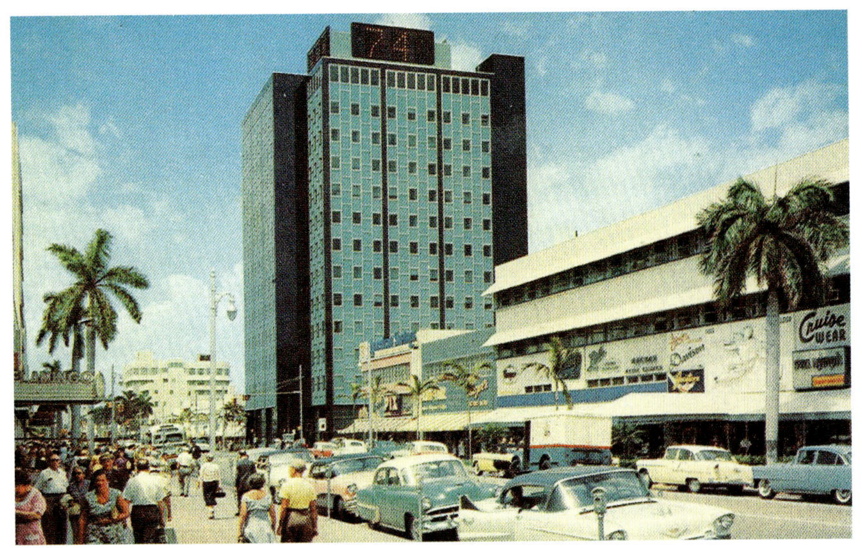

Lincoln Road, Miami, c. 1960

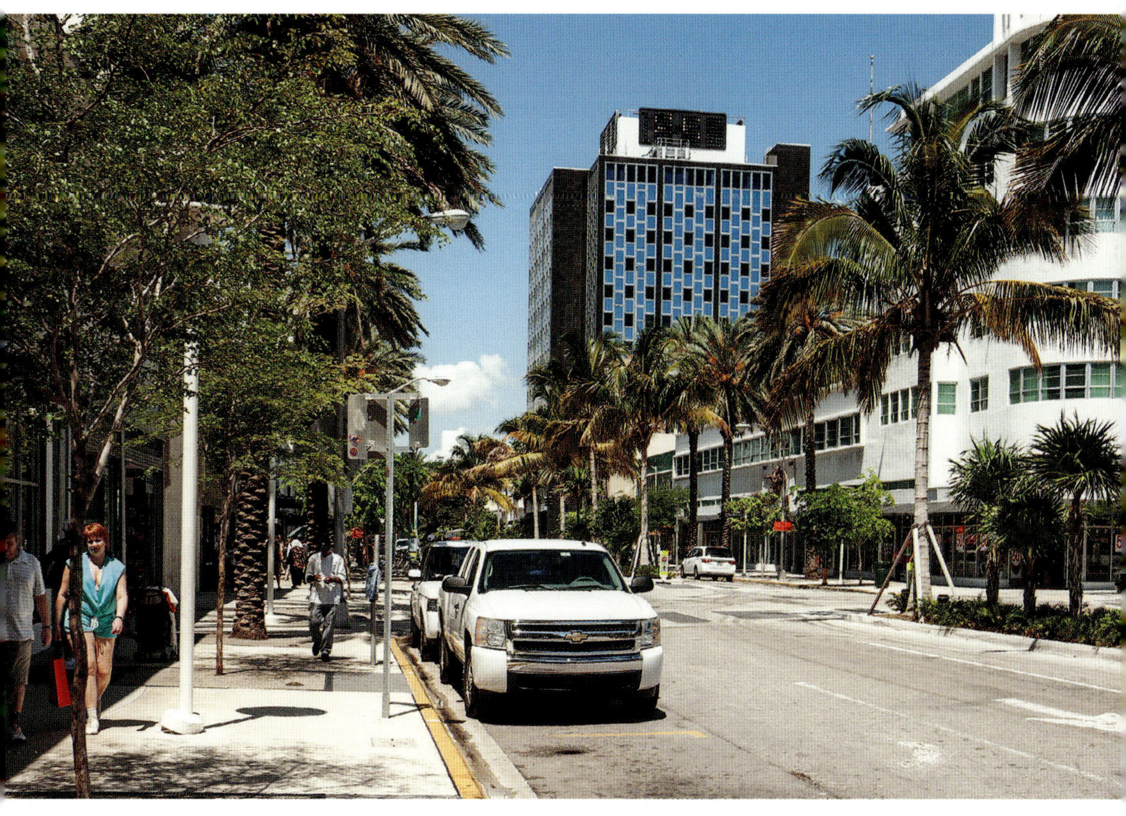

Colony Hotel, Ocean Drive, Miami, 1980

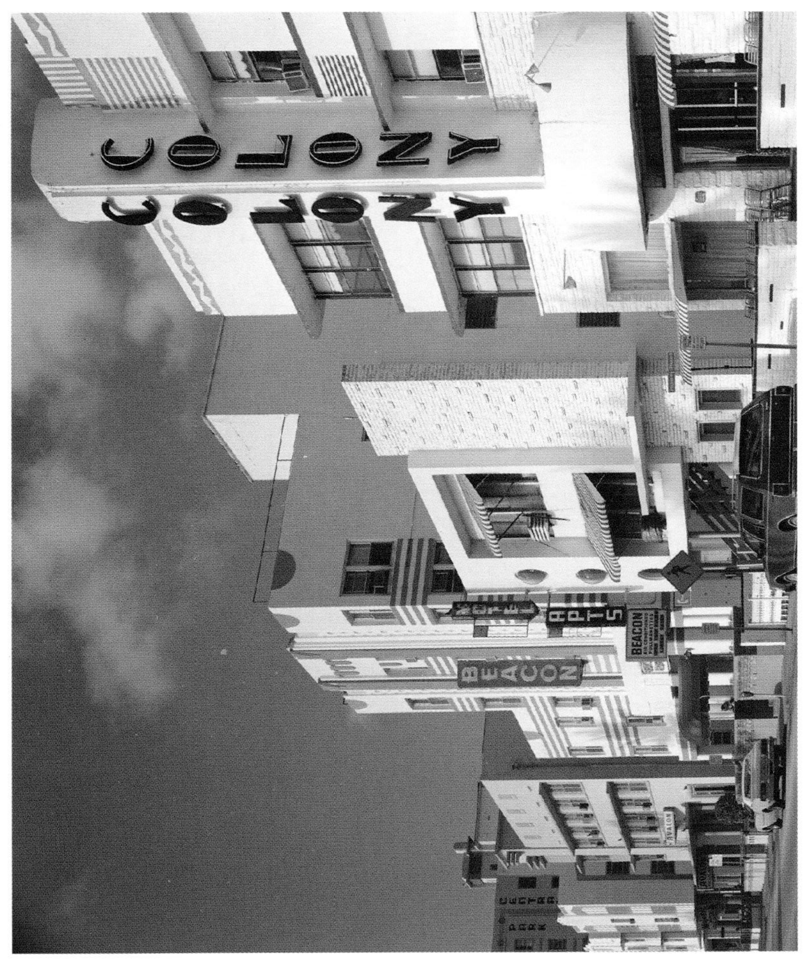

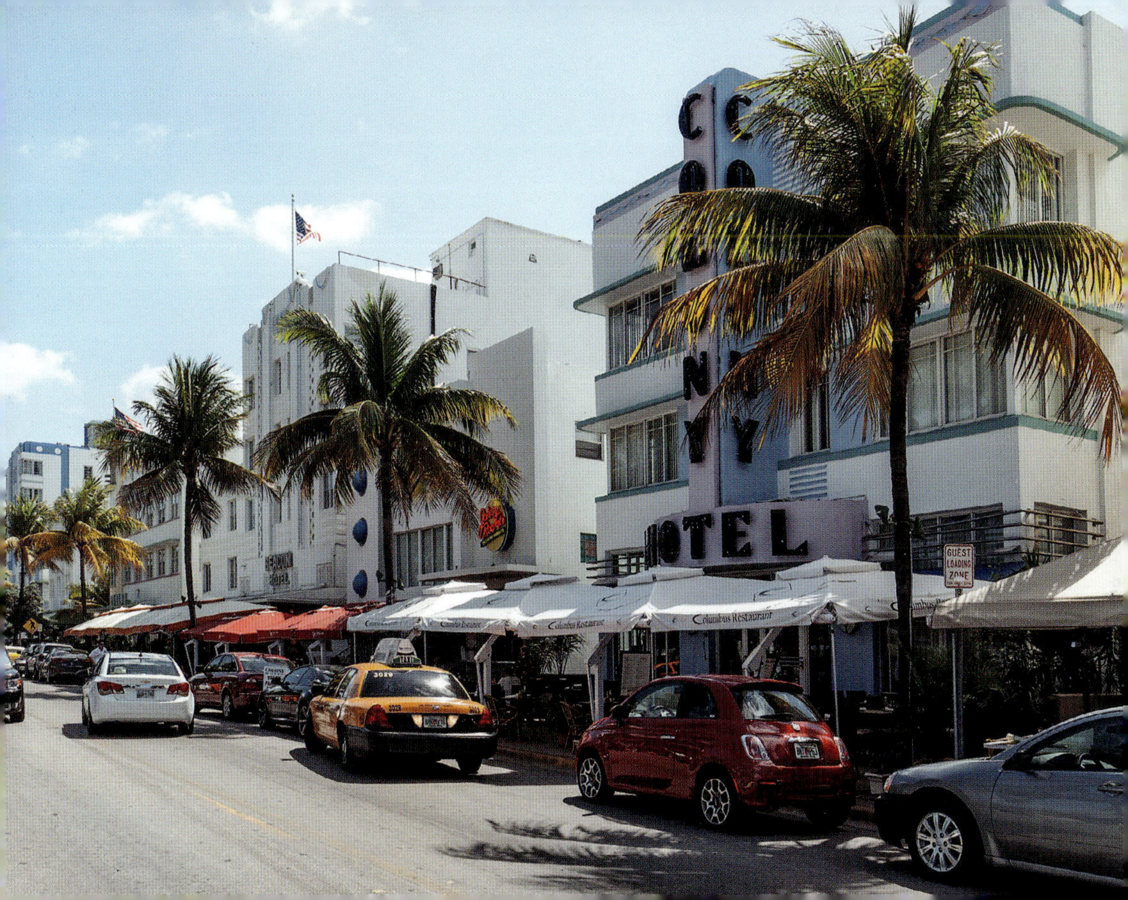
HOTEL
Columbus Restaurant
GUEST
LOADING
ZONE

Century Hotel, Ocean Drive, Miami, 1980

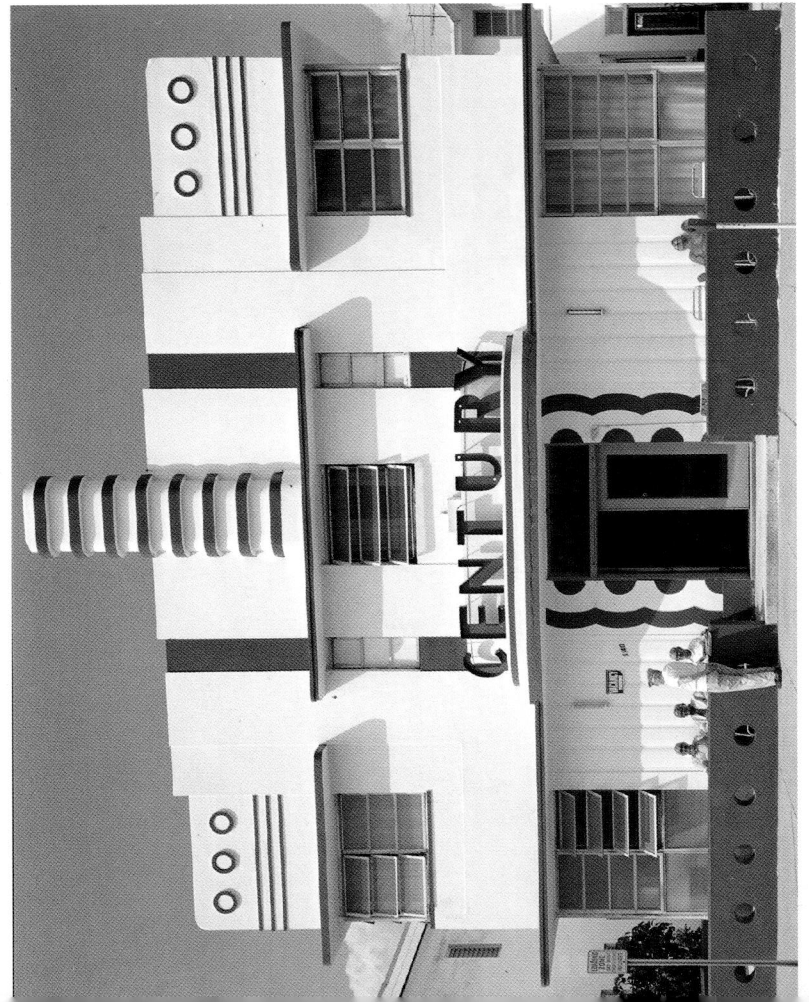

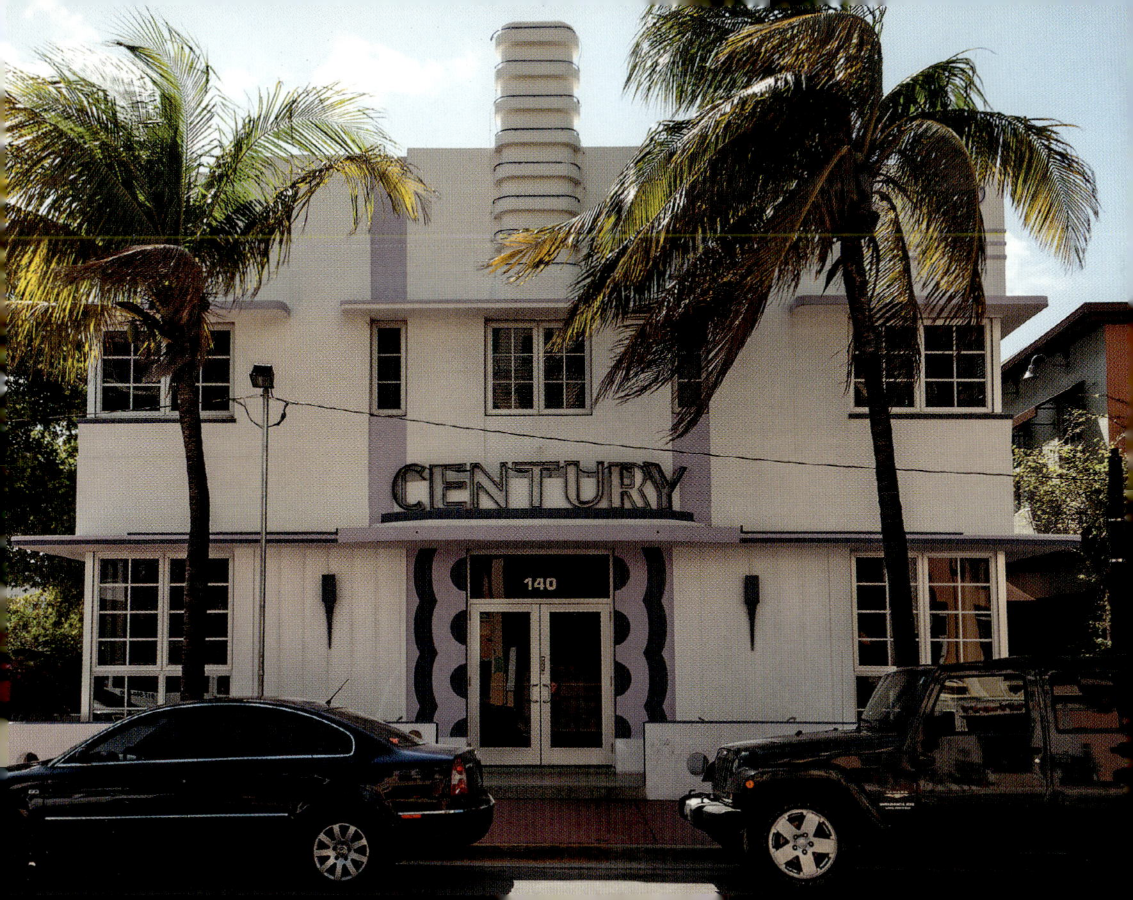
CENTURY
140

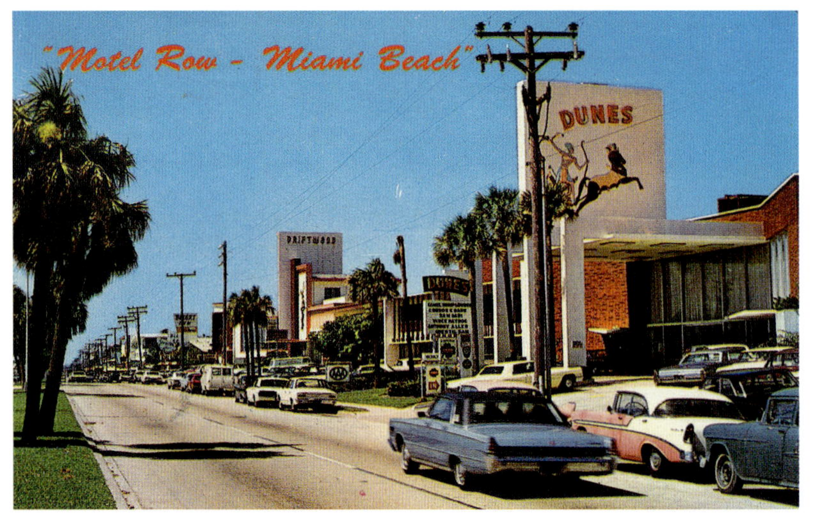

Collins Avenue at Sunny Isles Beach, Miami, c. 1970

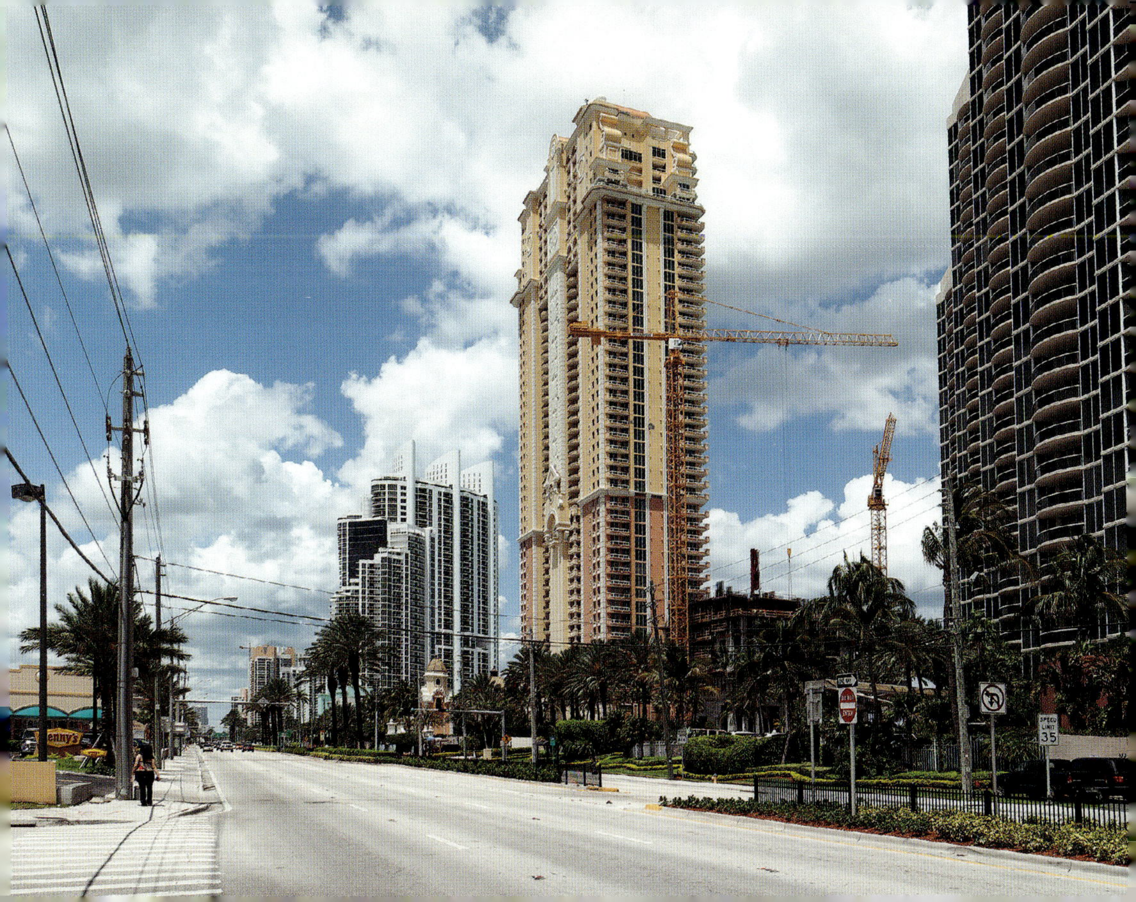
SPEED
LIMIT
35

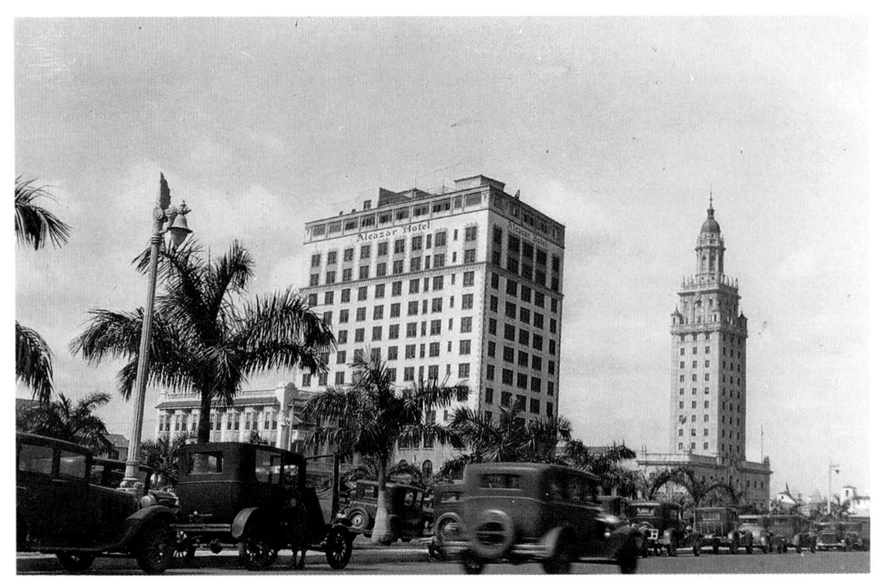

Biscayne Boulevard, Miami, 1932

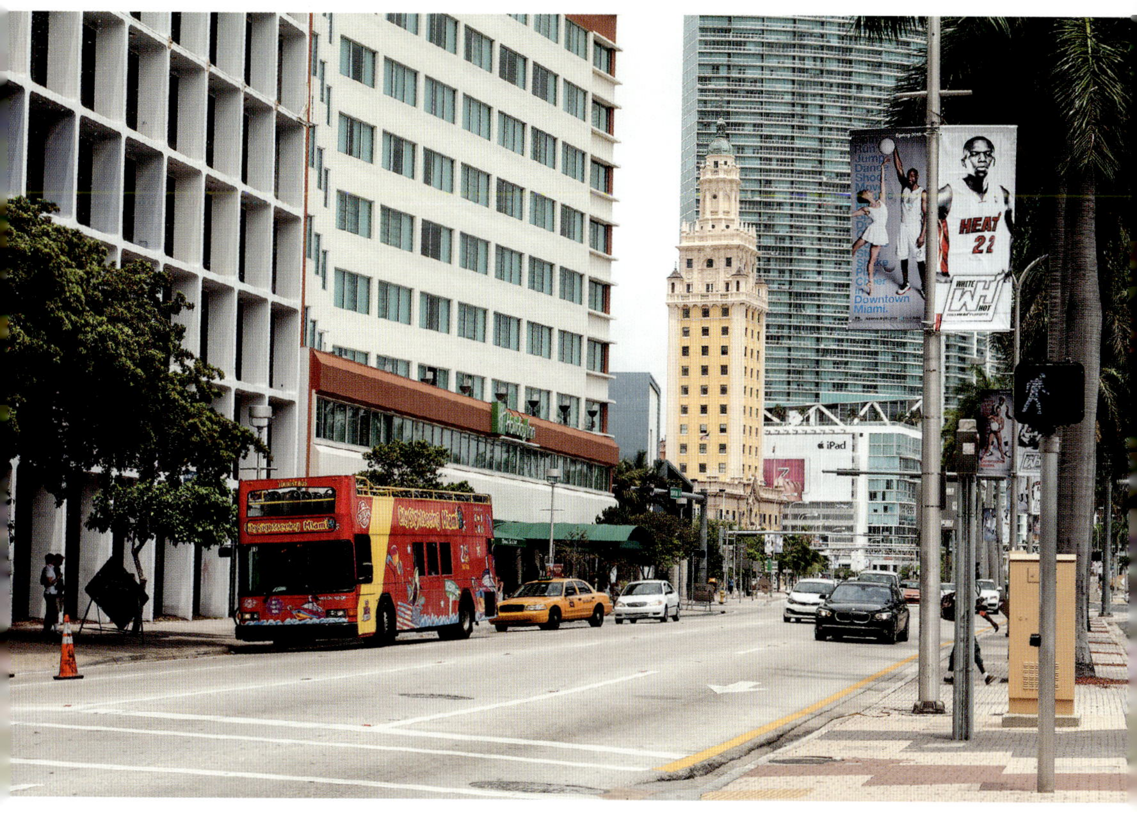
Downtown
Miami.
HEAT
22
iPad

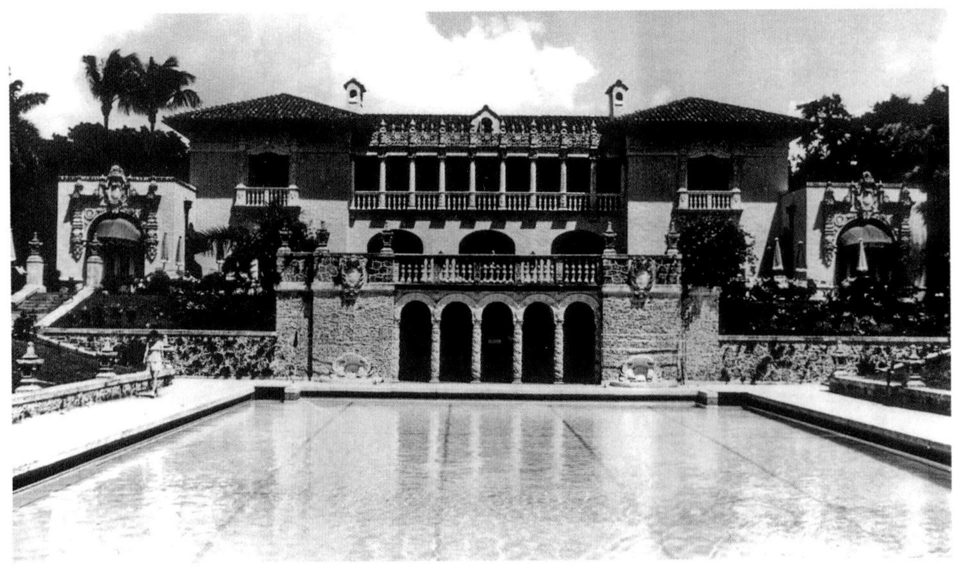

El Jardin (now Carrollton School), Miami, c. 1950

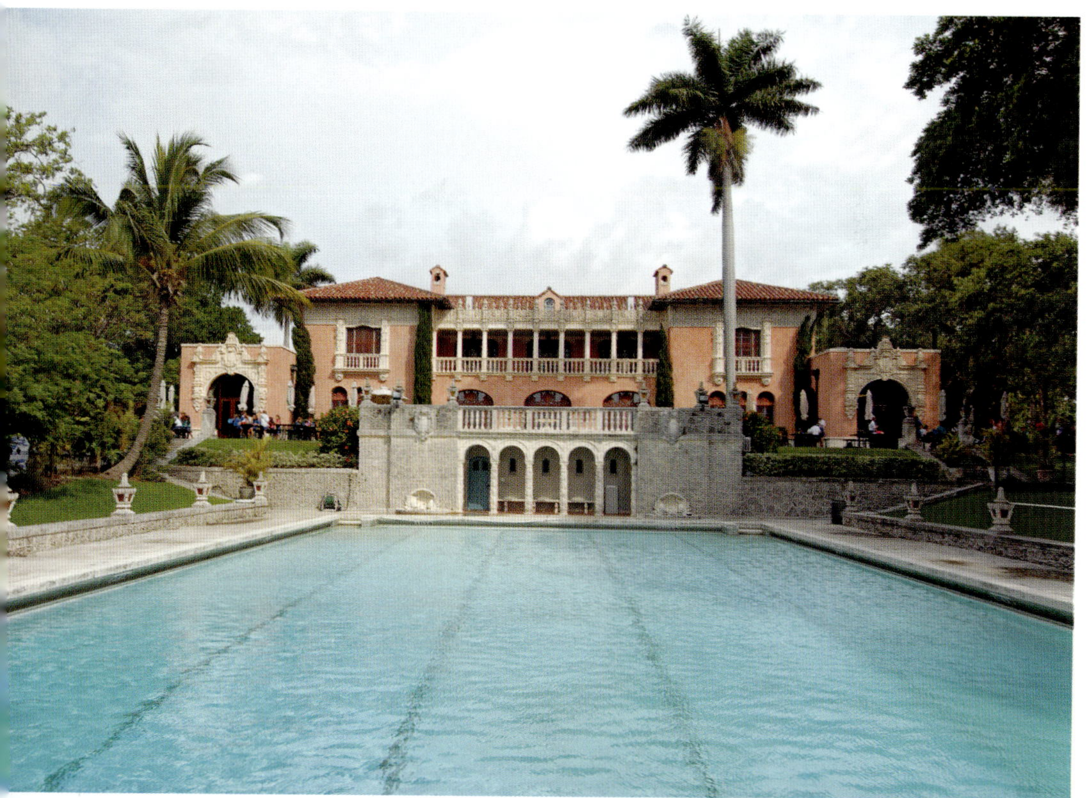

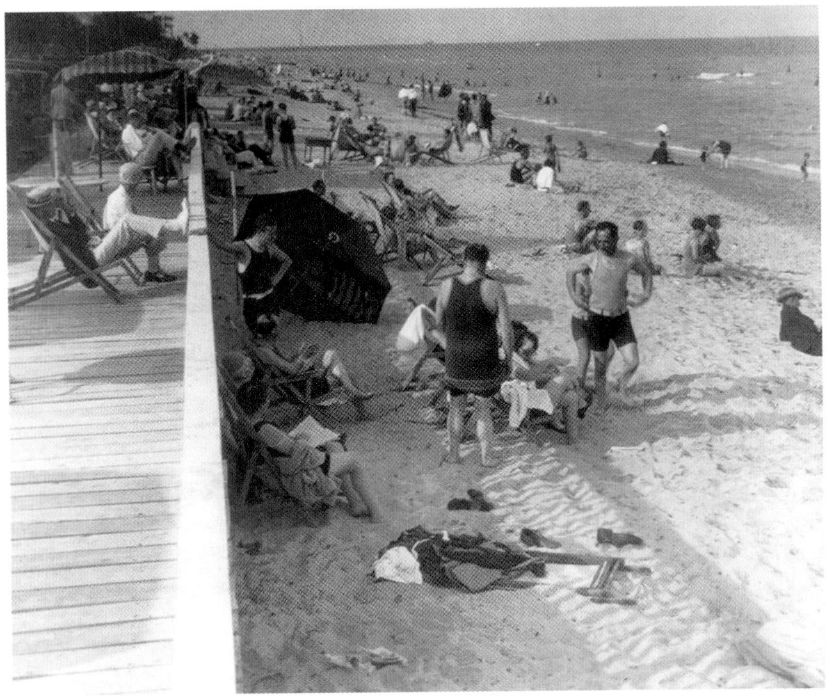

Beach Bathing, Miami, 1926

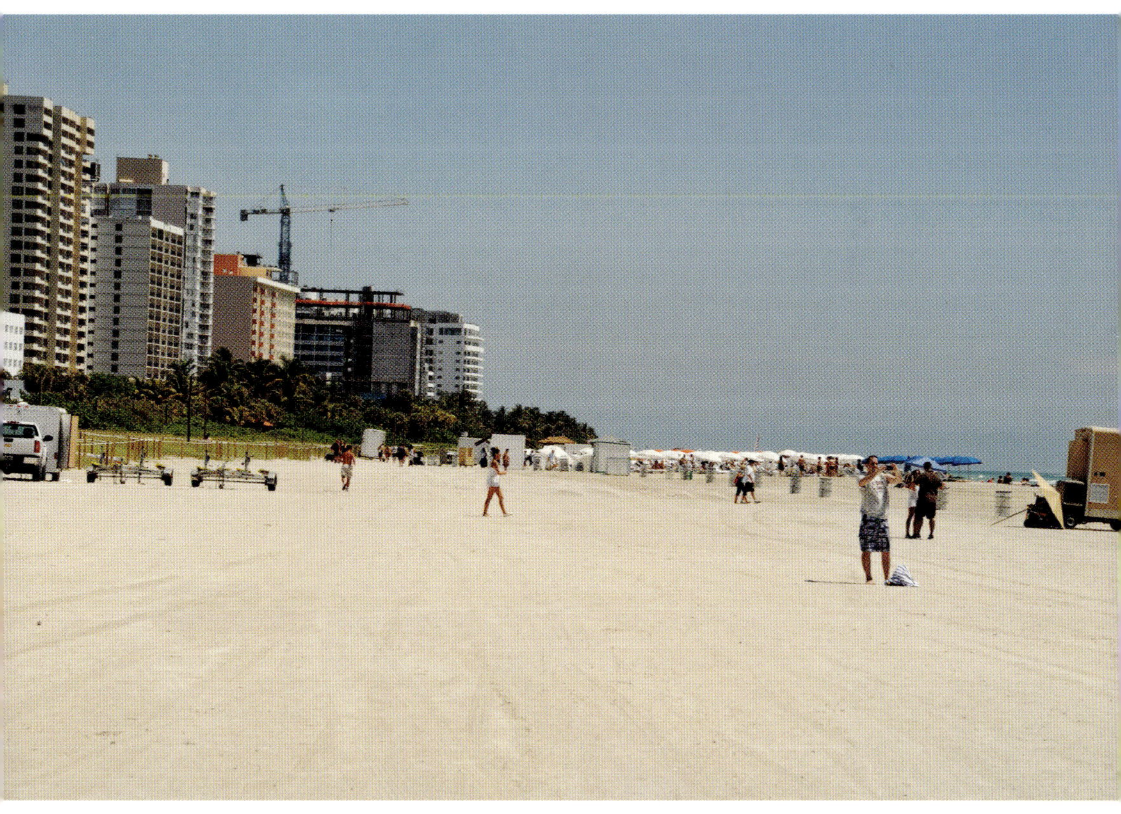

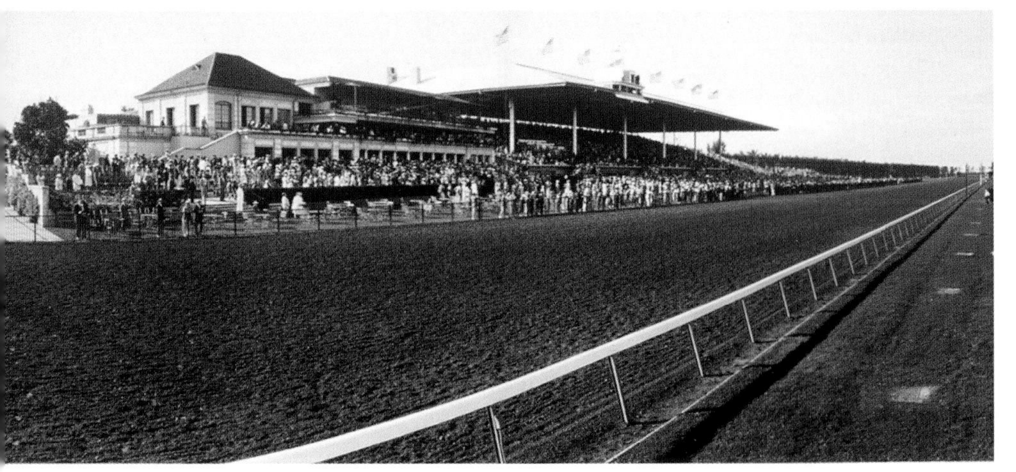

Hialeah Park Racetrack, Hialeah, 1937

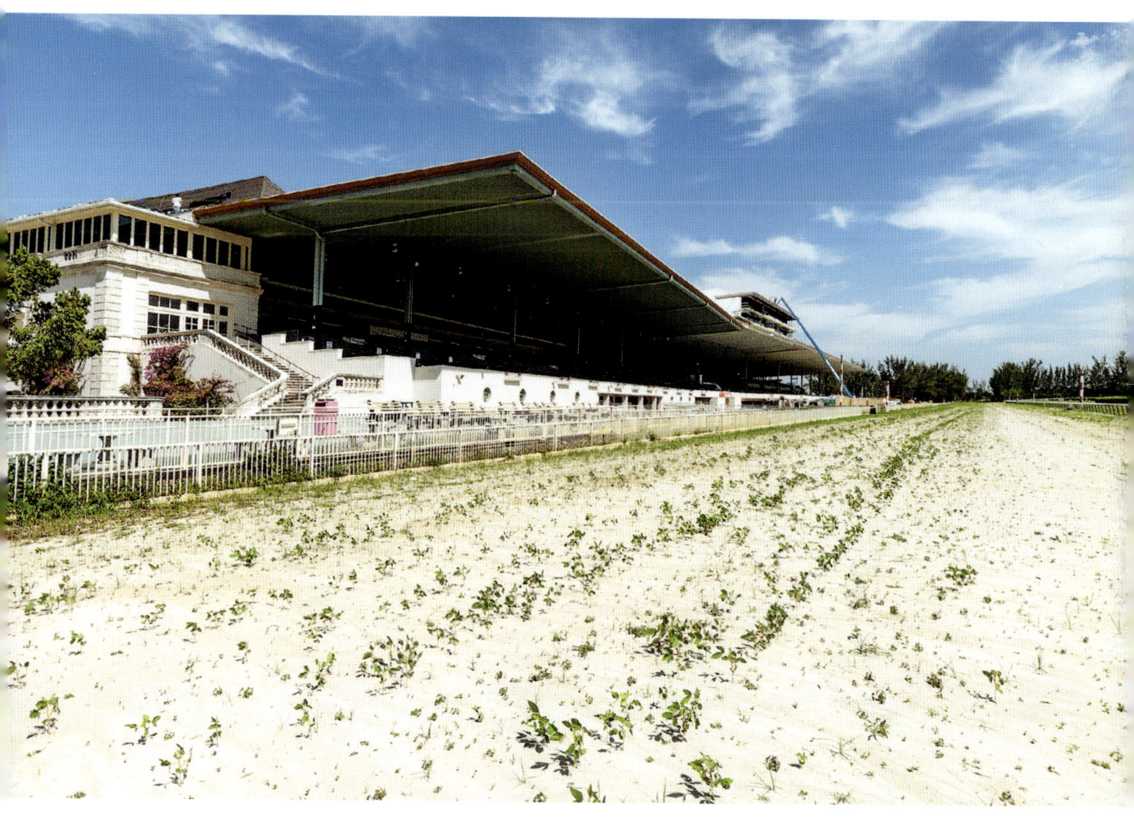

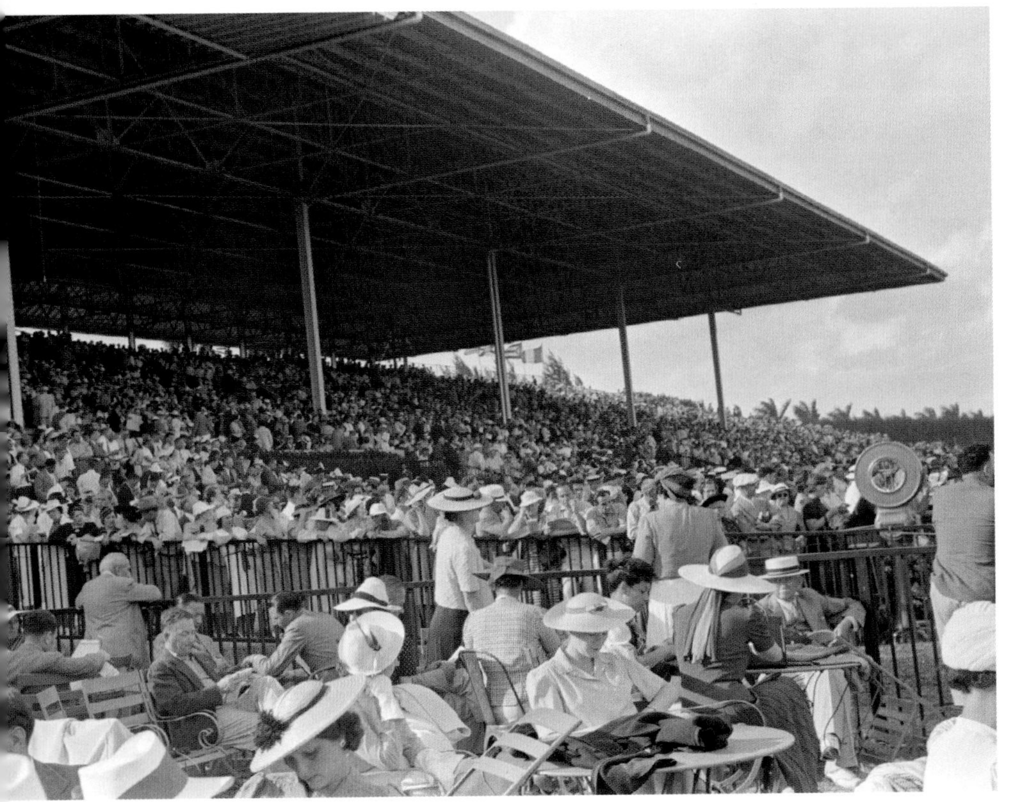

Hialeah Park Racetrack, Hialeah, 1939

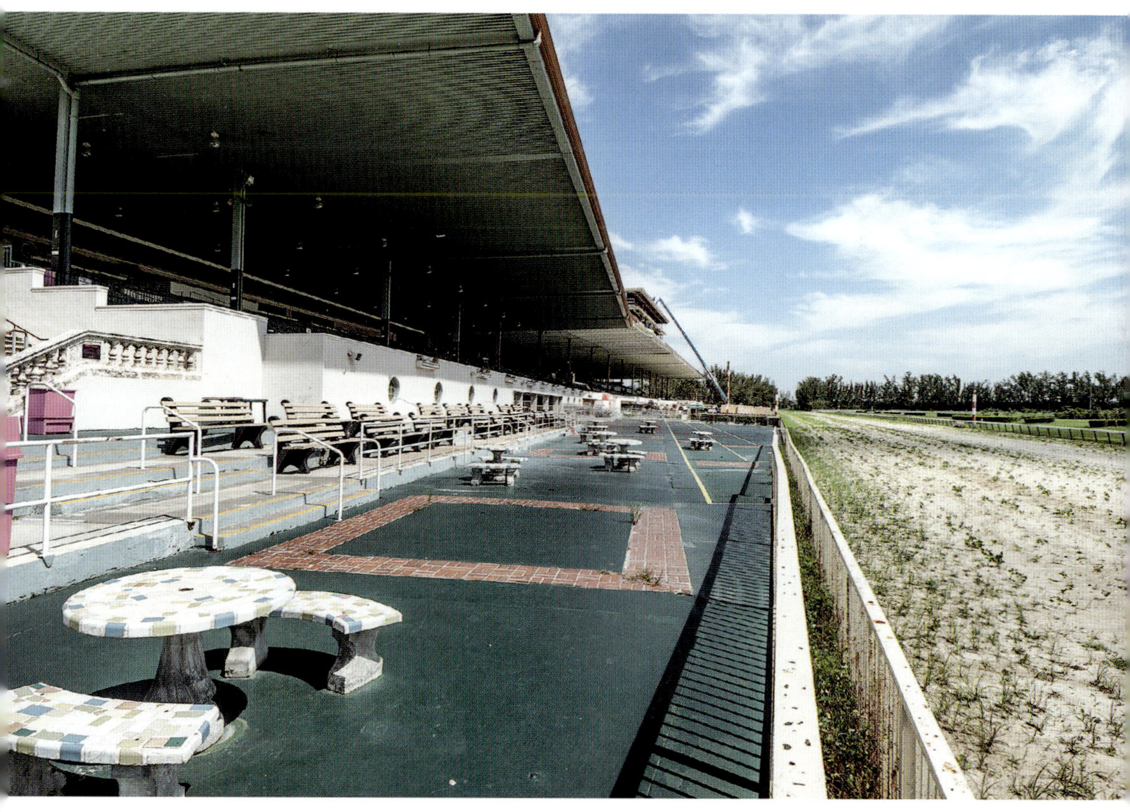

Hialeah Park Racetrack, Hialeah, 1939

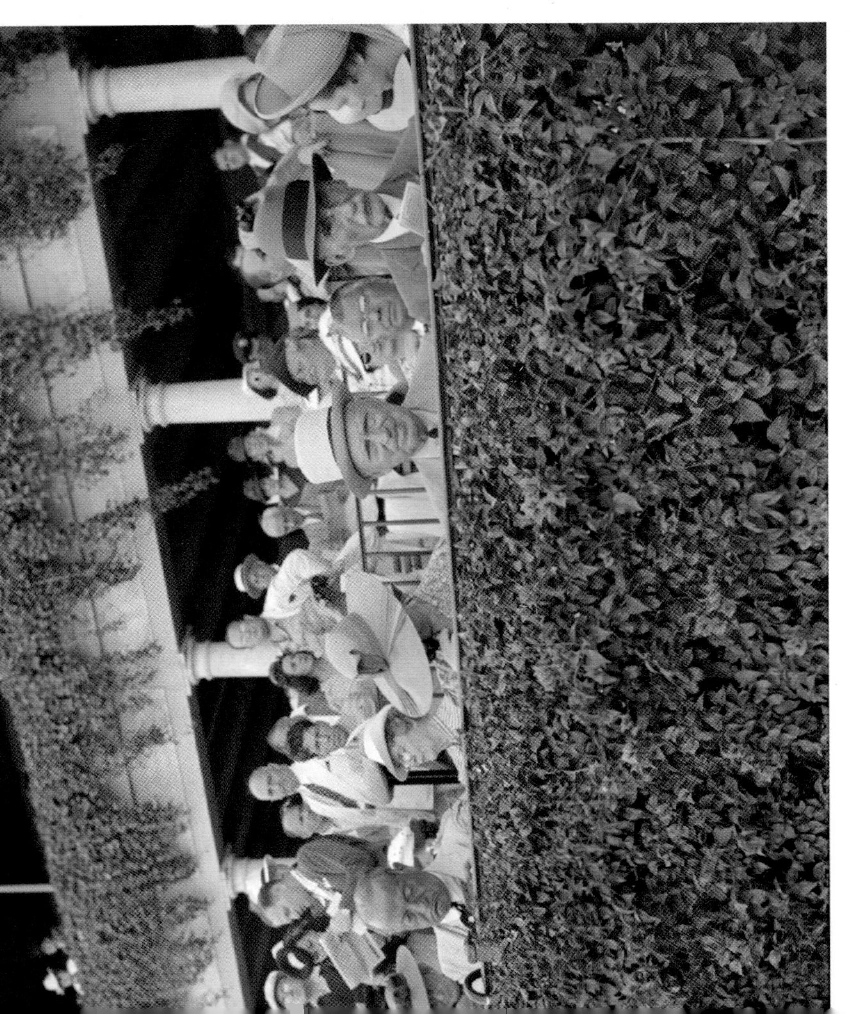

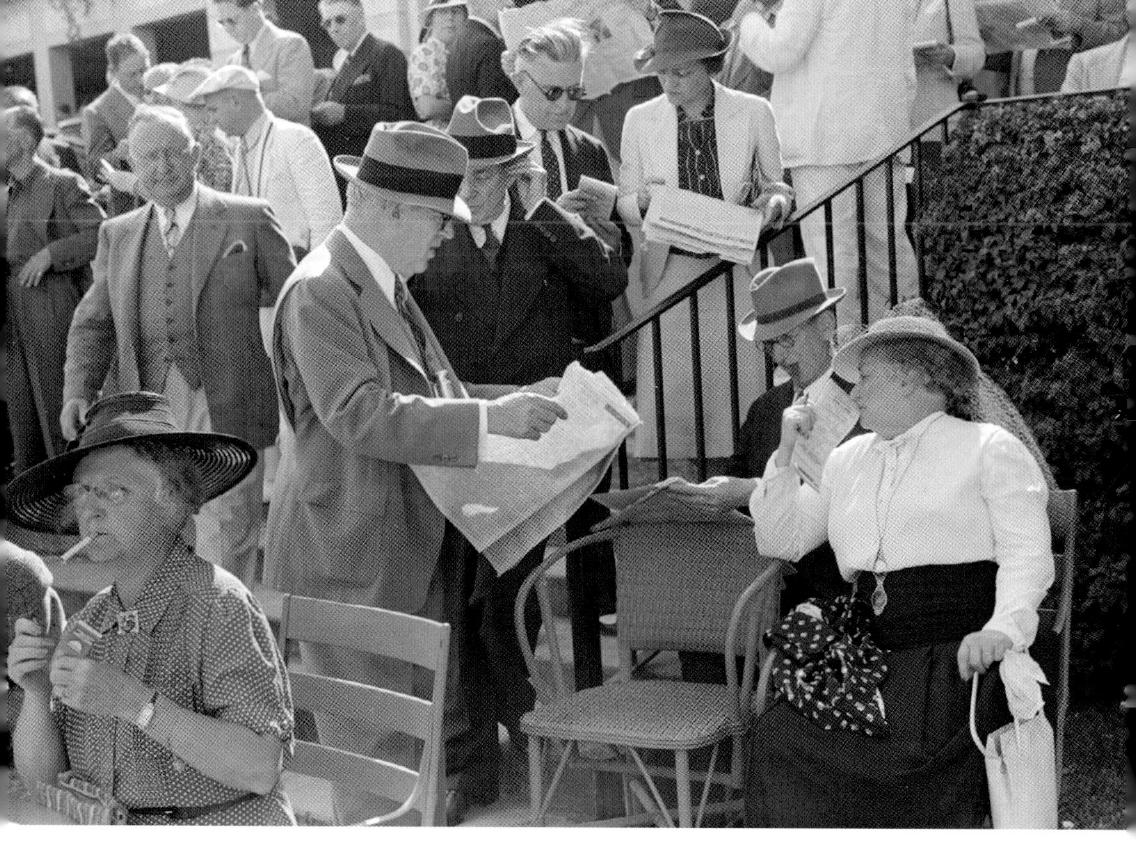

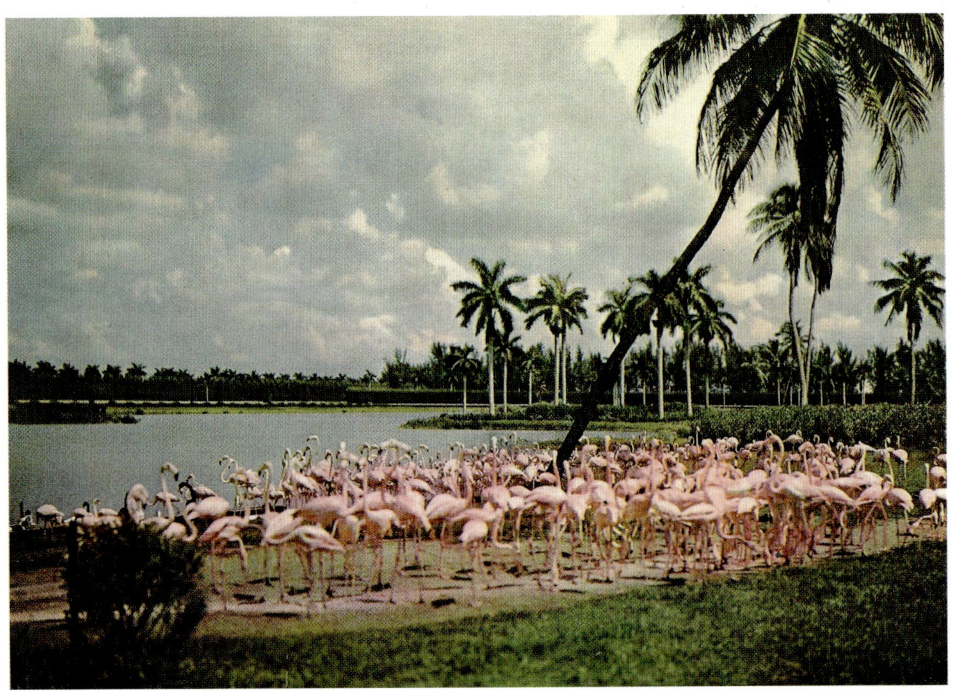

Hialeah Park Racetrack, Hialeah, 1955

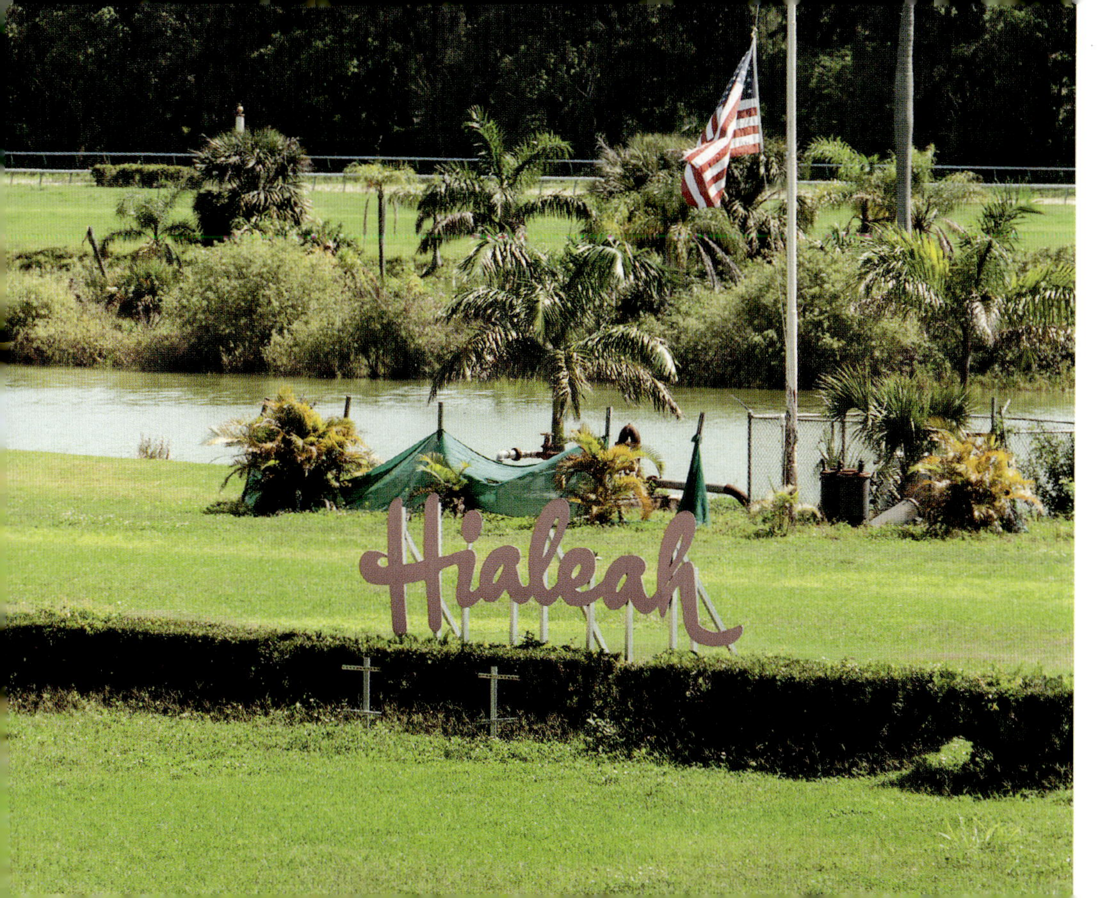
Hialeah

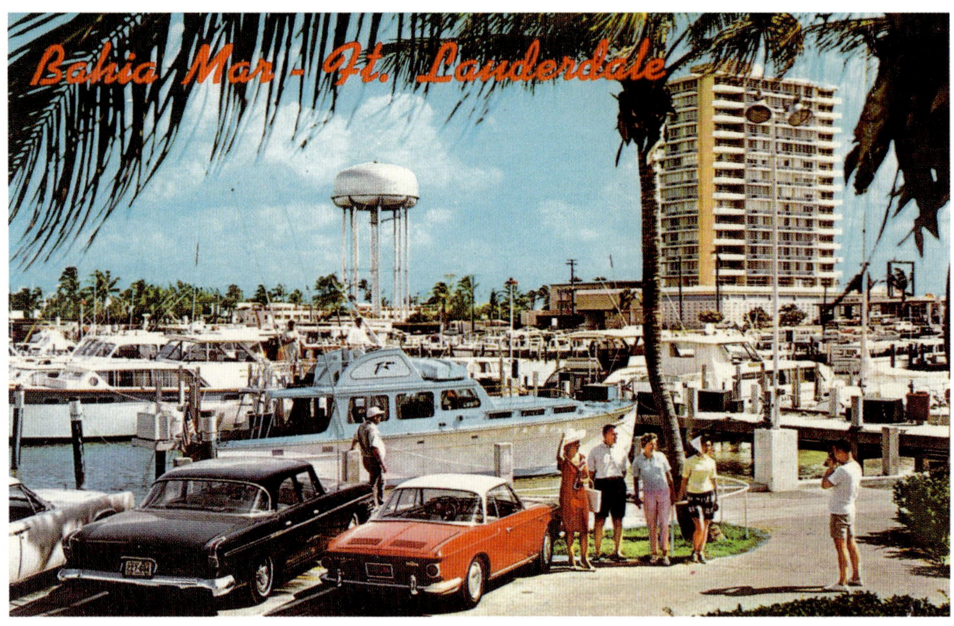

Bahia Mar Marina, Fort Lauderdale, c. 1960

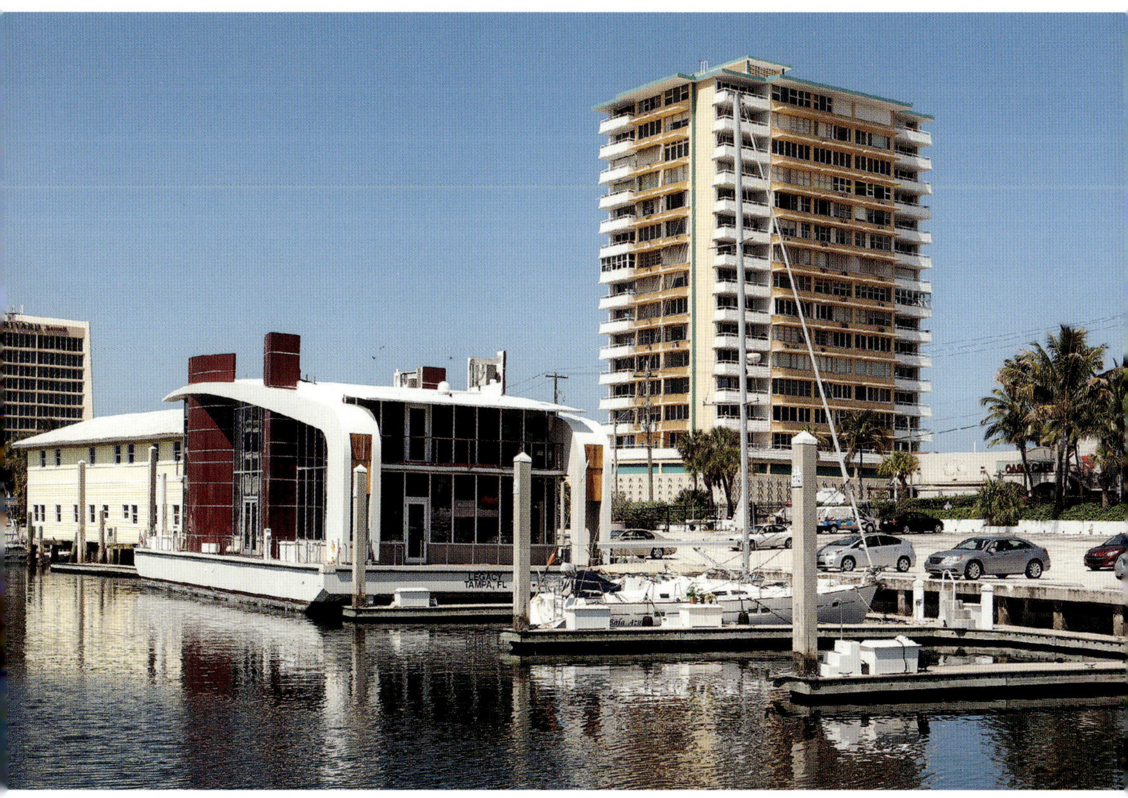
LEGACY
TAMPA, FL

Yankee Clipper (now Sheraton), Fort Lauderdale, c. 1955

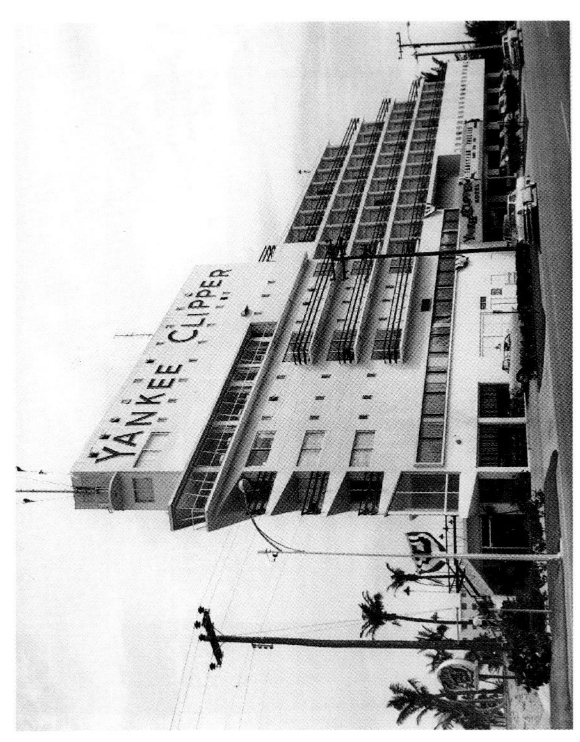

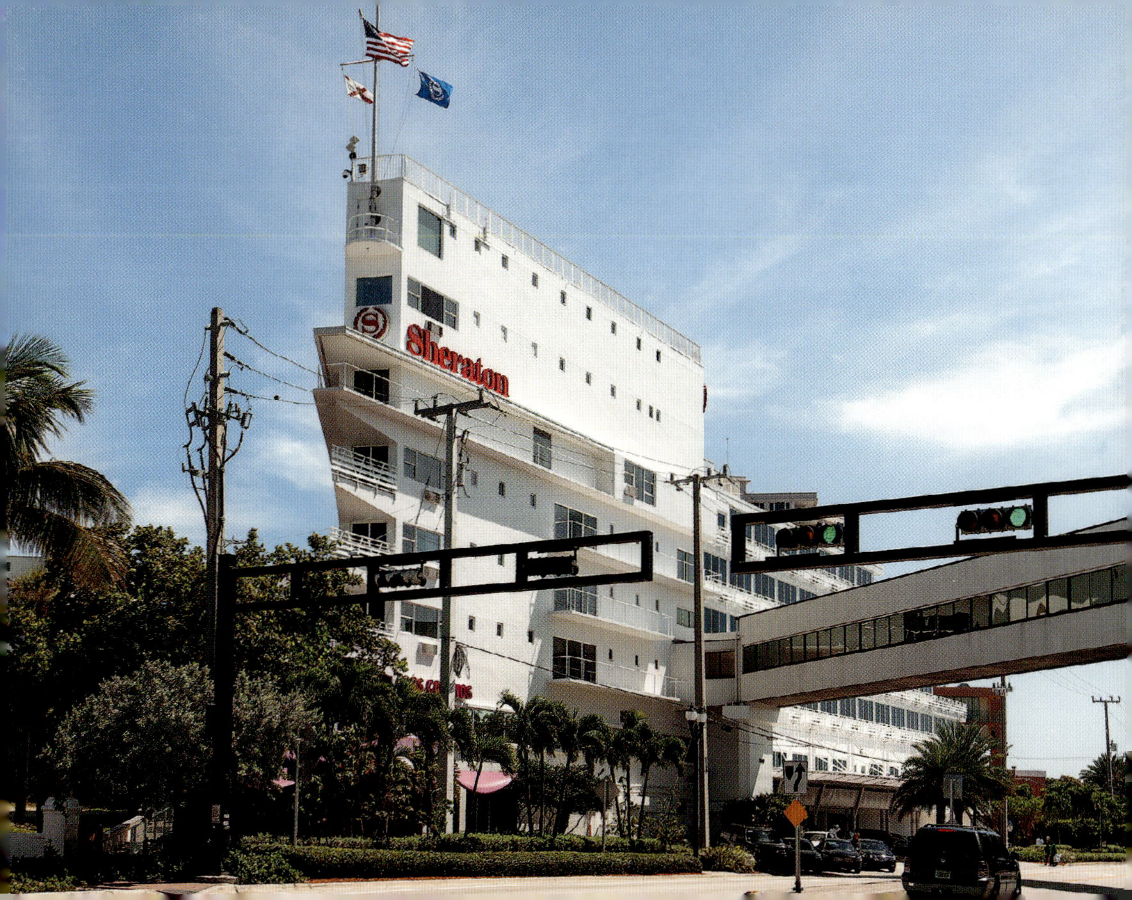
Sheraton

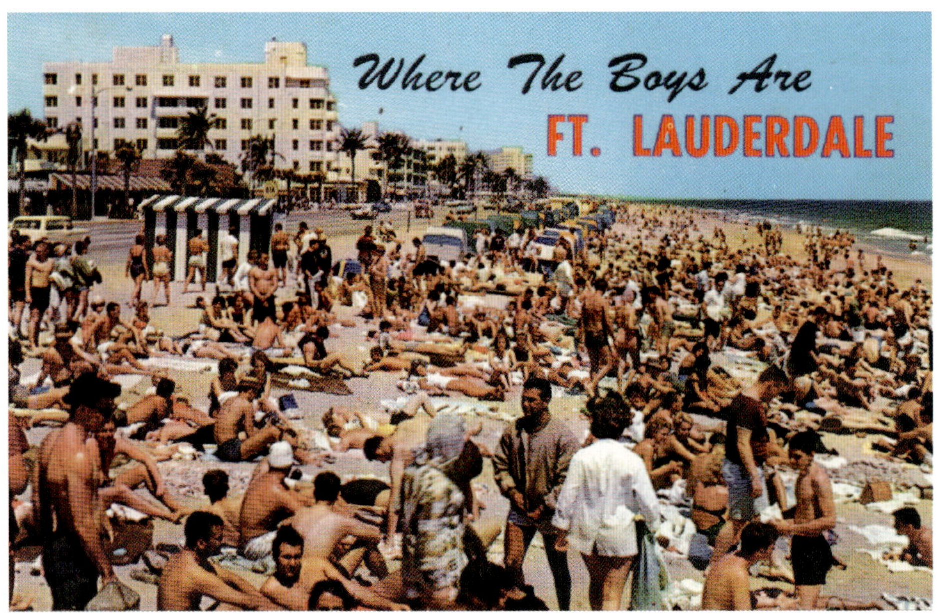

Fort Lauderdale Beach, c. 1965

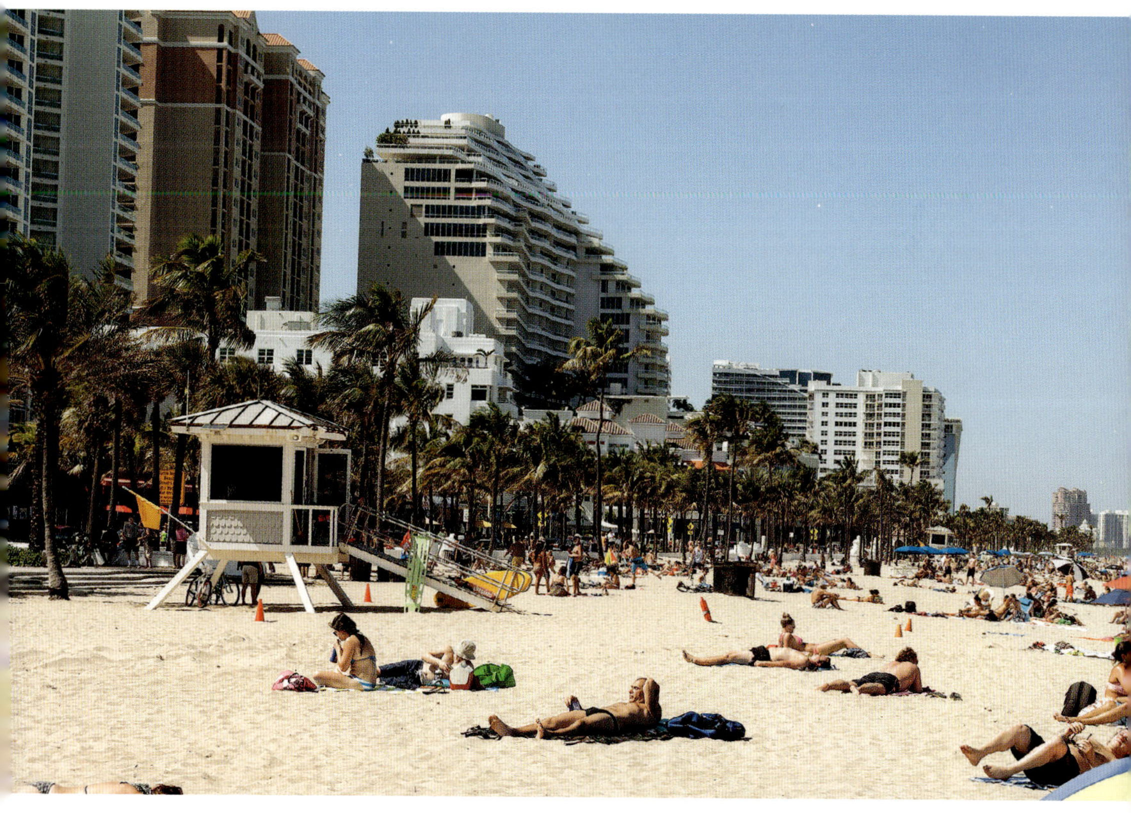

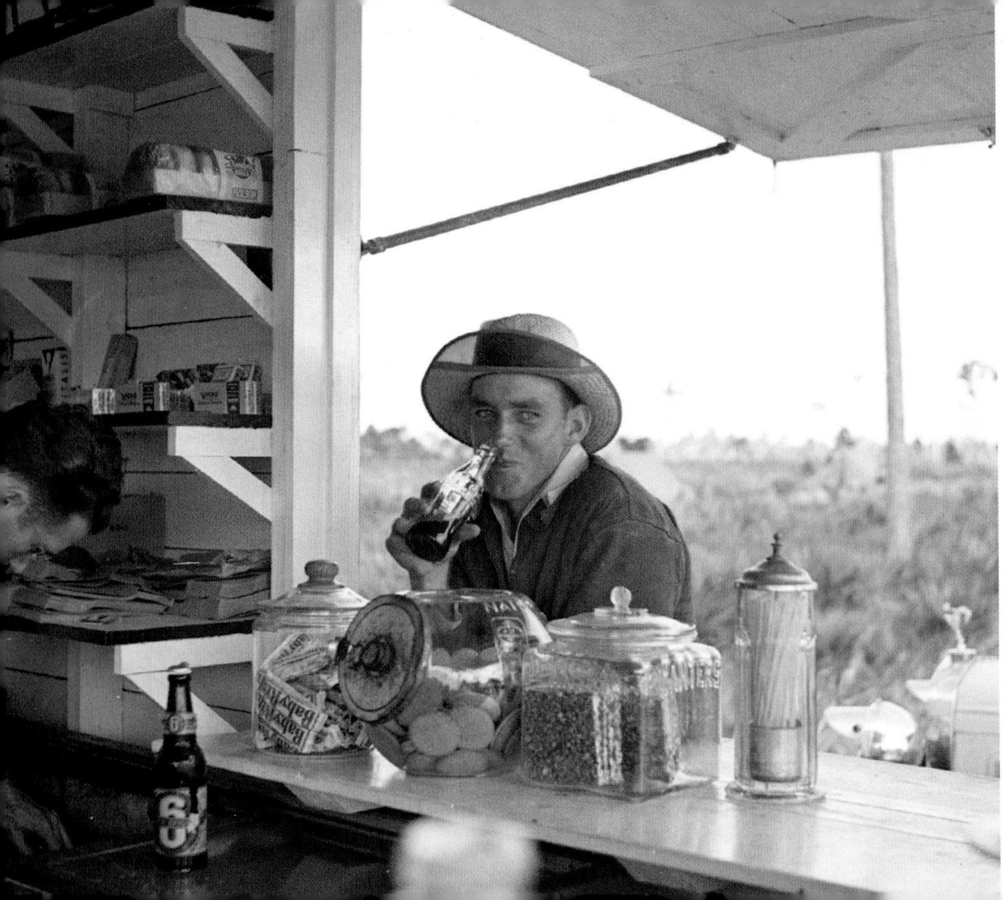

Packinghouse Worker, Deerfield Beach, 1937

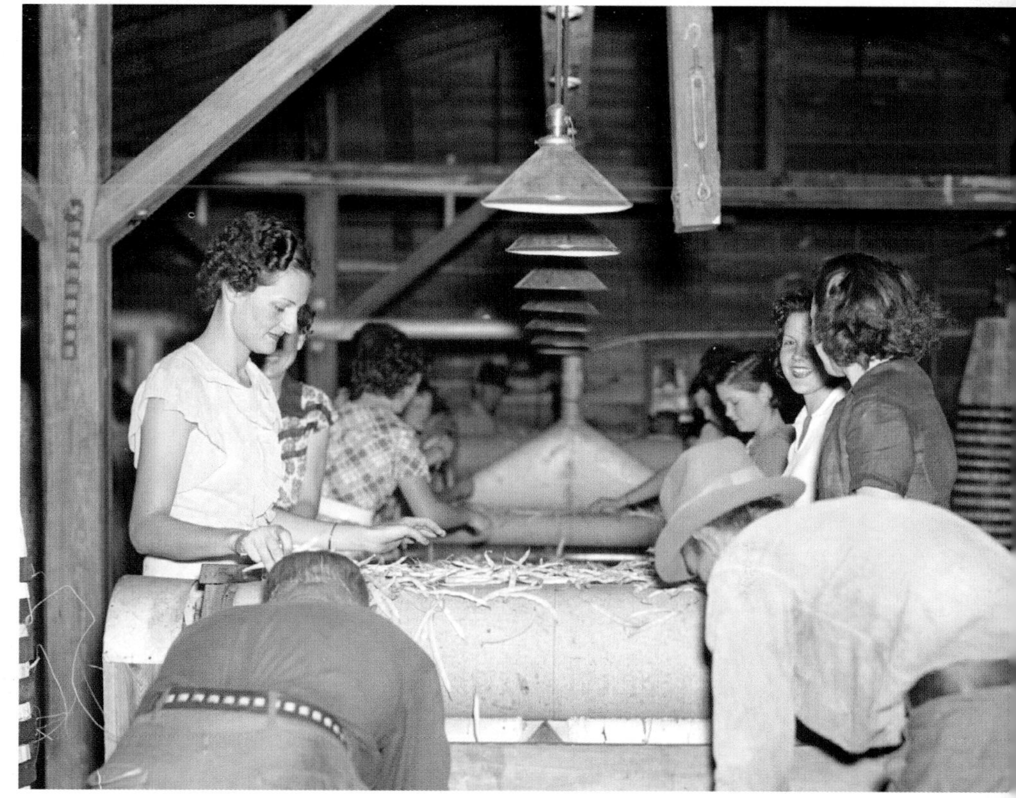

Vegetable Packing Plant, Deerfield Beach, 1937

Ask Mr. Foster Travel and Souvenir Shop, Palm Beach, 1902

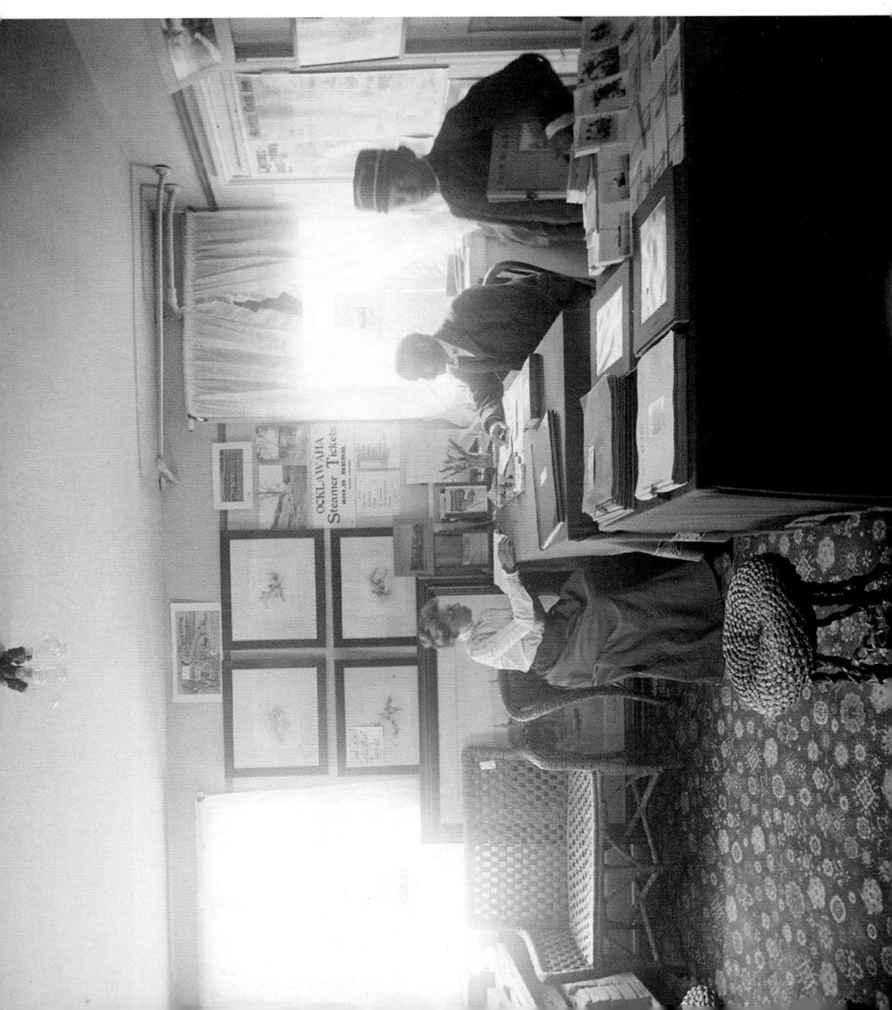

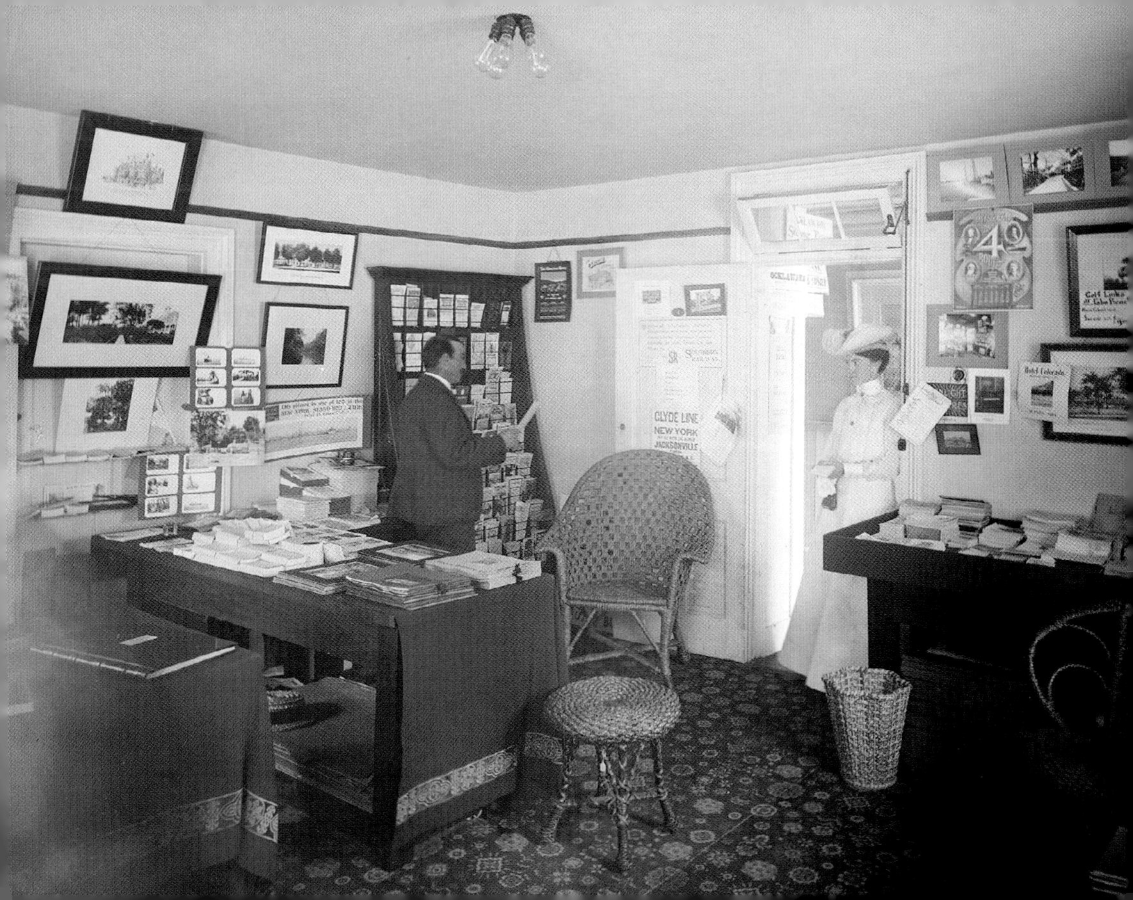
CLYDE LINE
NEW YORK
JACKSONVILLE

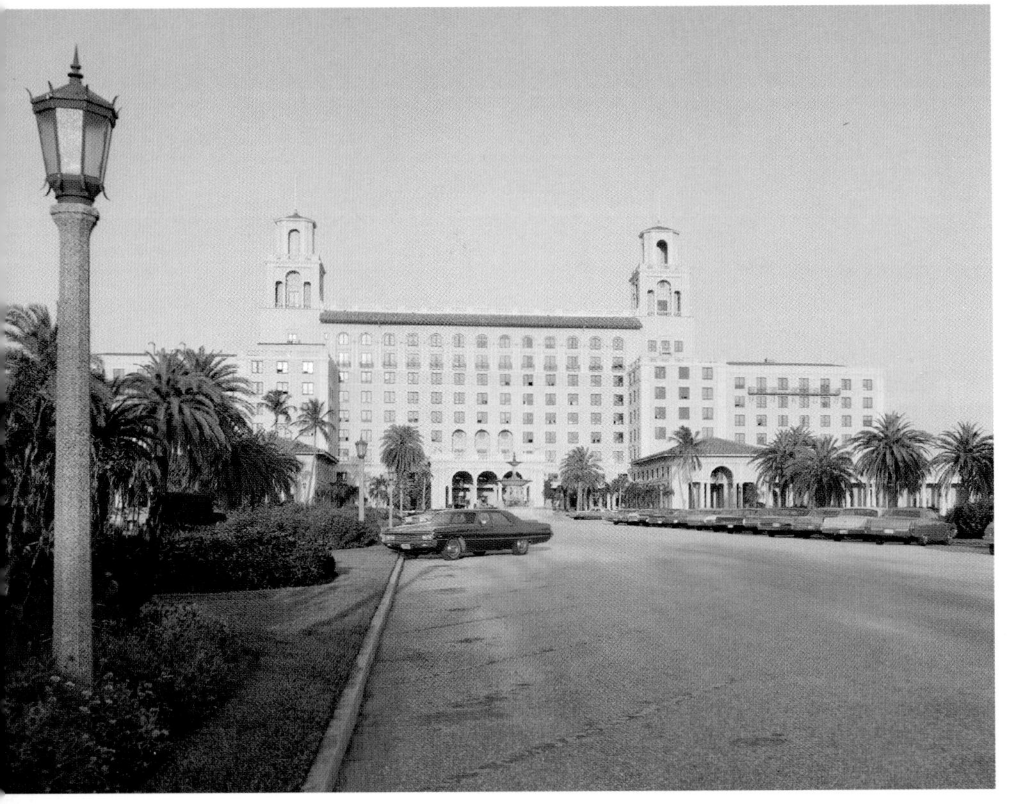

Breakers Hotel, Palm Beach, 1972

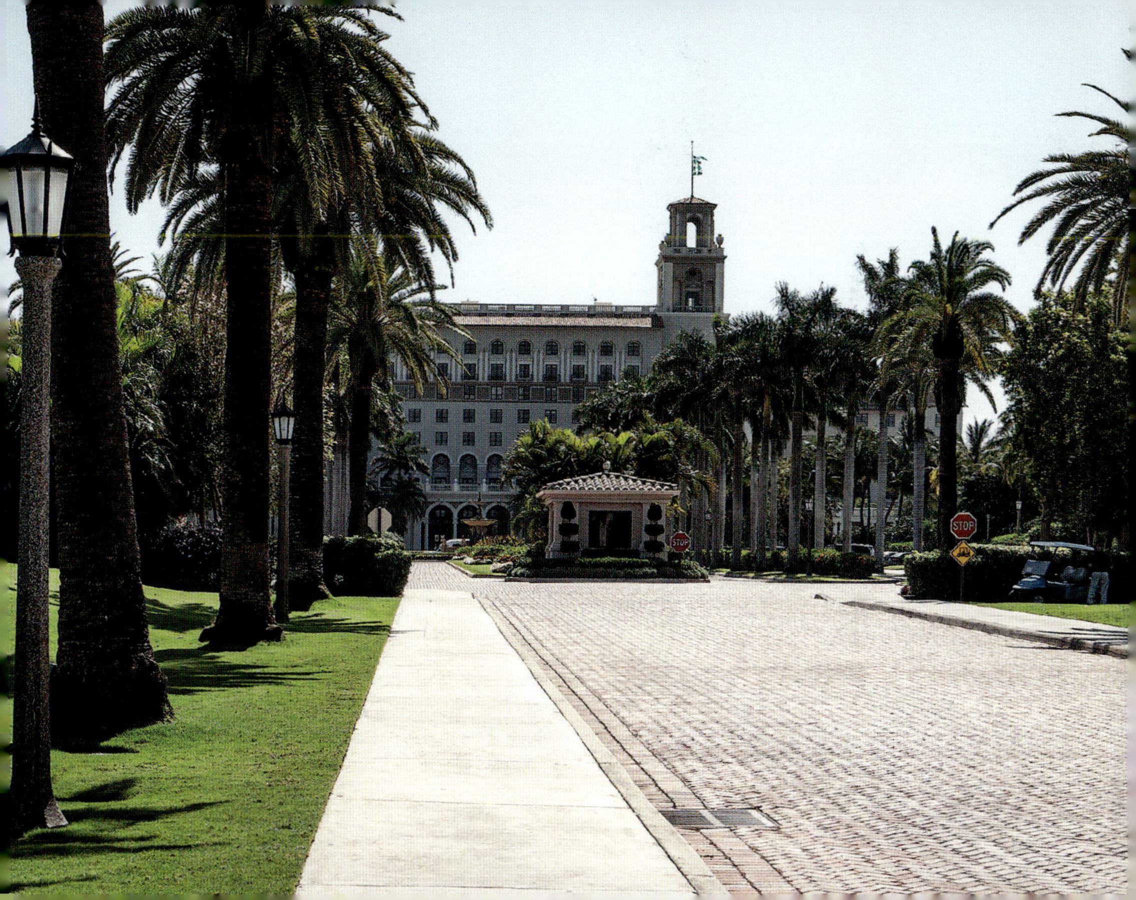
STOP
STOP

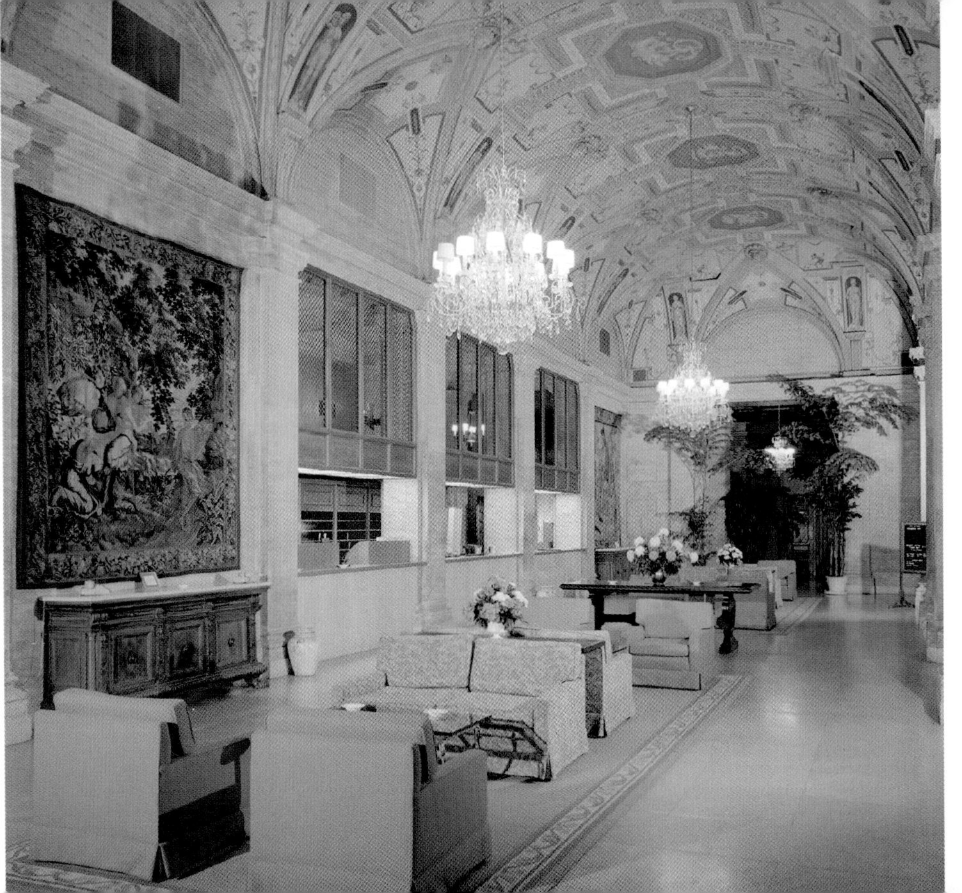

Breakers Hotel, Palm Beach, 1972

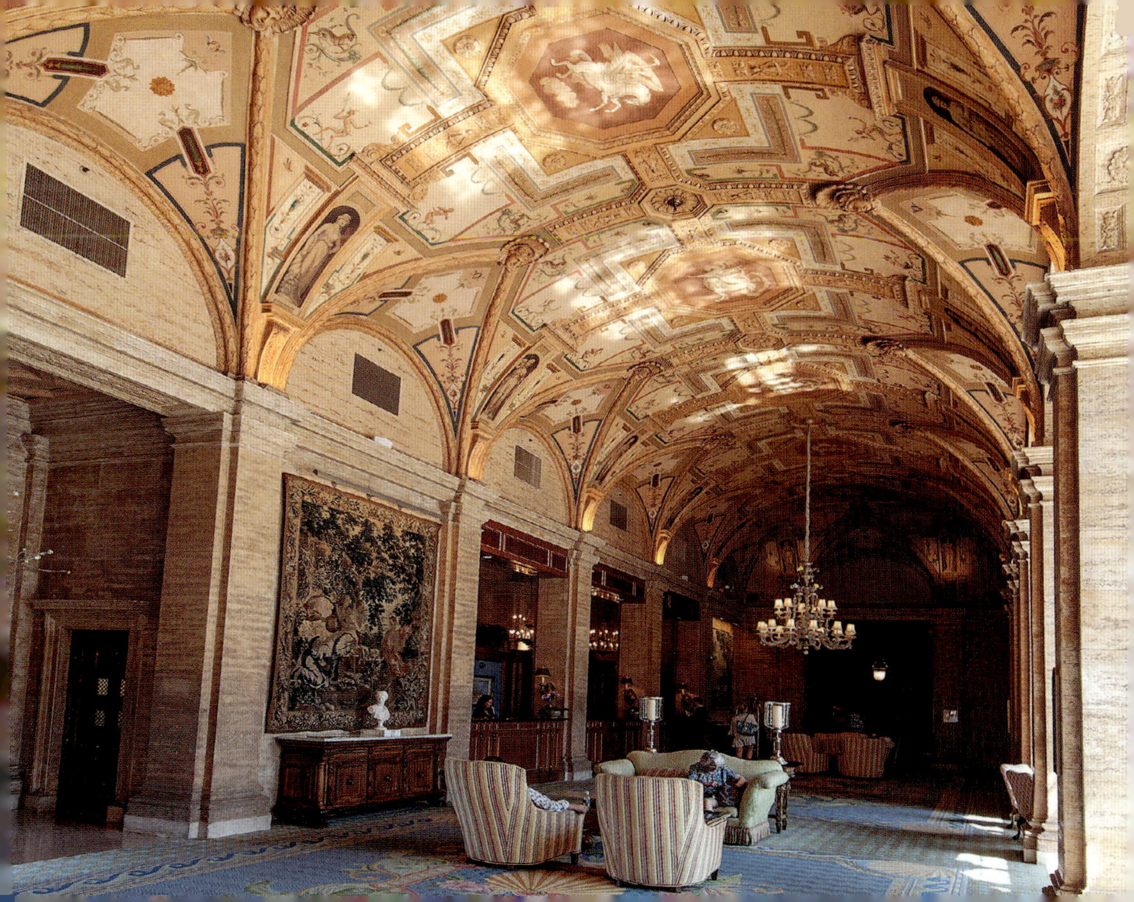

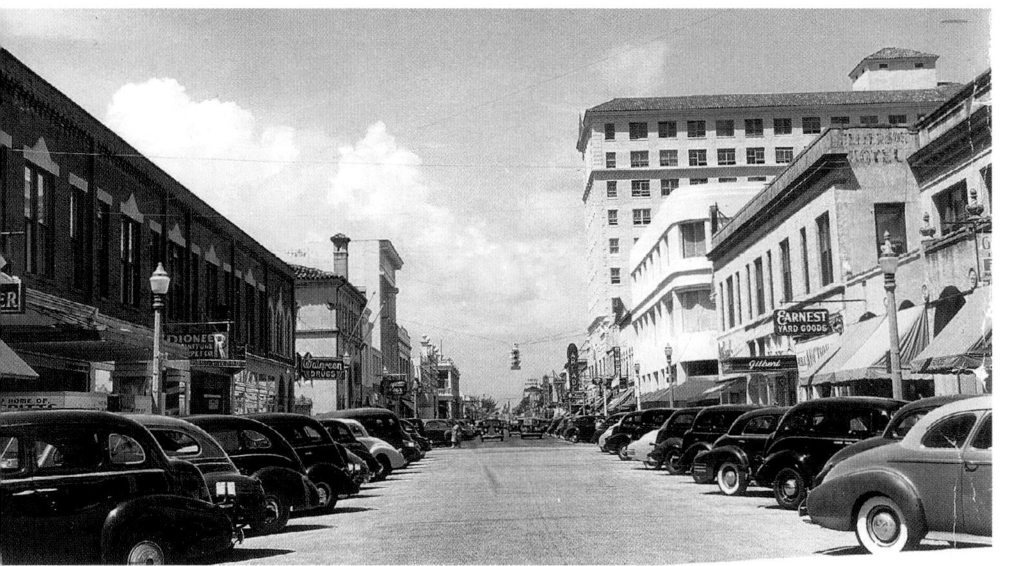

Clematis Street, Palm Beach, c. 1945

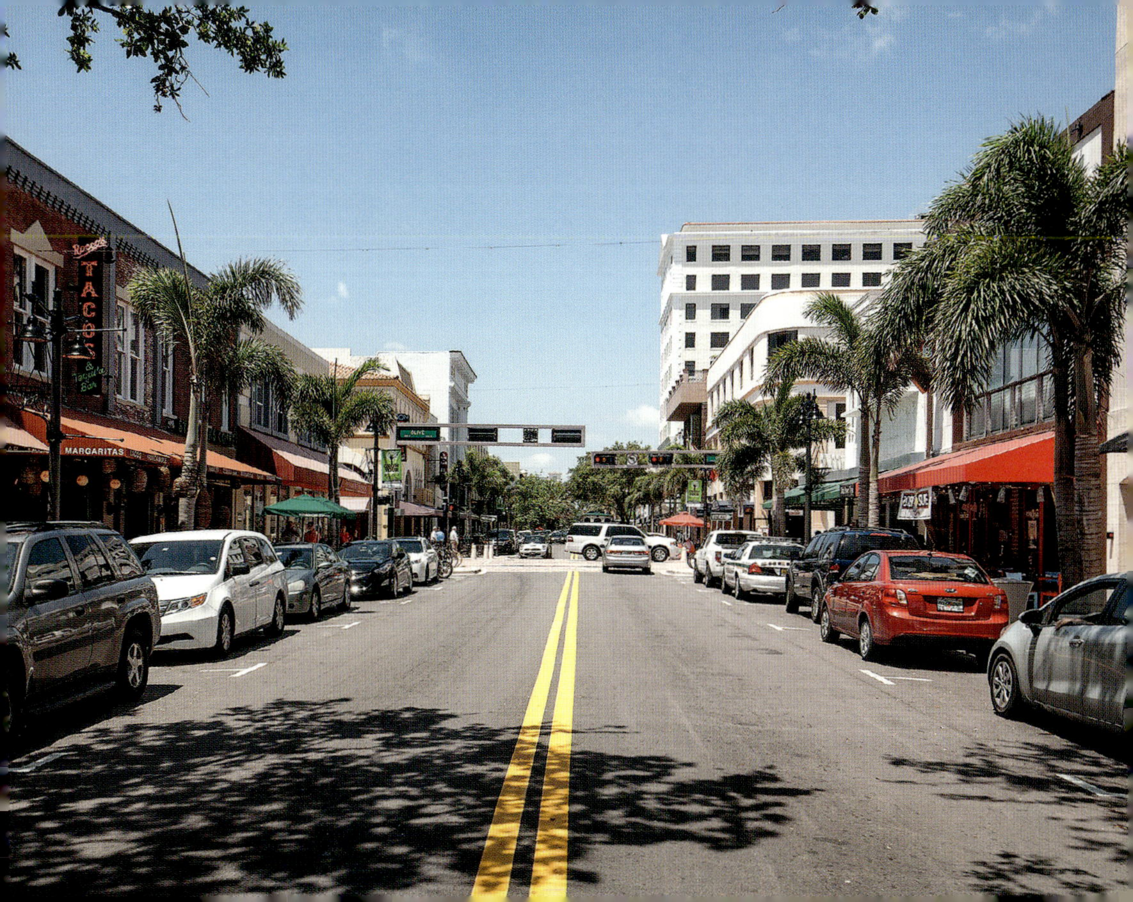
TACOS
MARGARITAS

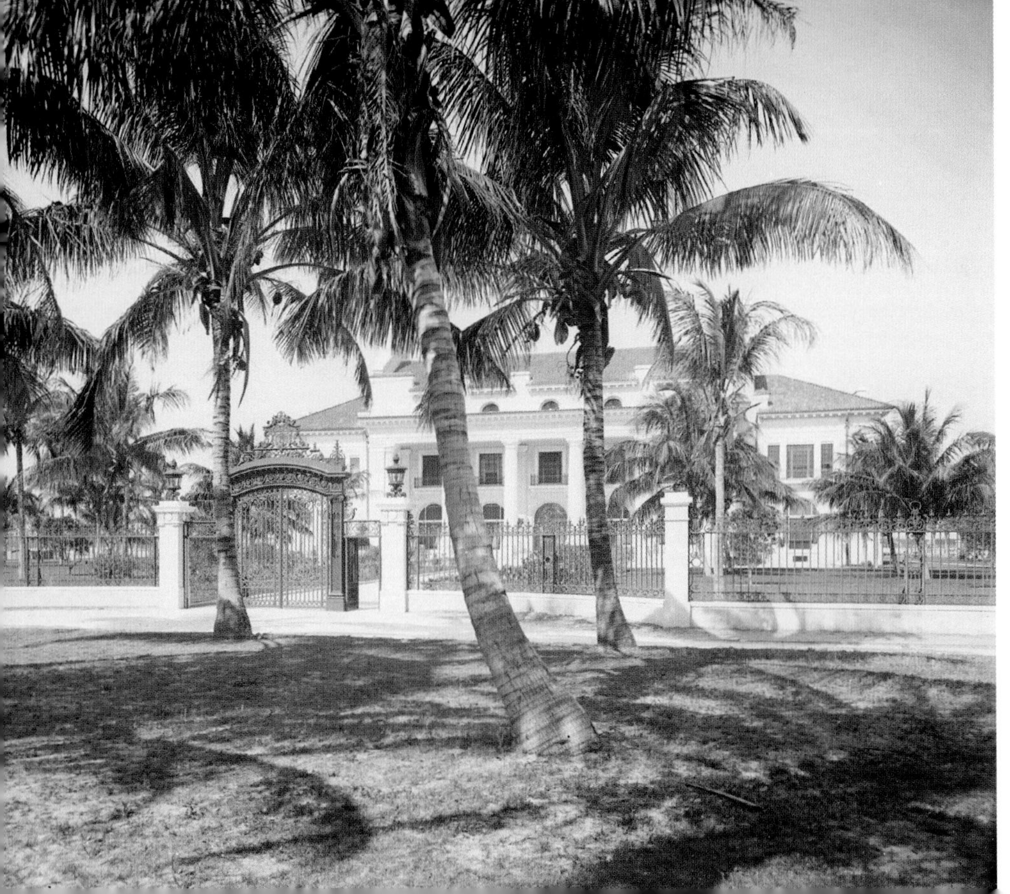

Flagler Museum, Palm Beach, 1908

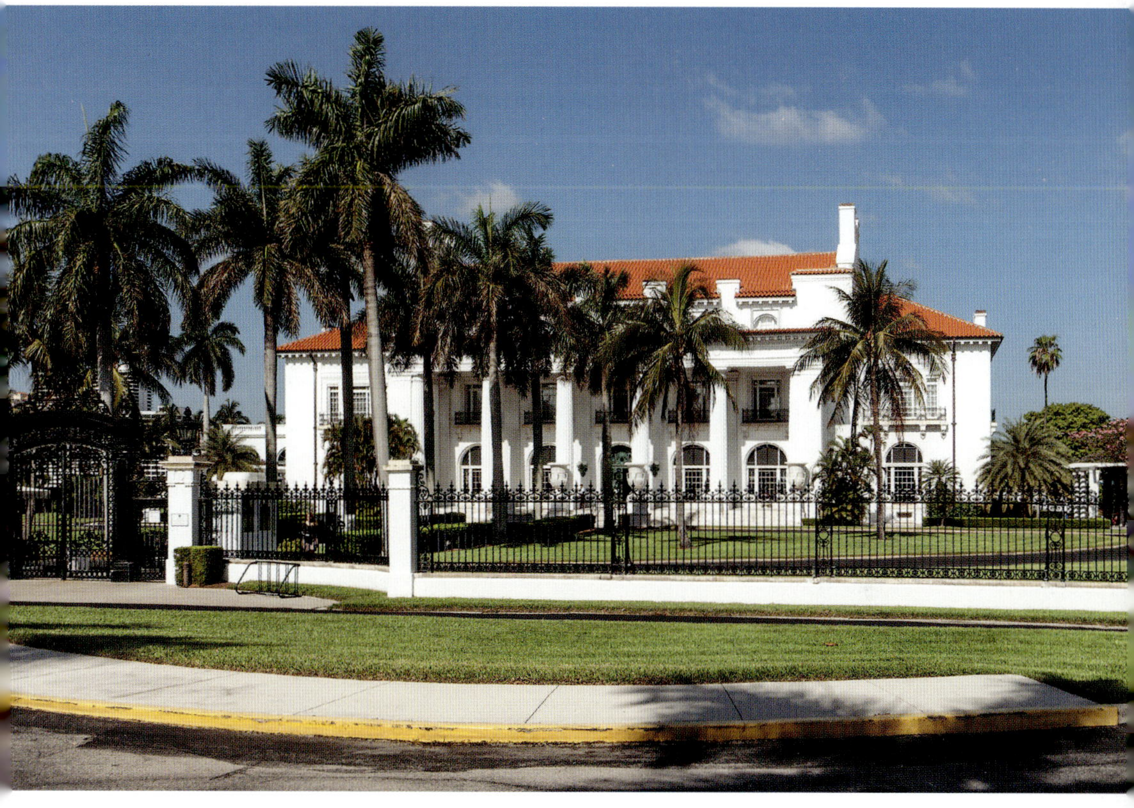

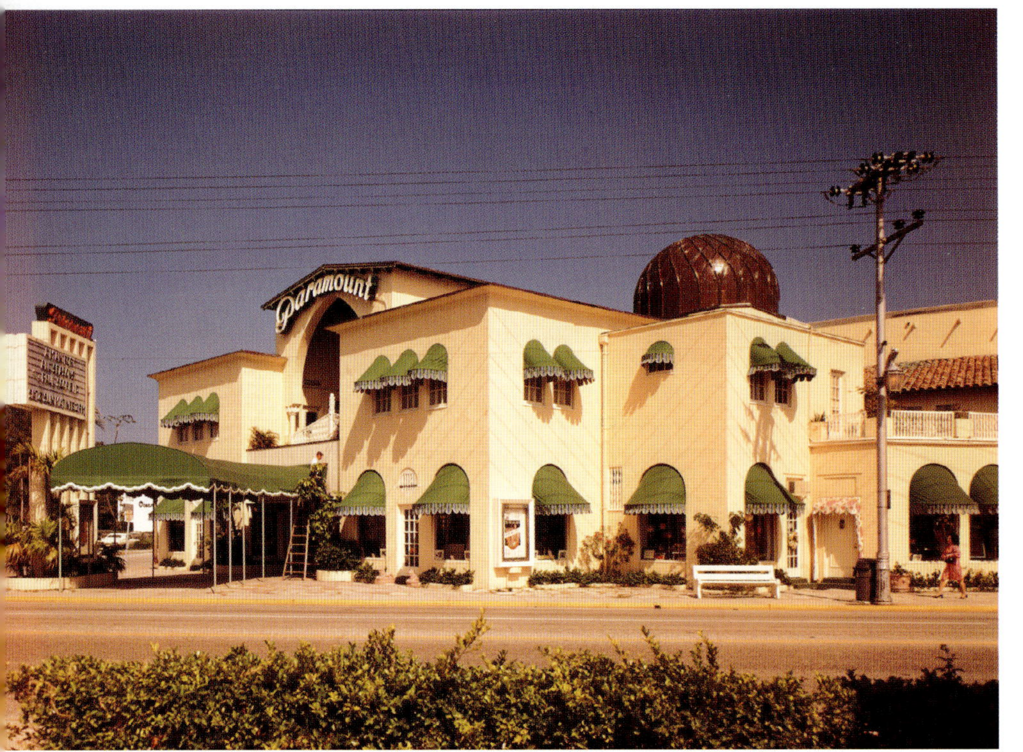

Paramount Theatre, Palm Beach, 1972

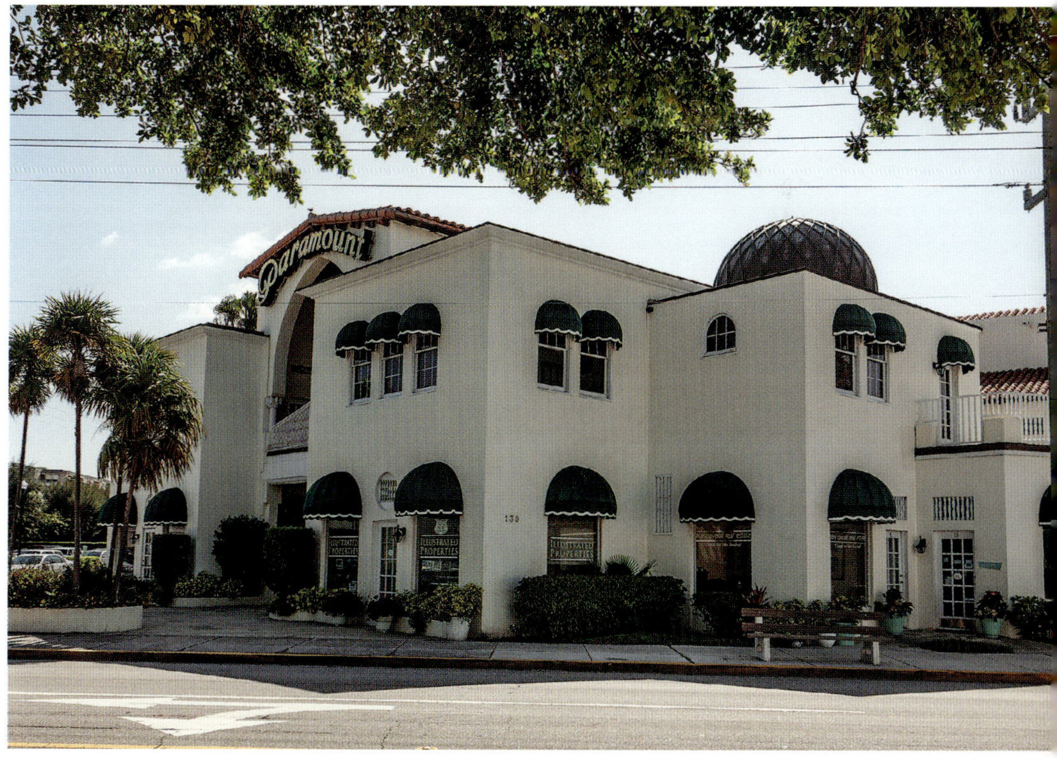
Paramount
139
ILLUSTRATED PROPERTIES
ILLUSTRATED PROPERTIES
ILLUSTRATED PROPERTIES

Hibiscus Avenue, Palm Beach, 1939

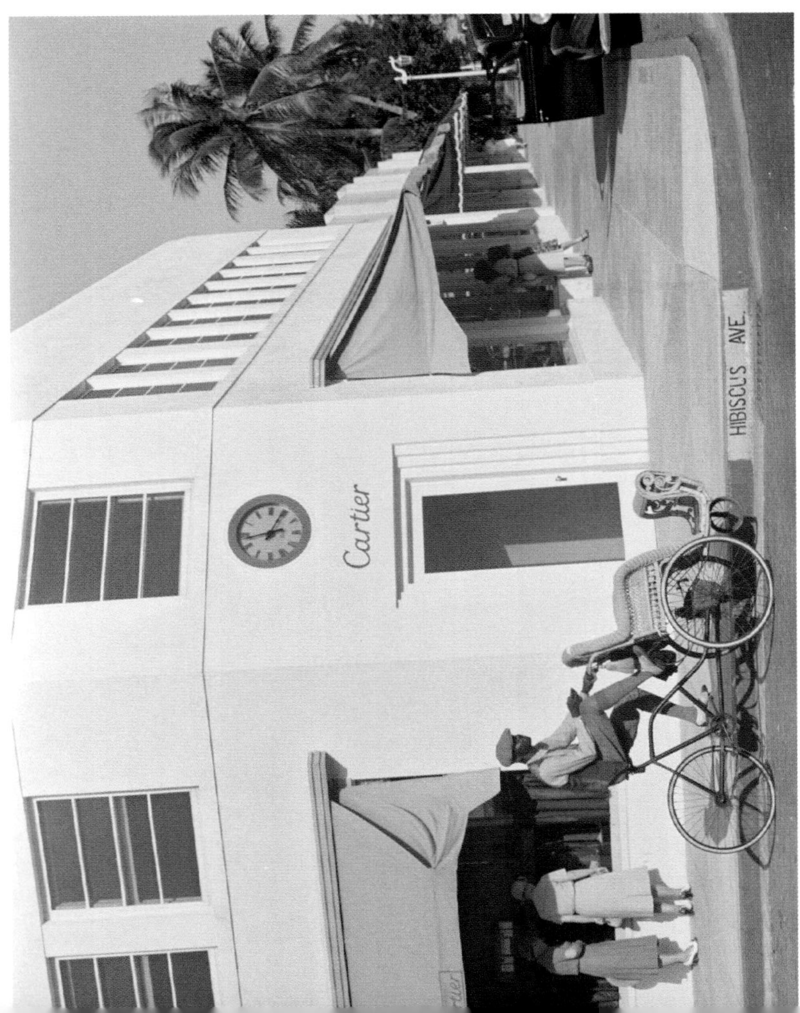

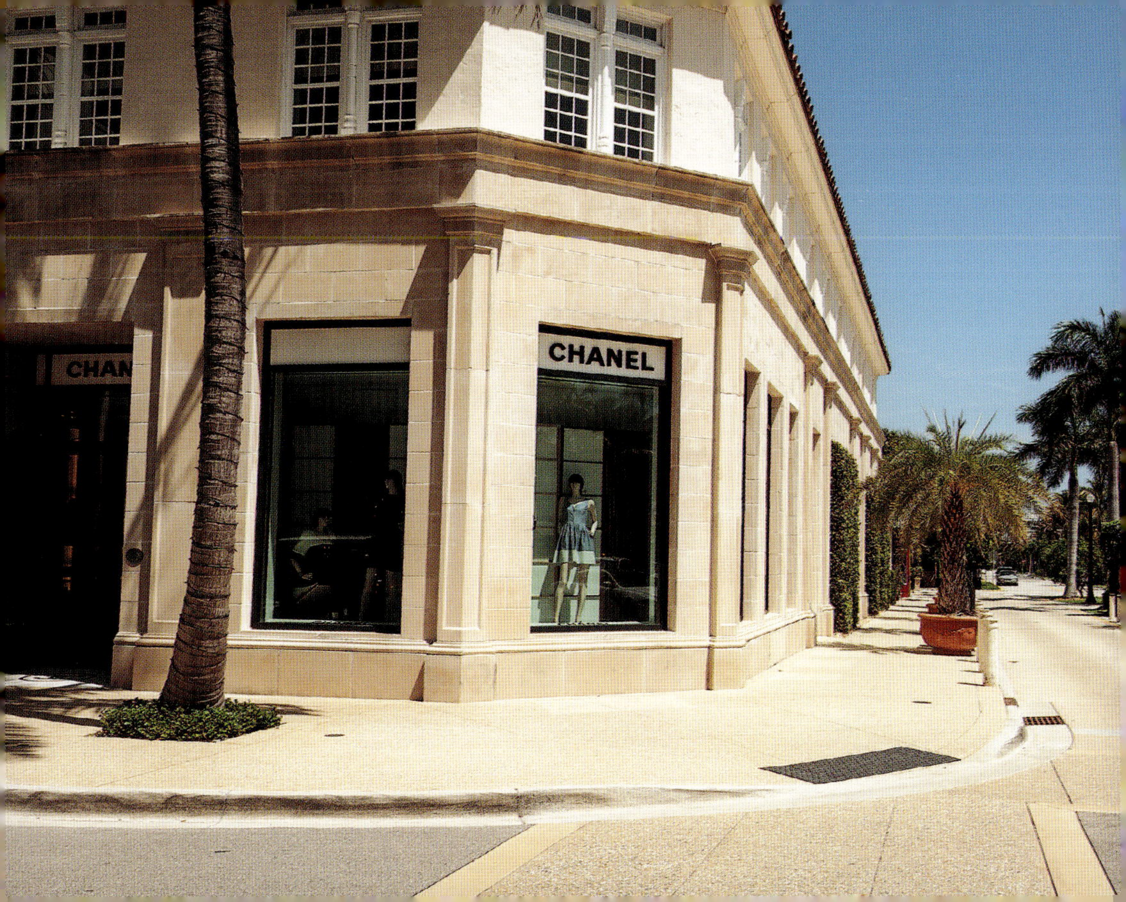
CHANEL
CHANEL

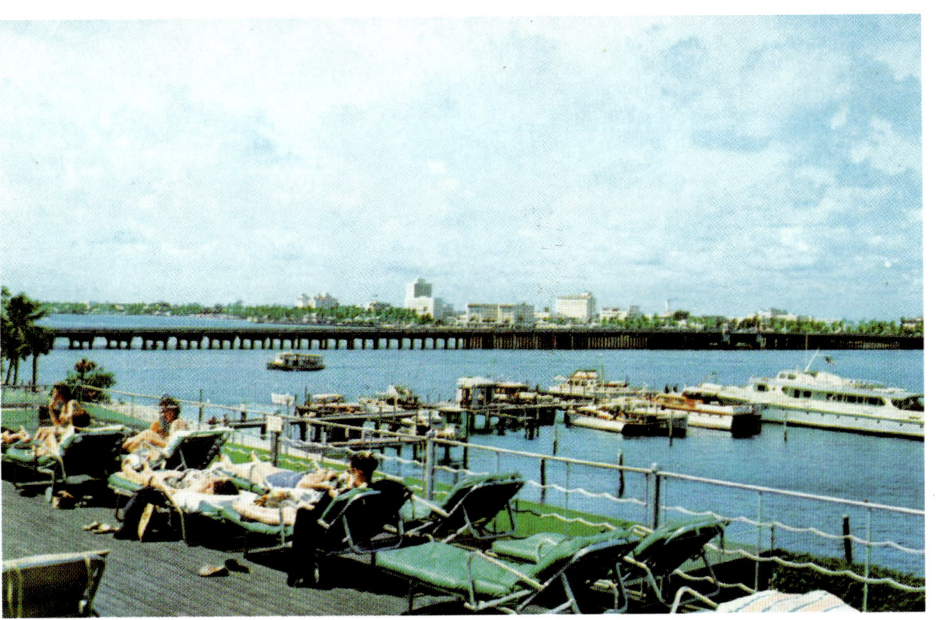

Flagler Bridge from the Biltmore Hotel, Palm Beach, c. 1965

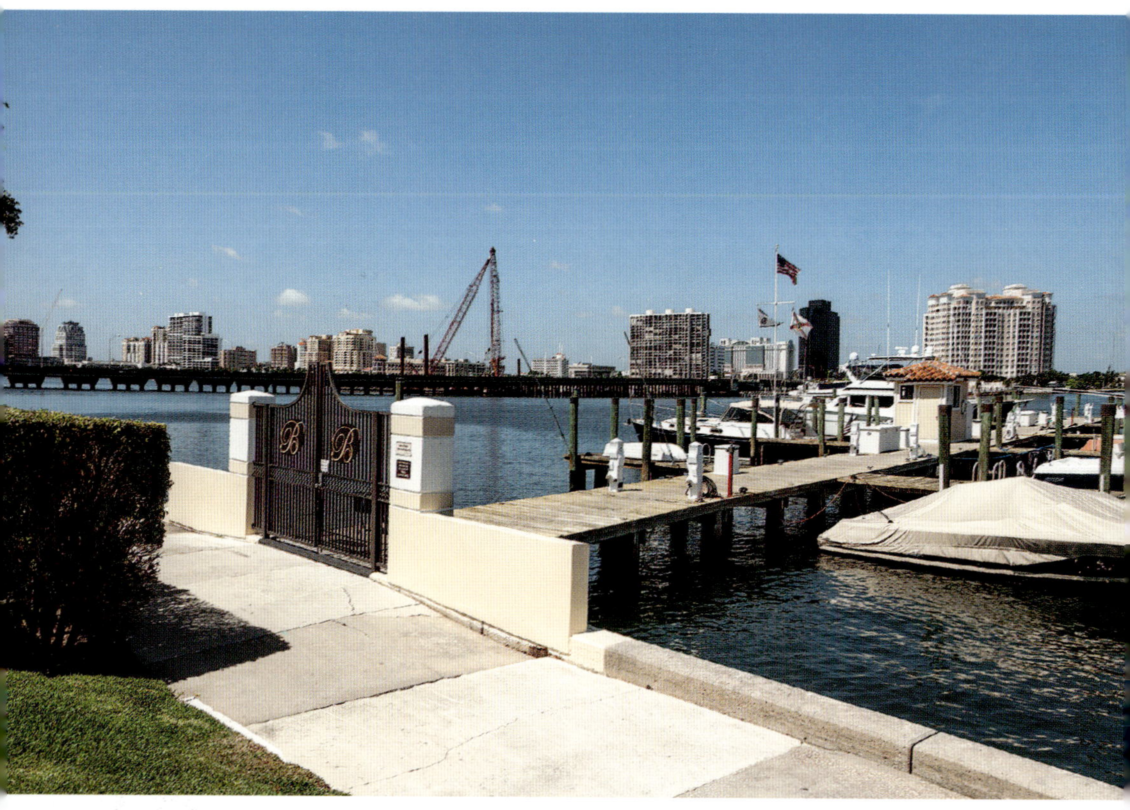

Bathers, Palm Beach, 1905

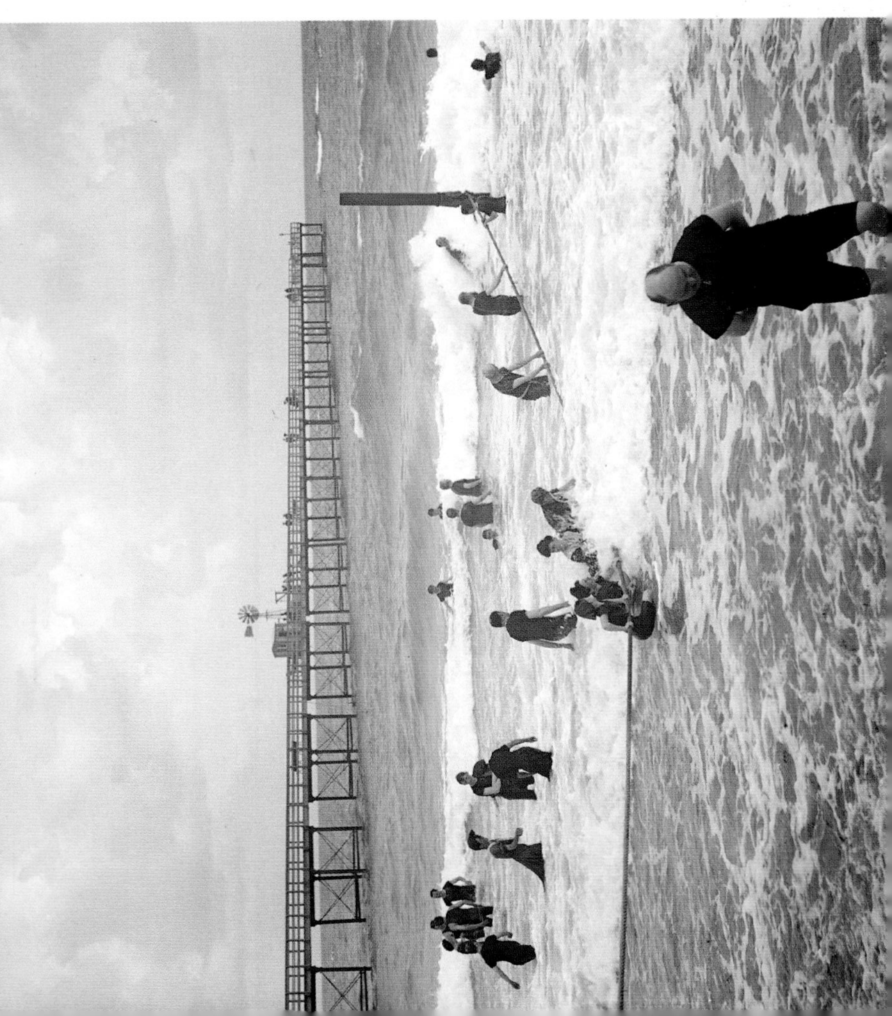

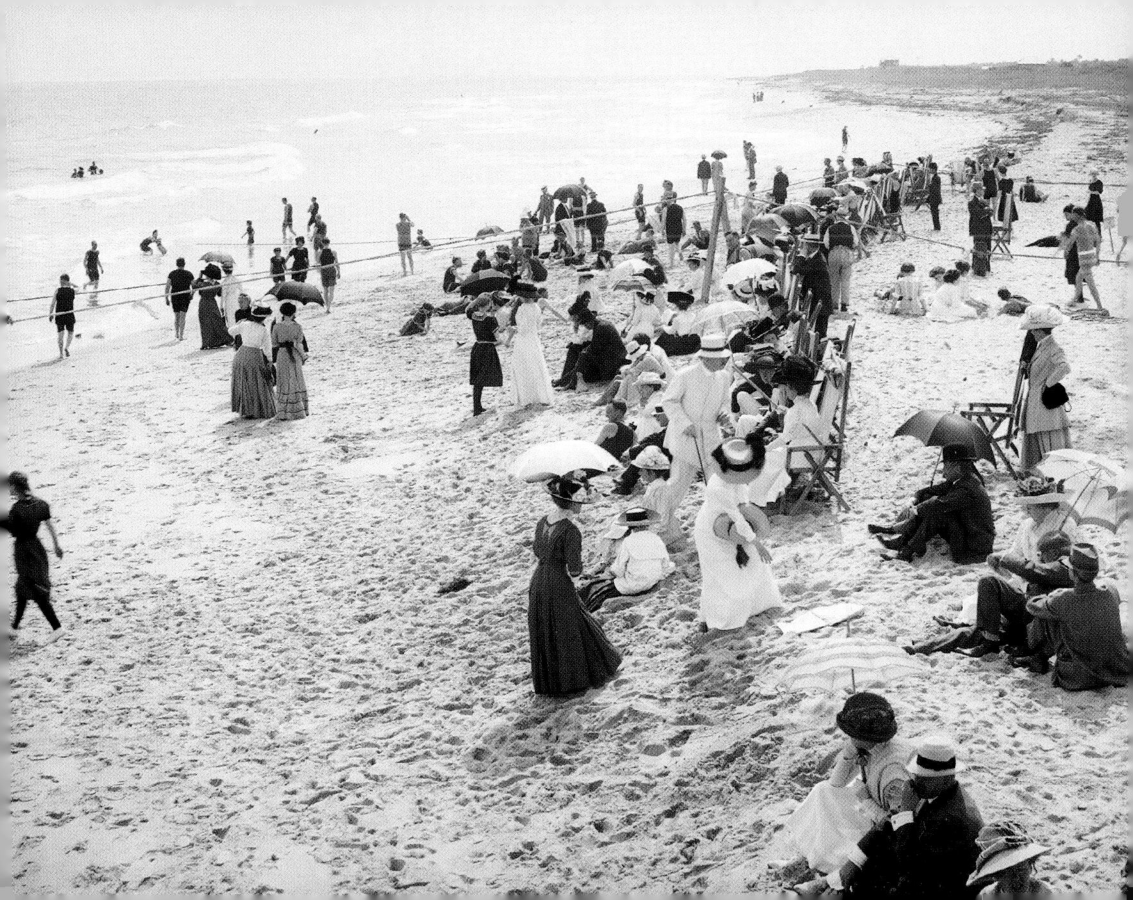

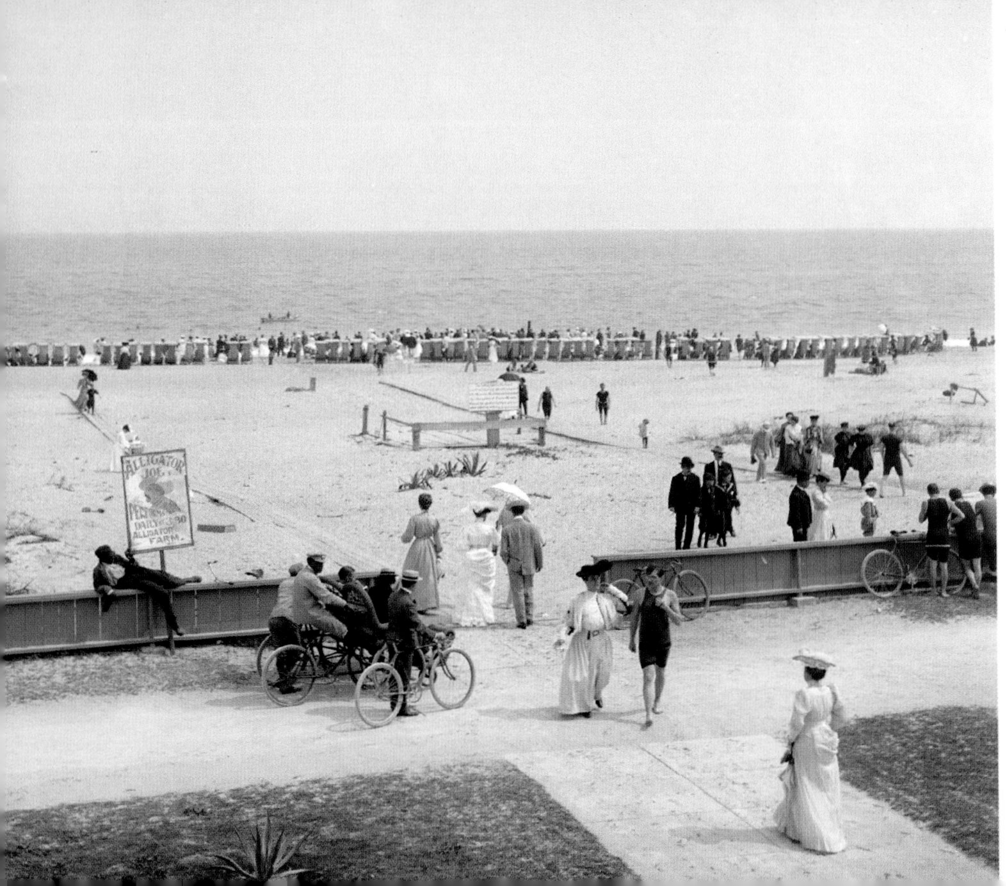

Bathers, Palm Beach, 1905

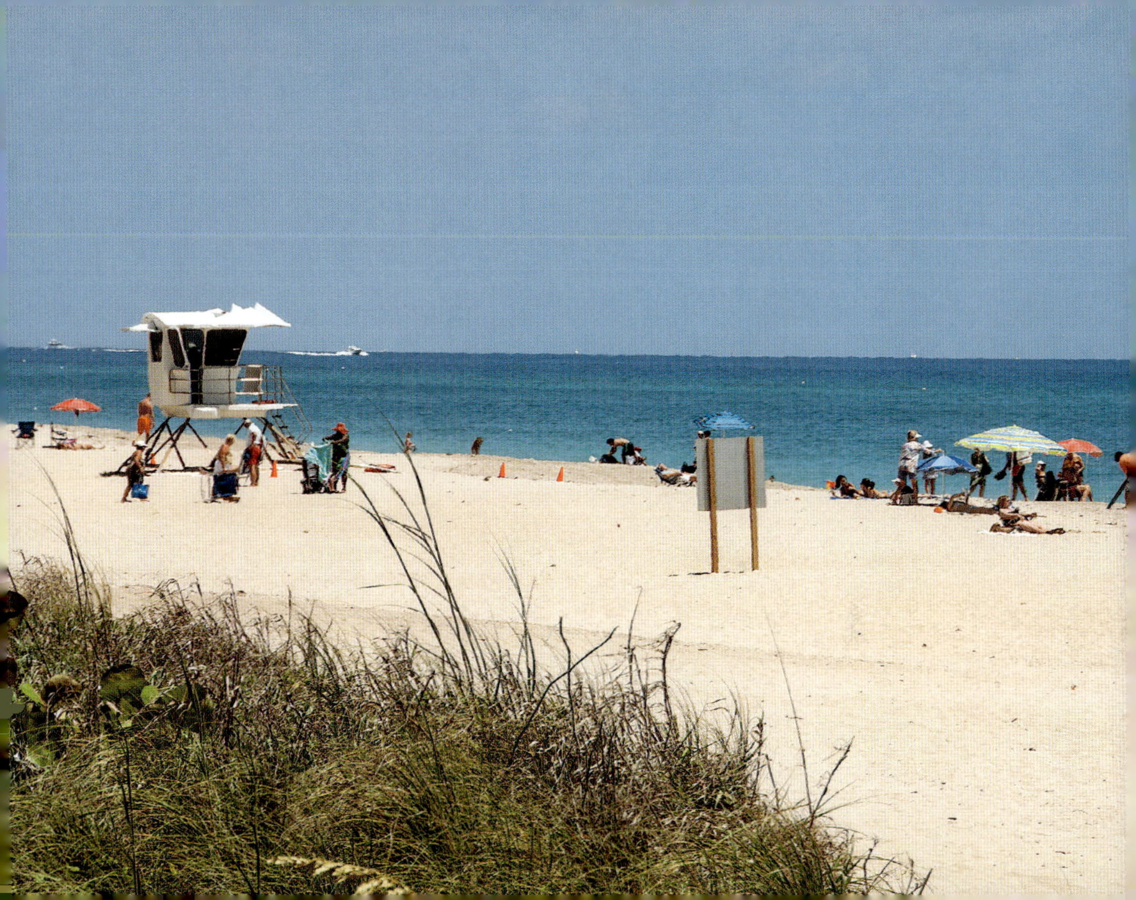

Cycle Paths, Palm Beach, c. 1905

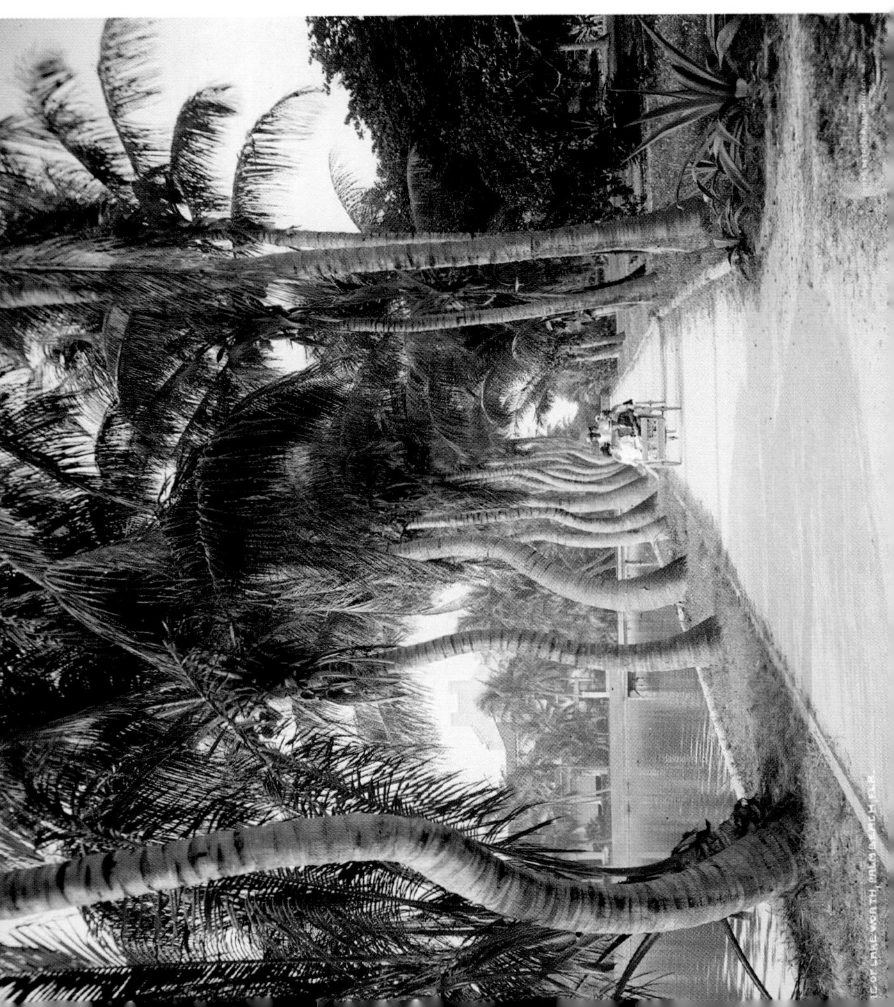

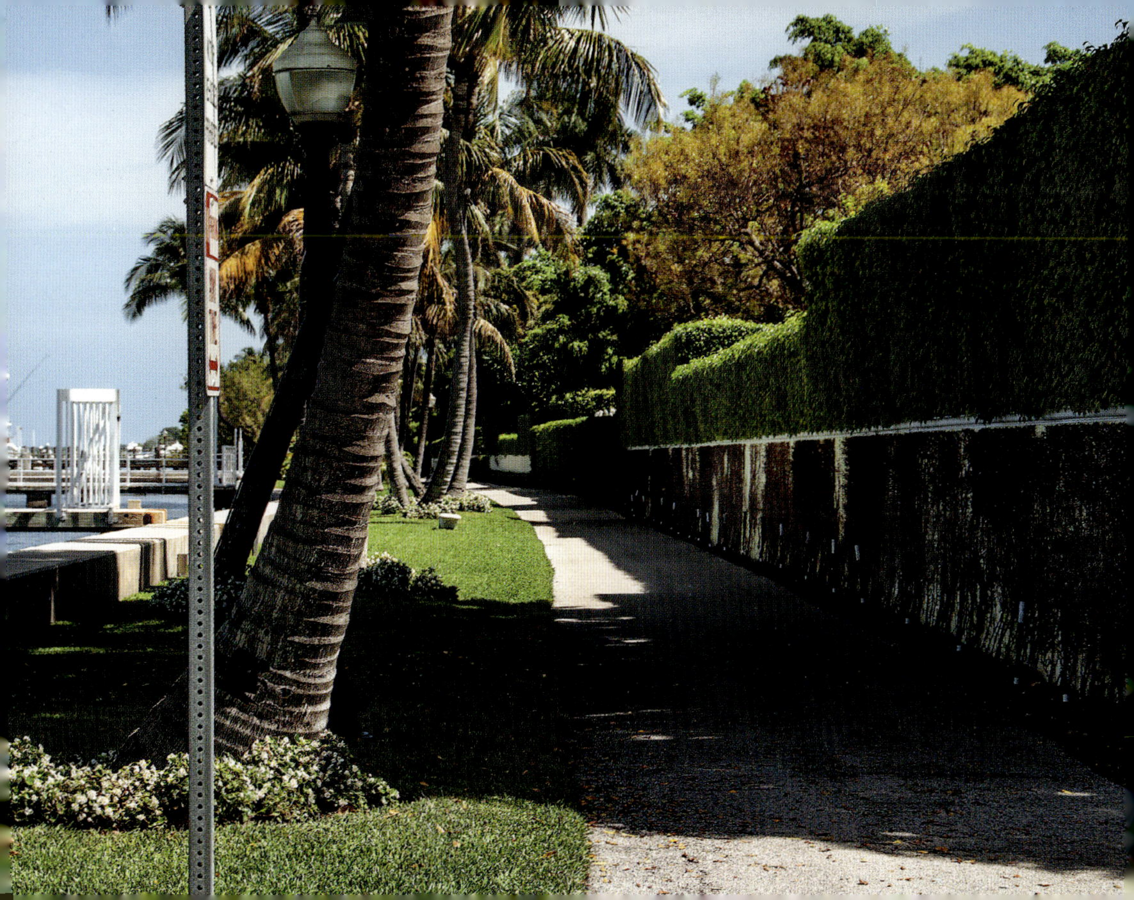

Cycle Paths, Palm Beach, c. 1905

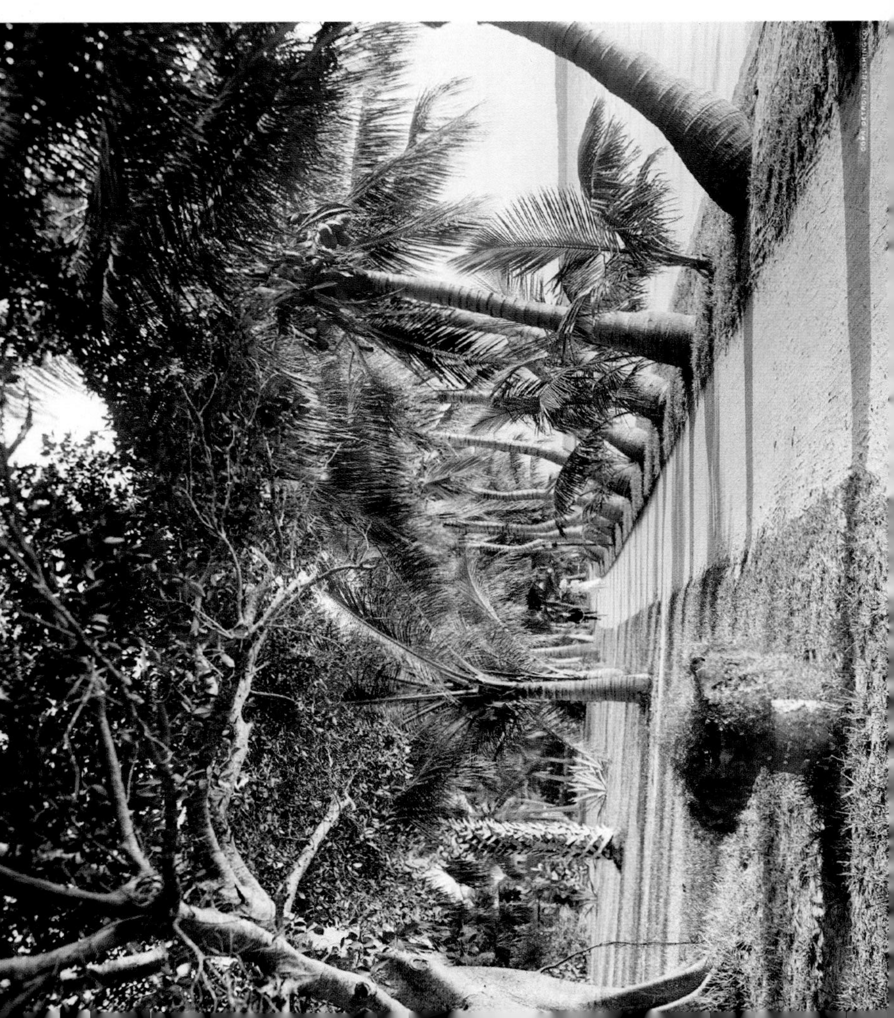

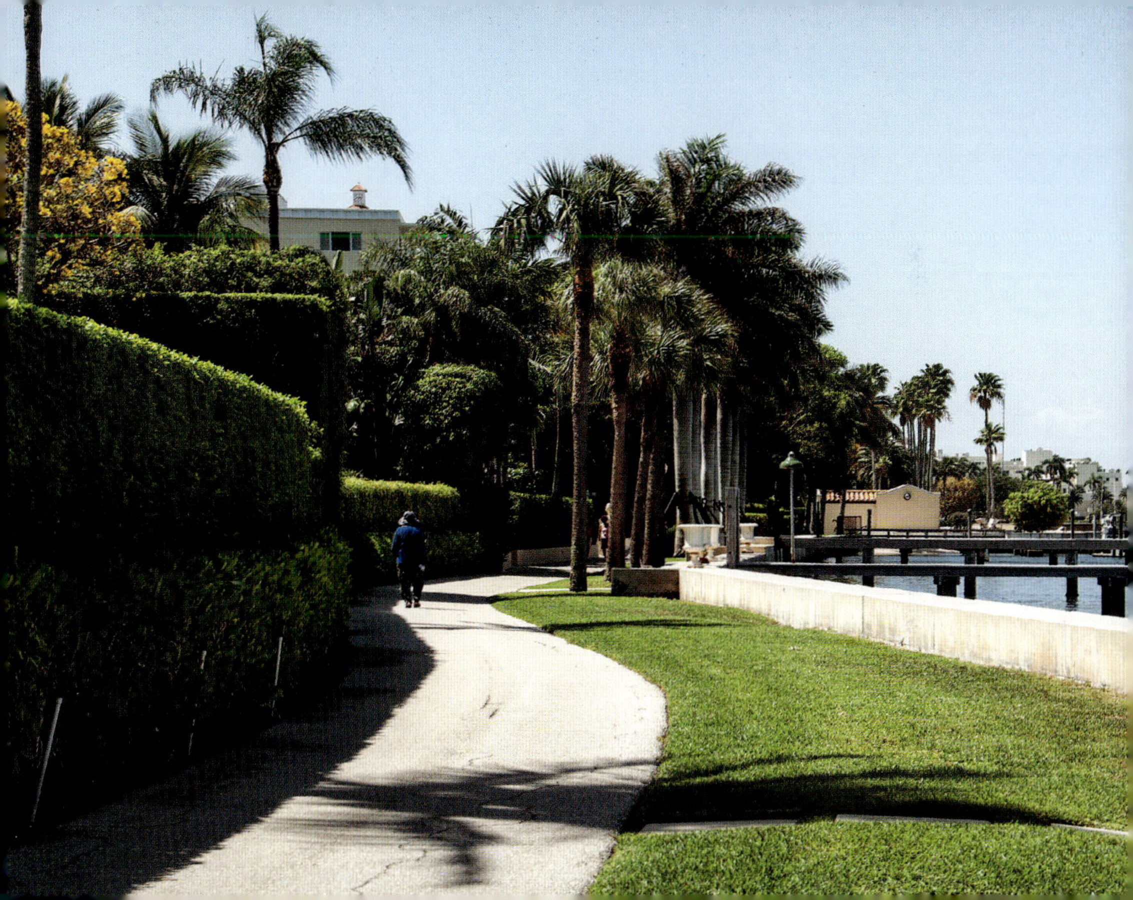

Golf Links, Palm Beach, 1904

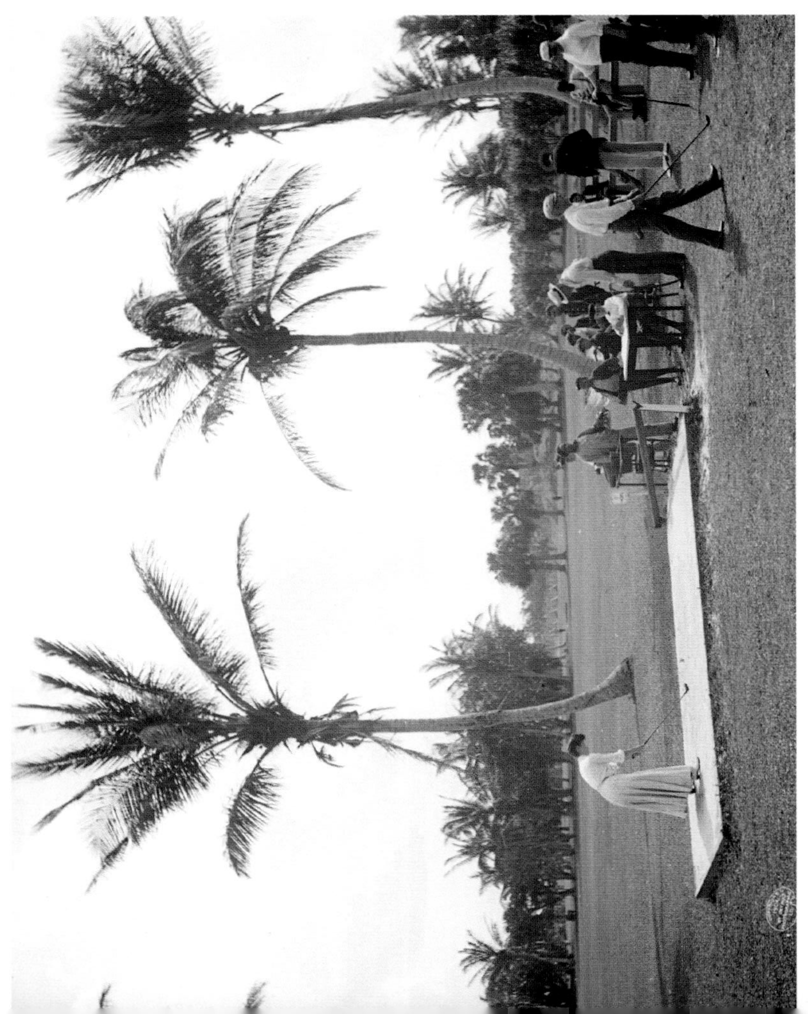

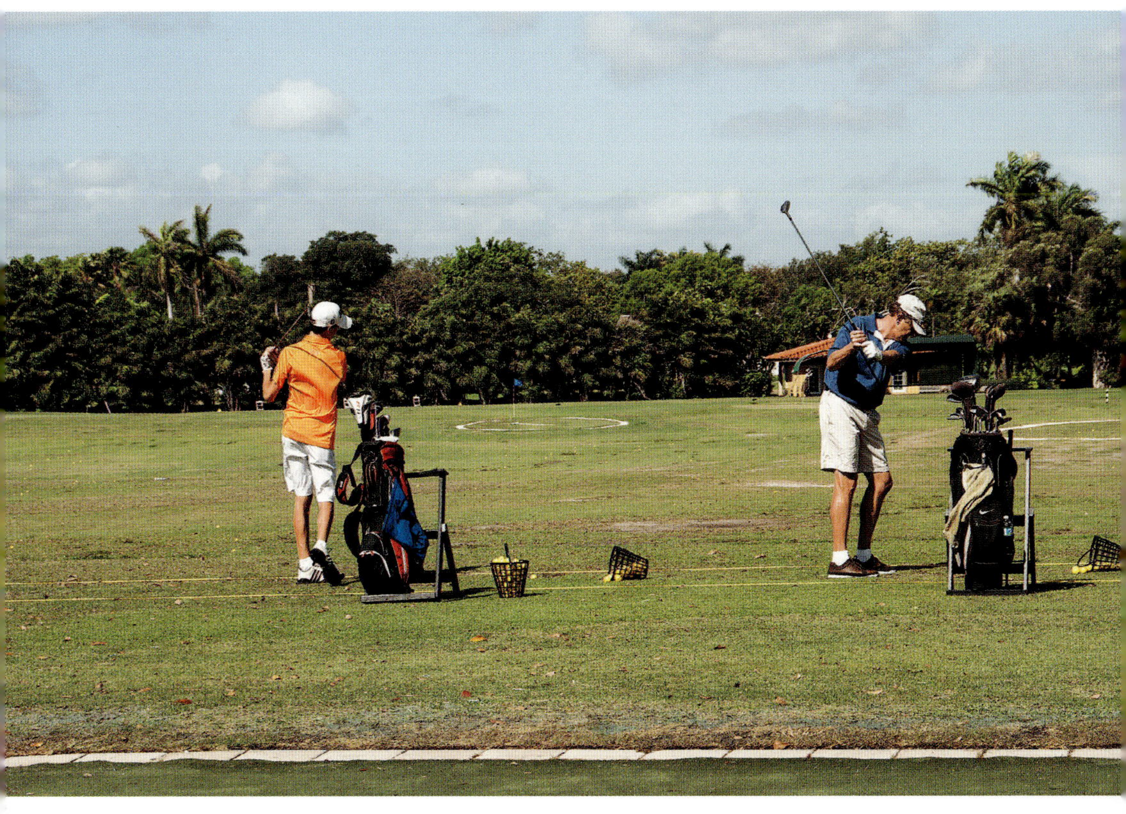

Fruit Packing Plant, Fort Pierce, 1937

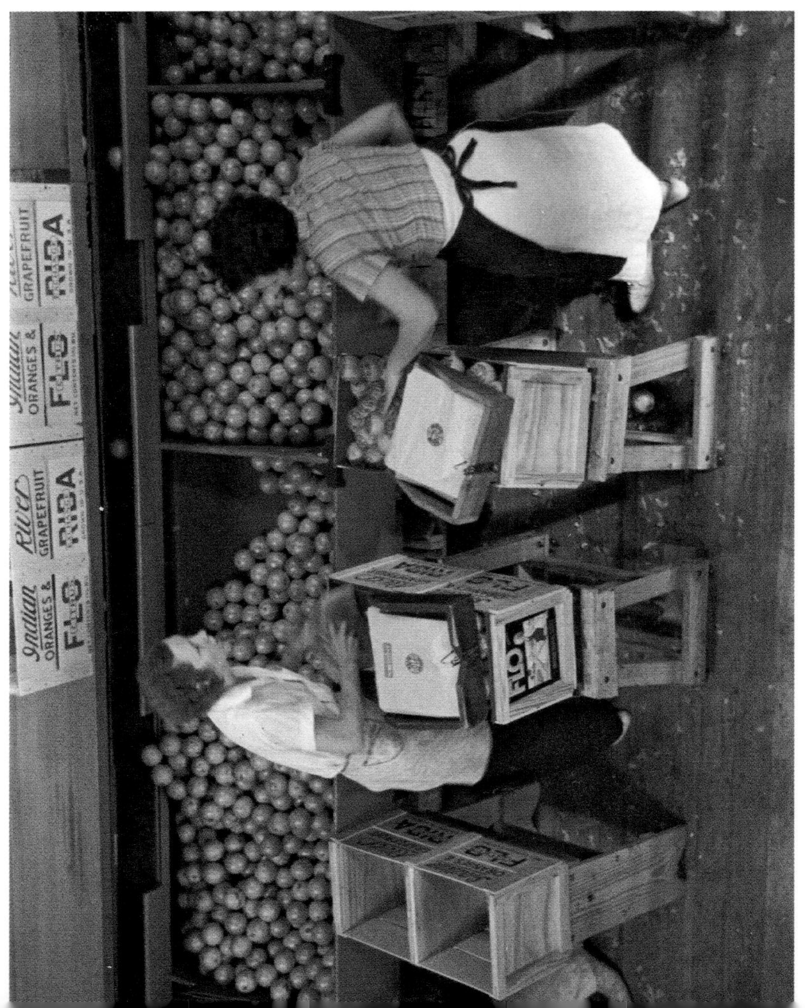

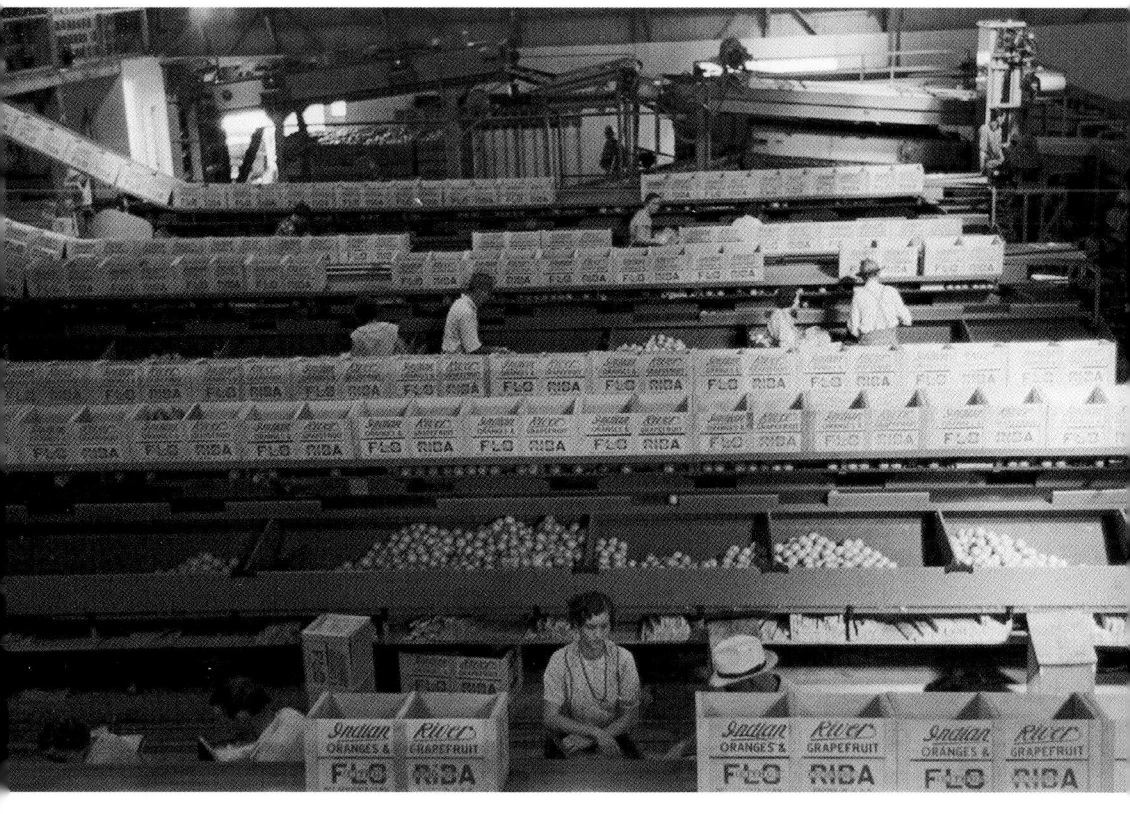
Indian
ORANGES &
FLO
River
GRAPEFRUIT
RIDA

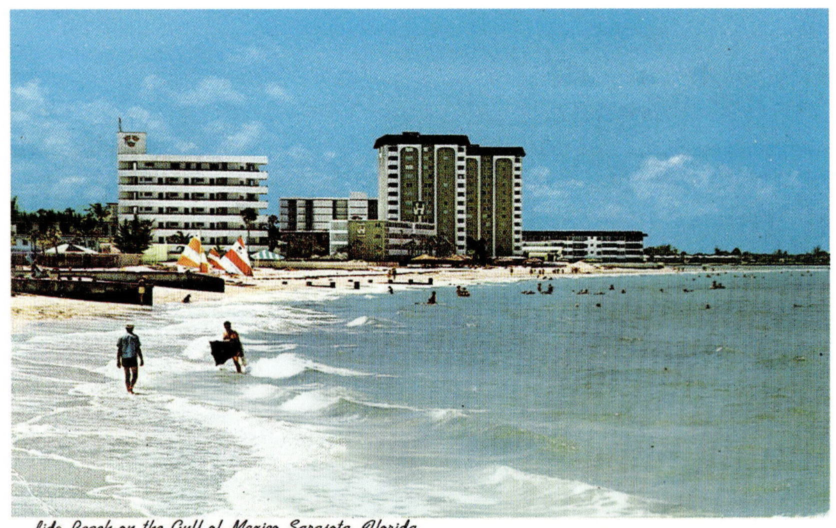

Lido Beach, Sarasota, c. 1970

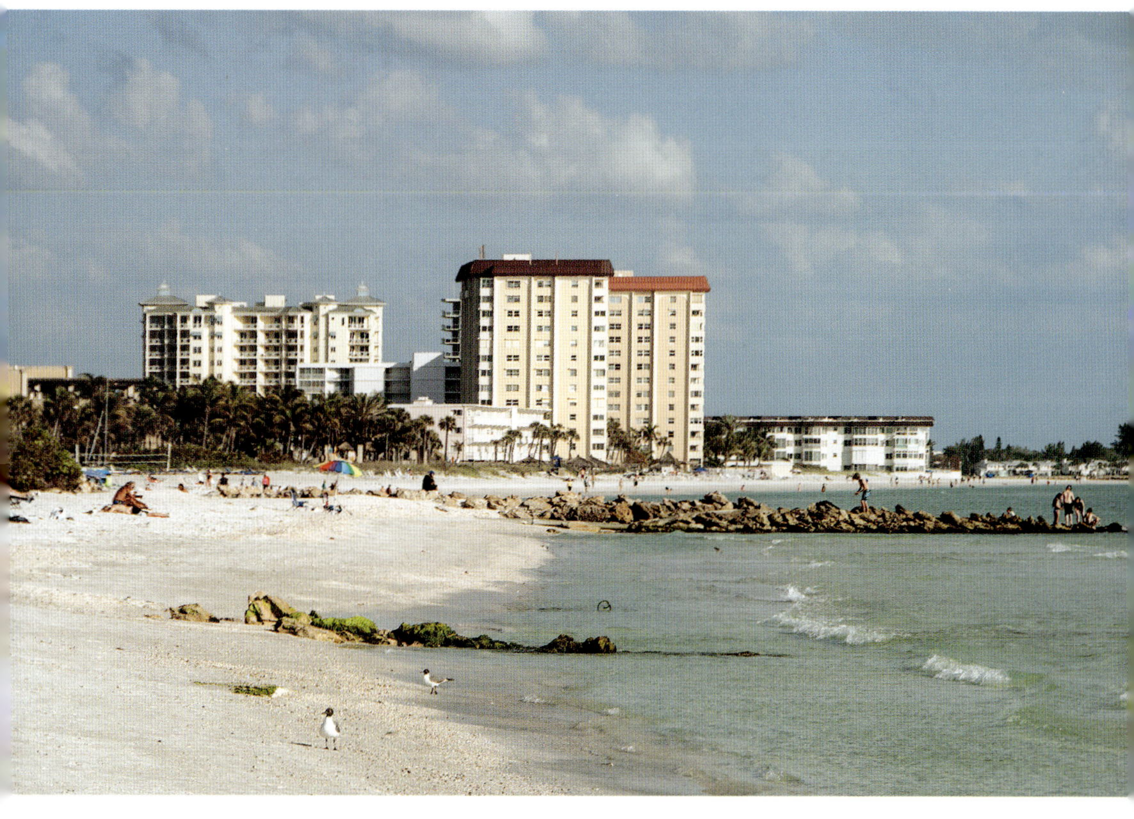

Ringling Mansion (now Museum), Sarasota, c. 1930

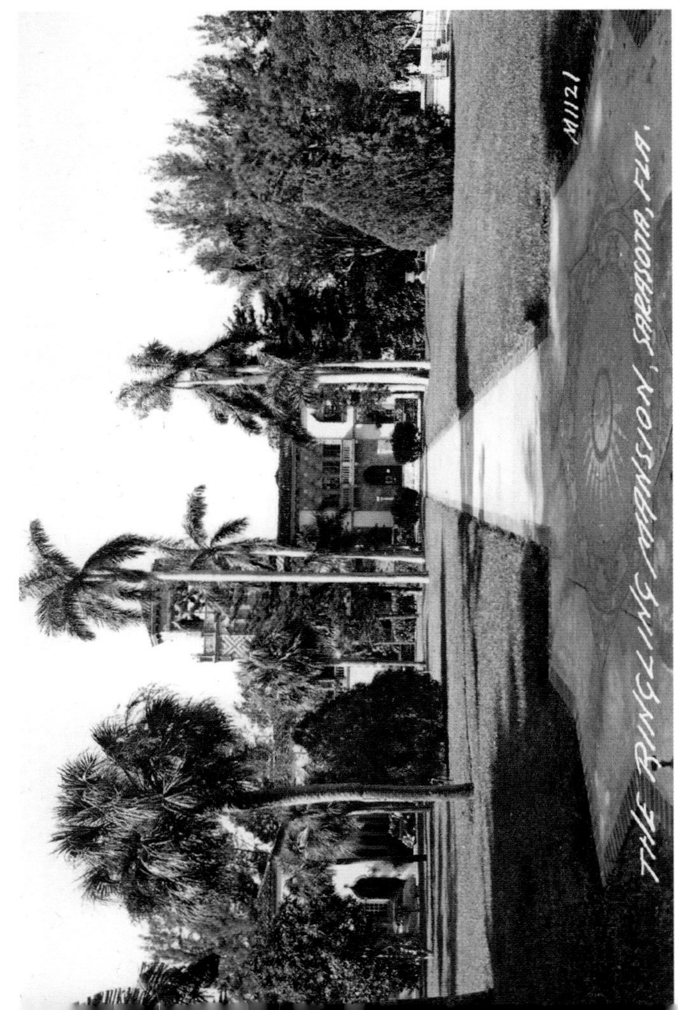

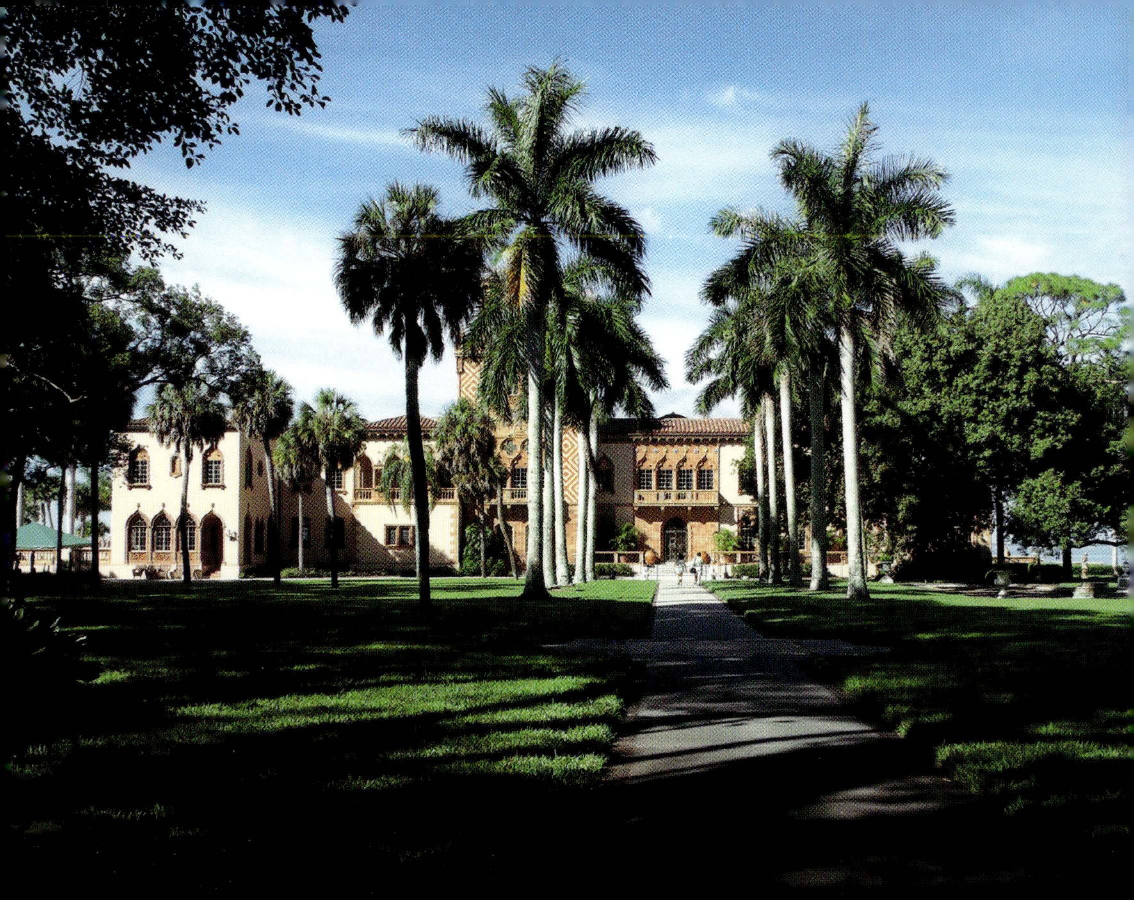

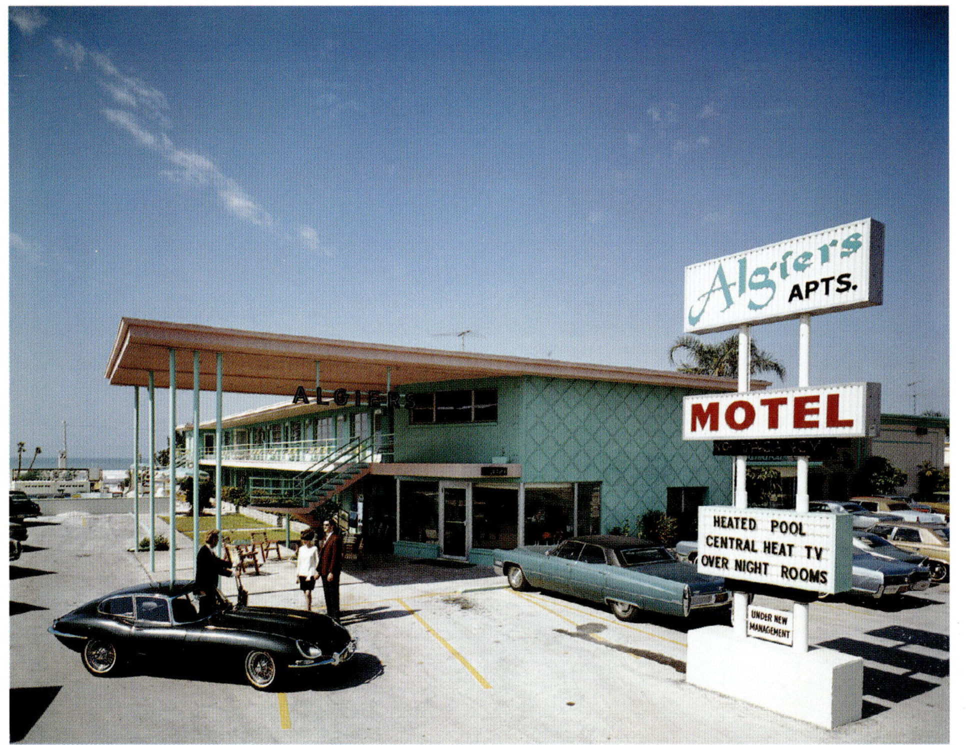

Algiers Apartments, Treasure Island, 1967

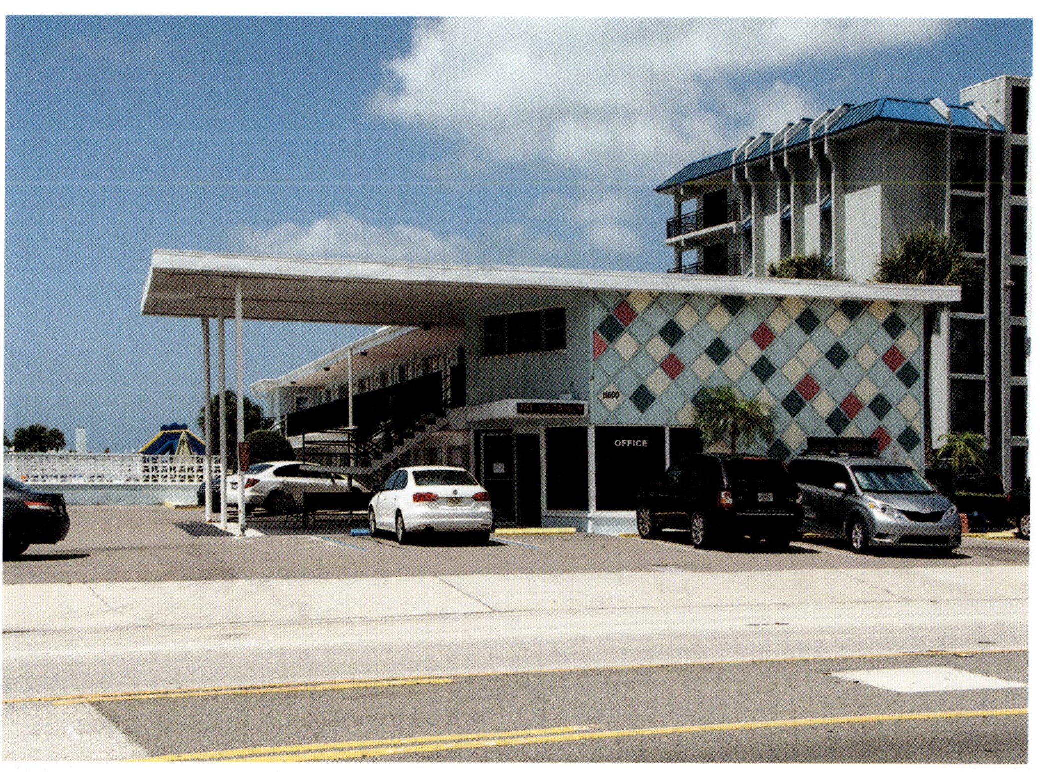
NO VACANCY
11600
OFFICE

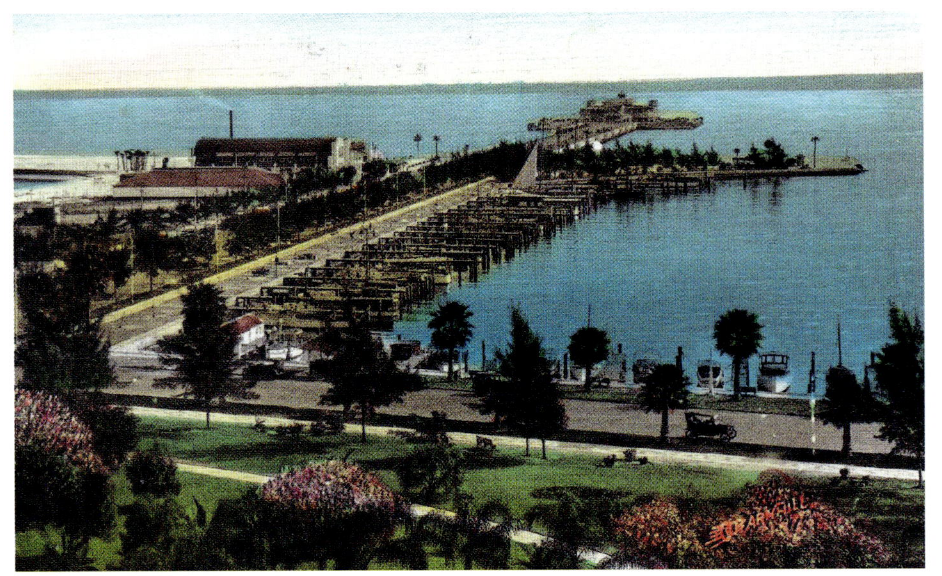

Pier, St. Petersburg, c. 1920

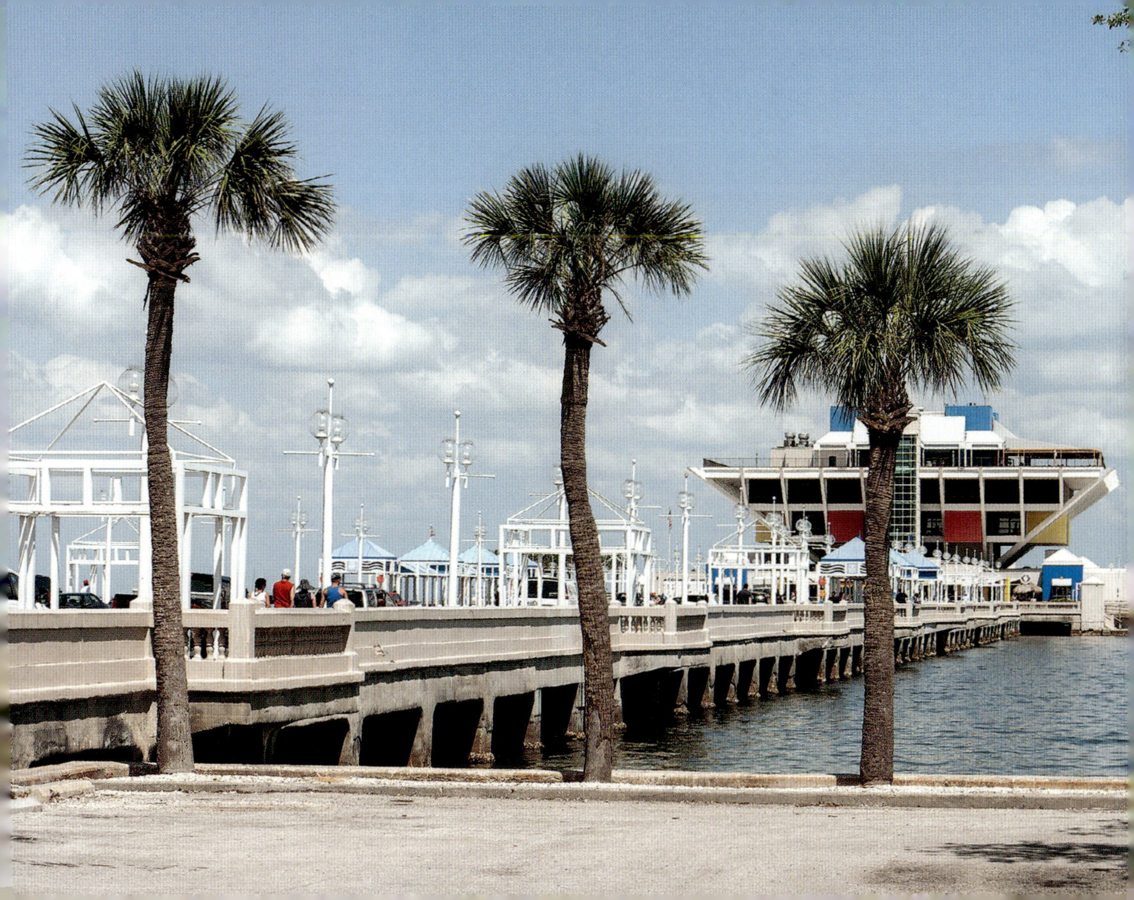

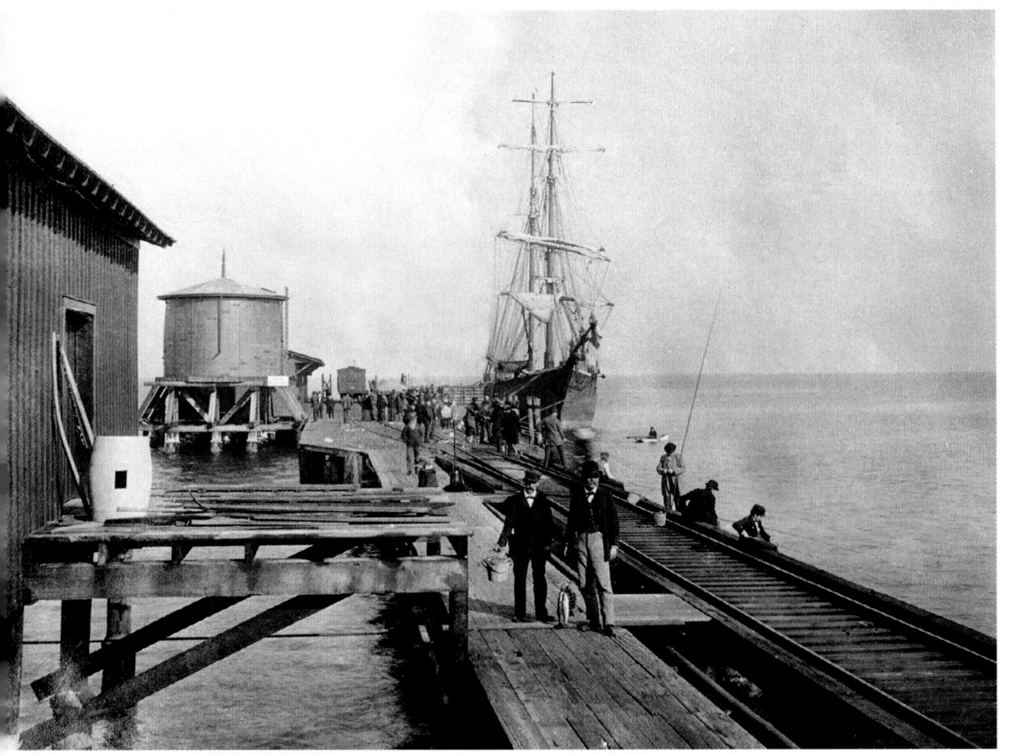

Pier, St. Petersburg, c. 1910

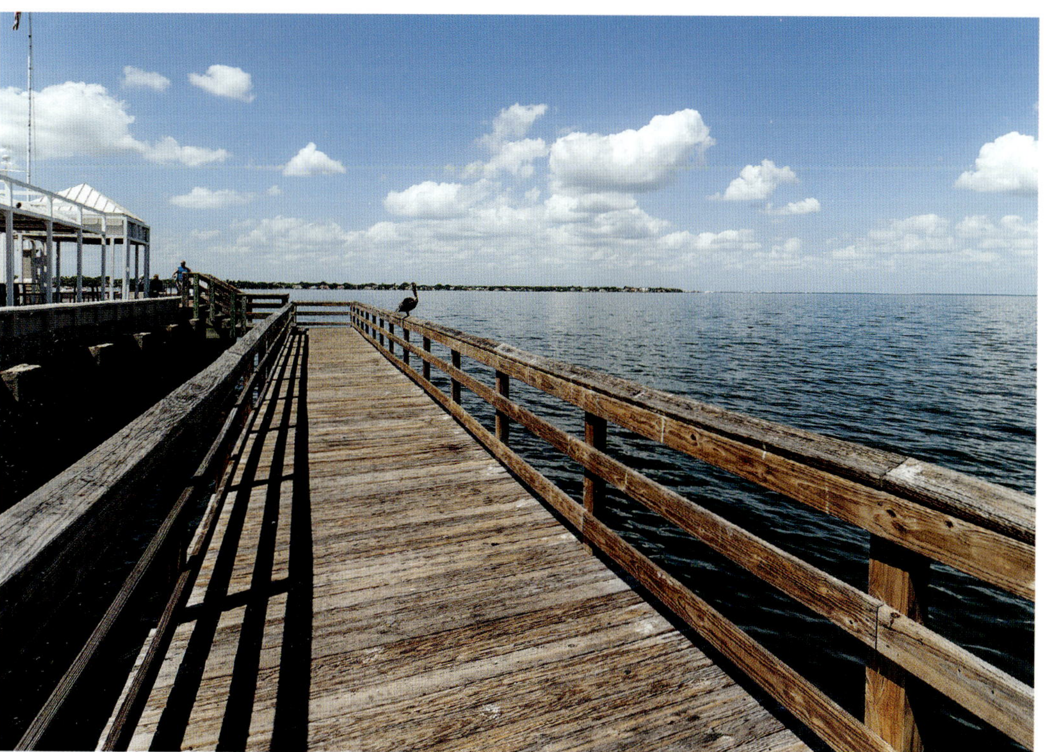

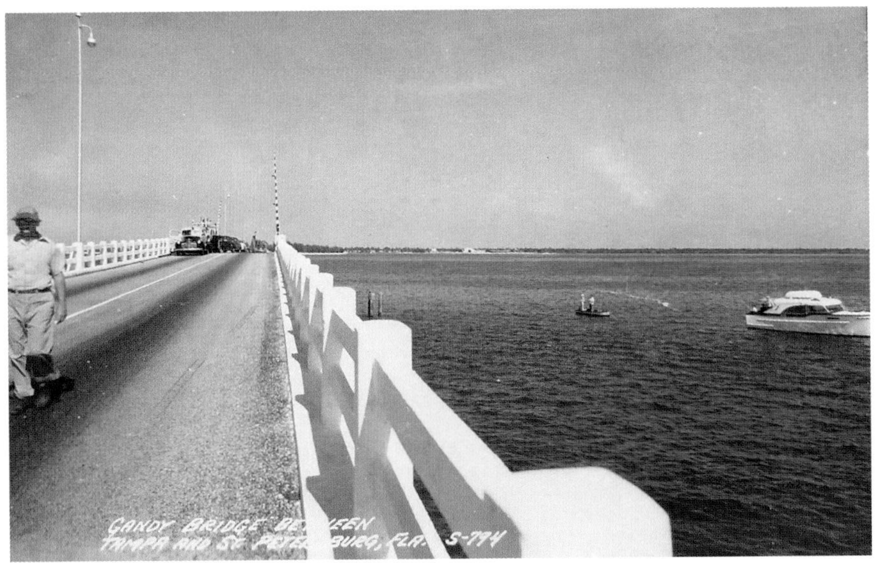

Gandy Bridge, St. Petersburg, 1952

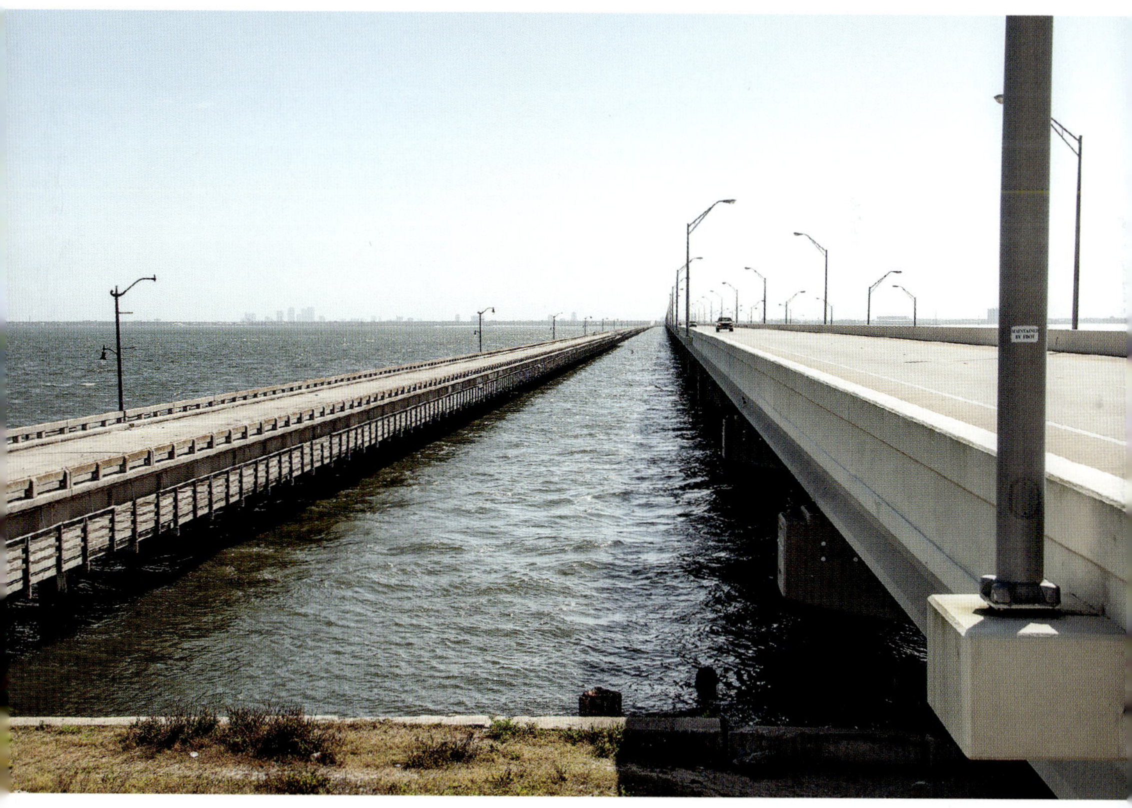

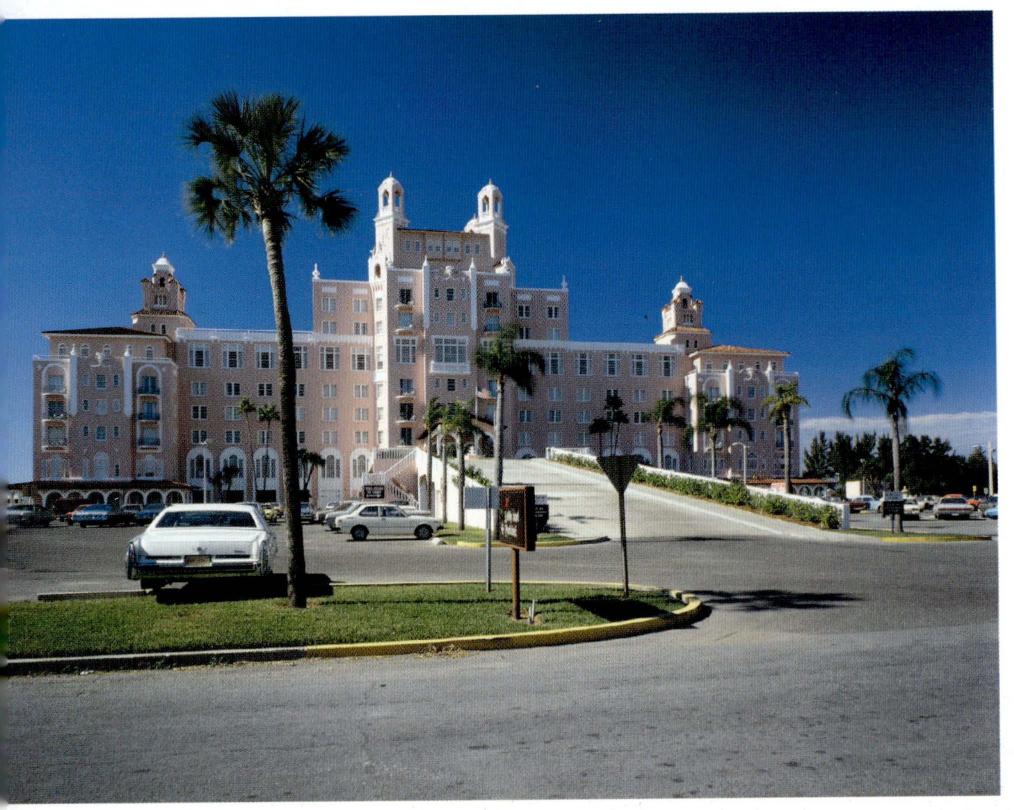

Don CeSar Hotel, St. Petersburg, c. 1975

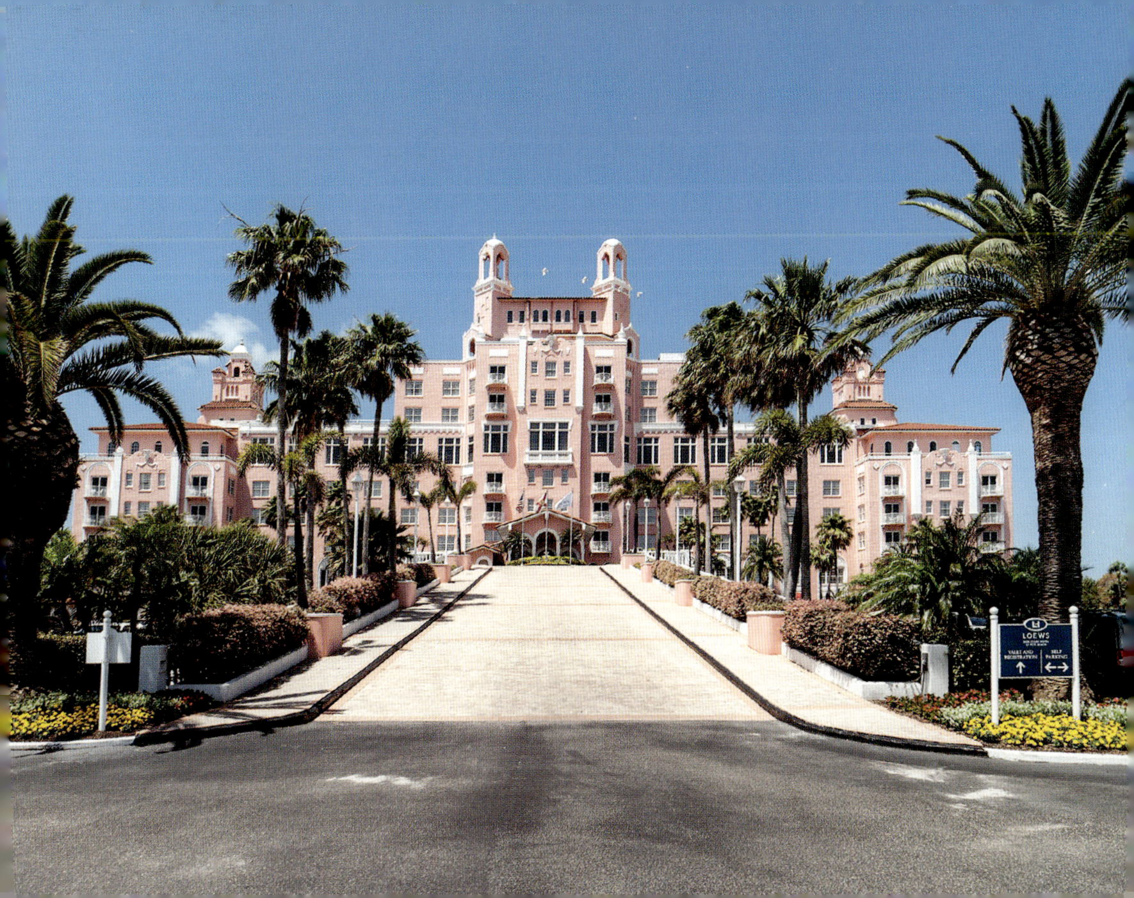
LOEWS

Coliseum, St. Petersburg, c. 1925

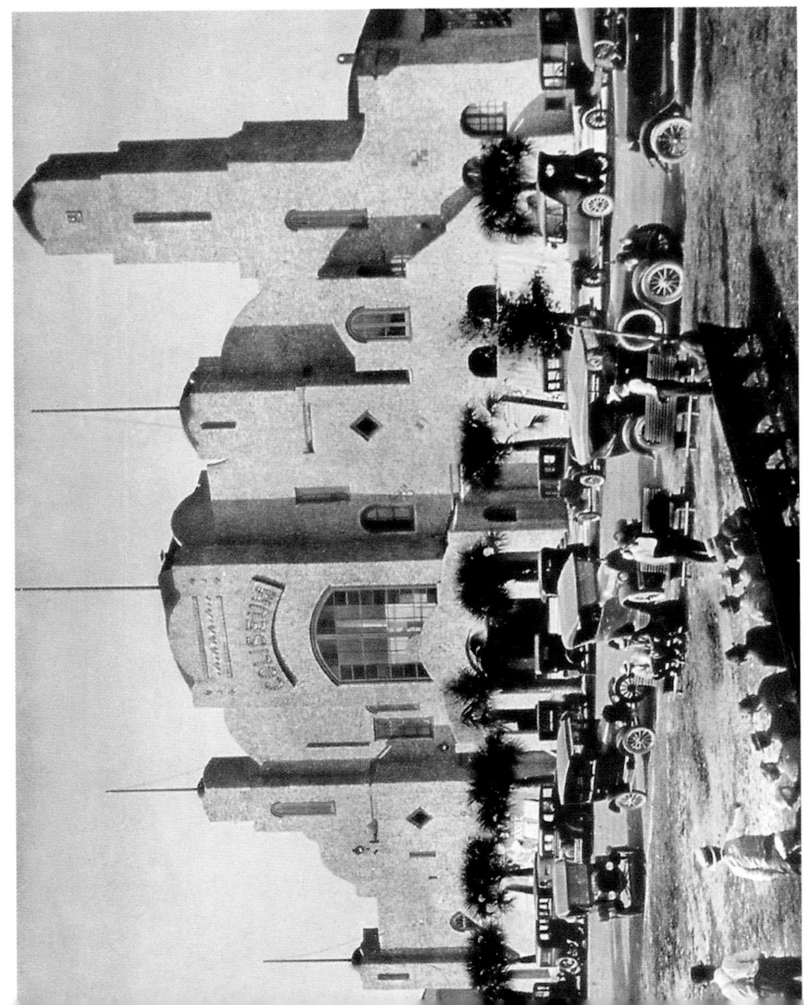

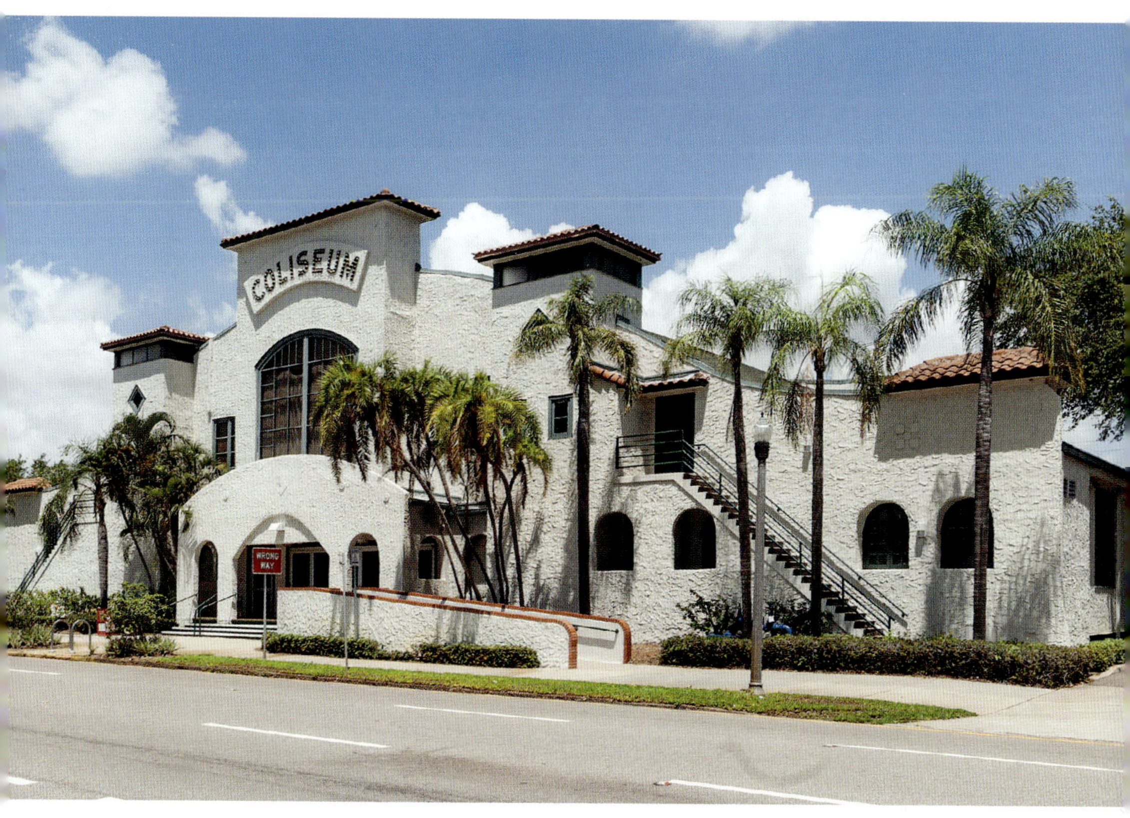
COLISEUM
WRONG WAY

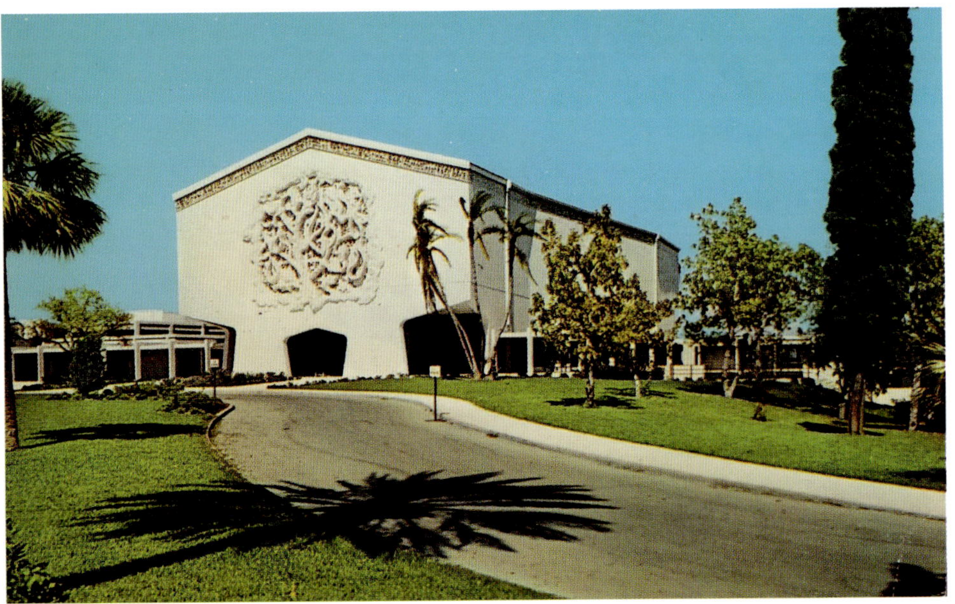

First Presbyterian Church, St. Petersburg, c. 1960

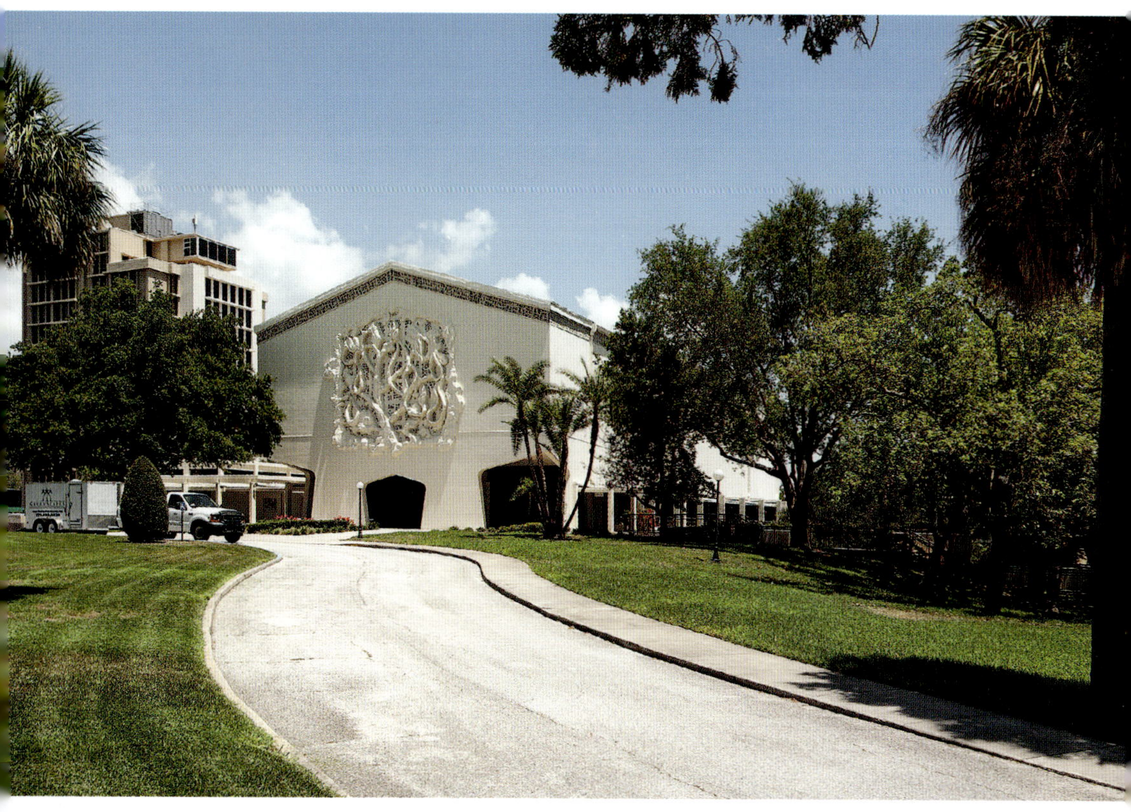

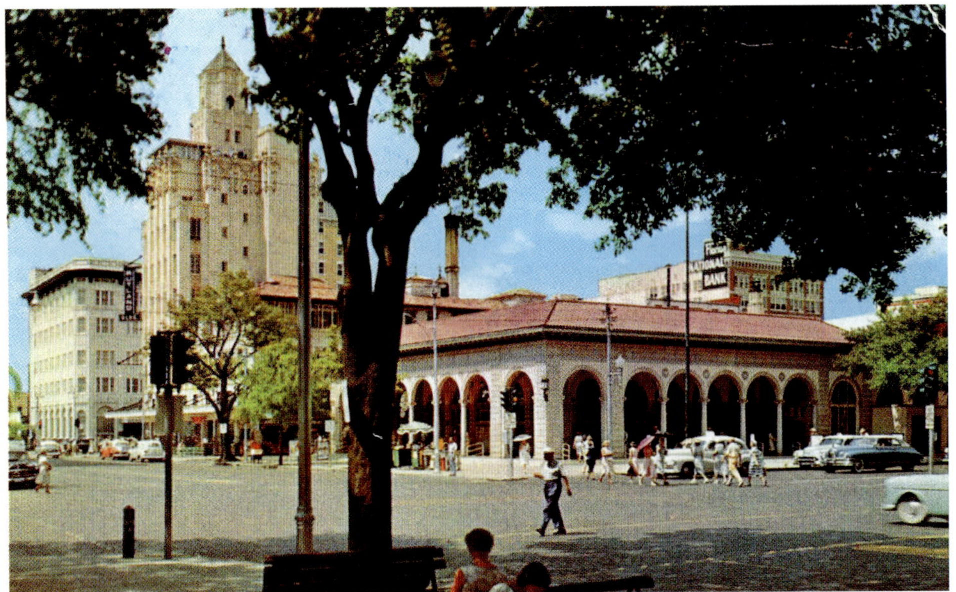

Post Office and the Rutland Building, St. Petersburg, c. 1955

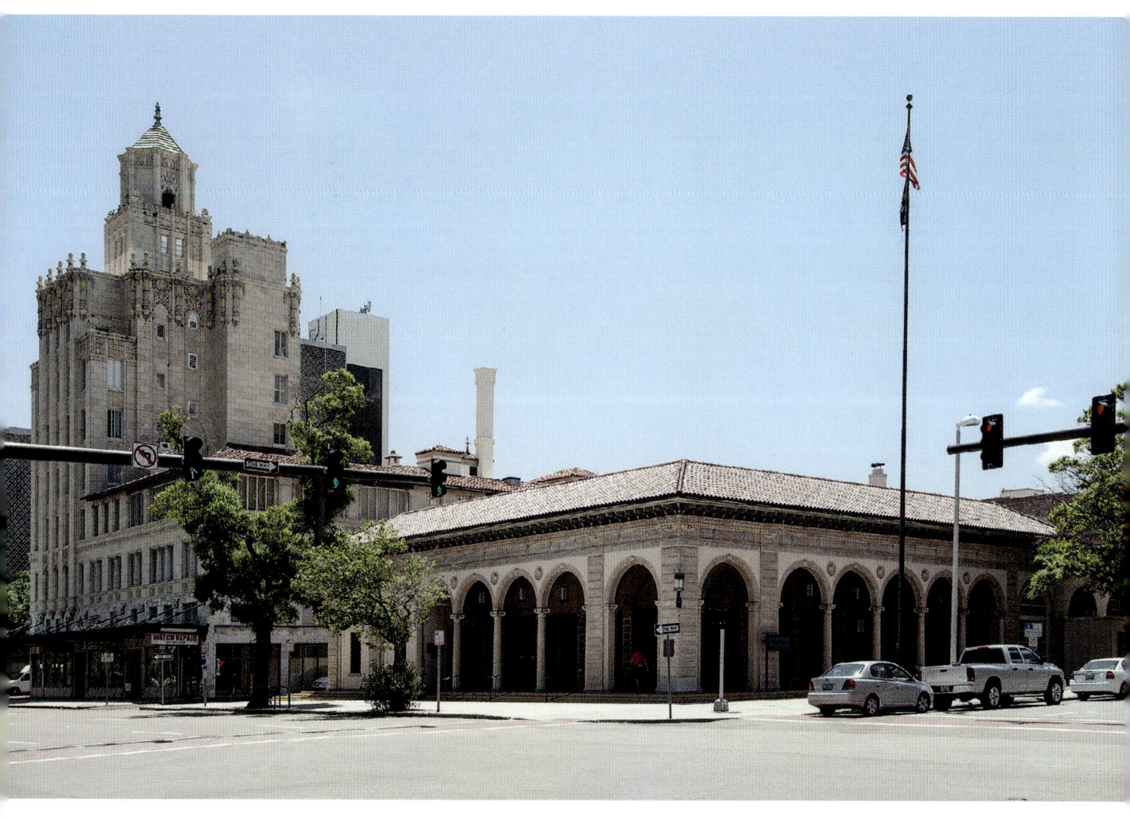
WATCH REPAIR
ONE WAY

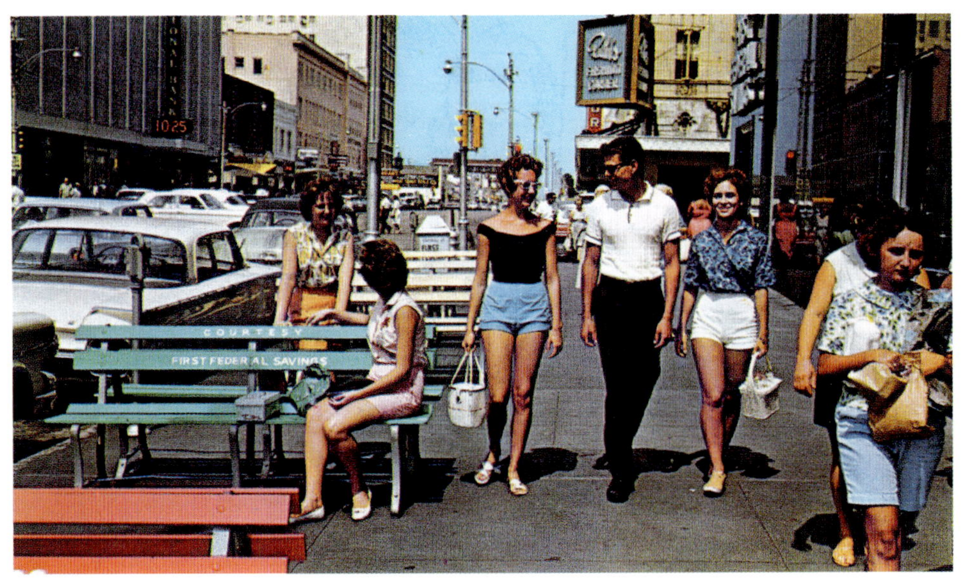

Central Avenue, St. Petersburg, c. 1960

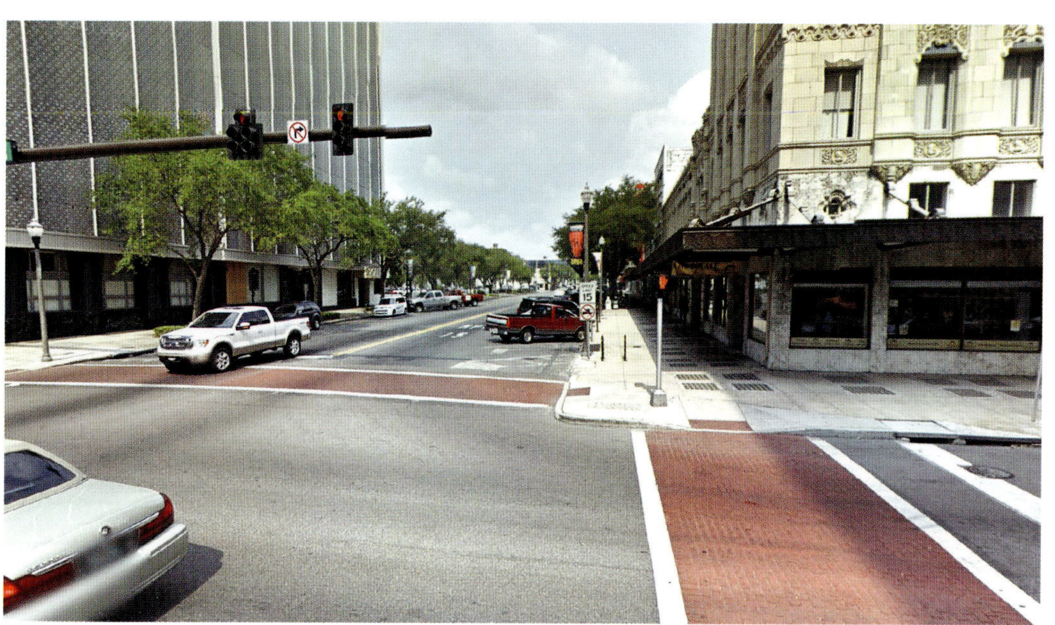
15

Central Avenue, St. Petersburg, c. 1975

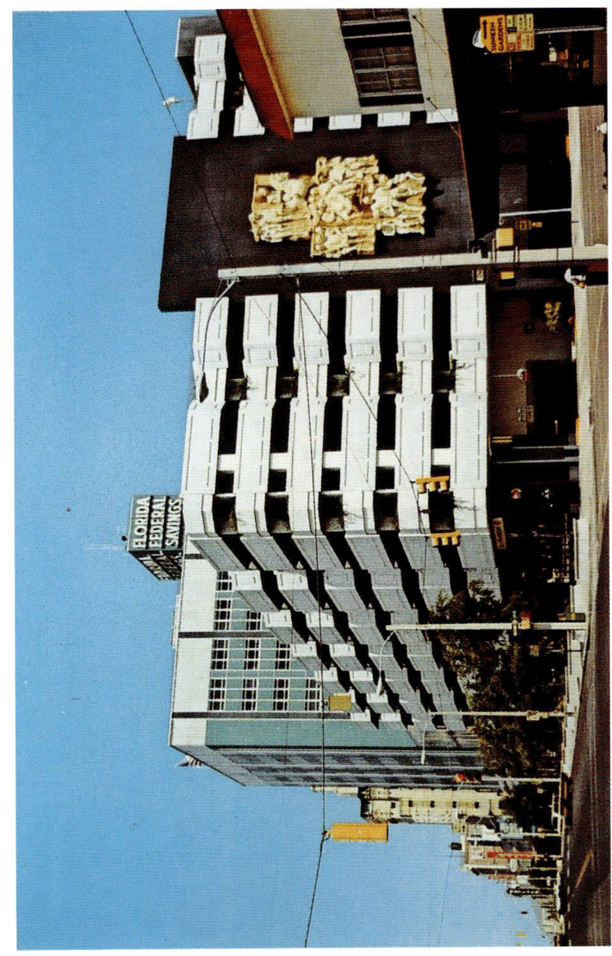

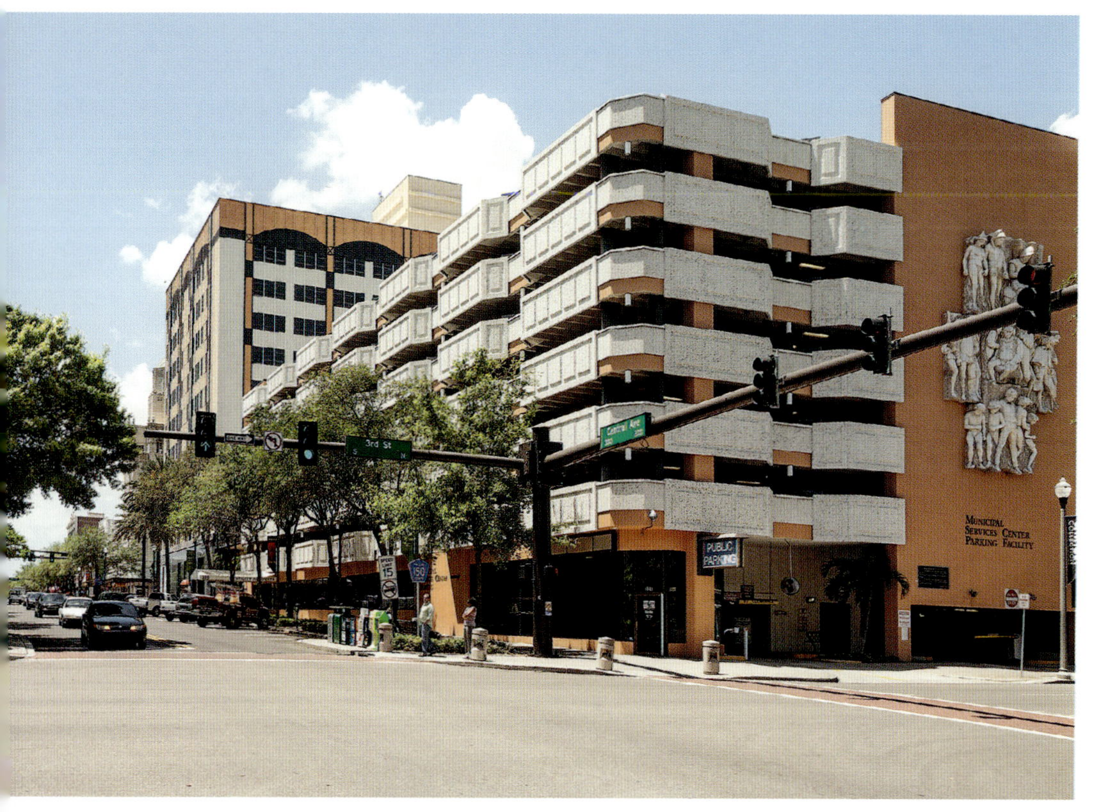
ONE WAY
3rd St
Central Ave
PUBLIC PARKING
Municipal Services Center Parking Facility

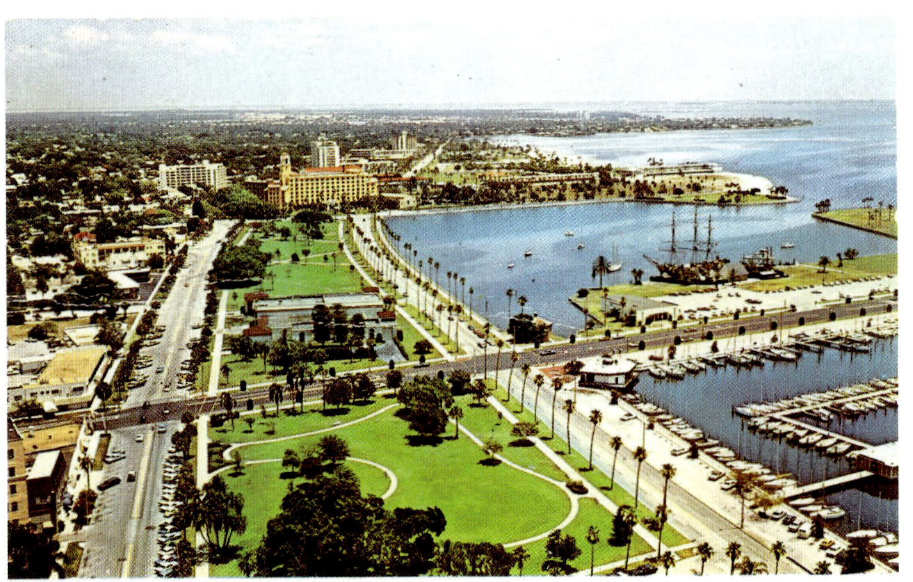

Beautiful Waterfront Park, St. Petersburg, Florida

Waterfronr Park, St. Petersburg, c. 1960

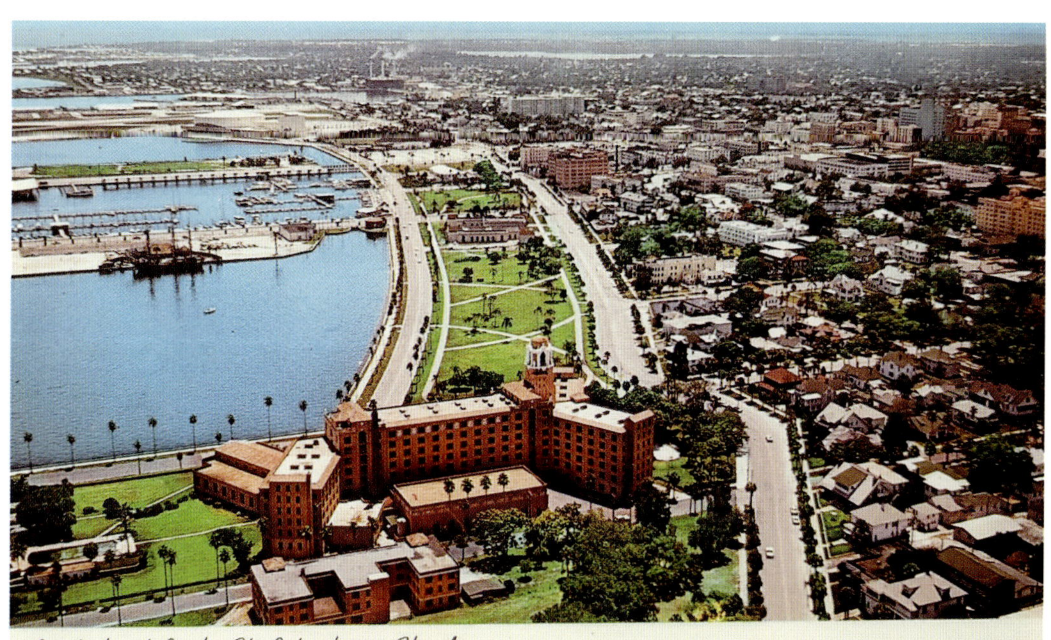

Waterfront Park, St. Petersburg, Florida

Band Shell, Williams Park, St. Petersburg, 1963

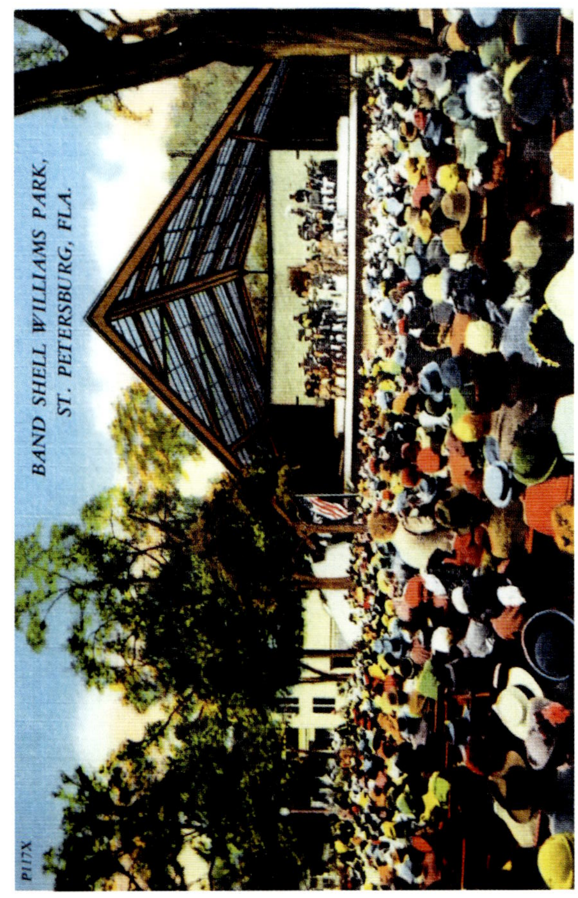

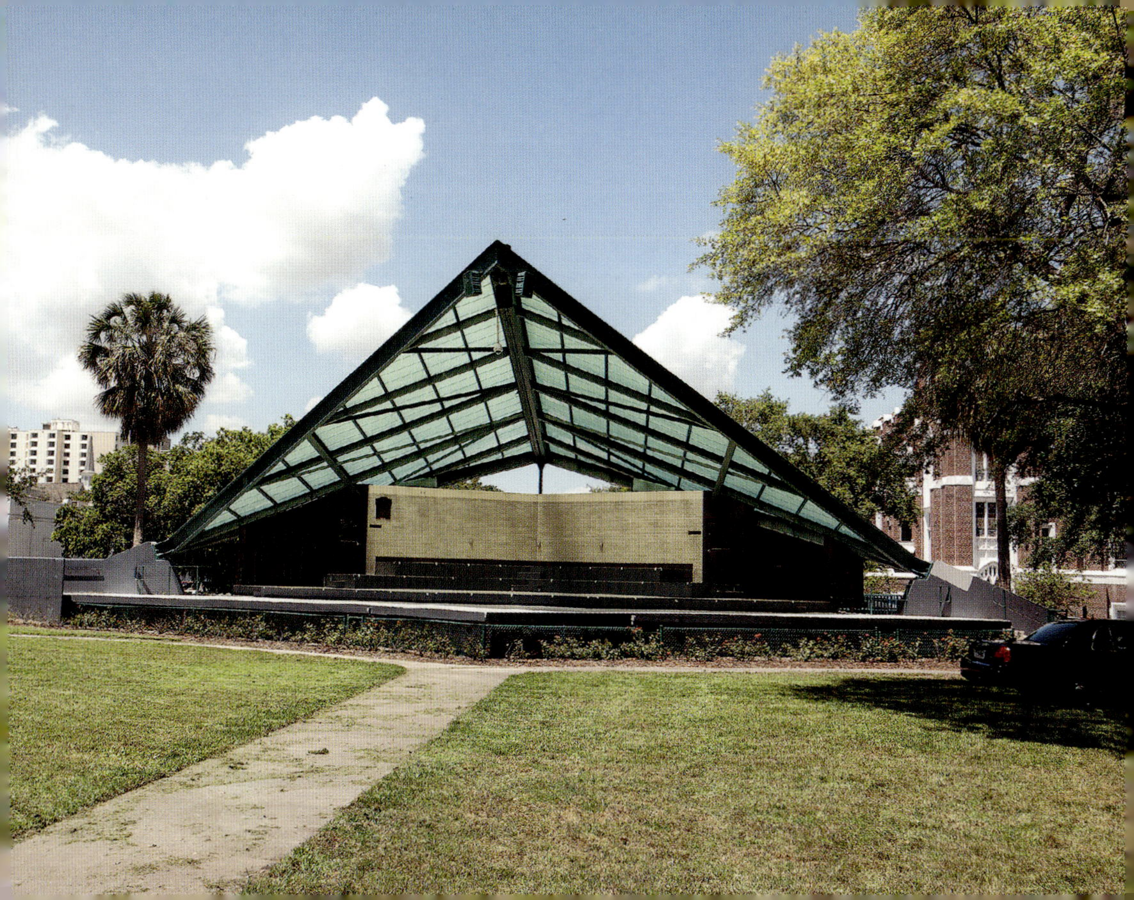

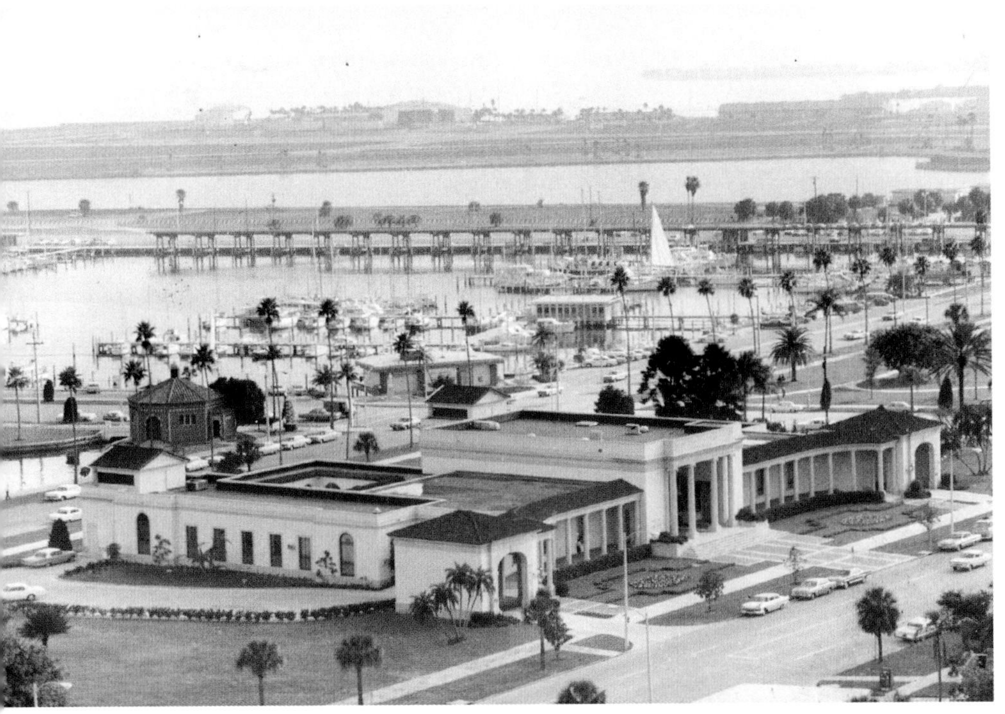

Museum of Fine Arts, St. Petersburg, 1967

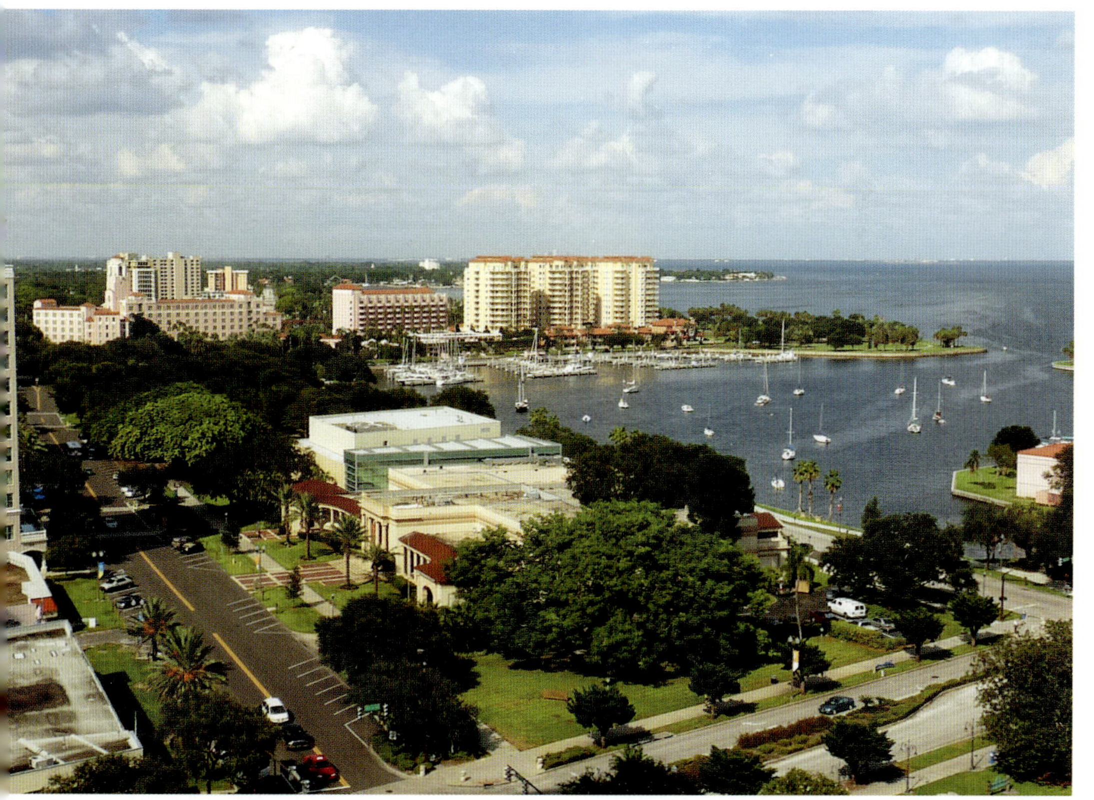

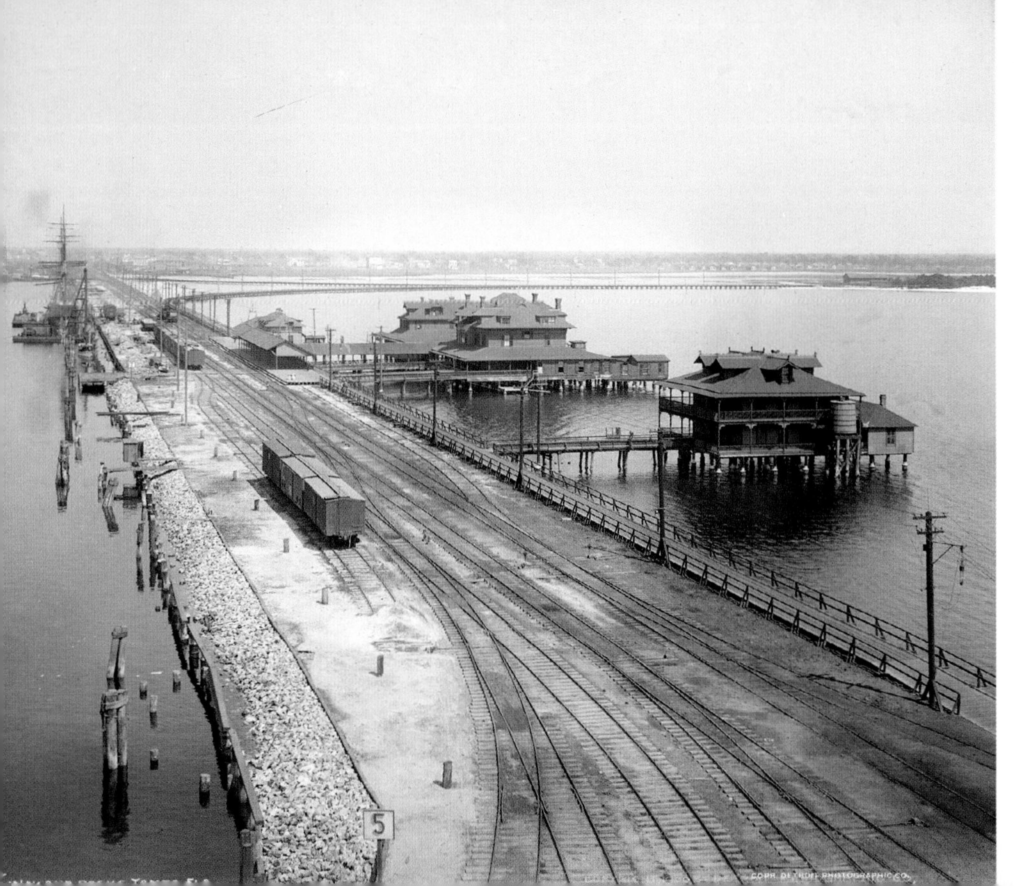

Pier and Docks (site of today's Picnic Island Park), Tampa, 1900

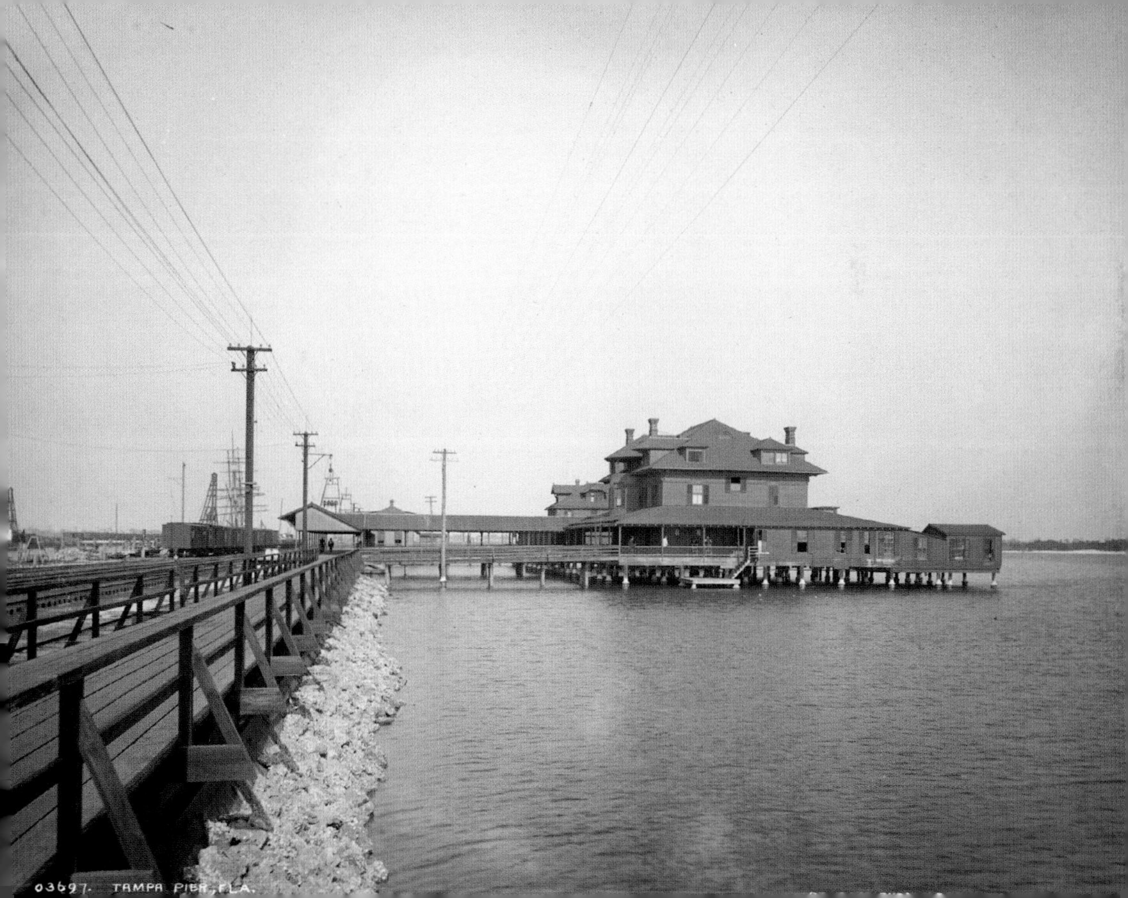
03697. TAMPA PIER, FLA.

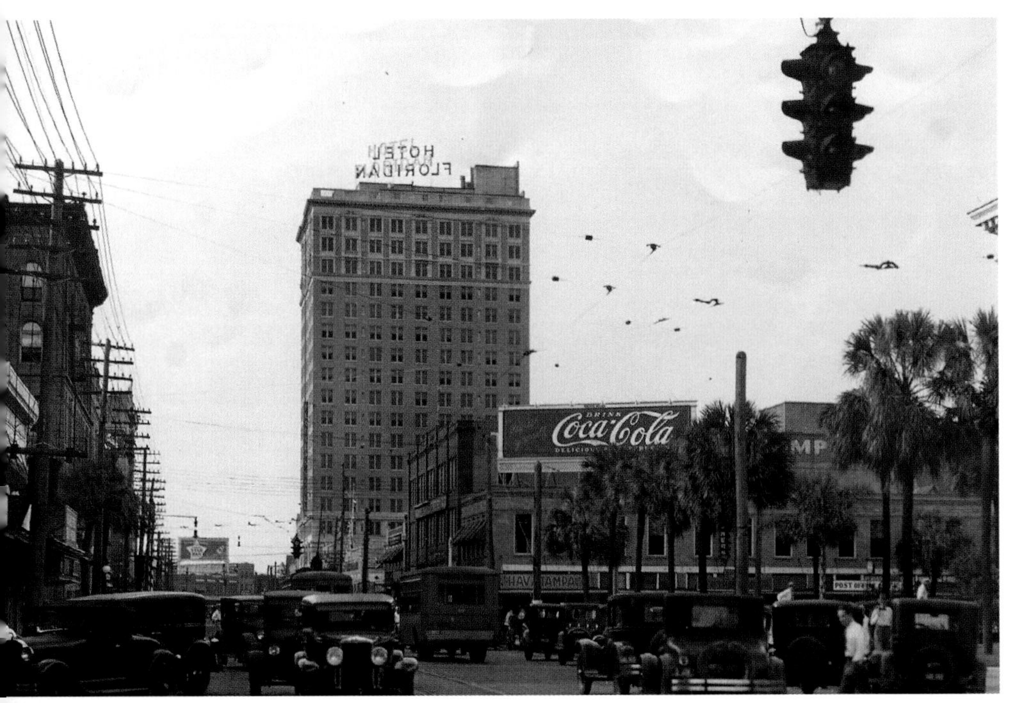

Hotel Floridan, Florida Avenue, Tampa, c. 1930

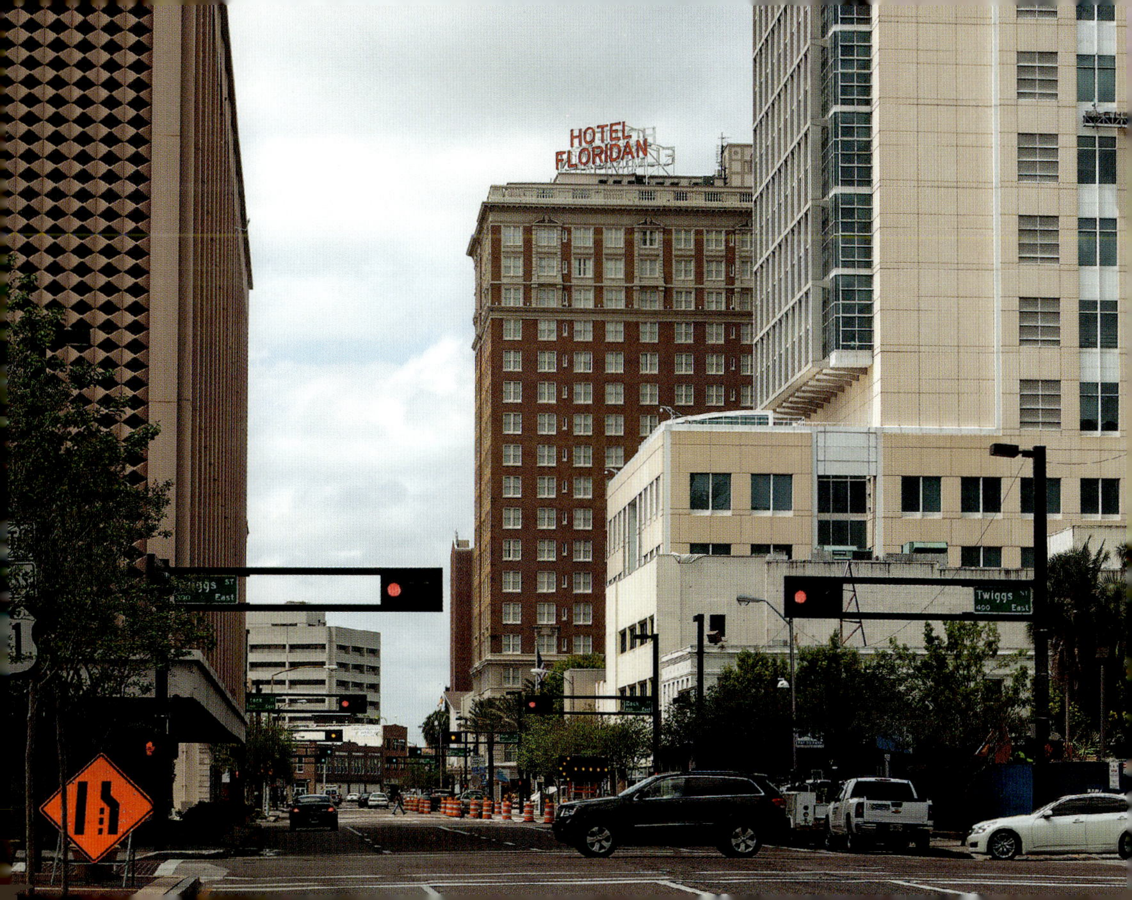
HOTEL
FLORIDAN
Twiggs St
400 East

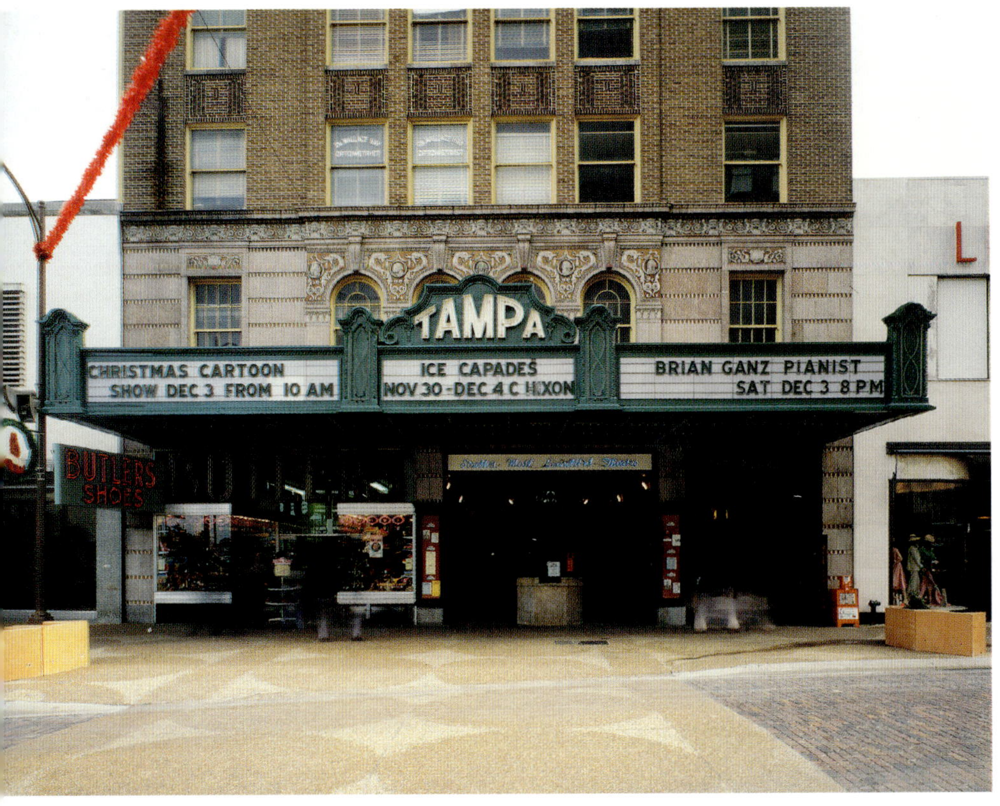

Tampa Theatre, Tampa, 1978

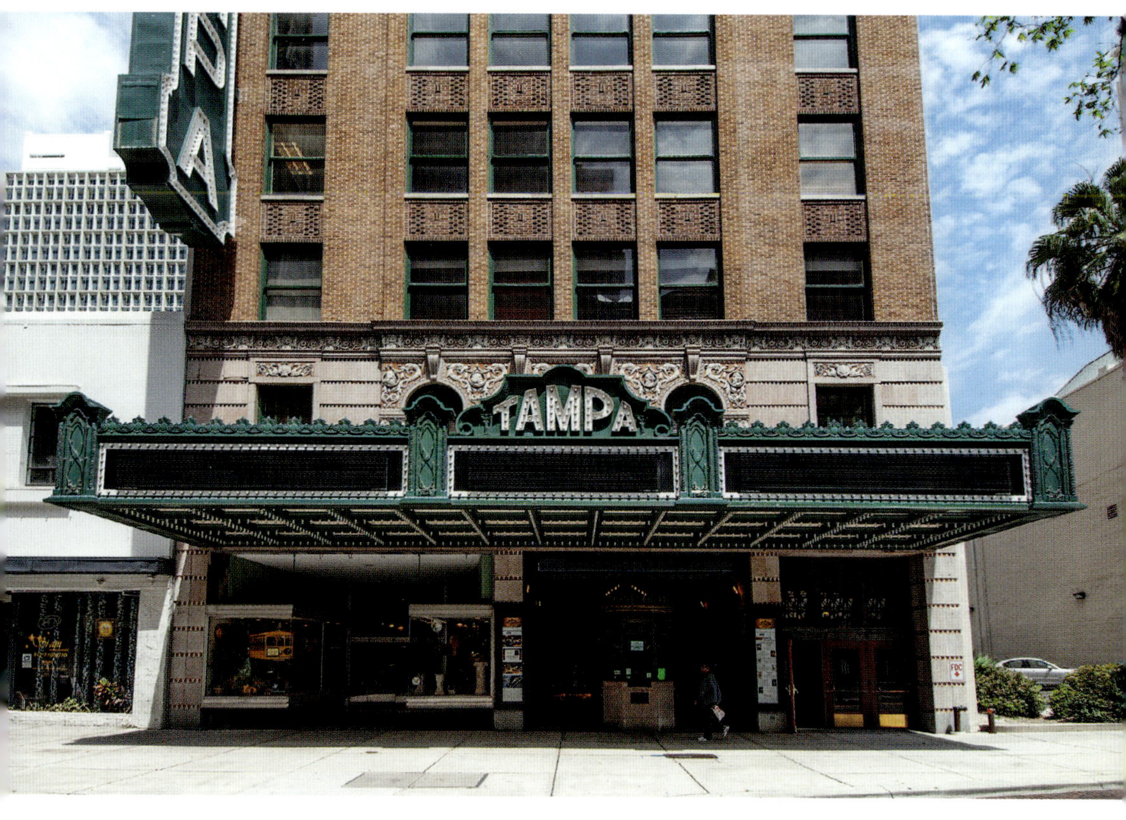
TAMPA

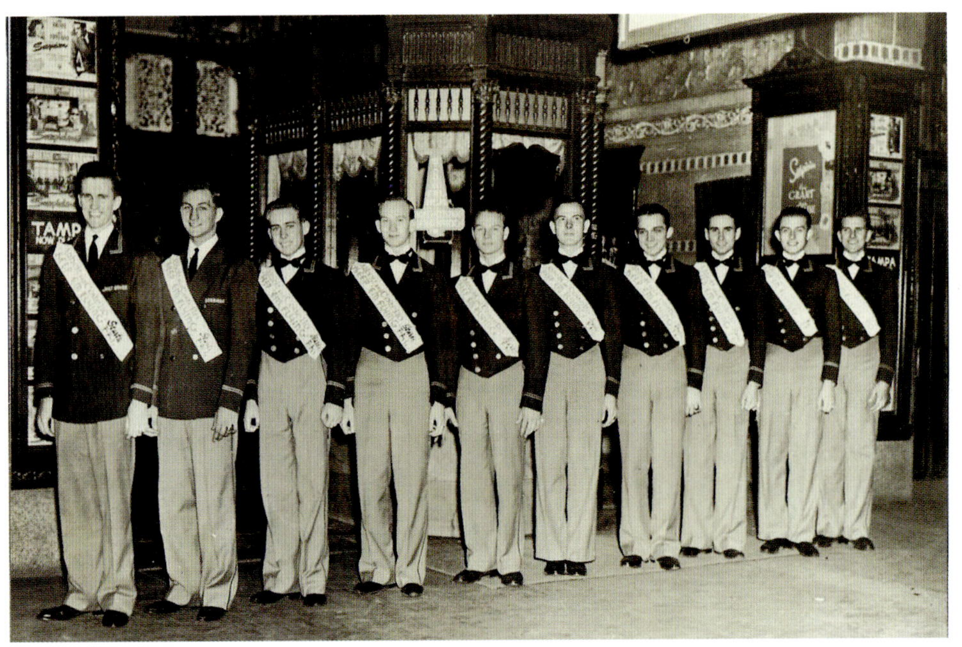

Tampa Theatre, Tampa, 1941

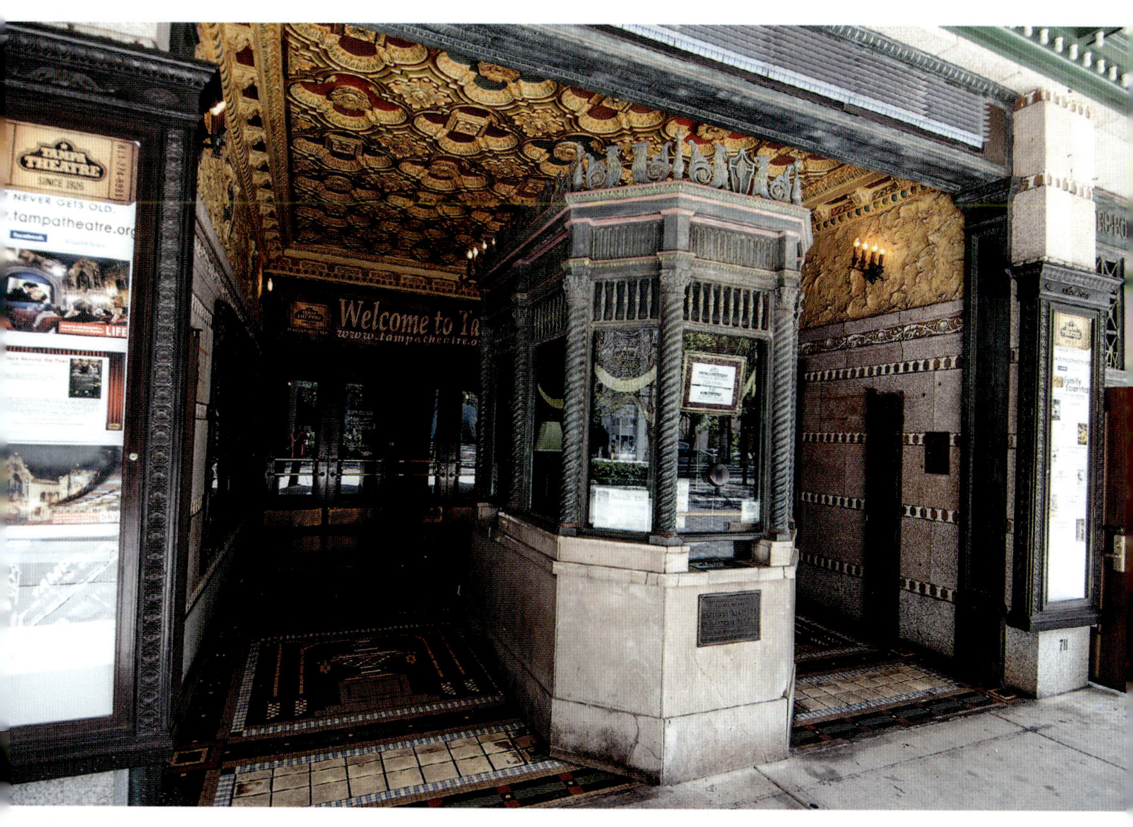
TAMPA THEATRE
SINCE 1926
NEVER GETS OLD.
LIFE
Welcome to
711

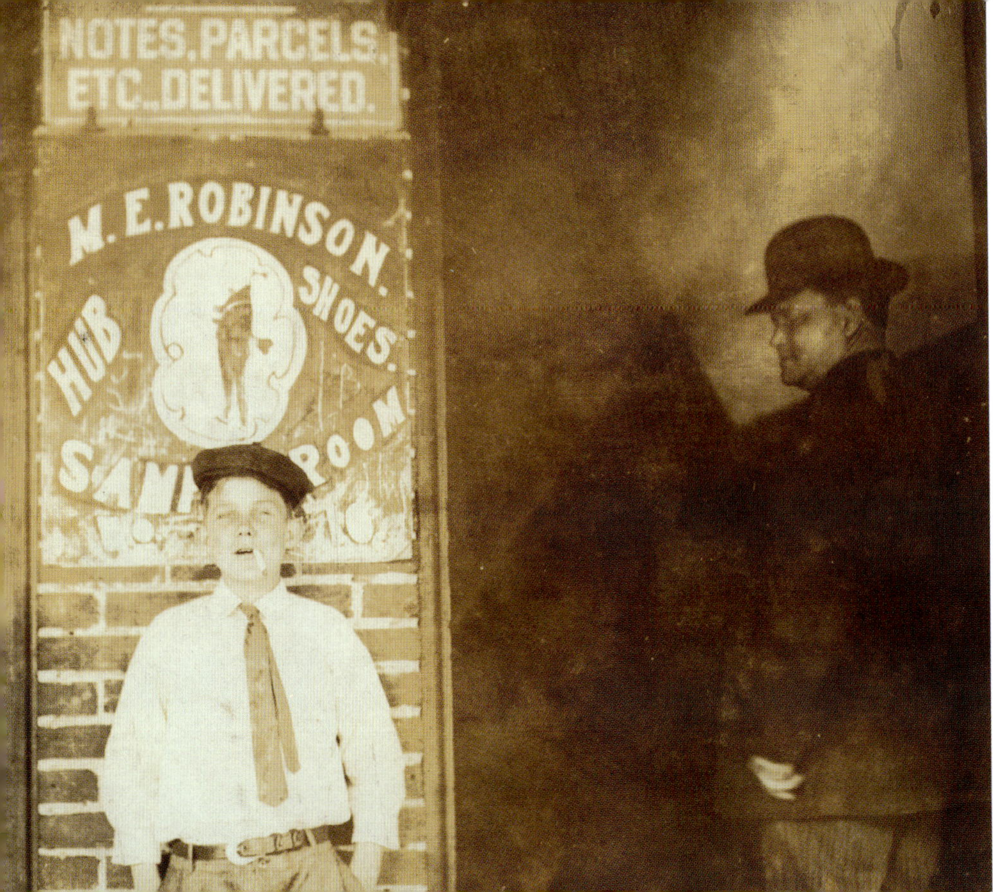

Western Union Messenger, Tampa, 1911

Tierra del Lago Cigar Company, Tampa, 1909

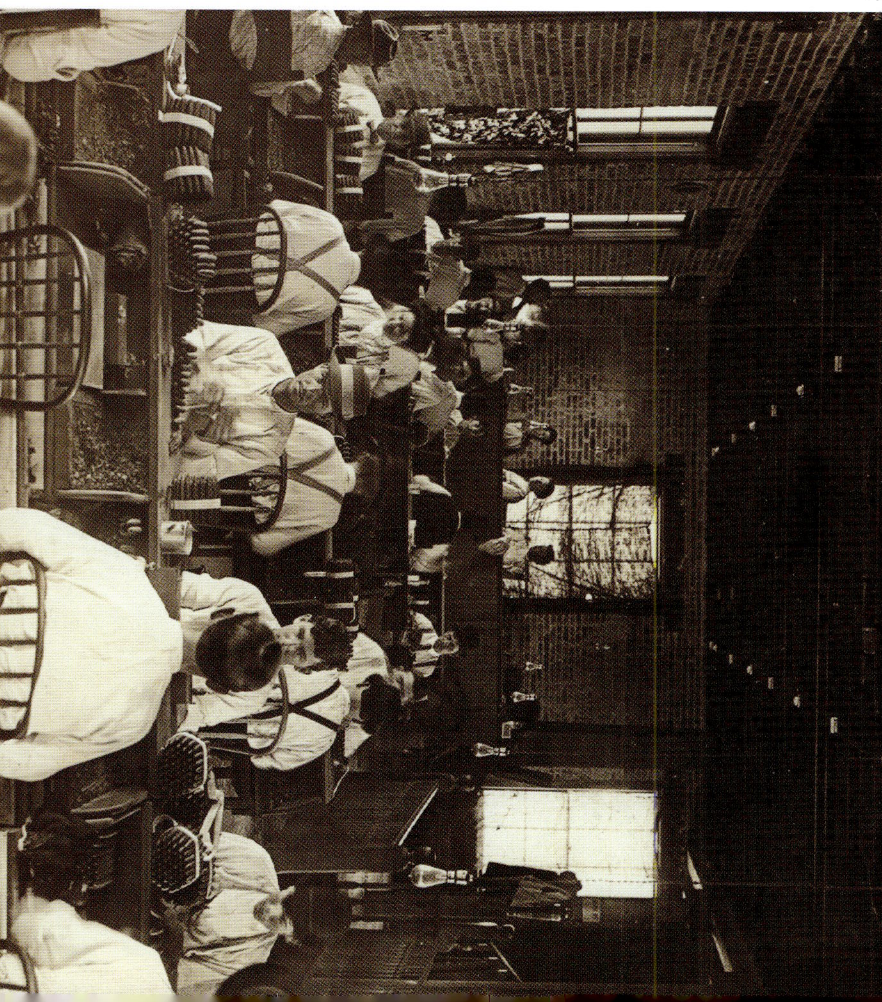

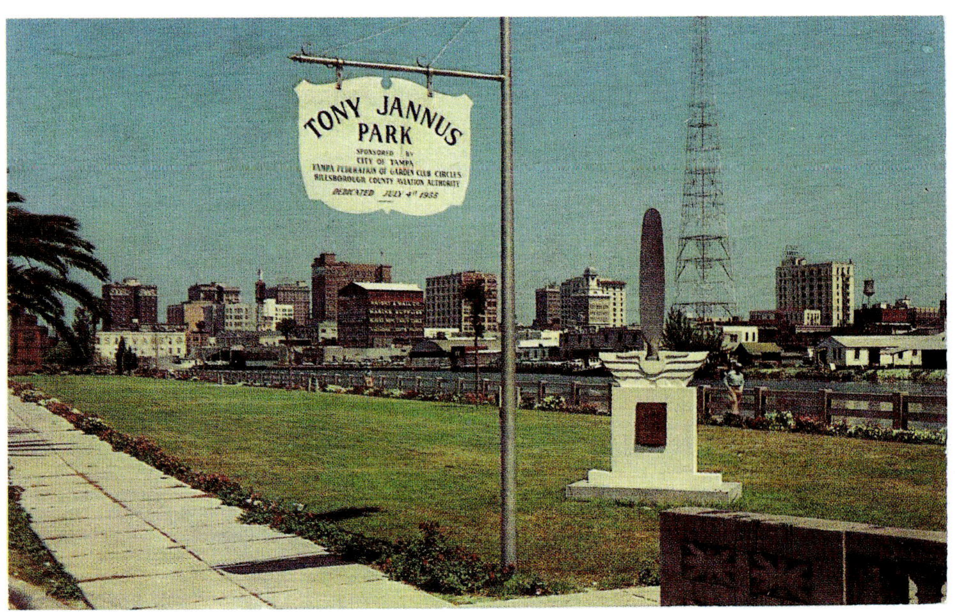

Tony Jannus Park, Tampa, 1963

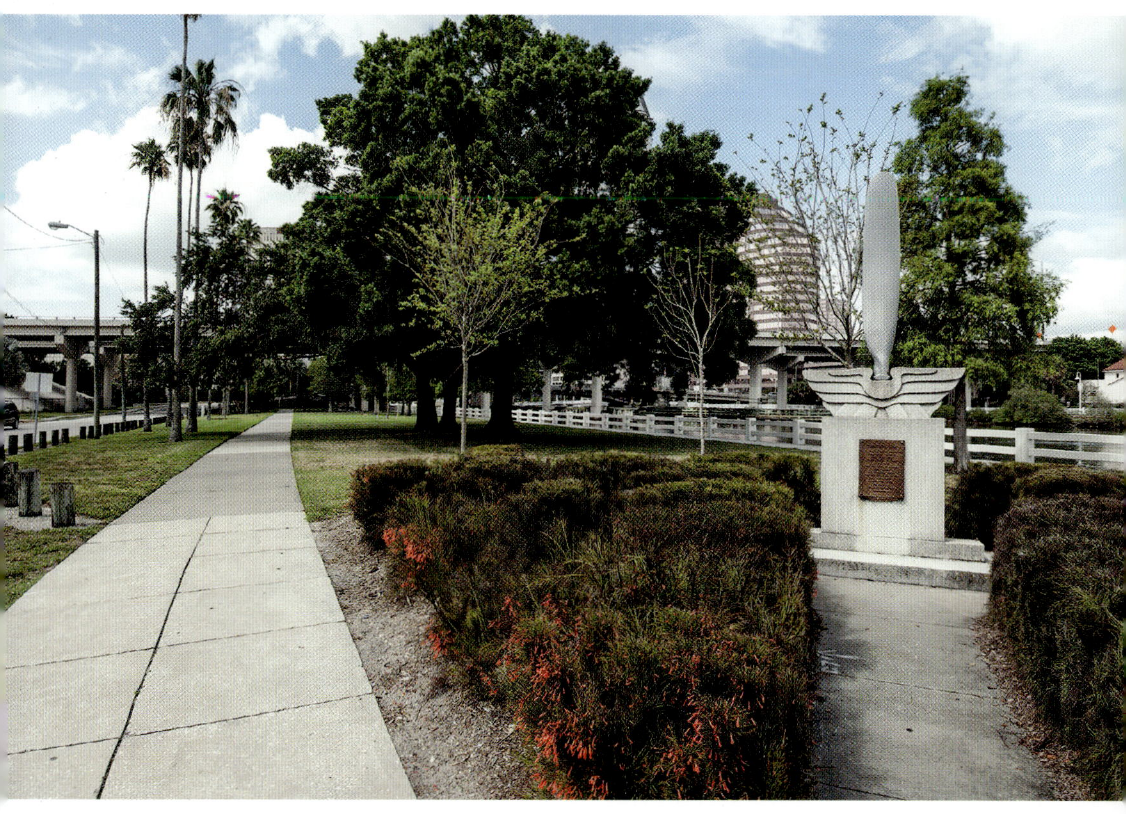

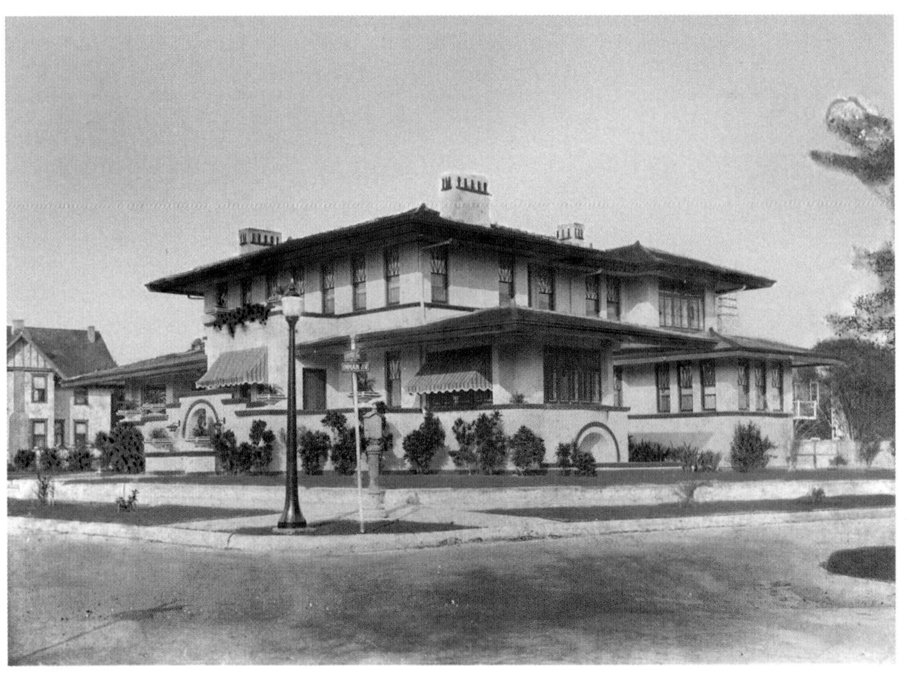

Leiman House, Tampa, c. 1920

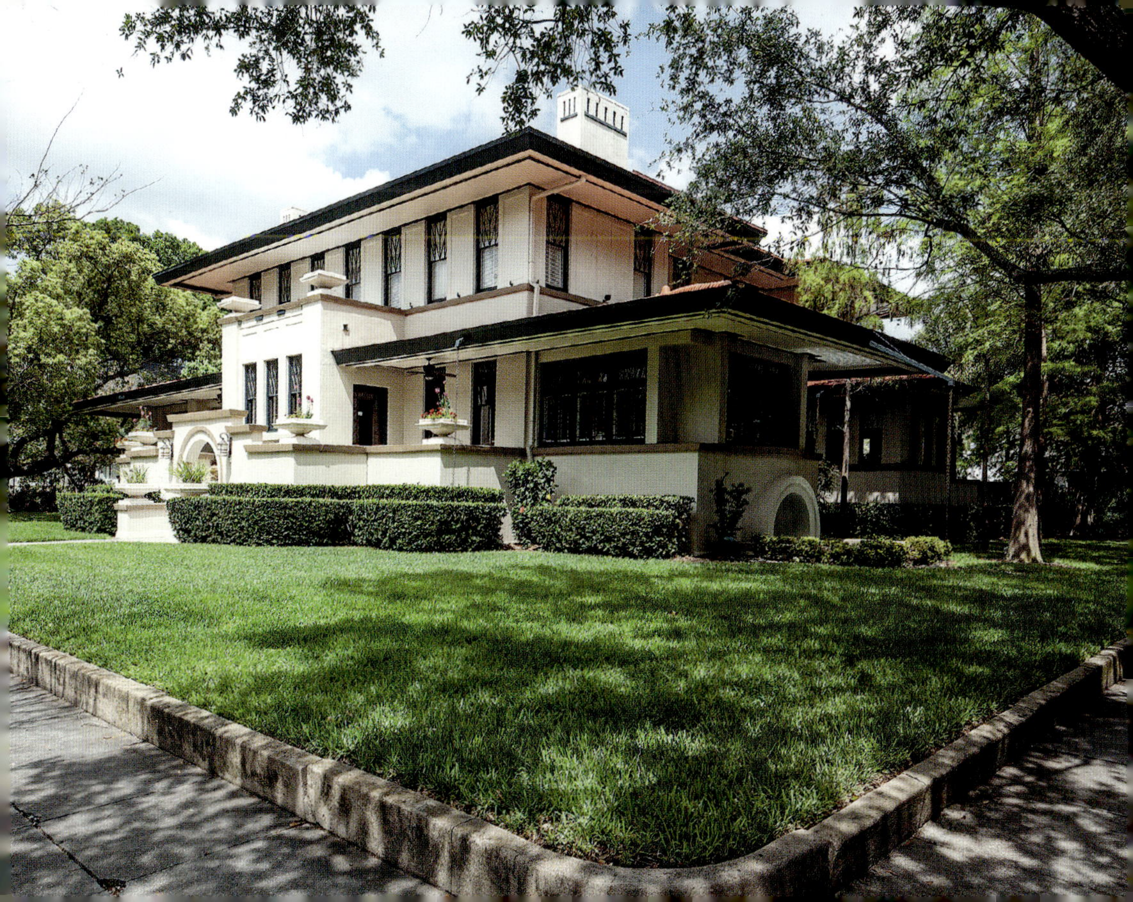

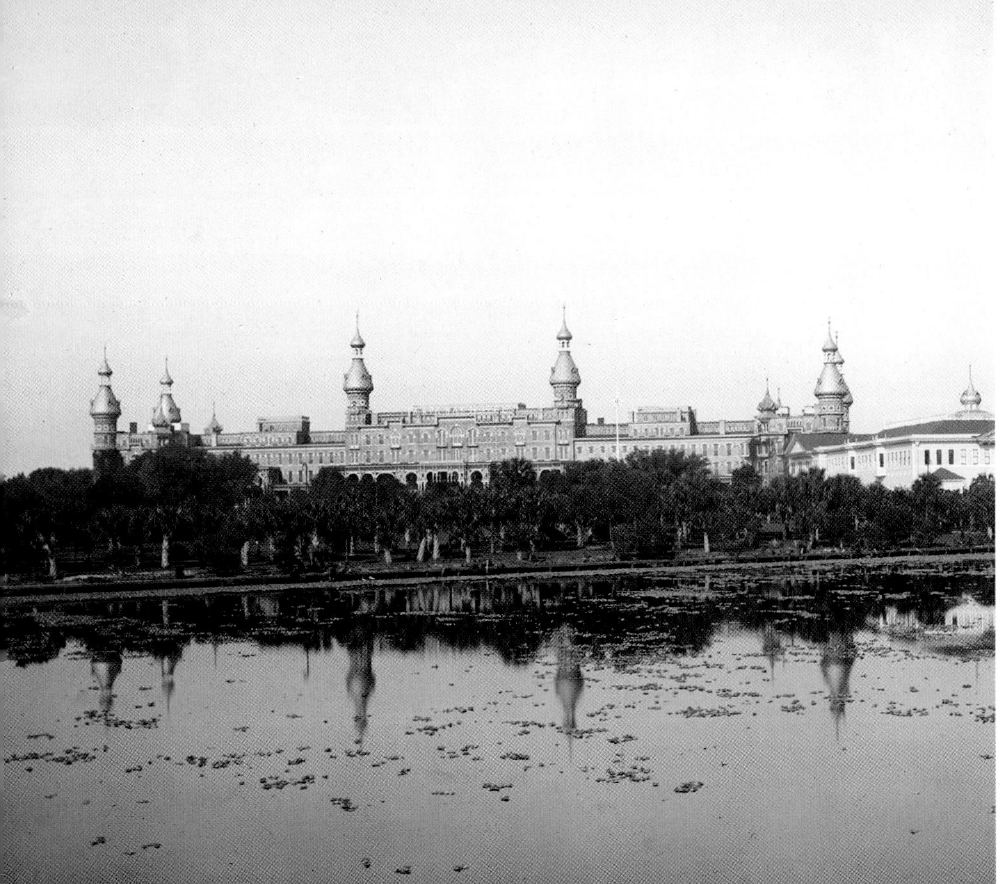

Tampa Bay Hotel (now University of Tampa), c. 1900

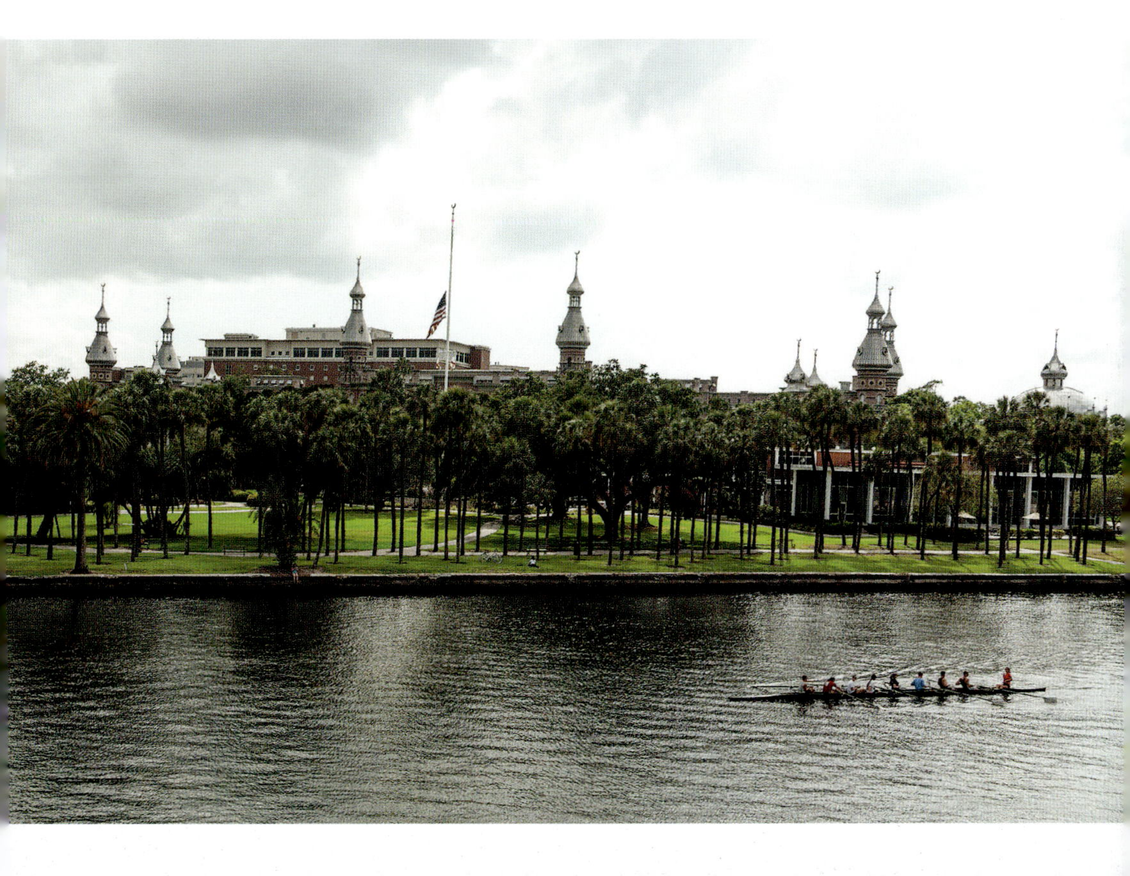

Tampa Bay Hotel (now University of Tampa), c. 1900

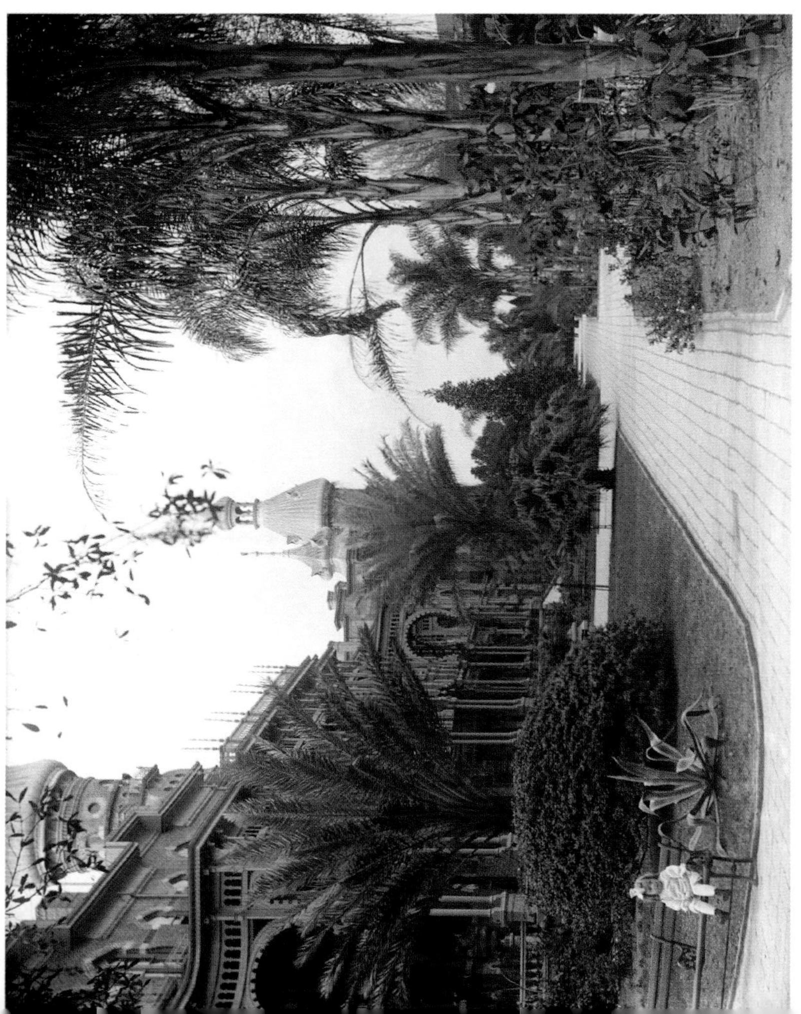

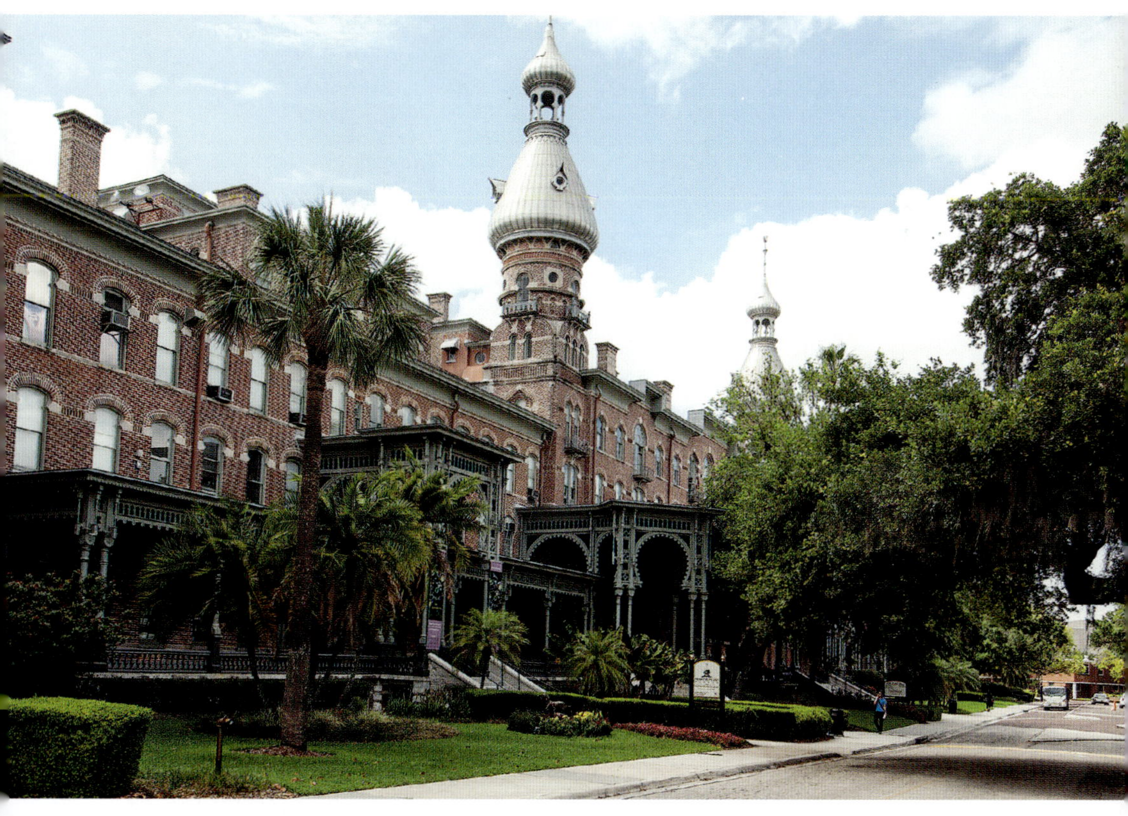

Tampa Bay Hotel (now University of Tampa), c. 1900

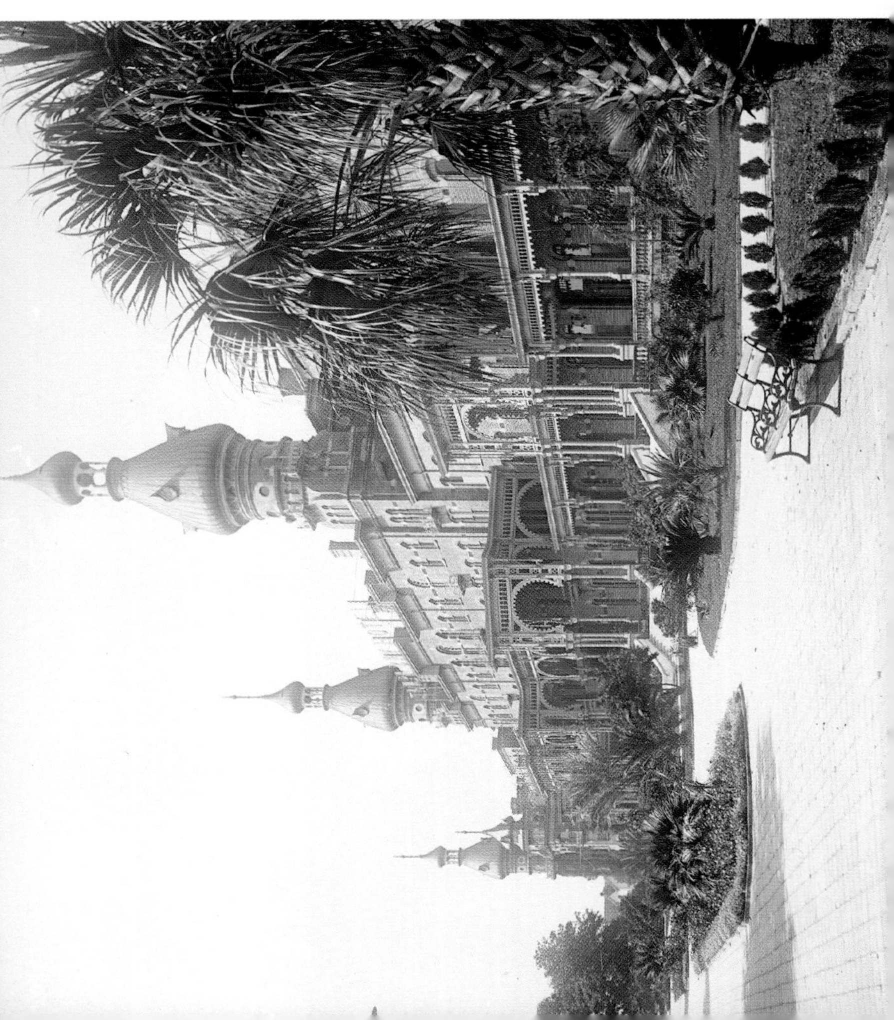

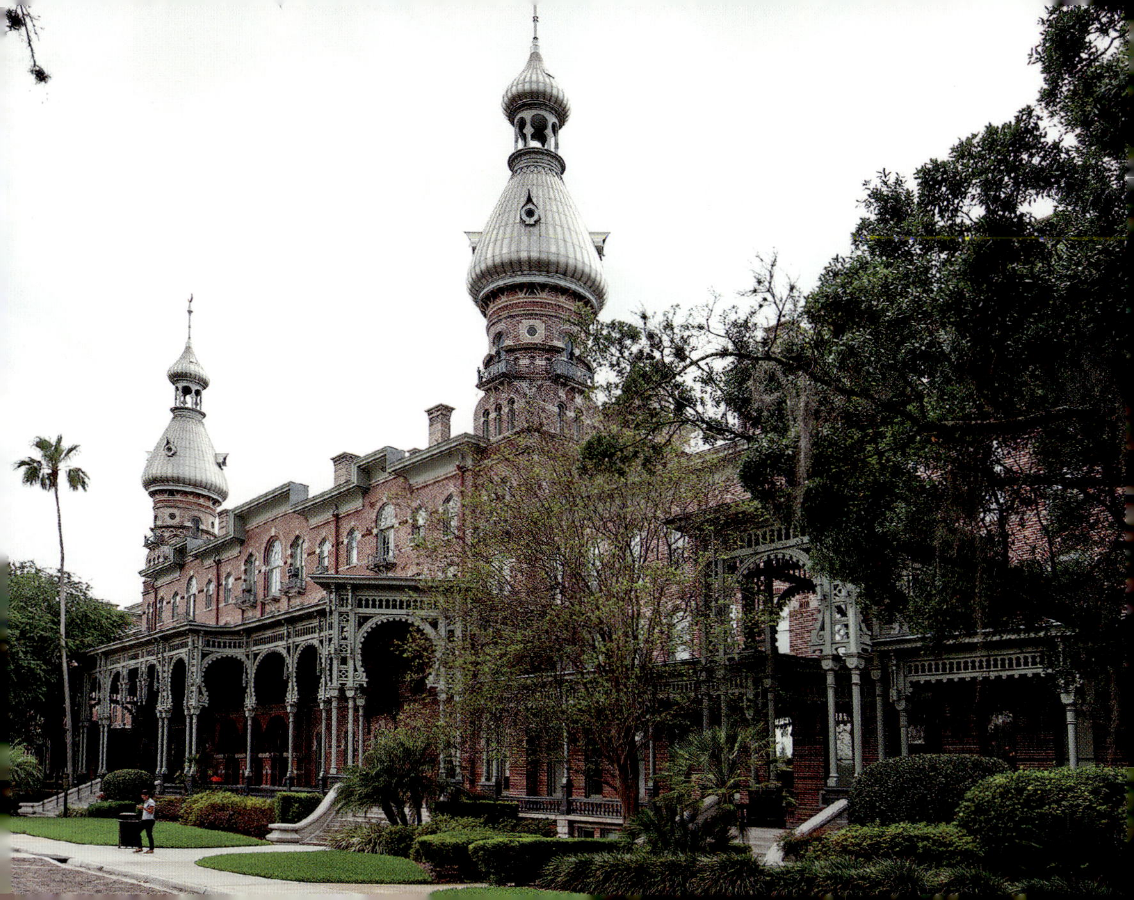

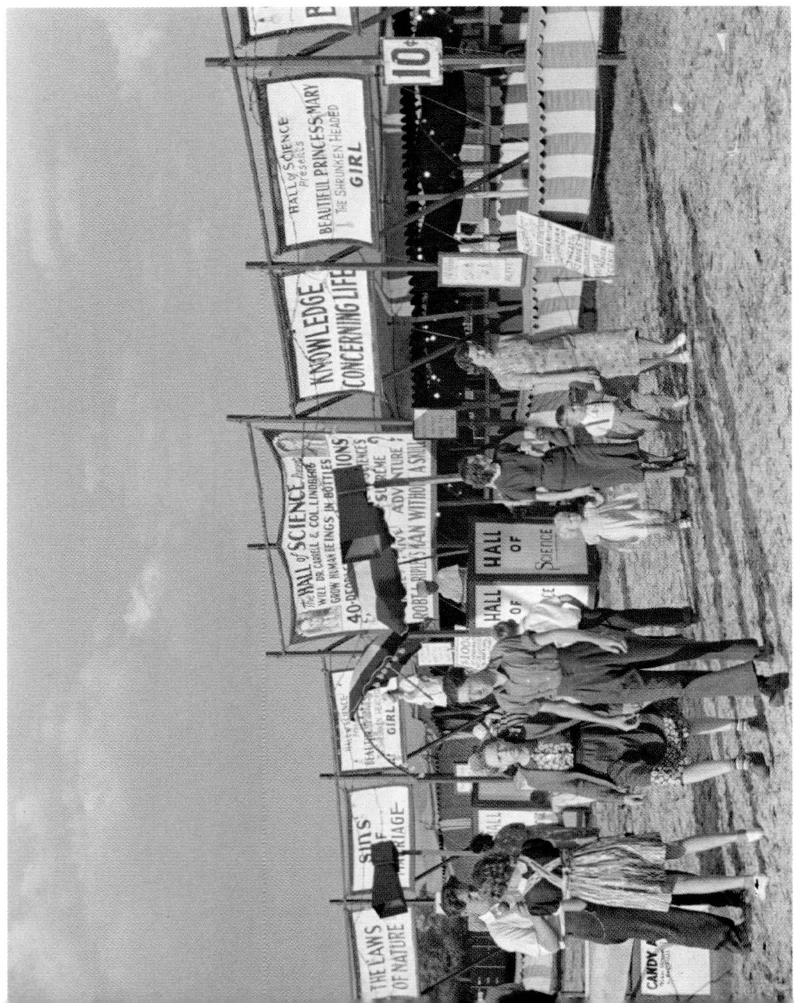

Florida Strawberry Festival, Plant City, 1939

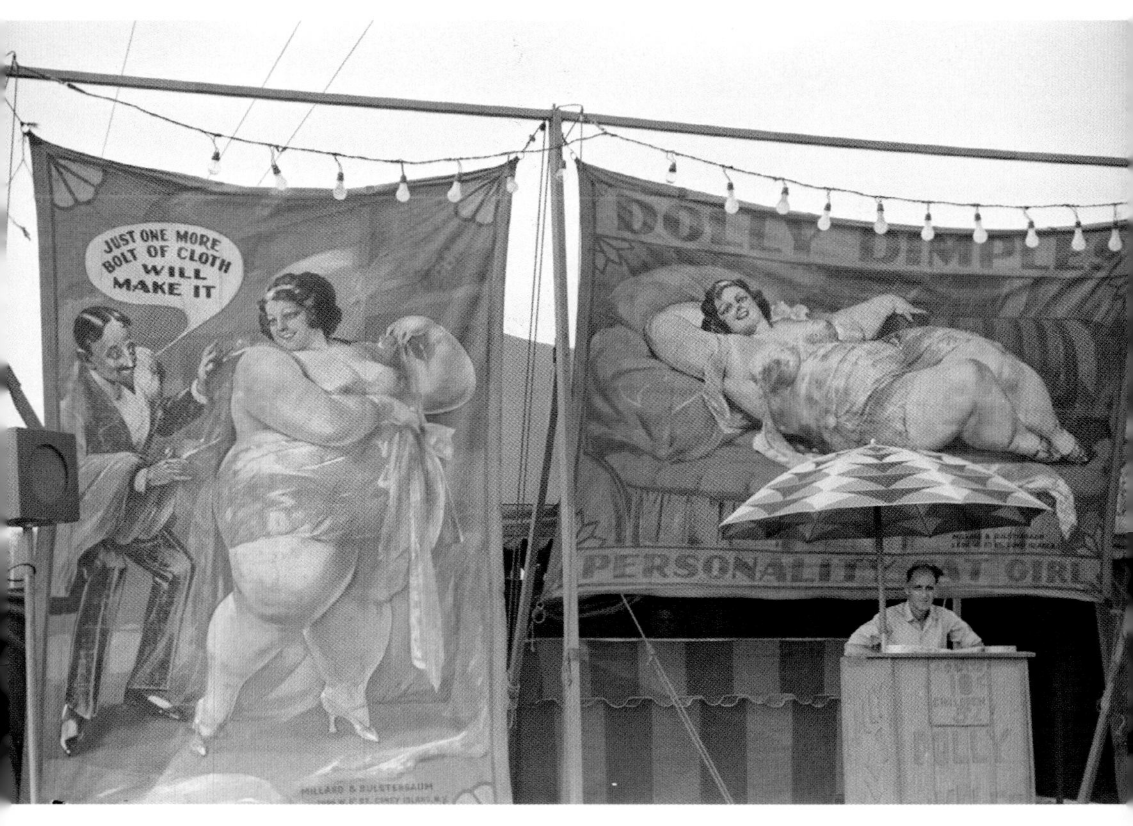
JUST ONE MORE BOLT OF CLOTH WILL MAKE IT
DOLLY DIMPLES
MILLARD & BULSTERBAUM
PERSONALITY

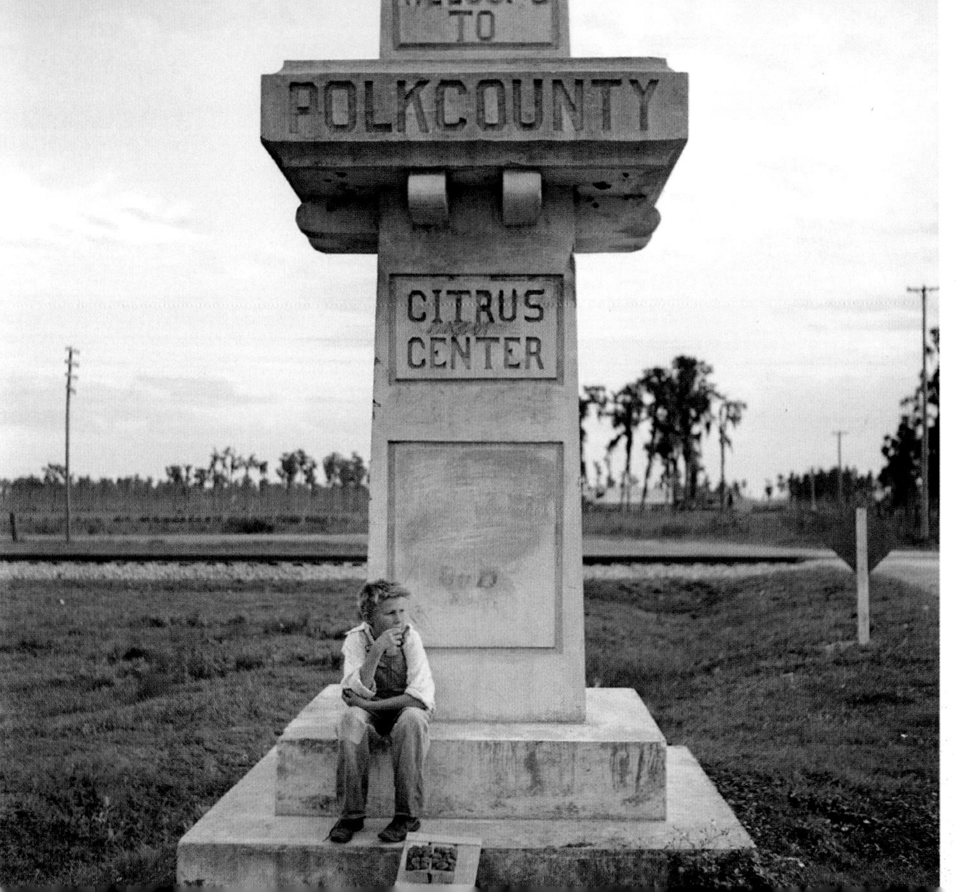

Welcome to Polk County; Fruit Canning Factory, Lakeland, 1937

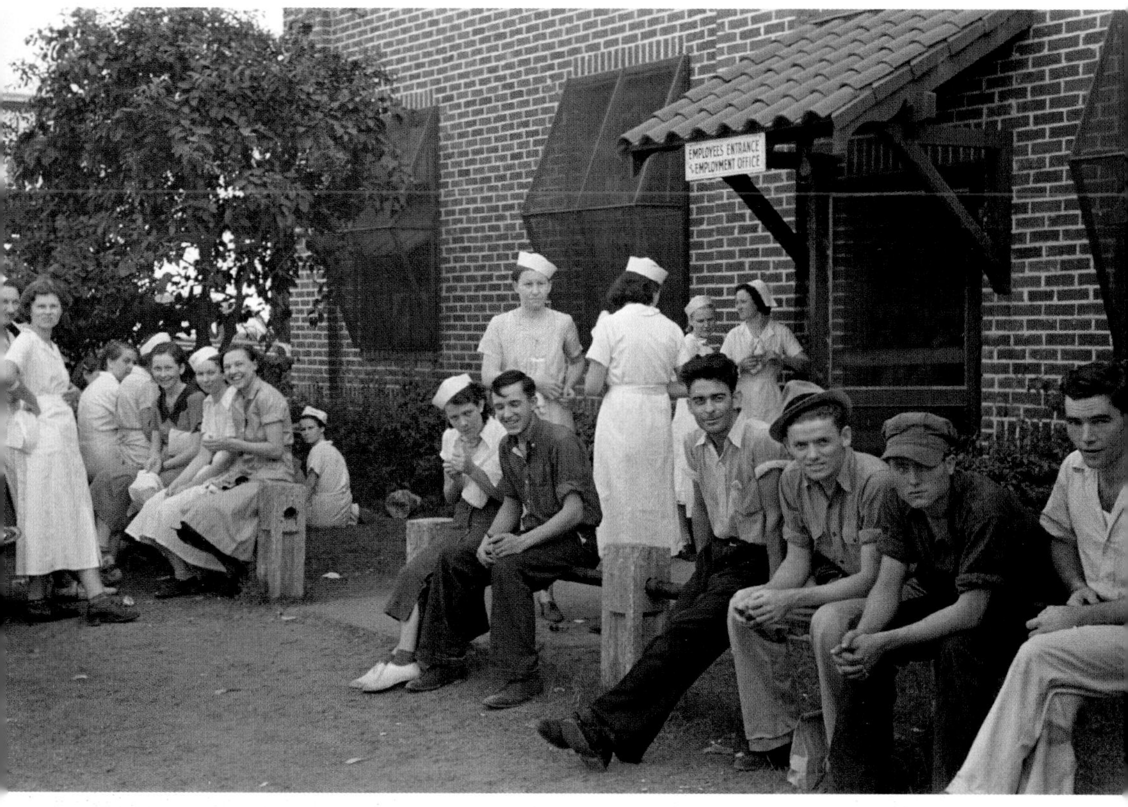
EMPLOYEES ENTRANCE
& EMPLOYMENT OFFICE

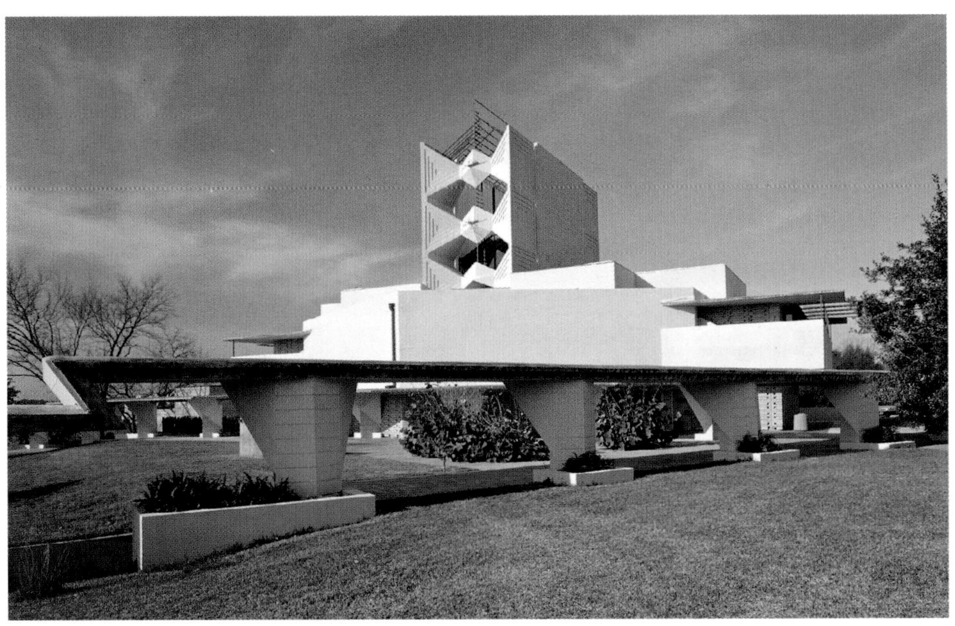

Annie Pfeiffer Chapel, Lakeland, 1979

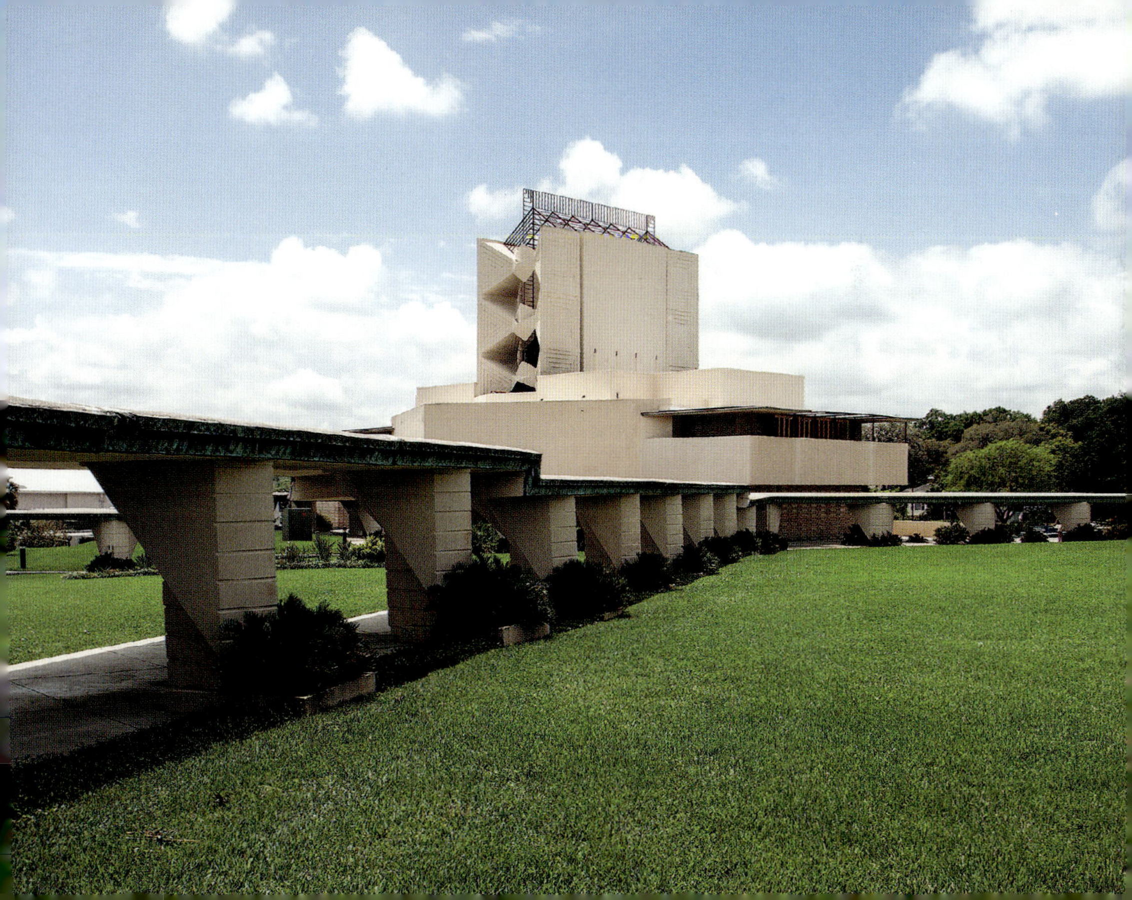

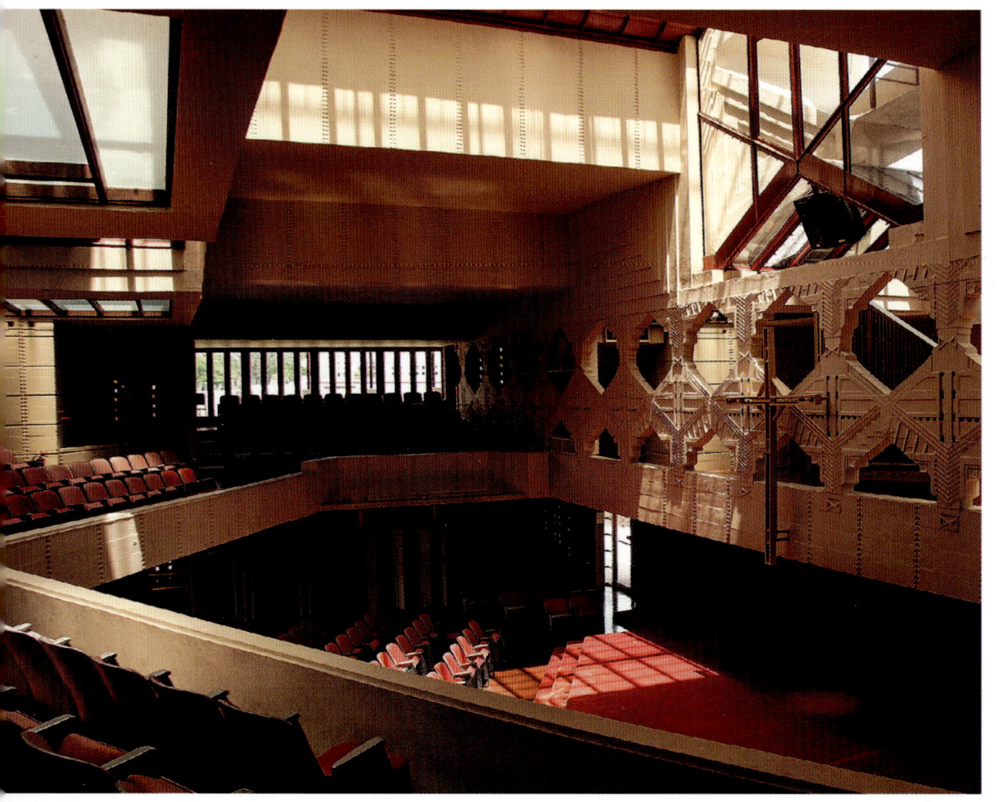

Annie Pfeiffer Chapel, Lakeland

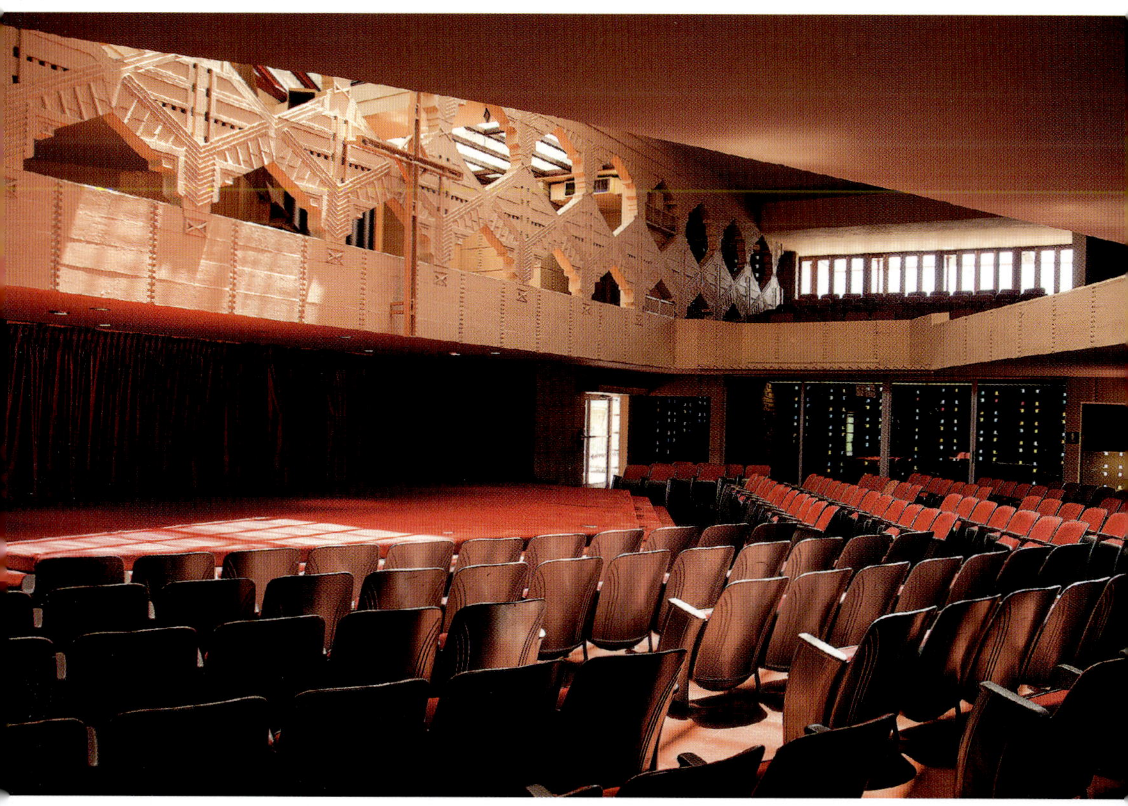

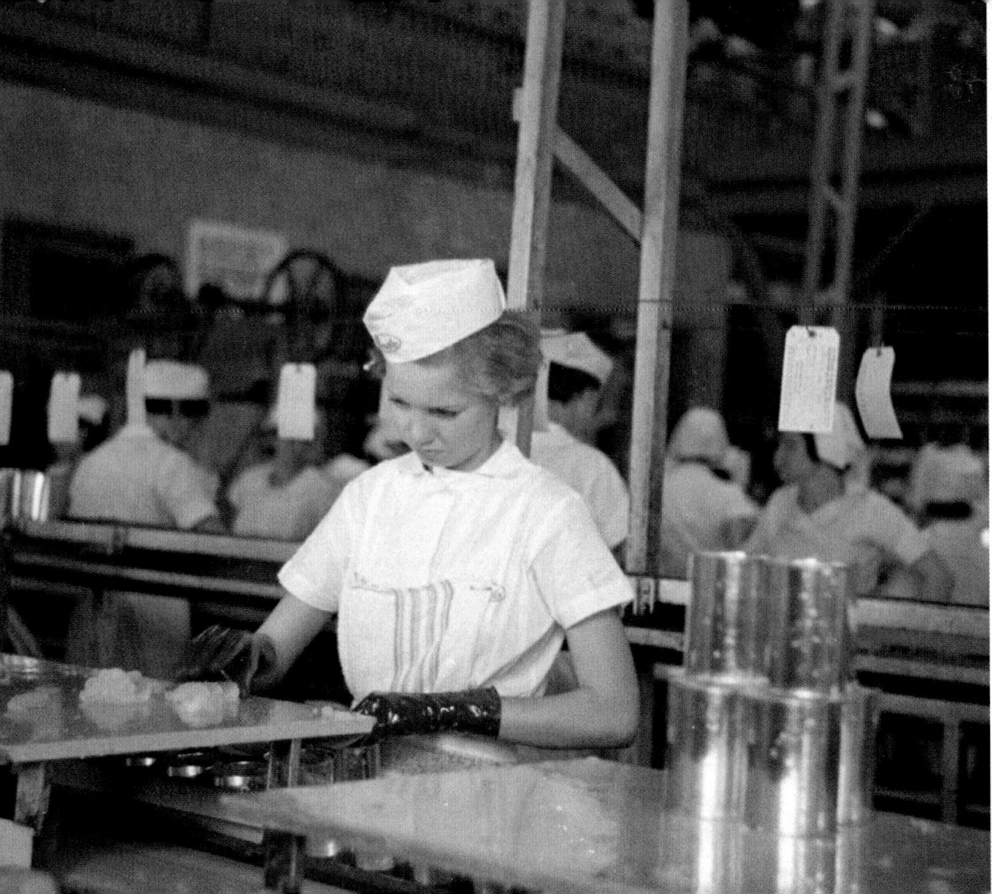

Fruit Canning Factory, Winter Haven, 1937

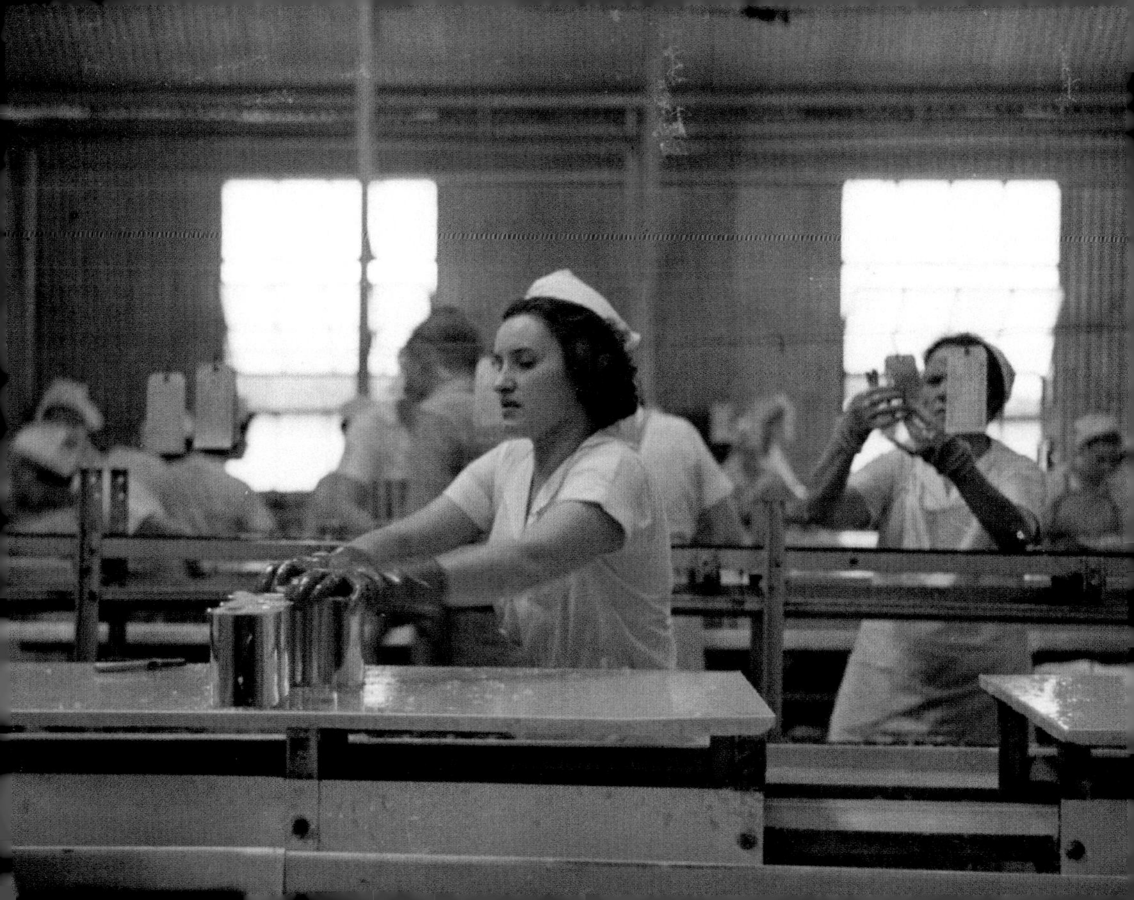

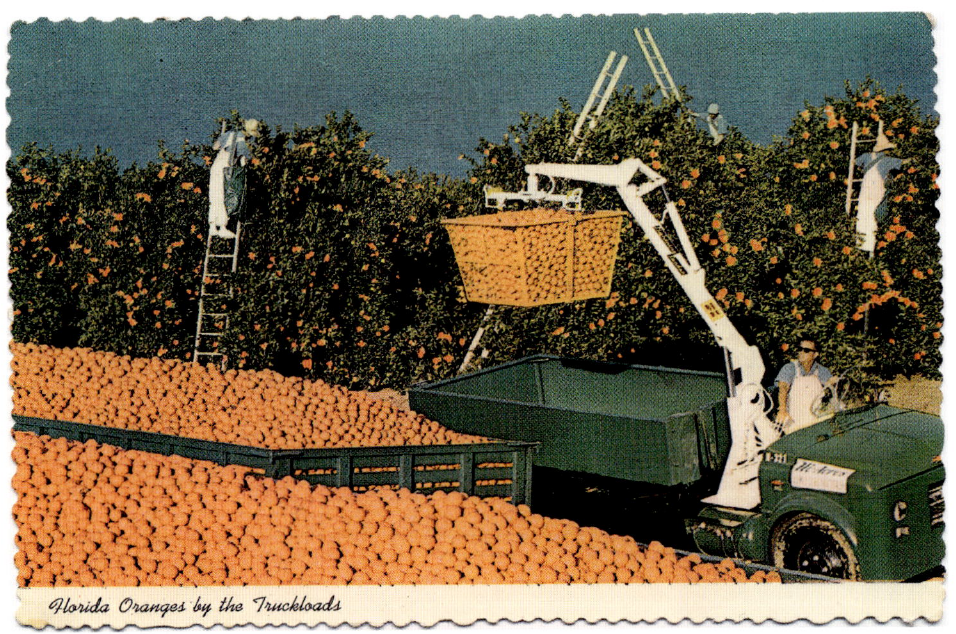

Orange Farm, Polk County, c. 1965

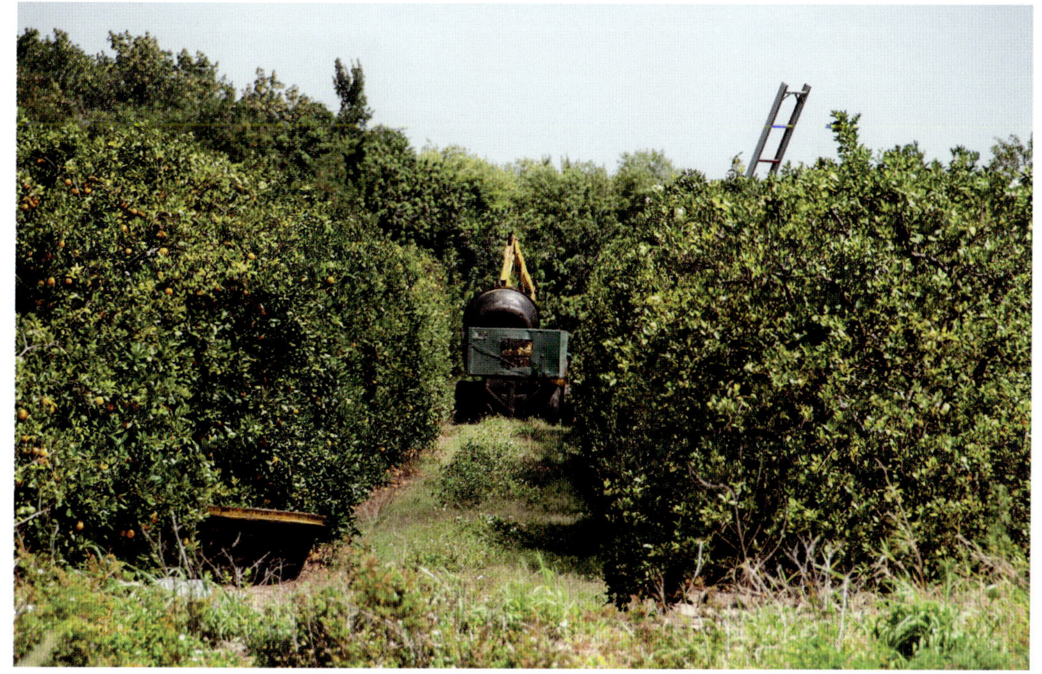

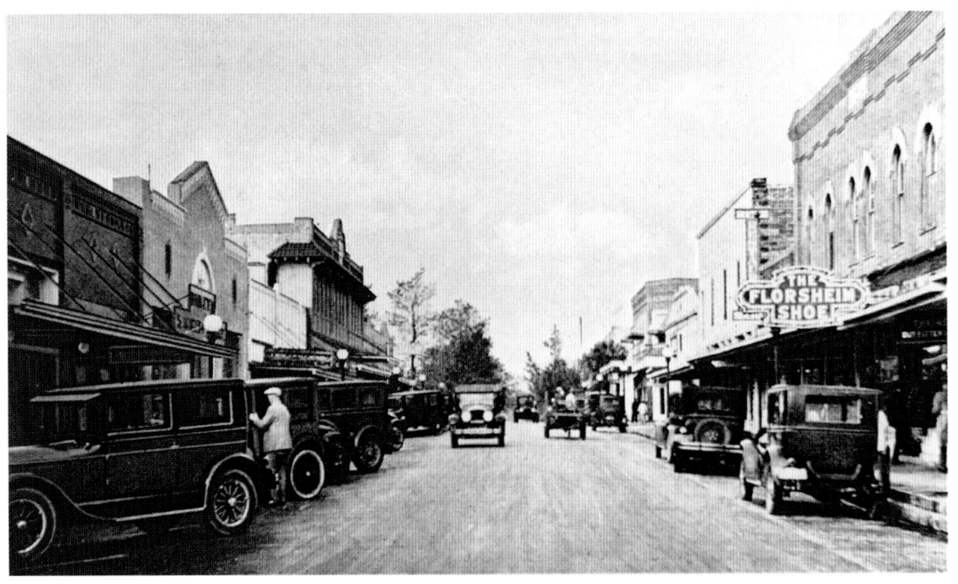

Tarpon Avenue, Tarpon Springs, c. 1925

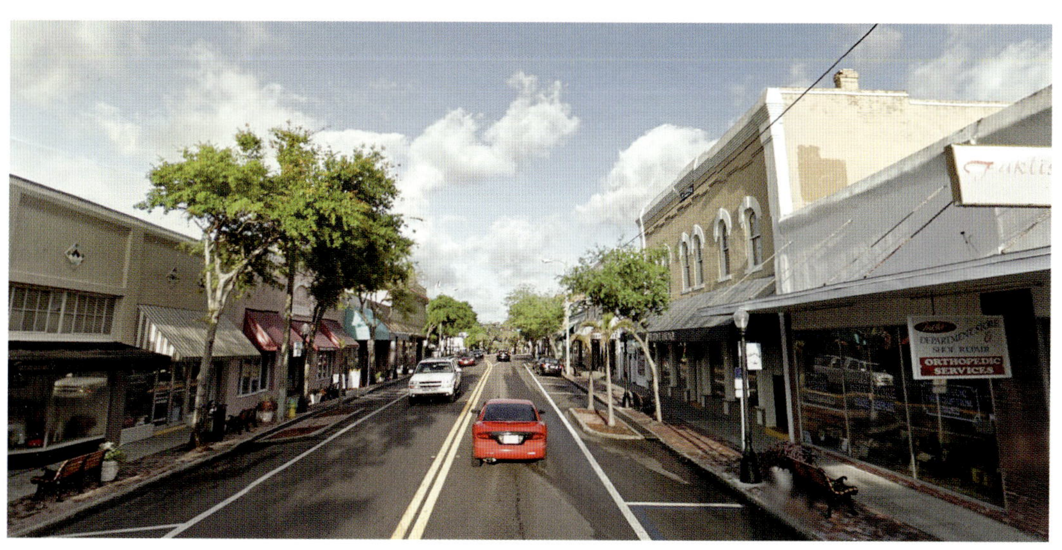
ORTHOPEDIC
SERVICES

Weeki Wachee Springs, Weeki Wachee, c. 1950

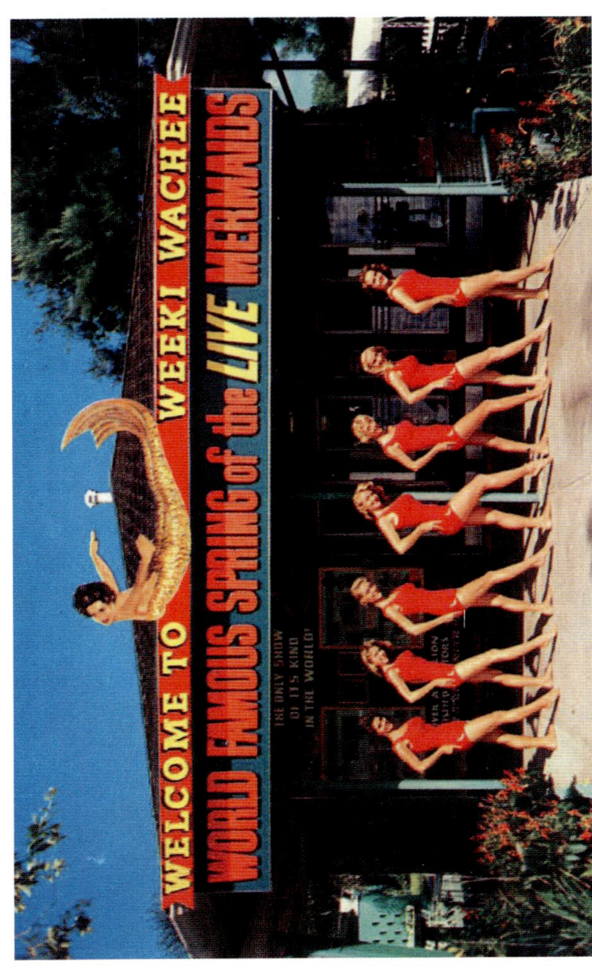

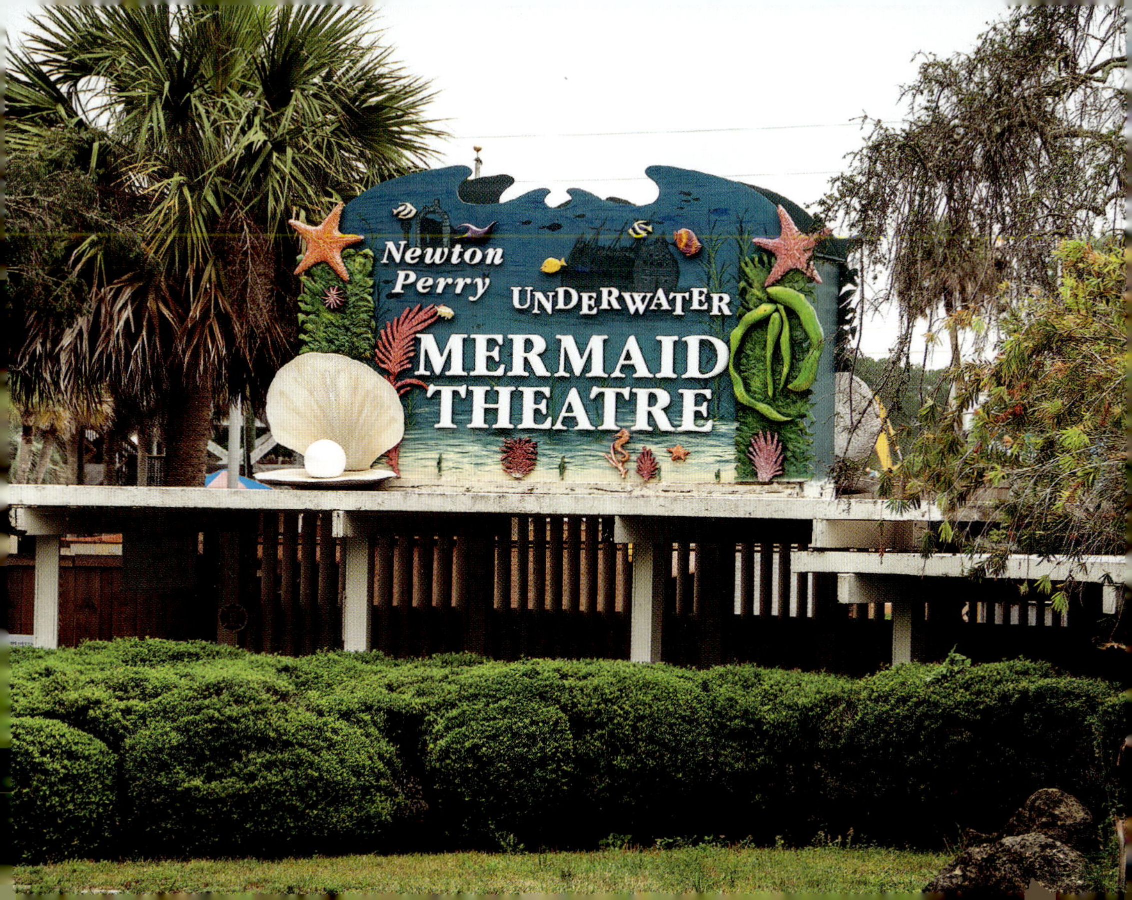
Newton
Perry
UNDERWATER
MERMAID
THEATRE

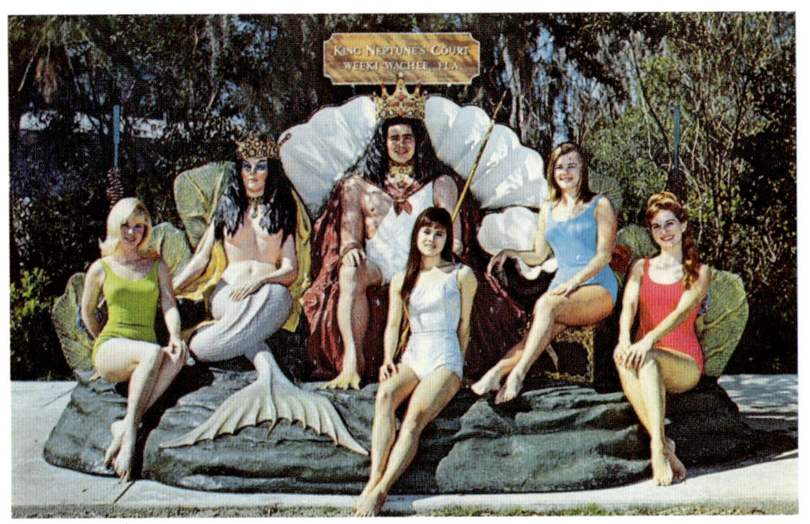

Weeki Wachee Springs, Weeki Wachee, c. 1965

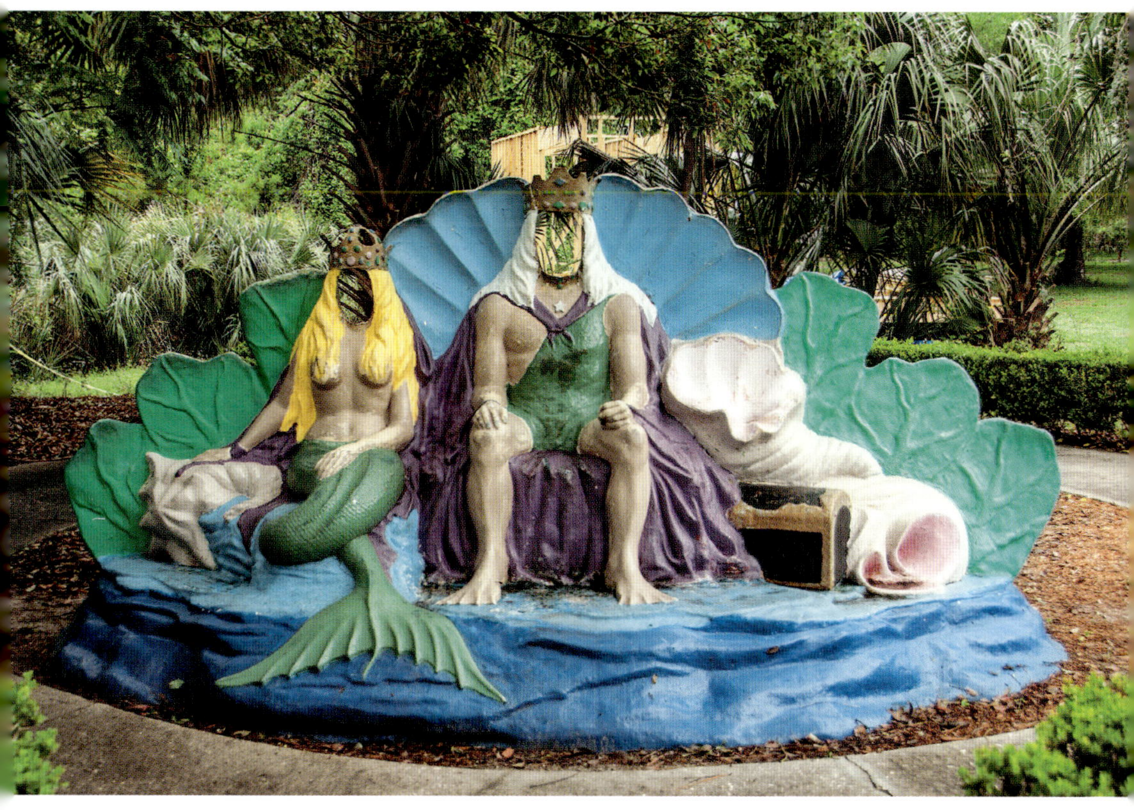

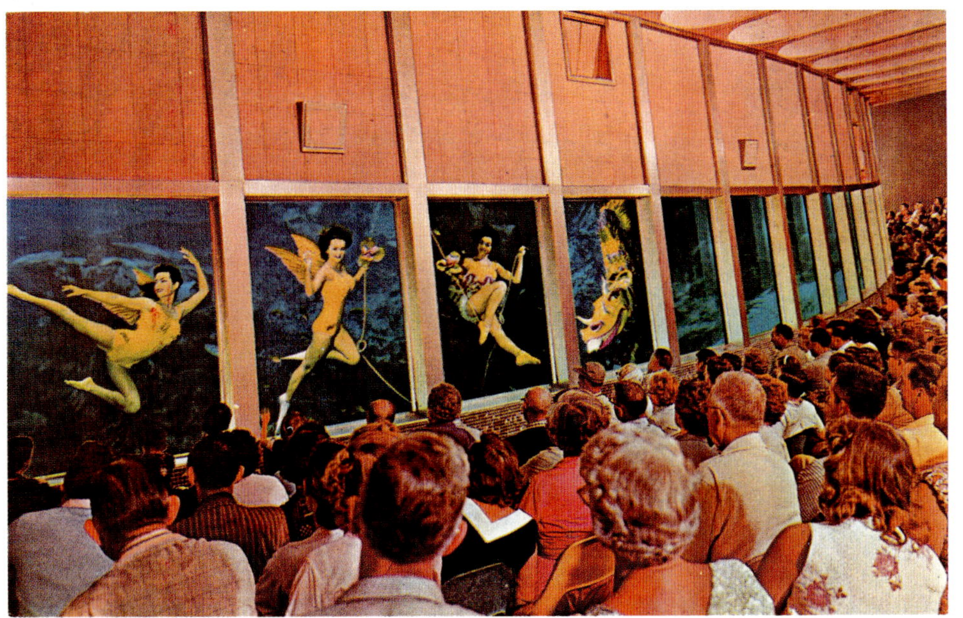

Weeki Wachee Springs, Weeki Wachee, c. 1965

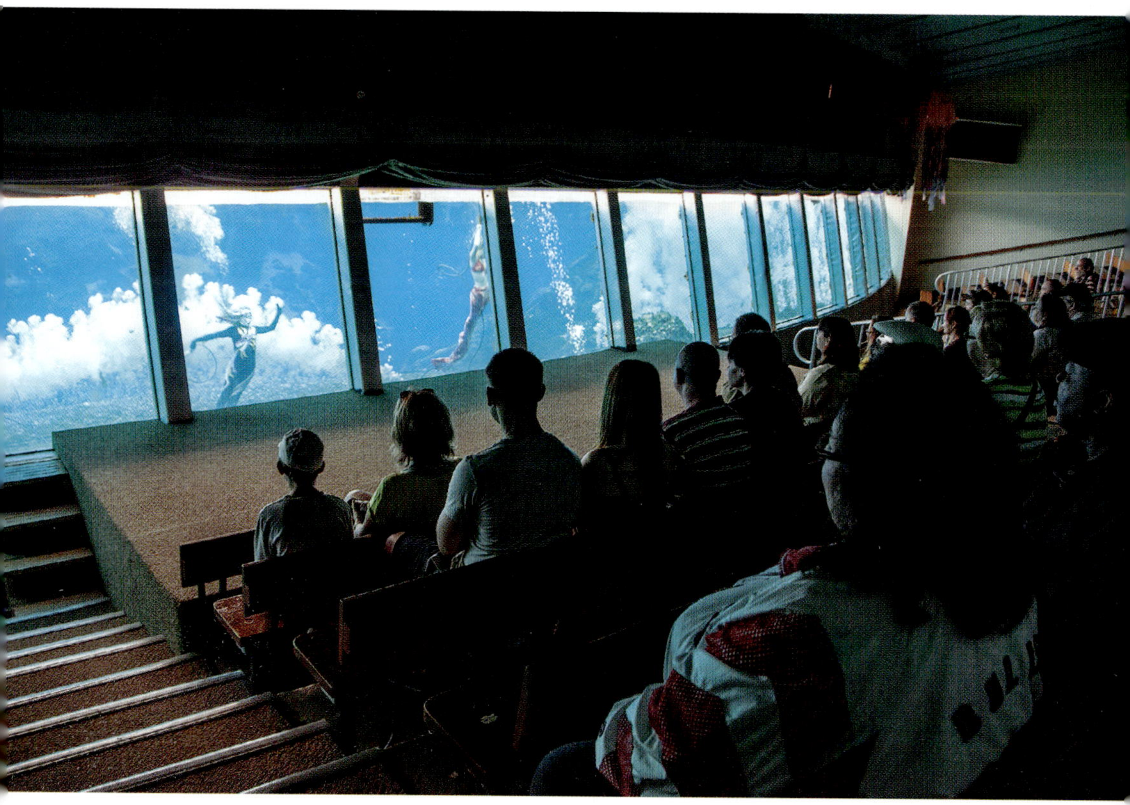

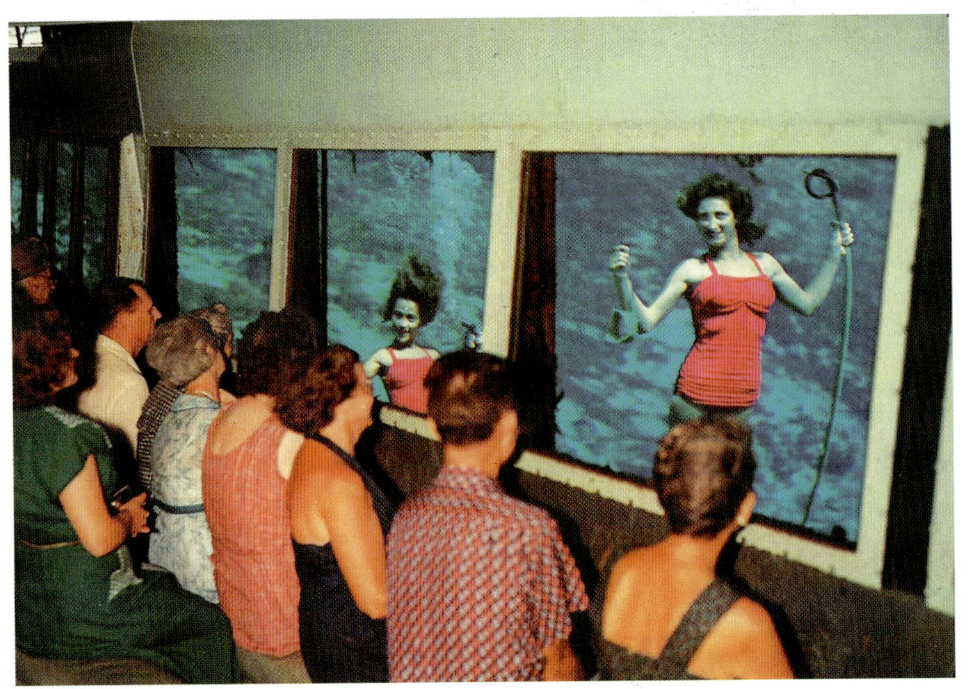

Weeki Wachee Springs, Weeki Wachee, c. 1965

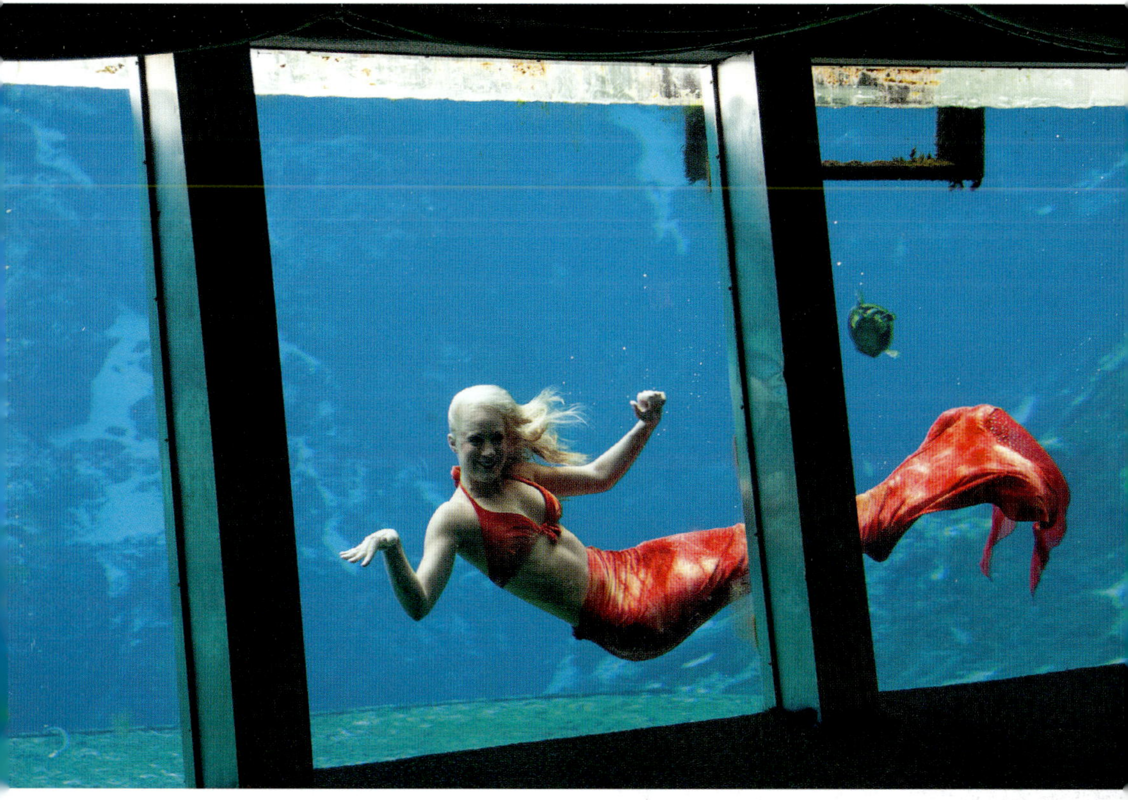

Silver Springs, 1902

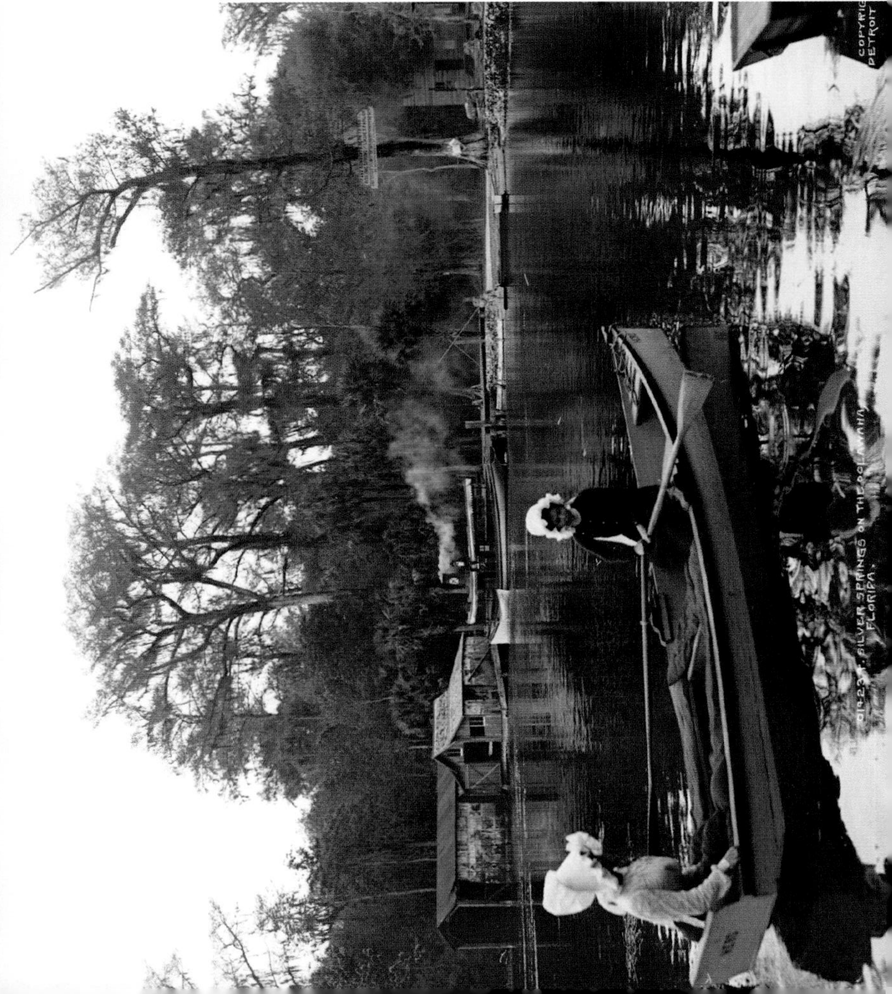

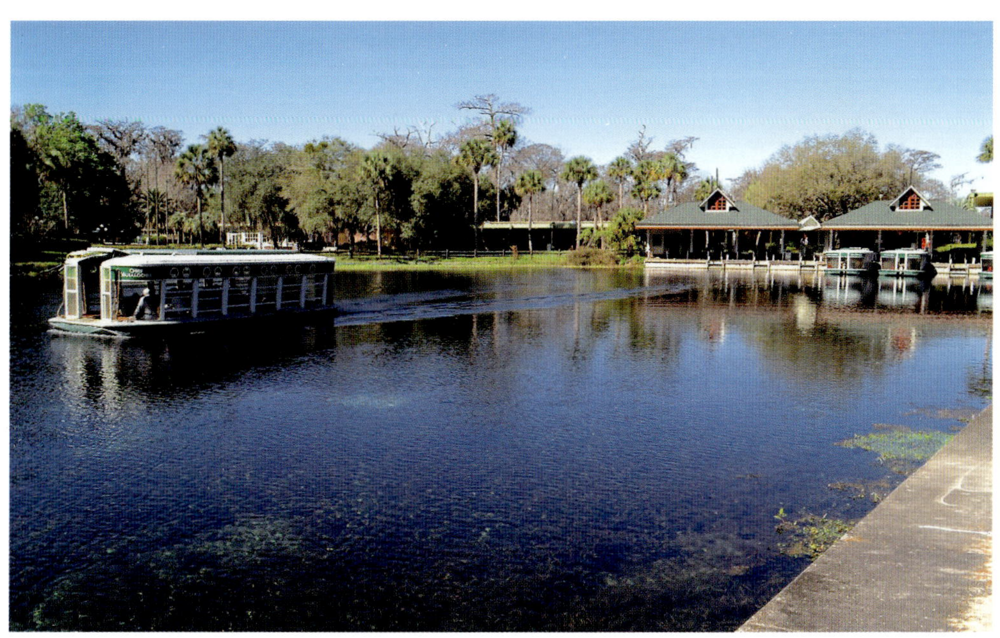

Silver Springs, 1900

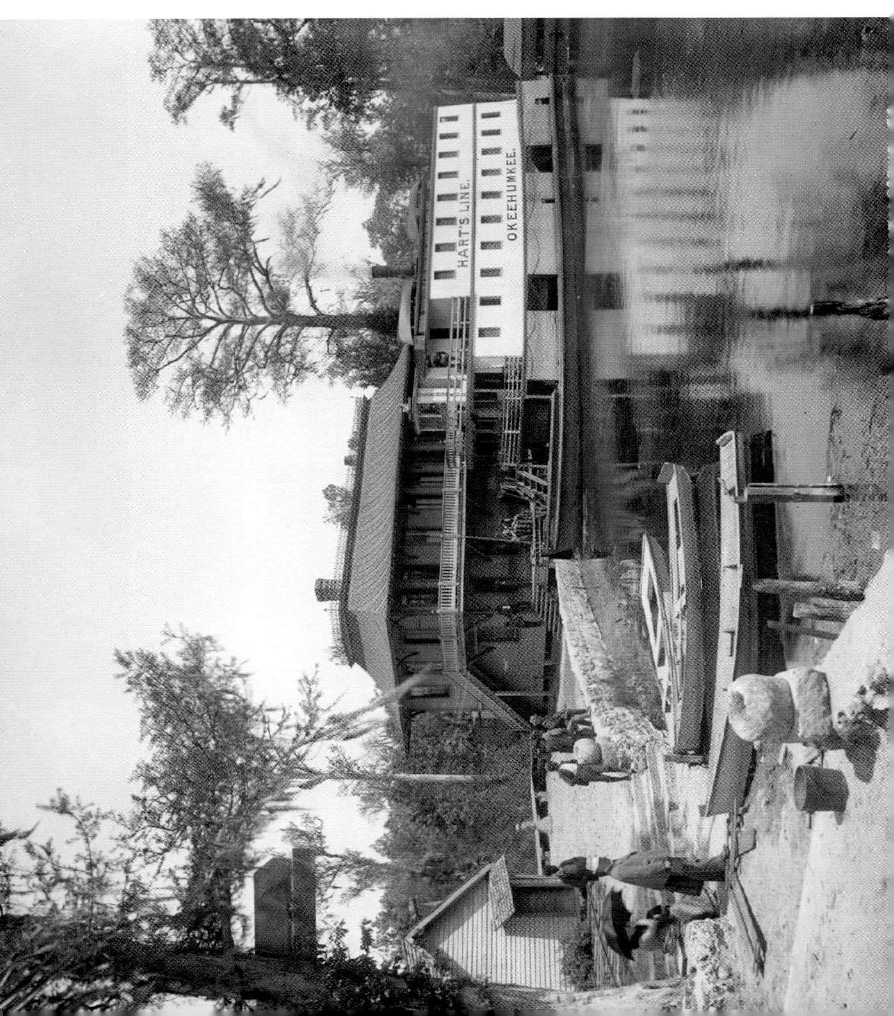

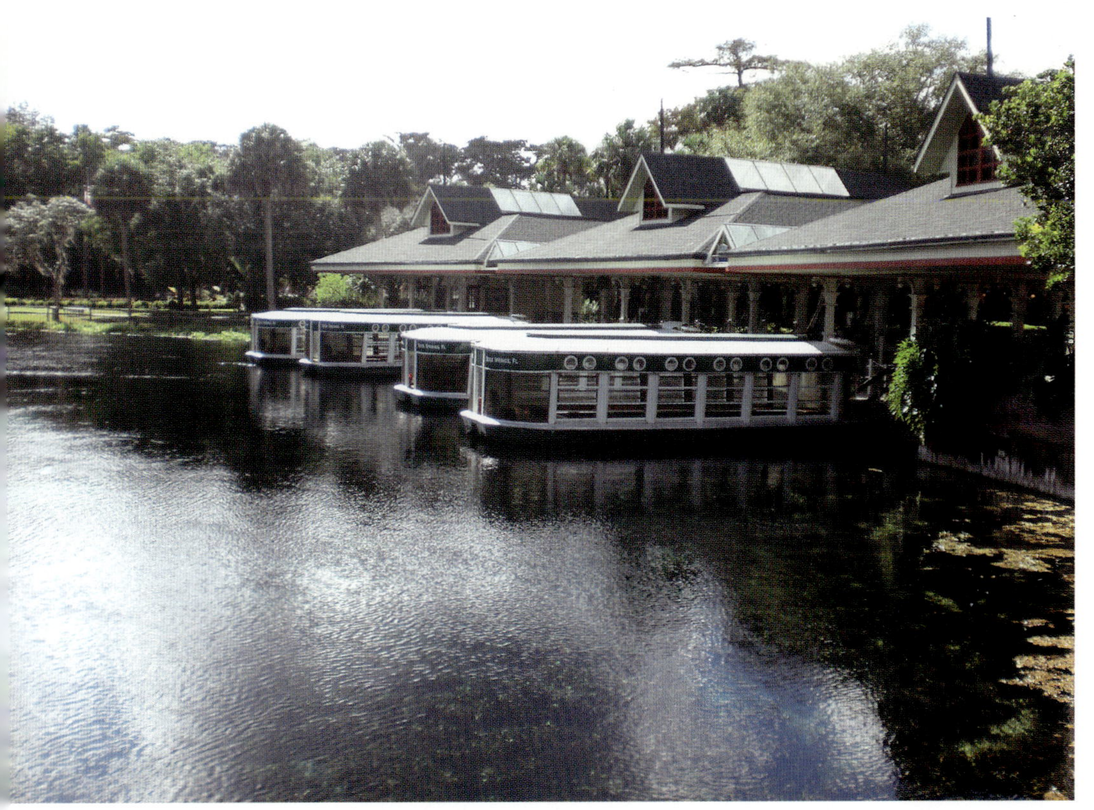

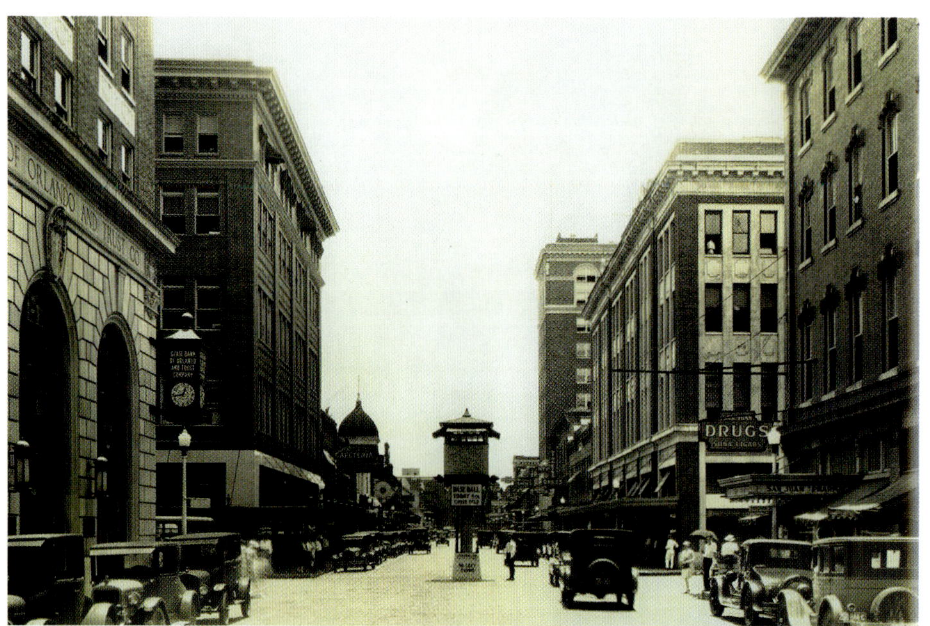

Orange Avenue, Orlando, 1927

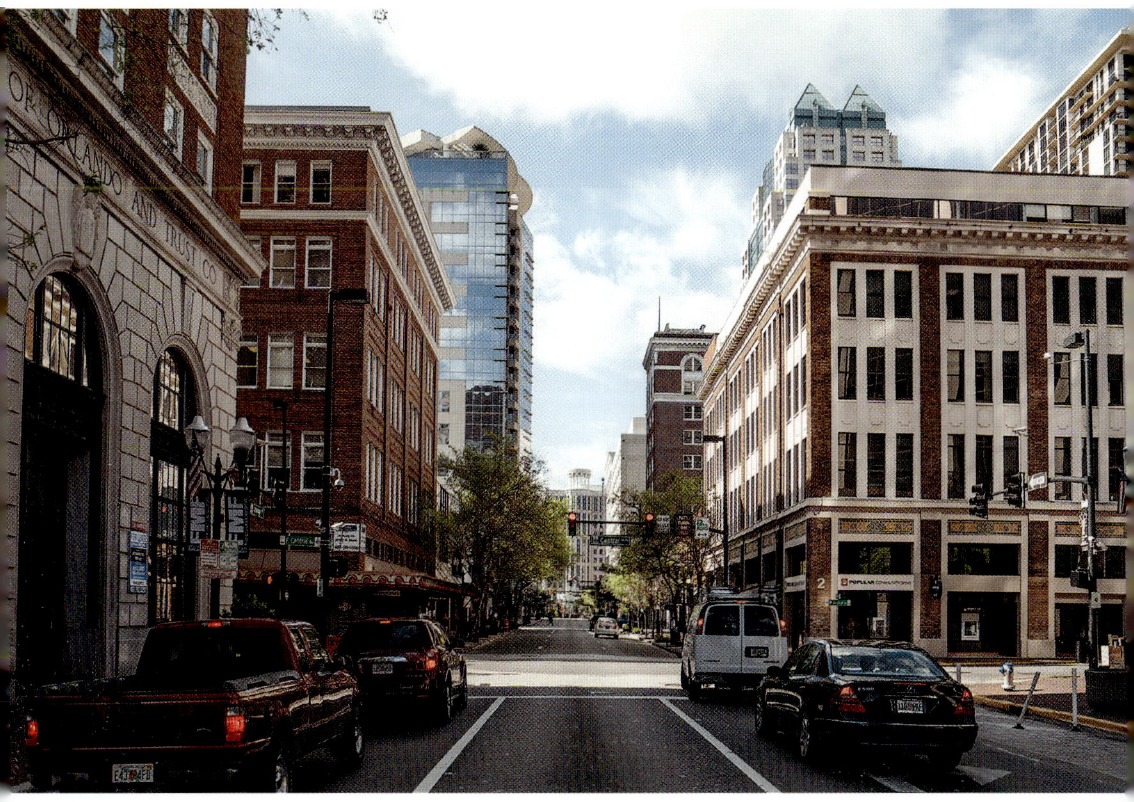
OF ORLANDO AND TRUST CO
POPULAR

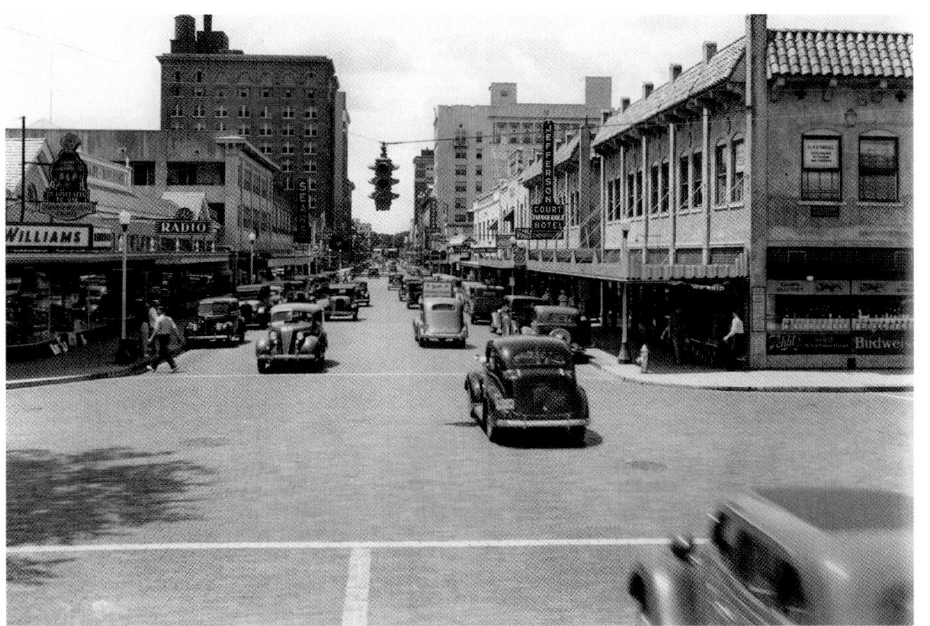

Orange Avenue, Orlando, 1937

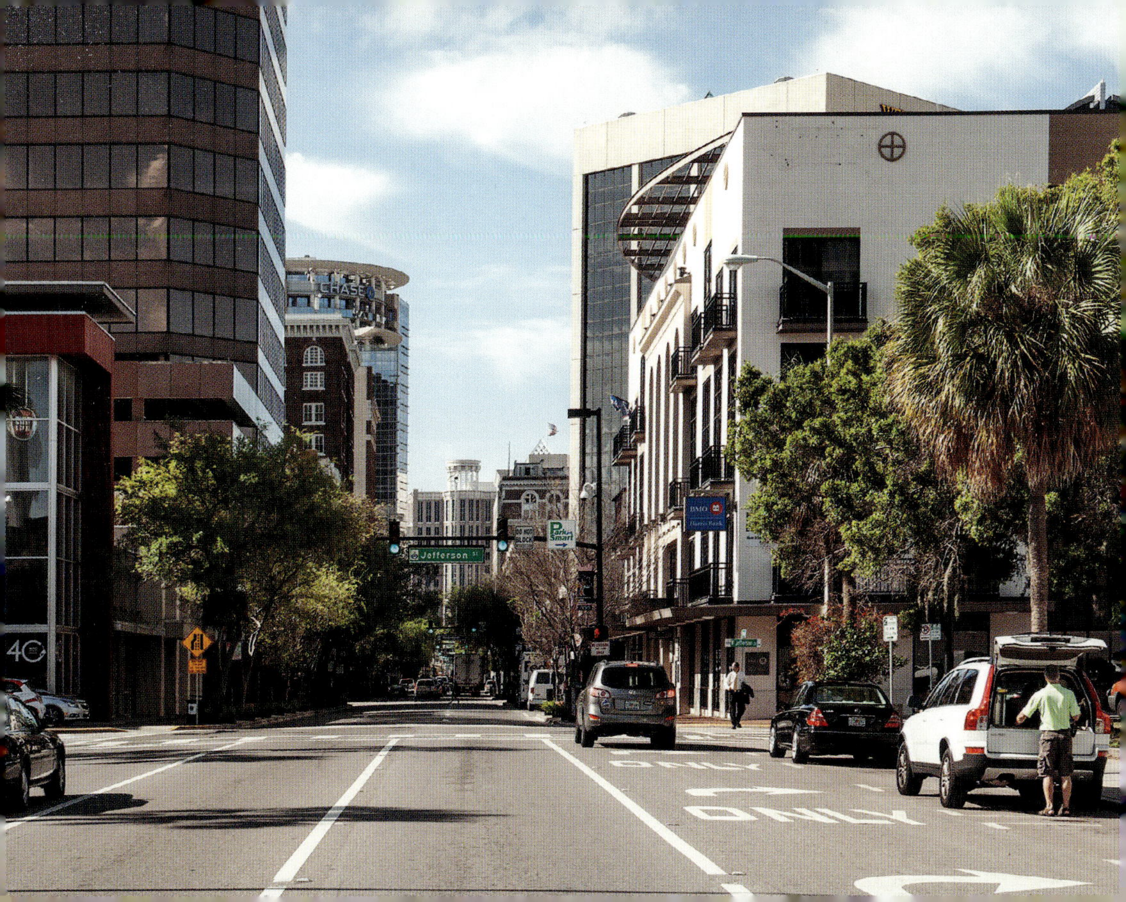
CHASE
Jefferson St
Park Smart
BMO
ONLY
ONLY

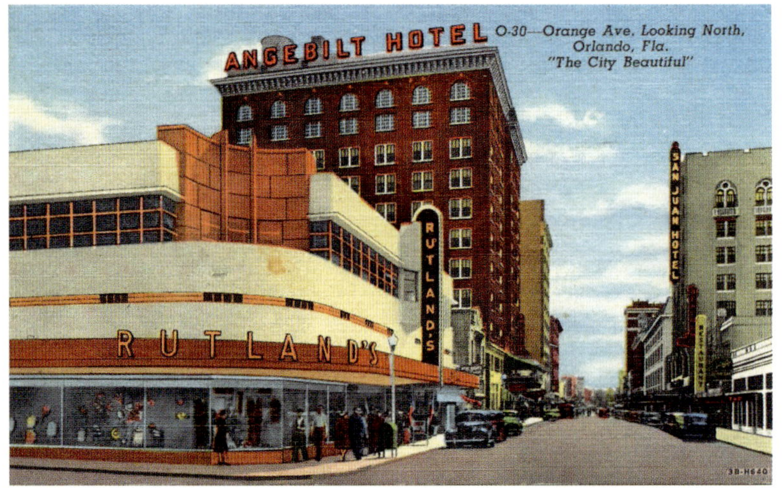

Orange Avenue, Orlando, c. 1940

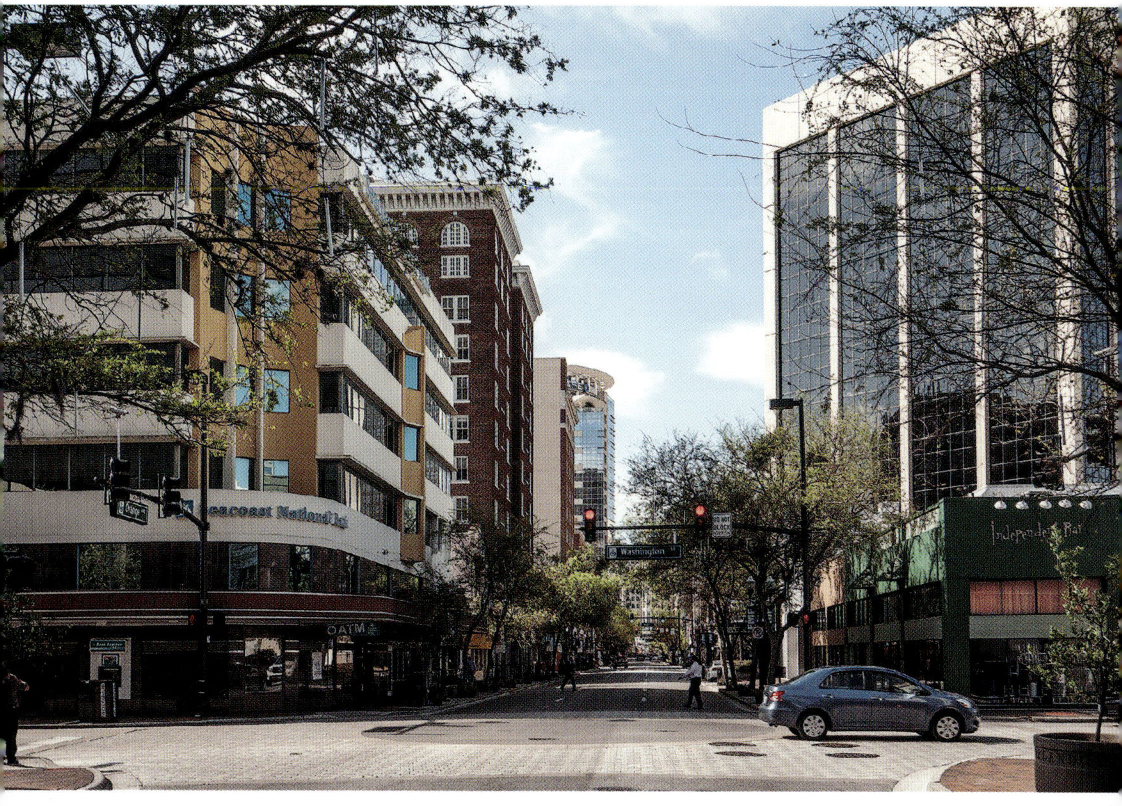
Washington
ATM

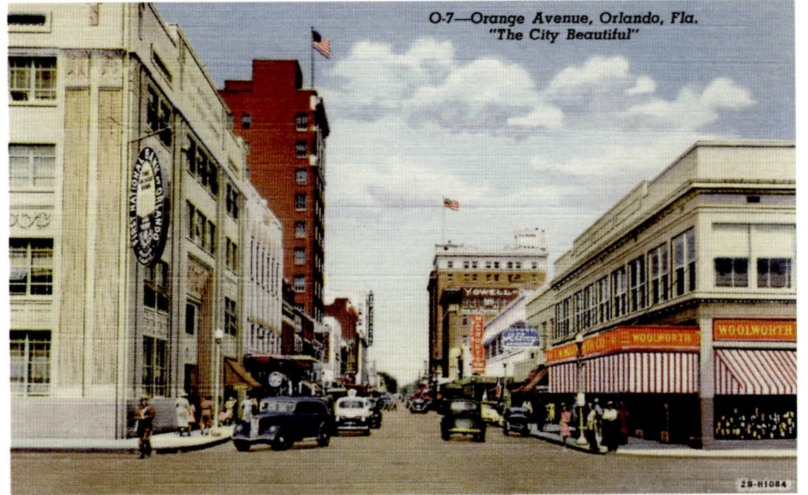

Orange Avenue, Orlando, c. 1940

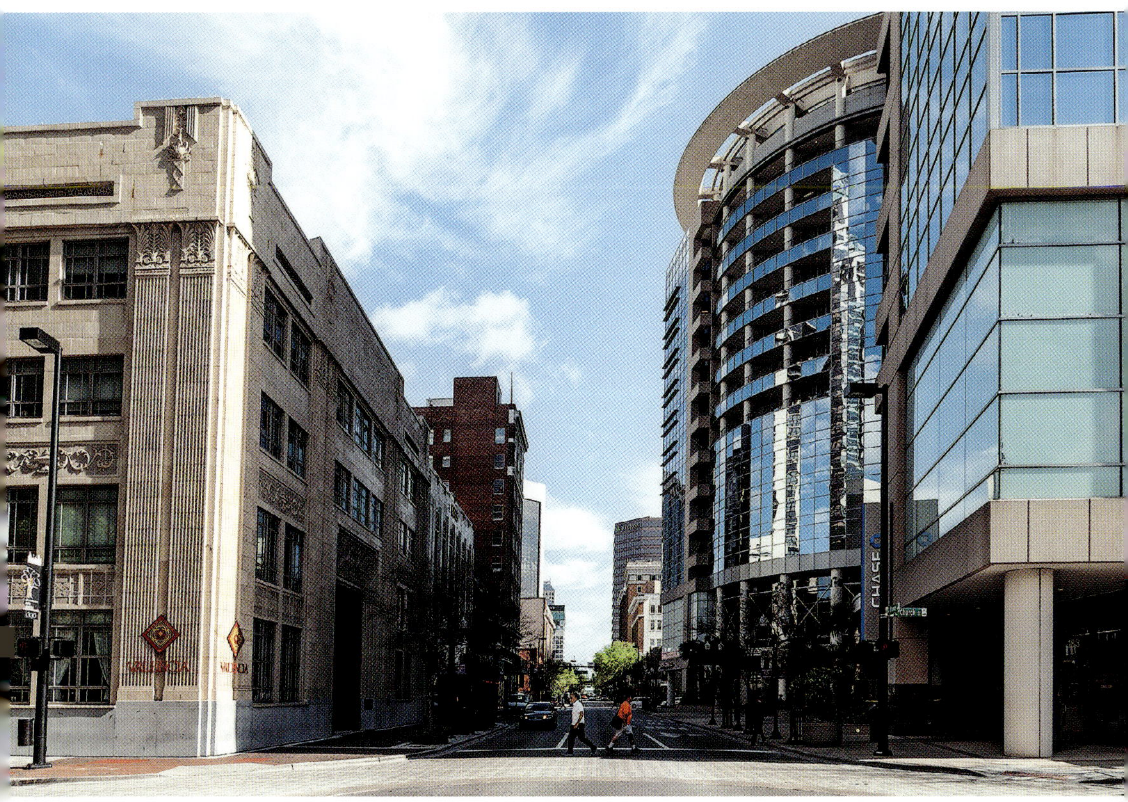
VALENCIA
CHASE

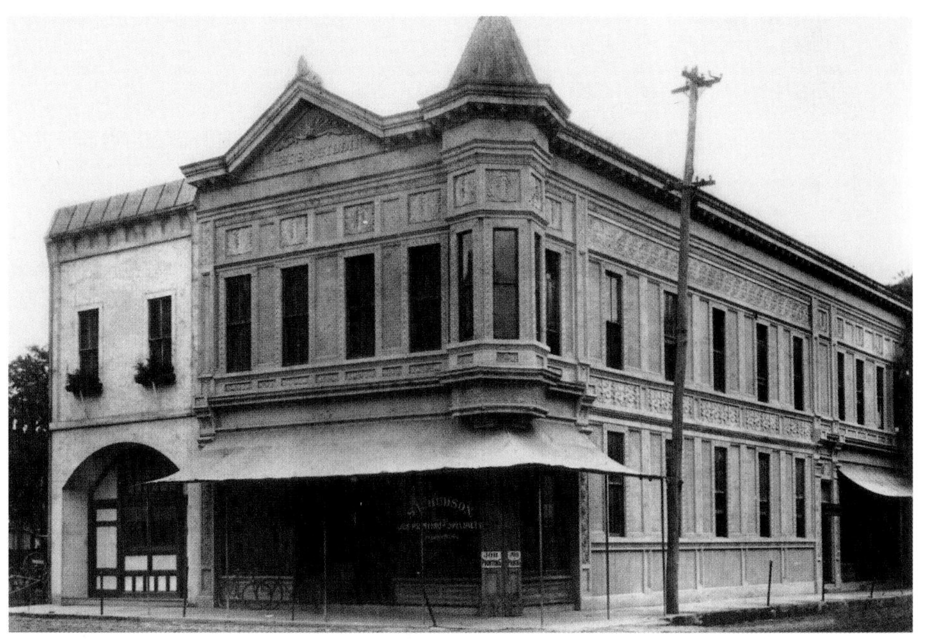

Rogers Building, Pine Street, Orlando, c. 1910

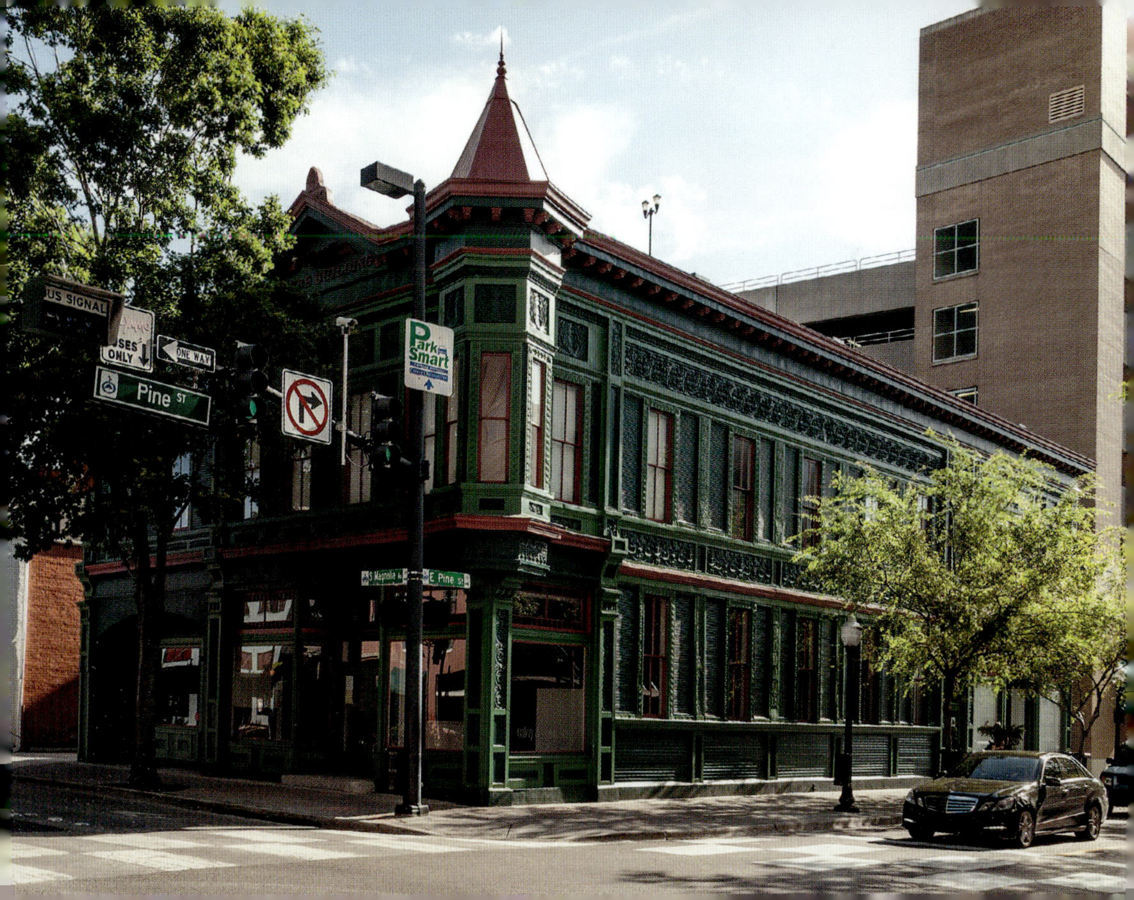
US SIGNAL
USES ONLY
ONE WAY
Pine ST
Park Smart
E Pine ST

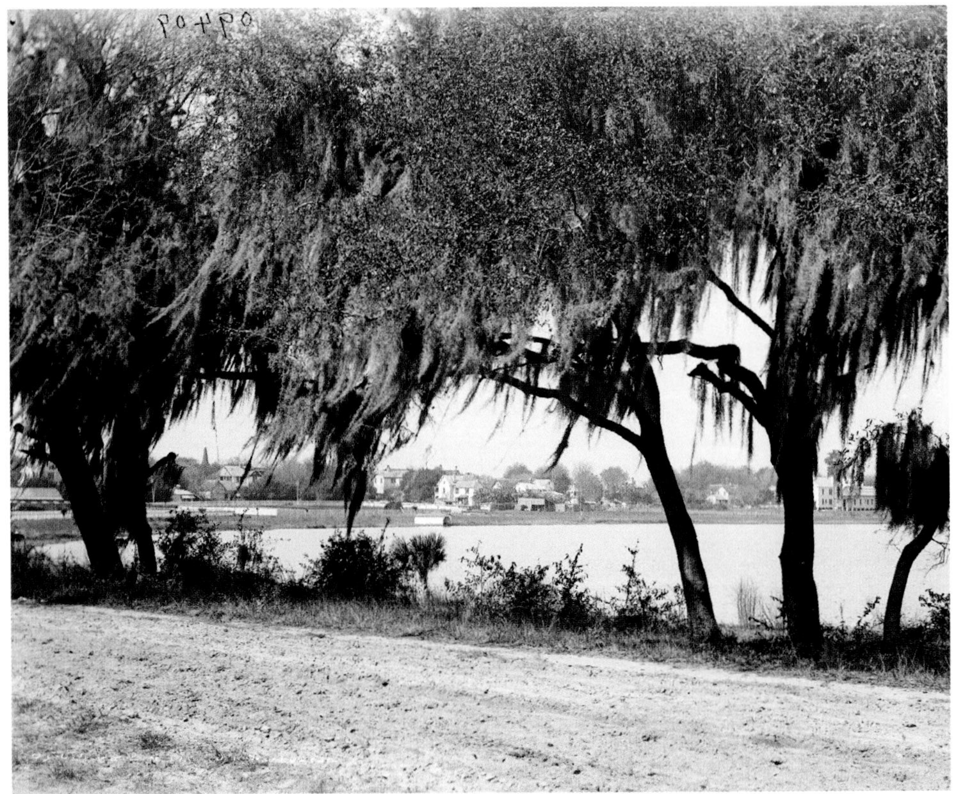

Lake Eola, Orlando, c. 1905

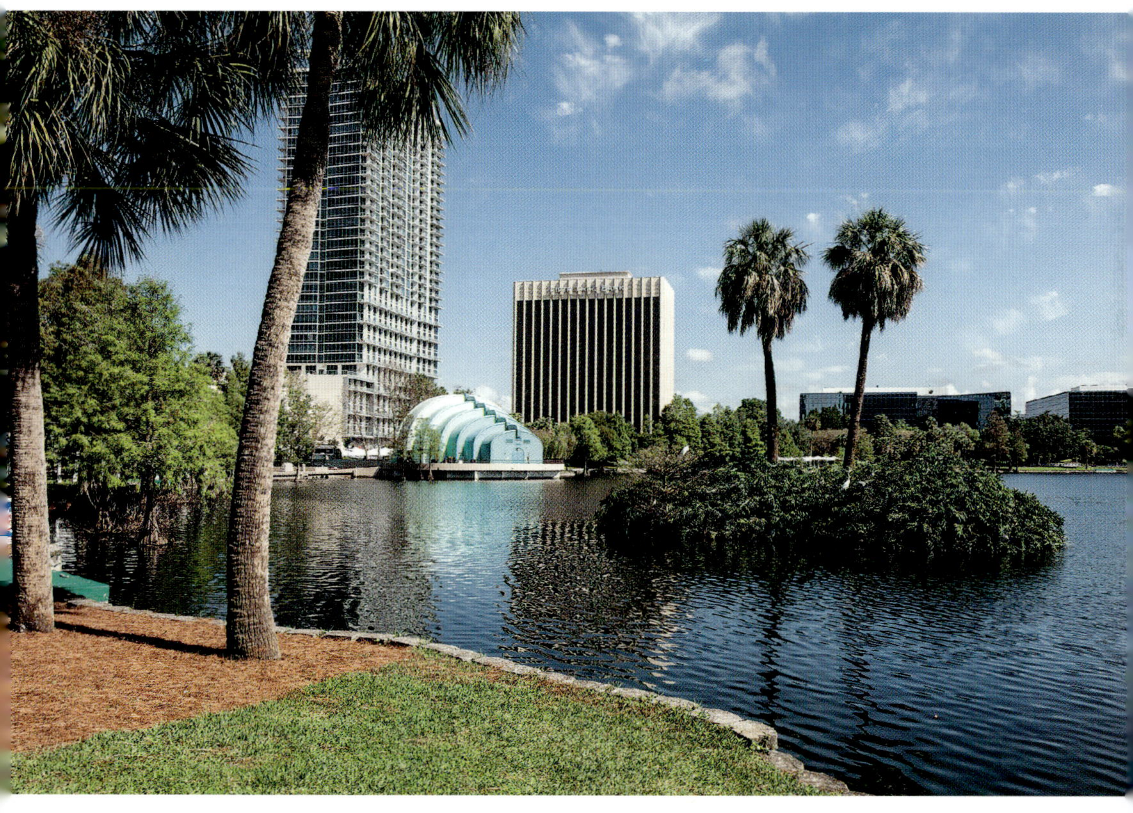

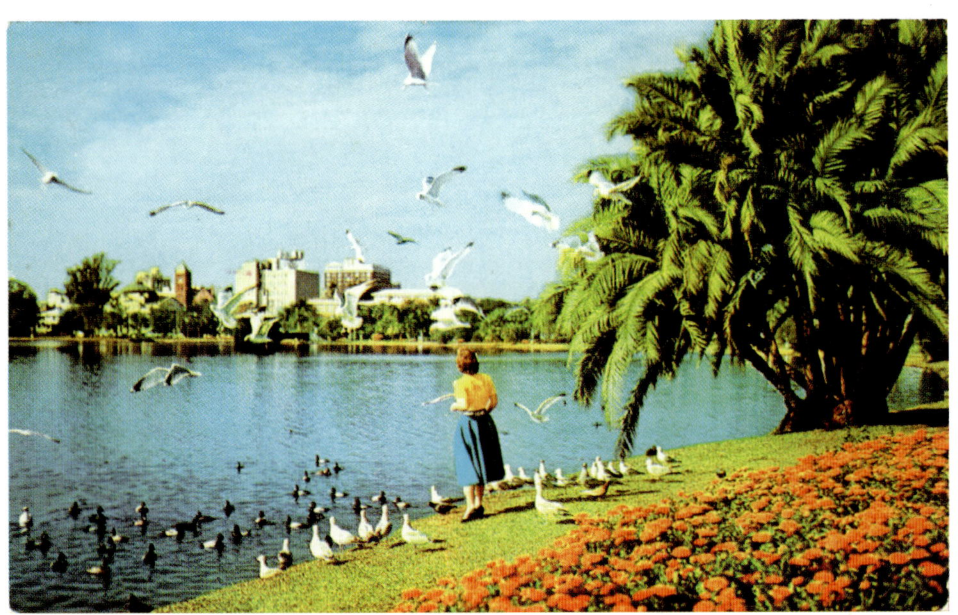

Lake Eola, Orlando, c. 1955

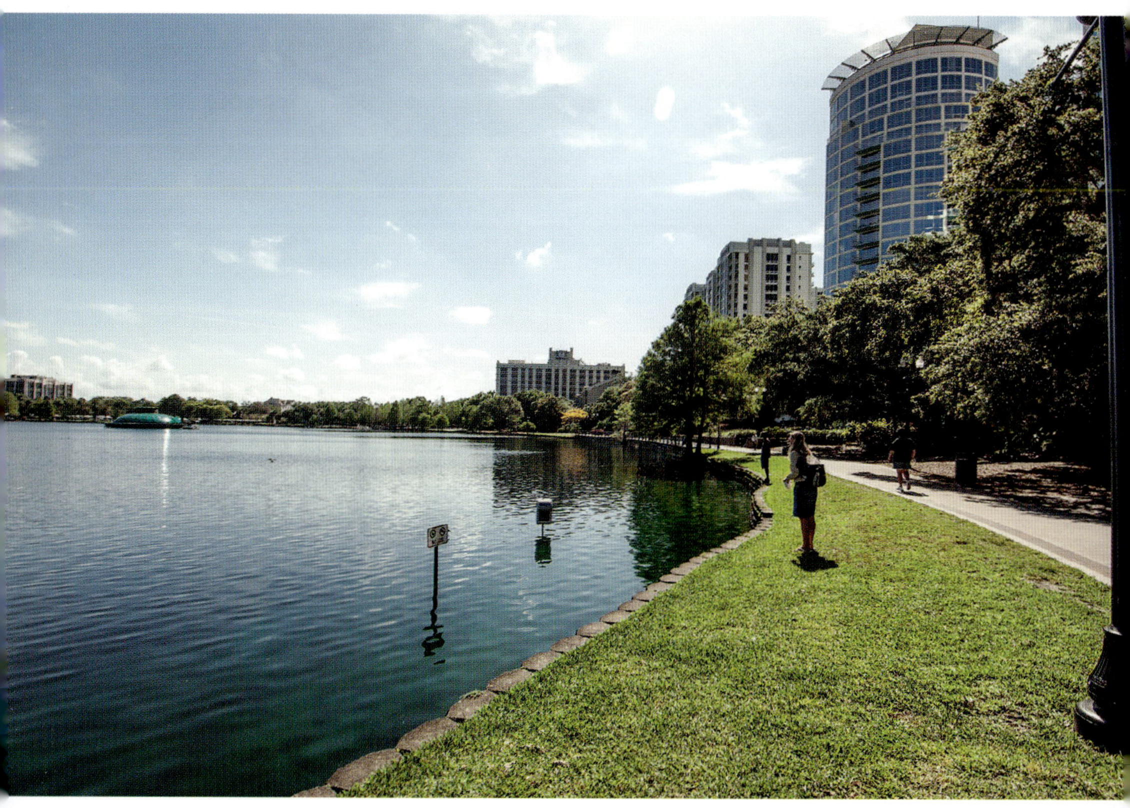

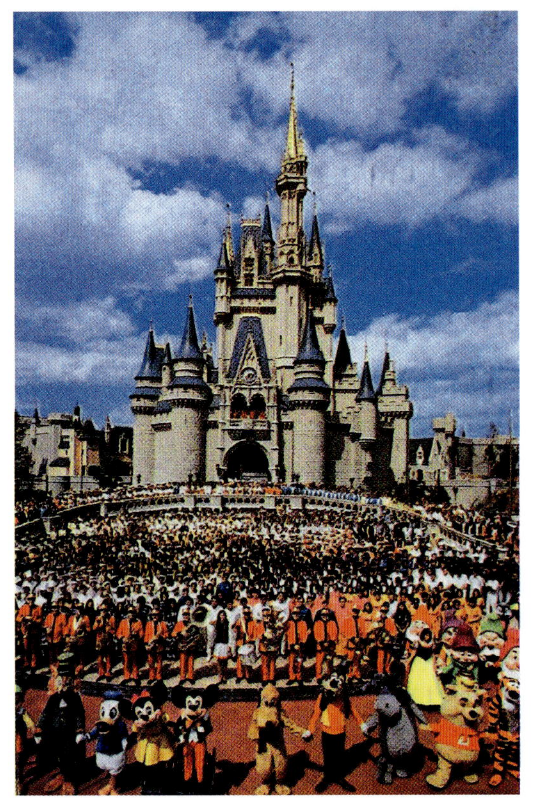

Cinderella Castle, Disney World, Orlando, 1971

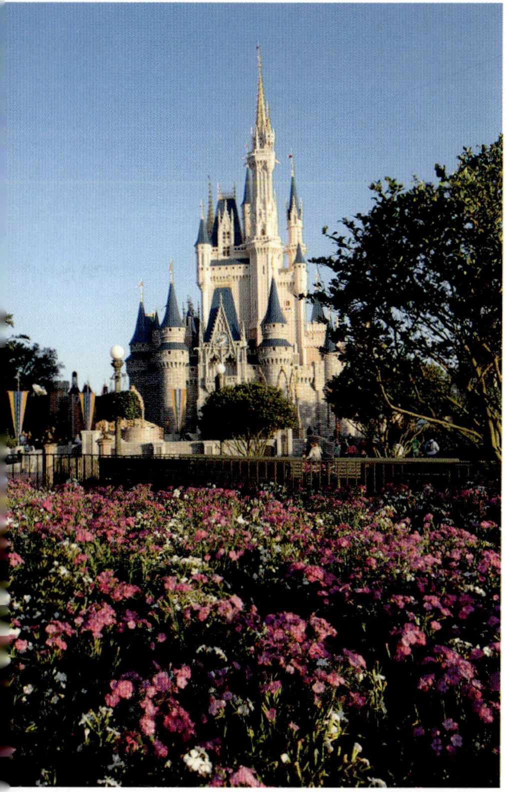

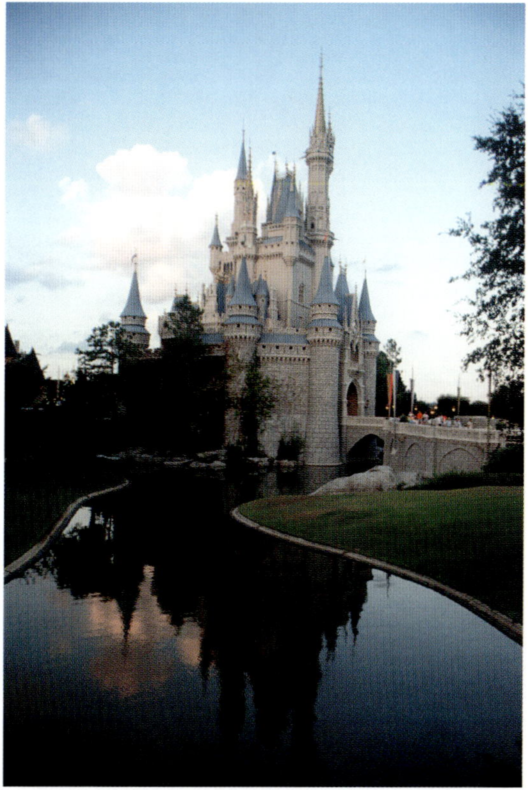

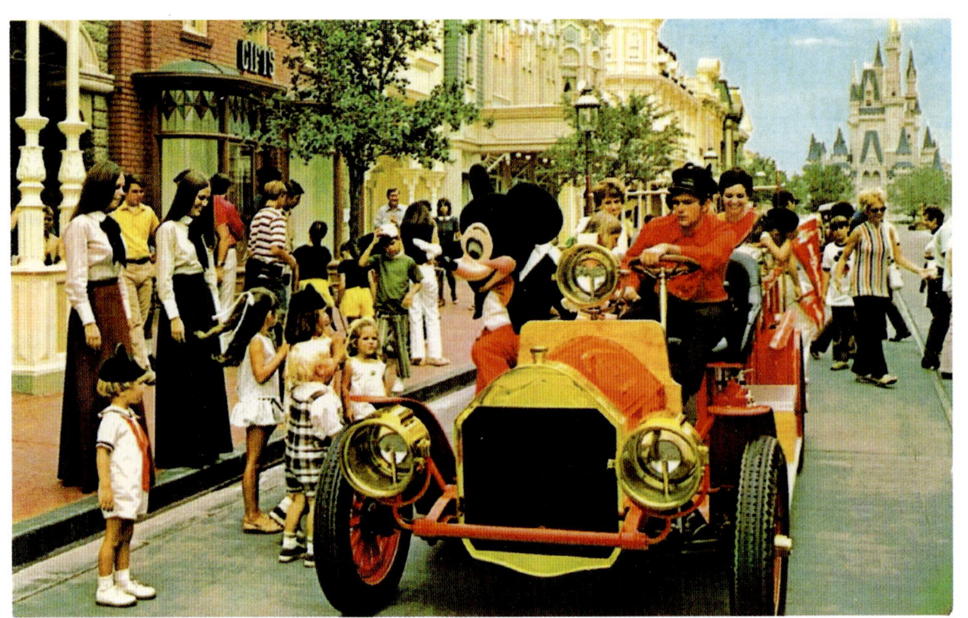

Magic Kingdom, Disney World, Orlando, 1971

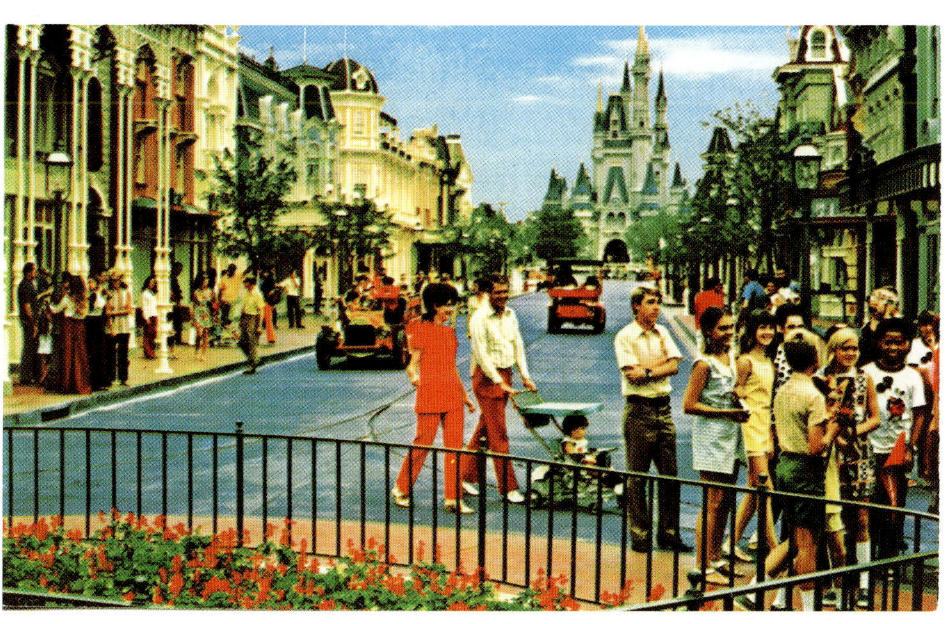

Magic Kingdom, Disney World, Orlando, 1971

Contemporary Resort and Monorail, Disney World, Orlando, 1971

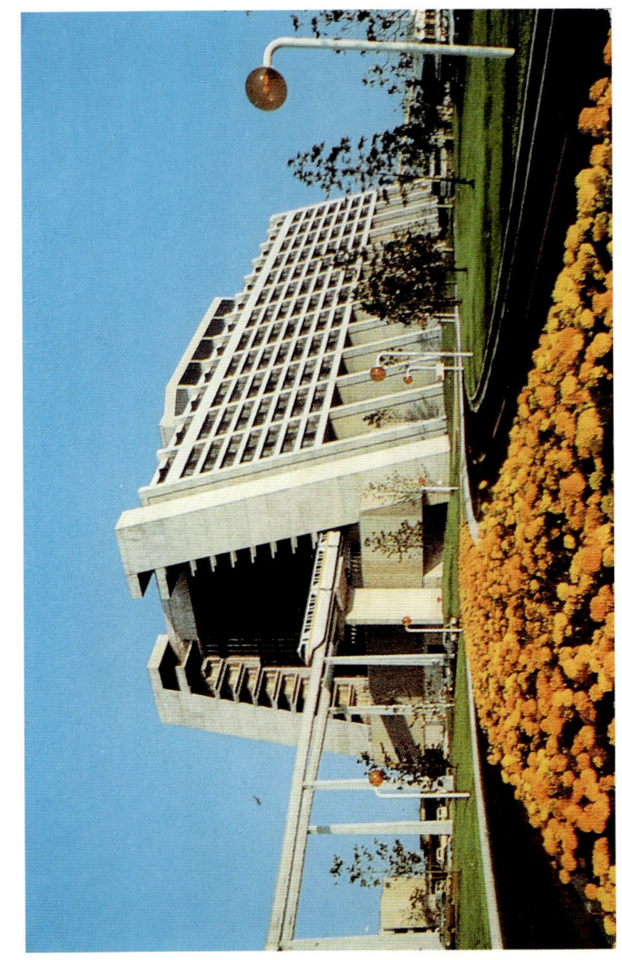

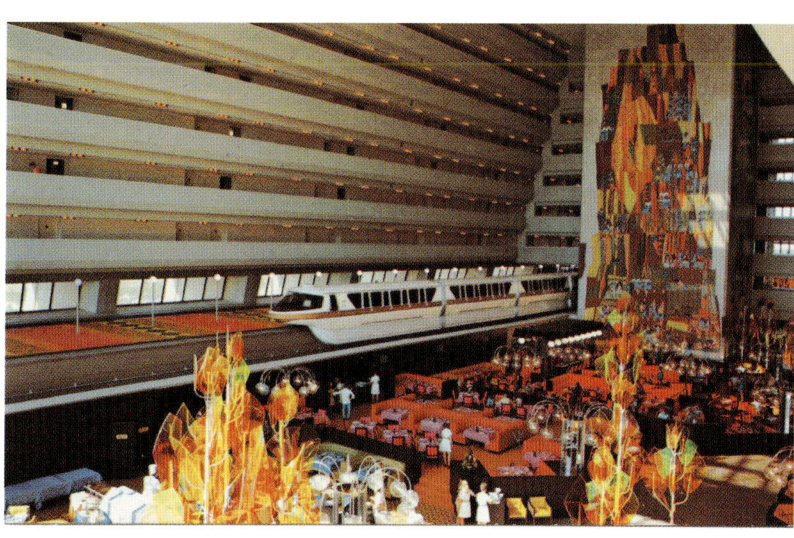

Contemporary Resort and Monorail, Disney World, Orlando, 1971

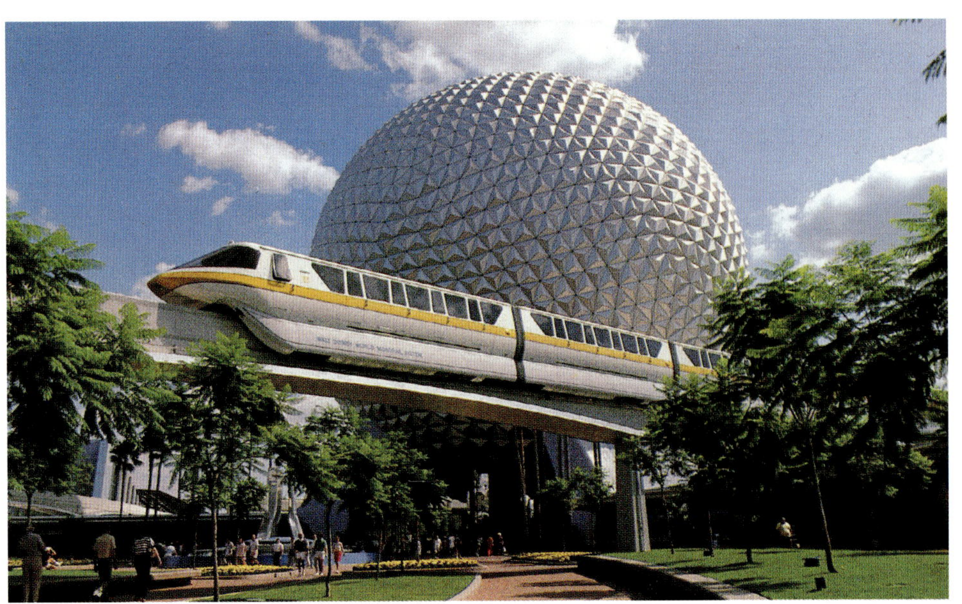

Monorail and Epcot Center, Walt Disney World, 1987

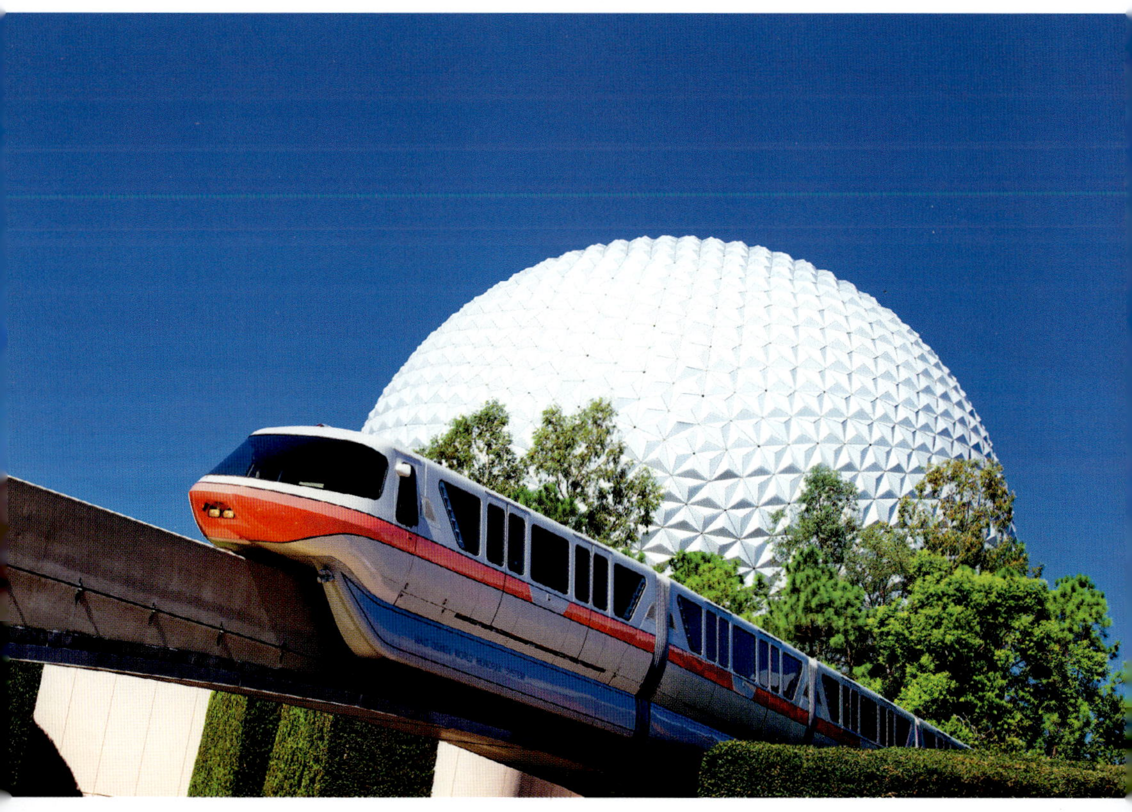

Monorail, Walt Disney World, c. 1990

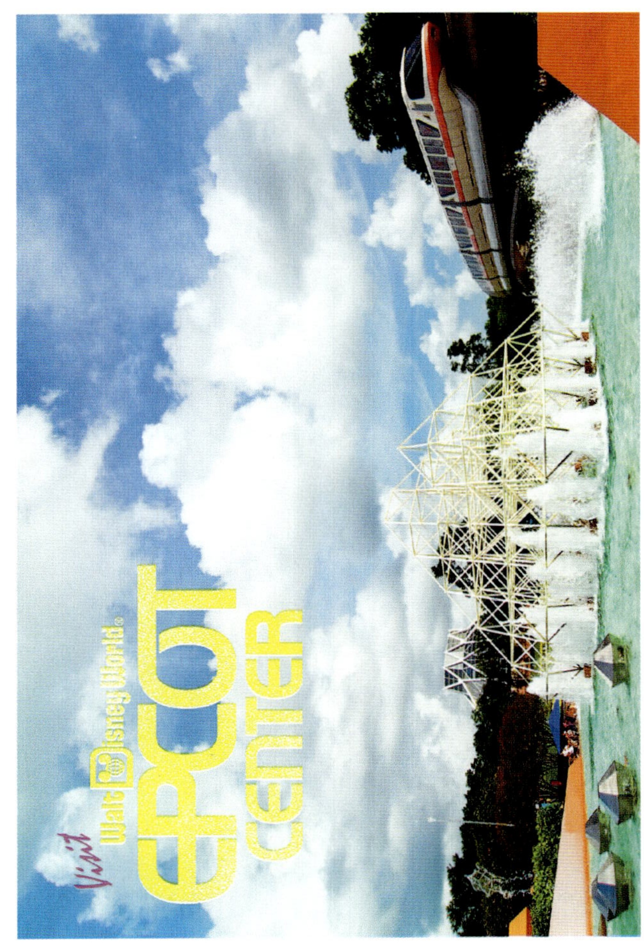

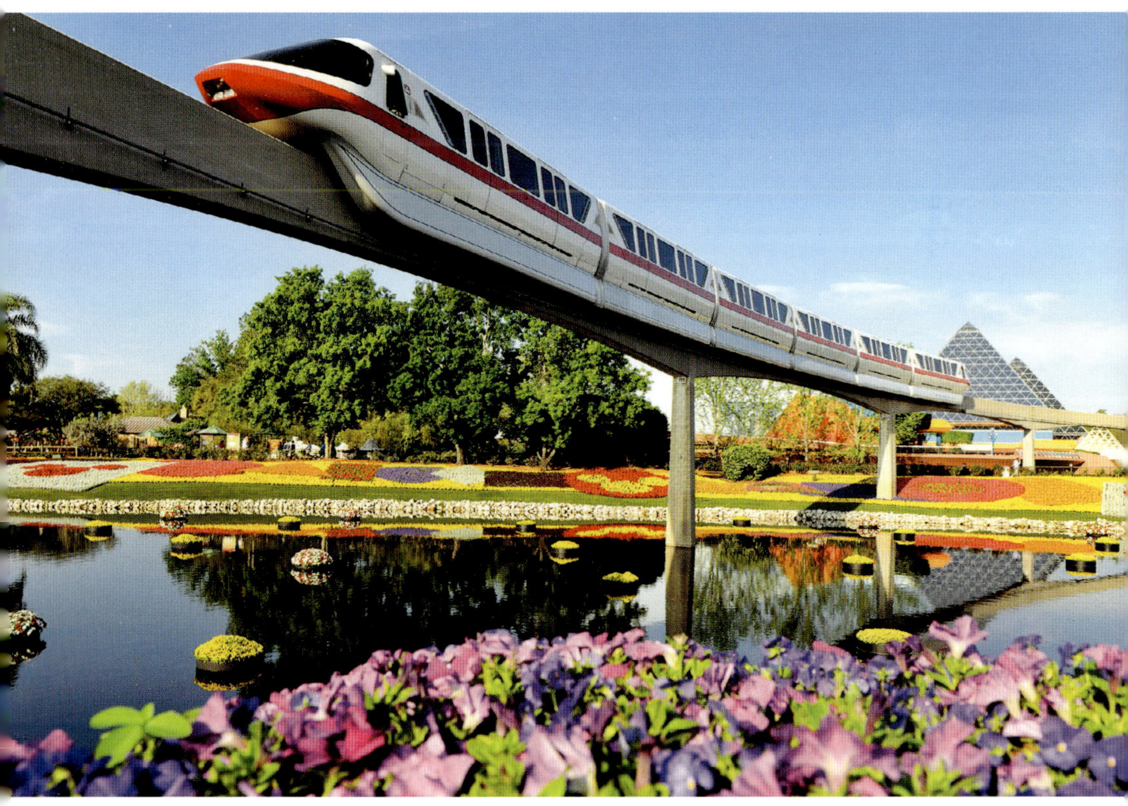

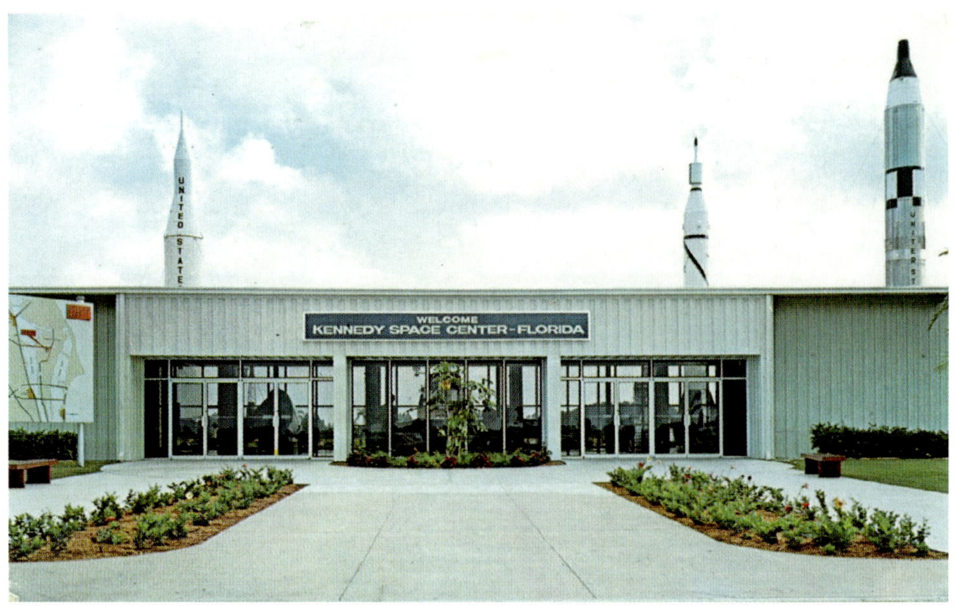

Kennedy Space Center, Cape Canaveral, 1975

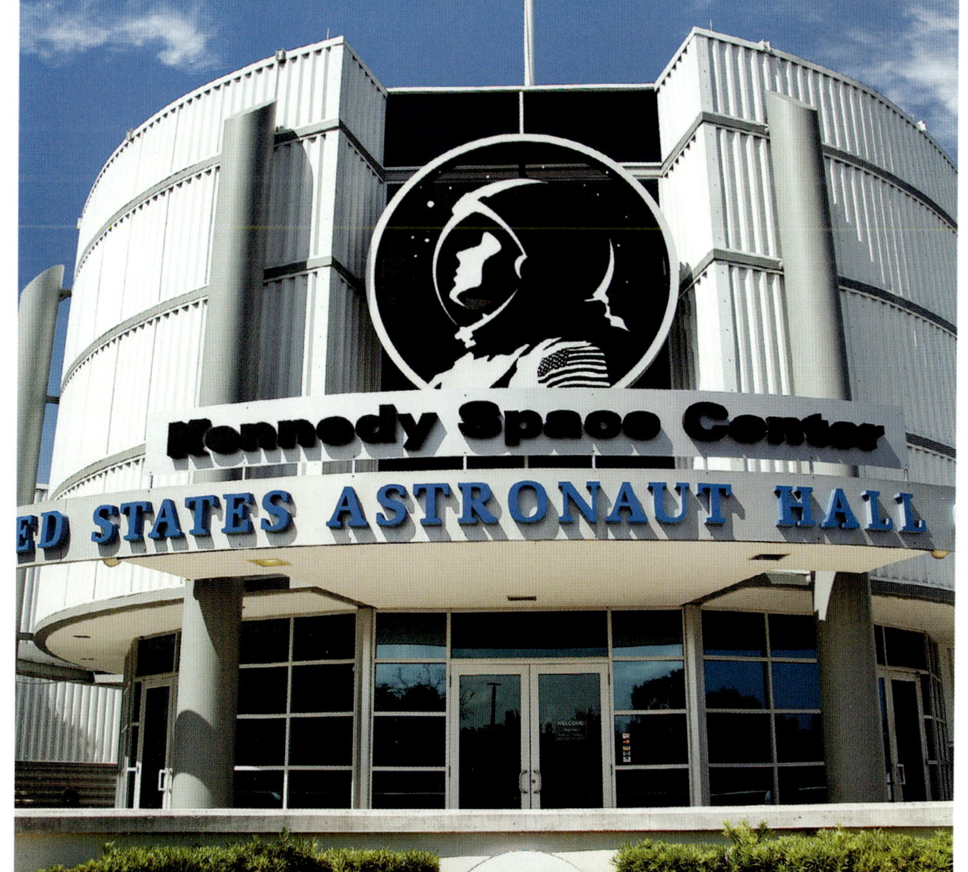
Kennedy Space Center
ED STATES ASTRONAUT HALL
Here we honor

Kennedy Space Center, Cape Canaveral, 1969

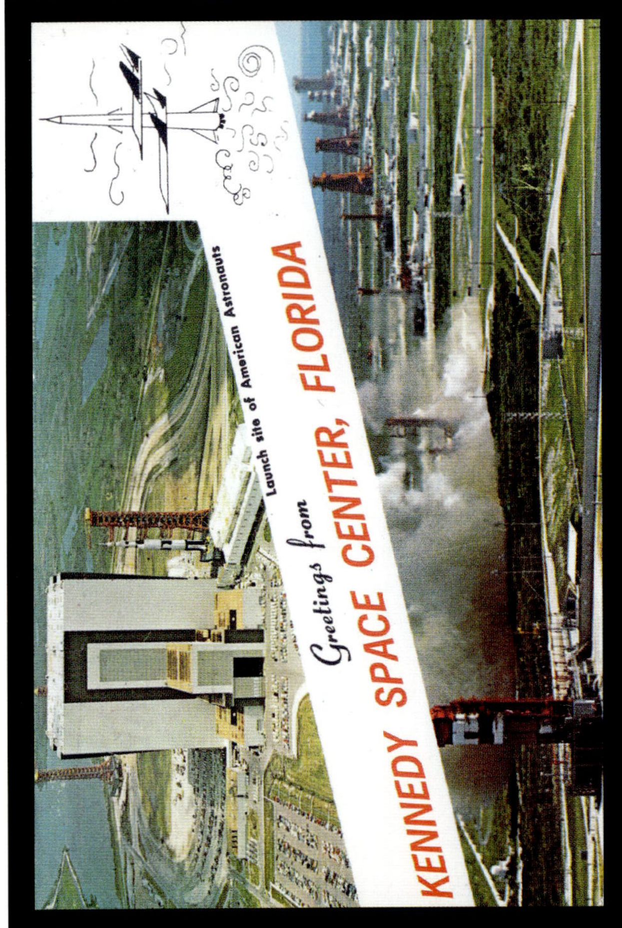

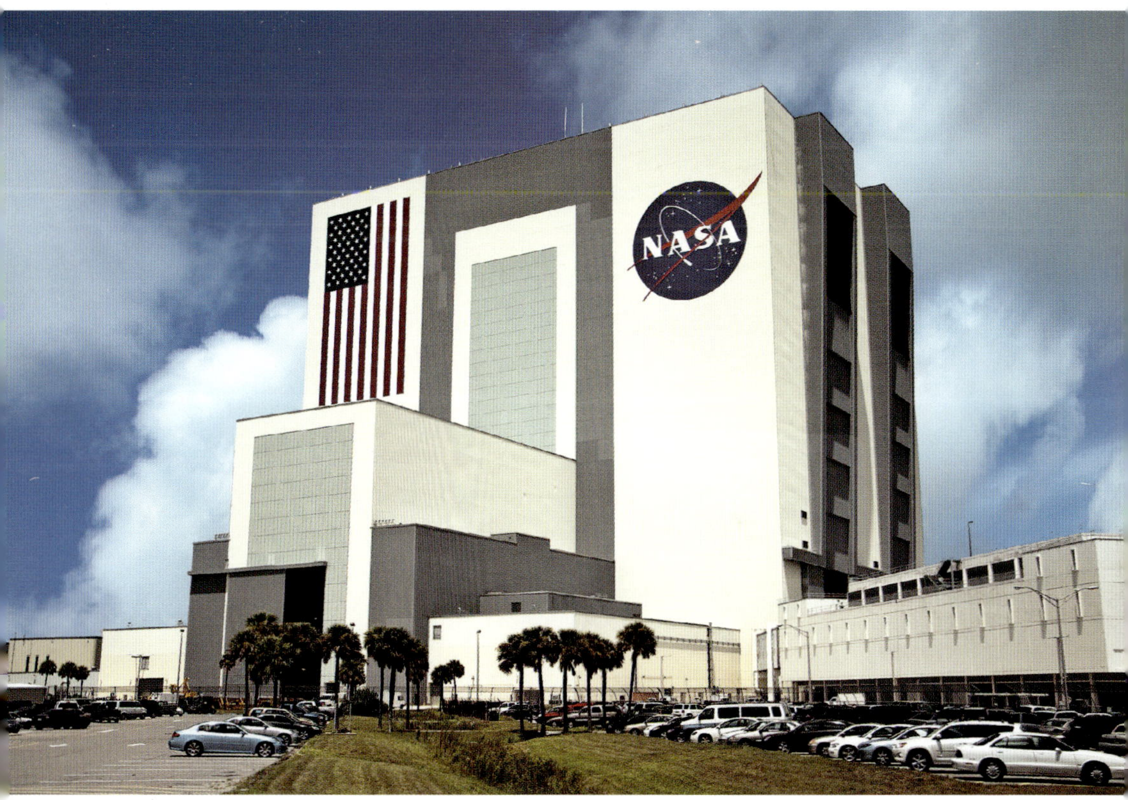
NASA

School of Technology, Stetson University, DeLand, 1904

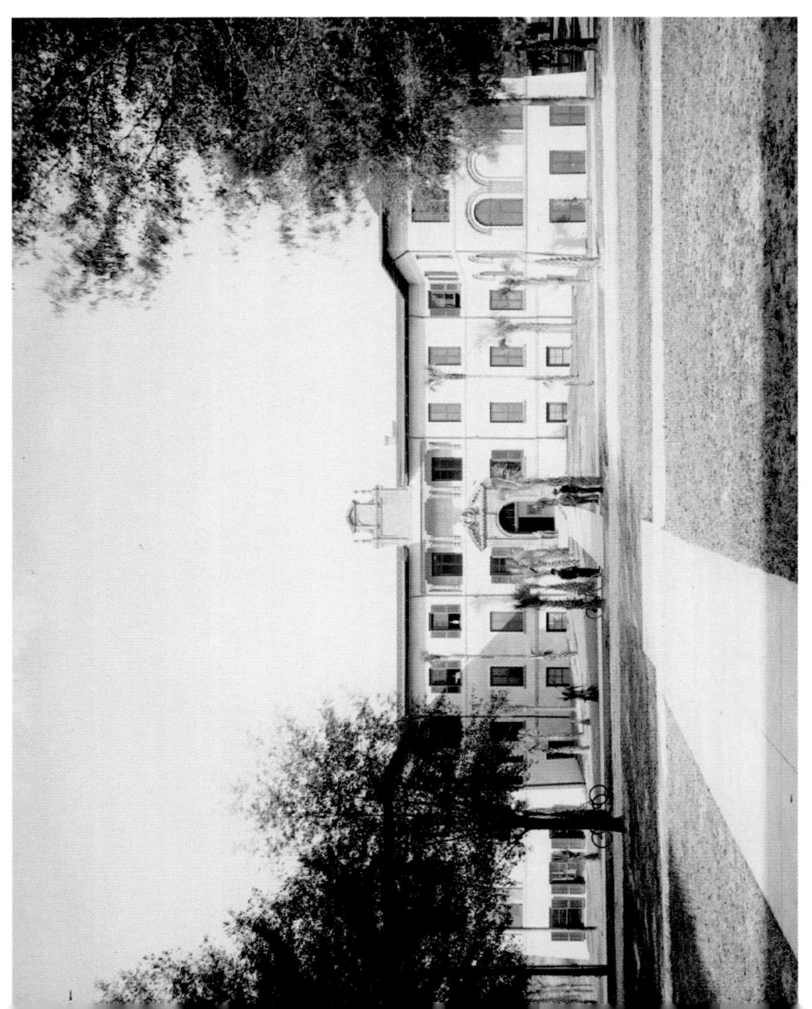

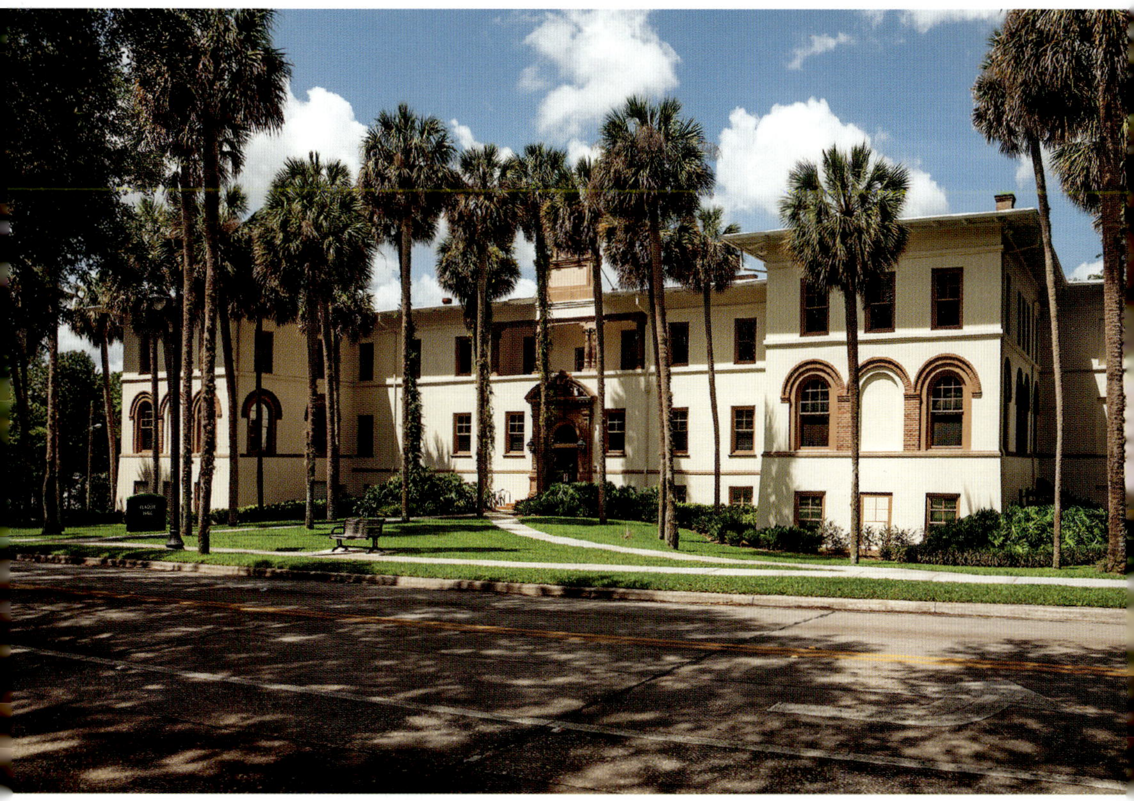

Chaudoin Hall, Stetson University, DeLand, 1904

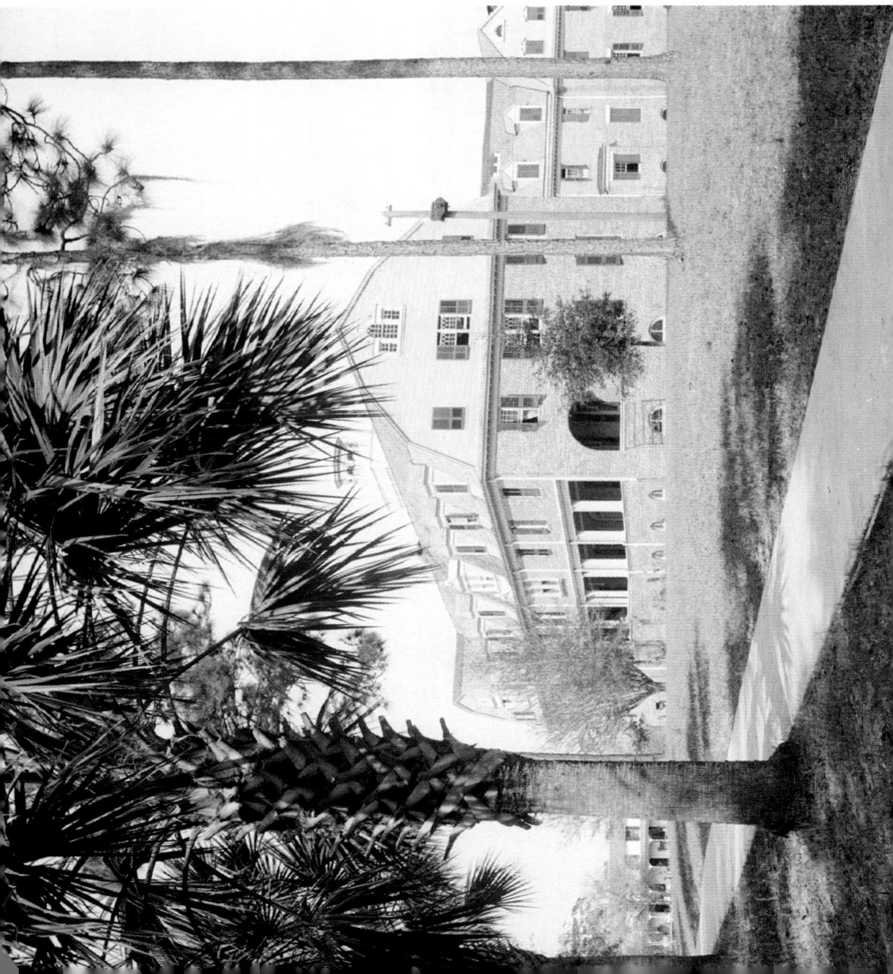

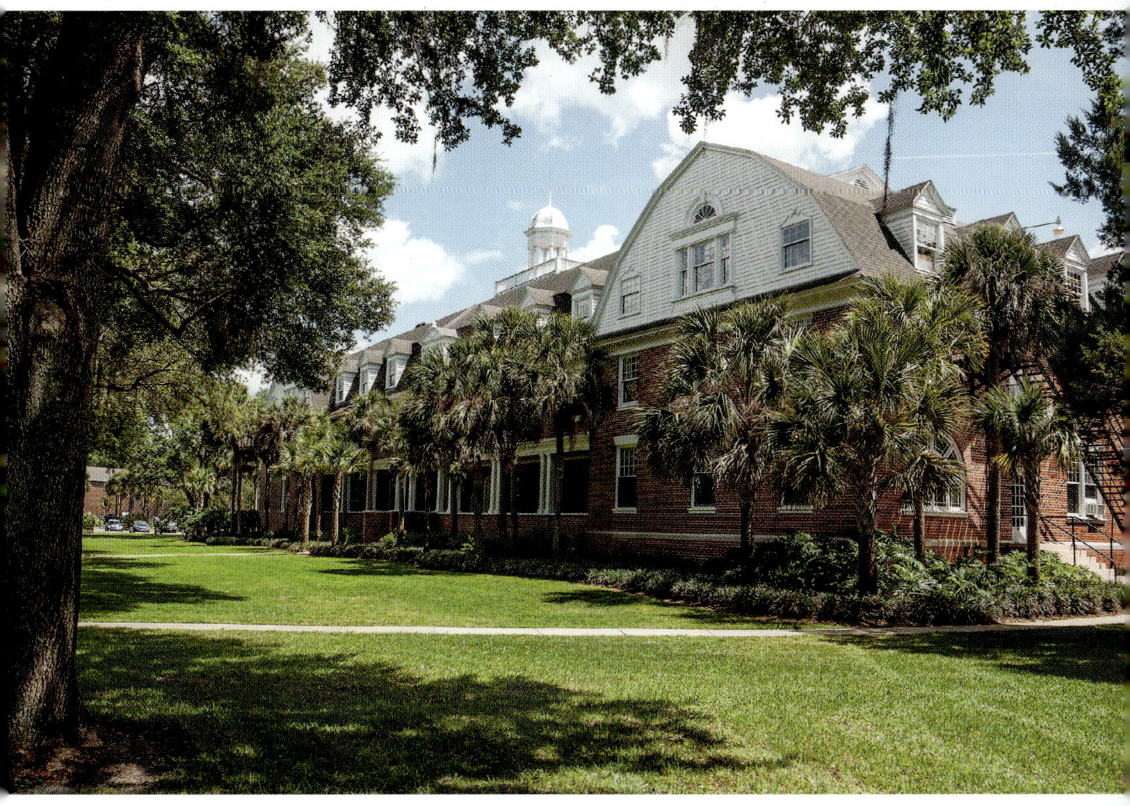

Elizabeth Hall, Stetson University, DeLand, 1904

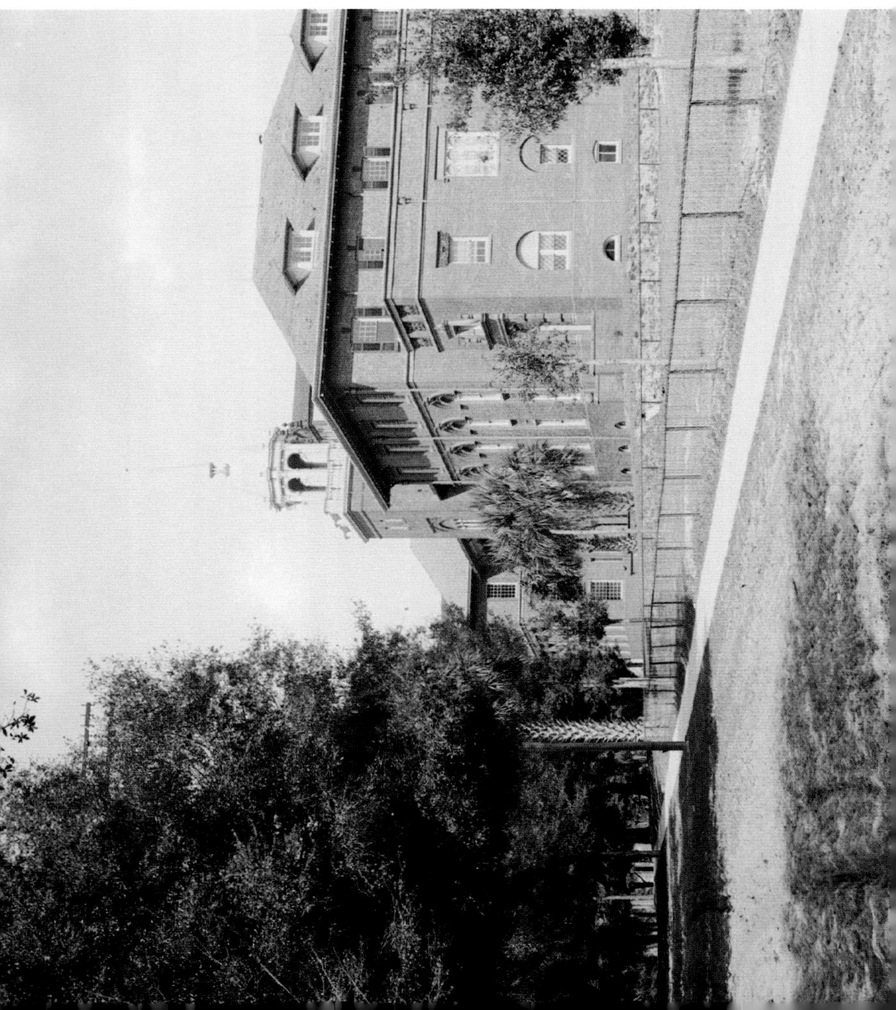

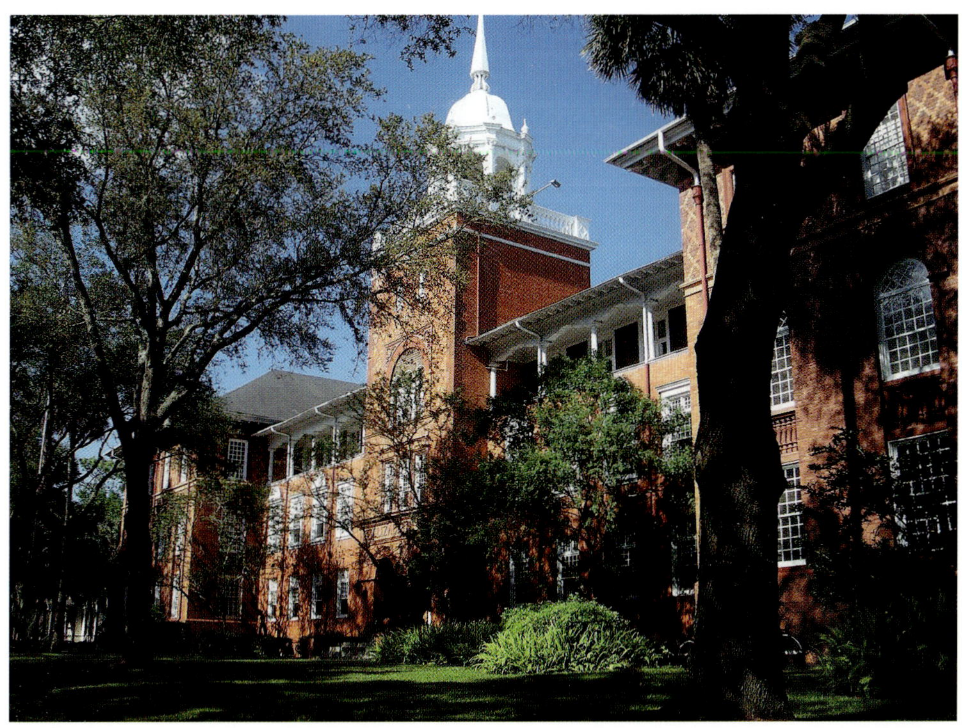

Sampson Hall, Stetson University, DeLand, 1912

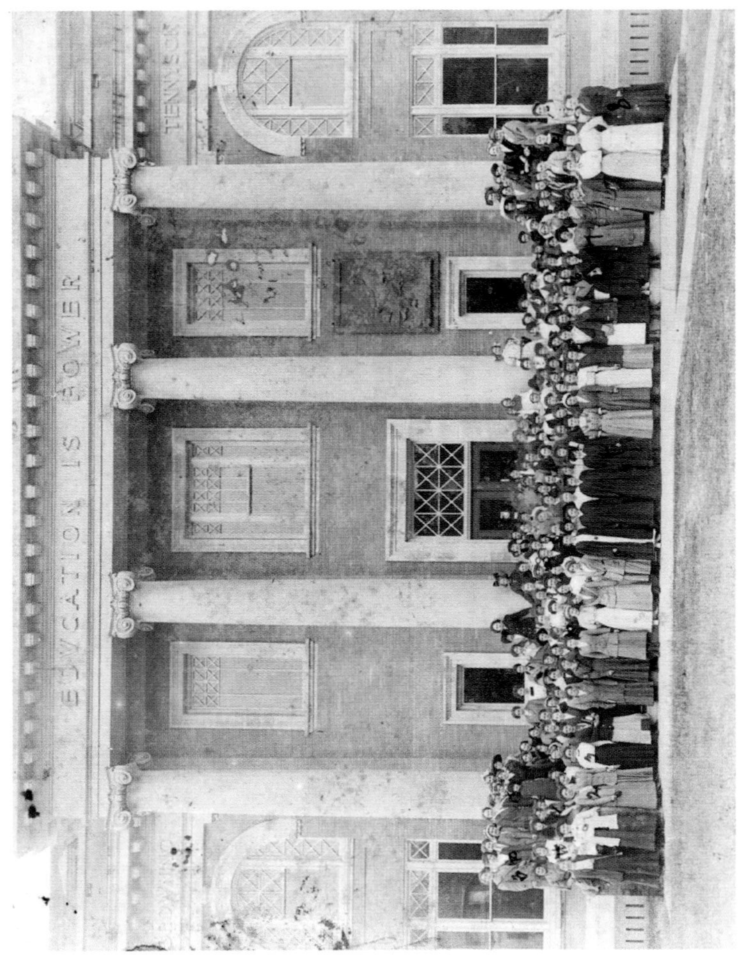

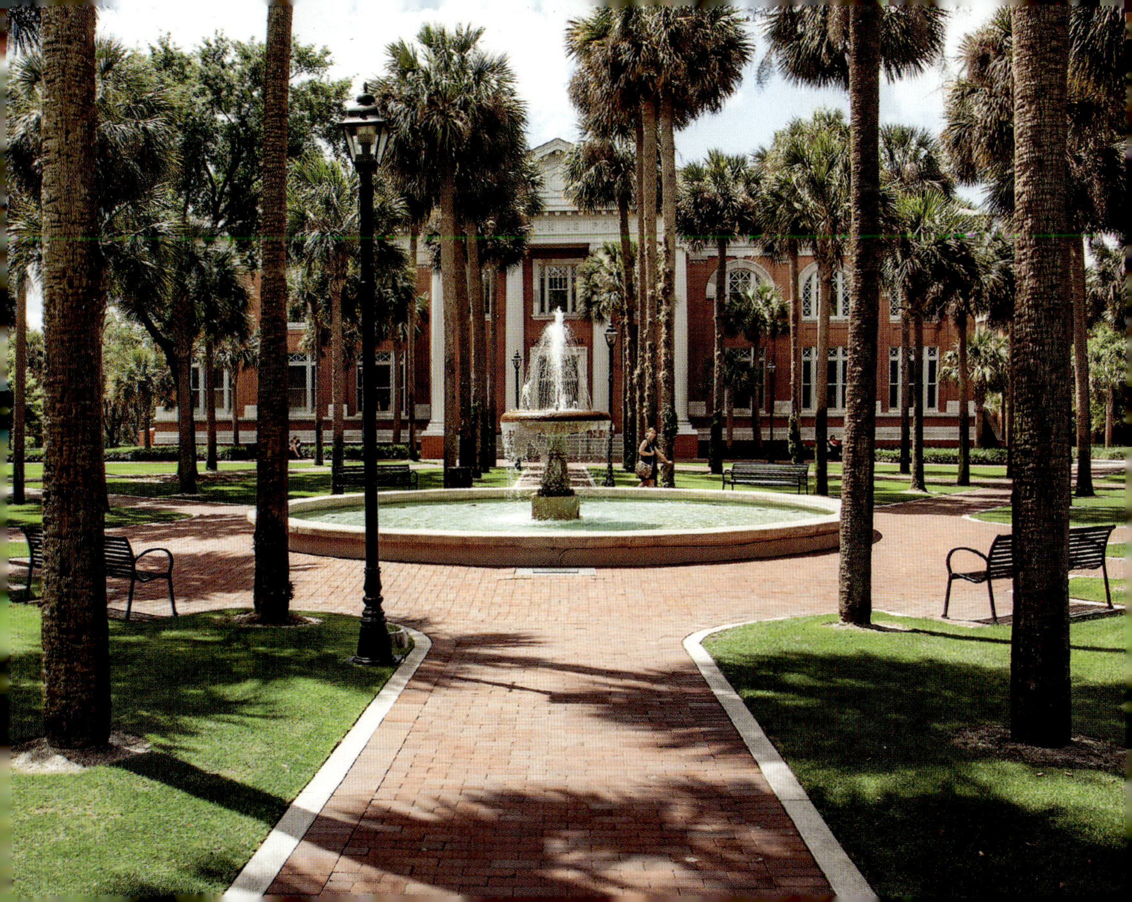

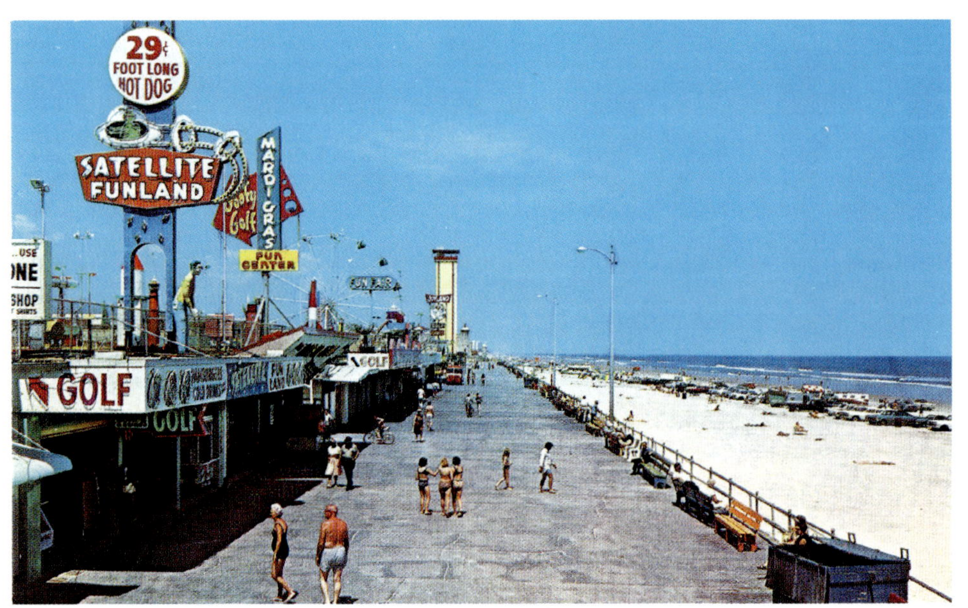

Daytona Beach, c. 1965

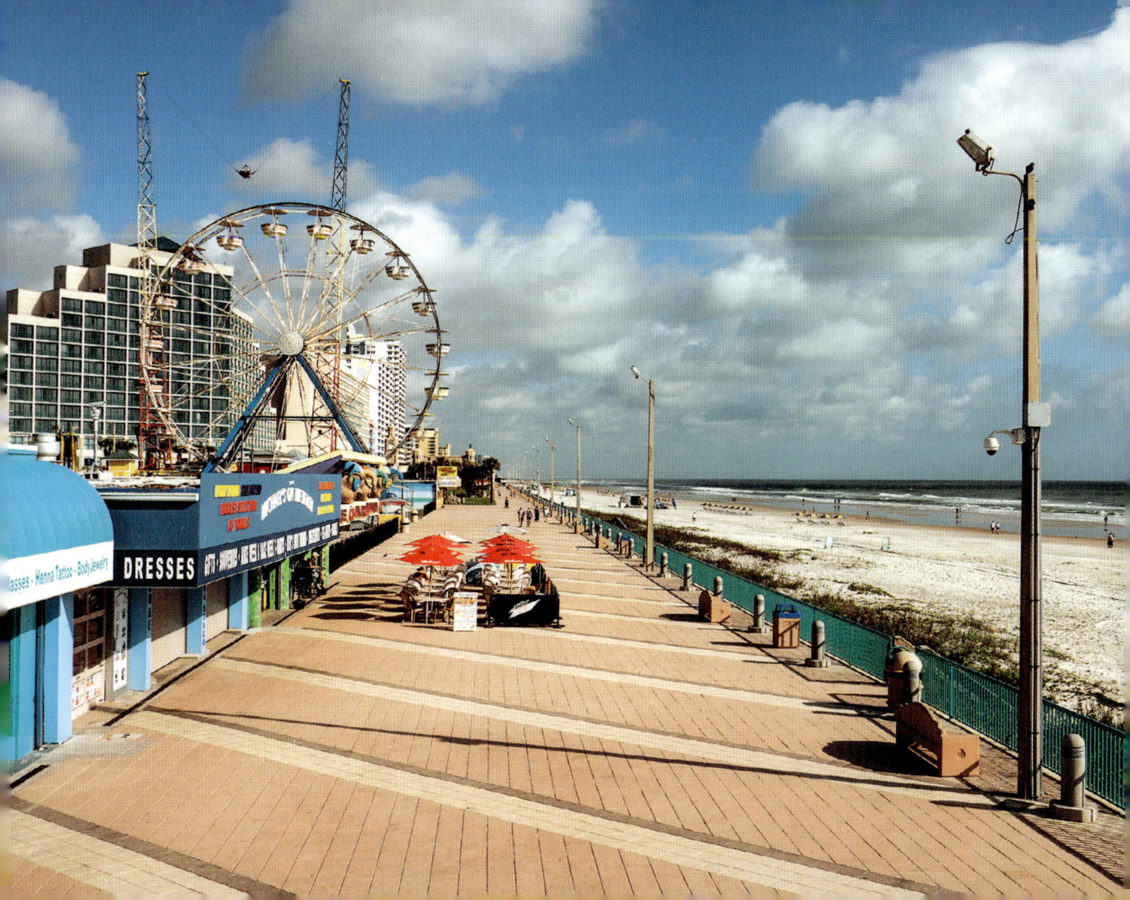

Henna Tattoo · Body Jewelry
DRESSES

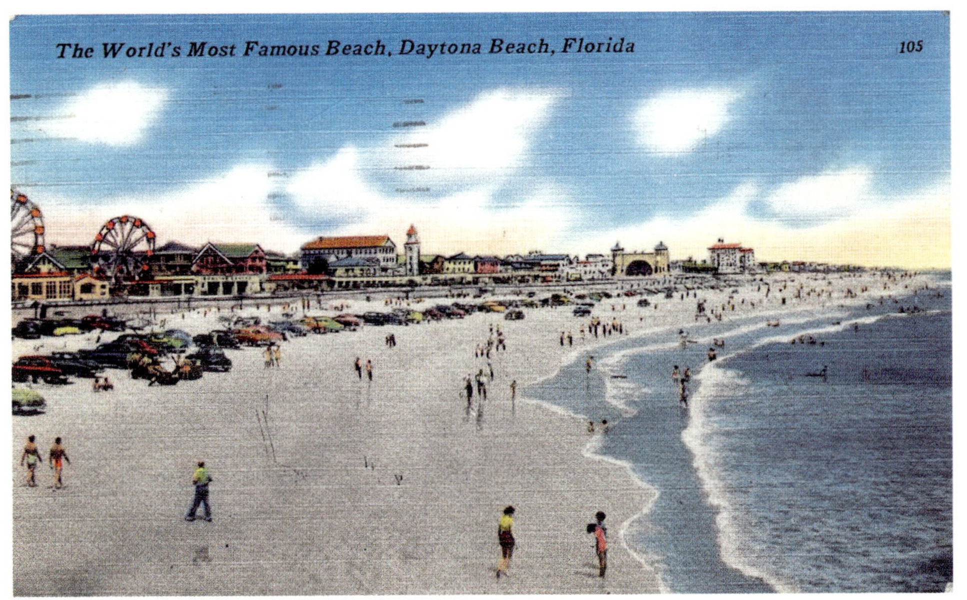

Daytona Beach, 1938

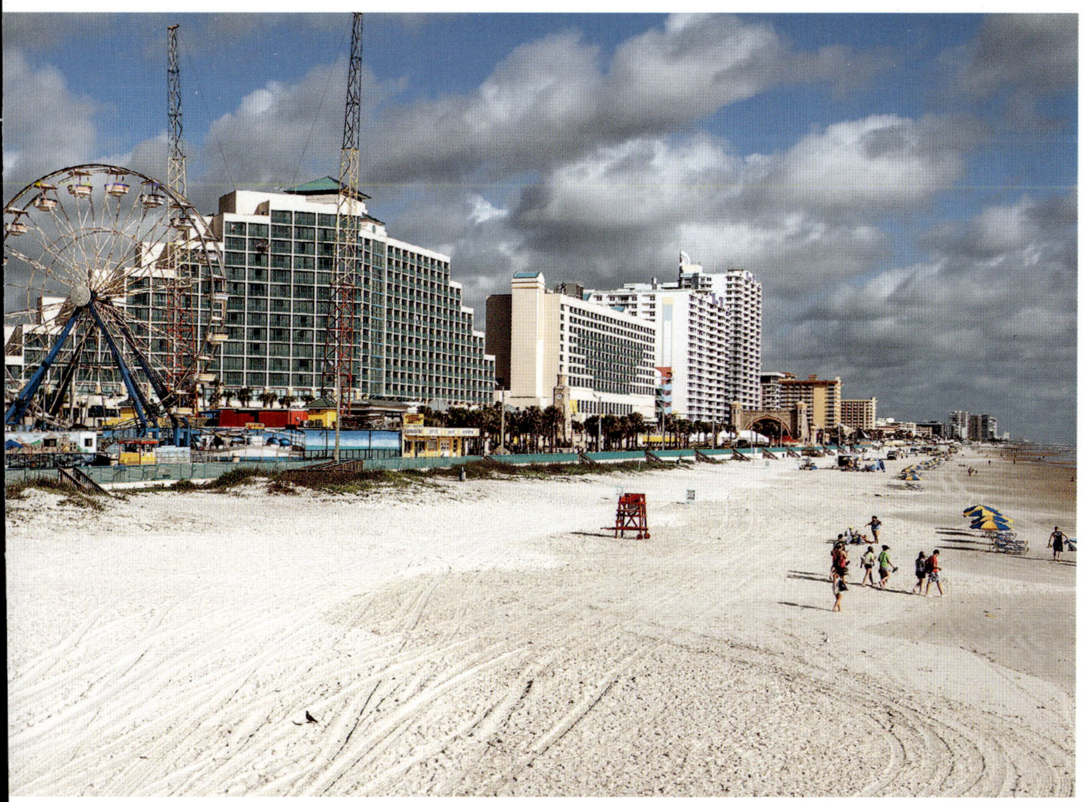

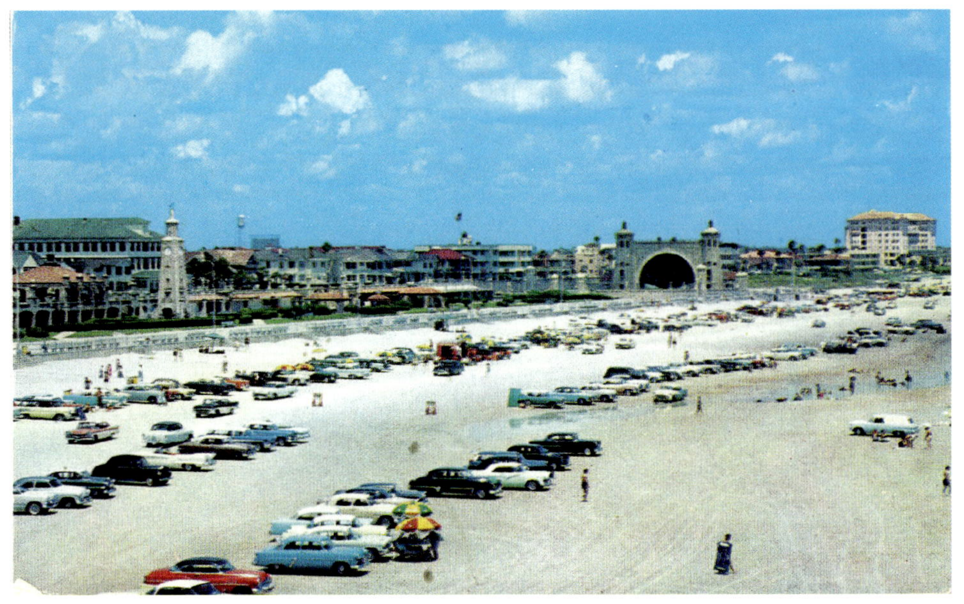

Daytona Beach, c. 1960

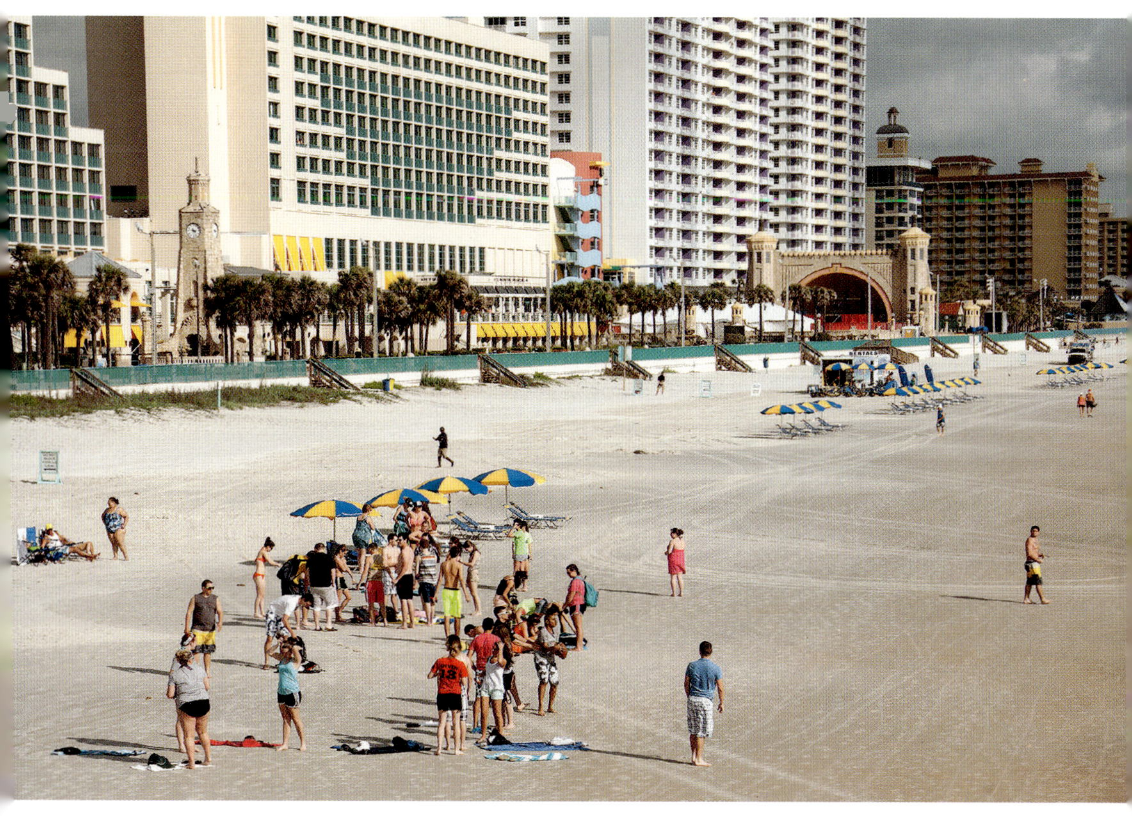

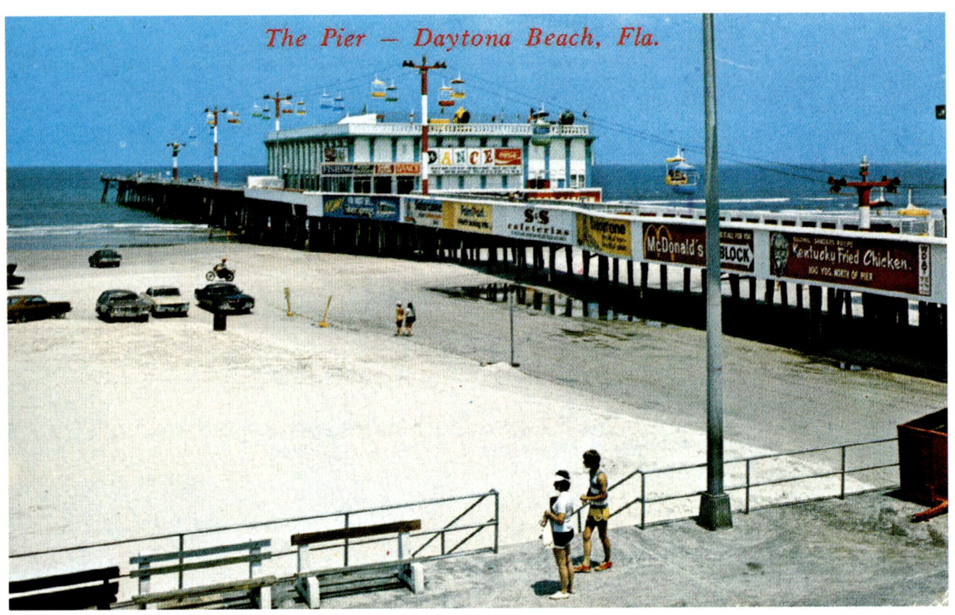

Daytona Beach, 1975

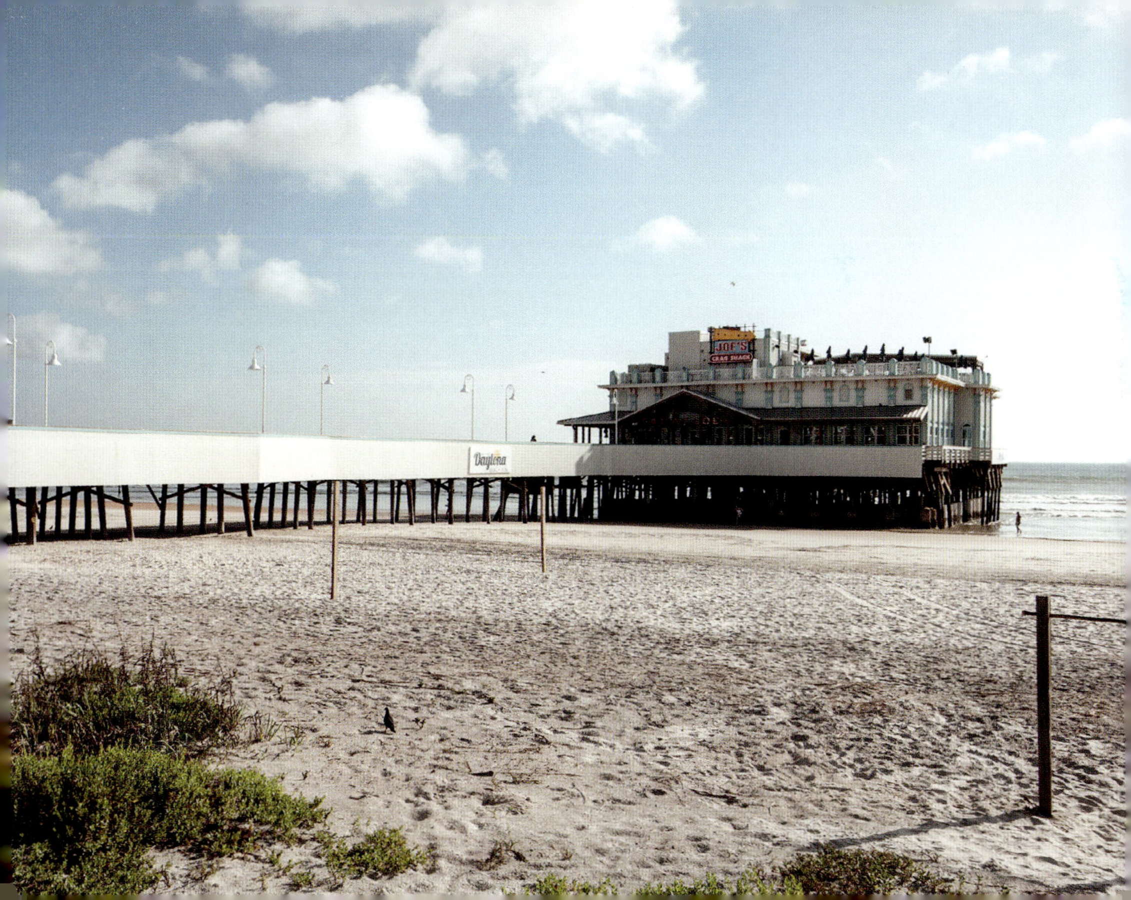
JOE'S
CRAB SHACK
Daytona

Daytona Beach, c. 1970

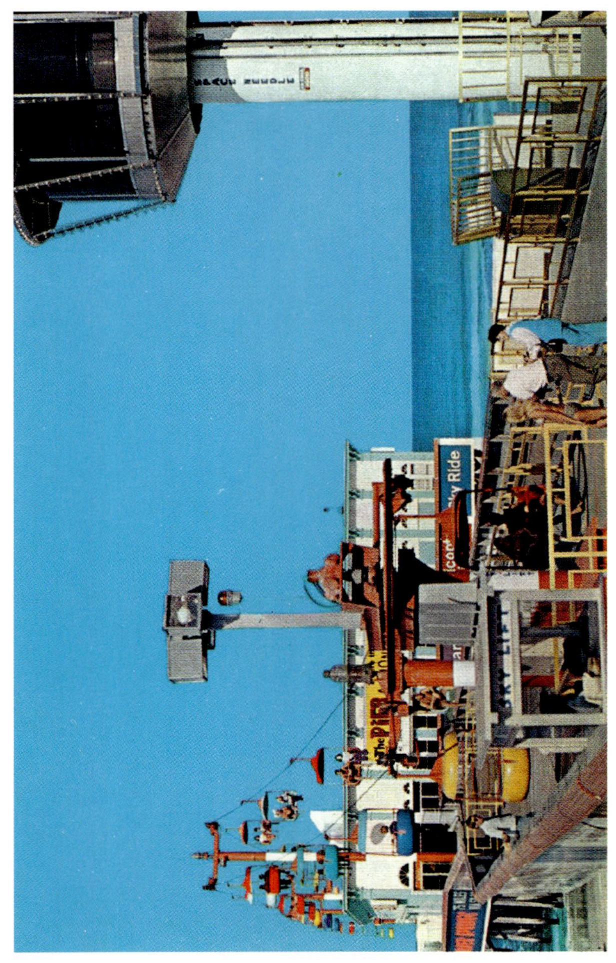

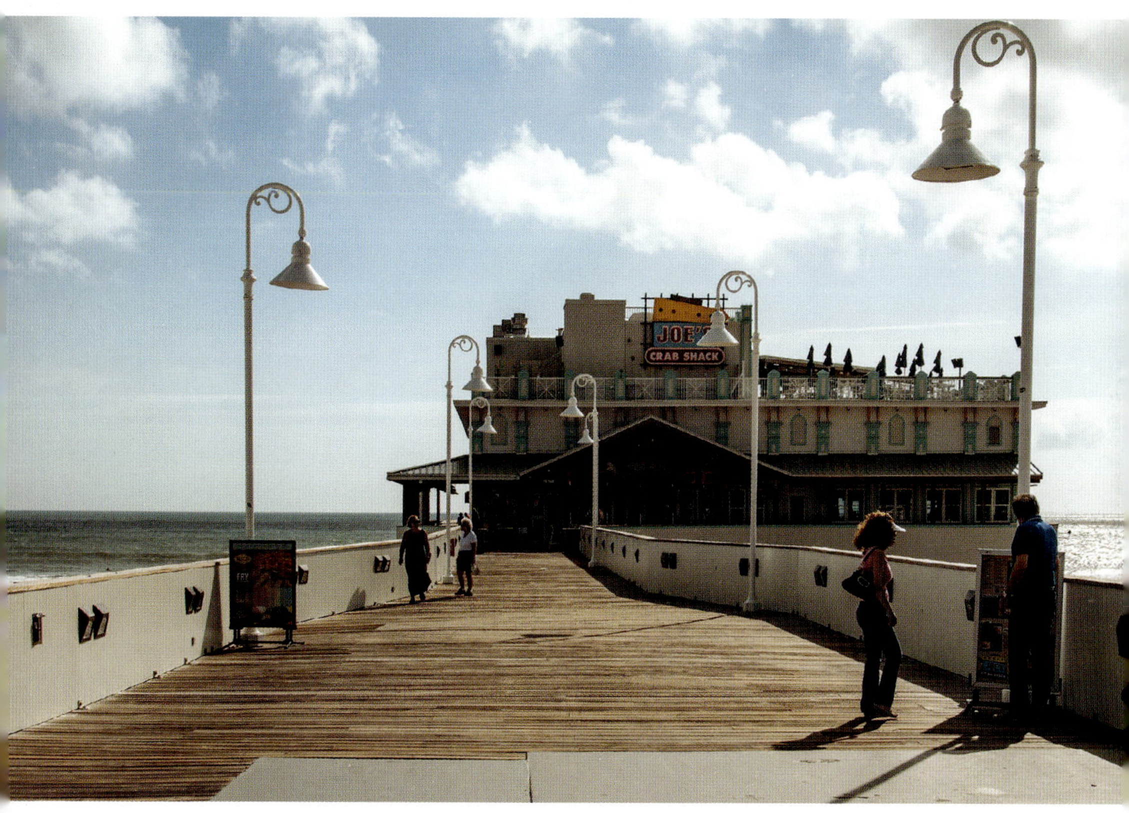
JOE'S
CRAB SHACK

Daytona Beach, 1904

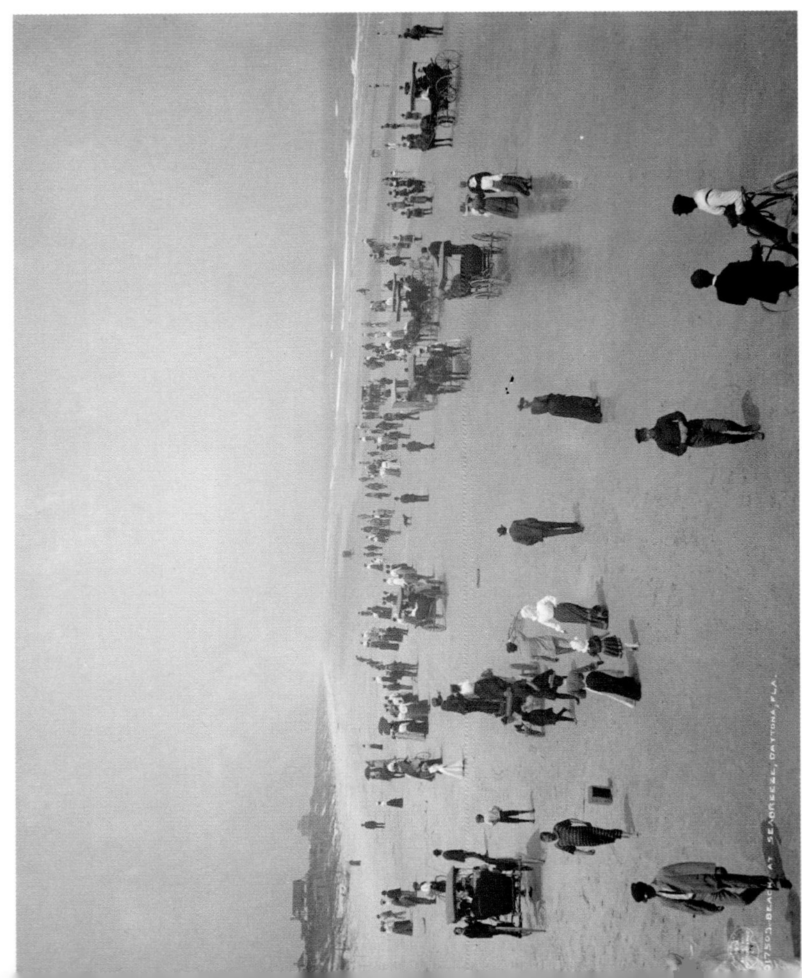

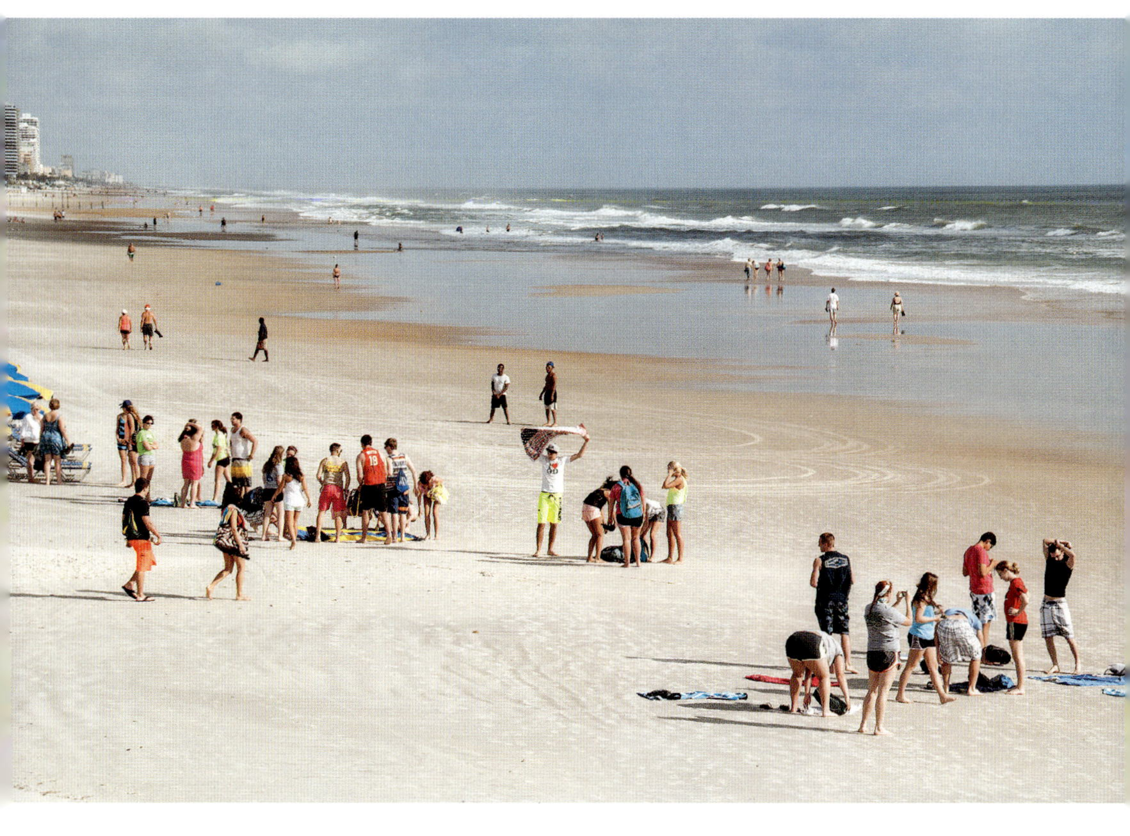

Beach Street, Daytona Beach, 1906

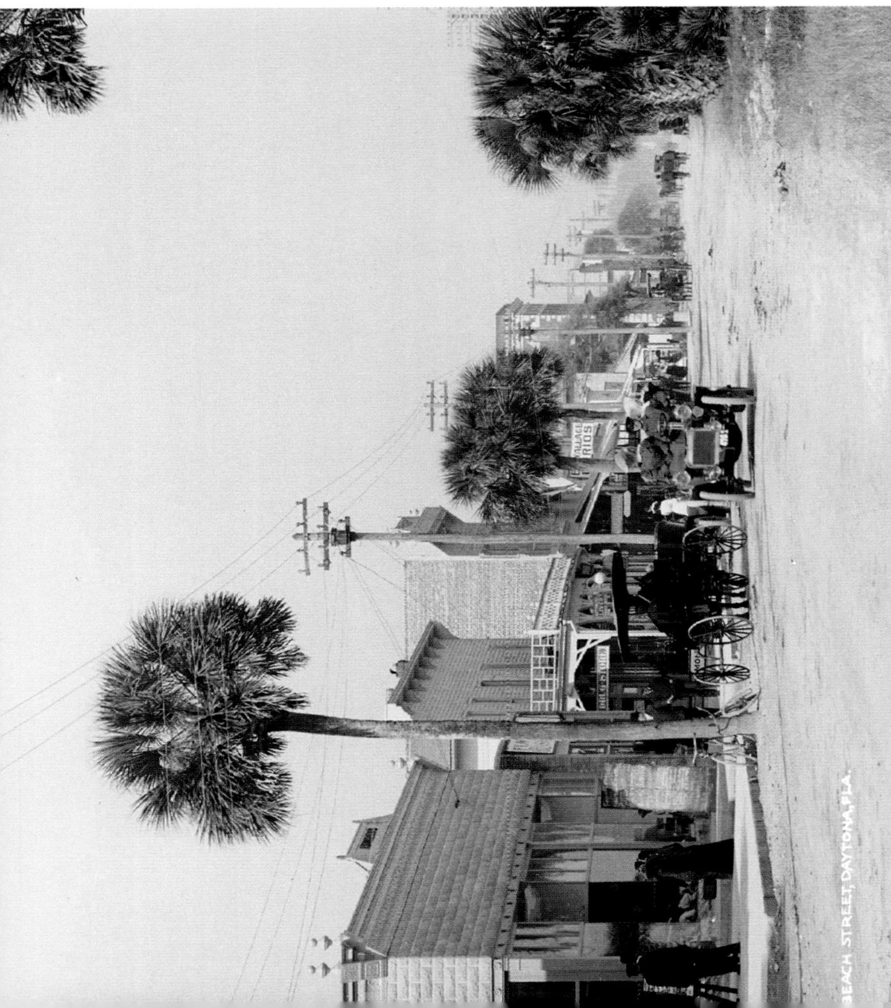

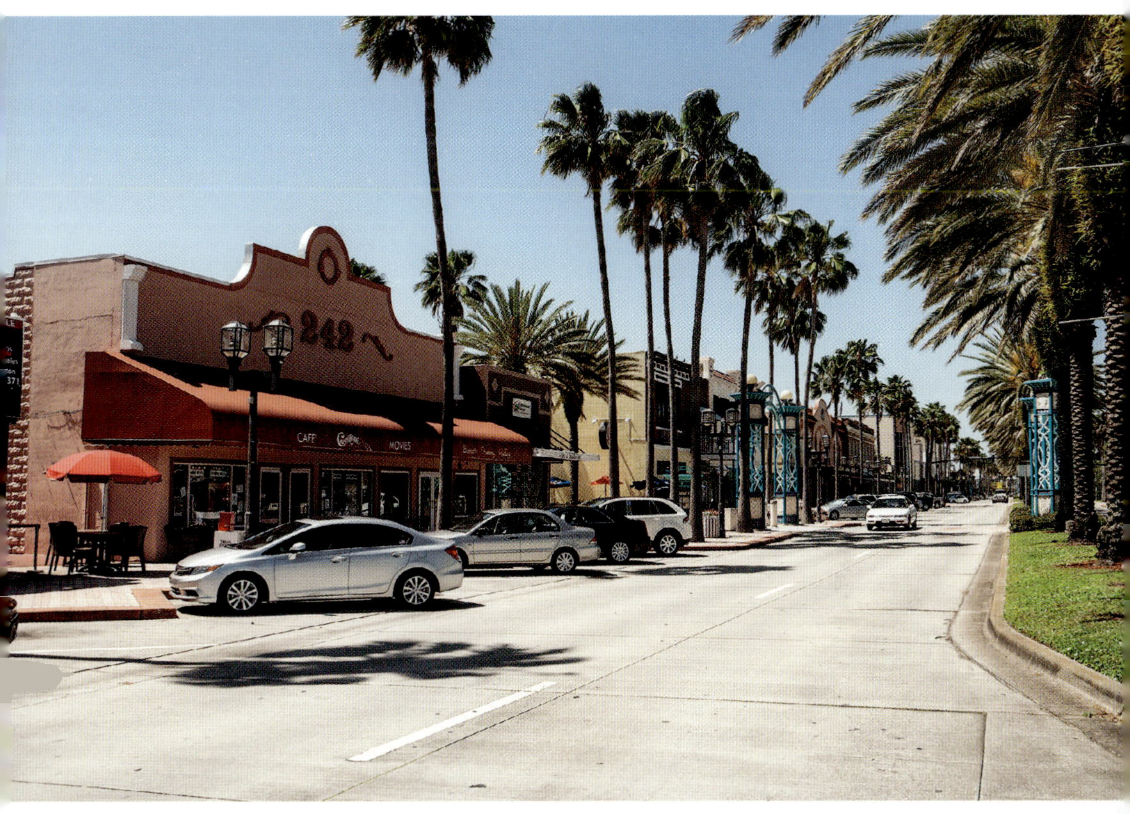
242
CAFE
MOVIES

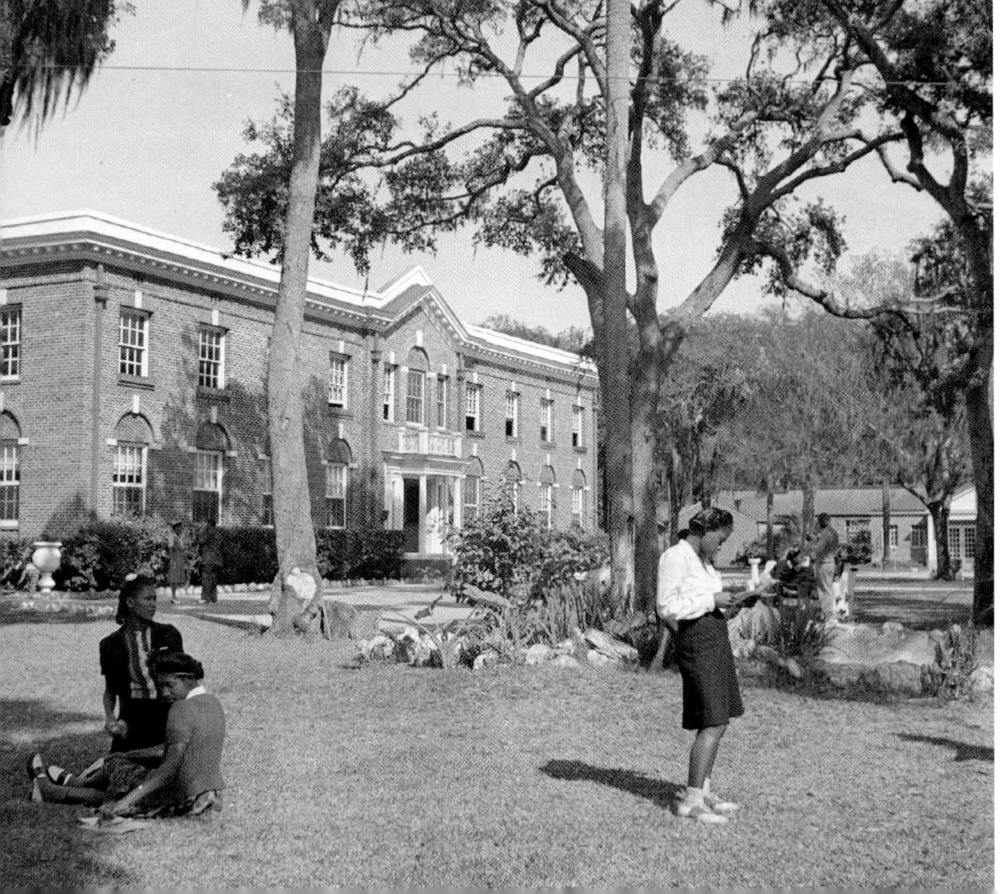

White Hall, Bethune-Cookman College, Daytona Beach, 1943

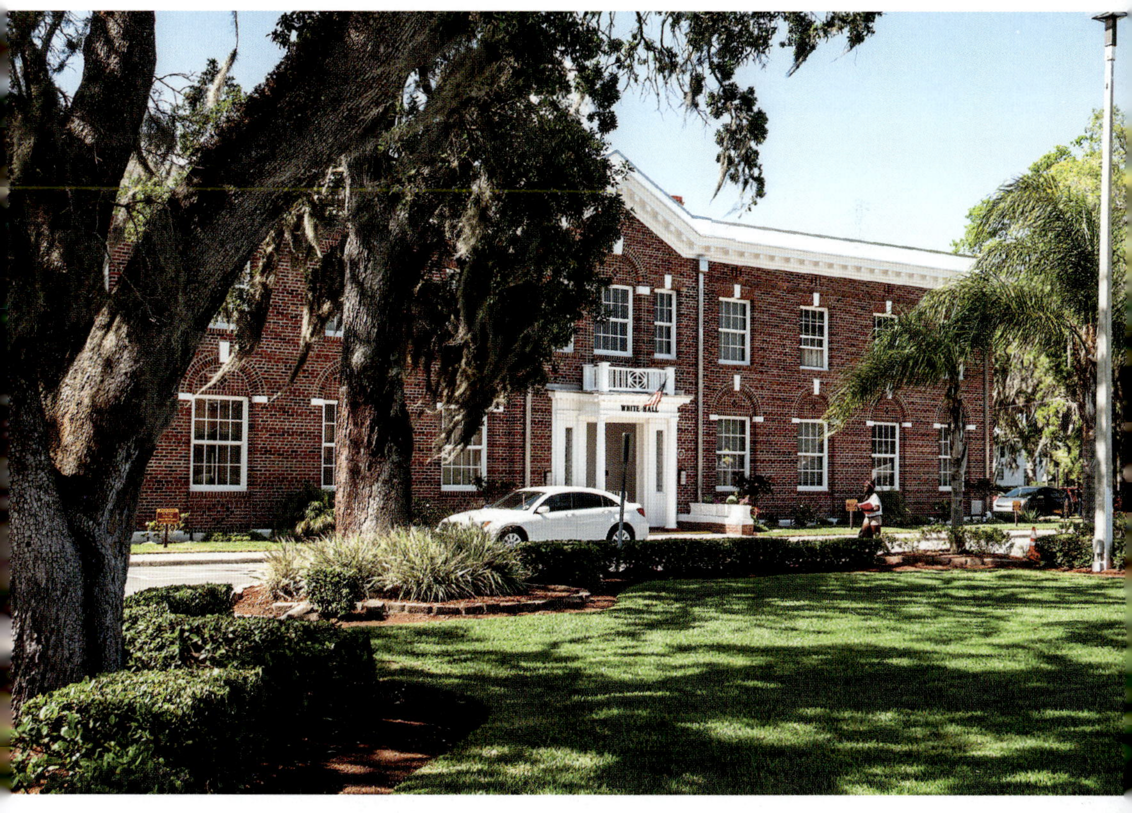
WHITE HALL

Mary McLeod Bethune at Bethune-Cookman College, Daytona Beach, 1943

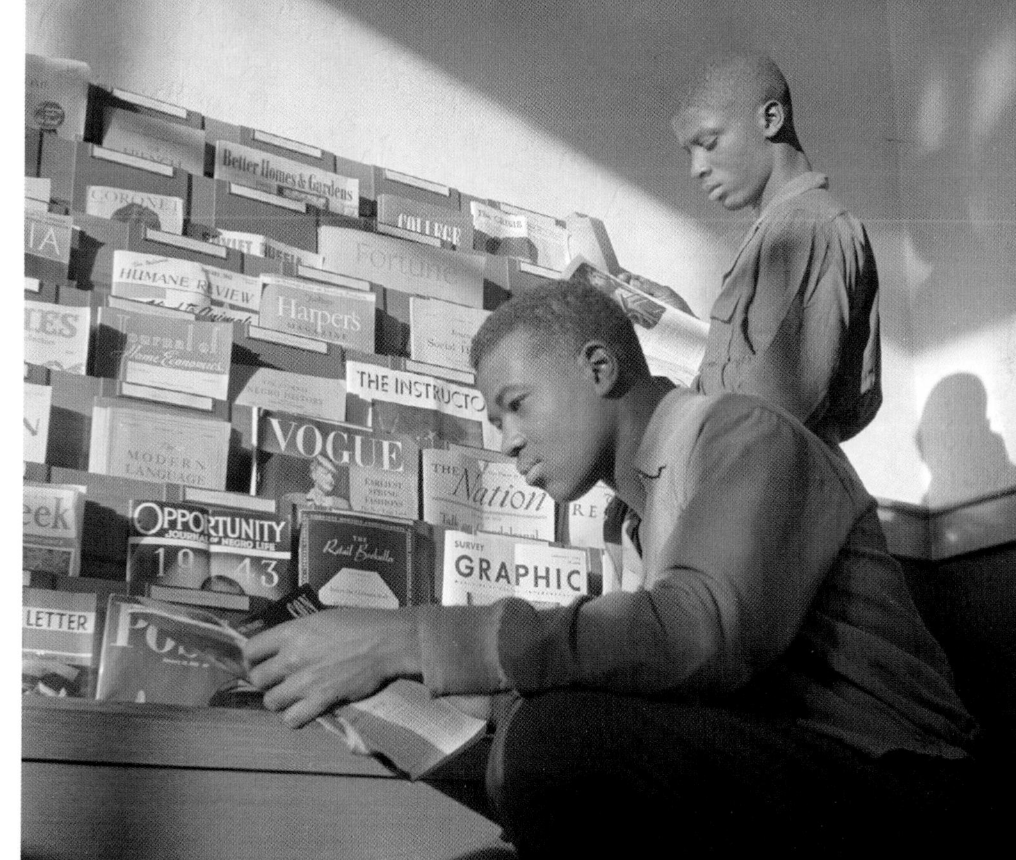

Bethune-Cookman College, Daytona Beach, 1943

Curtis Hall, Bethune-Cookman College, Daytona Beach, 1943

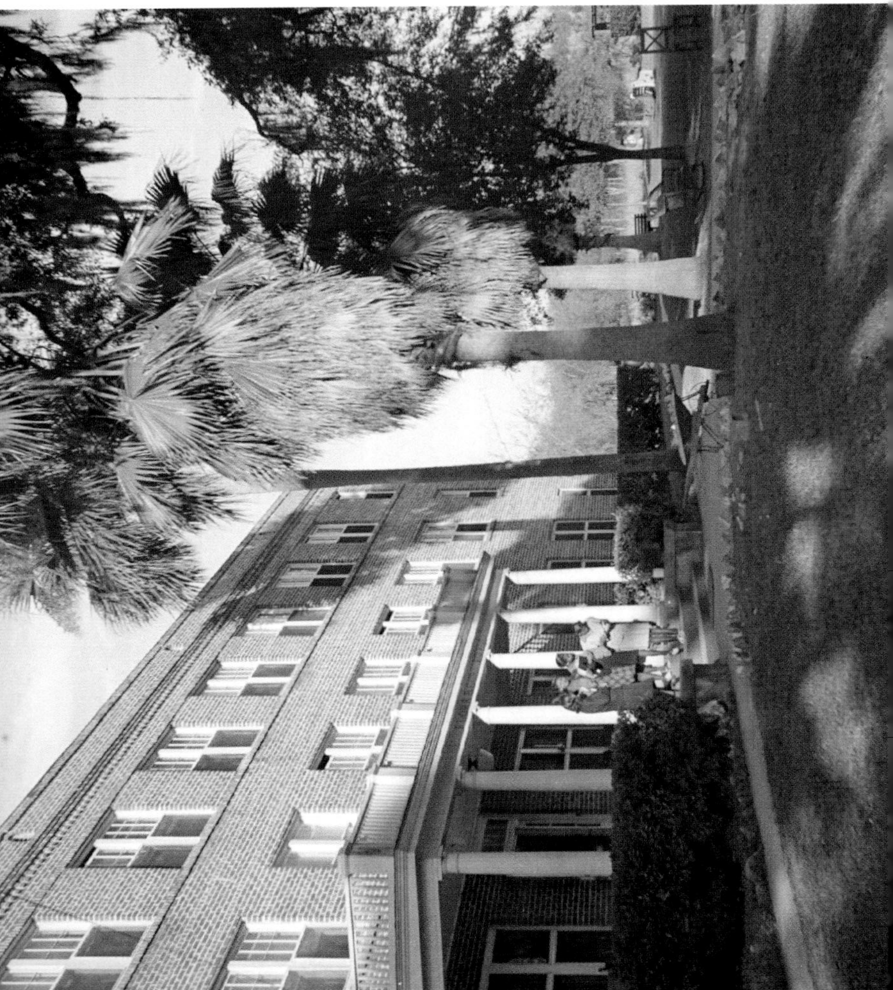

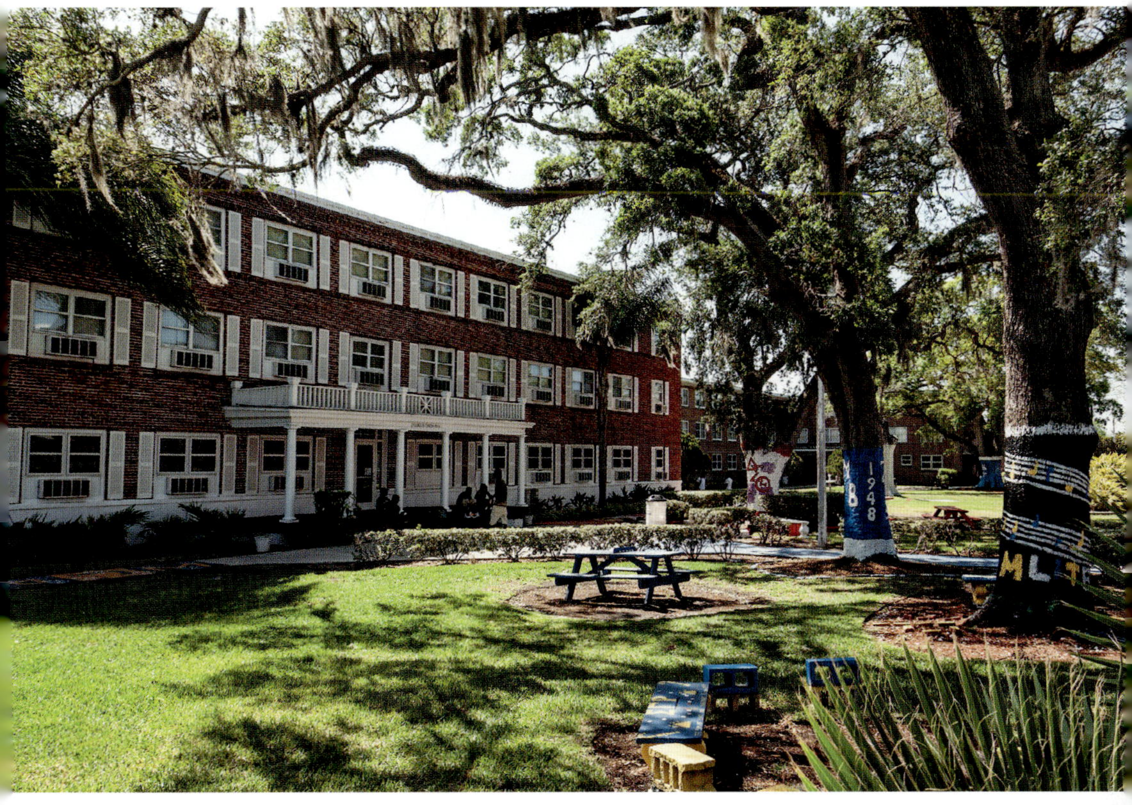
1948

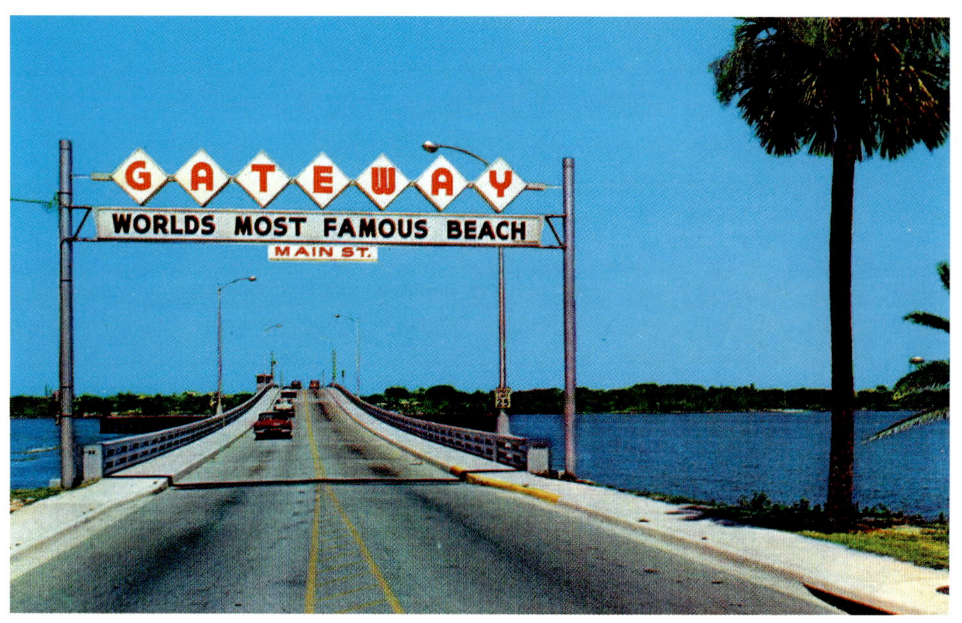

Main Street Bridge, Daytona Beach, c. 1965

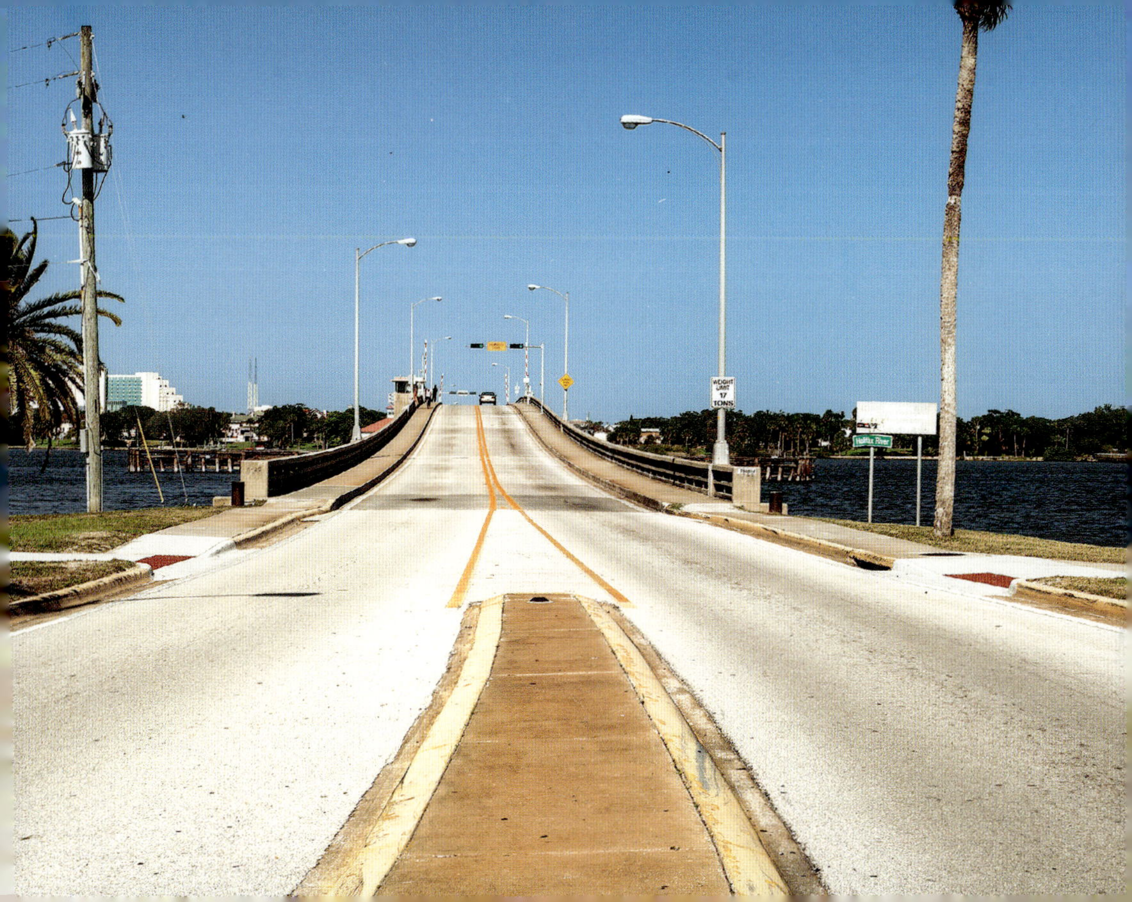
WEIGHT LIMIT 17 TONS
Halifax River

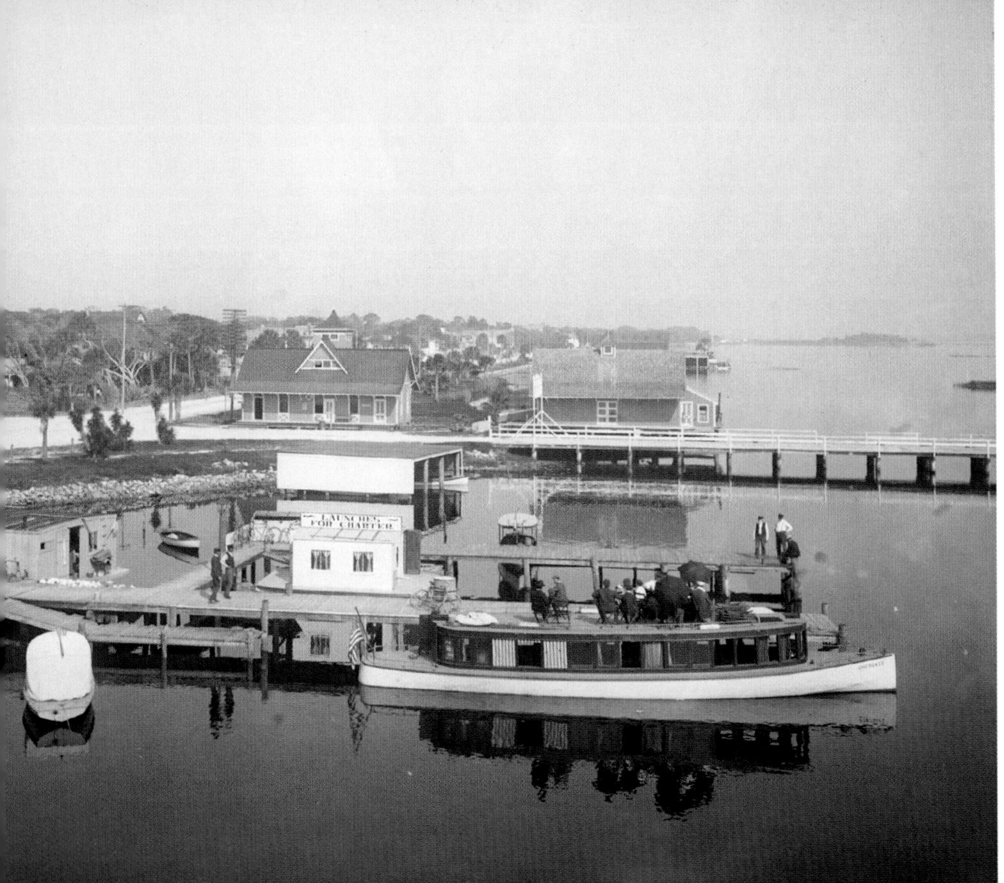

Waterfront, Daytona Beach, 1904

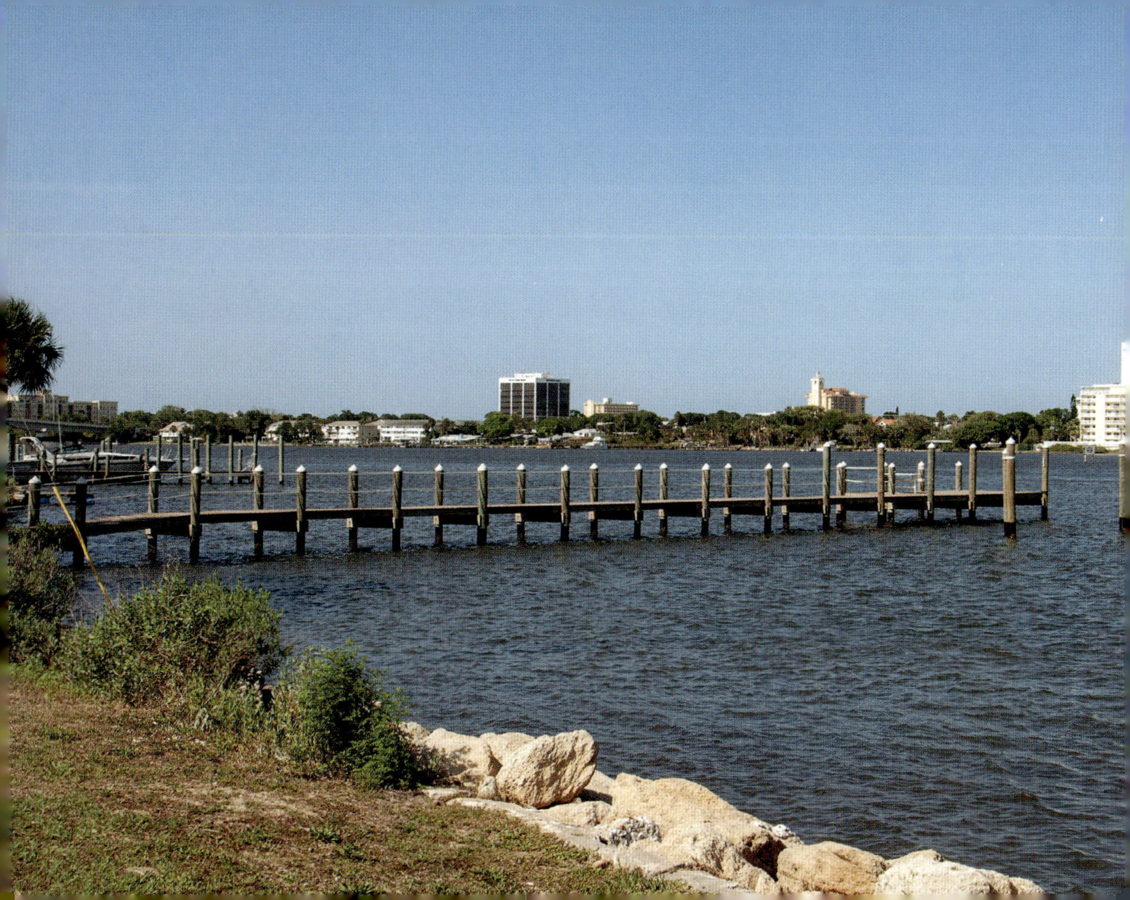

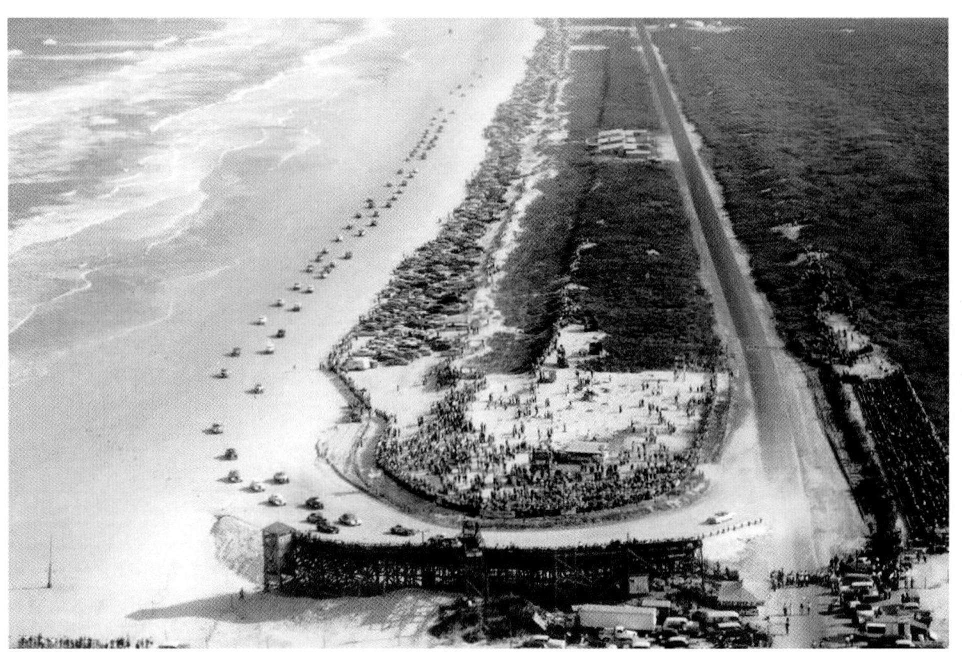

North Turn, Daytona Beach, 1958

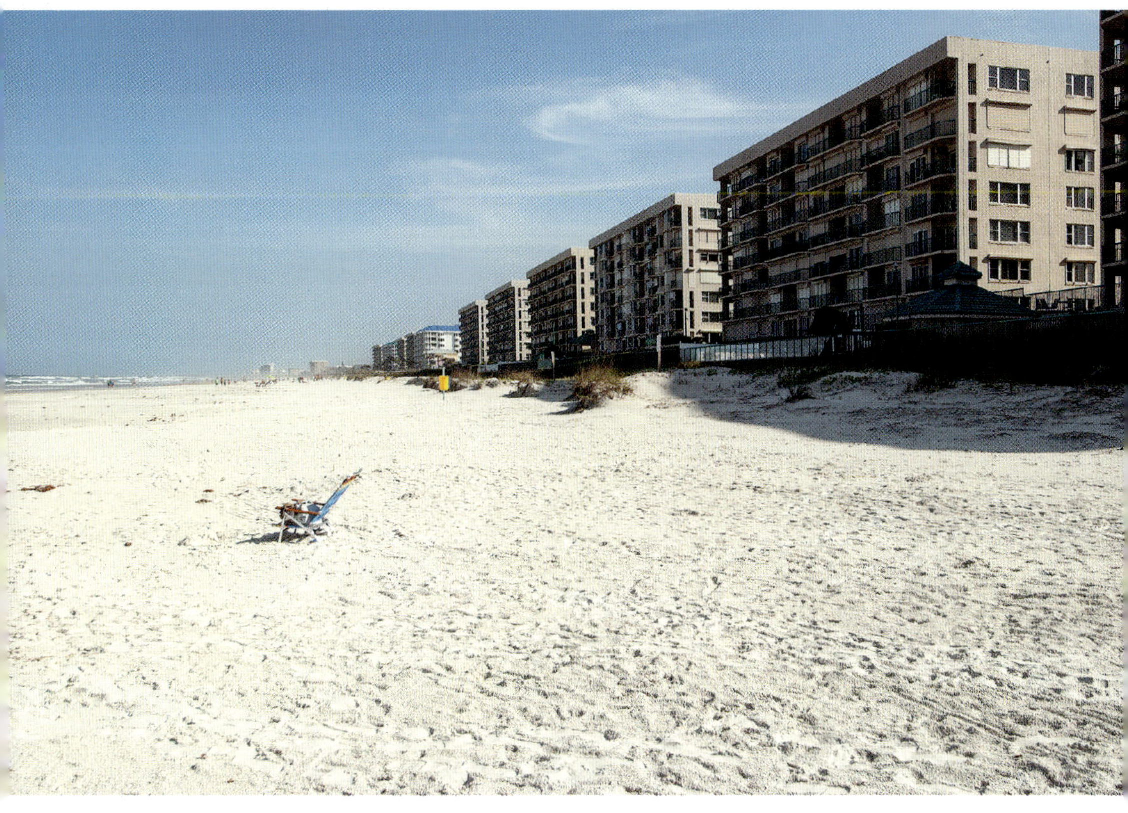

Daytona International Speedway, Daytona Beach, 1969

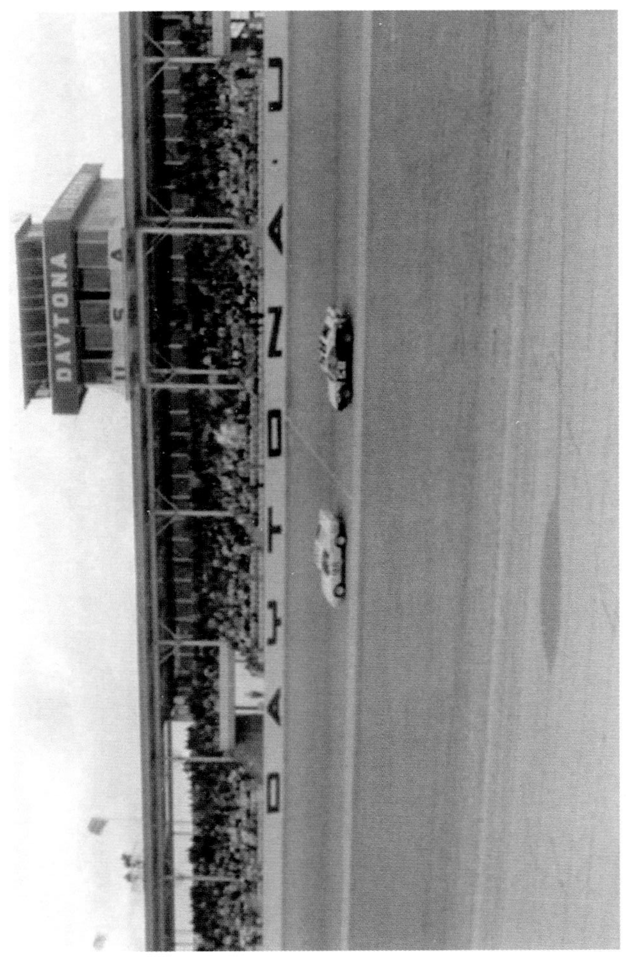

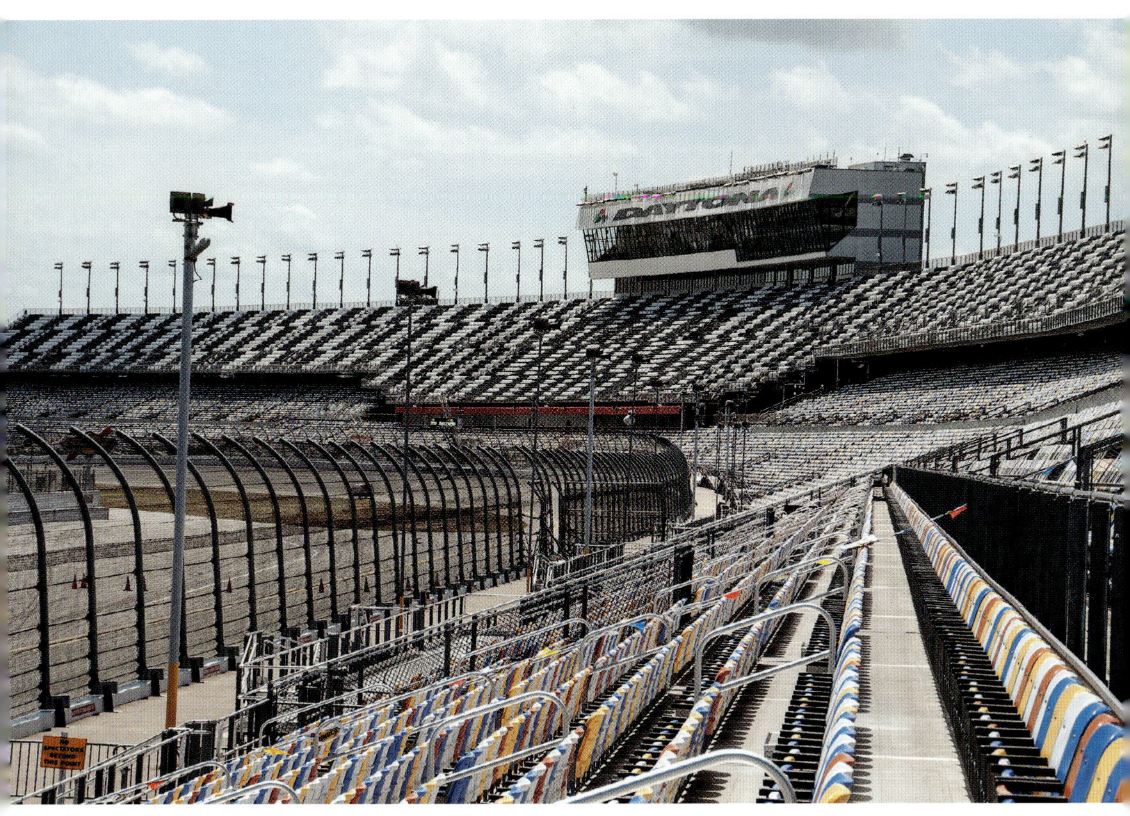
DAYTONA

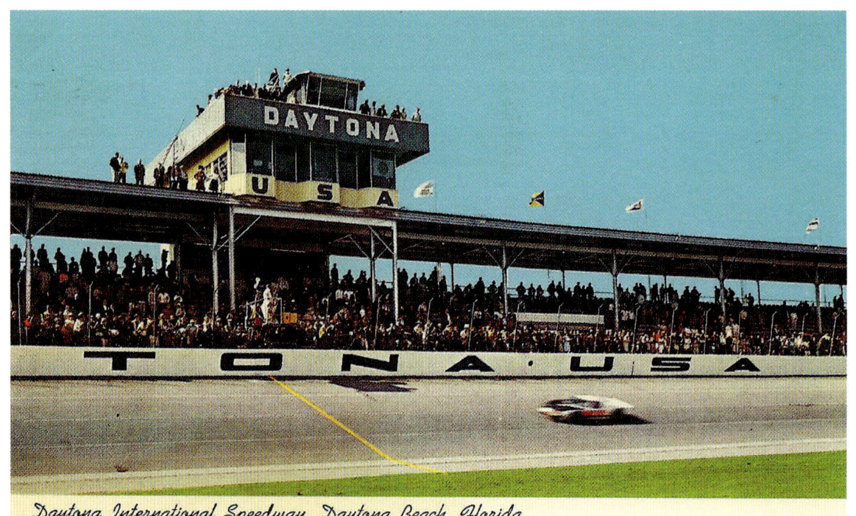

Daytona International Speedway, Daytona Beach, 1969

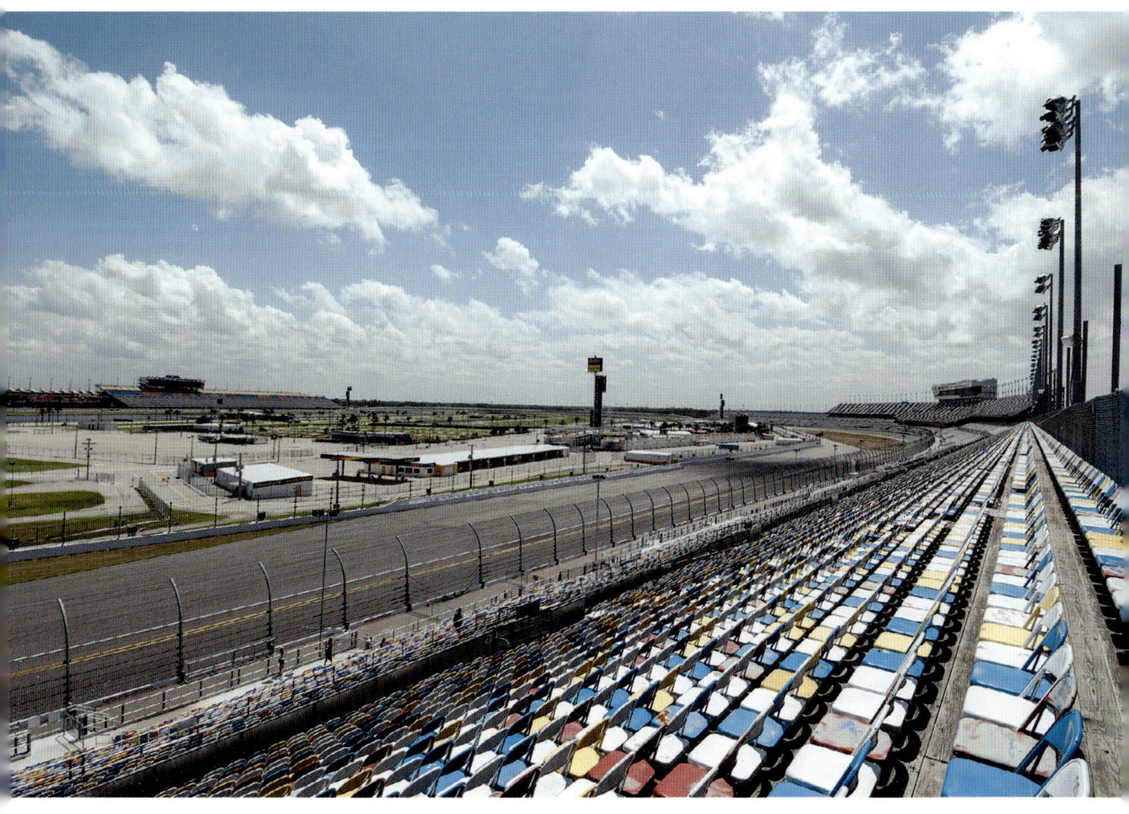

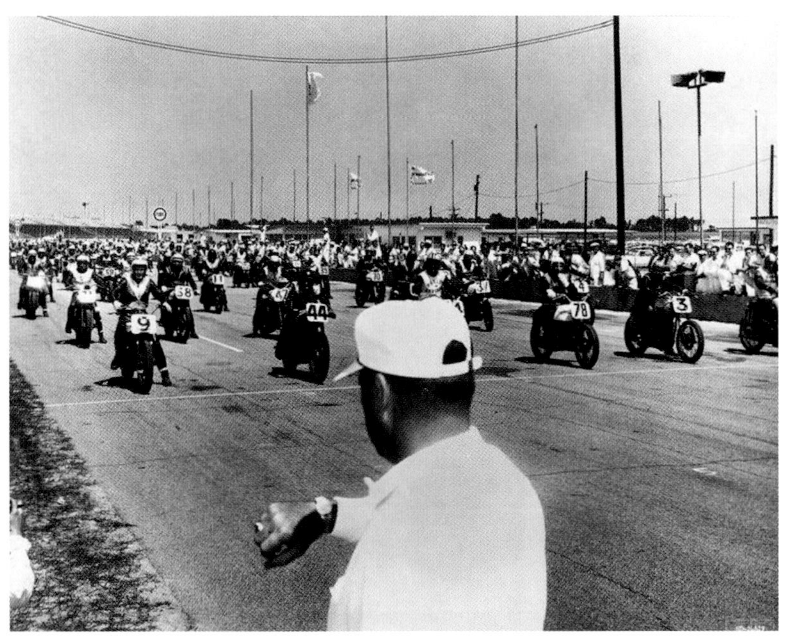

Daytona International Speedway, Daytona Beach, c. 1965

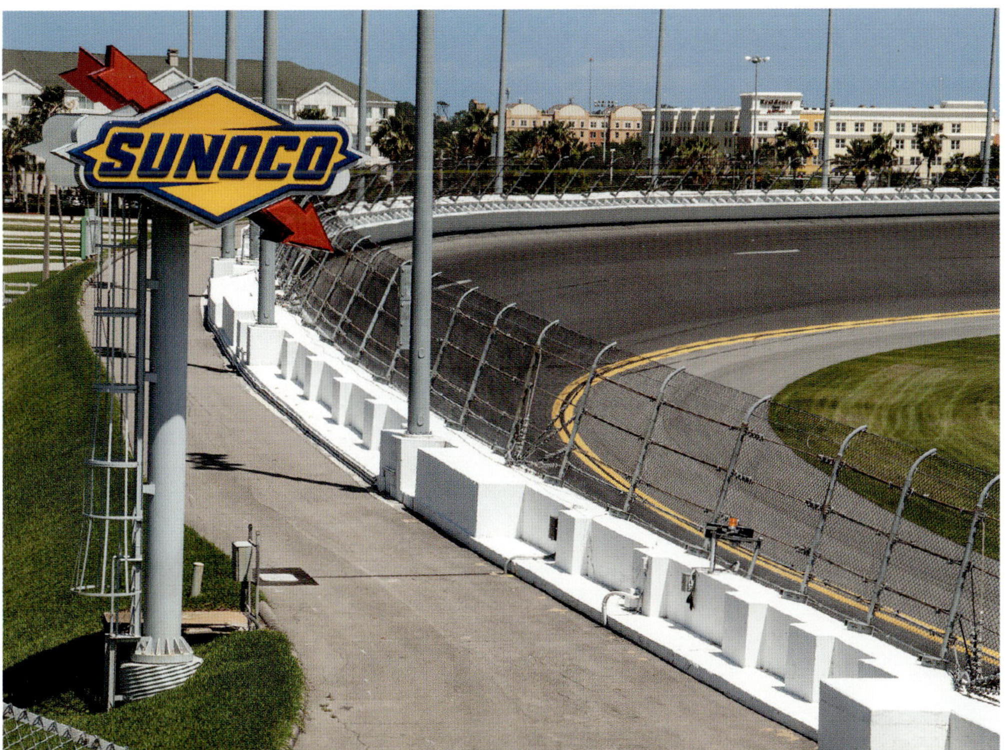
SUNOCO

Ormond Beach, c. 1885

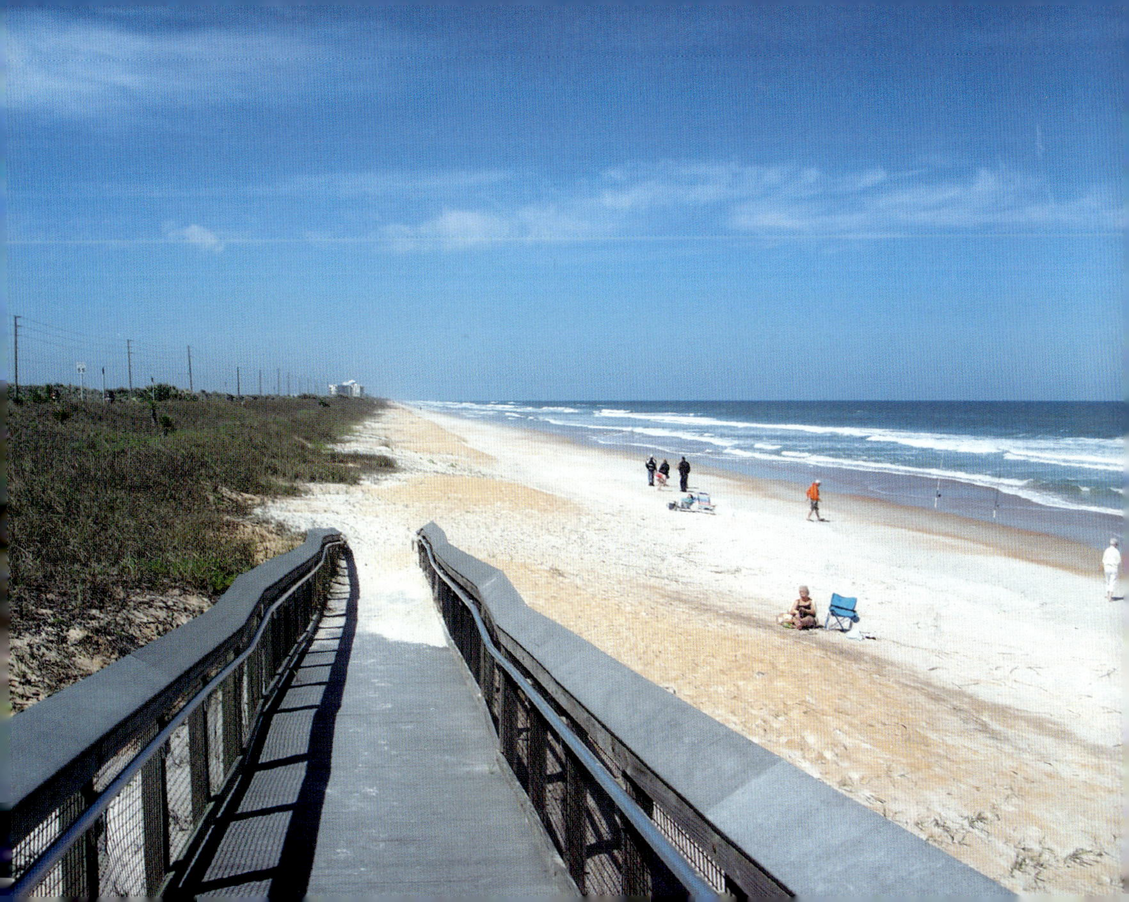

Tomoka State Park, c. 1895

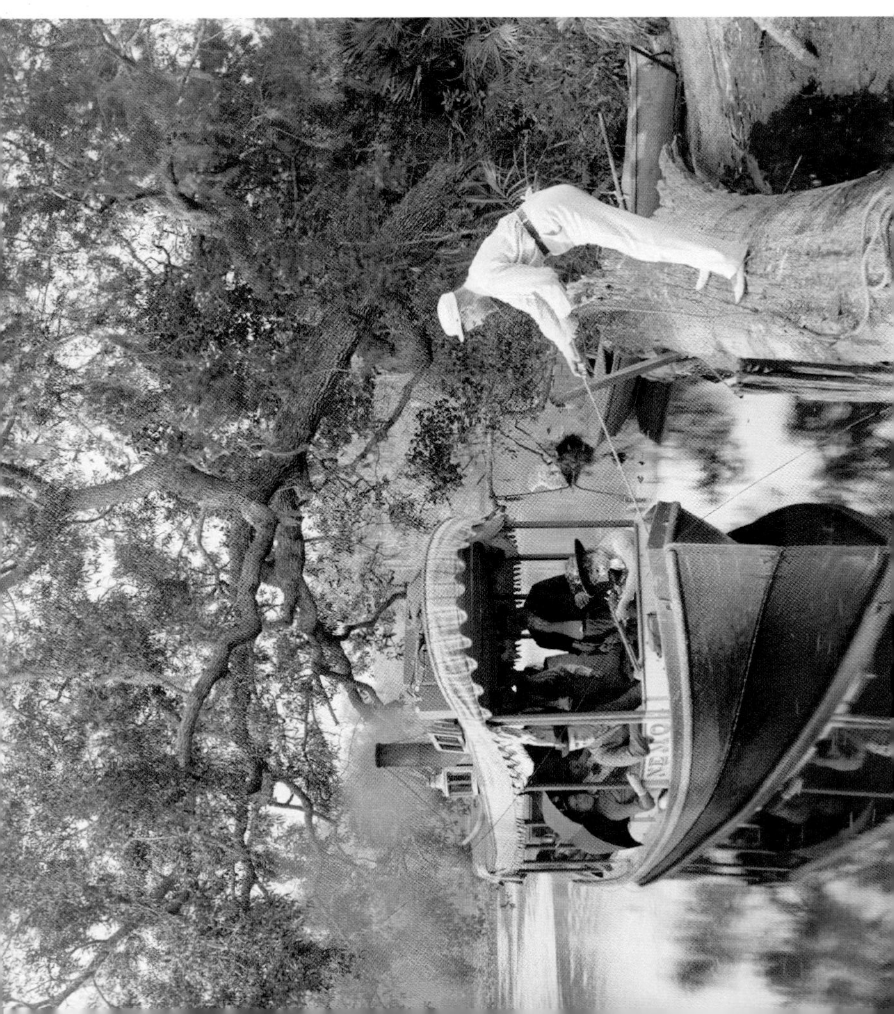

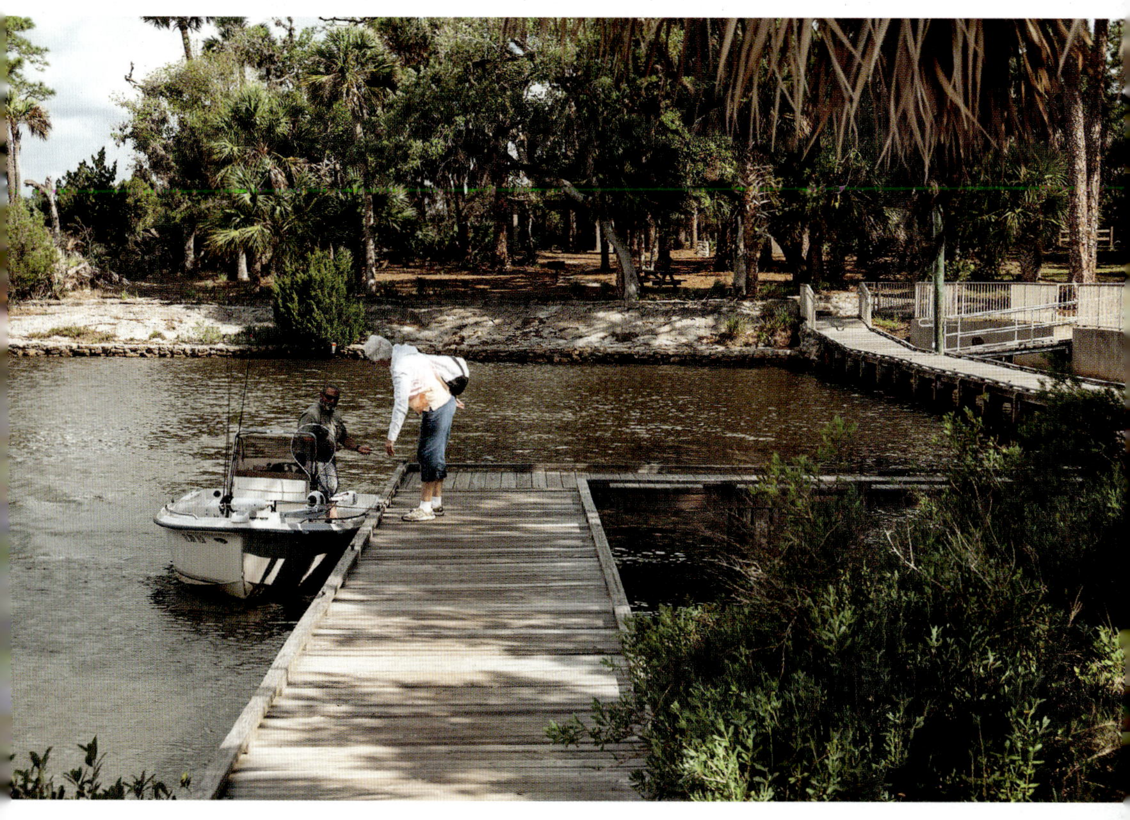

Tomoka State Park, c. 1895

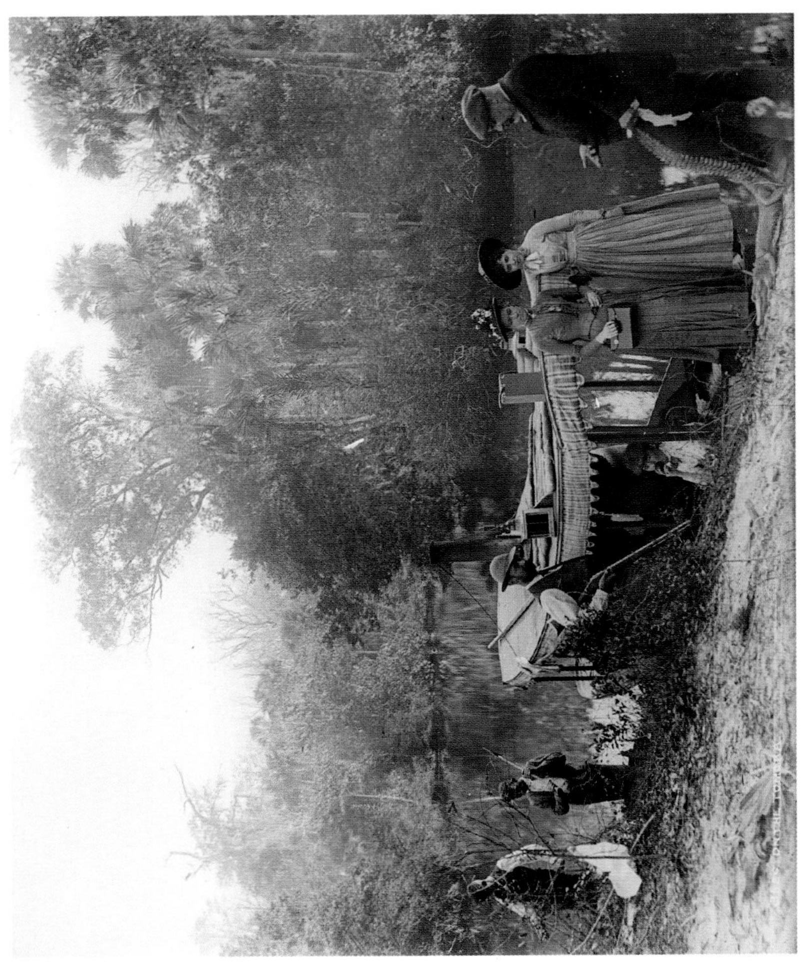

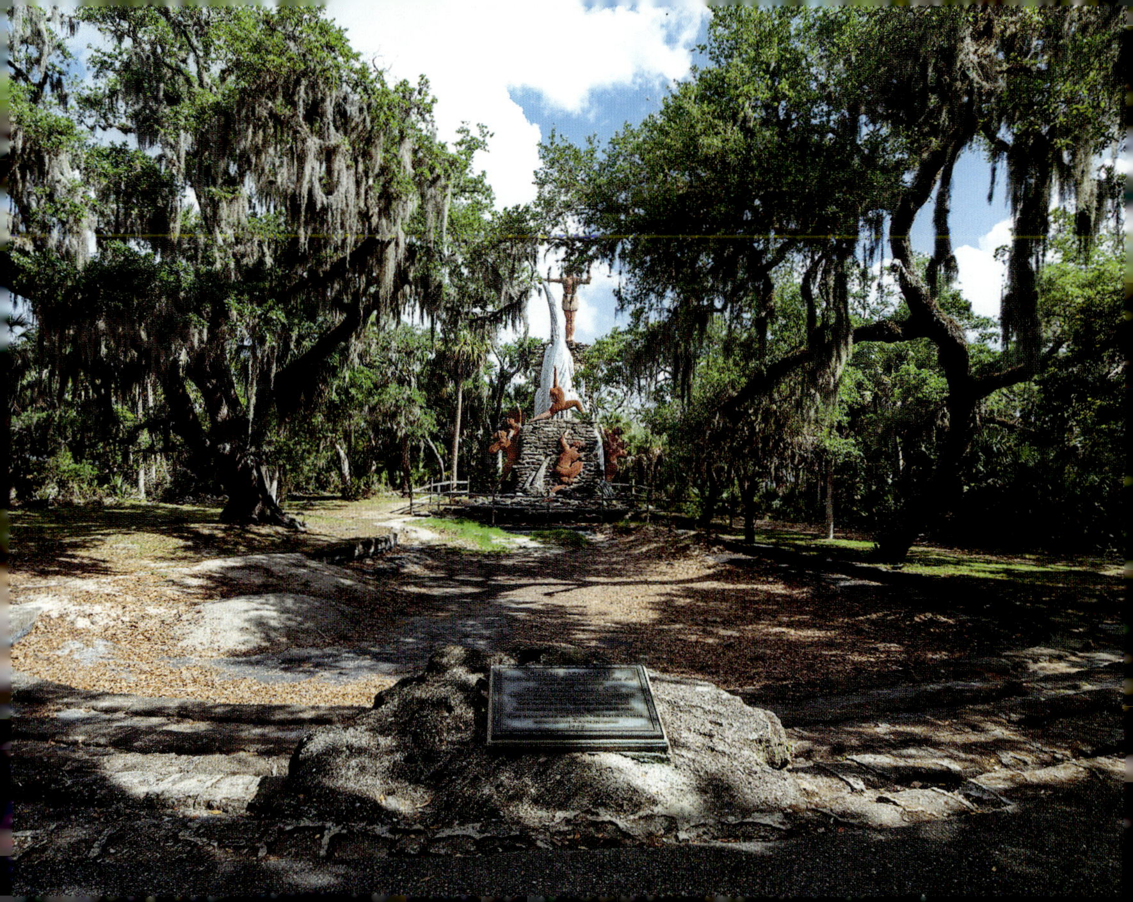

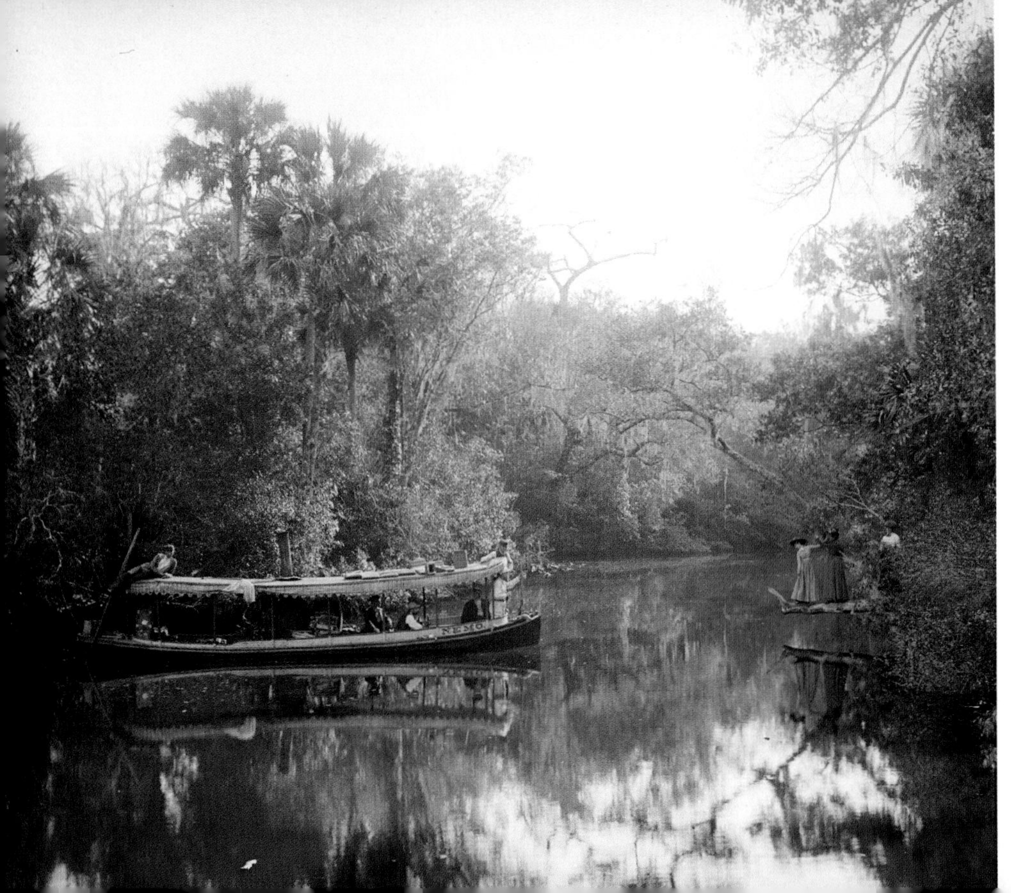

Tomoka State Park, c. 1895

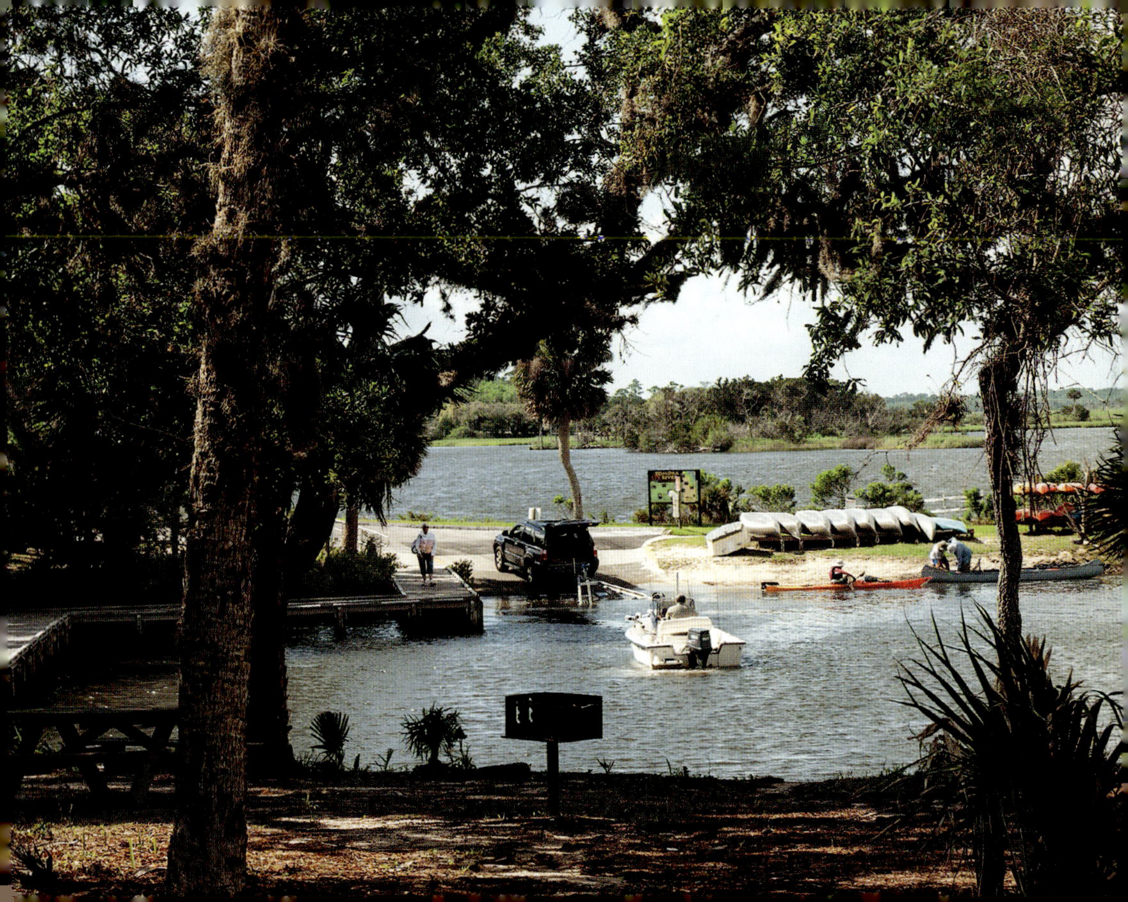

Tomoka State Park, c. 1895

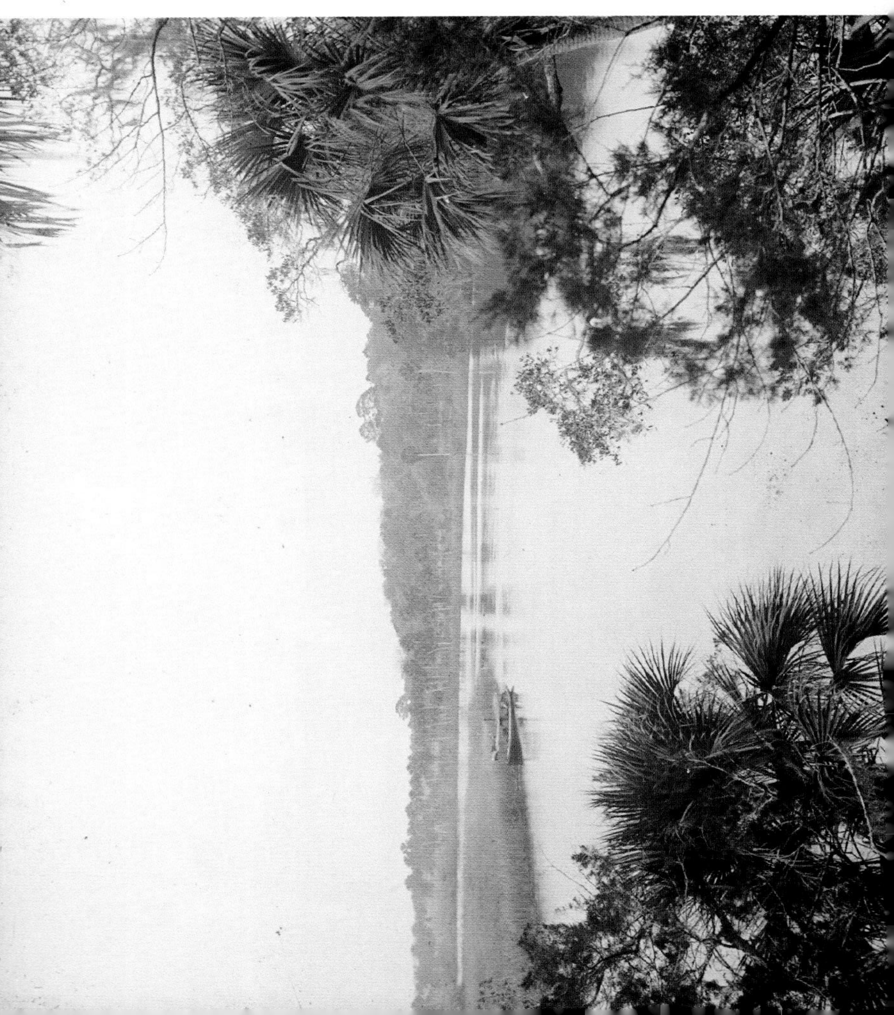

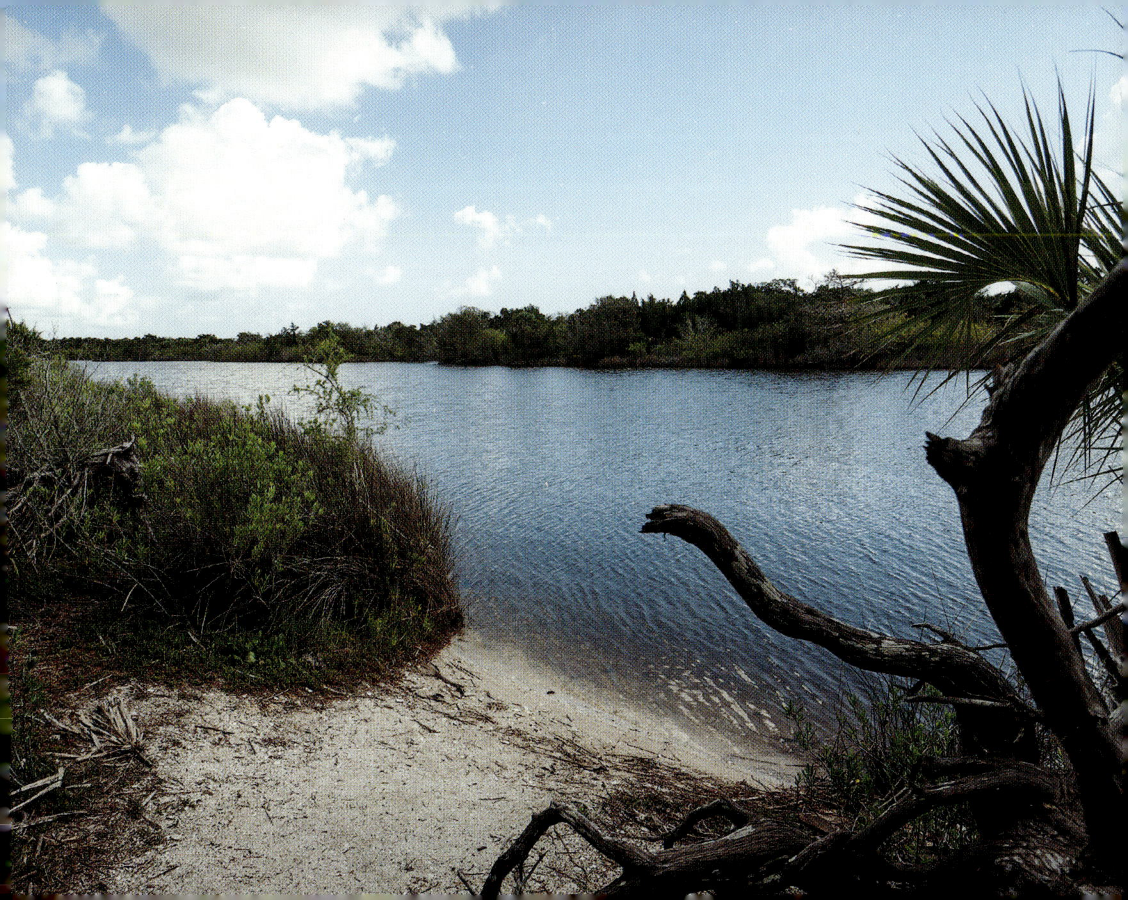

City Gates, St. Augustine, c. 1895

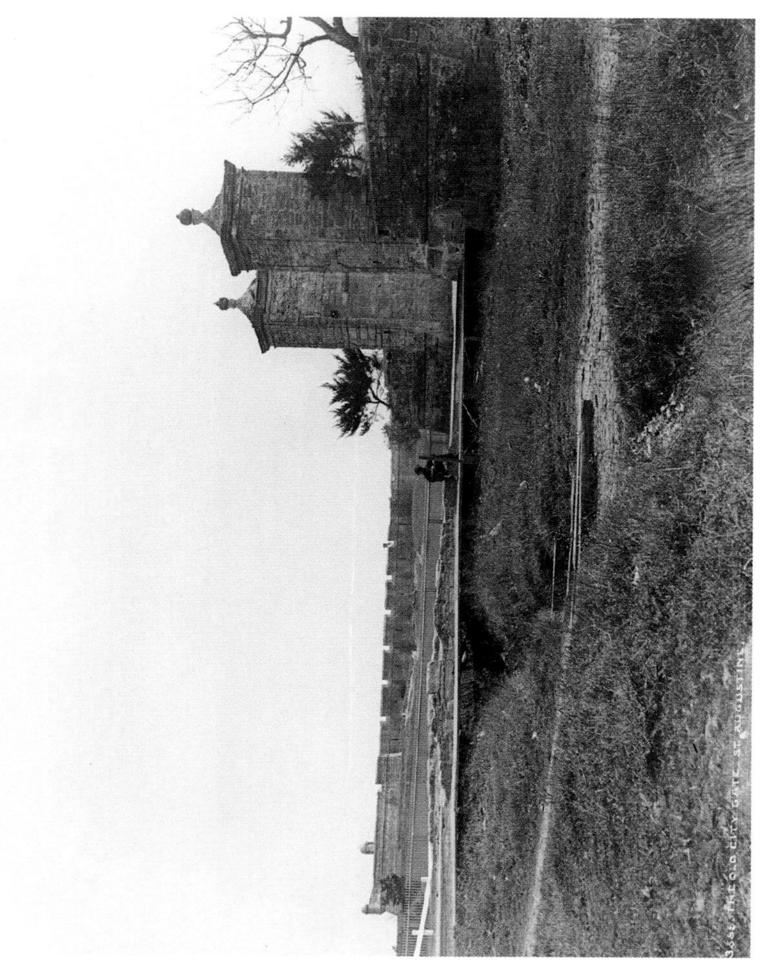

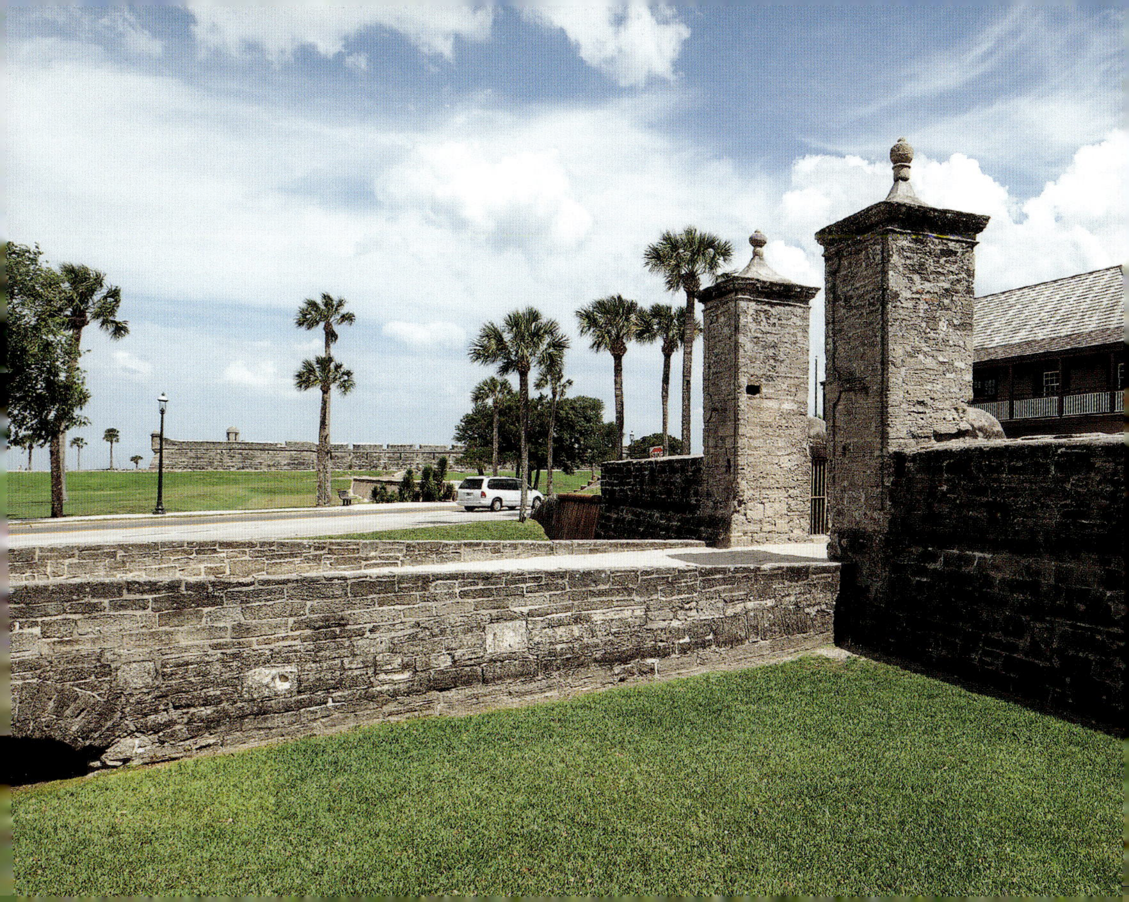

City Gates, St. Augustine, c. 1895

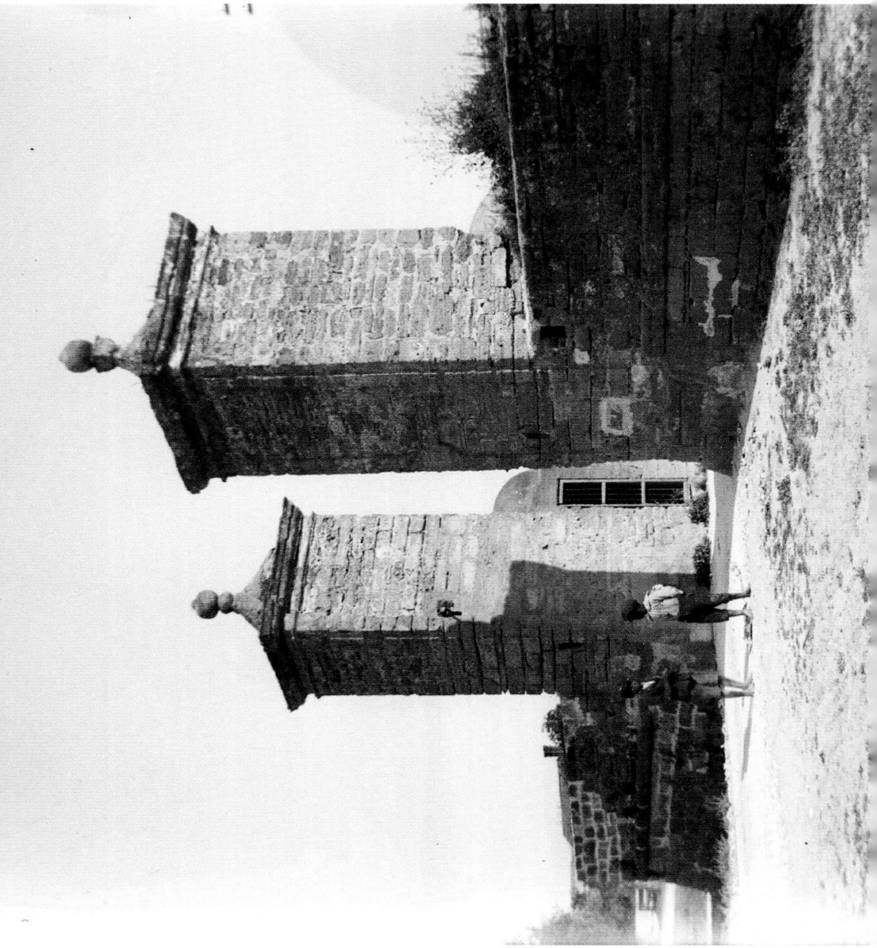

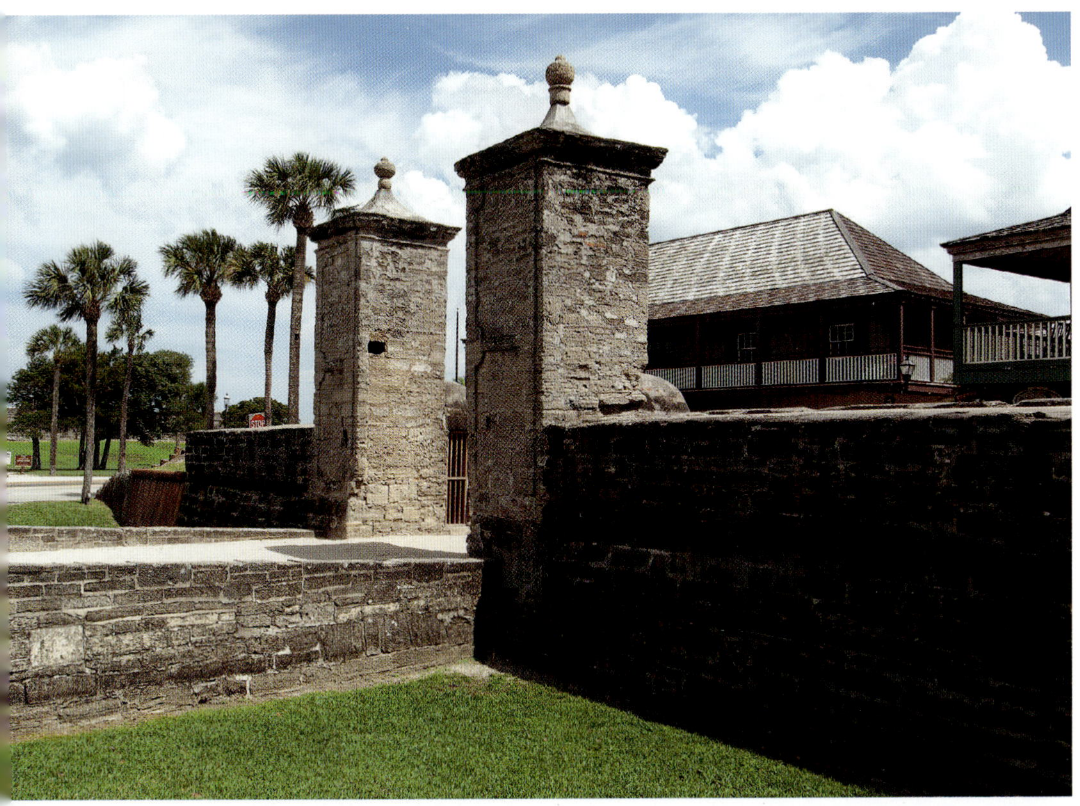

City Gates, St. Augustine, c. 1865

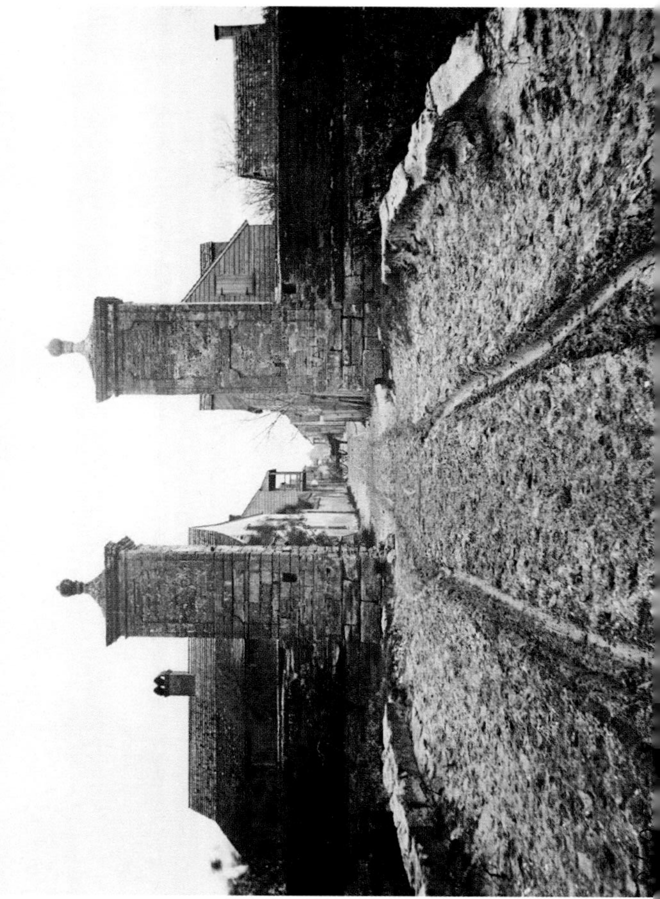

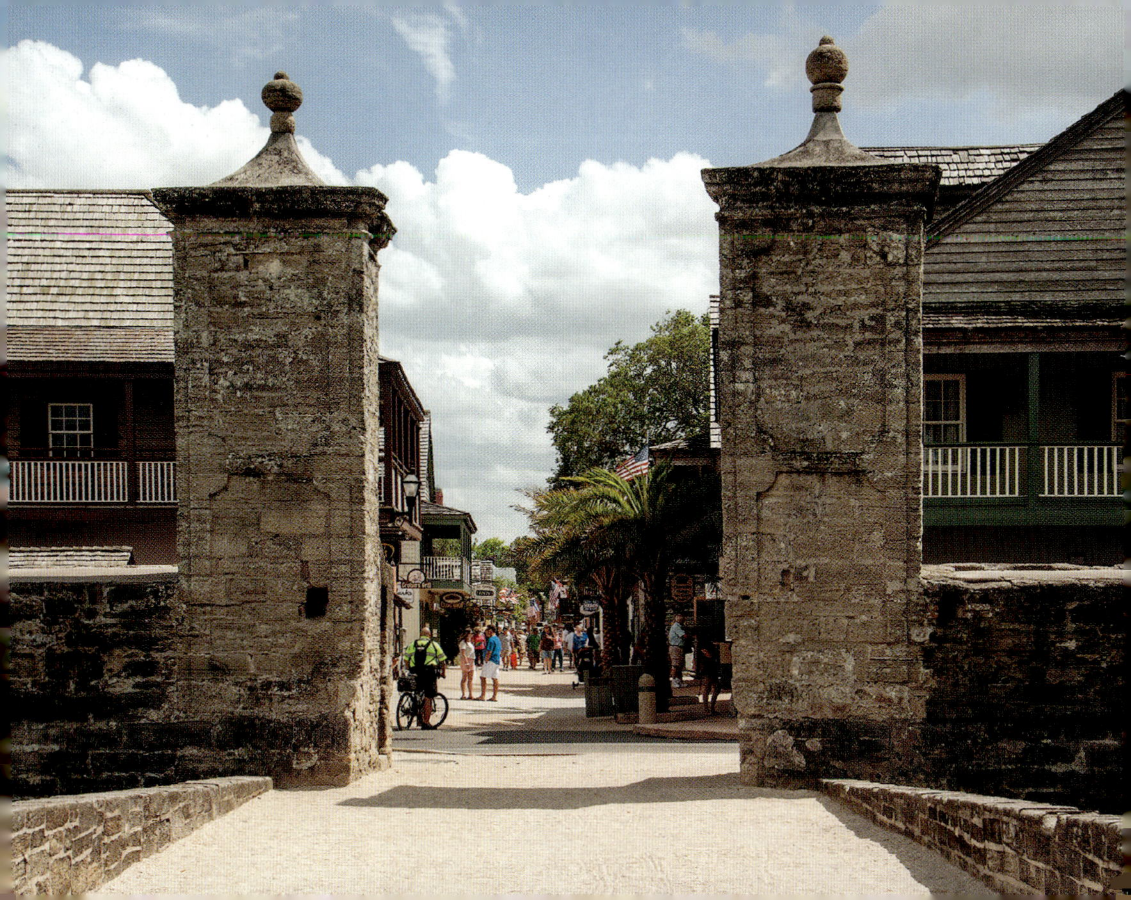

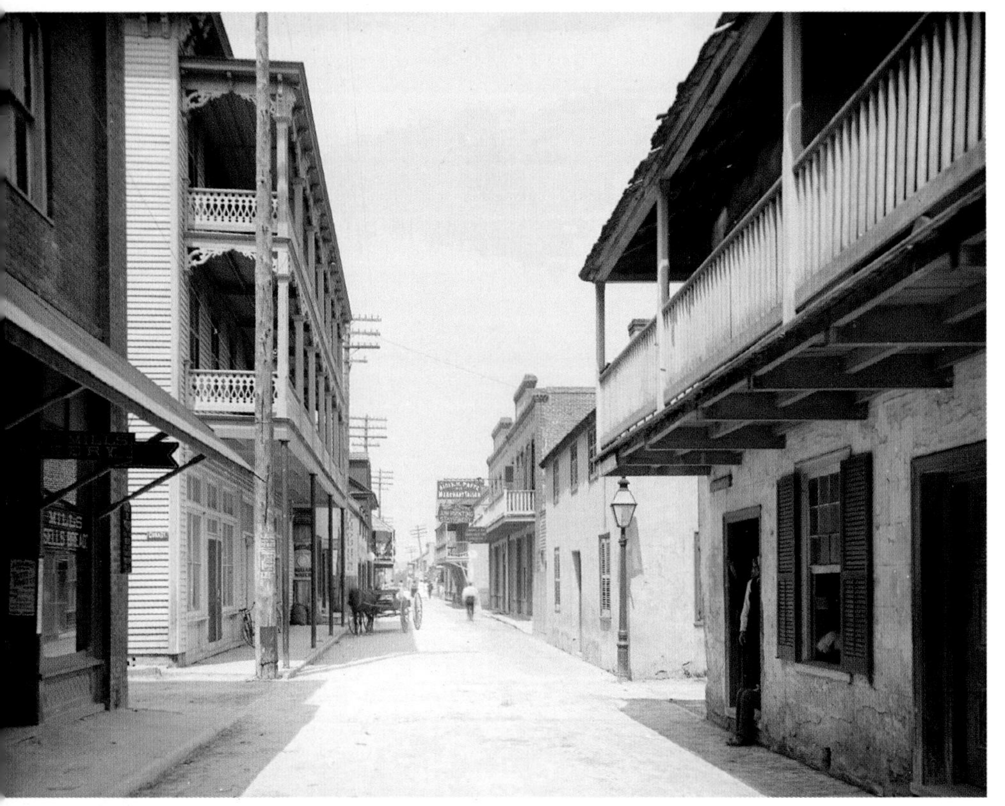

St. George Street, St. Augustine, c. 1905

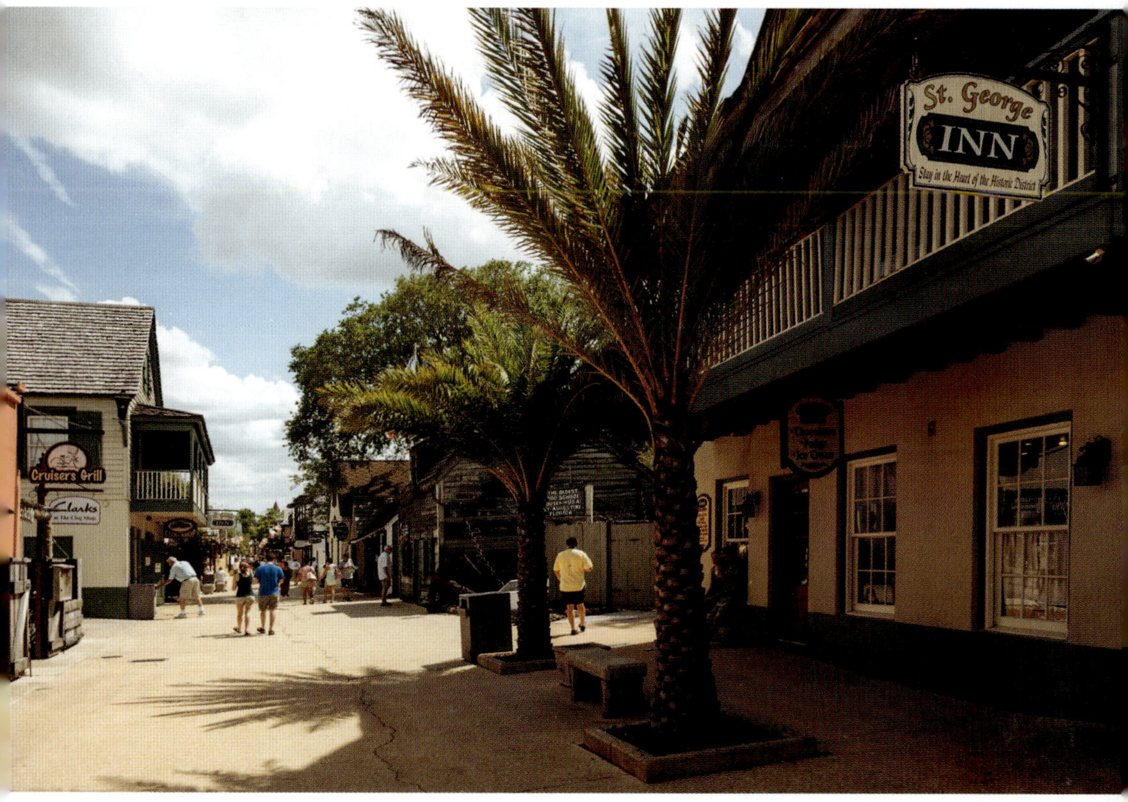
St. George
INN
Stay in the Heart of the Historic District
Cruisers Grill
Clarks

St. George Street, St. Augustine, c. 1895

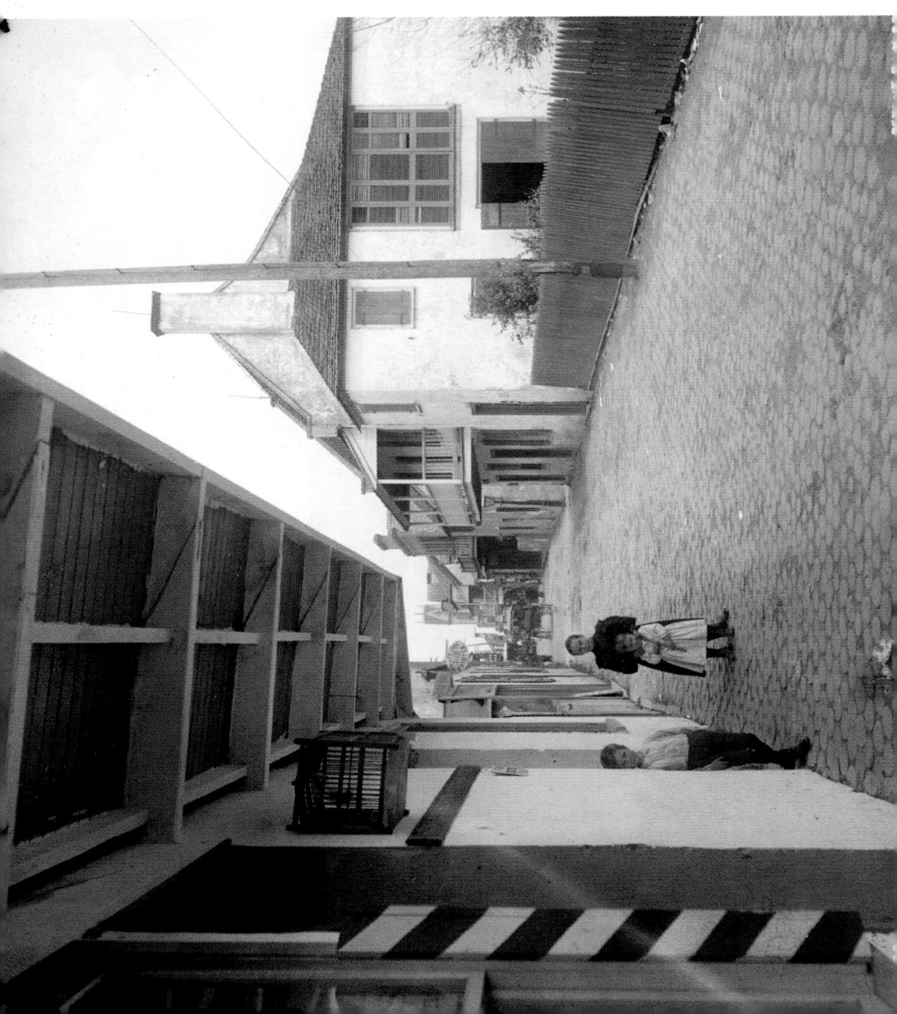

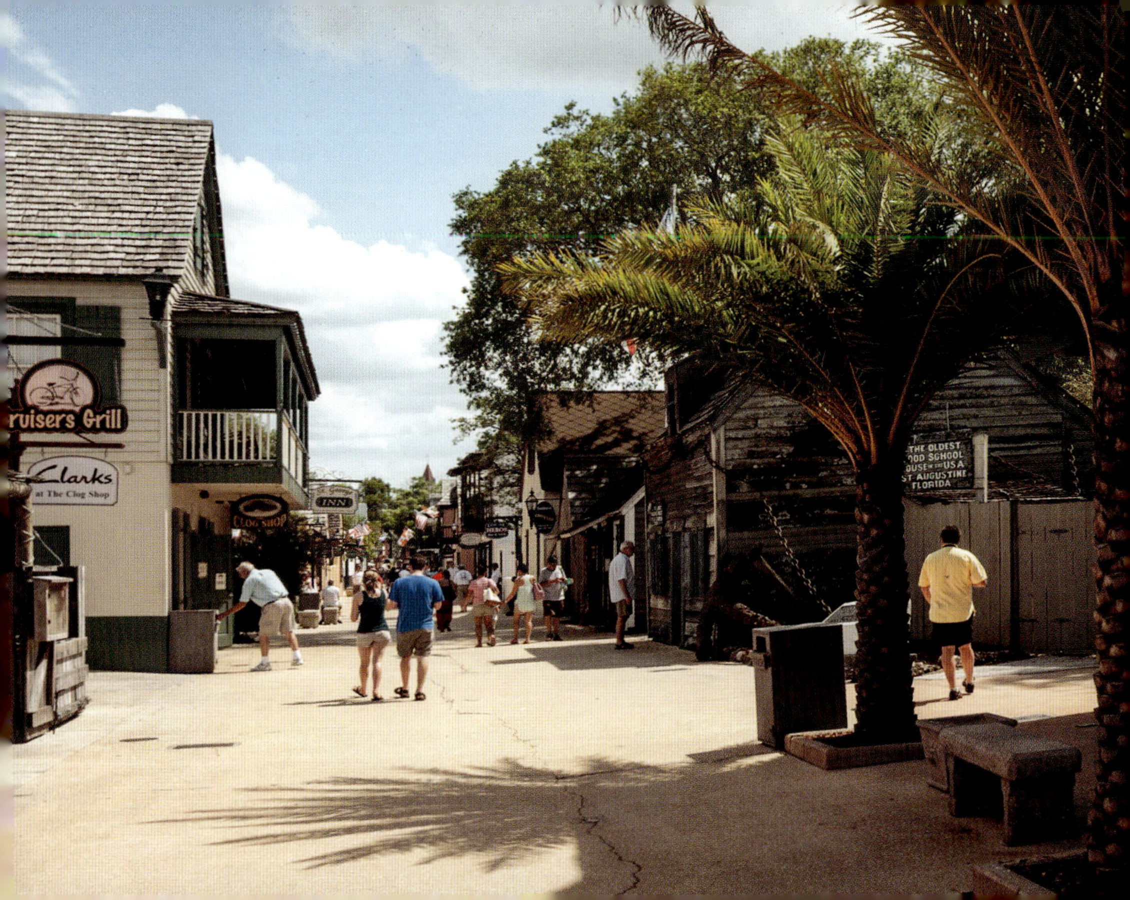
ruisers Grill
Clarks
at The Clog Shop
CLOG SHOP
INN
THE OLDEST
OOD SCHOOL
OUSE USA
ST AUGUSTINE
FLORIDA

St. George Street, St. Augustine, 1905

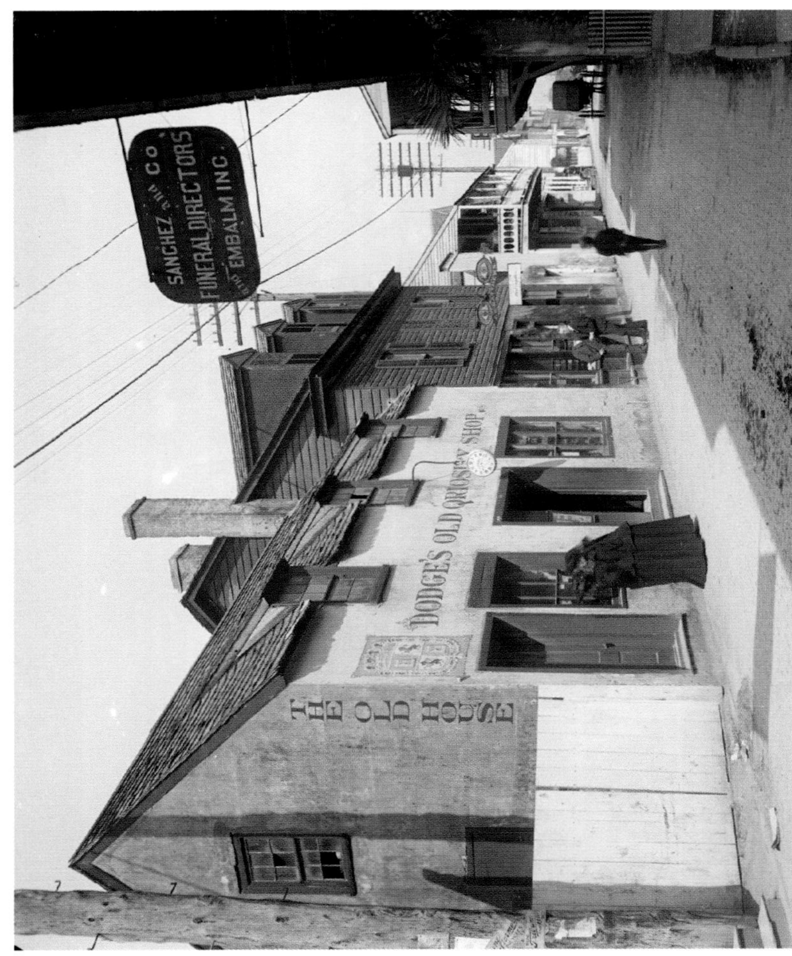

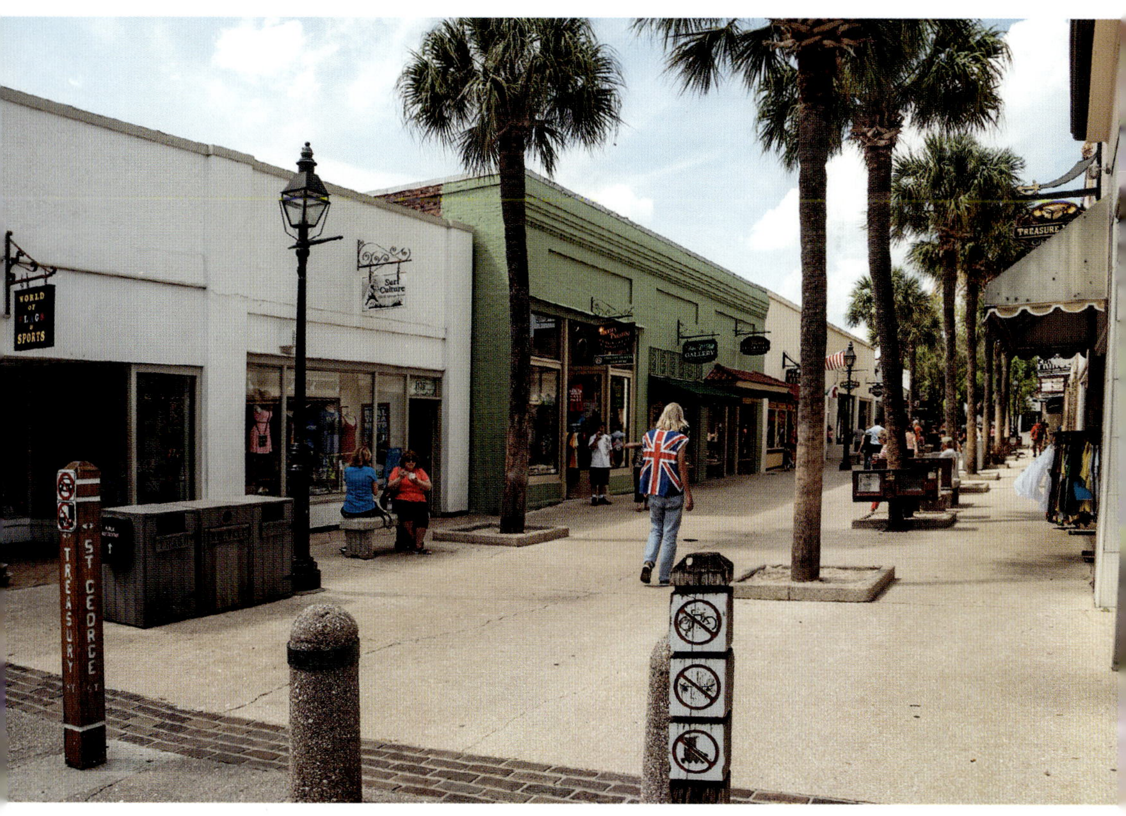
WORLD OF FLAGS & SPORTS
Surf Culture
GALLERY
TREASURE
TREASURY ST
ST GEORGE ST

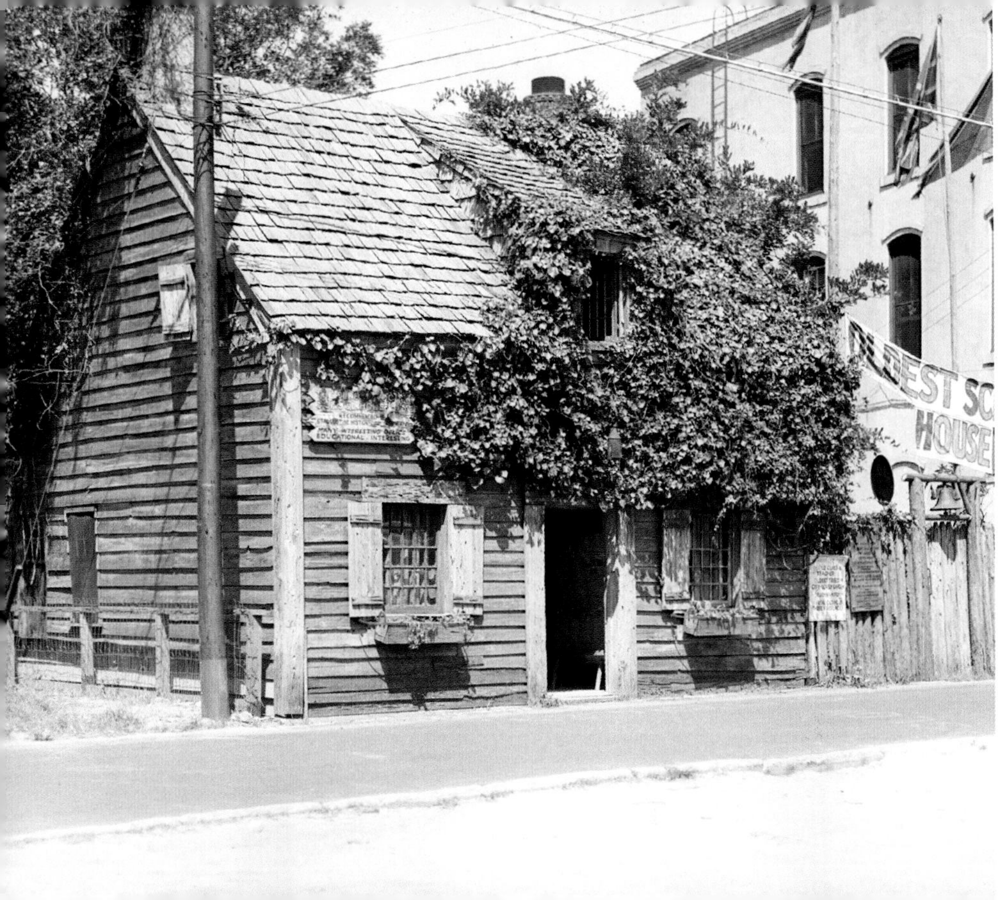

Oldest Wood Schoolhouse in USA, St. George Street, St. Augustine, 1937

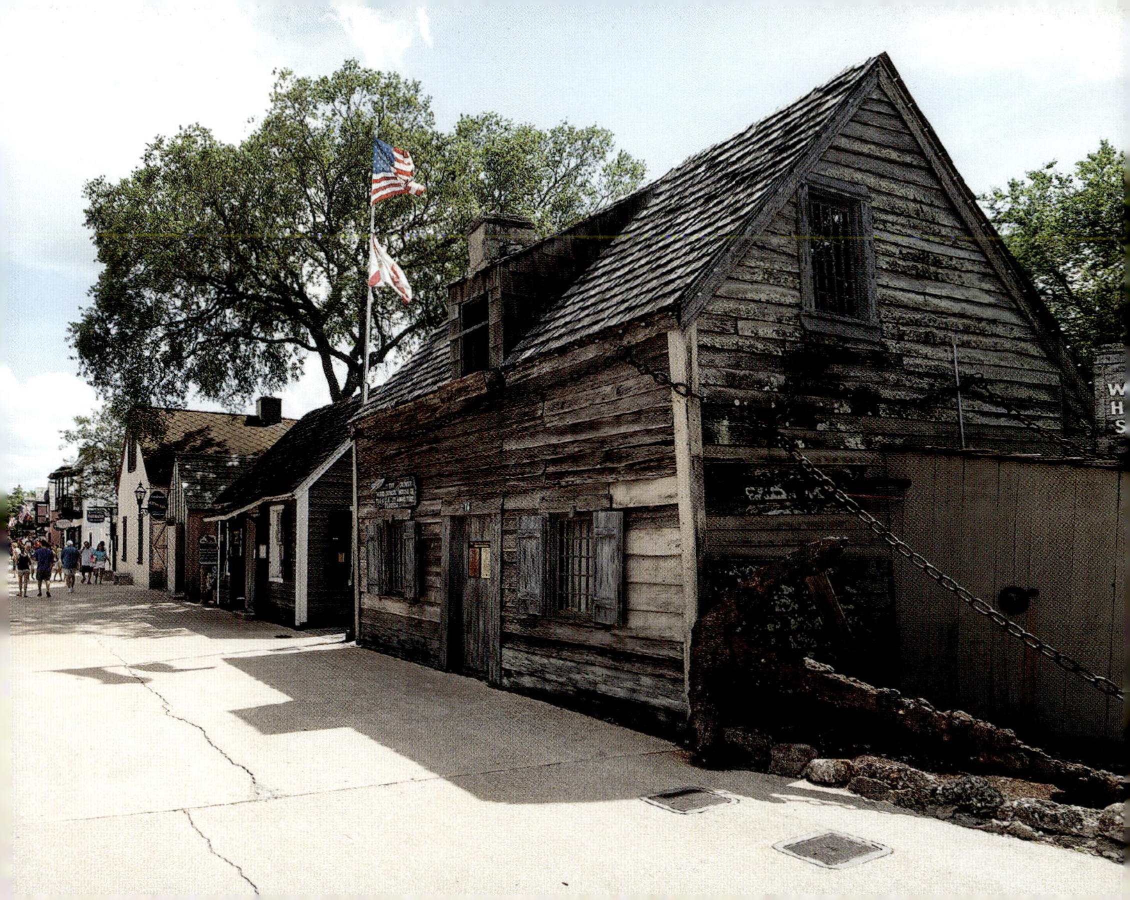

Prince Murat Coffee House, St. George Street, St. Augustine, 1938

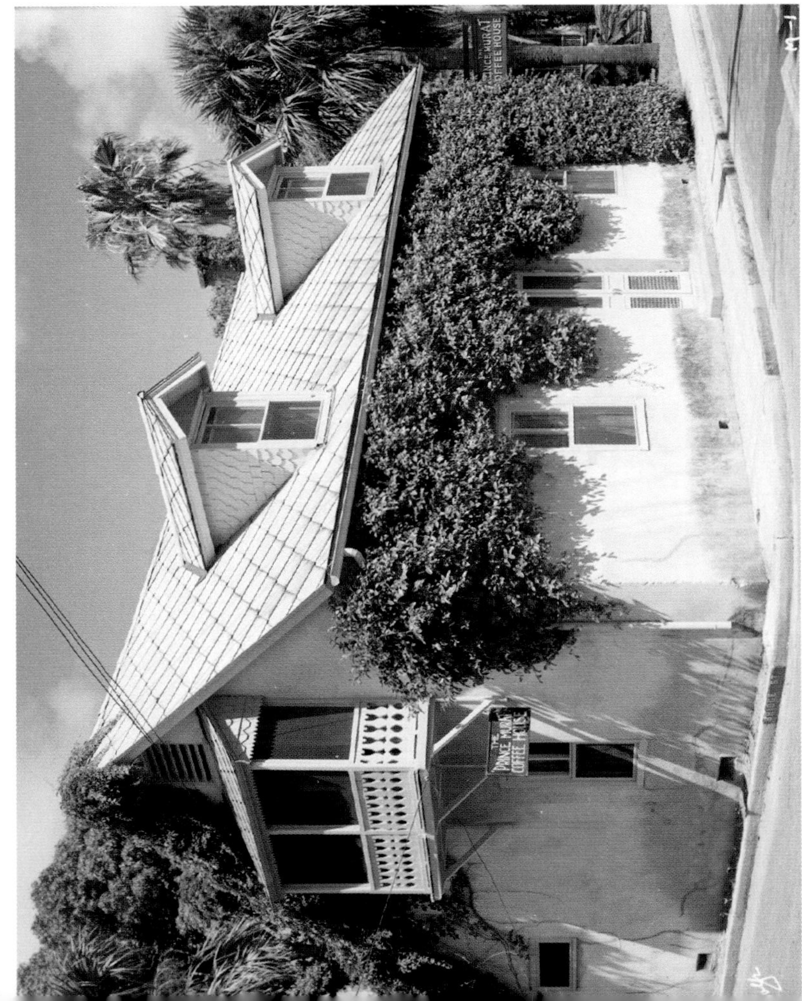

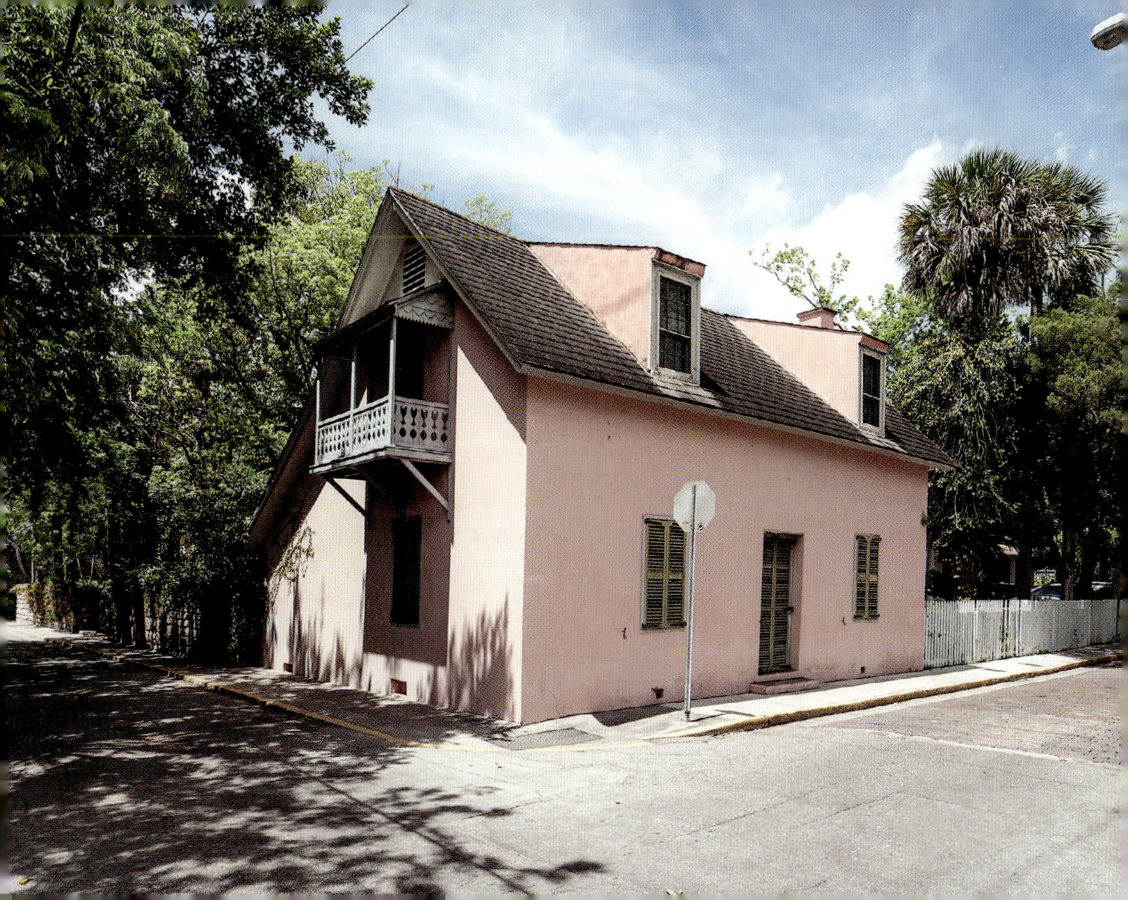

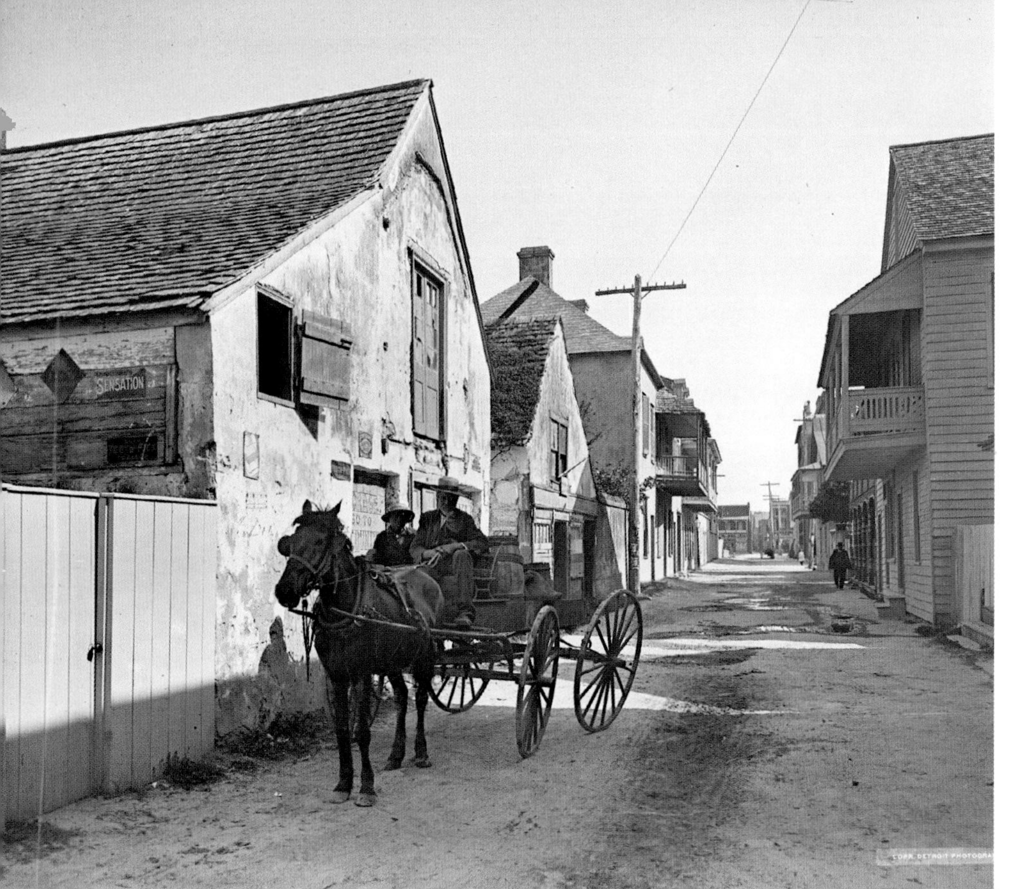

Charlotte Street, St. Augustine, 1901

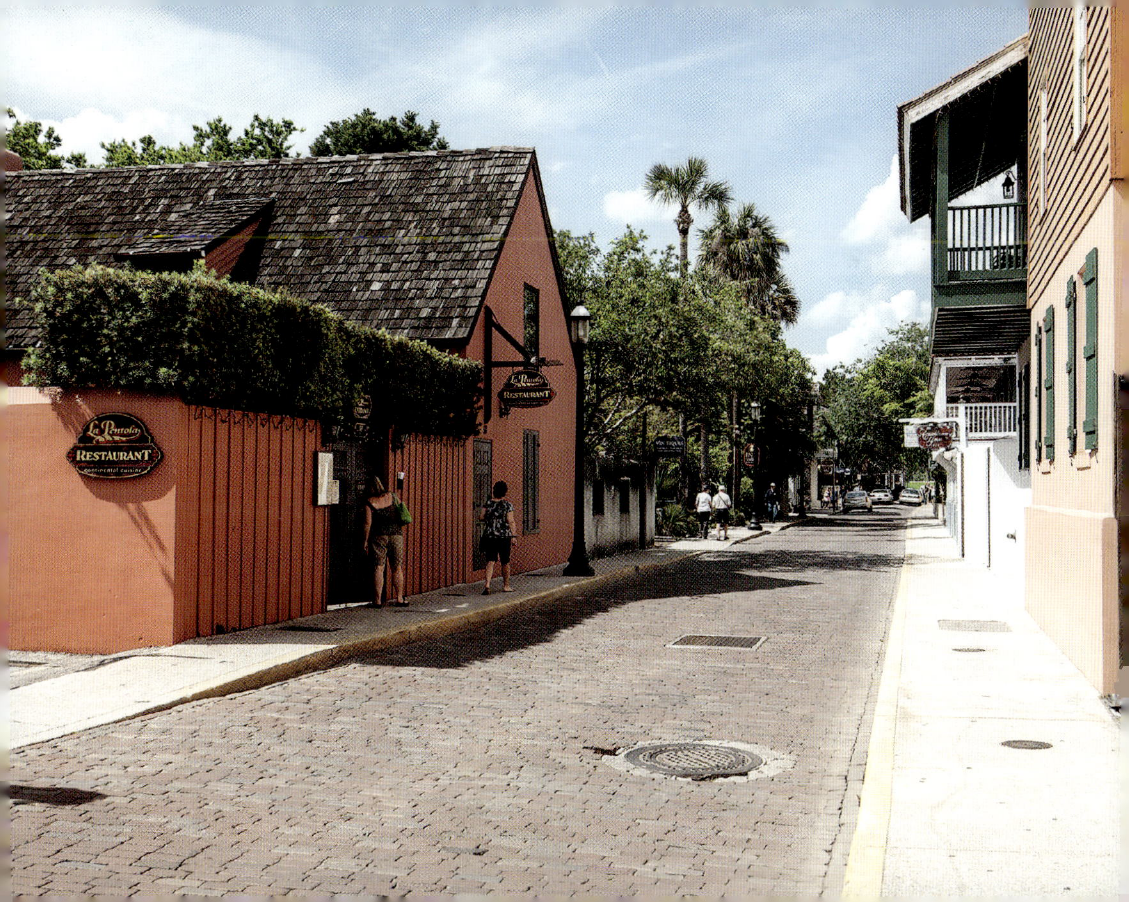
La Pentola
RESTAURANT
continental cuisine
La Pentola
RESTAURANT

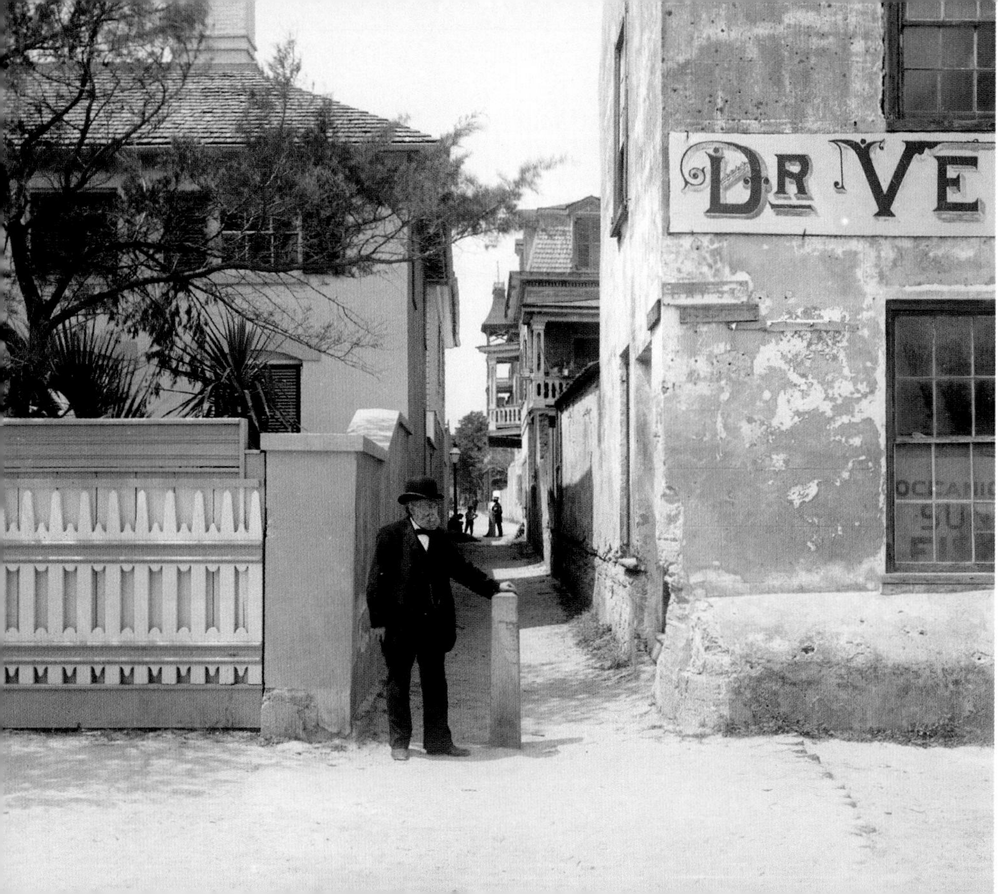

Treasury Street, St. Augustine, c. 1905

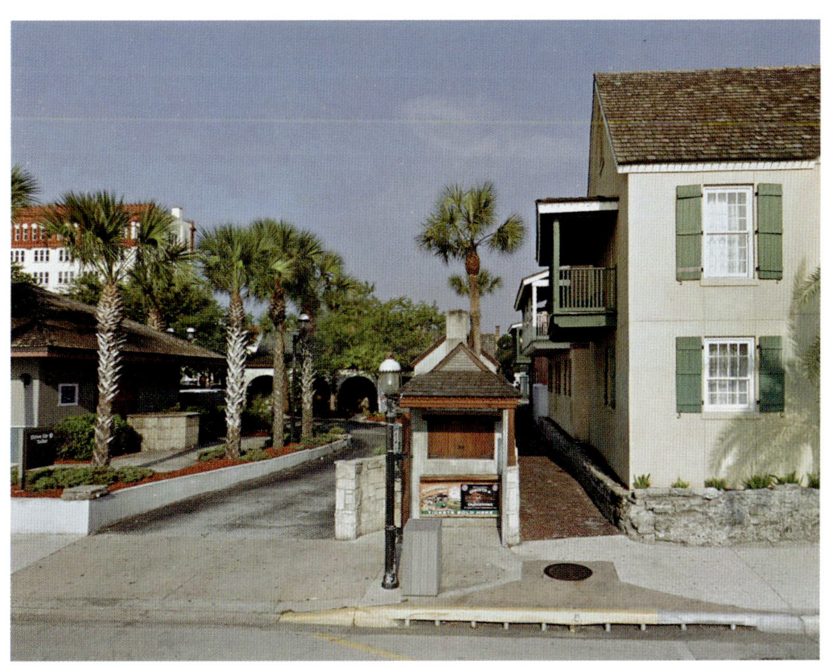

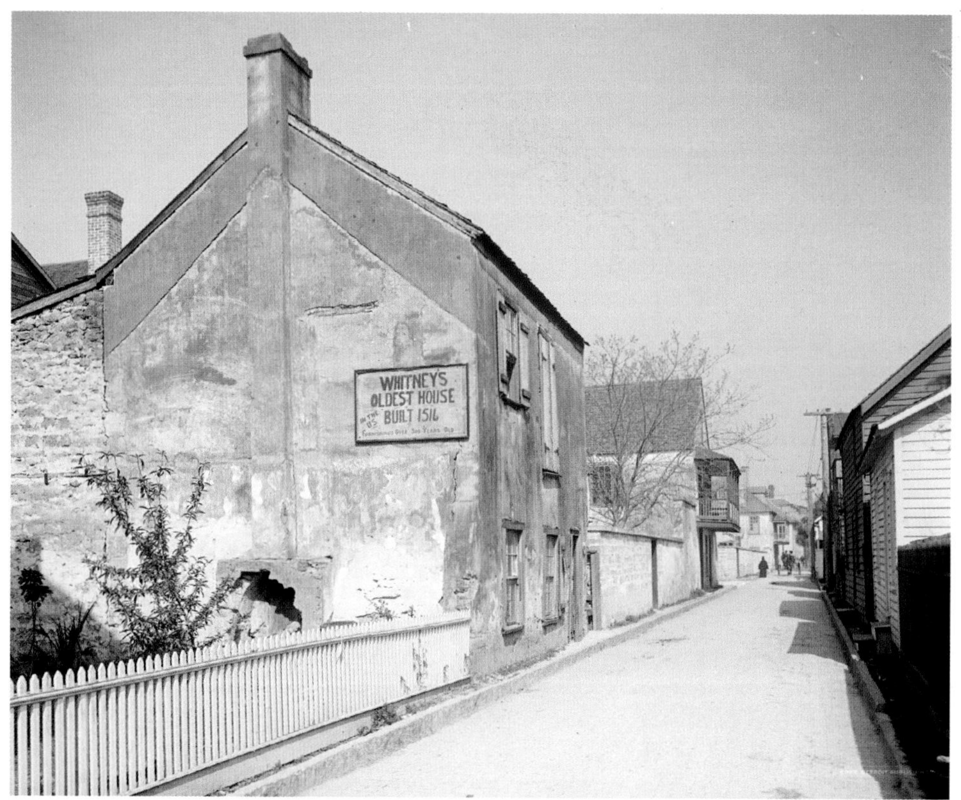

Aviles Street, St. Augustine, c. 1915

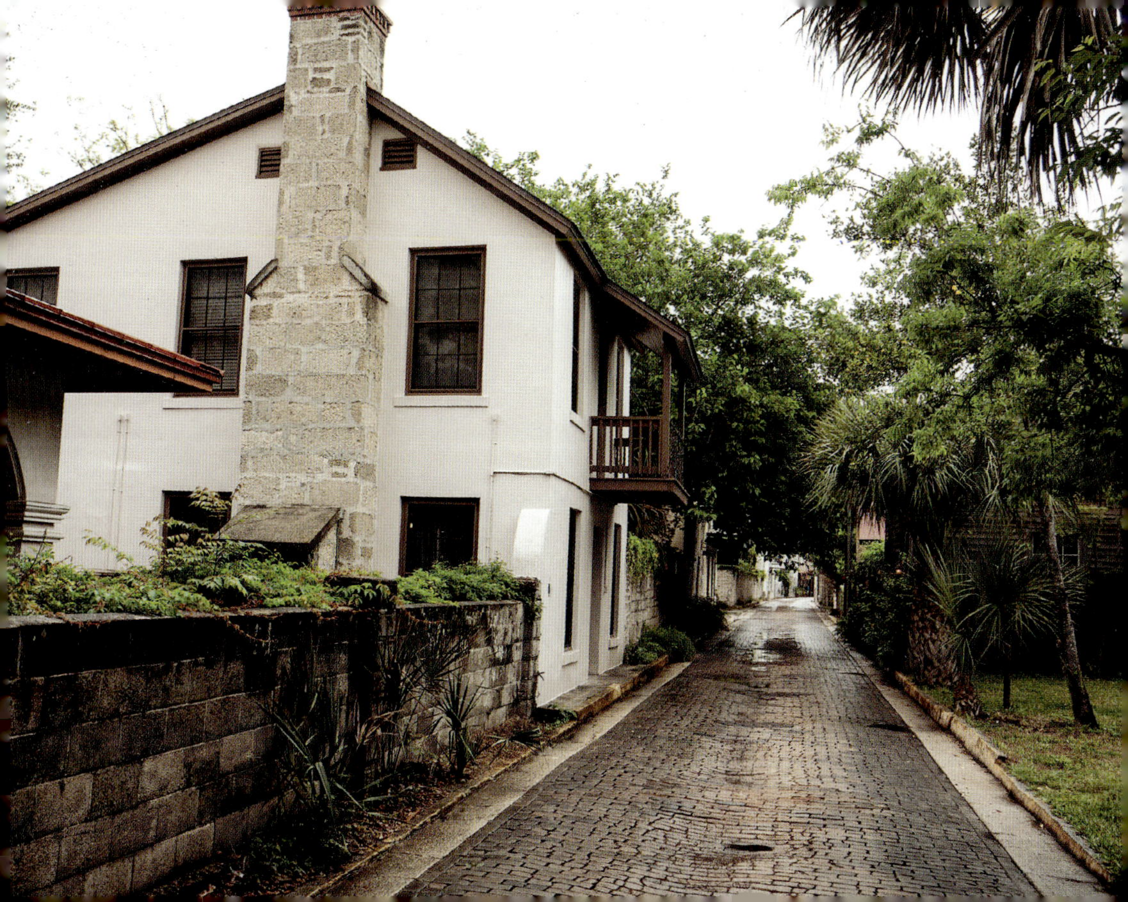

Oldest House in St. Augustine, St. Francis Street, c. 1905

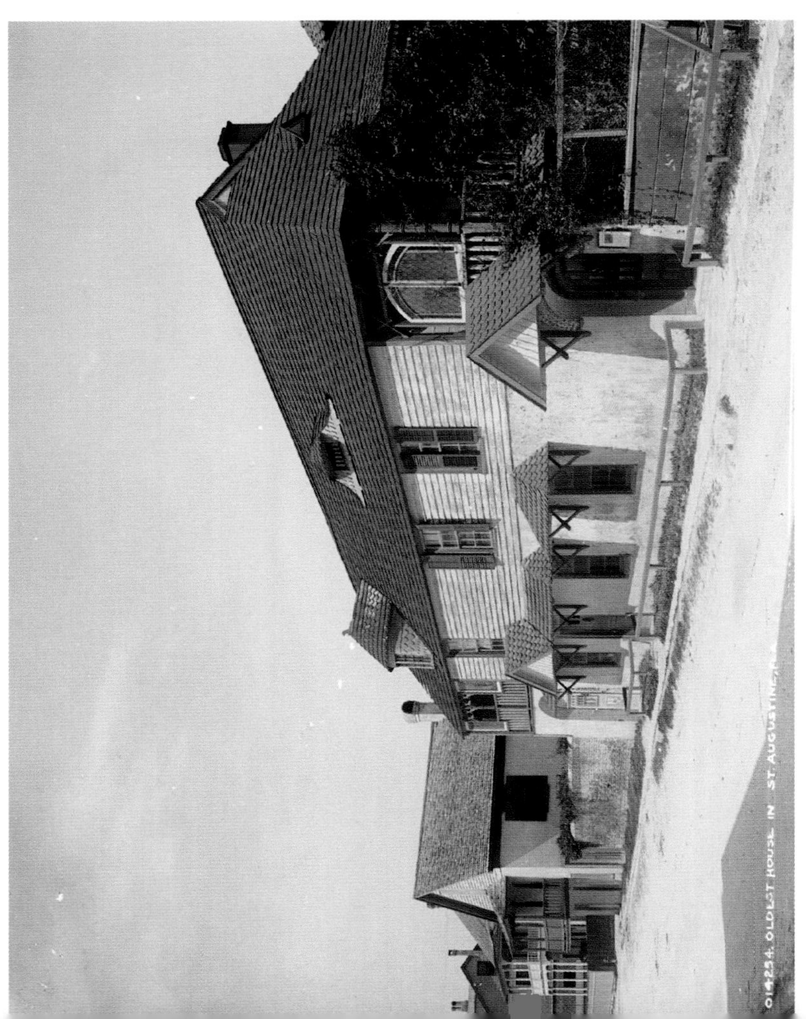

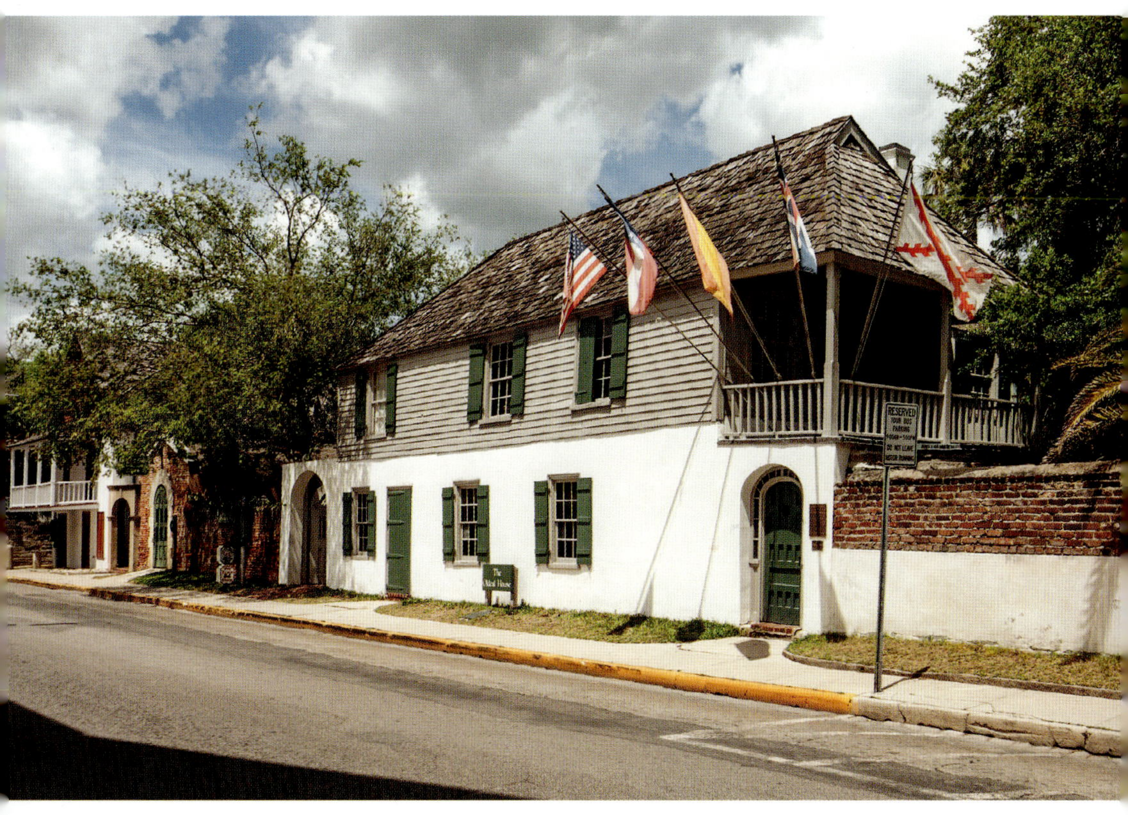
RESERVED
TOUR BUS
PARKING

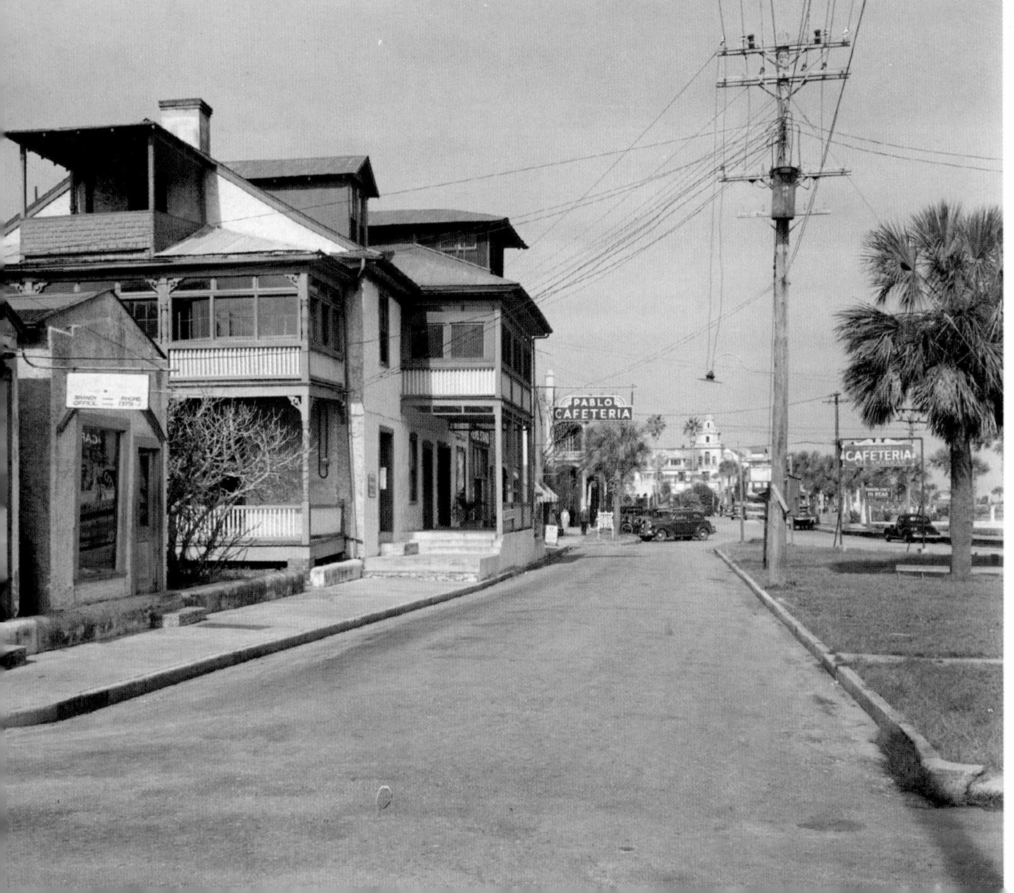

Marine Street, St. Augustine, 1937

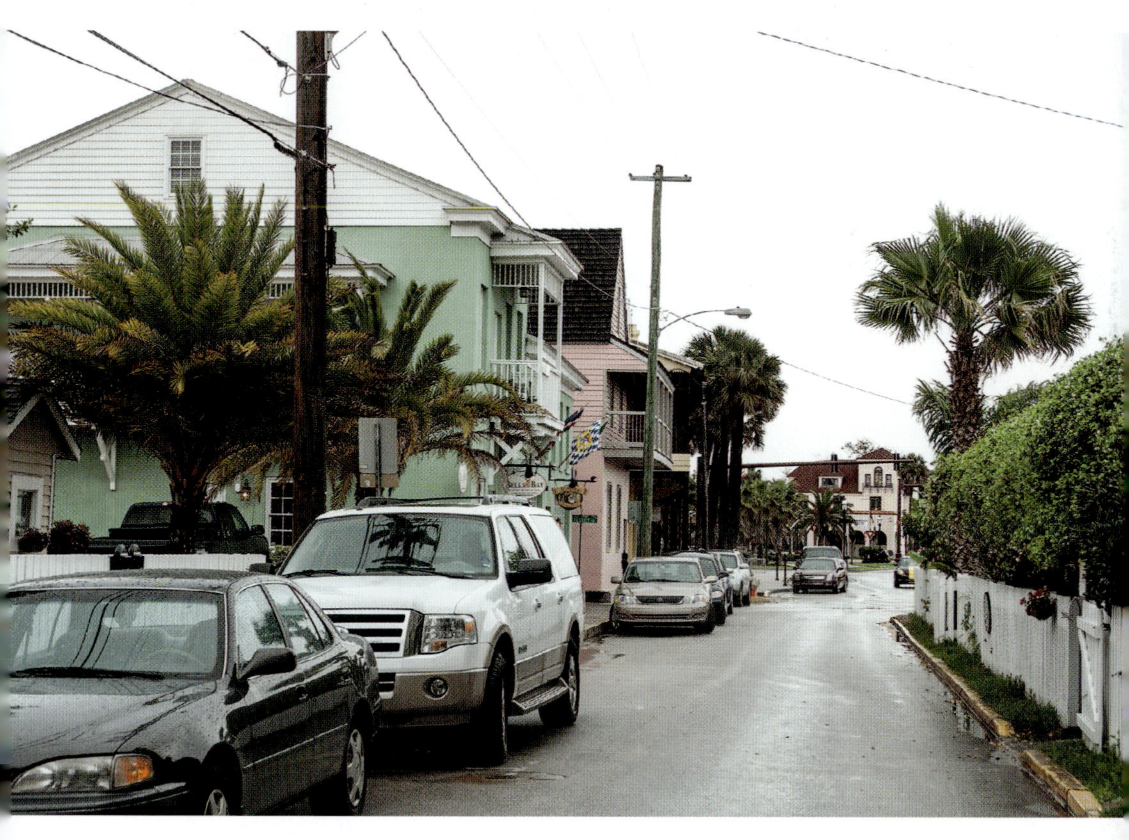

King Street at Avenida Menendez, St. Augustine, 1937

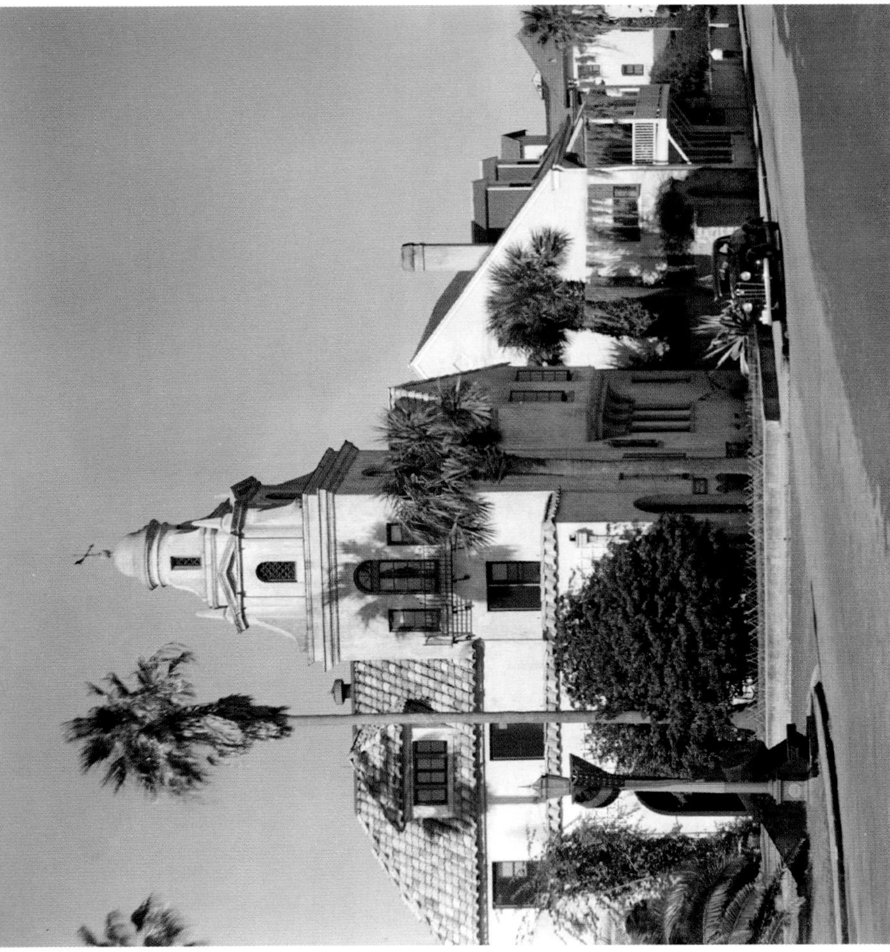

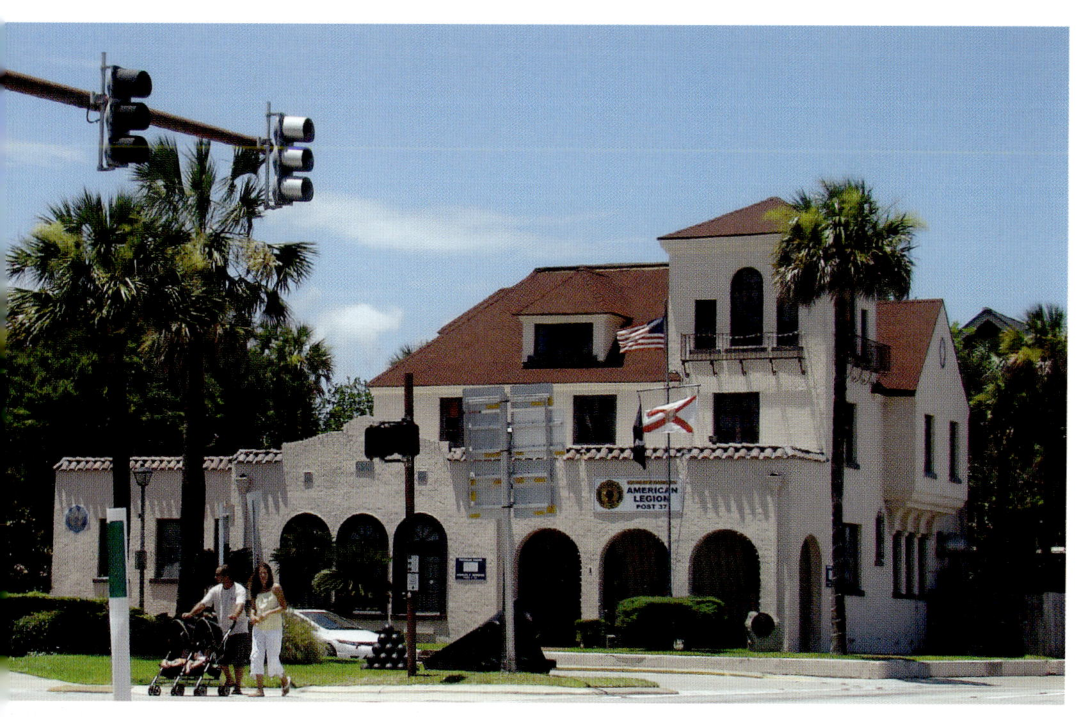
AMERICAN
LEGION
POST 37

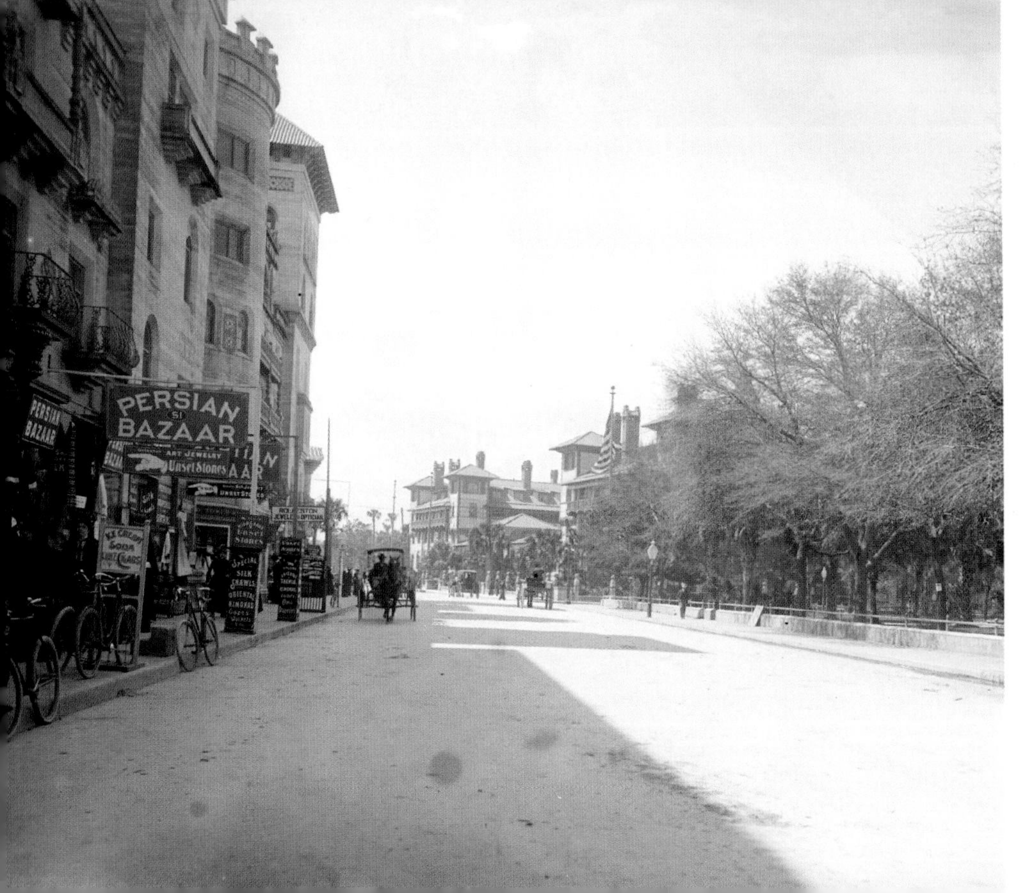

King Street, St. Augustine, c. 1900

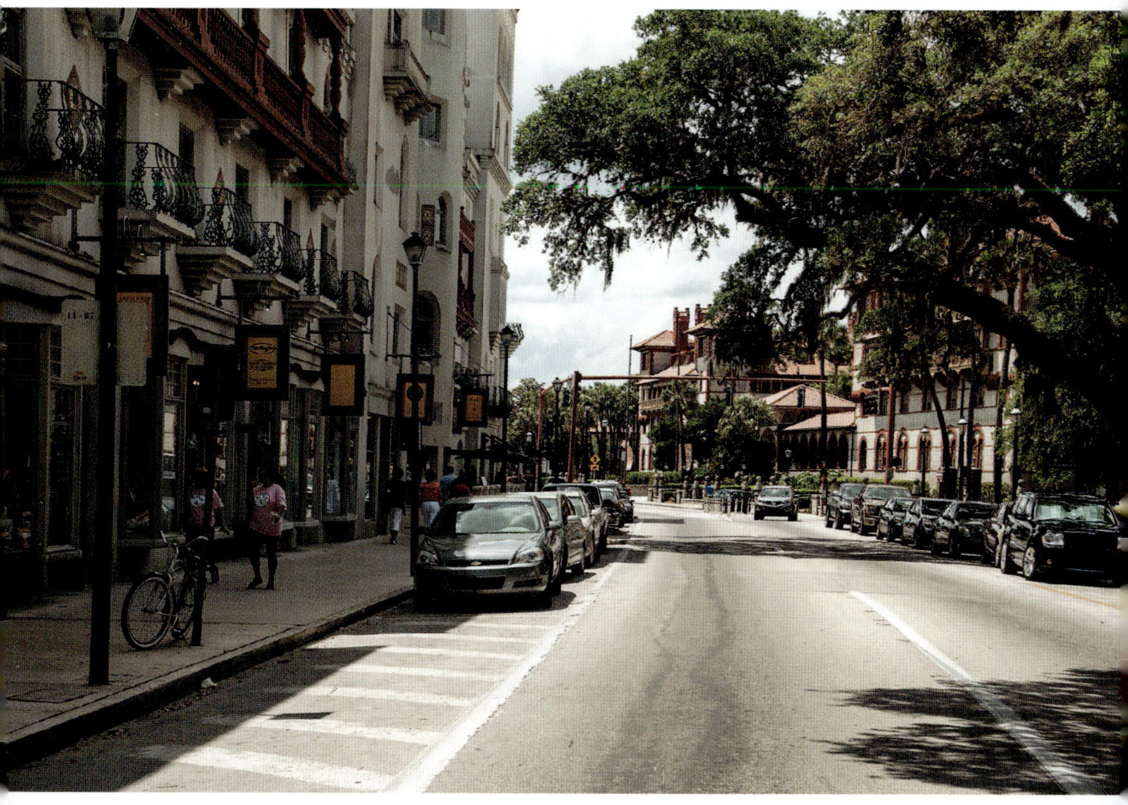

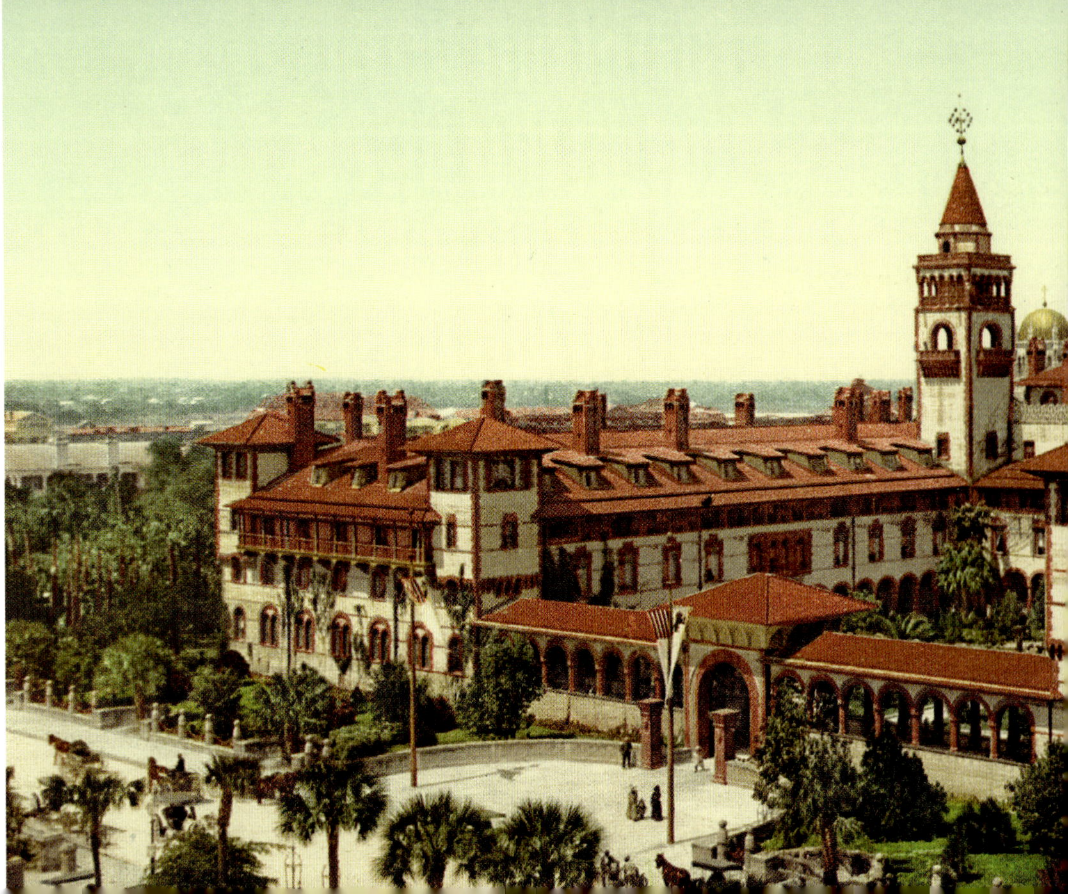

Ponce de León Hotel (now Flagler College), St. Augustine, 1902

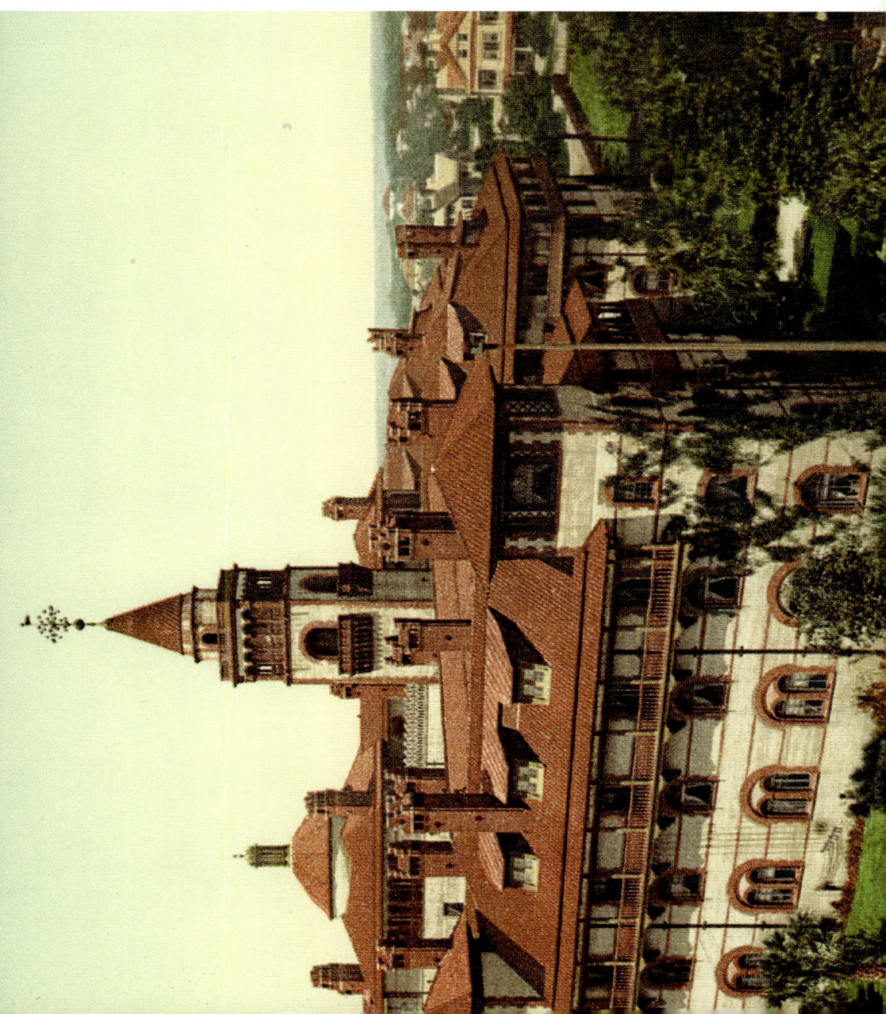

Ponce de León Hotel (now Flagler College), St. Augustine, c. 1895

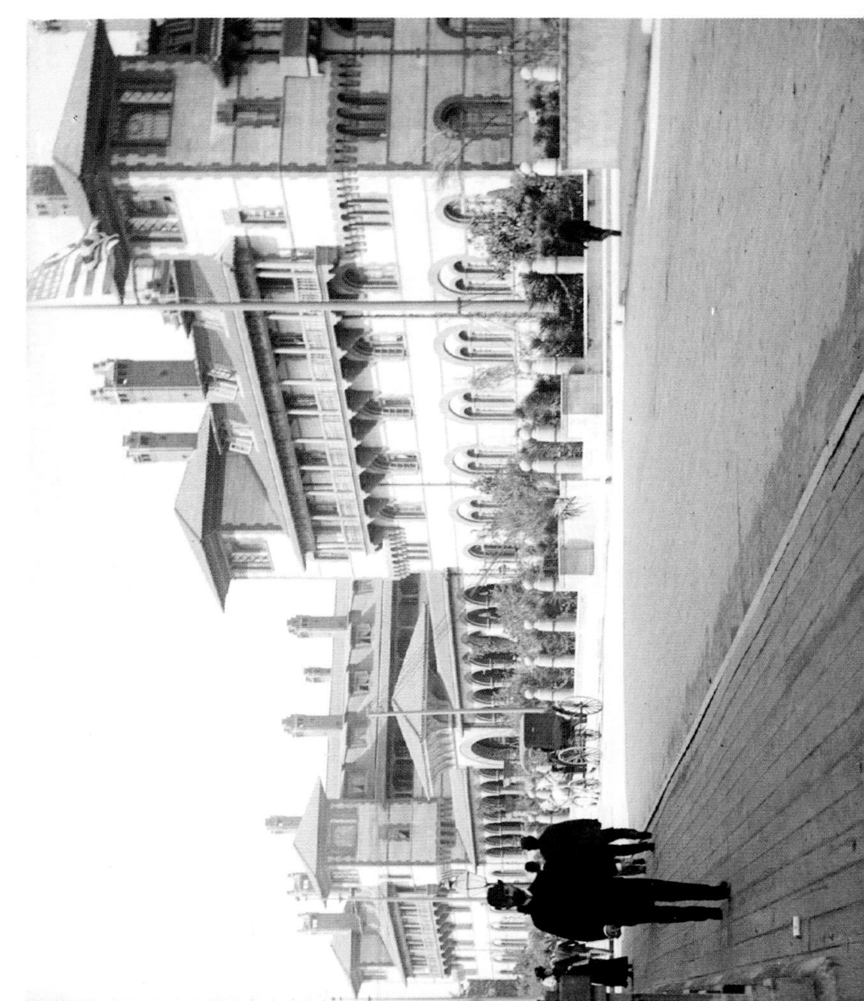

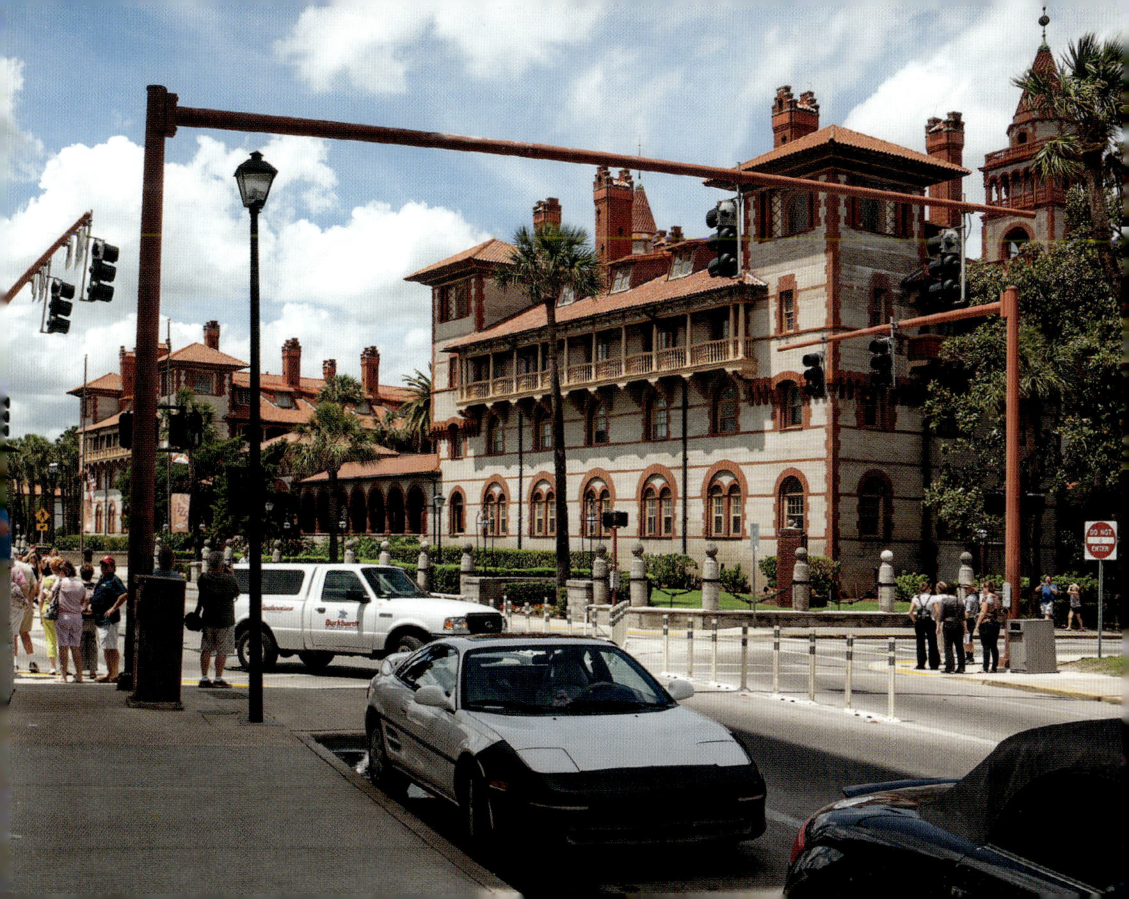
DO NOT ENTER

Ponce de León Hotel (now Flagler College), St. Augustine, 1937

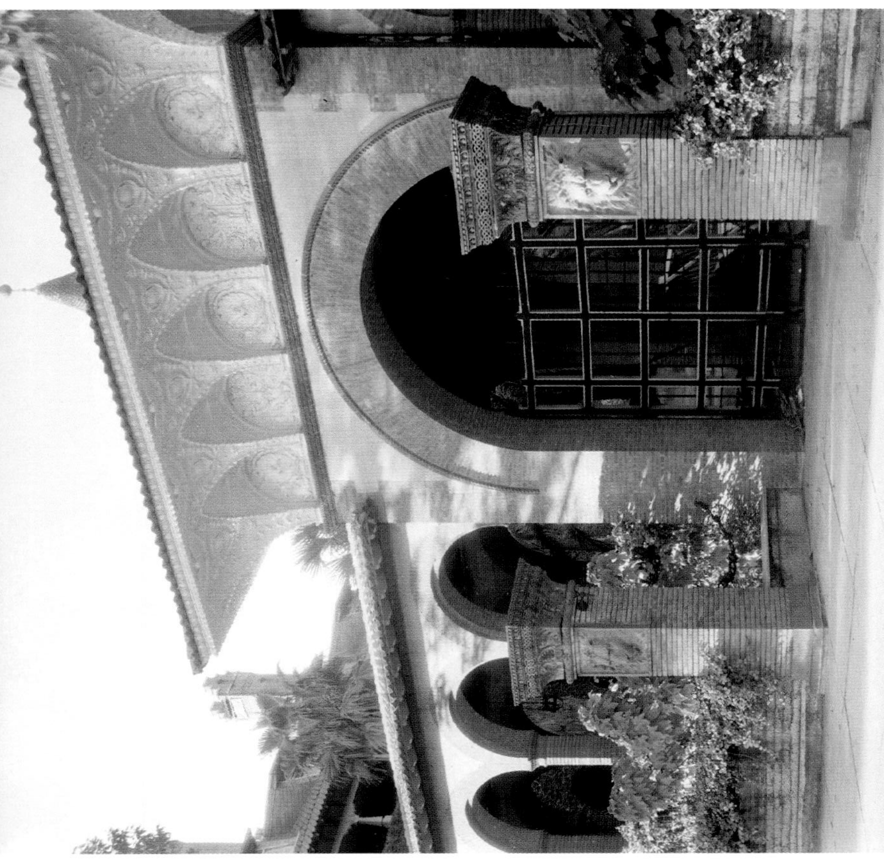

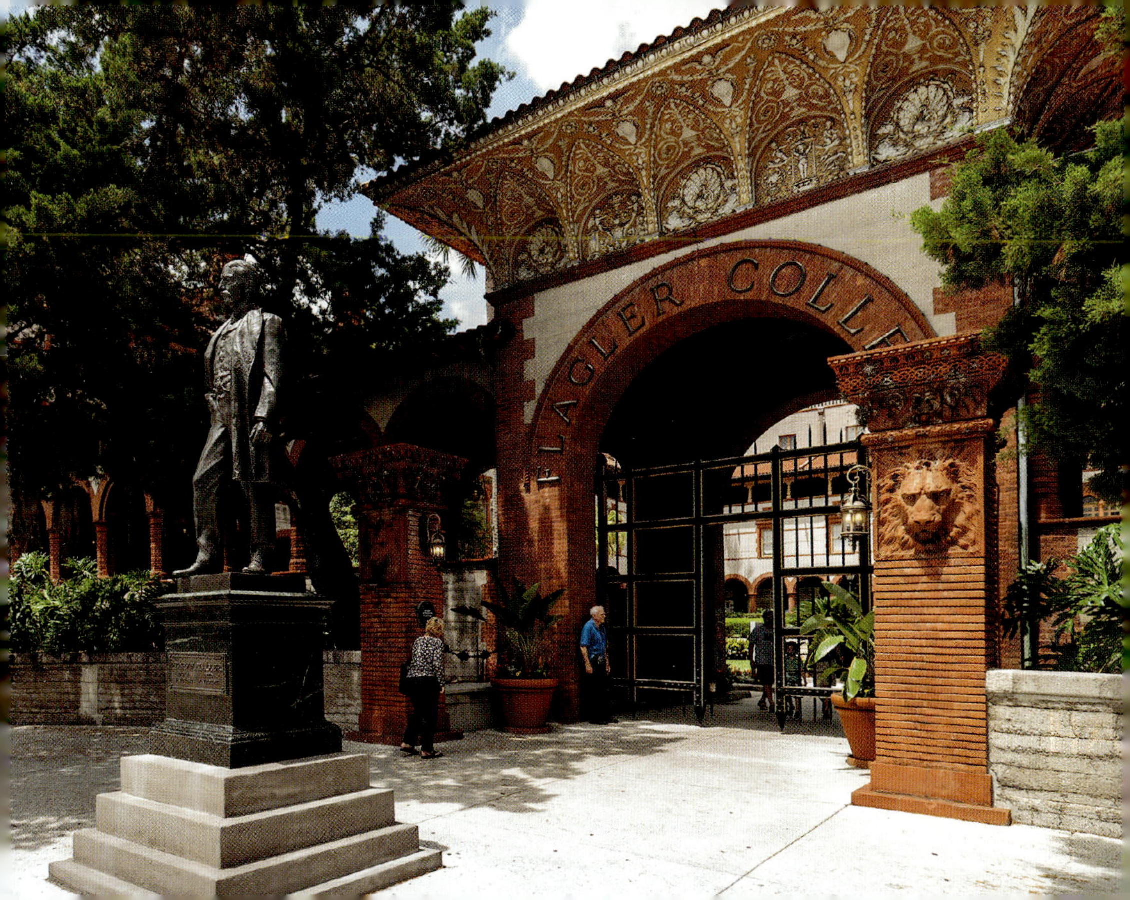
LAGLER COLLE

Ponce de León Hotel (now Flagler College), St. Augustine, c. 1910

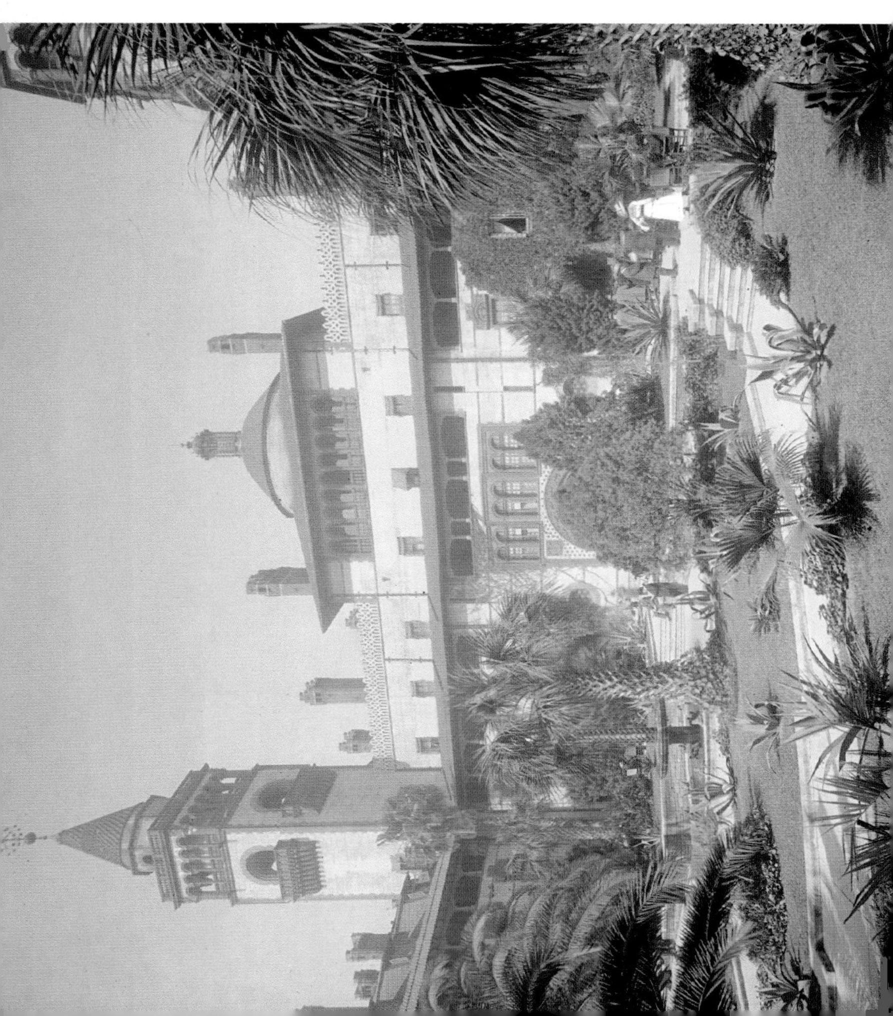

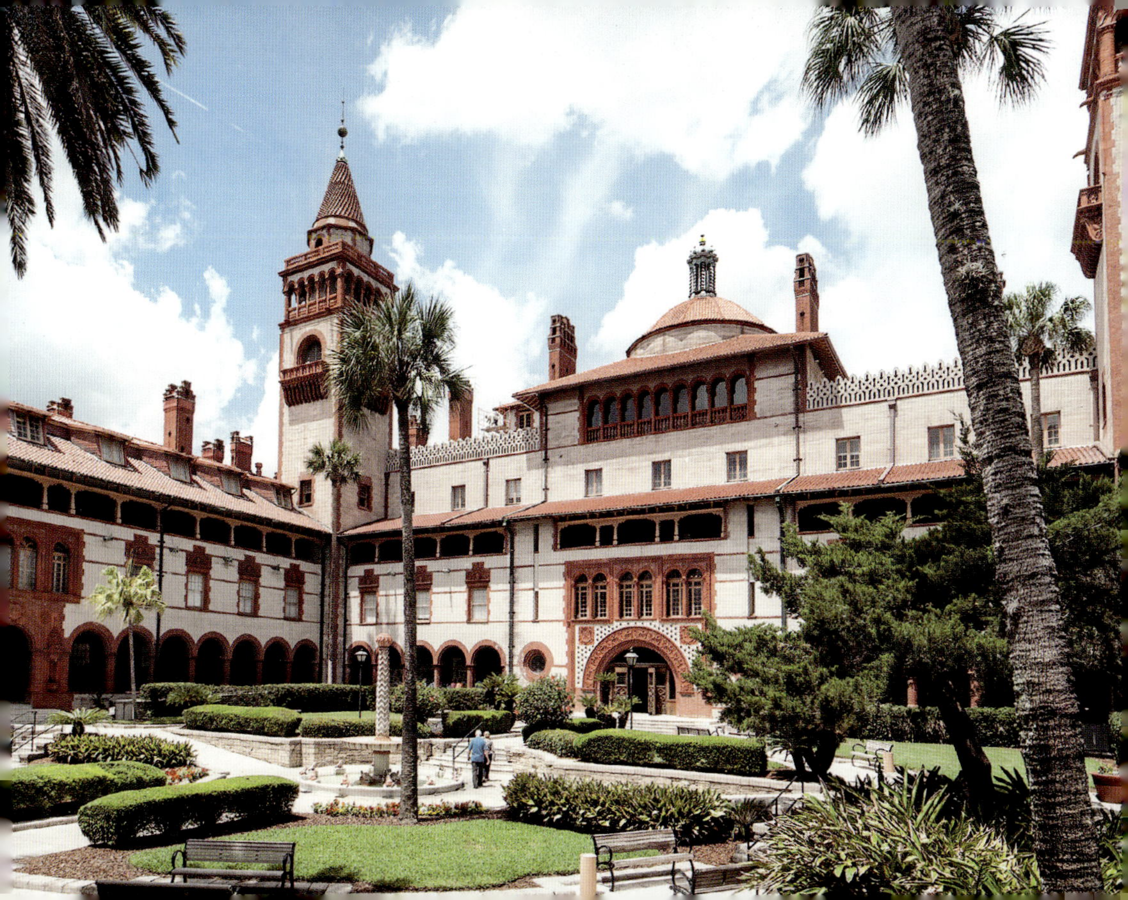

Ponce de León Hotel (now Flagler College), St. Augustine, 1905

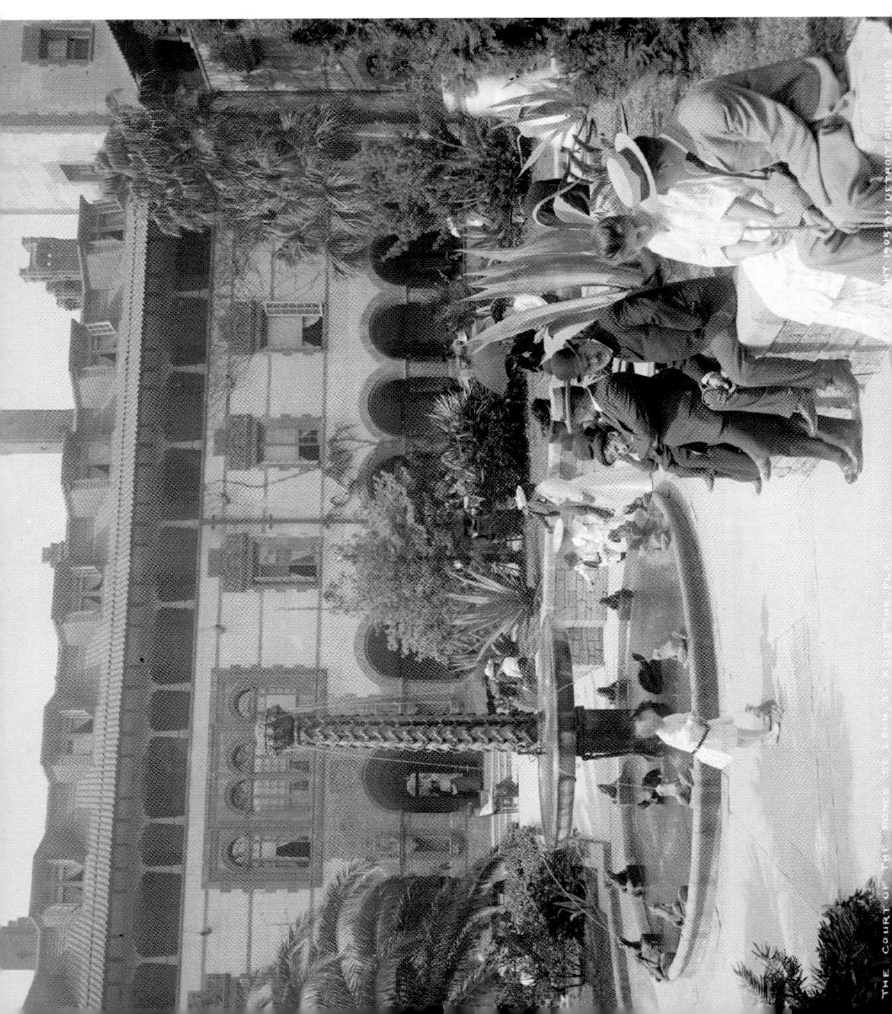

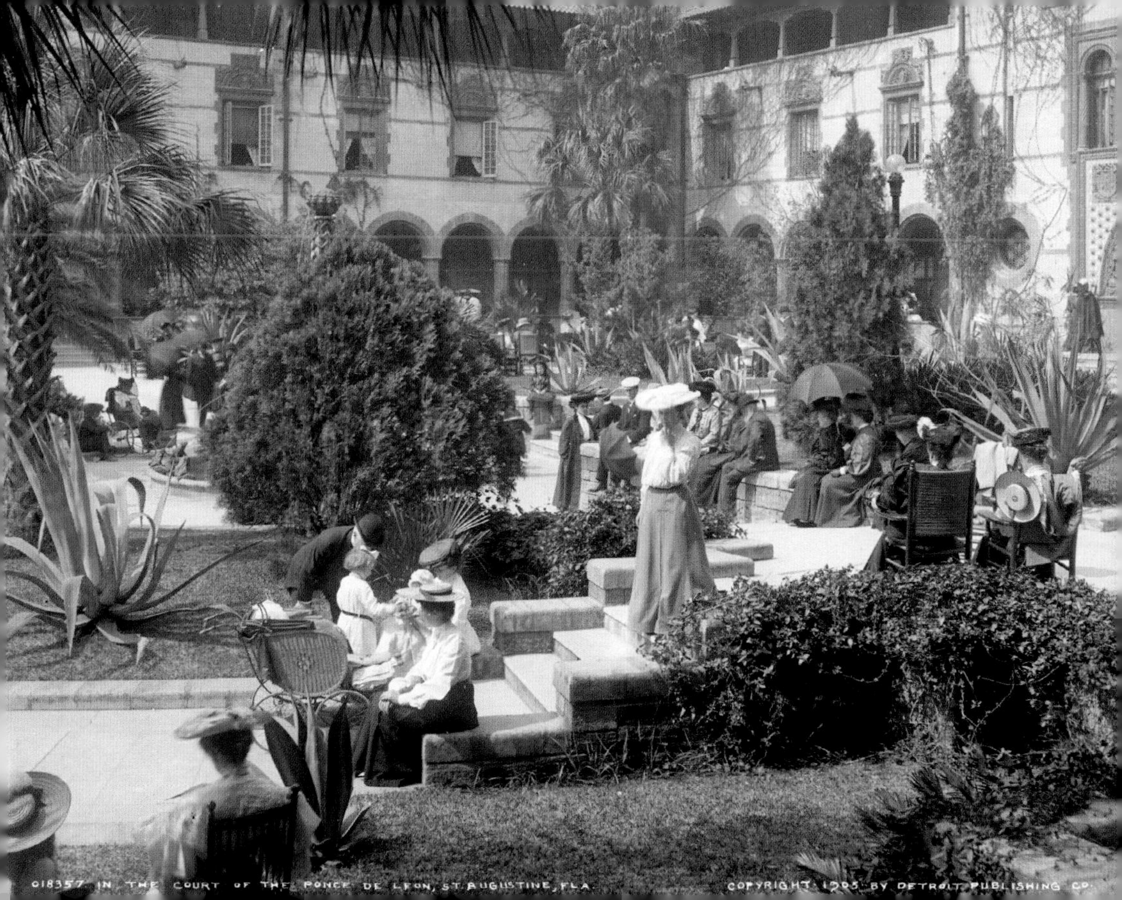
018357 IN THE COURT OF THE PONCE DE LEON, ST AUGUSTINE, FLA.
COPYRIGHT 1905 BY DETROIT PUBLISHING CO.

Ponce de León Hotel (now Flagler College), St. Augustine, c. 1905

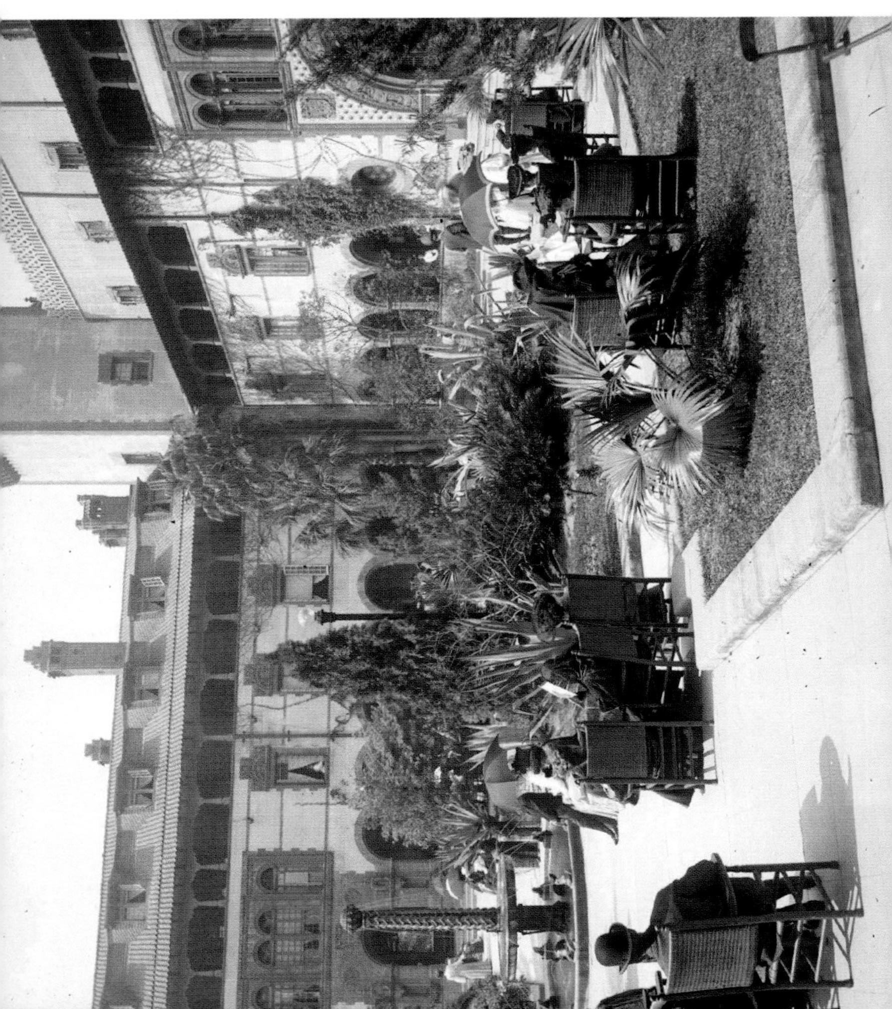

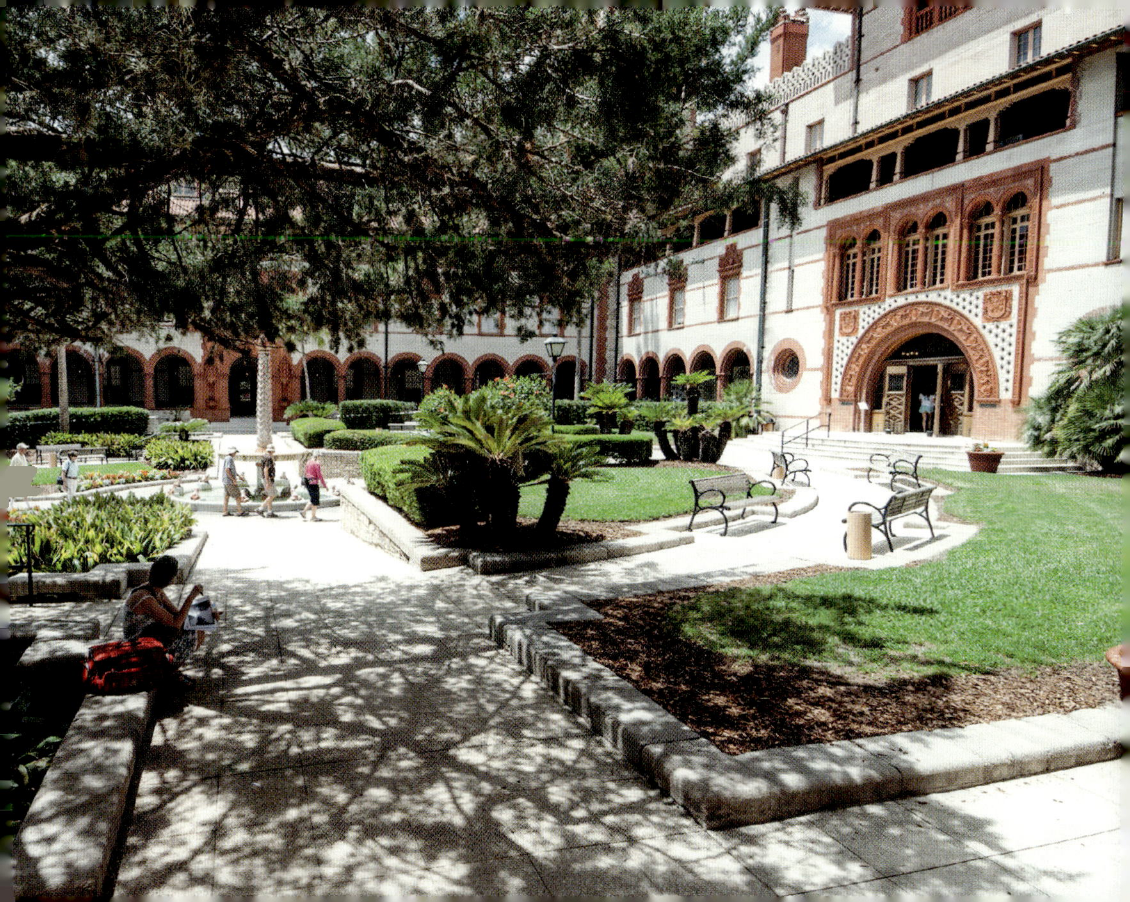

Ponce de León Hotel (now Flagler College), St. Augustine, c. 1895

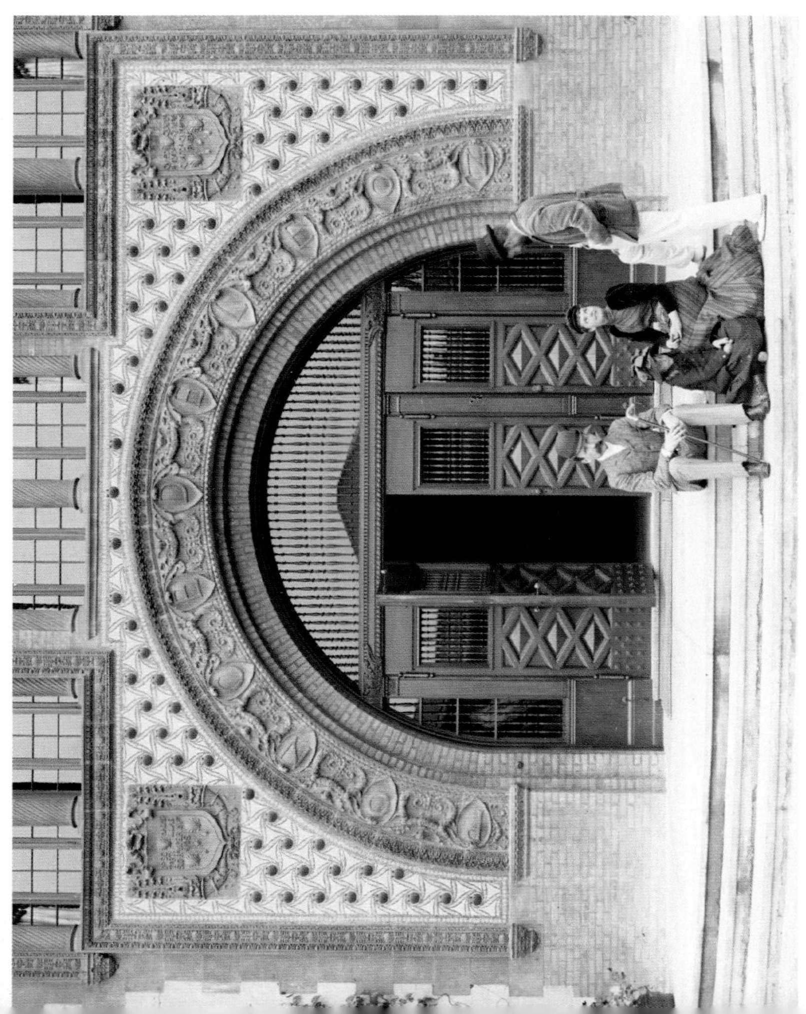

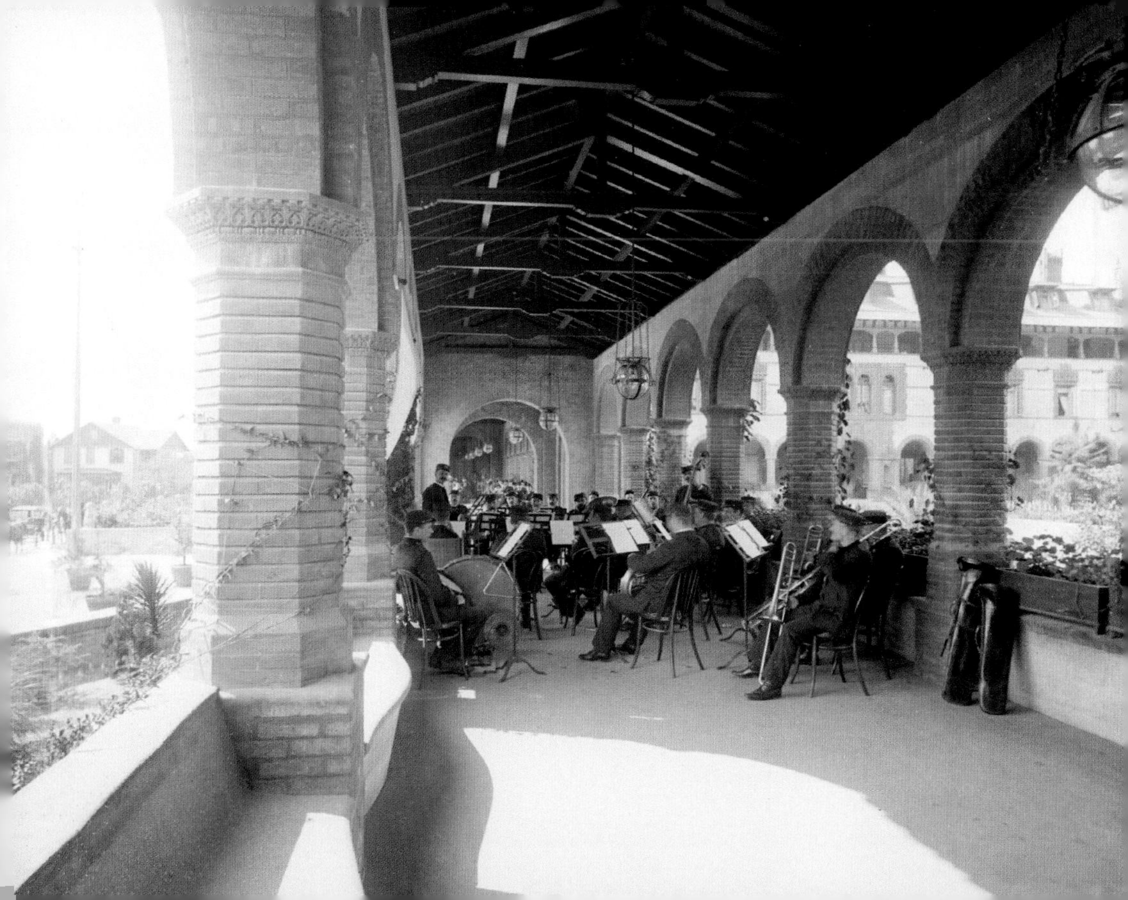

Ponce de León Hotel (now Flagler College), St. Augustine, c. 1895

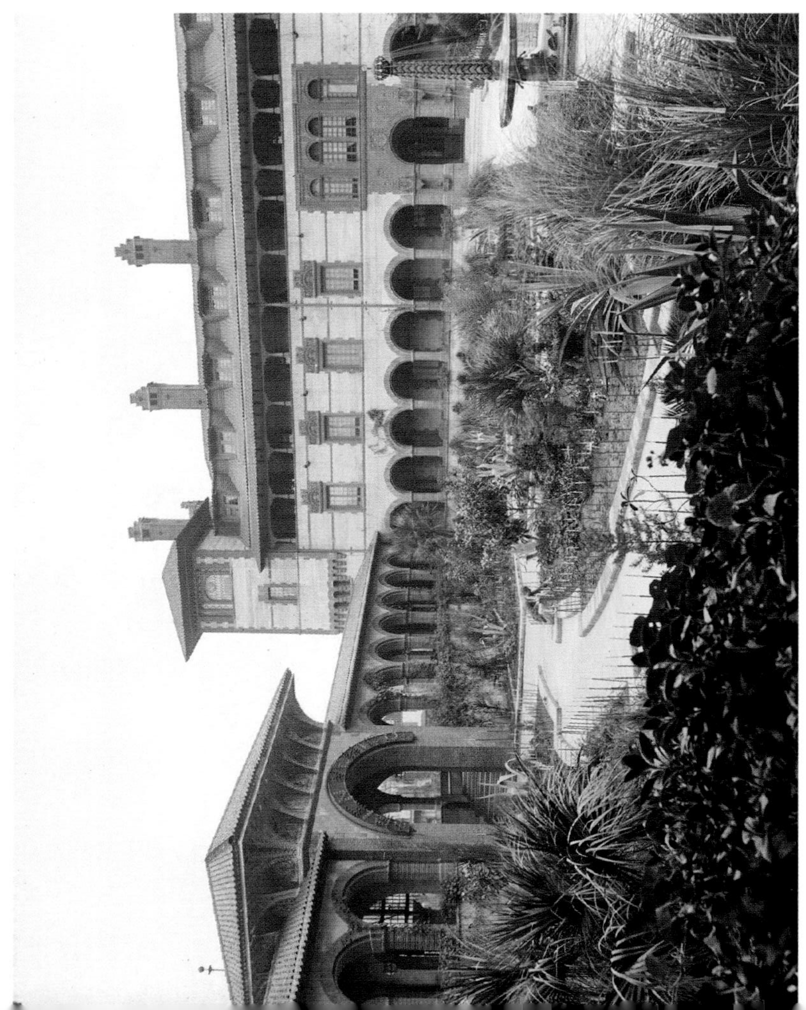

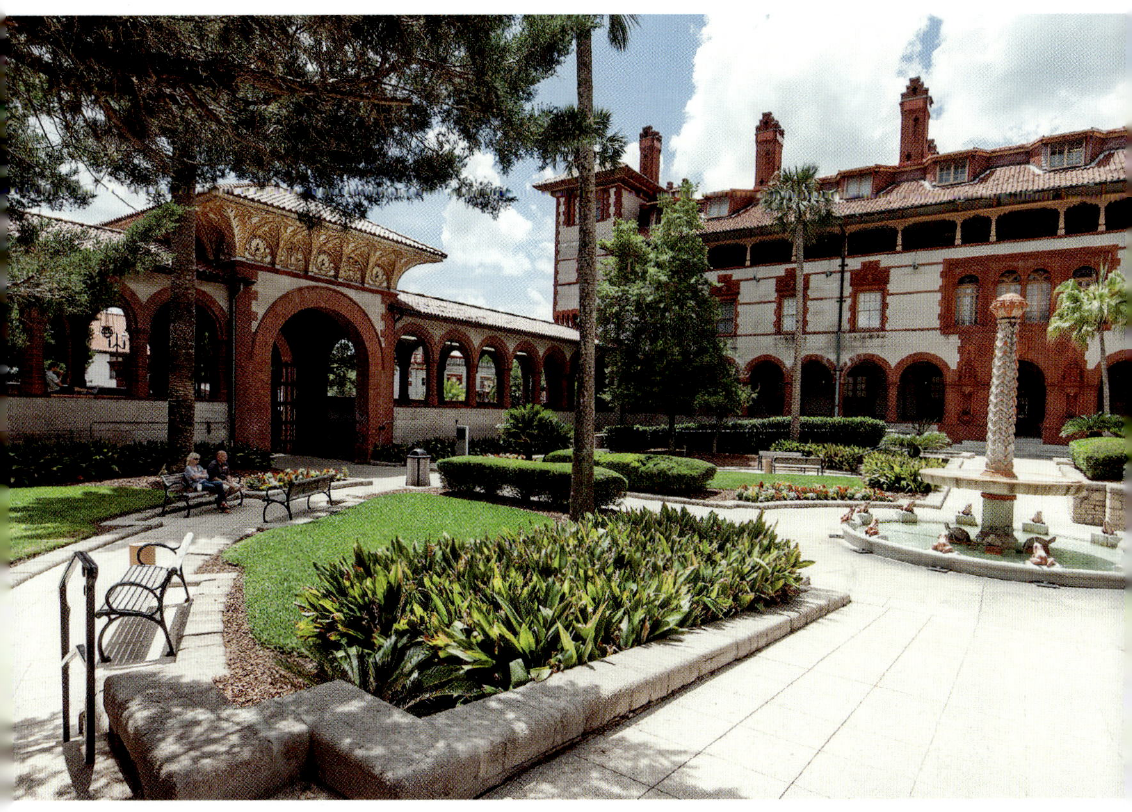

Ponce de León Hotel (now Flagler College), St. Augustine, c. 1895

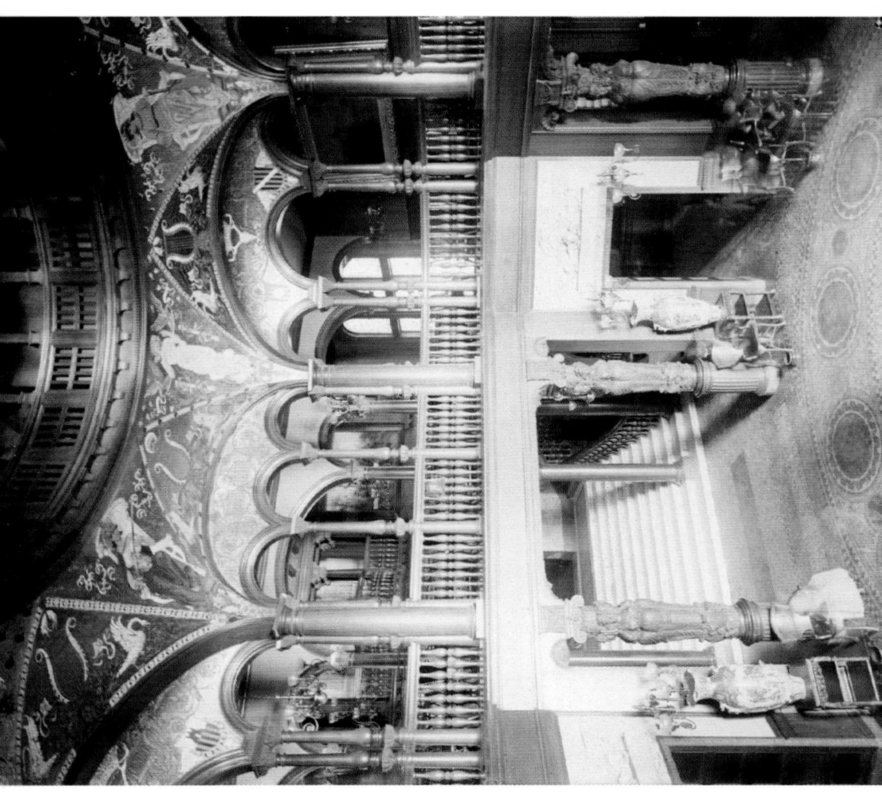

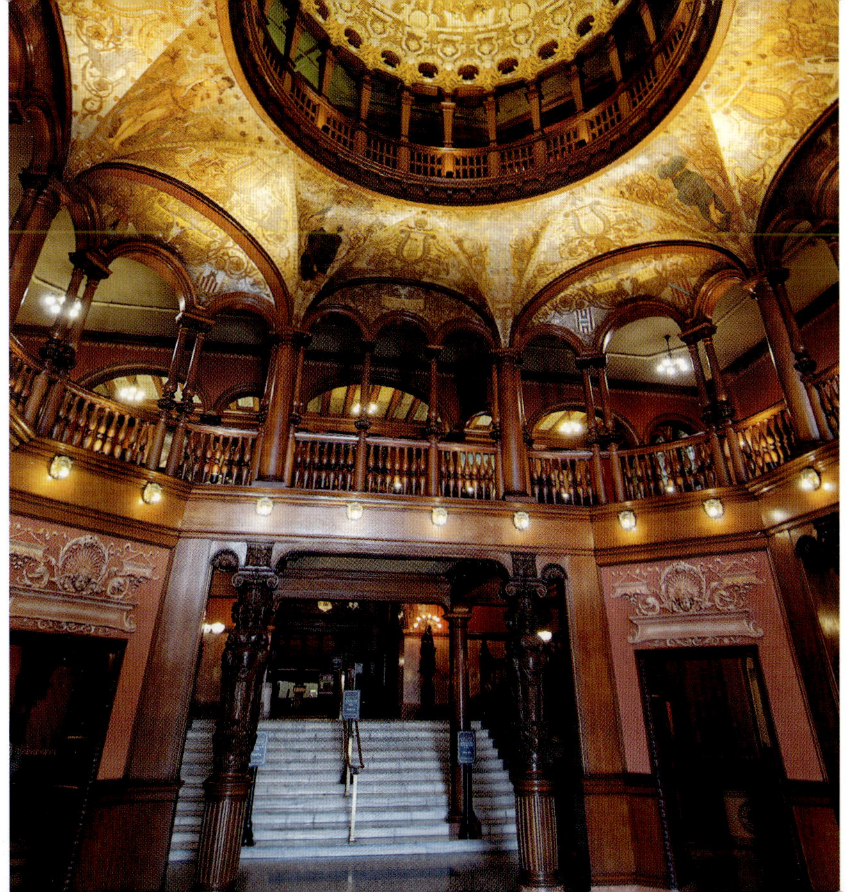

Old Market and Plaza, St. Augustine, c. 1895

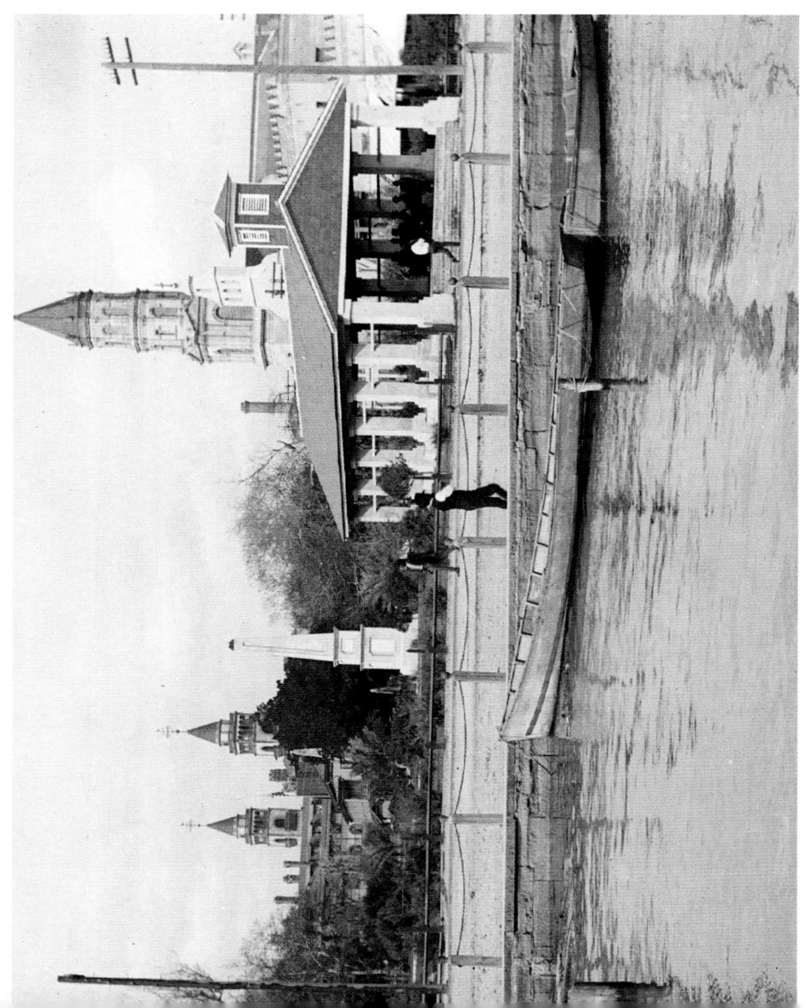

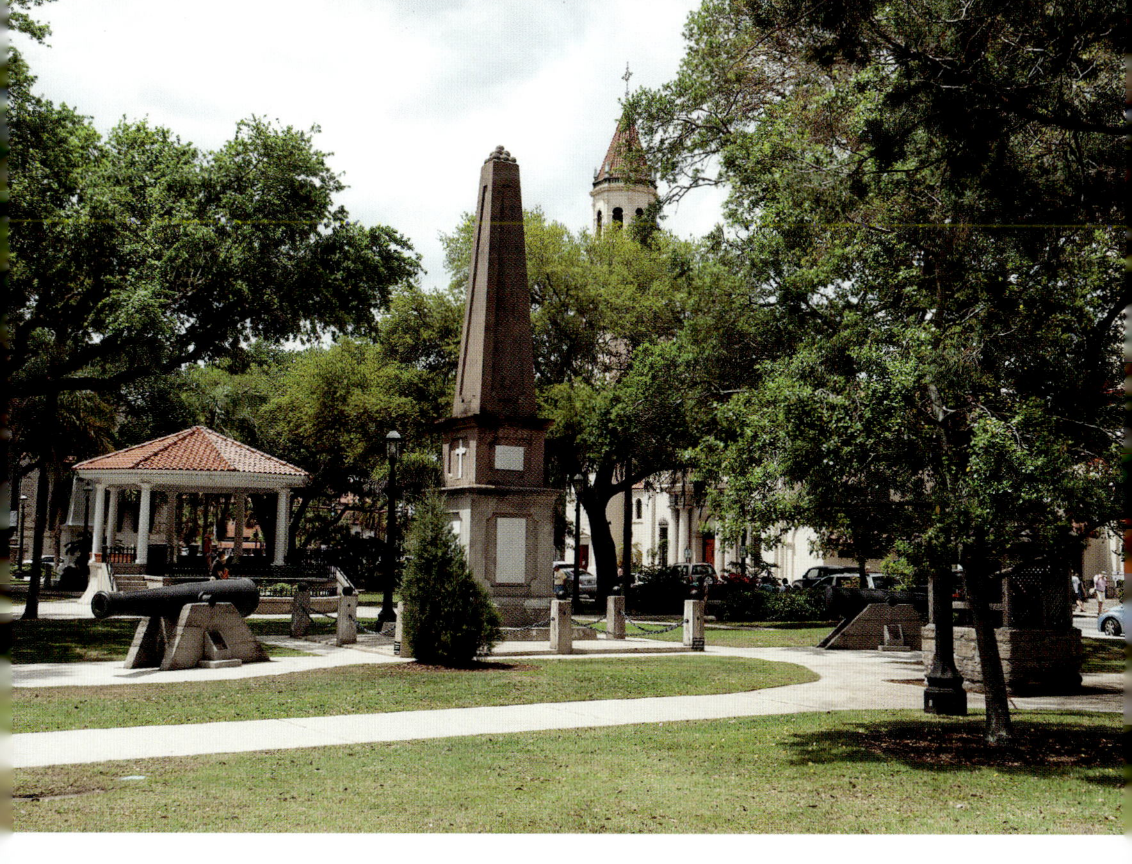

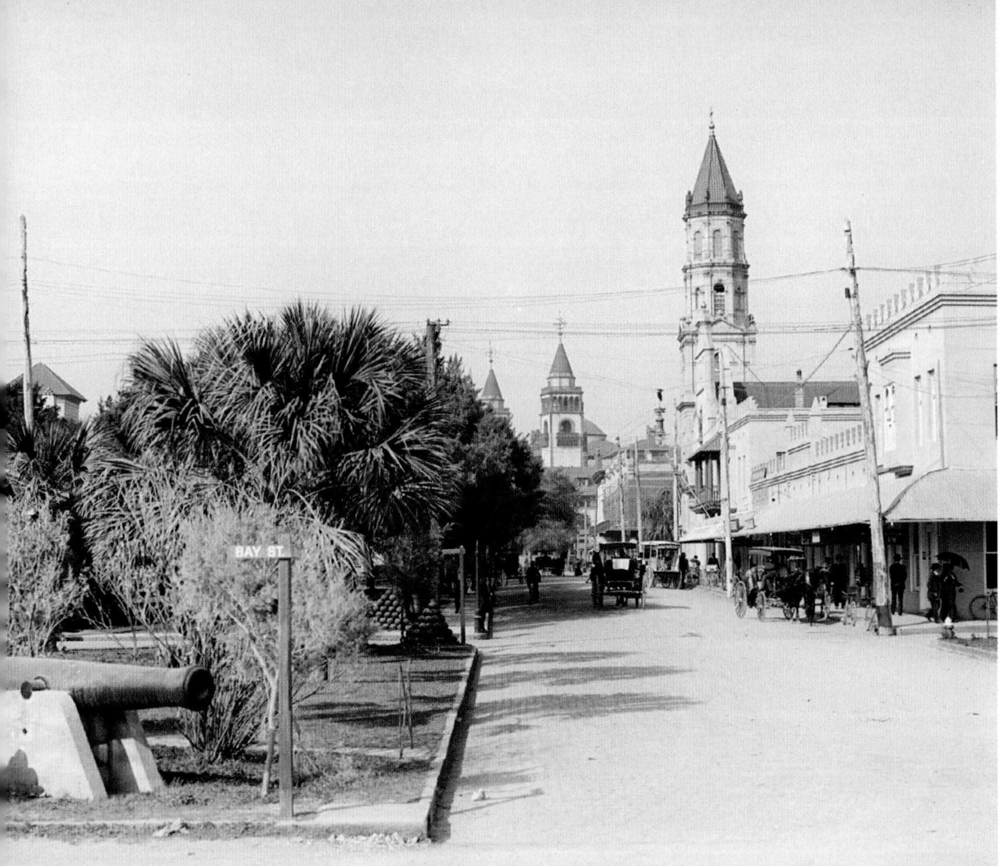

Cathedral Street, St. Augustine, c. 1905

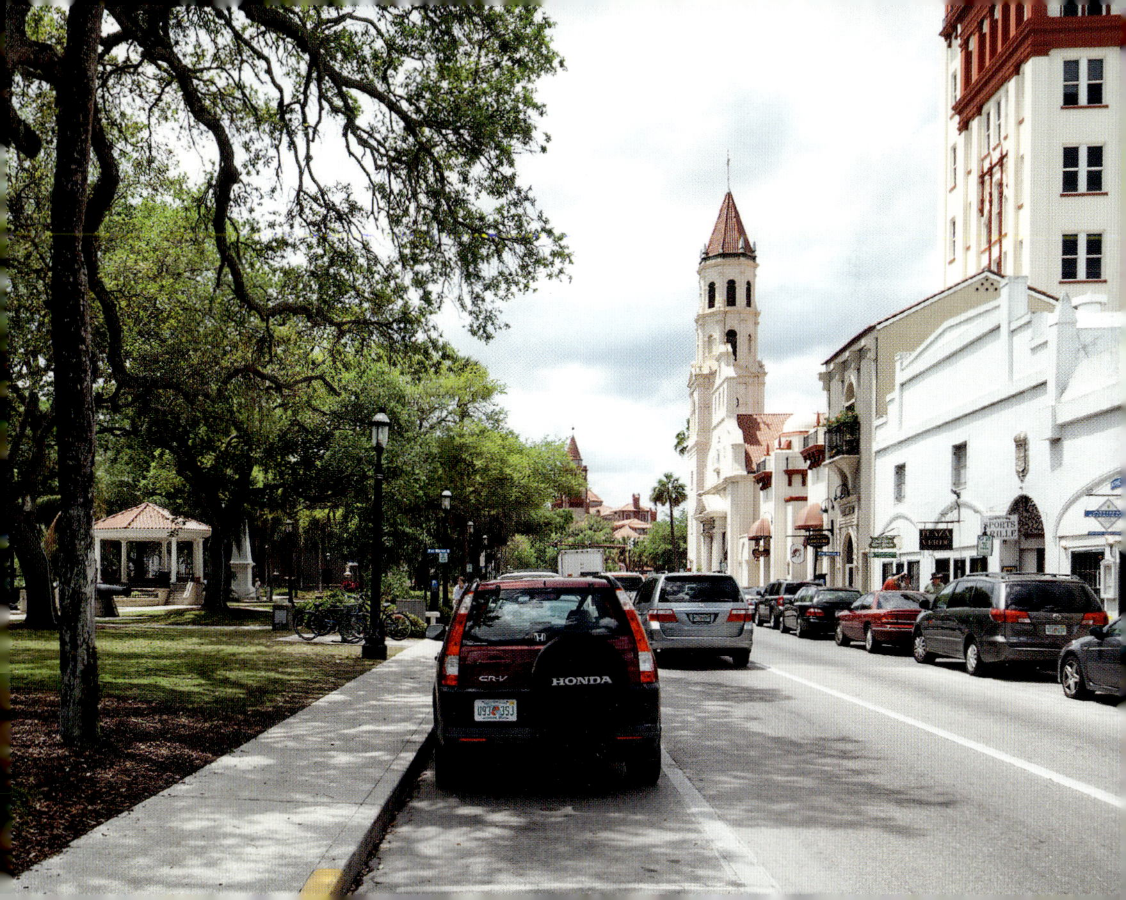
SPORTS
CR-V
HONDA

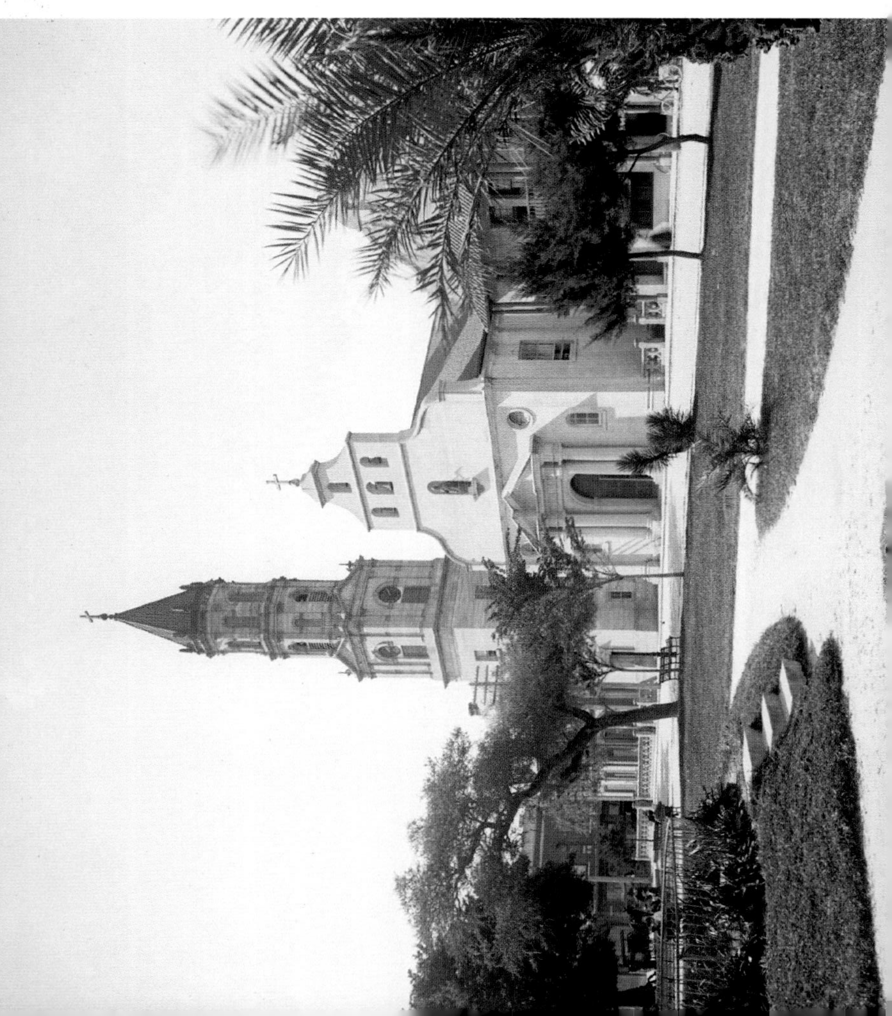

Cathedral, St. Augustine, 1901

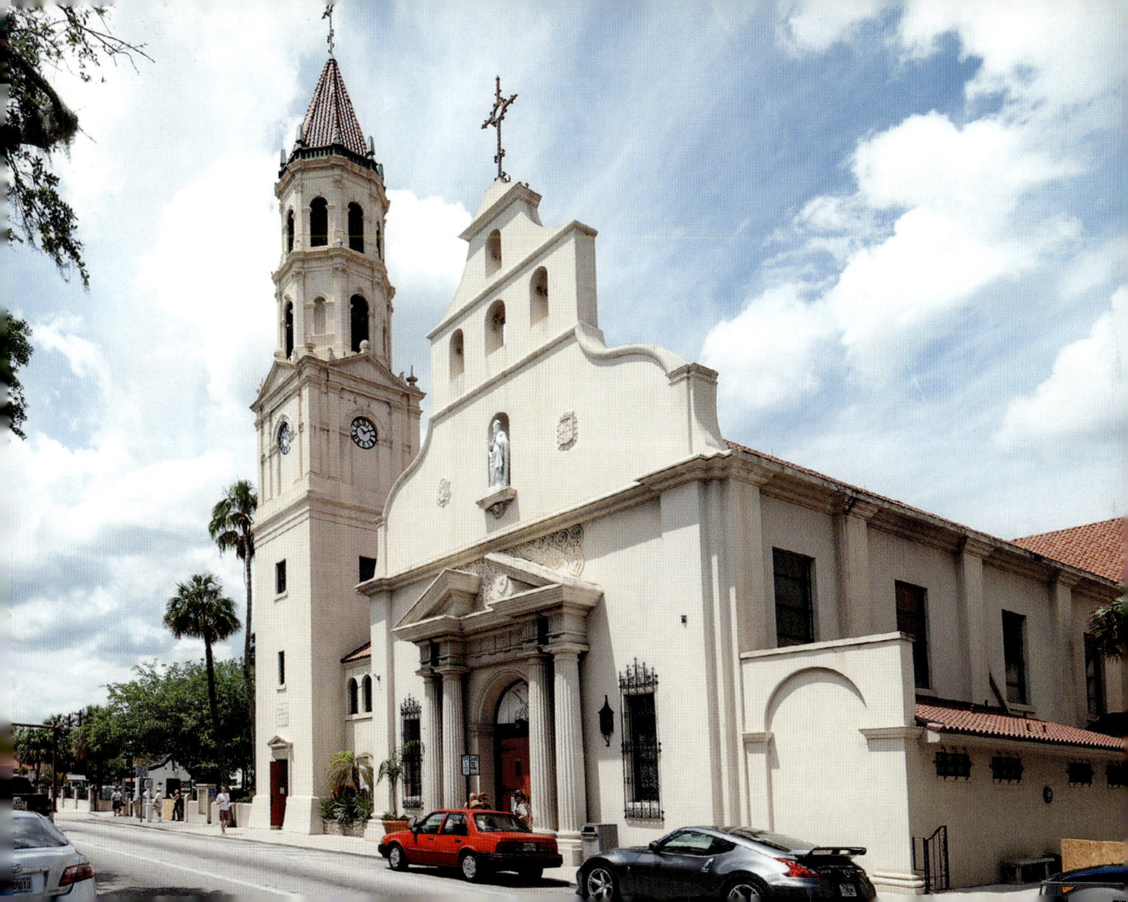

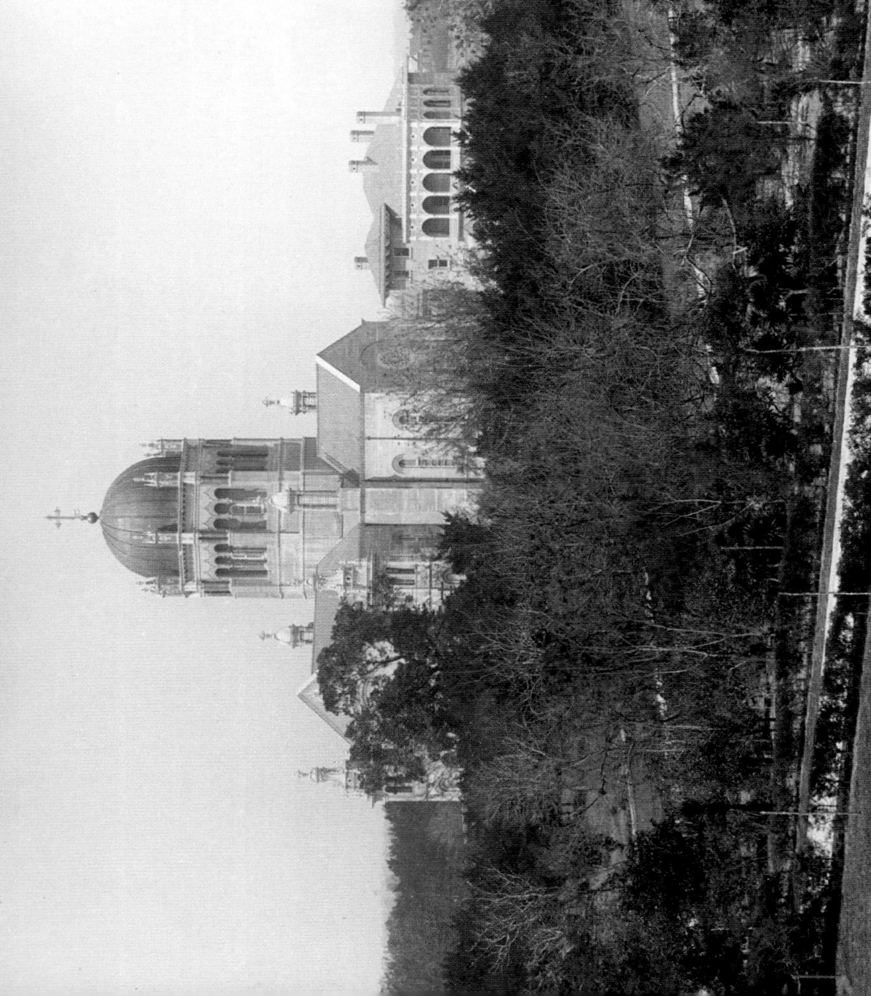

Memorial Presbyterian Church, St. Augustine, c. 1895

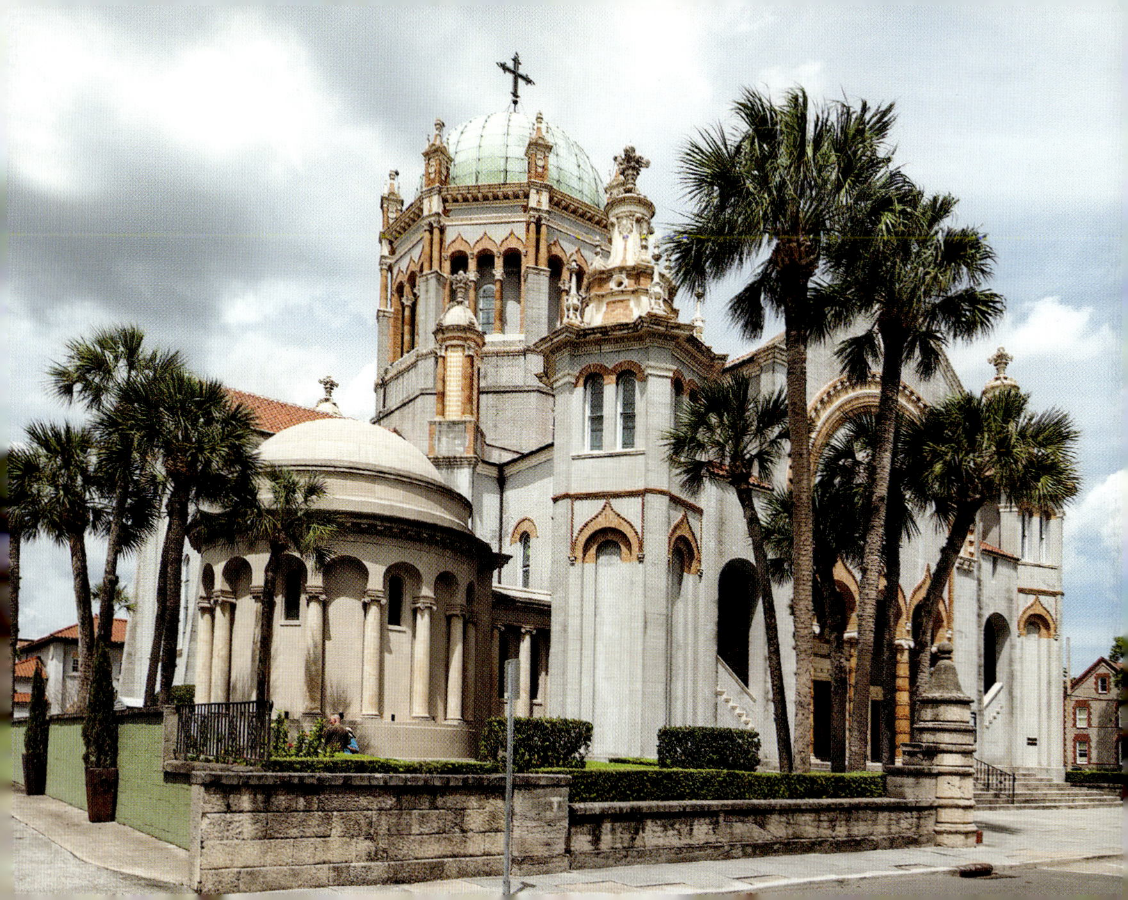

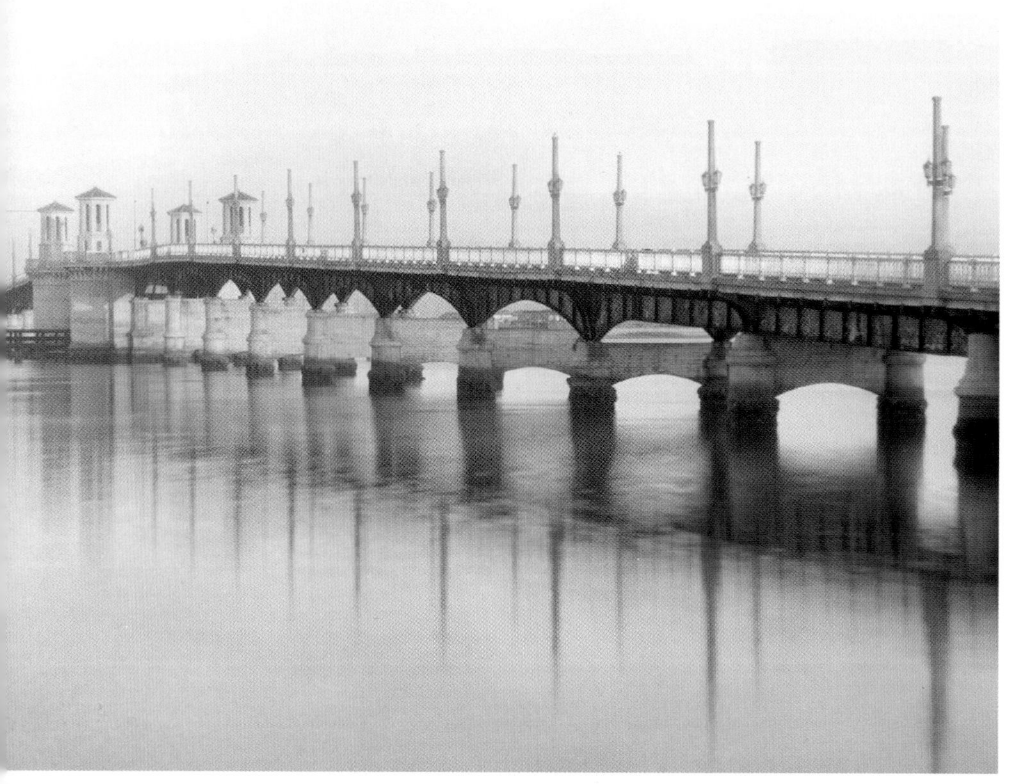

Bridge of Lions, St. Augustine, 1937

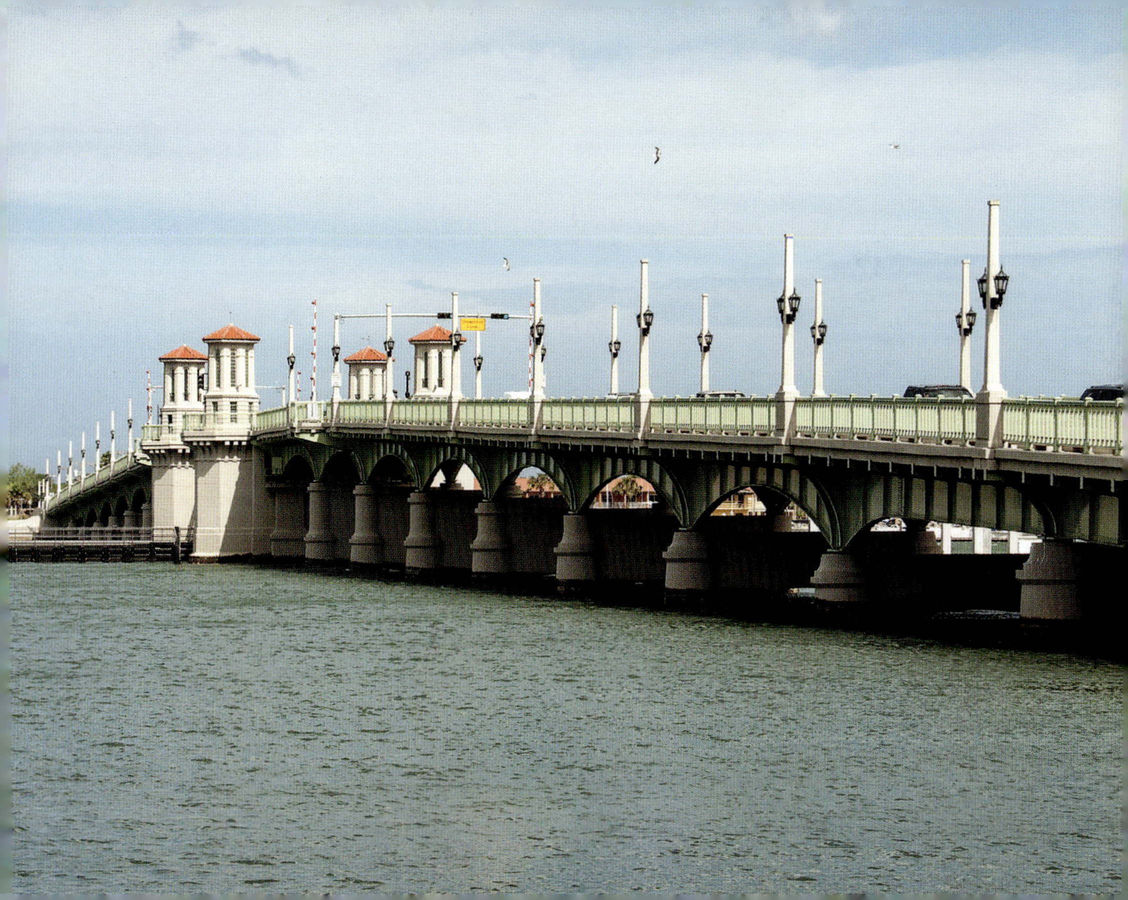

Bridge of Lions, St. Augustine, c. 1965

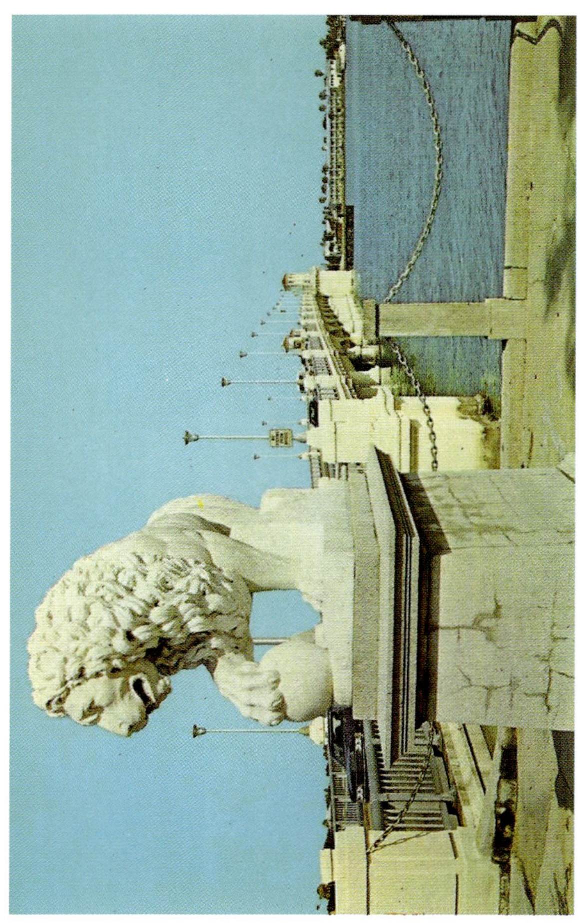

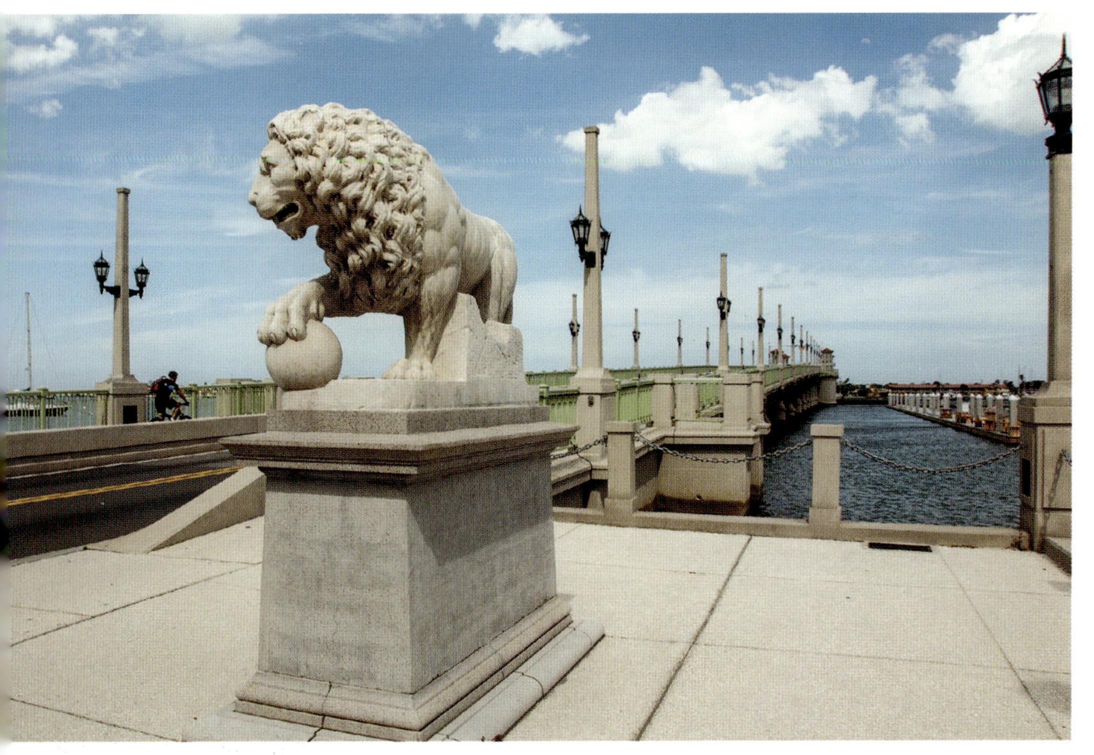

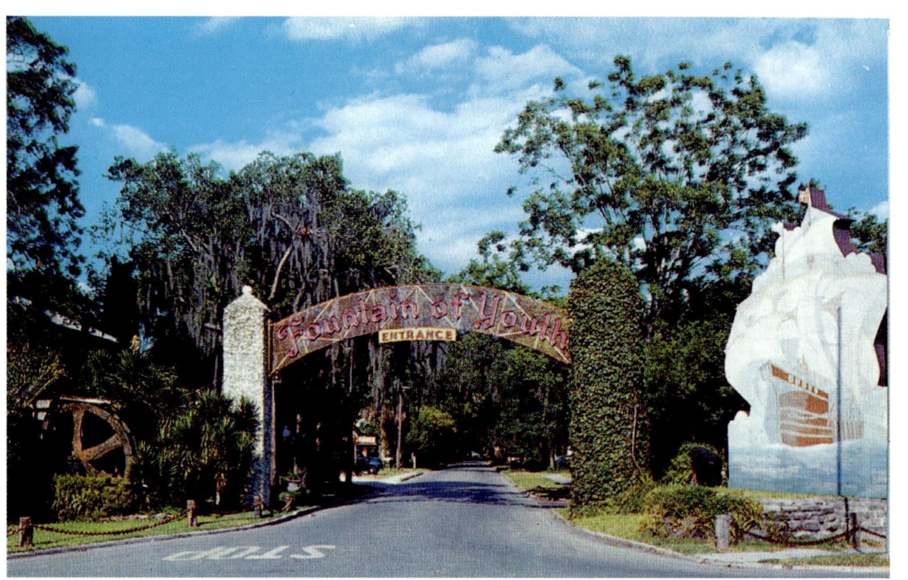

Fountain of Youth Archaeological Park, St. Augustine, c. 1965

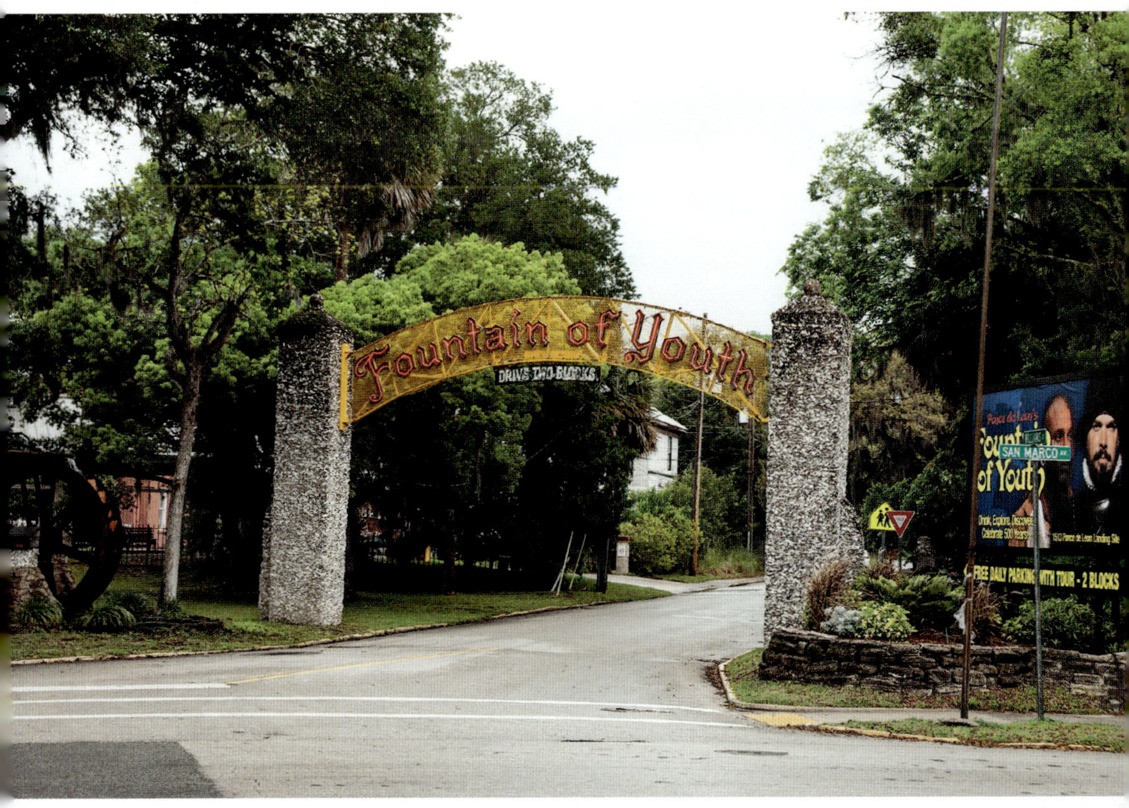
Fountain of Youth
DRIVE TWO BLOCKS
SAN MARCO AV
Celebrate 500 Years!
FREE DAILY PARKING WITH TOUR - 2 BLOCKS

Villa Zorayda, St. Augustine, 1904

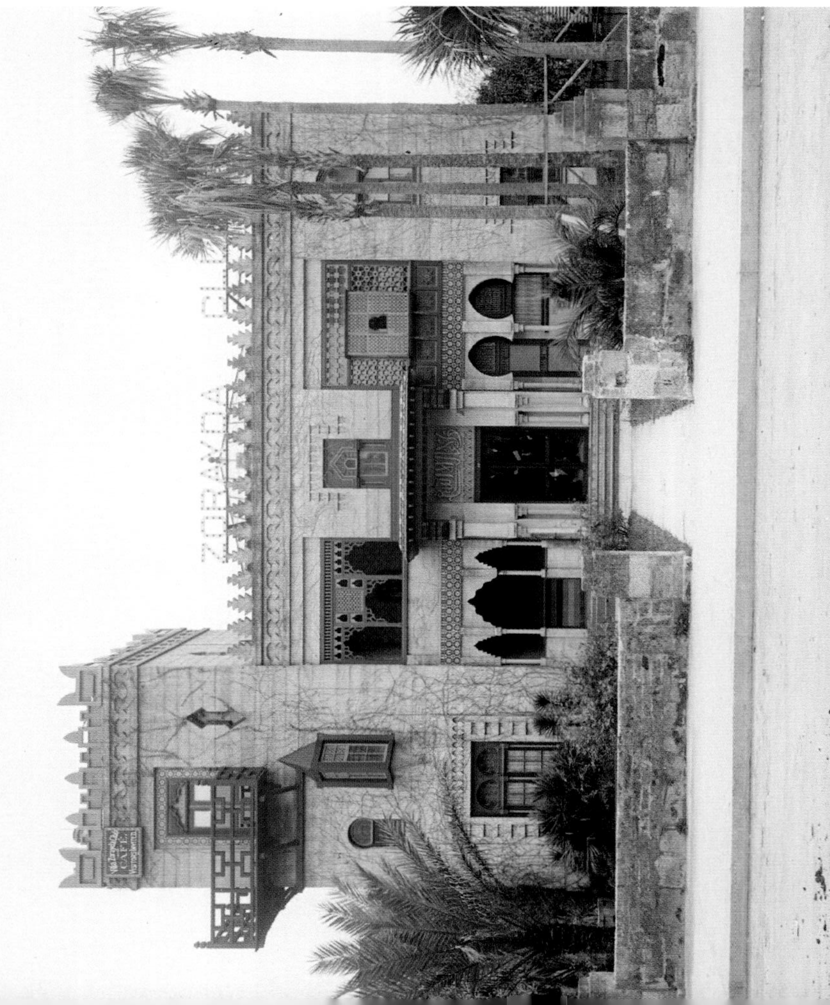

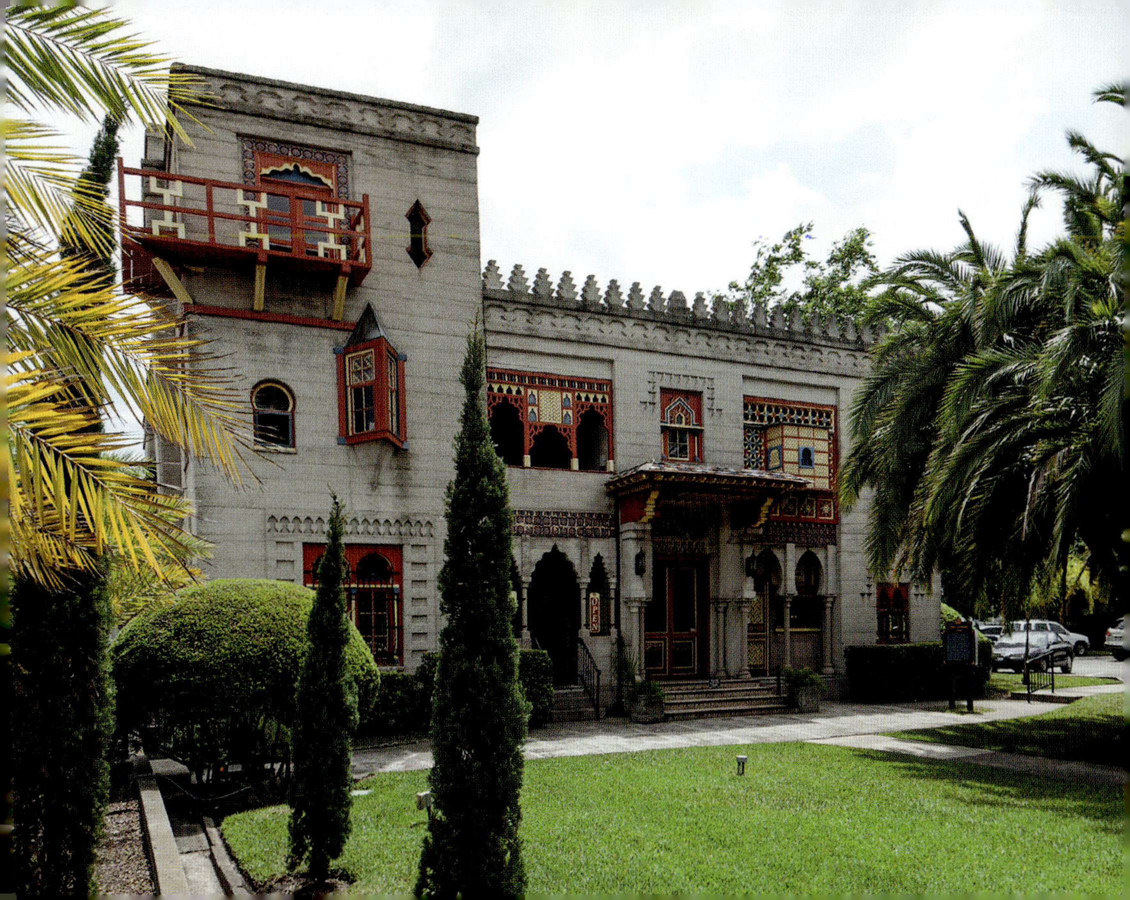
OPEN

Alcazar Hotel (now Lightner Museum), St. Augustine, c. 1905

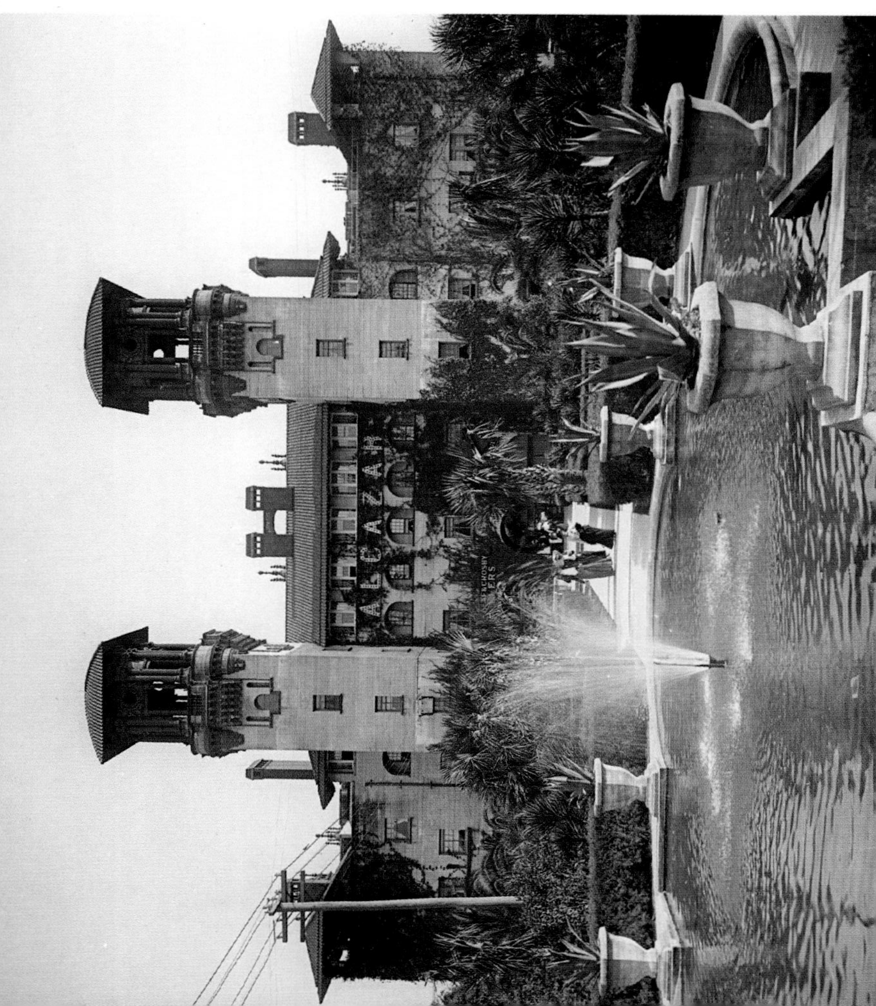

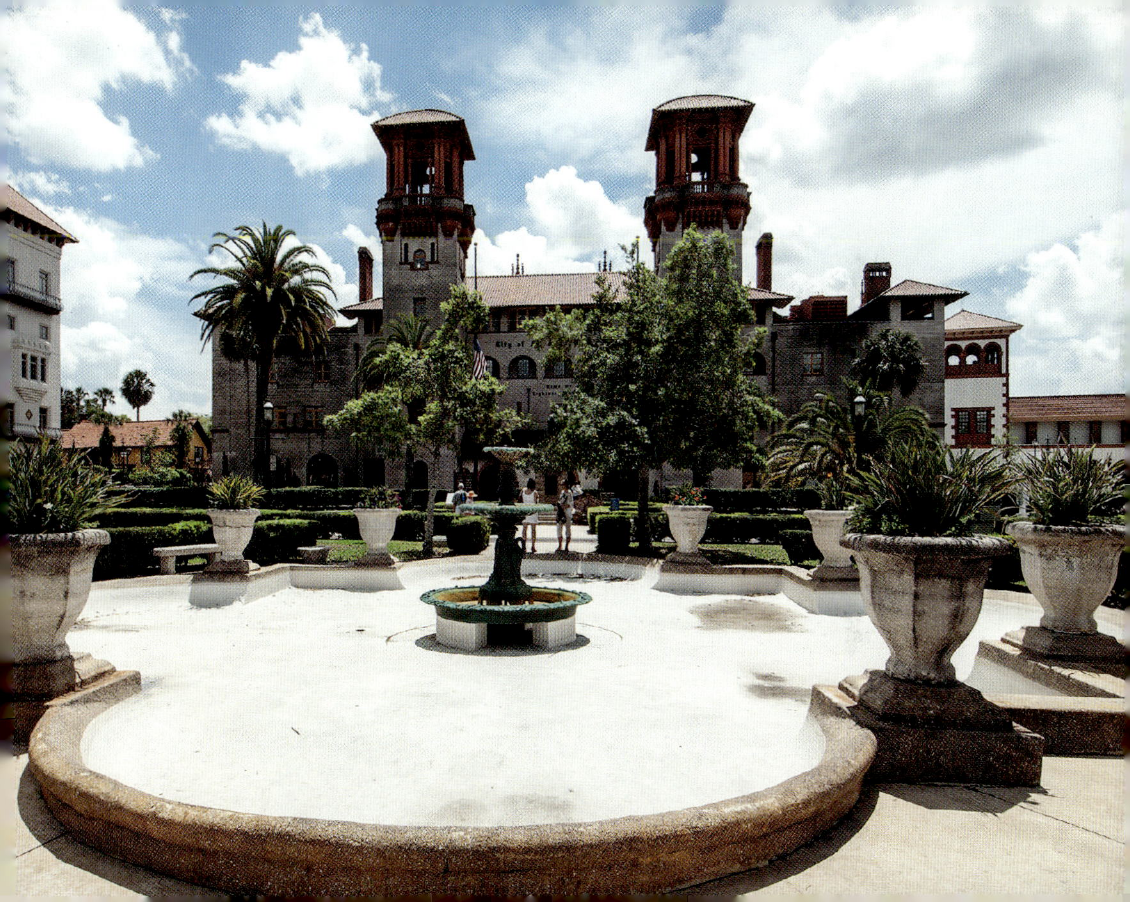

Alcazar Hotel (now Lightner Museum), St. Augustine, c. 1905

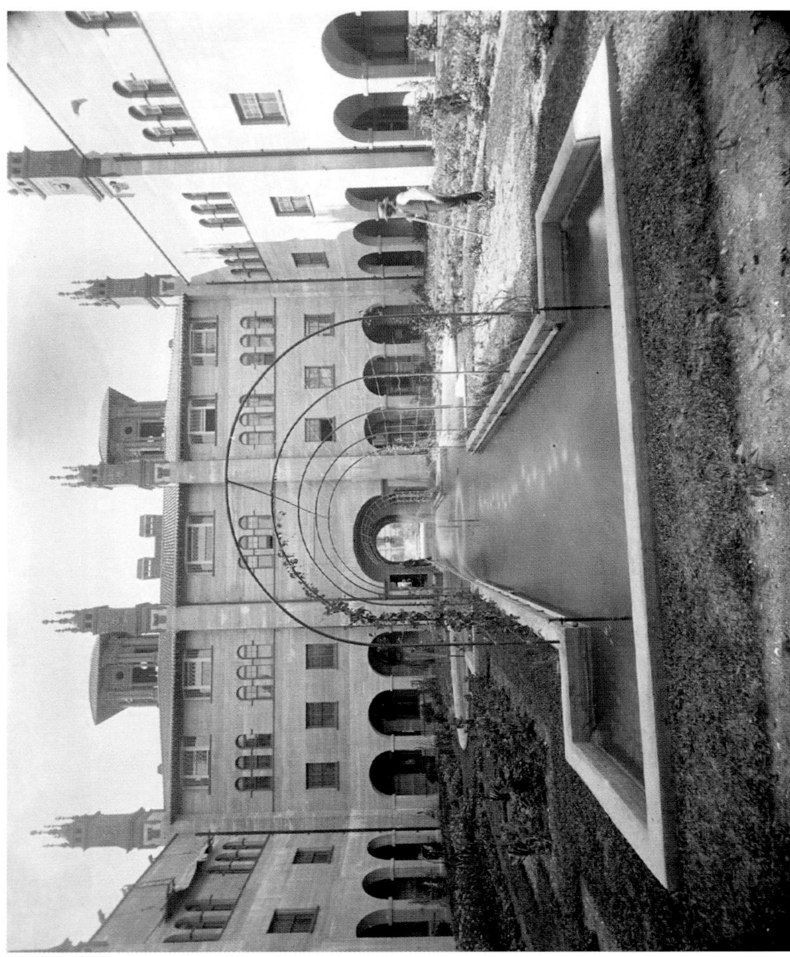

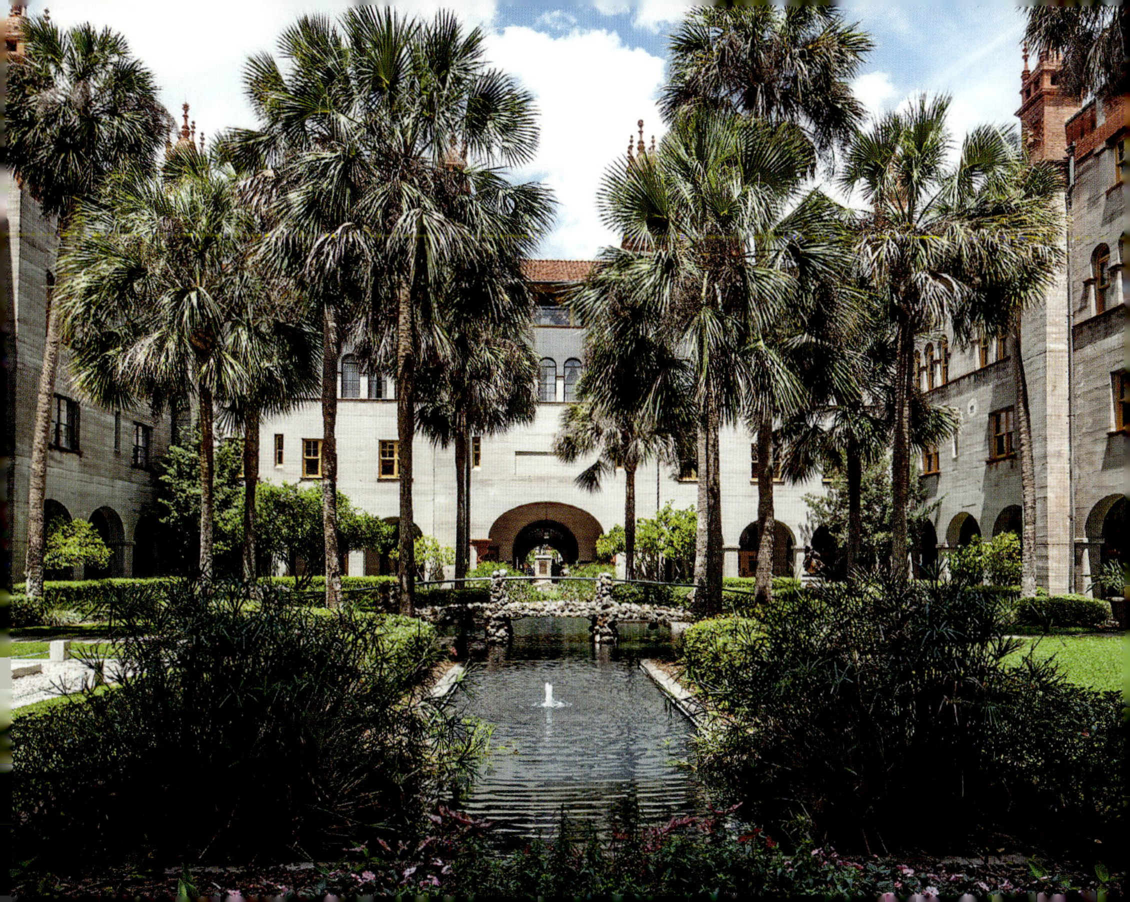

Alcazar Hotel, St. Augustine, 1927 (left), c. 1895 (right)

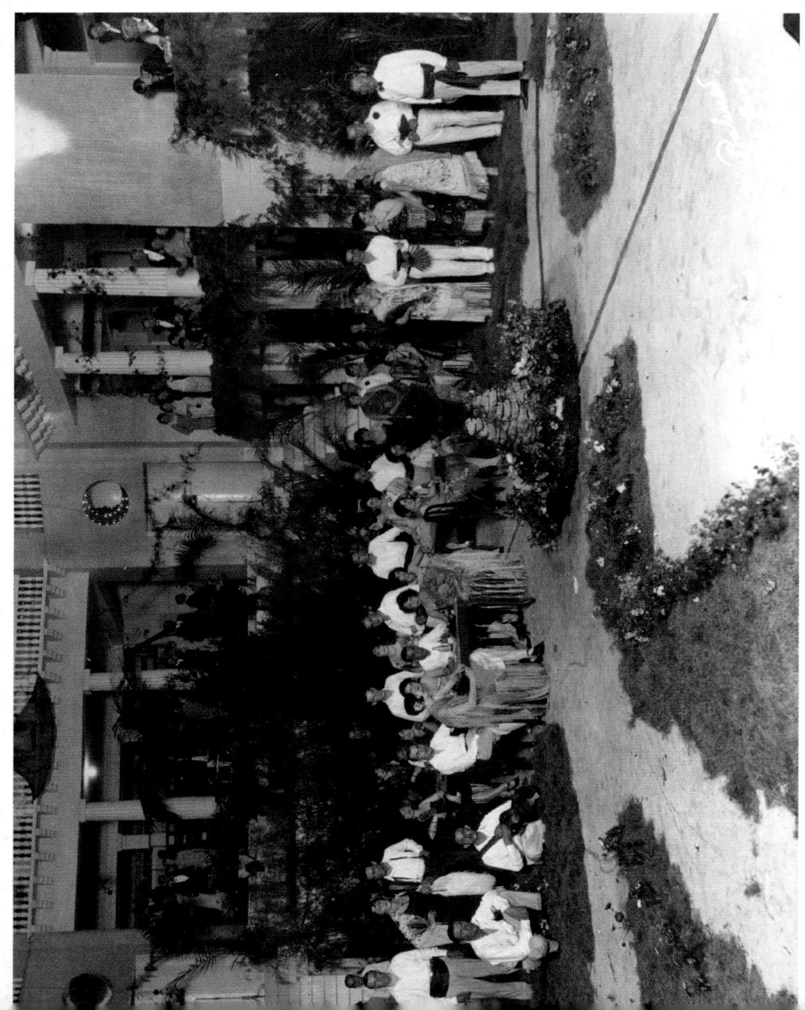

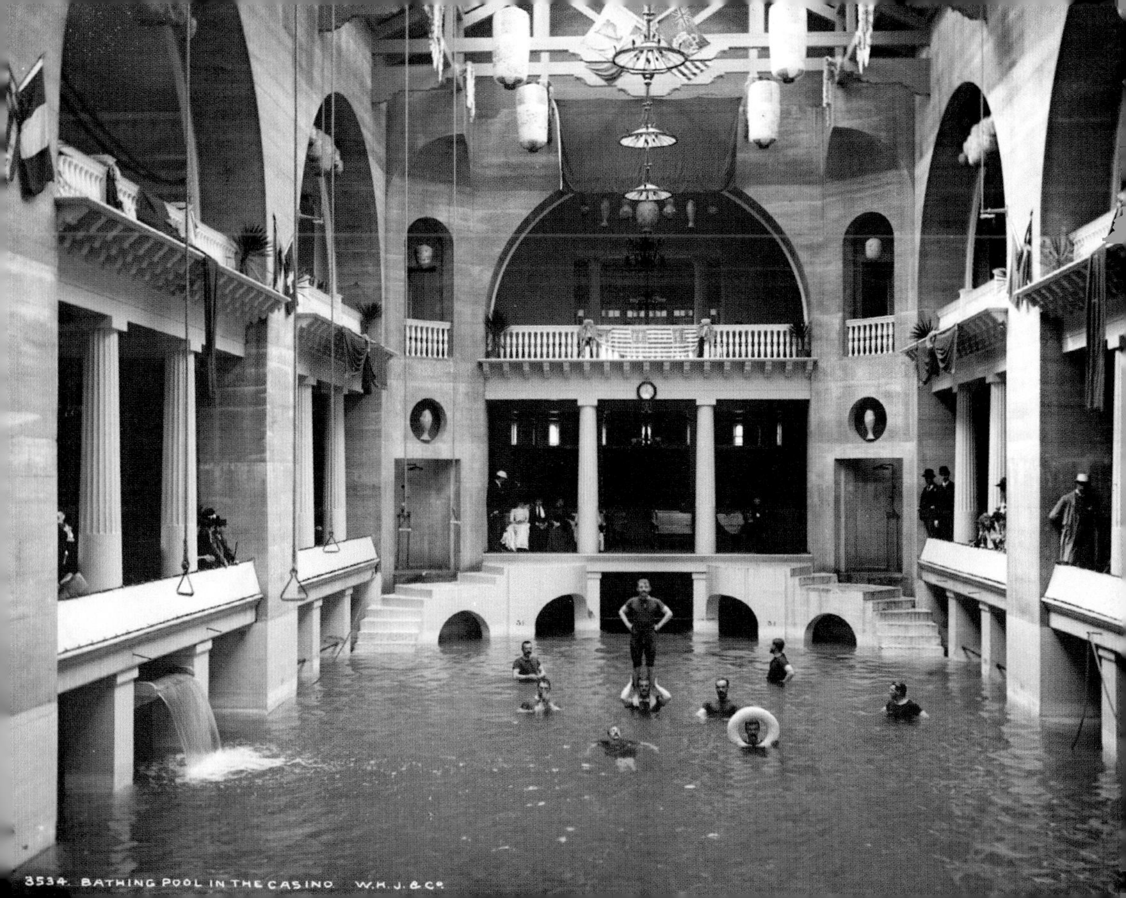
3534. BATHING POOL IN THE CASINO W.H.J. & Co.

Sea Wall, St. Augustine, c. 1895

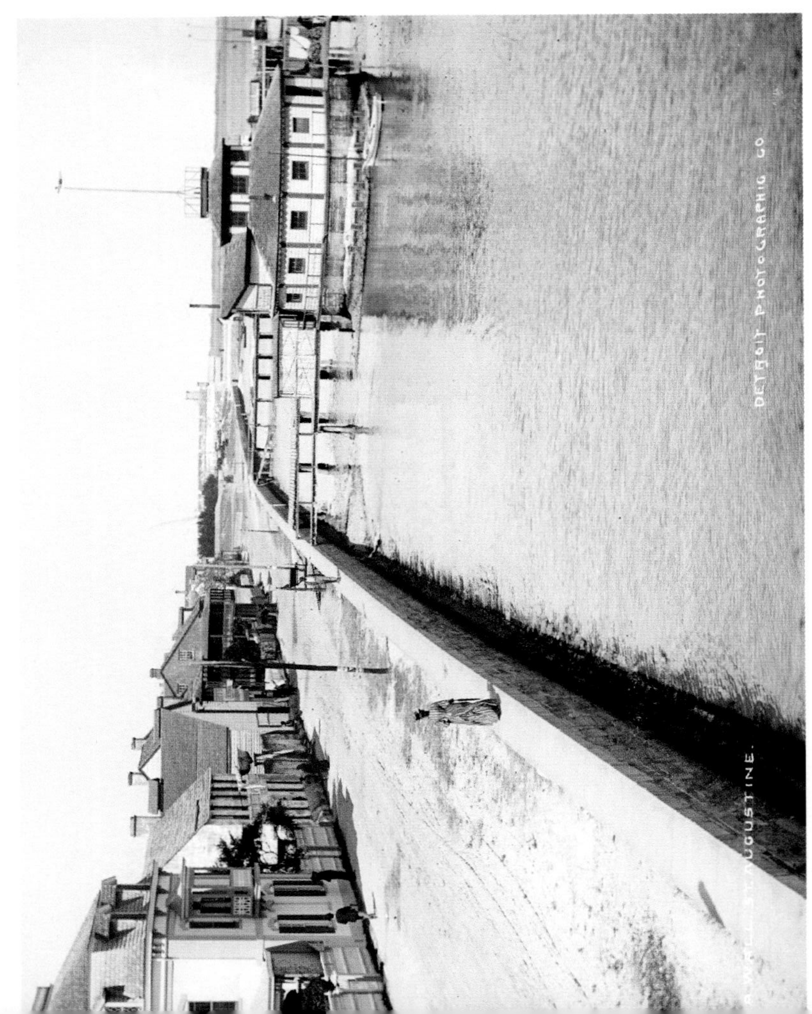

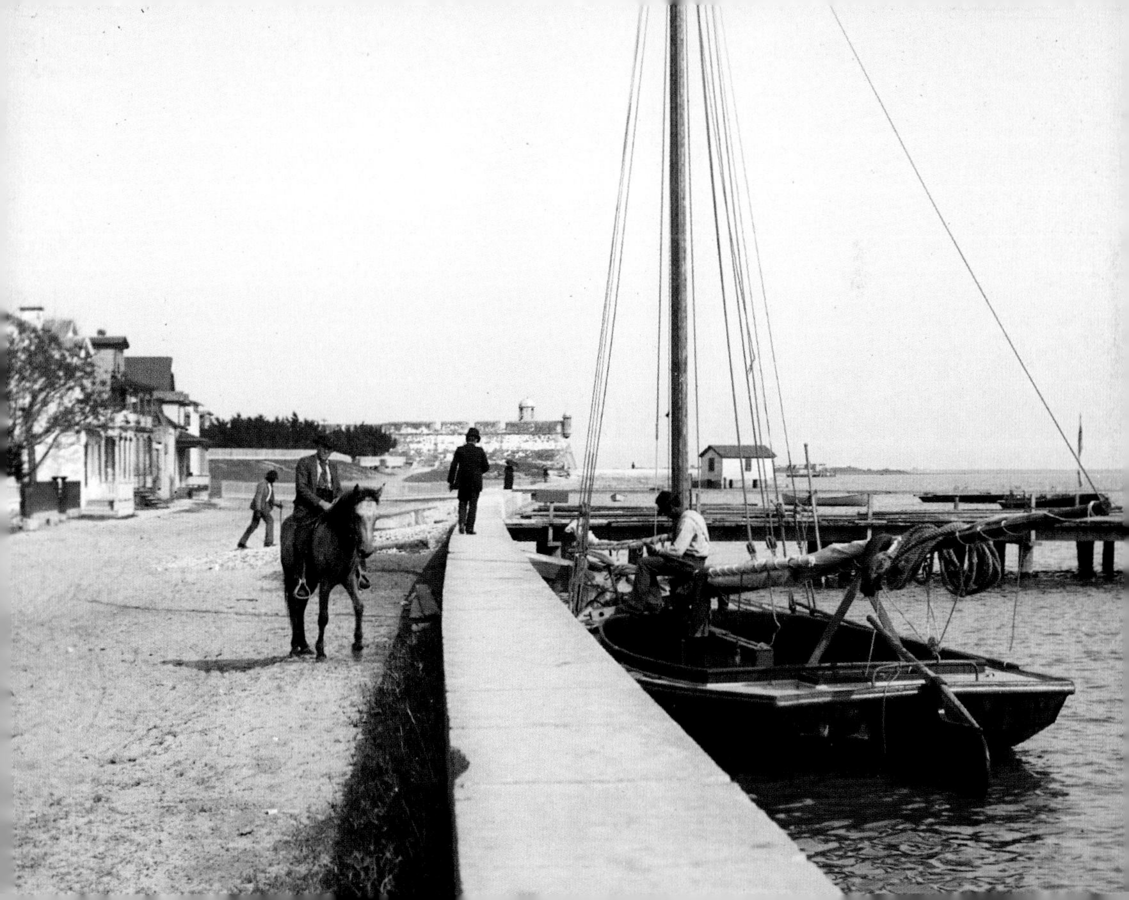

Castillo de San Marcos, St. Augustine, c. 1895

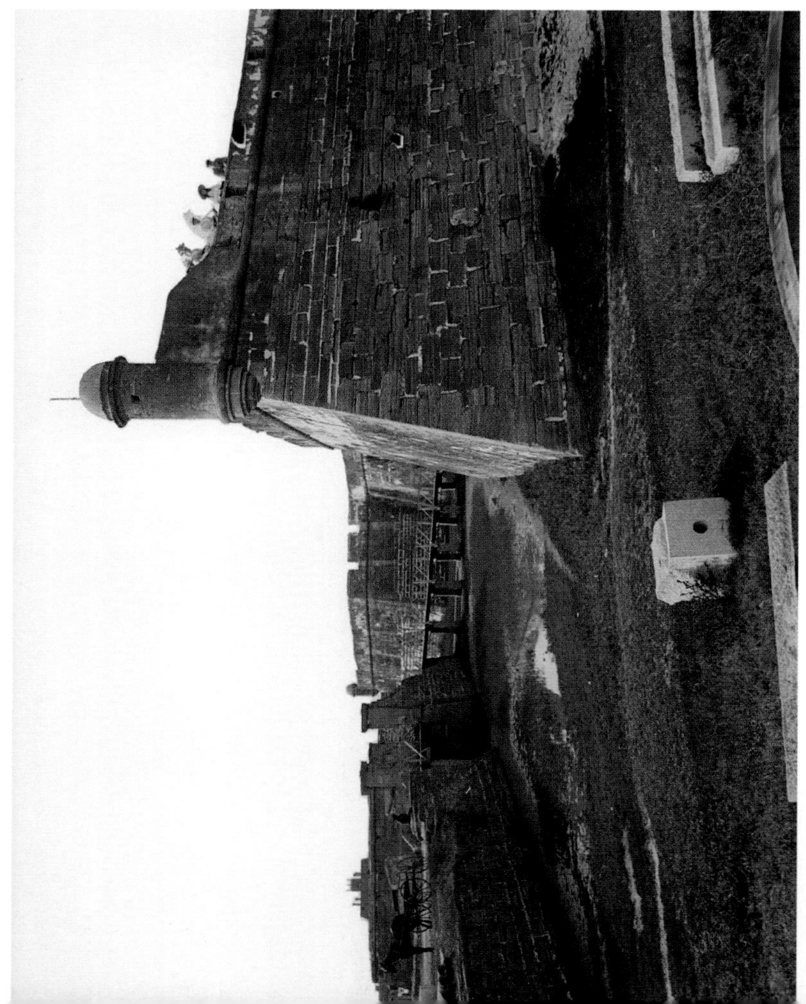

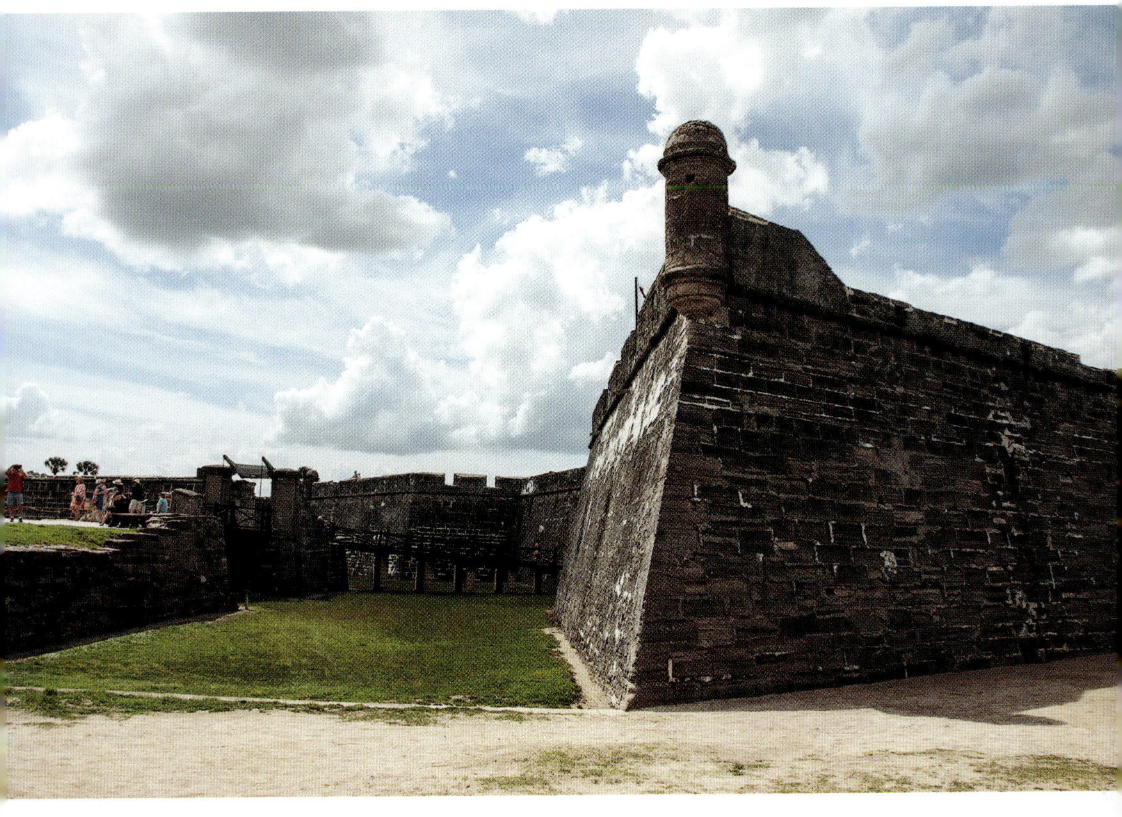

Castillo de San Marcos, St. Augustine, c. 1895

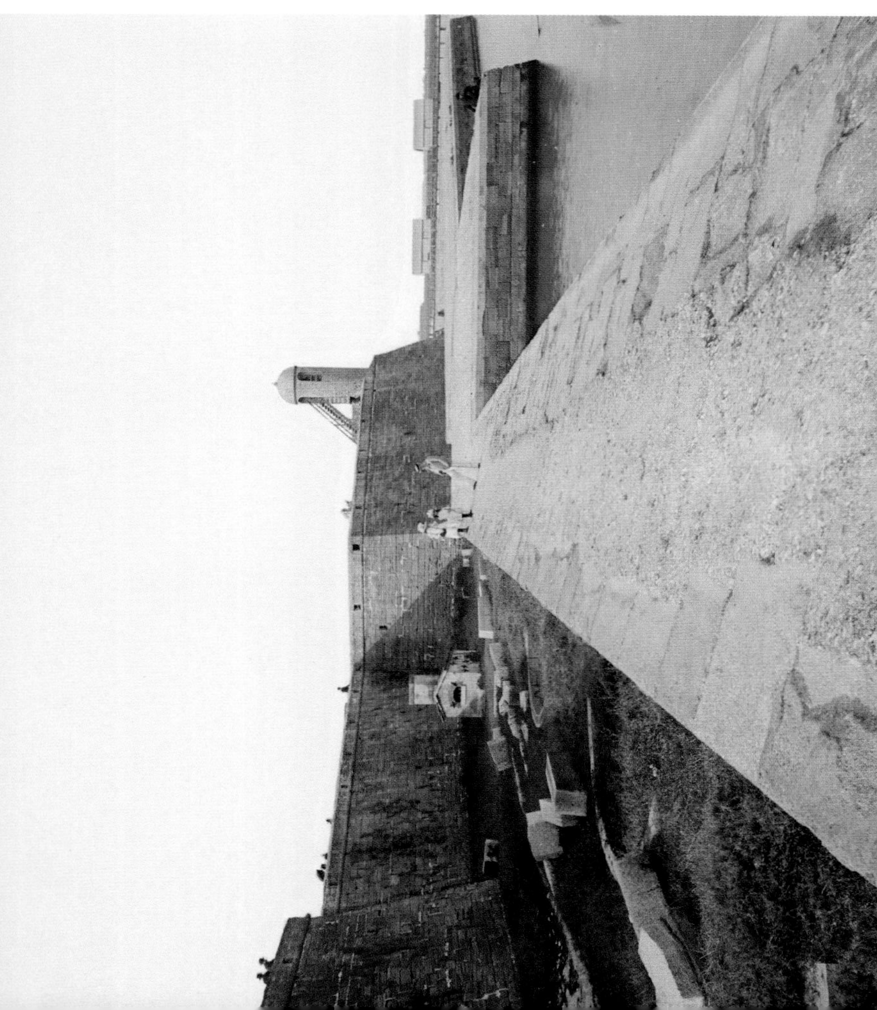

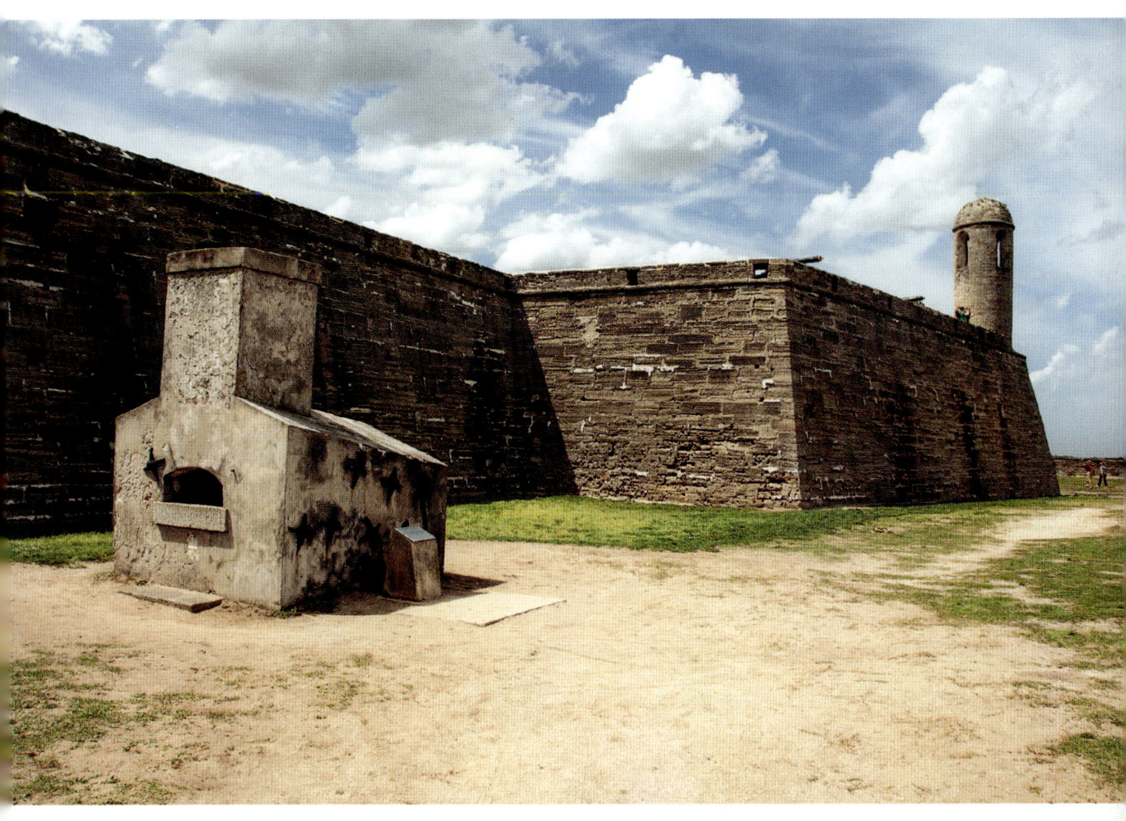

Castillo de San Marcos, St. Augustine, 1863

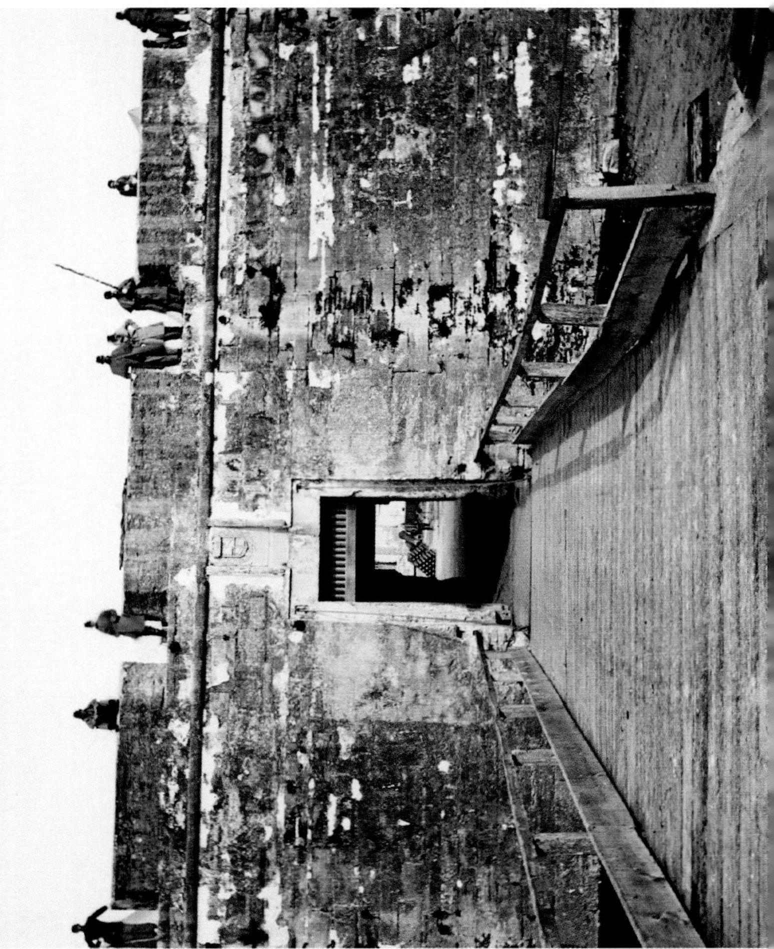

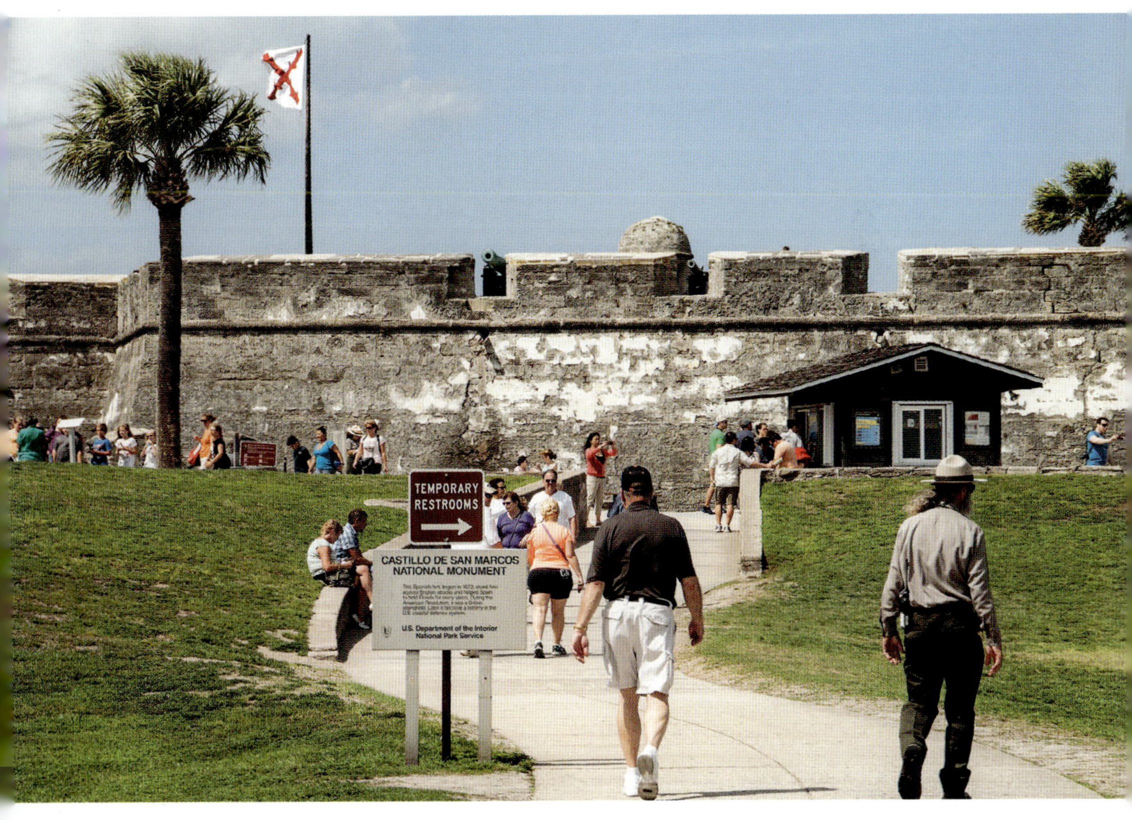
TEMPORARY
RESTROOMS
CASTILLO DE SAN MARCOS
NATIONAL MONUMENT
U.S. Department of the Interior
National Park Service

Anastasia Lighthouse, St. Augustine, 1902 (left), 1937 (right)

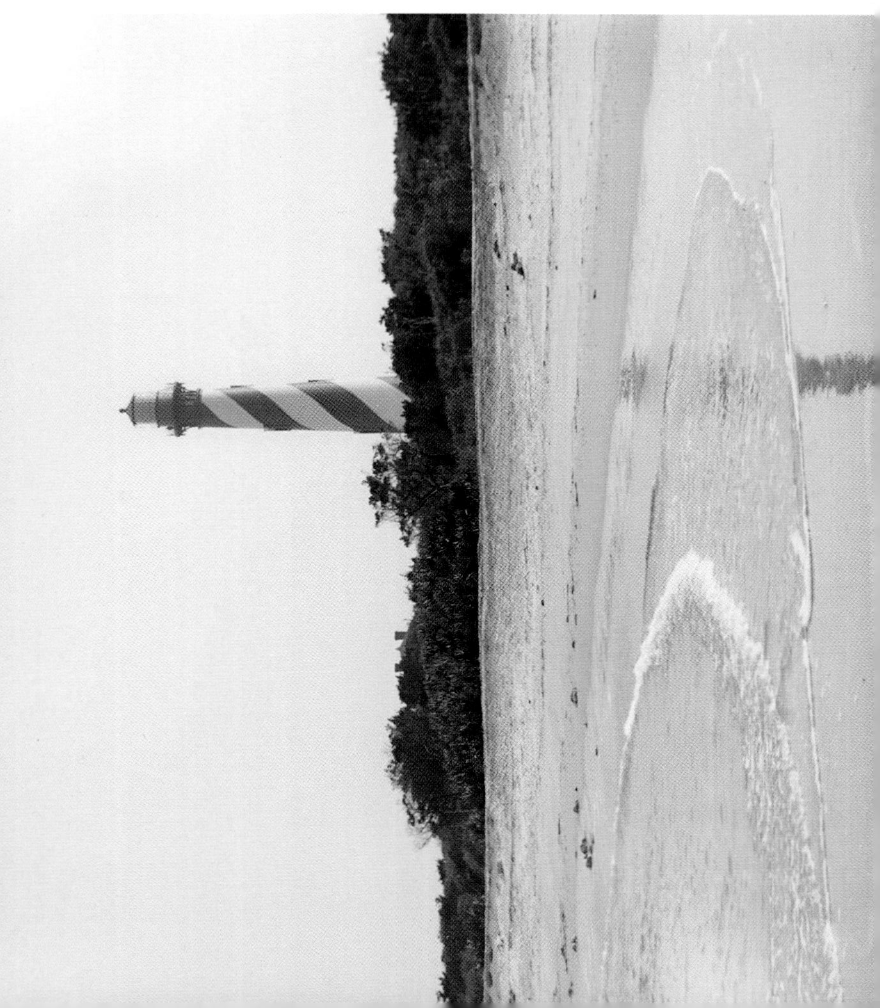

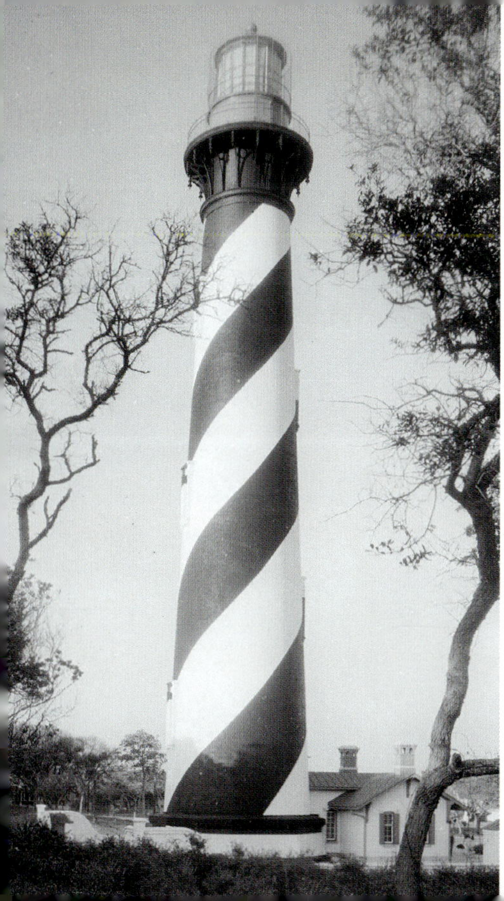

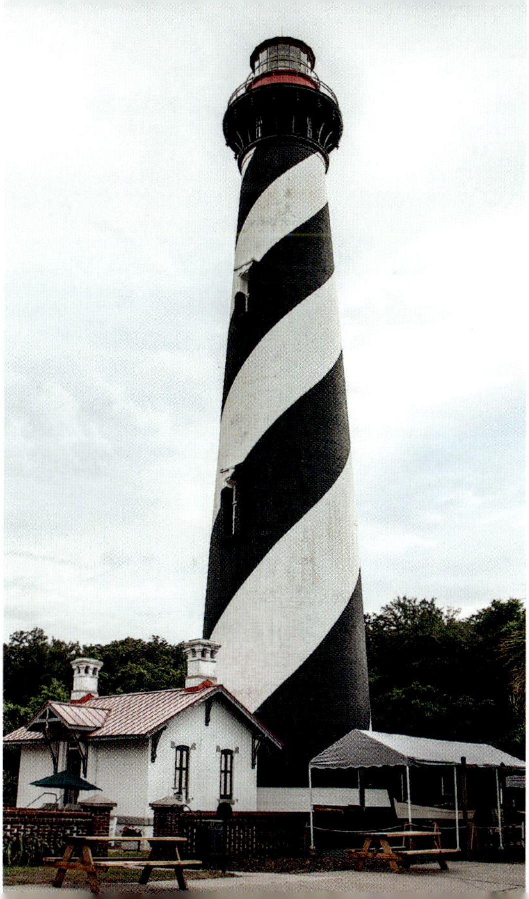

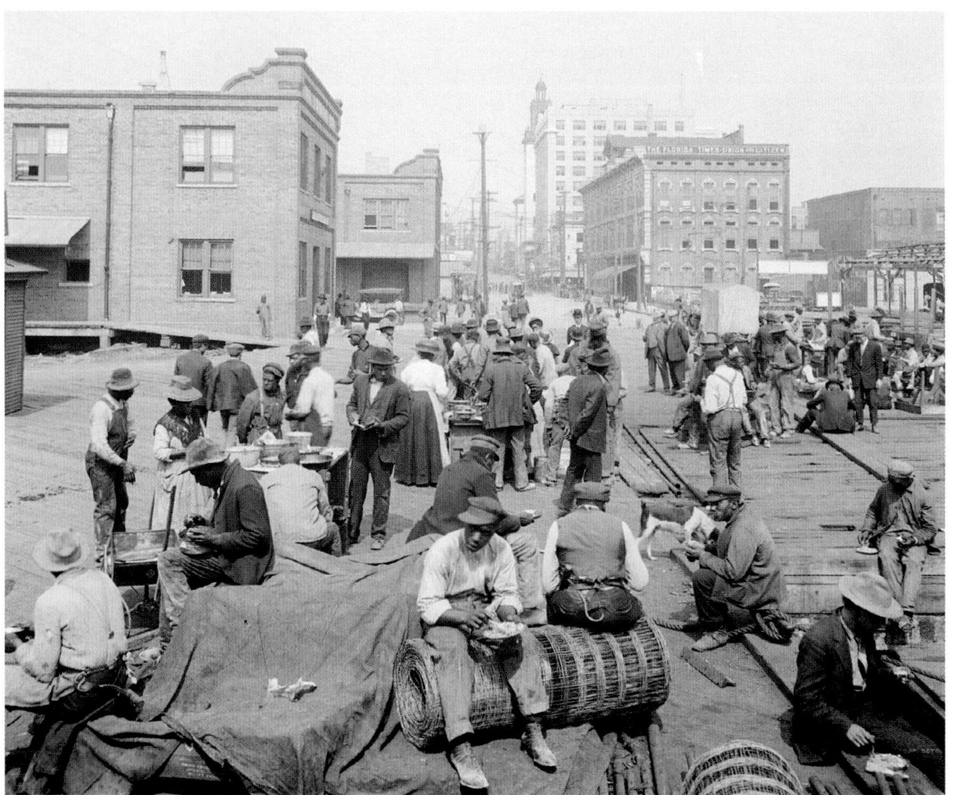

The Docks, Jacksonville, c. 1910

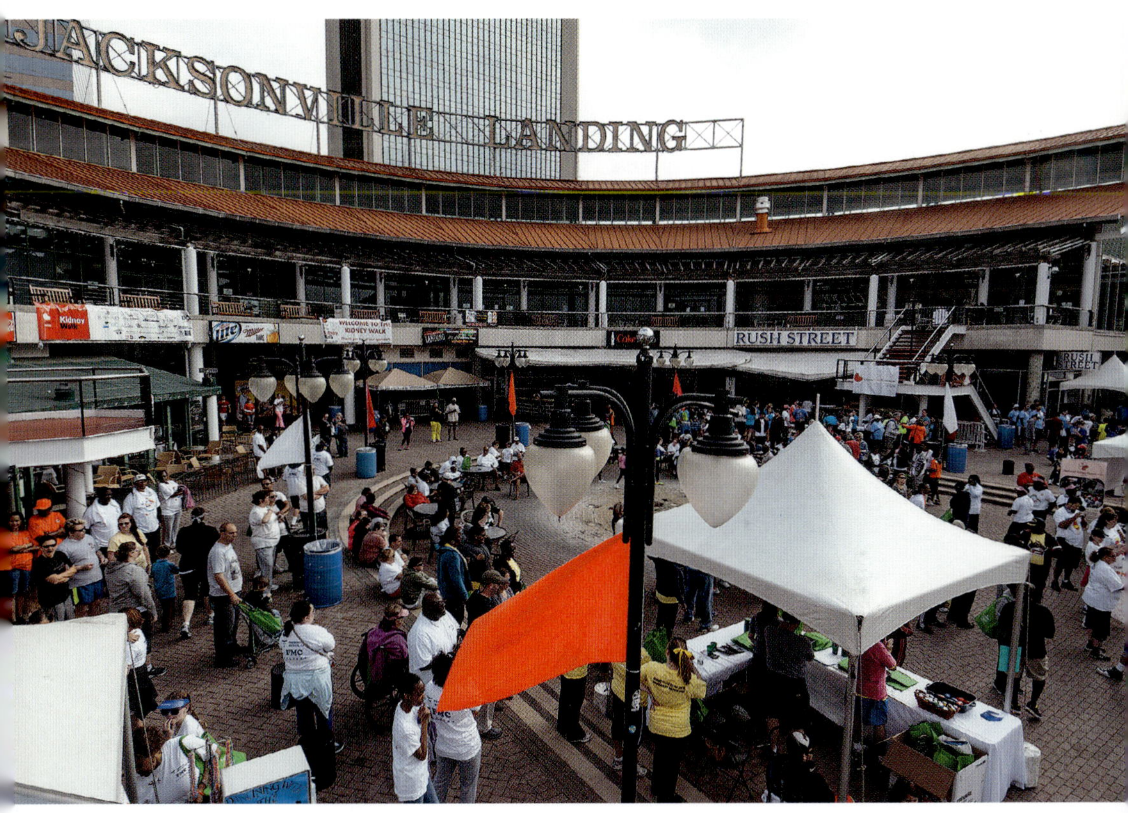
JACKSONVILLE LANDING
RUSH STREET
Kidney Walk
WELCOME TO THE KIDNEY WALK

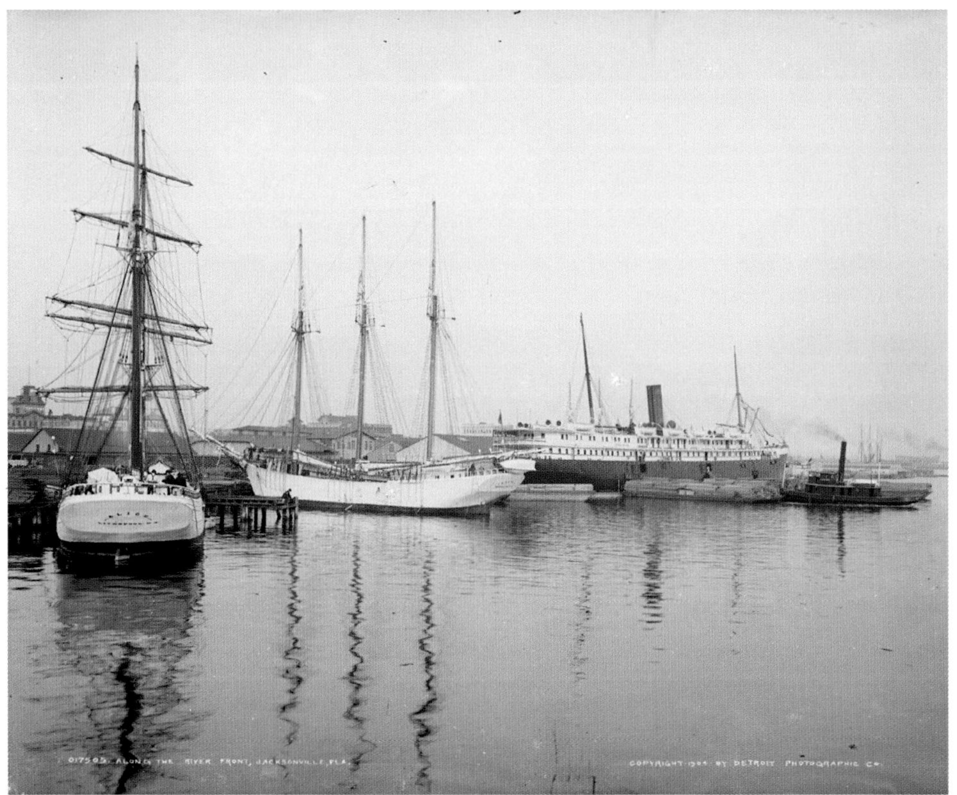

Riverfront, Jacksonville, 1904

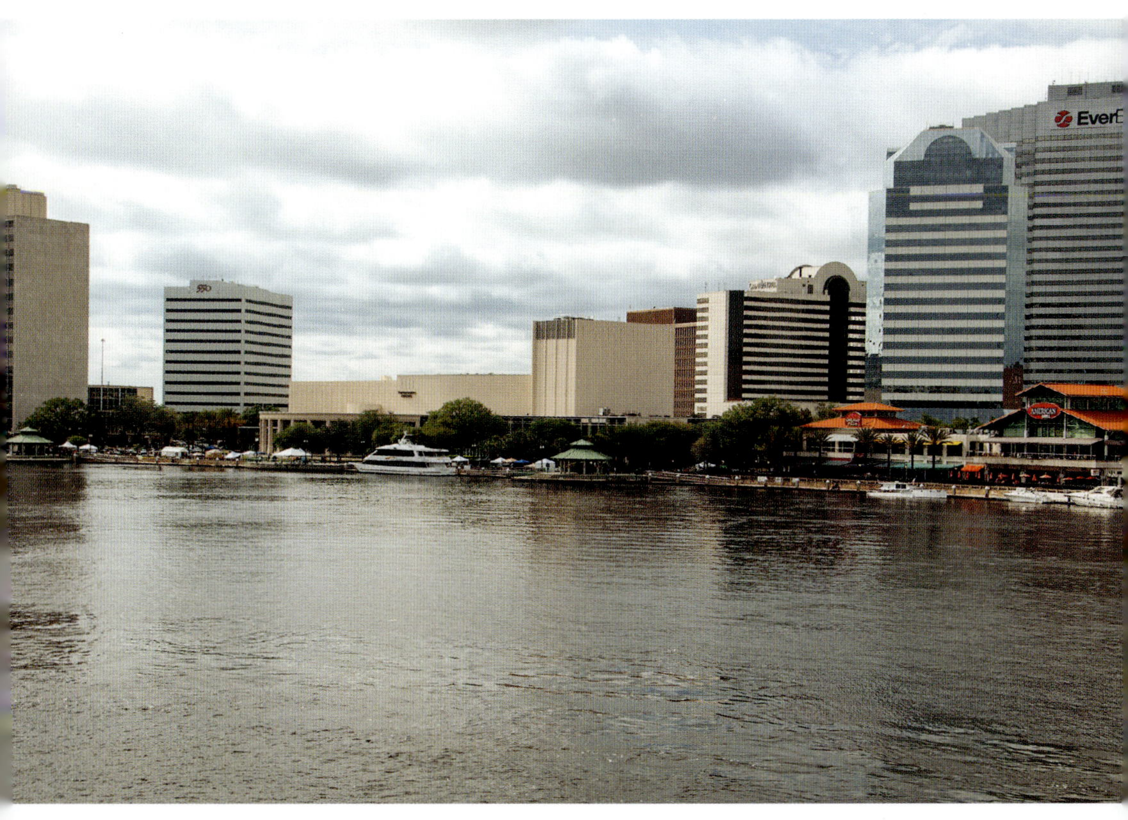

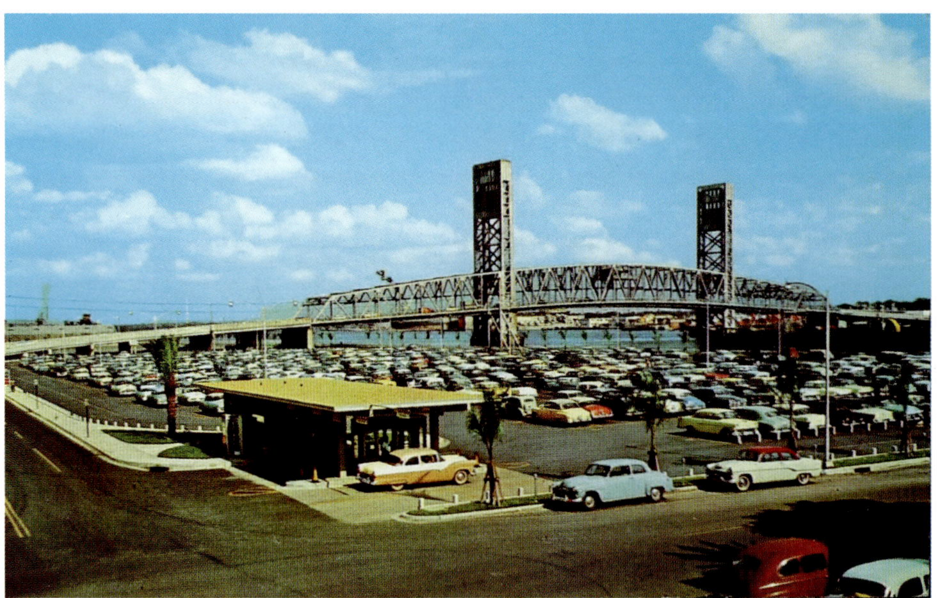

Main Street Bridge, Jacksonville, c. 1955

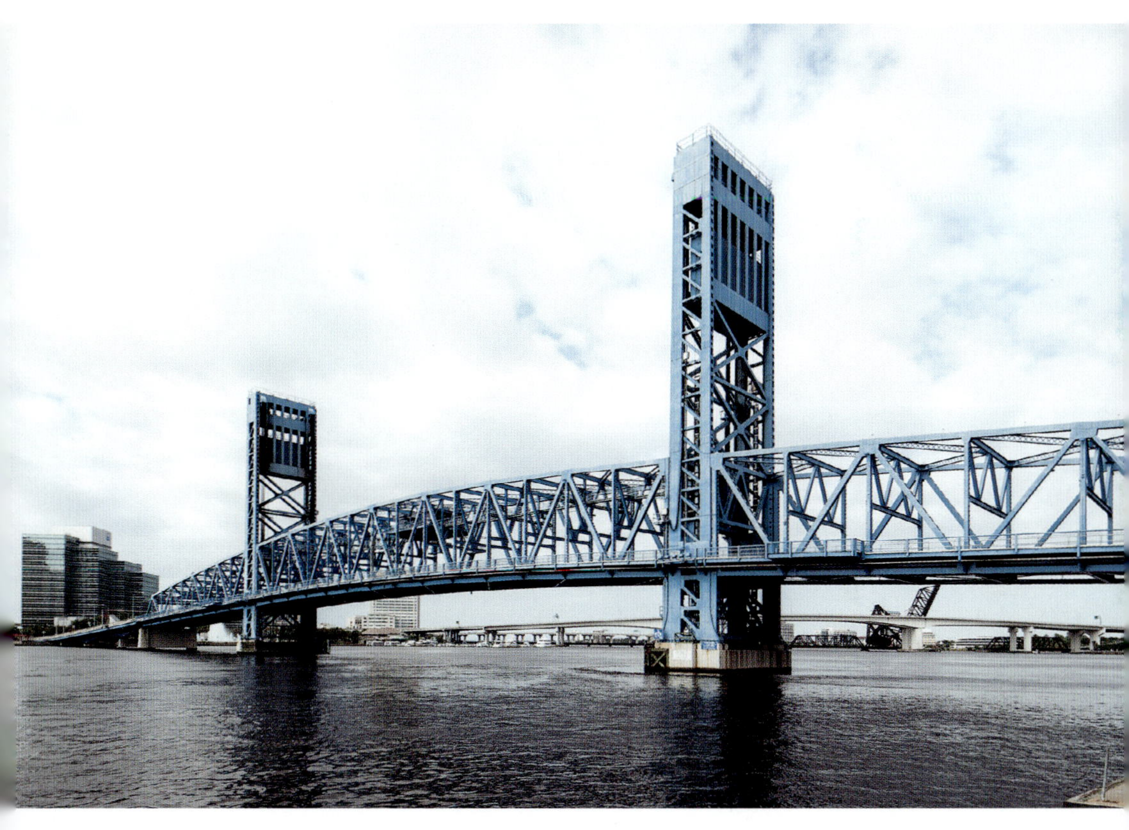

Windsor Hotel (demolished 1950), Hemming Plaza, Jacksonville, c. 1910

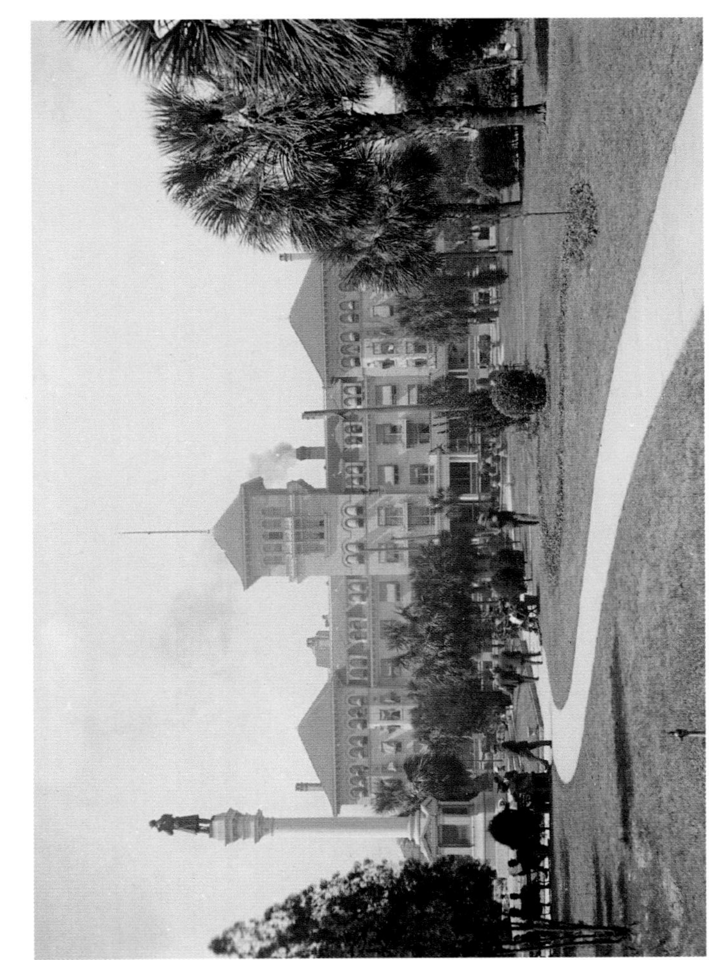

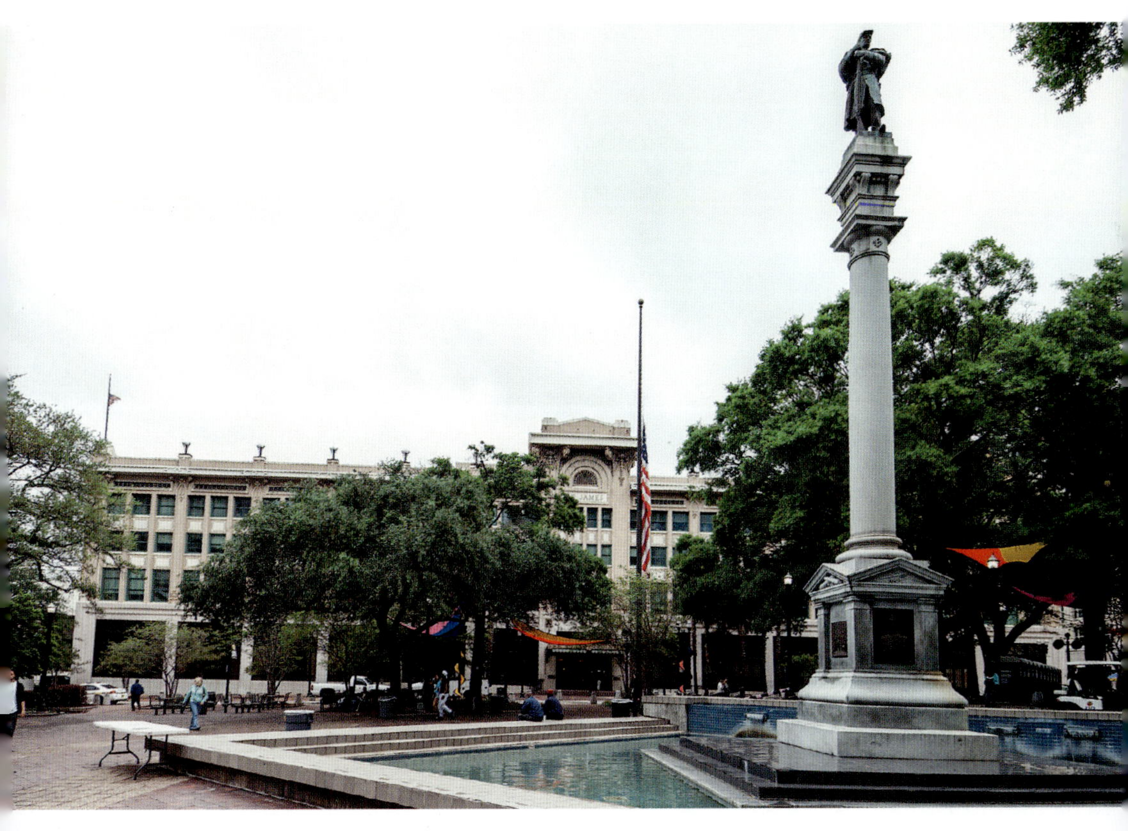
JAMES

Bisbee Building, Laura Street, Jacksonville, c. 1910

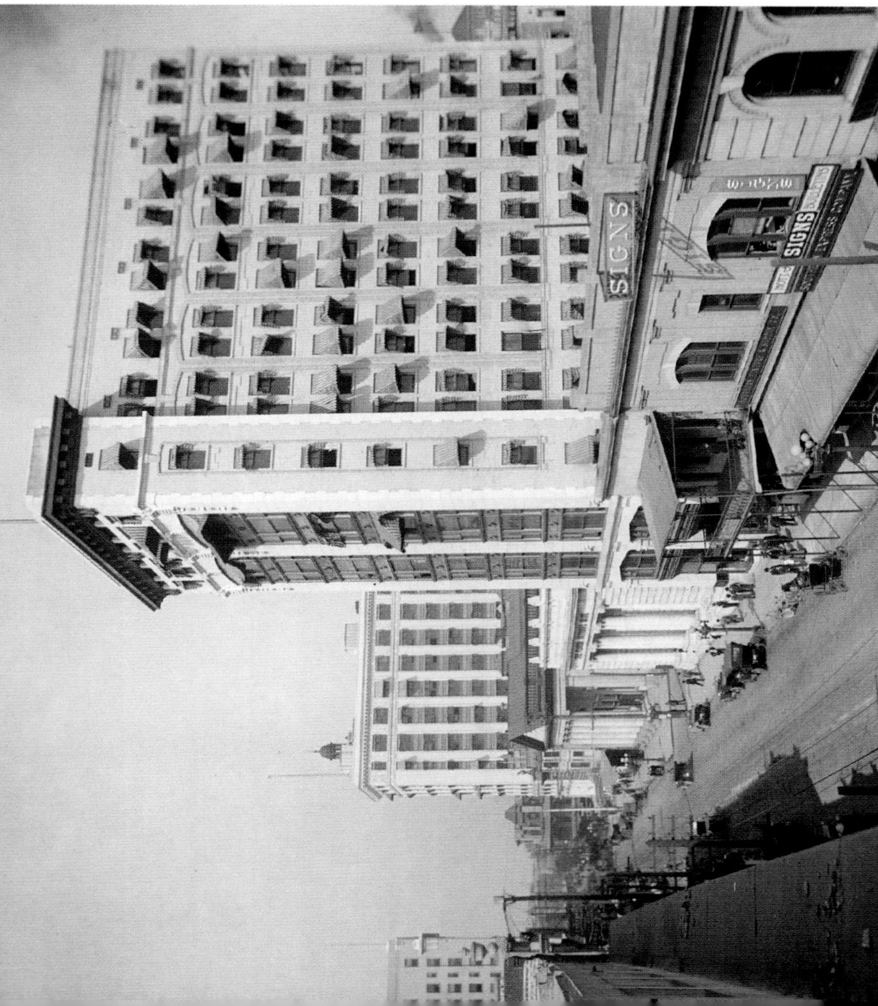

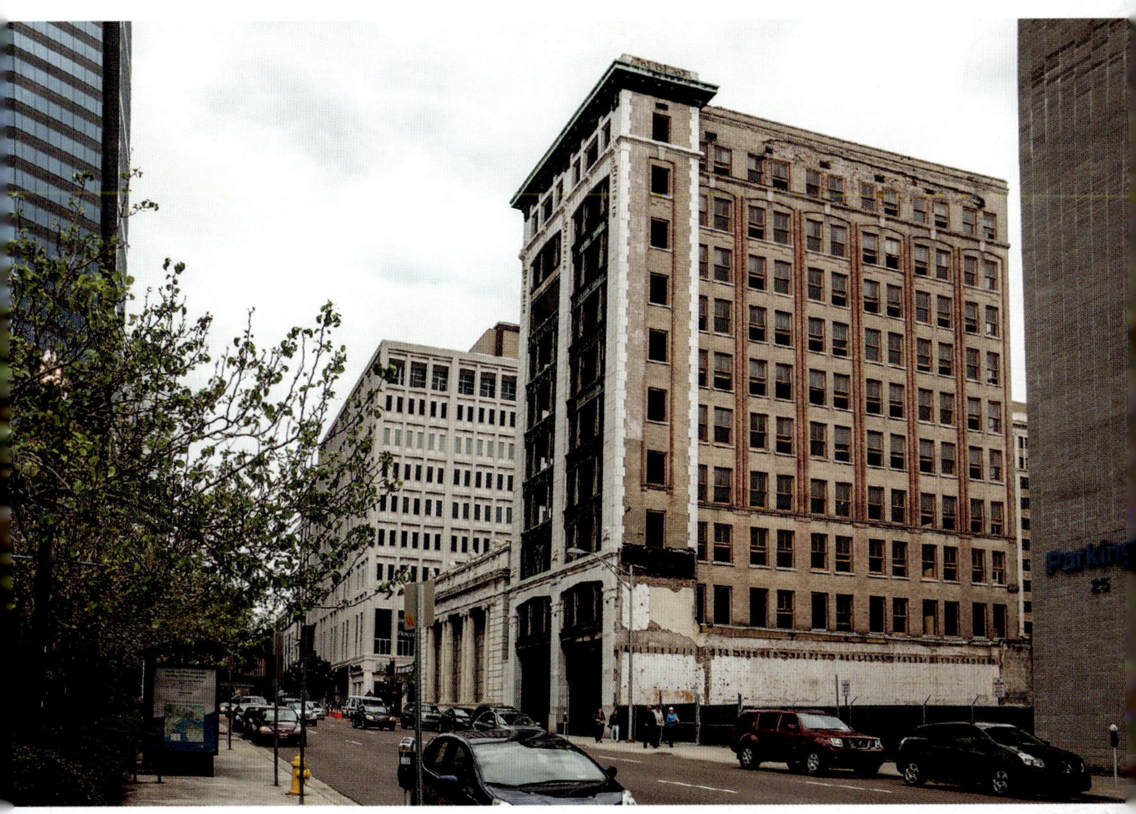
Parking
25

Laura Street, Jacksonville, c. 1915

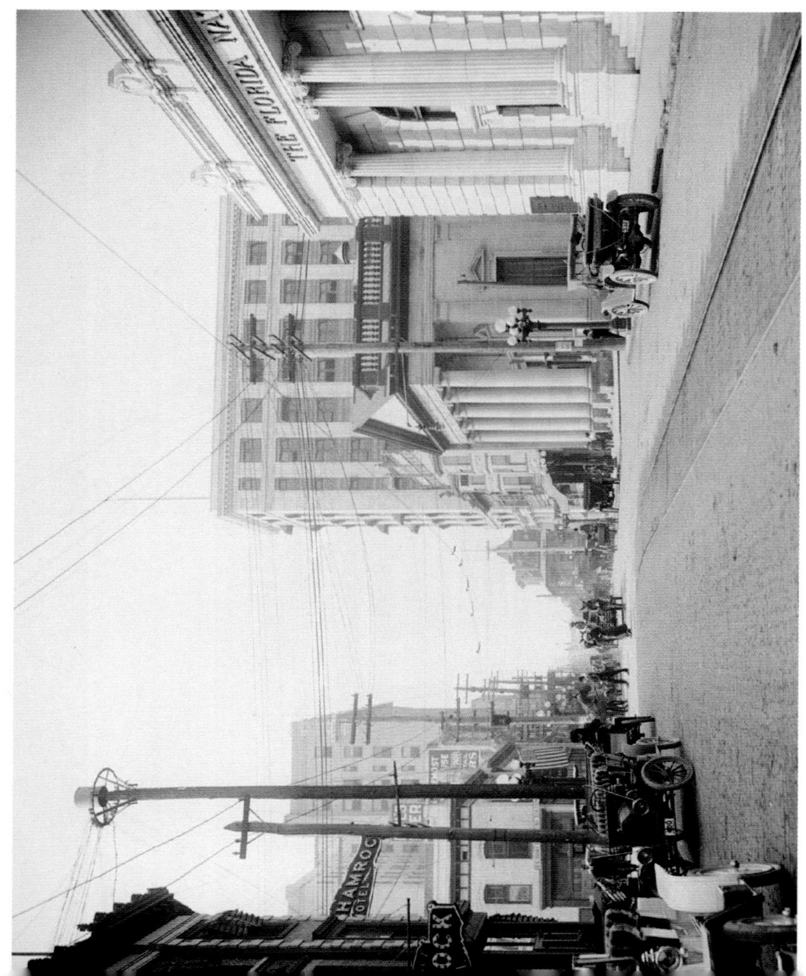

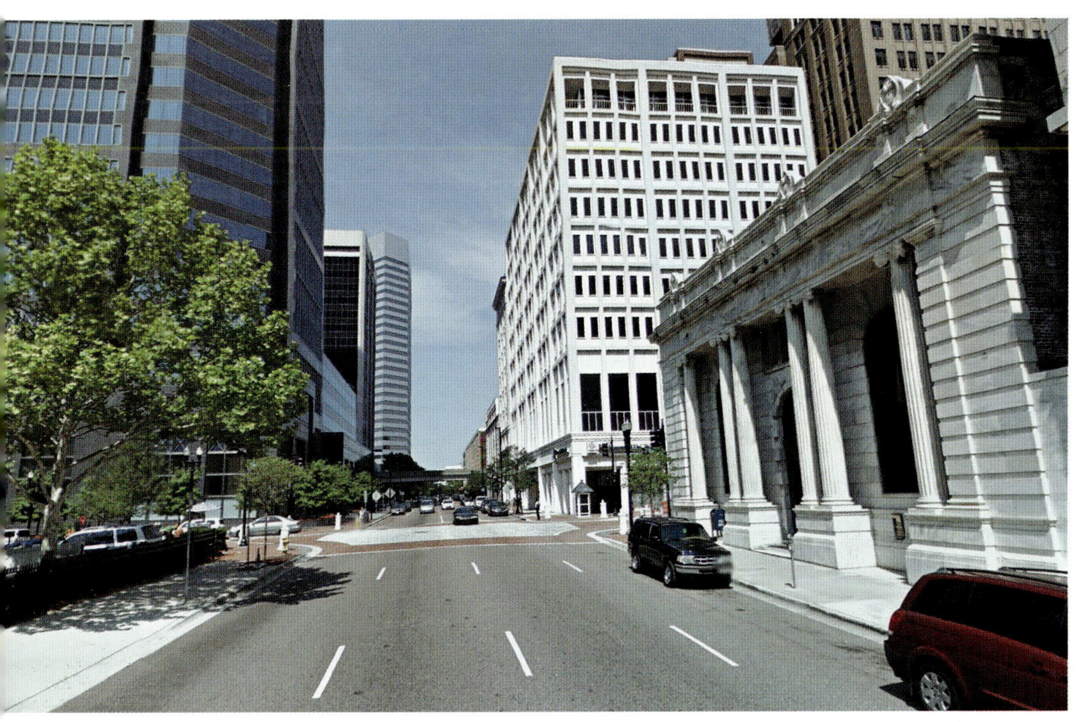

Morocco Temple, Newnan Street, Jacksonville, 1975

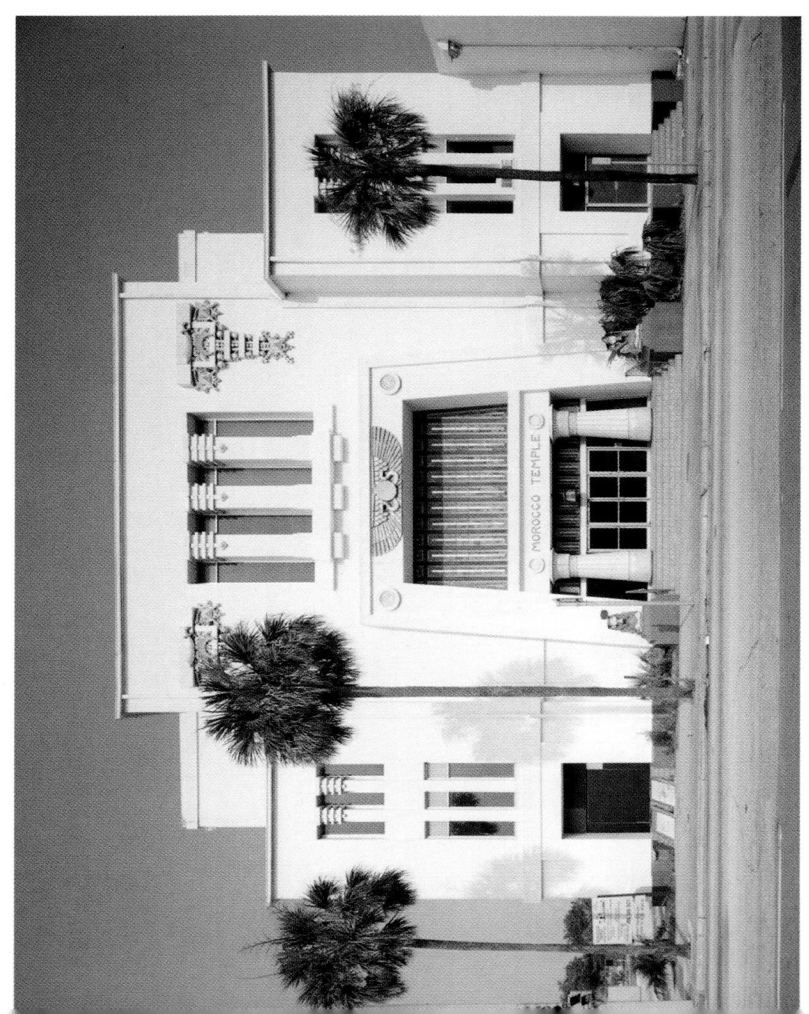

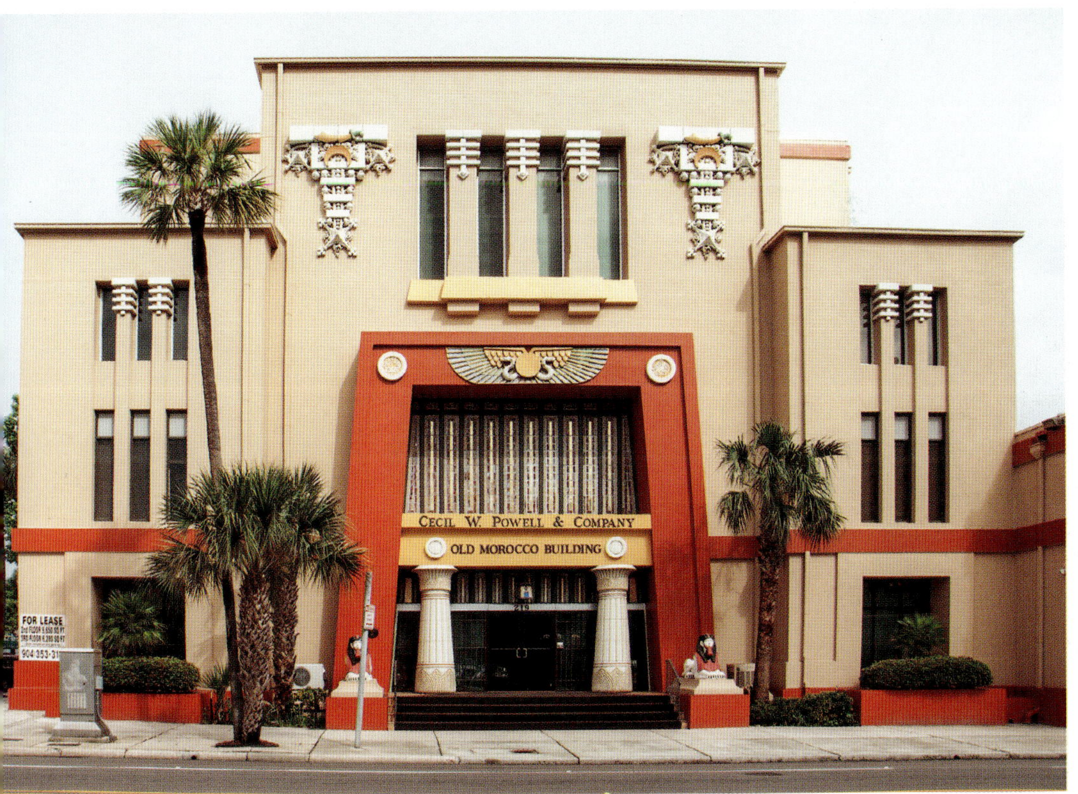
CECIL W. POWELL & COMPANY
OLD MOROCCO BUILDING
FOR LEASE

East Bay Street, Jacksonville, 1903

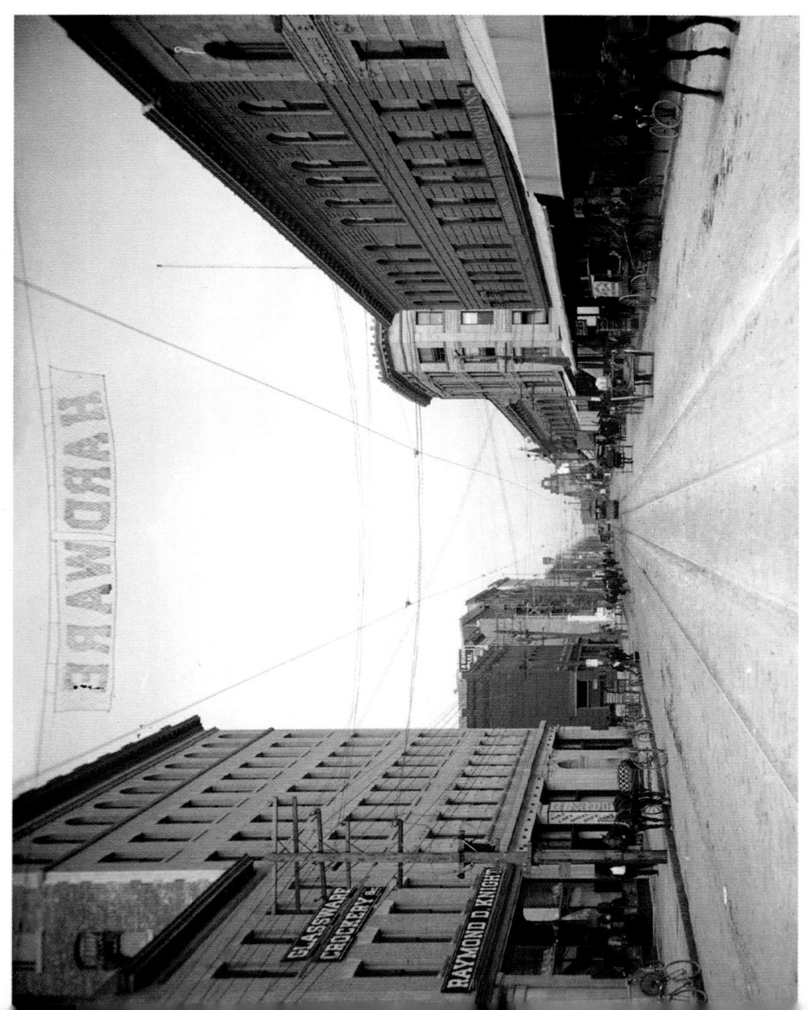

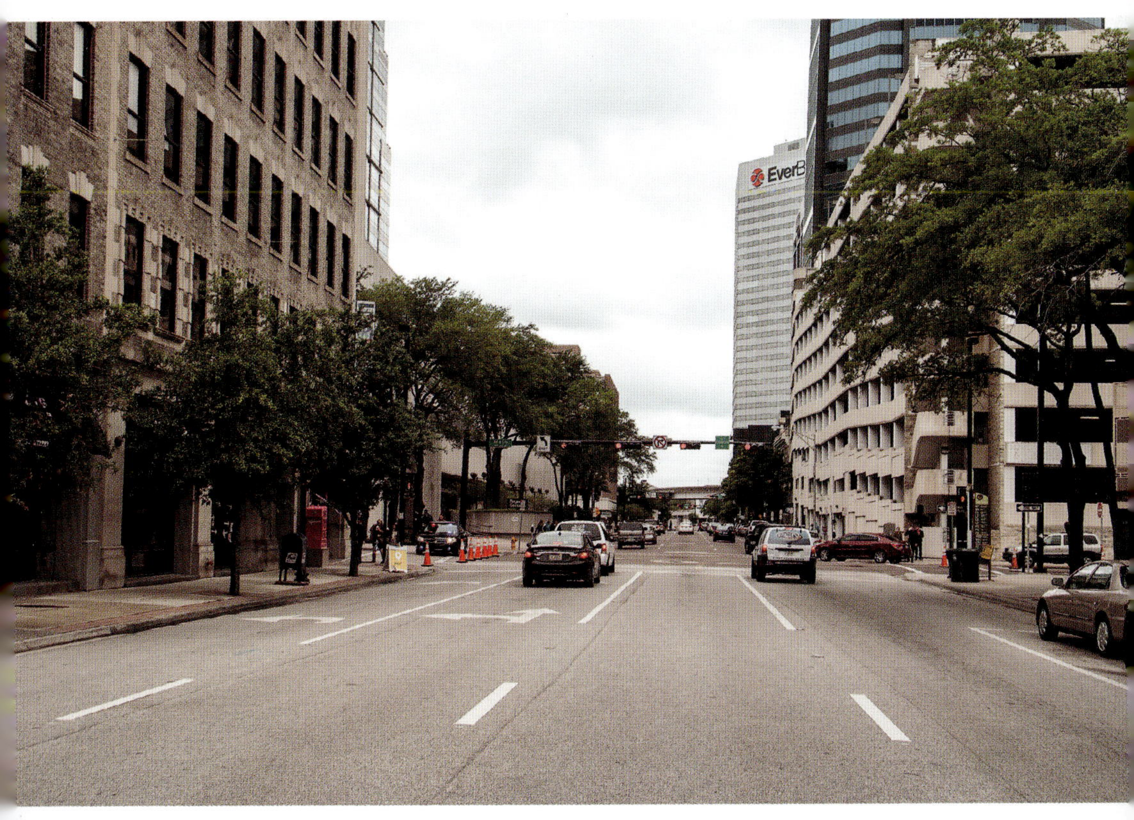
EverB

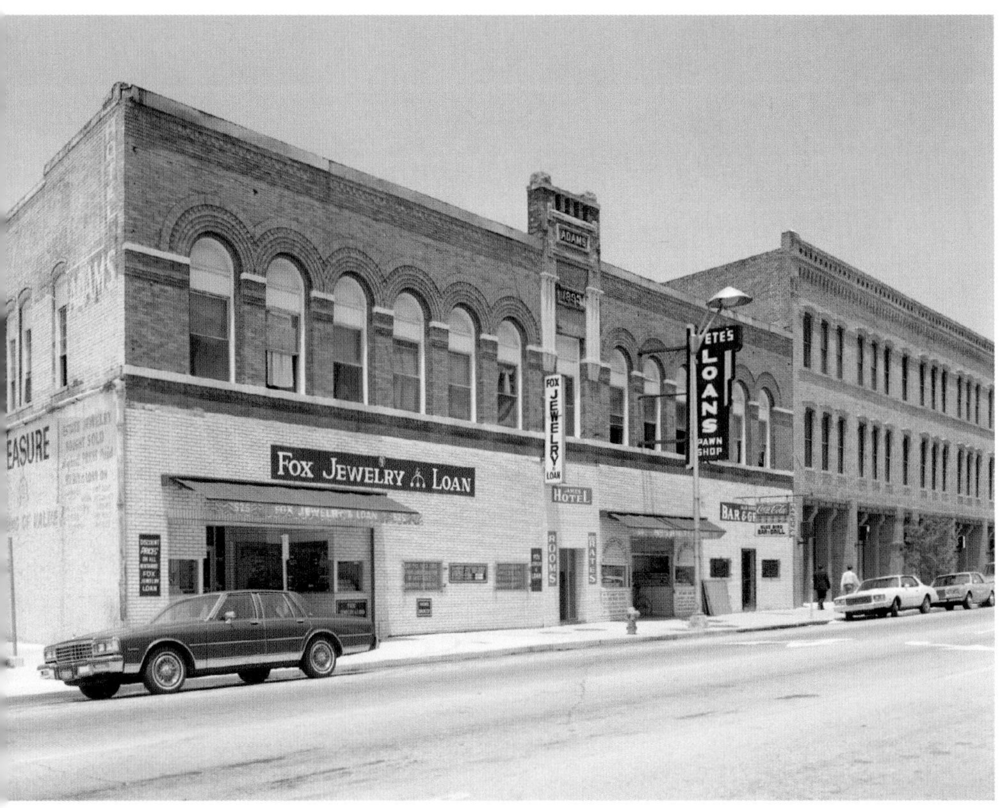

West Bay Street, Jacksonville, 1975

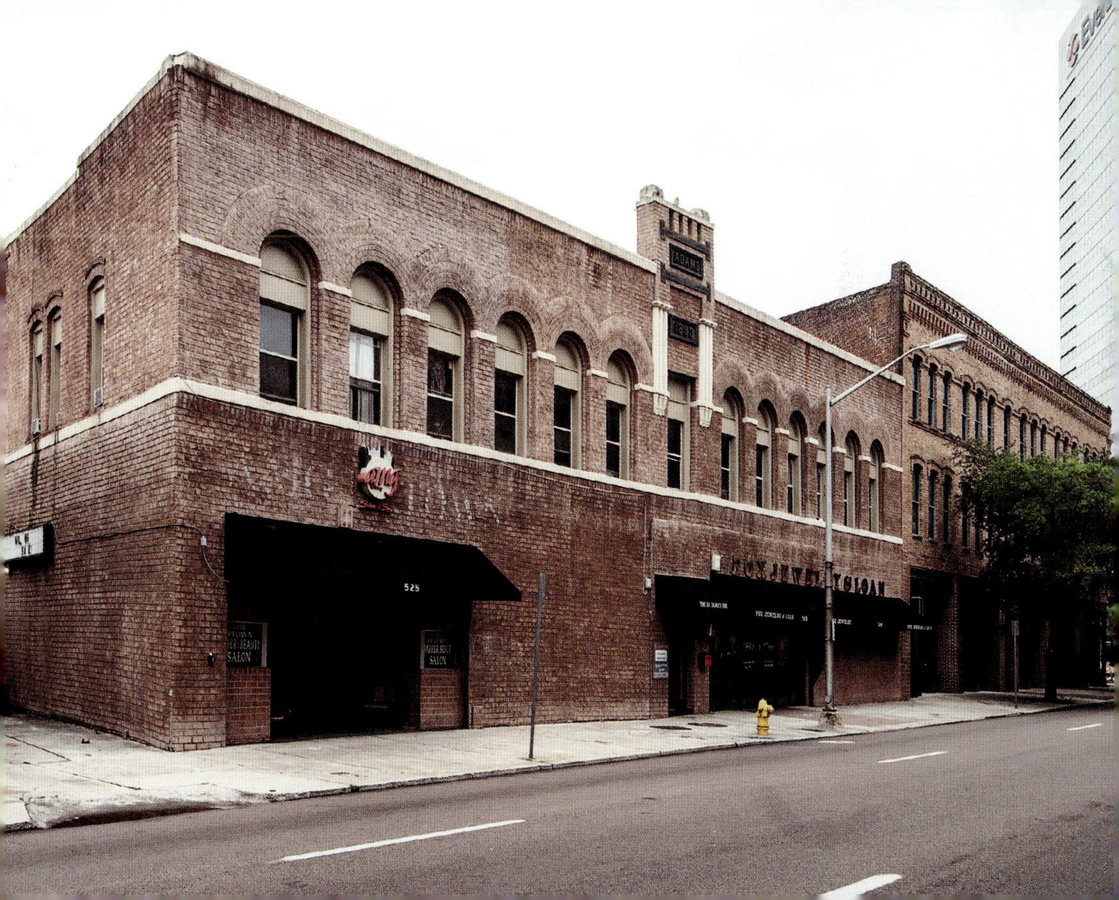
ADAMS
525
SALON
SALON

Riverside Park, Jacksonville, c. 1903

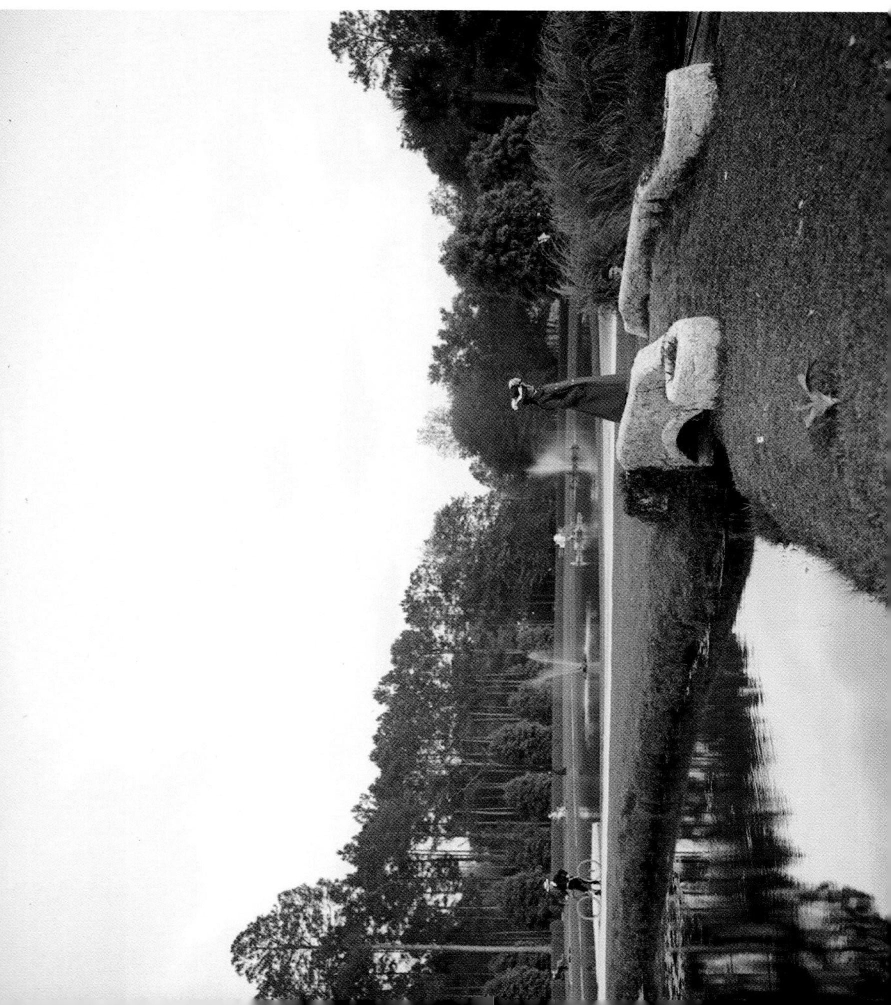

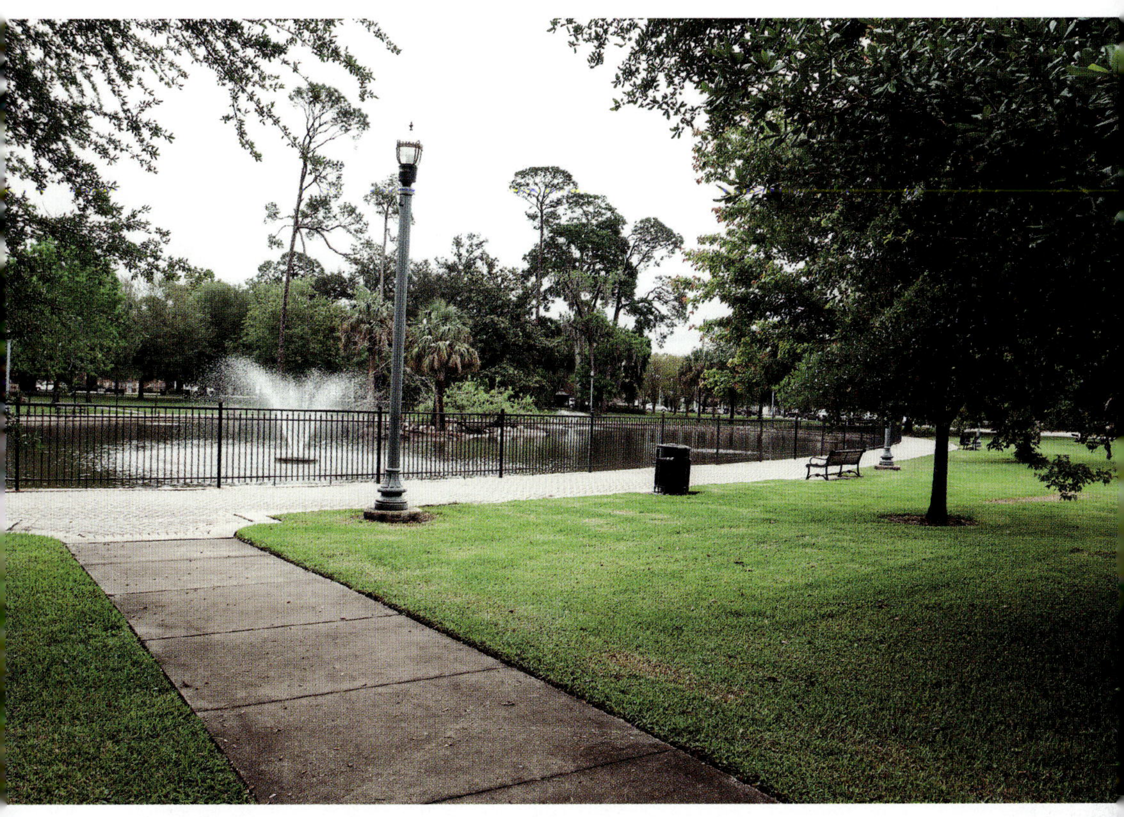

Florida State Capitol, Tallahassee, c. 1930

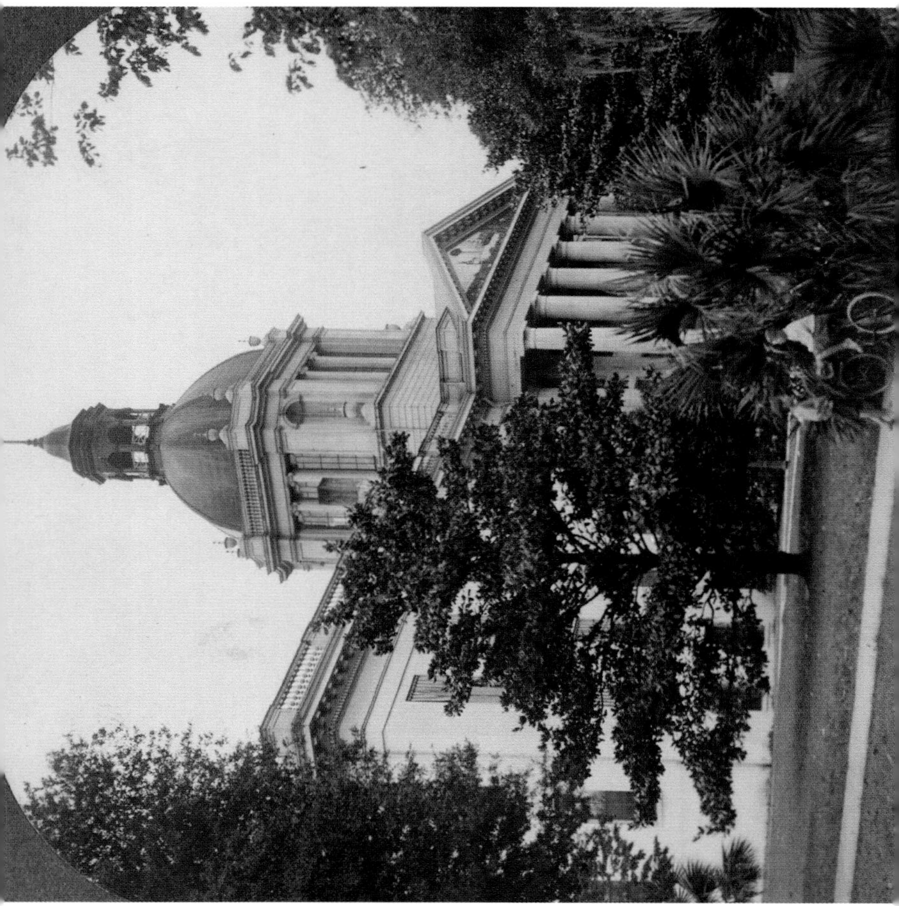

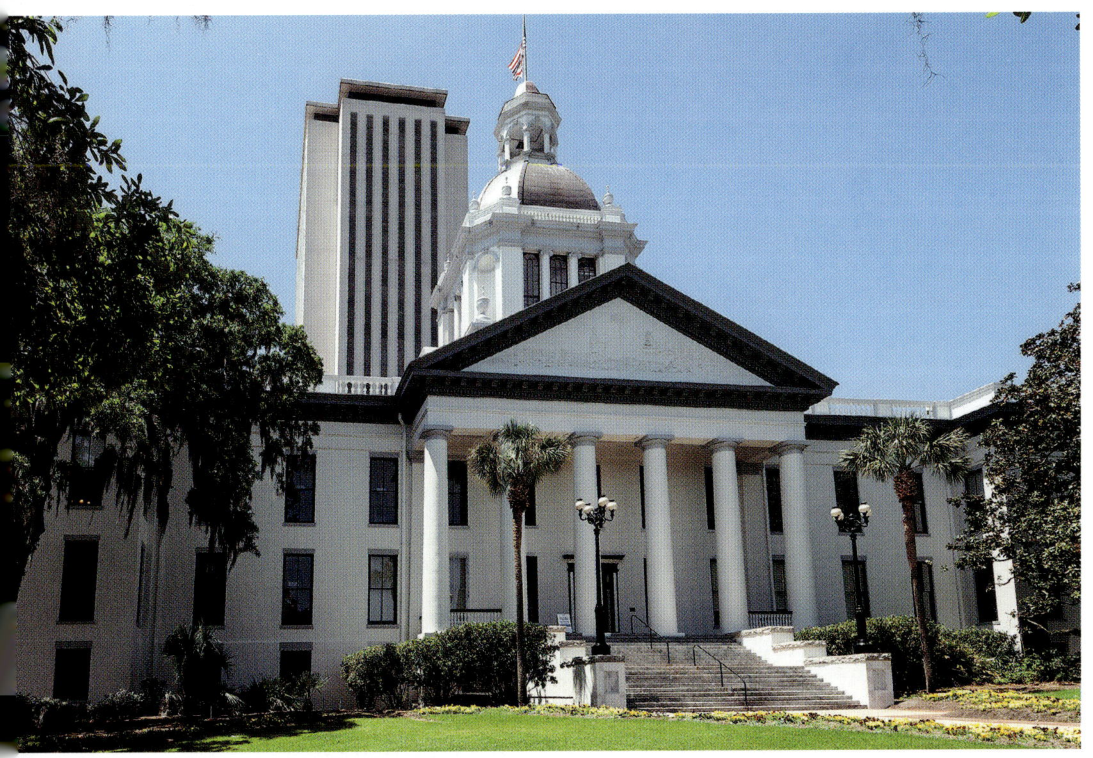

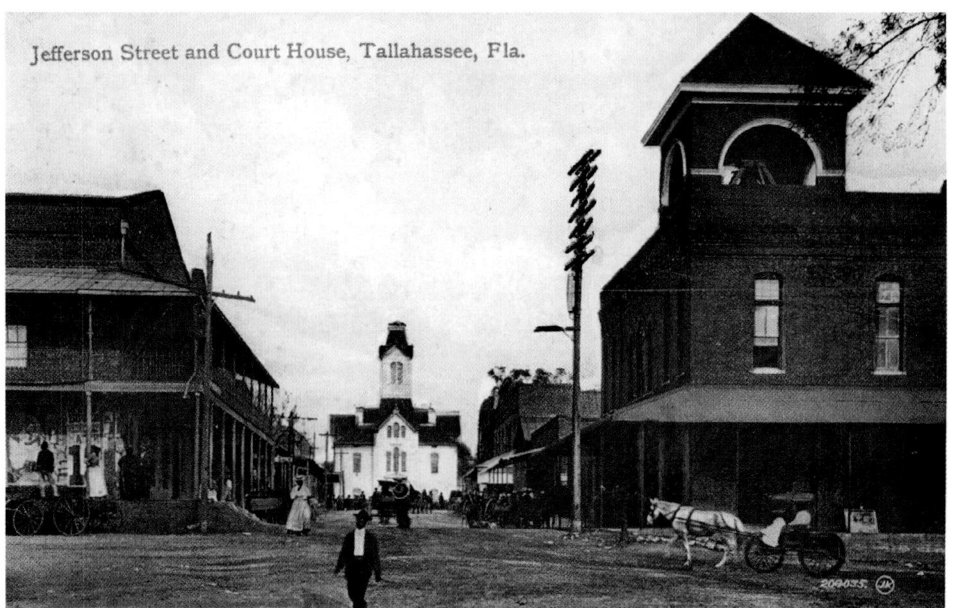

Jefferson Street and Old Court House, Tallahassee, c. 1900

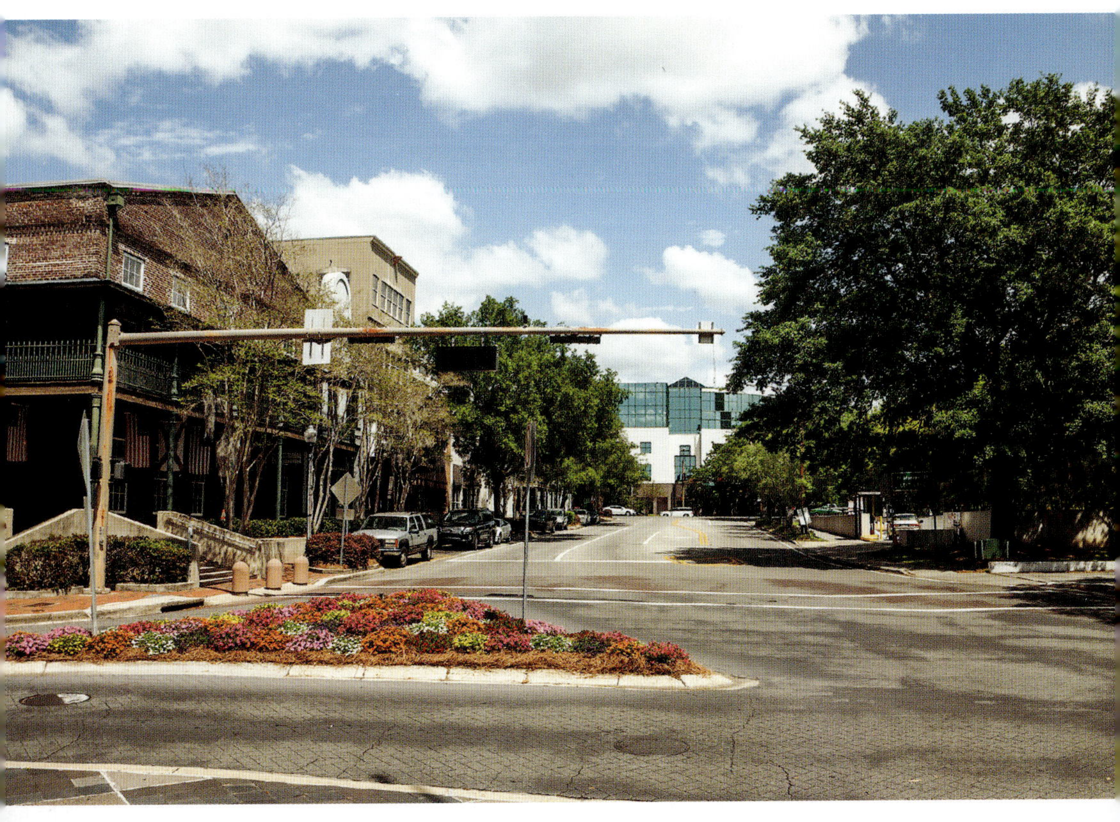

Bank of Florida Building, Apalachee Parkway, Tallahassee, 1962

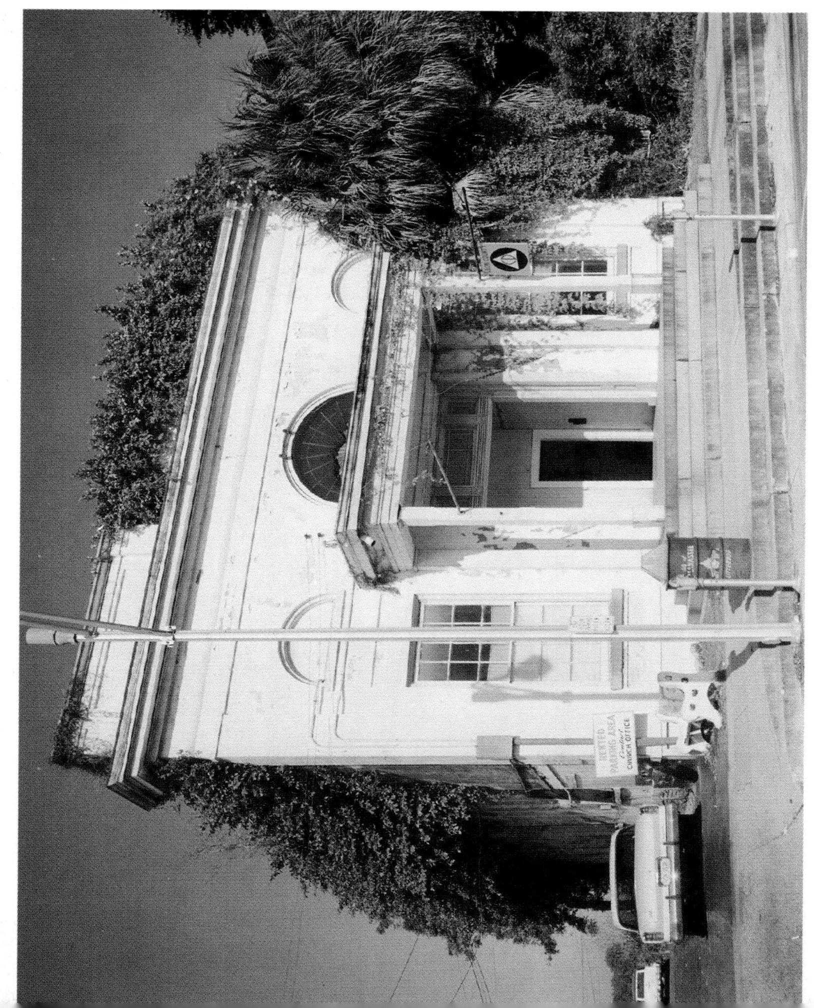

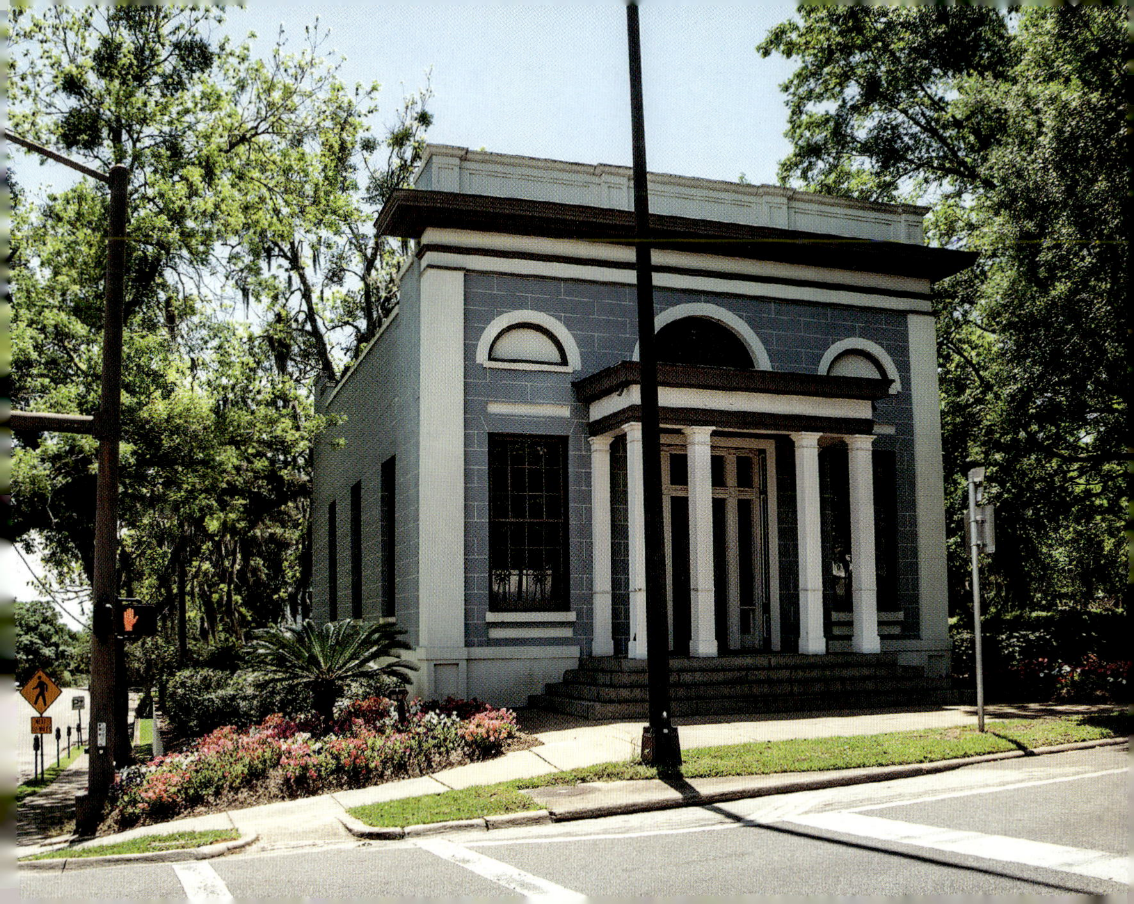

Government Street, Pensacola, 1912

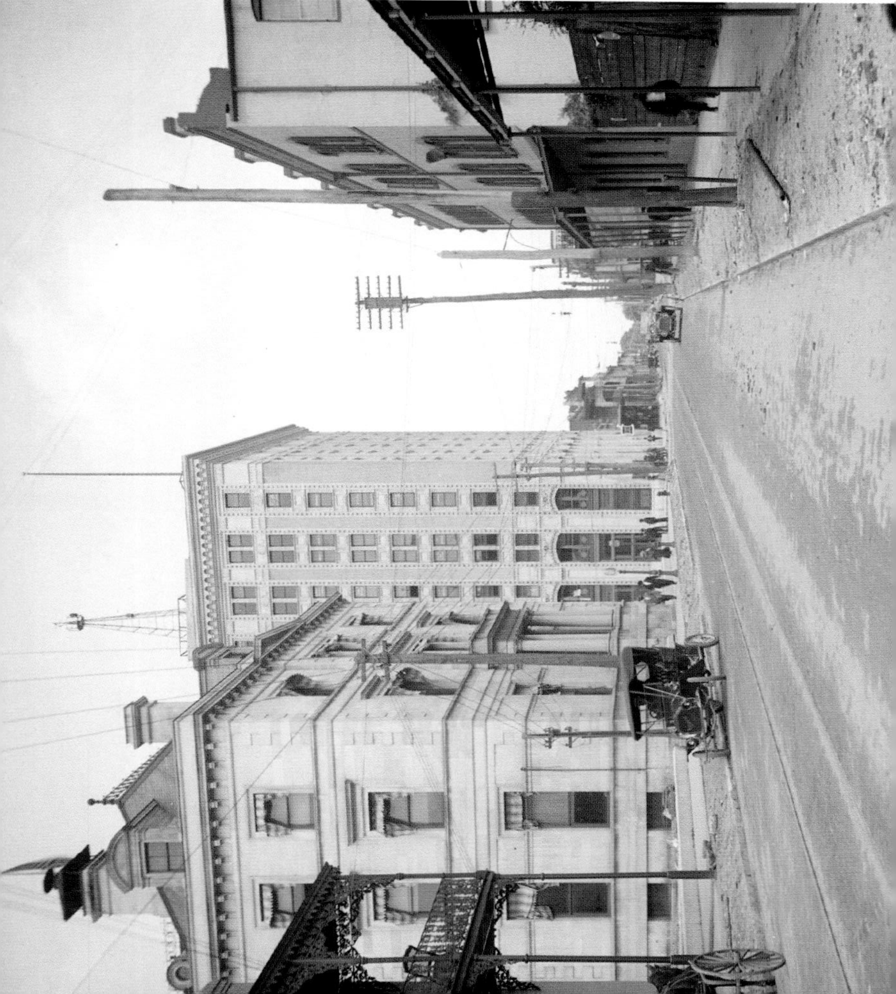

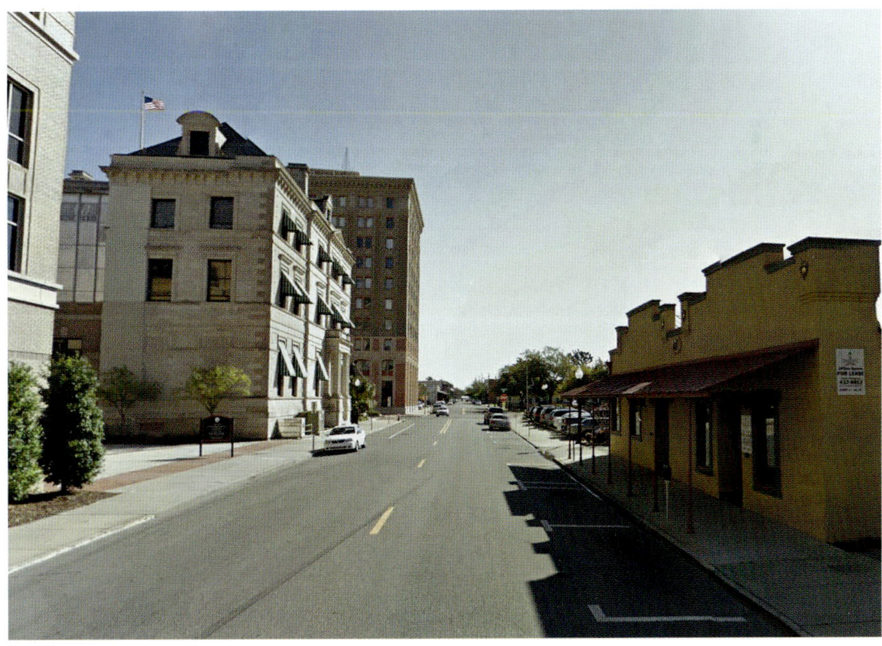

Palafox Street, Pensacola, 1912

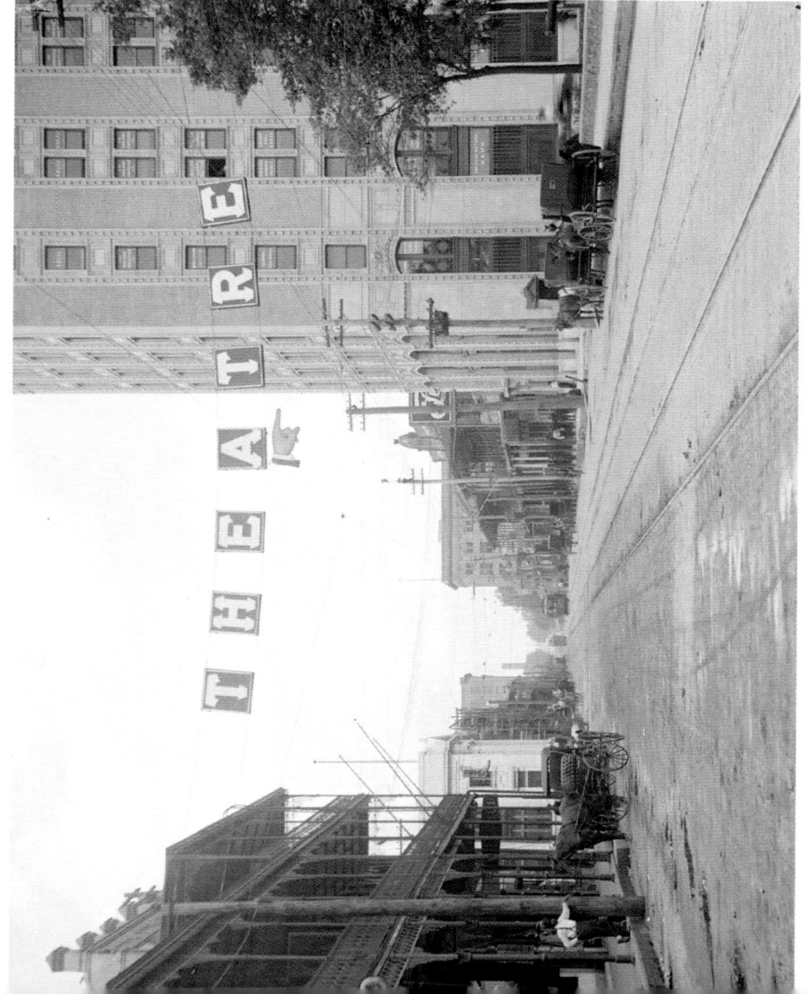

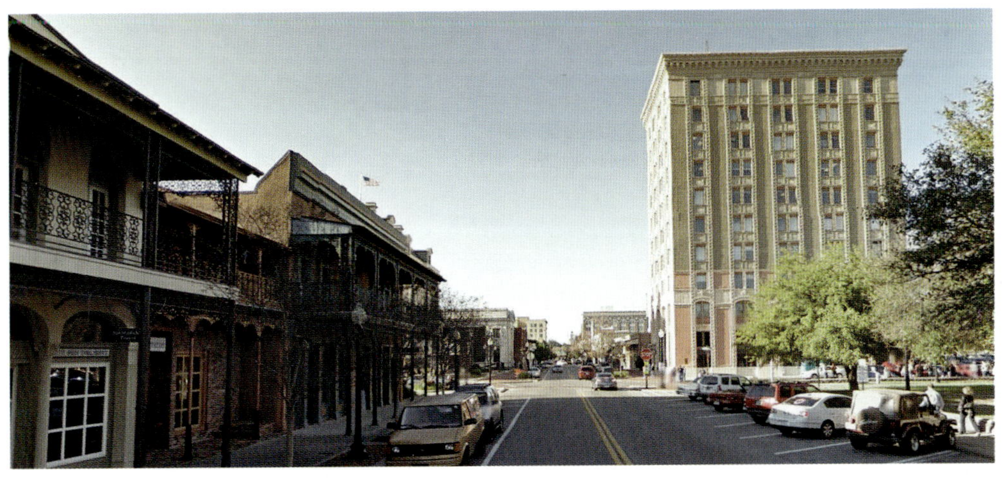

American National Bank, Palafox Street, Pensacola, 1912

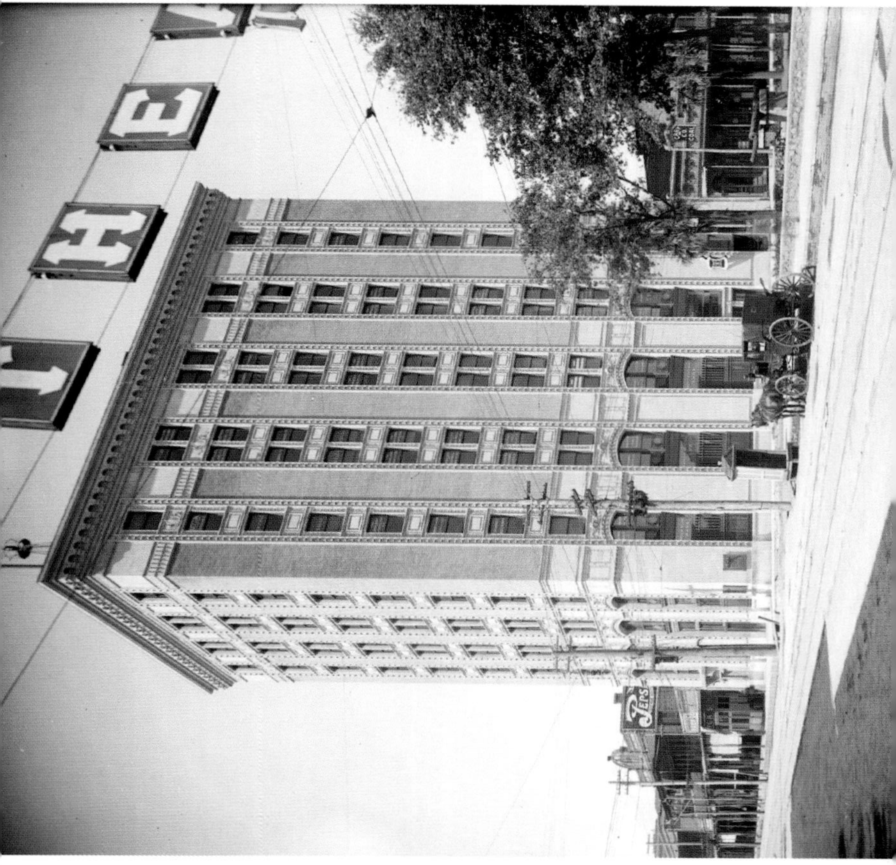

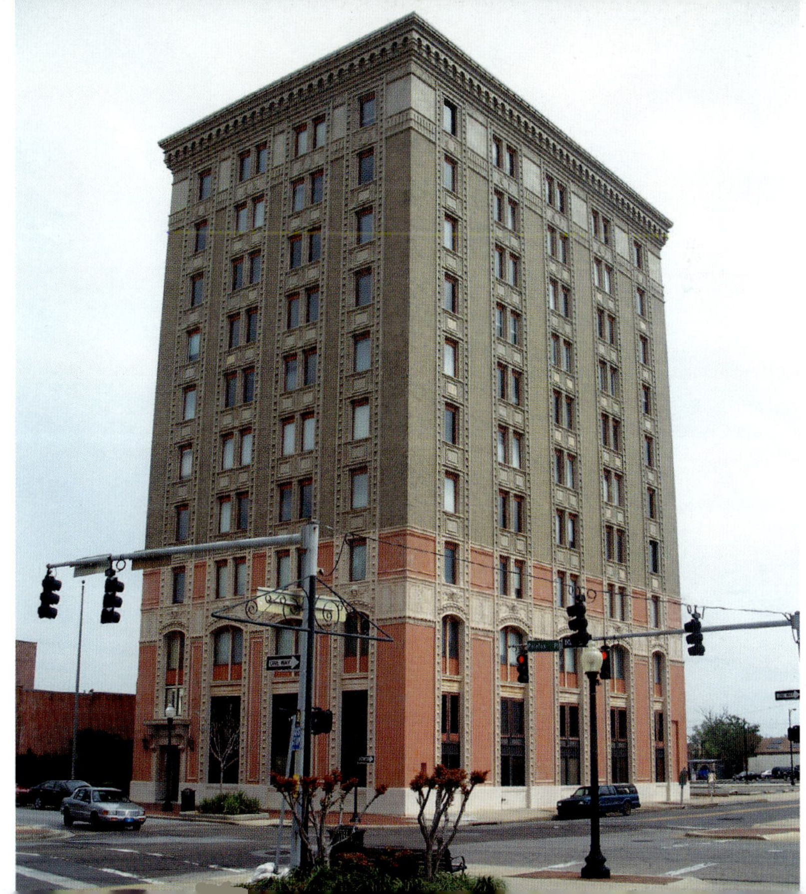
ONE WAY

Plaza Ferdinand, Pensacola, 1912 (left), 1909 (top right)

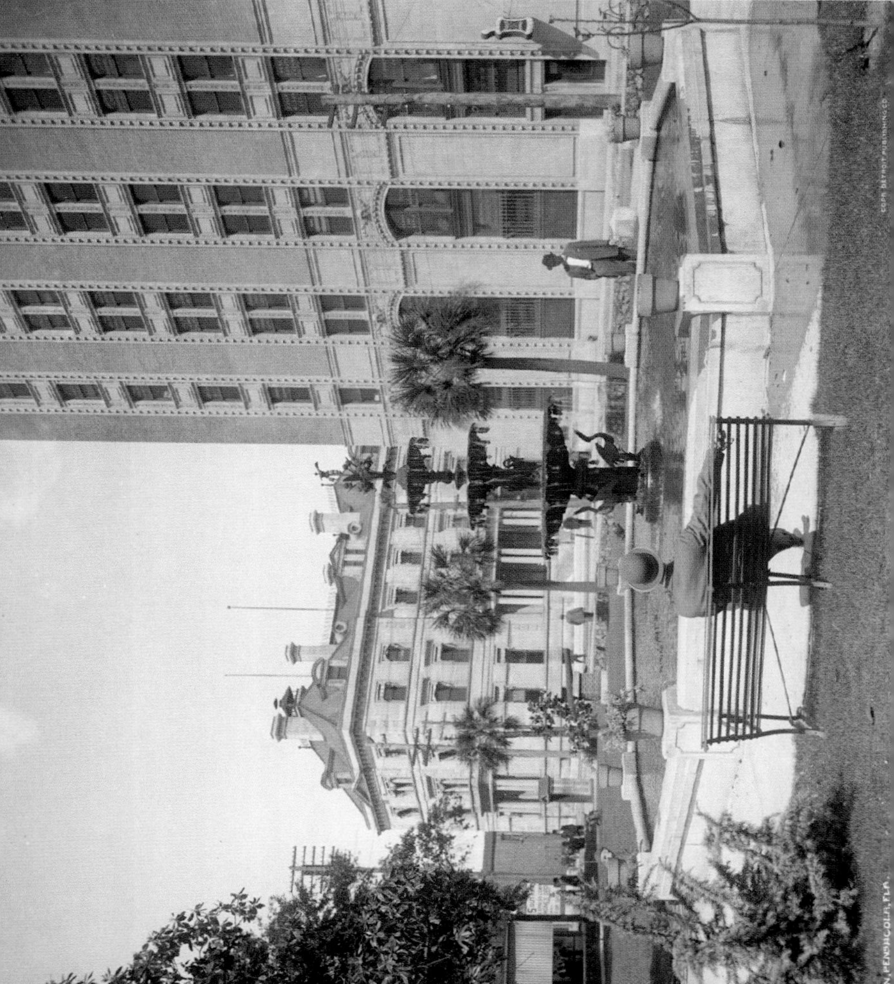

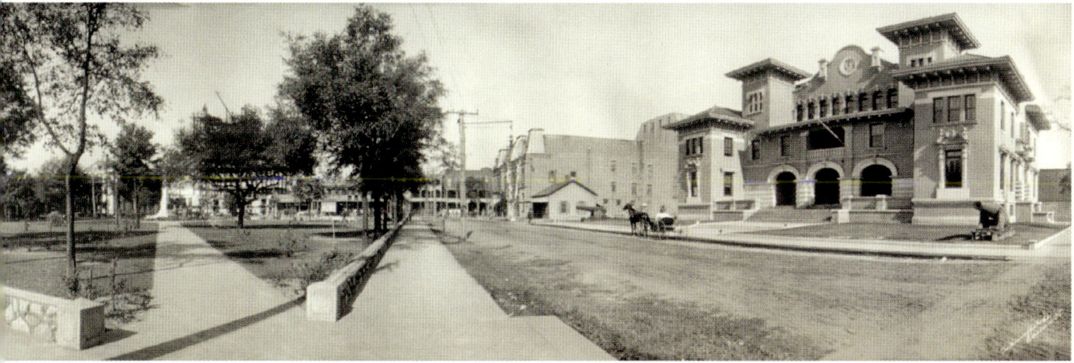

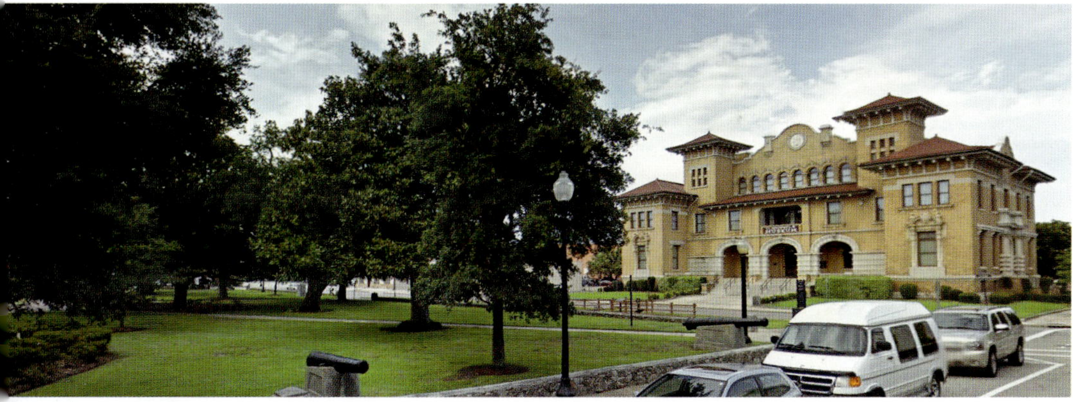

City Hall (now Florida State Museum), Pensacola, 1912

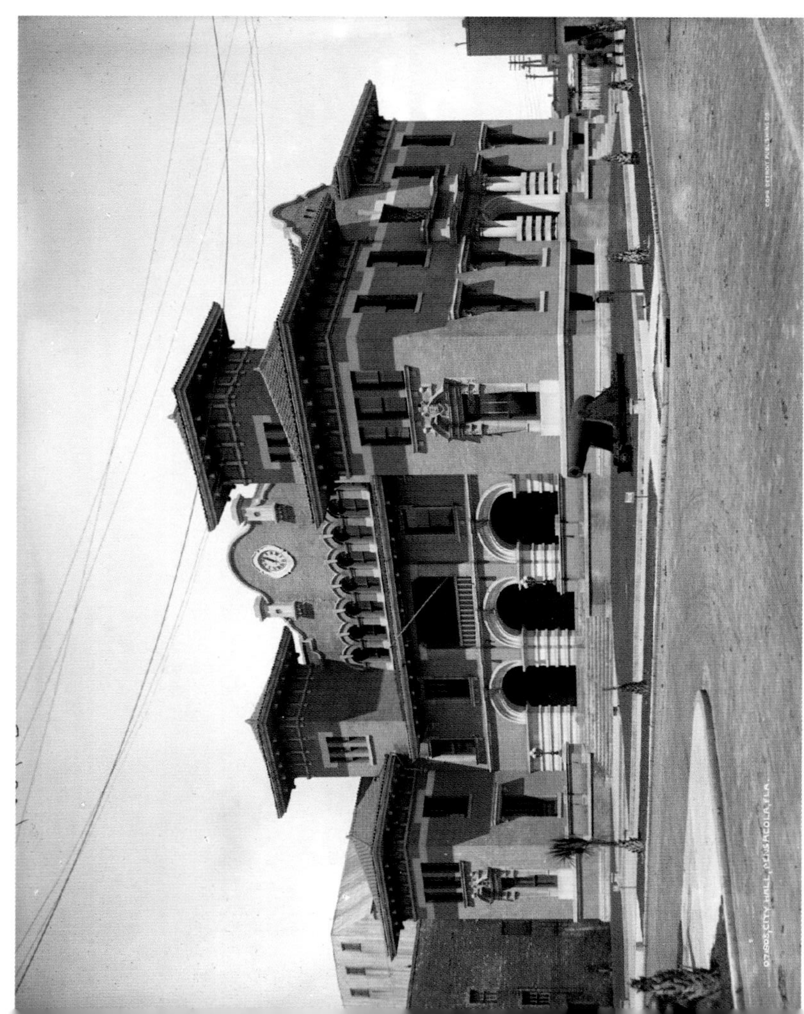

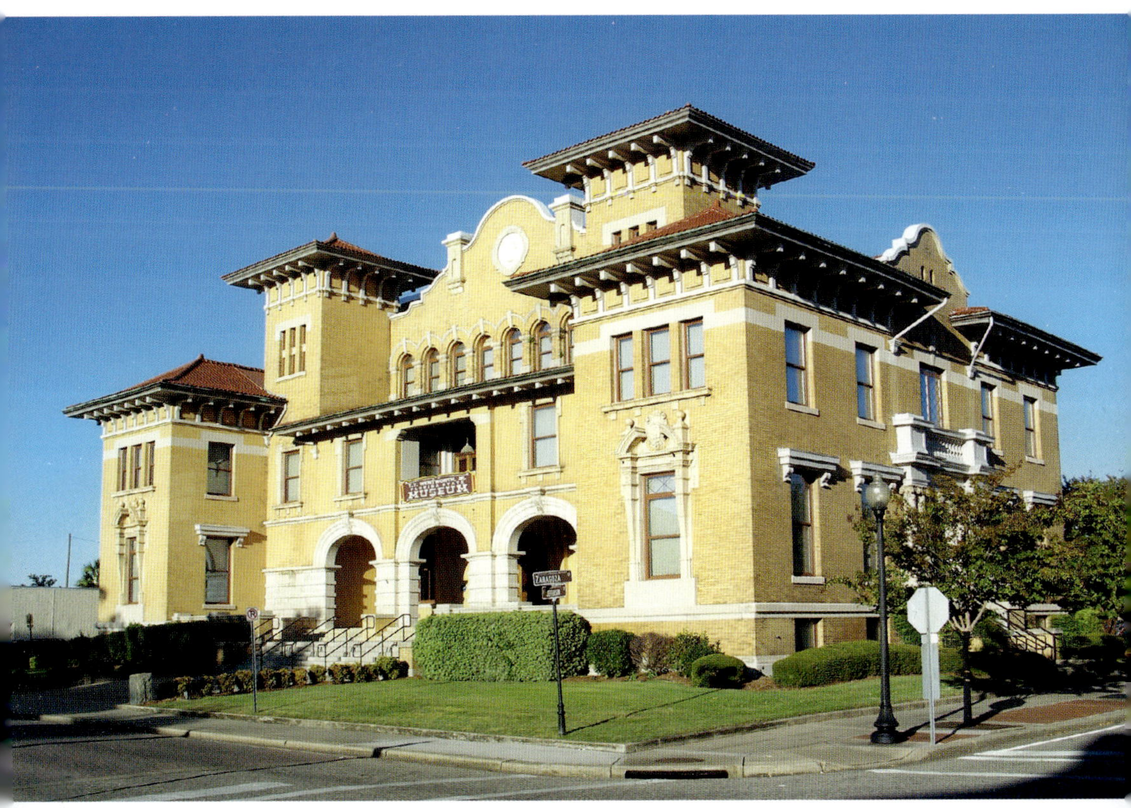
MUSEUM

U.S. Customs House and Post Office, Pensacola, 1912

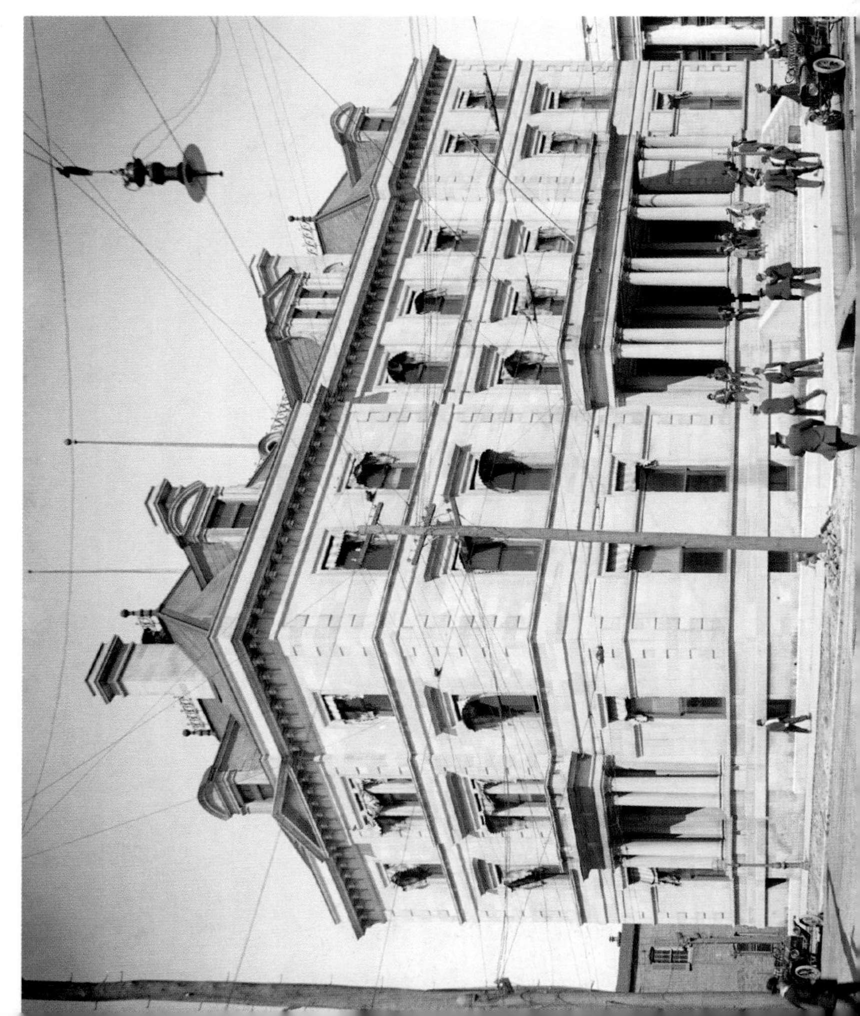

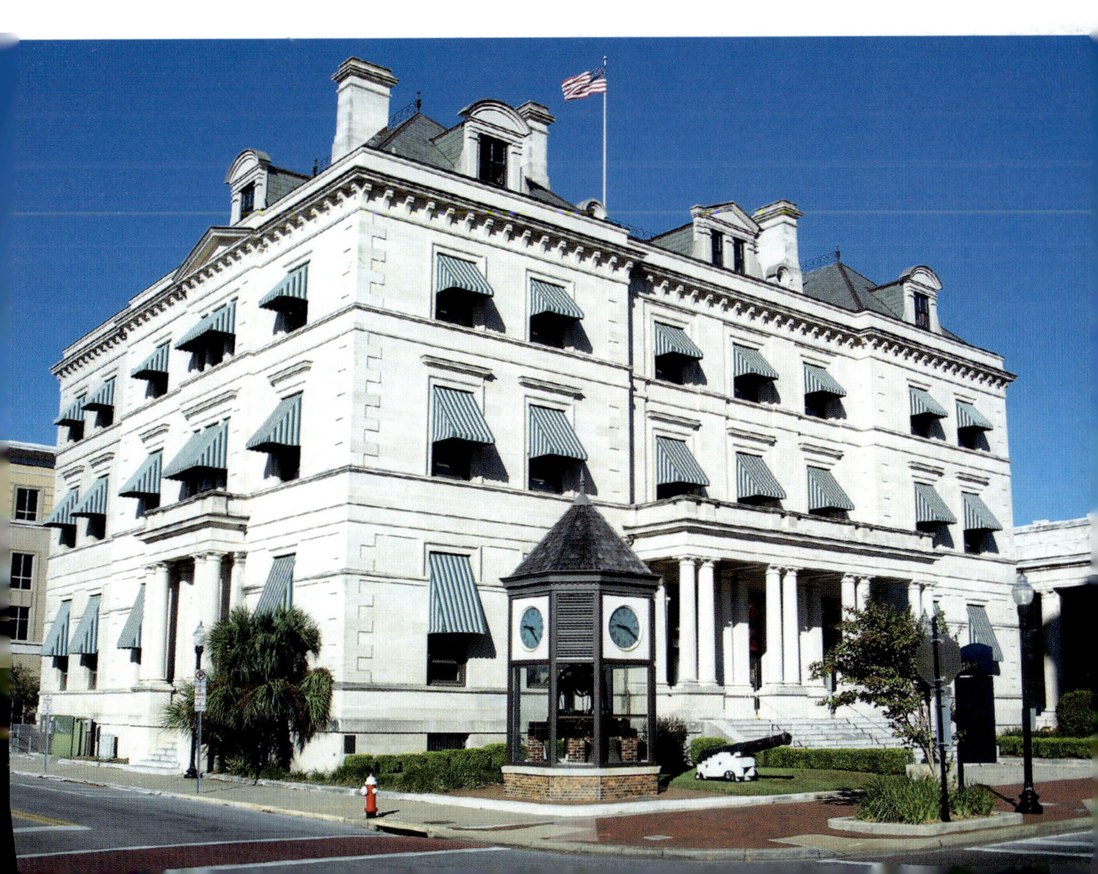

Acknowledgments

All "now" photographs are by David Watts, except for the following: Anova Image Library: 21, 131, 149, 157, 191, 201, 203, 301, 373, 389, 391, 395. Chad Hedstrom: 47. Walt Disney World: 219, 225, 227. Kennedy Space Center: 229, 231. Ebyabe: 237, 273, 393, 397, 399. Greenkayak: 309.

All "then" photographs are courtesy of the Library of Congress, except for the following: Anova Image Library: 6, 12, 14, 18, 22, 24, 26, 30, 40, 42, 44, 46, 48, 50, 52, 60, 64, 66, 68, 70, 76, 80, 90, 92, 94, 96, 106, 114, 128, 130, 134, 136, 138, 142, 144, 146, 148, 150, 152, 153, 154, 156, 160, 164, 168, 170, 188, 190, 192, 194, 196, 198, 204, 206, 208, 210, 212, 216, 238, 240, 242, 244, 246, 248, 260, 264, 266, 268, 270, 340, 342, 350, 366, 384. Harry F. Williams: 78. Corbis: 132. Walt Disney World: 218, 220–226. Kennedy Space Center: 228, 230.

Cover: Algiers Apartments, Treasure Island, 1967 (Corbis). Page 2: Rosie the Elephant at the Flamingo Hotel, Miami, 1923 (Library of Congress).

Researched, compiled and edited by David Salmo of Anova Books.